THE COMPLETE GUIDE TO NETWORKING AND NETWORK+, 2E

Michael W. Graves

THOMSON

DELMAR LEARNING

Australia • Canada • Mexico • Singapore • Spain • United Kingdom • United States

The Complete Guide to Networking and Network+, 2e

by Michael W. Graves

Vice President, Technology and Trades SBU:
Alar Elken

Editorial Director:
Sandy Clark

Senior Acquistions Editor:
Stephen Helba

Senior Channel Manager:
Dennis Williams

Senior Development Editor:
Michelle Ruelos Cannistraci

Marketing Director:
Dave Garza

Marketing Coordinator:
Stacey Wiktorek

Production Director:
Mary Ellen Black

Production Manager:
Andrew Crouth

Production Editor:
Dawn Jacobson

Art/Design Coordinator:
Francis Hogan

Senior Editorial Assistant:
Dawn Daugherty

Library of Congress Cataloging-in-Publication Data:

Library of Congress Control Number: 2005925897

The Complete Guide to Networking and Network+, 2e / Michael W. Graves

ISBN: 1418019445

NOTICE TO THE READER

Publisher does not warrant or guarantee any of the products described herein or perform any independent analysis in connection with any of the product information contained herein. Publisher does not assume, and expressly disclaims, any obligation to obtain and include information other than that provided to it by the manufacturer.

The reader is expressly warned to consider and adopt all safety precautions that might be indicated by the activities herein and to avoid all potential hazards. By following the instructions contained herein, the reader willingly assumes all risks in connection with such instructions.

The publisher makes no representation or warranties of any kind, including but not limited to, the warranties of fitness for particular purpose or merchantability, nor are any such representations implied with respect to the material set forth herein, and the publisher takes no responsibility with respect to such material. The publisher shall not be liable for any special, consequential, or exemplary damages resulting, in whole or part, from the readers' use of, or reliance upon, this material.

TABLE OF CONTENTS

CHAPER 2

CLIENTS AND SERVERS—WHO'S THE BOSS? 35

CHAPER 3:

THE HIGHWAYS AND BYWAYS OF THE NETWORK 63

PART 2: THE WORLD OF OSI

CHAPER 4

CHAPTER 7

THE NETWORK LAYER

CHAPTER 8

THE TRANSPORT LAYER

PART 3: THE NETWORKING PROTOCOLS

CHAPTER 13

THE OTHER PROTOCOLS

PART 4: PUTTING IT ALL TO WORK

CHAPTER 14

WORKING WITH REMOTE ACCESS

CHAPTER 15

CHAPTER 17

Chapter 18

Network Documentation and

Scheduled Maintenance

Chapter 19

Troubleshooting the Network

CHAPTER 20

APPENDICES

APPENDIX A

PREFACE

INTRODUCTION

Chances are extremely good that if you're reading this page right now, it's because you either already are a networking professional, or you have a desire to be one. Why? There are a lot of reasons for wanting to work with computers. One of those reasons is that it can be a financially rewarding field. It's also one of the fastest growing career fields. But for those of us who believe that variety is the spice of life, the sheer diversity of responsibilities and people that you work with is every bit as rewarding as the money.

Whatever your reasons for wanting a book of this nature may be, there is a lot in this book that will benefit virtually every level of reader. *The Complete Guide to Networking and Network+, 2e* can be used in three ways. As a *networking textbook*, it covers the basic networking theory taught in high-school, community college, or university networking technology courses. The simplified writing style makes it ideal for the beginning student with little or no background in networking, while the depth of coverage segues smoothly into intermediate/advanced level courses. The book provides not only background theory, but also explains the why's of using particular types of hardware. The OSI model is broken down into its seven separate layers and the book provides a detailed chapter on what goes on in each layer. Protocols, hardware, and troubleshooting are all handled in a similar manner.

As an *exam preparation reference*, the information in these pages provides all you need to know to study and successfully pass CompTIA's new 2005 Network+ certification exam. Each chapter addresses the objectives covered in the exam, while the text's descriptive and lively writing style makes learning fun and difficult concepts easier to understand.

Finally, as a *networking training guide*, the structure and organization of the book makes it a perfect candidate for the "five-day boot camp" environment. Chapters are structured so that each chapter can be read as a separate entity; you don't have to read the book straight through from beginning to end. The examples of real-life situations that network professionals will run into from time to time are useful tools in a professional training center setting.

However, once the class is over, this book won't have to go into hiding somewhere on a dusty shelf. Subject matter doesn't stop with the basics. Use it as a textbook today. Use it as a reference tomorrow.

ORGANIZATION

A basic knowledge of how to operate a personal computer is helpful, but not absolutely necessary. The first three chapters of this book act as an introduction to networking. In these hundred or so pages, the author starts with covering the basics and defines exactly what a network is and why it's important to build one.

From there, it starts to get a little more technical. The book begins to discuss networking theory, devoting chapters 4 through 10 to breaking the OSI model down layer by layer, until the reader has a clear understanding of how information starts at one device and travels over several hundred feet, or even several thousand miles, of wire, only to arrive perfectly intact at its destination.

Once networking theory is out of the way, the reader can concentrate on what the different networking protocols do, and when and where it is best use which protocol. Chapter 11 and Chapter 12 introduce the world of TCP/IP, and take the reader through a tour of some of the useful utilities that are a part of that suite. Chapter 13 covers the other protocols that show up on the Network+ exam, and in real life.

After that, you begin to get into the fun stuff, like interconnecting devices over remote connections (Chapter 14), setting security (Chapter 15), protecting your network from disaster (Chapter 16), planning and documenting networks (Chapter 17 and Chapter 18), and some good old-fashioned troubleshooting (Chapter 19). What kind of fun would this job be if, once in a while, we didn't get to fix something? The final chapter wraps things up with a brief discussion of the Internet (you can find out who *really* invented it!) in Chapter 20.

FEATURES

As you browse through the pages of *The Complete Guide to Networking and Network+, 2e*, a few key qualities should pop out at you right away. Chapters are logically organized so that the reader learns how data moves across the network in basically the same order as a computer system prepares data for transport, and how the infrastructure moves it. The author's light-handed approach to presenting the information makes the material easier to read and much easier to learn. There are hundreds of high-quality illustrations that supplement the text and dozens of tables that organize information into an easy to understand format. Advice on troubleshooting is supplemented by the field experiences of the author himself.

The text includes the following features:

1. Network+ Objectives mapped to the textbook are placed in the Introduction.

2. Each chapter begins with a list identifying the **Objectives** to be covered for the Network+ Exam.

3. Networking is full of acronyms and technical terms that you need to understand, so each chapter integrates **Buzz Words**, **Tricky Terminology**, and **Acronym Alerts** to introduce and reinforce key terminology.

4. **Exam Notes** for the student are given throughout the text providing helpful hints in preparing for the Network+ Exam.

5. **Sidebars** offer interesting insights into the life of a networking professional.

6. A **Chapter Summary** provides a quick refresher and review key points from the text.

7. Each chapter concludes with two sets of questions, called **Brain Drain** and **64K$ Questions**. The first set is a series of challenging, essay-oriented questions, and the second set consists of a set of multiple-choice, true/false, and short answer review questions.

8. A comprehensive **Glossary** and **Answers to Odd-Numbered Questions** are placed at the end of the book.

9. A CD in the back of the book includes **video clips** from the *Networking Fundamentals Video Series and Network+ Video Series* and **additional practice test questions**.

10. **View the Video** icon at the end of selected chapters identifies when to refer to the accompanying CD, which reinforces concepts learned through animations and demonstrations.

SUPPLEMENTS

Lab Manual

The lab manual includes a set of 15 lab exercises ranging from installing an operating system to exercises on backup and recovery.
(ISBN:1418019453)

e-resource **CD**

The following instructional aids are available all on one CD.

- **Textbook Solutions** includes answers to all end-of-chapter review questions
- **Lab Manual Solutions** includes answers to all lab exercise review questions.
- **ExamView Testbank** includes over 700 questions in a variety of formats, including multiple-choice, true/false, matching and more.
- **PowerPoint Presentation Slides** highlight key concepts from each chapter and can be used as handouts or as a springboard for lecture and discussion.
- **Image Library** includes all images from the textbook so instructors can customize handouts, tests, and power point presentations.

(ISBN: 1418019488)

Online Companion

The Online Companion features additional information on preparing for the Network+ Exam, including online quizzes and an Ask the Author section. Please visit www.delmarlearning.com/certification.

ABOUT THE AUTHOR

Michael Graves has been working in the computer industry ever since the days of 80286. He holds CompTIA's A+, Network+, Server+, and INet+ Certifications and is an Accredited Compaq Technician. Mr. Graves has taught classes at Champlain College, Essex Technical Center and Northwest Technical Center in Vermont and currently works with the Department of Homeland Security.

ACKNOWLEDGMENTS

This may come as a bit of a surprise to some, but someone like myself doesn't just sit down at the keyboard, start typing one day, and have a book of this nature just pop out the other end. There are a lot of very talented people who worked very hard on this project, and without their dedication, support, and assistance, this book never would have happened.

First off, let me thank my agent, Djana Pearson Morris of Pearson, Morris & Belt Literary Agency. She doesn't know the meaning of the word "can't." Nor does she know how to fail.

The editorial crew that pieced the manuscript together after I finished butchering it was nothing short of phenomenal. Debbie Abshier, founder and president of Abshier House, has put together one of the finest editorial crews I have ever worked with: Joell Smith-Borne, Christy Pierce, Kim Heusel, and Debbie Berman. Joell Smith-Borne took my clunky prose and crafted it into sentences that made sense. By the time she was done, one could almost be led to believe that I know how to write!

Last, but most importantly, I want to thank my parents, Mr. Leonard Graves and Mrs. Thelma Graves, for all the support they've given me throughout a very long and not always enjoyable project. They never stopped believing in me. I may never be able to fill your shoes, Mom and Dad, but you sure give me the right goal to shoot for. I love you both.

INTRODUCING THE NEW NETWORK+

The *Computing Technology Industry Association* (CompTIA) has been administering certification exams in the computing industry for over a decade now. It started with venerable A+ Certification for computer hardware professionals and has been constantly adding new fields of study to its repertoire. Network+ is not a new certification. It's been around for several years. However, in 2005, CompTIA revamped the exam to recognize changes in the industry, and well, quite frankly, to make it a bit more challenging.

Network+ is a certification that tells the world that you know your way around a network. This, of course, doesn't make their certification unique. Microsoft, Novell, and Cisco all have exams designed to prove that point. These proprietary exams cover the operating system aspect of networking quite well. The difference is that CompTIA's exam is vendor neutral. Network+ deals with the physical and theoretical aspects of networking. By passing this exam, you're demonstrating that you can work in pretty much any environment they throw at you.

Many, such as myself, who have taken the majority of CompTIA's exams, consider Network+ to be one of the harder exams, if not the hardest, of all that CompTIA offers. If you think about it, this only makes sense. For a certification to gain respect, it must demonstrate that the possessor of that certificate has demonstrated a superior knowledge of the subject in question. Certification is supposed to prove that you're one of the leaders of the pack, not just one of the pack.

It would appear that CompTIA has achieved its goal of making the certification respectable. Novell and Lotus have both accepted the Network+ certification as partial fulfillment of one of the steps in their own certification programs for some time. Recently, Microsoft joined the ranks. Starting late in 2001, Network+ became one of the exams accepted toward the new MCSA certification offered by Microsoft.

A number of colleges and universities have begun offering college credit for Network+ certification. But most importantly, there are very few major corporations who *don't* accept the certificate as proof of competency for employment purposes. 3Com Corporation, Compaq Computers, IBM, Intel, Lotus, Microsoft, and Novell are just a few of the companies that publicly acknowledge that they look for the Network+ certification when interviewing potential employees.

And isn't that what it's all about?

ON CERTIFICATION AND TESTING

If you're really new to this whole certification procedure, you might be asking yourself just why you're going through all this trouble. After all, you know everything there is to know about building networks, don't you? You probably even have a small network set up in your own house. I know I do.

The point is, a potential employer isn't going to take the word of every Tom, Dick, and Mary that comes through the door saying, "I'm the greatest network engineer this town has ever seen!" Employers want some sort of proof, and they sure don't want to take the time and effort to generate their own testing programs (although some companies do). The majority of companies put their faith in one of the established programs of certification.

This concept of certification is certainly not unique to the computer industry. Most industries have had certification programs in place for many years. Electricians, plumbers, dental assistants, and virtually every other profession you can think of maintains some form of certification procedure.

CompTIA's certification programs have been around for about as long as any other in our industry. They are trusted and respected by a vast majority of companies that hire information technology (IT) professionals. In fact, many companies prefer CompTIA certifications to vendor-specific programs for the very reason that they are *not* vendor specific.

ABOUT THE EXAM

Network+ exams are offered at either Thomson Prometric or VUE authorized testing centers. Questions are offered as multiple choice options on a desktop computer connected into a testing network. Questions are drawn from a bank of questions in a database and follow a simple formula. CompTIA has determined that the average test should contain certain percentages of questions that pertain to particular subjects. CompTIA refers to each specific exam topic as a *domain area.* **Table 1.1** lists those domain areas and their relative weight on the exam.

The testing software used by CompTIA prevents the exam itself from being confusing. Directions for each type of question offered are displayed on the screen. The directions will let you know when multiple answers are appropriate. The testing software even provides a nice little tutorial that takes you through a few sample questions. If you choose to take advantage of the tutorial, the questions you'll see do not relate to the Network+ exam in any way, shape, or form, but they do give you an idea of how to take the test. If you really have a problem with the software, proctors are nearby and available to help. But don't bother asking them what the correct answer is. They won't tell you even if they know.

When you think you're finally finished, you'll have an opportunity to review your questions and answers. I highly recommend that you take advantage of that opportunity. It is very likely that a question that comes up later in the exam will jog something in your memory that helps you with one you had trouble with earlier. By reviewing the questions, you might realize that you misinterpreted a question or simply checked the wrong box. While reviewing, however, don't make the mistake of second-guessing yourself. It's just as easy to talk yourself out of a correct response as it is to recognize a bonehead answer when you see one.

Table 1.1 Exam Contents (Domain area percentages)

Network+ Domain Area	% of Exam Coverage
Domain 1.0, Media and Topologies	20%
Domain 2.0, Protocols and Standards	20%
Domain 3.0, Network Implementation	25%
Domain 4.0, Network Support	35%
Total	100%

THE TEST OBJECTIVES

The exam is broken down into four areas of study, or domains. In order to better prepare you for passing the exam, I have put together the following outline using information extracted from CompTIA's web site at www.comptia.org. Unfortunately, I found that organizing a book based directly on this outline would lead to a disjointed and very confusing book. Therefore, I have chosen to present the material in a way that I have found enables students to grasp the information most quickly. I have chosen to take a systematic approach to networking theory, using the concepts of the *Open Systems Interconnect* (OSI) networking model developed by the International Standards Organization (ISO) as the foundation for this book. However, all topics targeted by CompTIA will be covered in detail.

The following outline tells you what *Chapters* cover each of the topics covered on the exam. Note that in many cases, a topic might be covered on more than one place.

DOMAIN 1.0: MEDIA AND TOPOLOGIES – 20%

1.1   Recognize the following logical or physical network topologies given a diagram, schematic or description:

Star *(Chapters 1 and 6)*
Bus *(Chapters 1 and 6)*
Mesh *(Chapters 1 and 6)*
Ring *(Chapters 1 and 6)*

1.2   Specify the main features of 802.2 (Logical Link Control), 802.3 (Ethernet), 802.5 (token ring), 802.11 (wireless), and FDDI (Fiber Distributed Data Interface) networking technologies, including:

Speed *(Chapters 1 and 5)*
Access method (CSMA/CA (Carrier Sense Multiple Access/Collision Avoidance) and CSMA/CD))
   (Chapters 1 and 7)
(Carrier Sense Multiple Access/Collision Detection)) *(Chapter 7)*
Topology *(Chapters 1 and 6)*
Media *(Chapters 1 and 5)*

1.3   Specify the characteristics (For example: speed, length, topology, and cable type) of the following cable standards:

10BASE-T and 10BASE-FL *(Chapter 6)*
100BASE-TX and 100BASE-FX *(Chapter 6)*
1000BASE-T, 1000BASE-CX, 1000BASE-SX and 1000BASE-LX *(Chapter 6)*
10 GBASE-SR, 10 GBASE-LR and 10 GBASE-ER *(Chapter 6)*

1.4   Recognize the following media connectors and describe their uses:

RJ-11 (Registered Jack) *(Chapters 1 and 3)*
RJ-45 (Registered Jack) *(Chapters 1 and 3)*
F-Type *(Chapter 3)*
ST (Straight Tip) *(Chapter 3)*
SC (Subscriber Connector or Standard Connector) *(Chapter 3)*
IEEE 1394 (FireWire) *(Chapter 3)*

Fiber LC (Local Connector) *(Chapter 3)*
MT-RJ (Mechanical Transfer Registered Jack) *(Chapter 3)*
USB (Universal Serial Bus) *(Chapter 3)*

1.5   Recognize the following media types and describe their uses:

Category 3, 5, 5e, and 6 *(Chapter 3)*
UTP (Unshielded Twisted Pair) *(Chapter 3)*
STP (Shielded Twisted Pair) *(Chapter 3)*
Coaxial cable *(Chapter 3)*
SMF (Single Mode Fiber) optic cable *(Chapter 3)*
MMF (Multimode Fiber) optic cable *(Chapter 3)*

1.6   Identify the purposes, features and functions of the following network
      components:

Hubs *(Chapter 1 and Lab Manual)*
Switches *(Chapters 1 and 6)*
Bridges *(Chapters 1 and 6)*
Routers *(Chapters 1, 7, 11, 13, and 17)*
Gateways *(Chapters 7 and 15)*
CSU/DSU (Channel Service Unit/Data Service Unit) *(Chapters 1 and 14)*
NICs (Network Interface Card) *(Chapter 1 and Lab Manual)*
ISDN (Integrated Services Digital Network) adapters *(Chapters 1 and 14)*
WAPs (Wireless Access Point) *(Chapters 1 and 5)*
Modems *(Chapter 14)*
Transceivers (media converters) *(Chapters 3 and 14)*
Firewalls *(Chapter 15)*

1.7   Specify the general characteristics (For example: carrier speed, frequency,
      transmission type and topology) of the following wireless technologies:

802.11 (Frequency hopping spread spectrum) *(Chapters 3 and 5)*
802.11x (Direct sequence spread spectrum) *(Chapters 3 and 5)*
Infrared *(Chapters 3 and 5)*
Bluetooth *(Chapter 14)*

1.8   Identify factors which affect the range and speed of wireless service
      (For example: interference, antenna type and environmental factors).
      (Chapters 3 and 5)

DOMAIN 2.0: PROTOCOLS AND STANDARDS – 20%

2.1   Identify a MAC (Media Access Control) address and its parts.
      (Chapter 13)

2.2   Identify the seven layers of the OSI (Open Systems Interconnect) model and their functions. *(Chapters 4 and 10)*

2.3   Identify the OSI (Open Systems Interconnect) layers at which the following network components operate:

Hubs *(Chapter 5)*
Switches *(Chapter 6)*
Bridges *(Chapter 7)*
Routers *(Chapter 7)*
NICs (Network Interface Card) *(Chapter 5)*
WAPs (Wireless Access Point) *(Chapter 14)*

2.4   Differentiate between the following network protocols in terms of routing, addressing schemes, interoperability and naming conventions:

IPX/SPX (Internetwork Packet Exchange/Sequence Packet Exchange) *(Chapters 7 and 13)*
NetBEUI (Network Basic Input/Output System Extended User Interface) *(Chapter 13 and Lab Manual)*
AppleTalk/AppleTalk over IP (Internet Protocol) *(Chapter 13)*
TCP/IP (Transmission Control Protocol/Internet Protocol) *(Chapters 11 and 12)*

2.5   Identify the components and structure of IP (Internet Protocol) addresses (IPv4, IPv6) and the required setting for connections across the Internet. *(Chapter 11)*

2.6   Identify classful IP (Internet Protocol) ranges and their subnet masks (For example: Class A, B and C). *(Chapter 11)*

2.7   Identify the purpose of subnetting. *(Chapter 11)*

2.8   Identify the differences between private and public network addressing schemes. *(Chapter 11)*

2.9   Identify and differentiate between the following IP (Internet Protocol) addressing methods:

Static *(Chapter 11)*
Dynamic *(Chapter 11)*
Self-assigned (APIPA (Automatic Private Internet Protocol Addressing)) *(Chapter 11)*

2.10 Define the purpose, function and use of the following protocols used in the TCP/IP (Transmission Control Protocol/Internet Protocol) suite:

TCP (Transmission Control Protocol) *(Chapters 8, 11, and 12)*

UDP (User Datagram Protocol) *(Chapters 8 and 11)*
FTP (File Transfer Protocol) *(Chapter 8)*
SFTP (Secure File Transfer Protocol) *(Chapter 8)*
TFTP (Trivial File Transfer Protocol) *(Chapter 8)*
SMTP (Simple Mail Transfer Protocol) *(Chapters 10 and 11)*
HTTP (Hypertext Transfer Protocol) *(Chapter 11)*
HTTPS (Hypertext Transfer Protocol Secure) *(Chapter 11)*
POP3/IMAP4 (Post Office Protocol version 3/Internet Message Access Protocol version 4)
  (Chapters 11 and 20)
Telnet *(Chapter 11)*
SSH (Secure Shell) *(Chapters 11 and 15)*
ICMP (Internet Control Message Protocol) *(Chapter 11)*
ARP/RARP (Address Resolution Protocol/Reverse Address Resolution Protocol)
  (Chapter 11)
NTP (Network Time Protocol) *(Chapter 11)*
NNTP (Network News Transport Protocol) *(Chapter 11)*
SCP (Secure Copy Protocol) *(Chapter 11)*
LDAP (Lightweight Directory Access Protocol) *(Chapter 2)*
IGMP (Internet Group Multicast Protocol) *(Chapter 11)*
LPR (Line Printer Remote) *(Chapter 14)*

2.11 Define the function of TCP/UDP (Transmission Control Protocol/User Datagram Protocol) ports. *(Chapters 8 and 11)*

2.12 Identify the well-known ports associated with the following commonly used services and protocols:

20 FTP (File Transfer Protocol) *(Chapter 8)*
21 FTP (File Transfer Protocol) *(Chapter 8)*
22 SSH (Secure Shell) *(Chapter 8)*
23 Telnet *(Chapter 8)*
25 SMTP (Simple Mail Transfer Protocol) *(Chapter 8)*
53 DNS (Domain Name Service) *(Chapter 8)*
69 TFTP (Trivial File Transfer Protocol) *(Chapter 8)*
80 HTTP (Hypertext Transfer Protocol) *(Chapter 8)*
110 POP3 (Post Office Protocol version 3) *(Chapter 8)*
119 NNTP (Network News Transport Protocol) *(Chapter 8)*
123 NTP (Network Time Protocol) *(Chapter 8)*
143 IMAP4 (Internet Message Access Protocol version 4) *(Chapter 8)*
443 HTTPS (Hypertext Transfer Protocol Secure) *(Chapter 8)*

2.13 Identify the purpose of network services and protocols (For example: DNS (Domain Name Service), NAT (Network Address Translation), ICS (Internet Connection Sharing), WINS (Windows Internet Name Service),

SNMP (Simple Network Management Protocol), NFS (Network File System), Zeroconf (Zero configuration), SMB (Server Message Block), AFP (Apple File Protocol), LPD (Line Printer Daemon) and Samba). *(Chapters 11 and 13)*

2.14 Identify the basic characteristics (For example: speed, capacity and media) of the following WAN (Wide Area Networks) technologies:

Packet switching *(Chapter 14)*
Circuit switching *(Chapter 14)*
ISDN (Integrated Services Digital Network) *(Chapter 14)*
FDDI (Fiber Distributed Data Interface) *(Chapter 14)*
T1 (T Carrier level 1)/E1/J1 *(Chapter 14)*
T3 (T Carrier level 3)/E3/J3 *(Chapter 14)*
OCx (Optical Carrier) *(Chapter 14)*
X.25 *(Chapter 14)*

2.15 Identify the basic characteristics of the following internet access technologies:

xDSL (Digital Subscriber Line) *(Chapter 14)*
Broadband Cable (Cable modem) *(Chapter 14)*
POTS/PSTN (Plain Old Telephone Service/Public Switched Telephone Network) *(Chapter 14)*
Satellite *(Chapter 14)*
Wireless *(Chapter 14)*

2.16 Define the function of the following remote access protocols and services:

RAS (Remote Access Service) *(Chapter 14)*
PPP (Point-to-Point Protocol) *(Chapters 6 and 14)*
SLIP (Serial Line Internet Protocol) *(Chapters 6 and 14)*
PPPoE (Point-to-Point Protocol over Ethernet) *(Chapter 14)*
PPTP (Point-to-Point Tunneling Protocol) *(Chapter 14)*
VPN (Virtual Private Network) *(Chapter 14)*
RDP (Remote Desktop Protocol) *(Chapter 14)*

2.17 Identify the following security protocols and describe their purpose and function:

IPSec (Internet Protocol Security) *(Chapter 15)*
L2TP (Layer 2 Tunneling Protocol)
SSL (Secure Sockets Layer) *(Chapter 15)*
WEP (Wired Equivalent Privacy) *(Chapter 15)*
WPA (Wi-Fi Protected Access) *(Chapter 15)*
802.1x *(Chapter 15)*

2.18 Identify authentication protocols (For example: CHAP (Challenge Handshake Authentication Protocol), MS-CHAP (Microsoft Challenge Handshake Authentication Protocol), PAP (Password Authentication Protocol), RADIUS (Remote Authentication Dial-In User Service), Kerberos and EAP (Extensible Authentication Protocol)). *(Chapter 14)*

DOMAIN 3.0: NETWORK IMPLEMENTATION – 25%

3.1 Identify the basic capabilities (For example: client support, interoperability, authentication, file and print services, application support and security) of the following server operating systems to access network resources:

UNIX/Linux/Mac OS X Server *(Chapter 2)*
Netware *(Chapter 2)*
Windows *(Chapter 2)*
Appleshare IP (Internet Protocol) *(Chapter 2)*

3.2 Identify the basic capabilities needed for client workstations to connect to and use network resources (For example: media, network protocols and peer and server services). *(Chapter 2)*

3.3 Identify the appropriate tool for a given wiring task (For example: wire crimper, media tester/certifier, punch down tool or tone generator). *(Chapters 3 and 19)*

3.4 Given a remote connectivity scenario comprised of a protocol, an authentication scheme, and physical connectivity, configure the connection. Includes connection to the following servers:

UNIX/Linux/MAC OS X Server *(Chapter 14)*
Netware *(Chapter 14)*
Windows *(Chapter 14)*
Appleshare IP (Internet Protocol) *(Chapter 14)*

3.5 Identify the purpose, benefits and characteristics of using a firewall. *(Chapter 15)*

3.6 Identify the purpose, benefits and characteristics of using a proxy service. *(Chapter 15)*

3.7 Given a connectivity scenario, determine the impact on network functionality of a particular security implementation (For example: port blocking/filtering, authentication and encryption). *(Chapters 7, 8, 9, 10, 15, and 17)*

3.8 Identify the main characteristics of VLANs (Virtual Local Area Networks). *(Chapter 15)*

3.9 Identify the main characteristics and purpose of extranets and intranets.

3.10 Identify the purpose, benefits and characteristics of using antivirus software. *(Chapters 16 and 18)*

3.11 Identify the purpose and characteristics of fault tolerance:
    Power *(Chapter 16)*
    Link redundancy *(Chapter 16)*
    Storage *(Chapter 16)*
    Services *(Chapter 16)*

3.12 Identify the purpose and characteristics of disaster recovery:
    Backup/restore *(Chapter 16)*
    Offsite storage *(Chapter 16)*
    Hot and cold spares *(Chapter 16)*
    Hot, warm and cold sites *(Chapter 16)*

DOMAIN 4.0: NETWORK SUPPORT – 35%

4.1 Given a troubleshooting scenario, select the appropriate network utility from the following:
    Tracert/traceroute *(Chapters 11 and 19)*
    ping *(Chapters 11 and 19)*
    arp *(Chapters 11 and 19)*
    netstat *(Chapters 11 and 19)*
    nbtstat *(Chapters 11 and 19)*
    ipconfig/ifconfig *(Chapters 11 and 19)*
    winipcfg *(Chapters 11 and 19)*
    nslookup/dig *(Chapters 11 and 19)*

4.2 Given output from a network diagnostic utility (For example: those utilities listed in objective 4.1), identify the utility and interpret the output. *(Chapters 12 and 19)*

4.3 Given a network scenario, interpret visual indicators (For example: link LEDs (Light Emitting Diode) and collision LEDs (Light Emitting Diode)) to determine the nature of a stated problem. *(Chapter 19)*

4.4 Given a troubleshooting scenario involving a client accessing remote network services, identify the cause of the problem (For example: file services, print services, authentication failure, protocol configuration, physical connectivity and SOHO (Small Office/Home Office) router). *(Chapters 2 and 19)*

4.5 Given a troubleshooting scenario between a client and the following server environments, identify the cause of a stated problem:

UNIX/Linux/Mac OS X Server *(Chapter 2)*
Netware *(Chapter 2)*
Windows *(Chapter 2 and Lab Manual)*
Appleshare IP (Internet Protocol) *(Chapters 2 and 13)*

4.6 Given a scenario, determine the impact of modifying, adding or removing network services (For example: DHCP (Dynamic Host Configuration Protocol), DNS (Domain Name Service) and WINS (Windows Internet Name Service)) for network resources and users. *(Chapters 12 and 19)*

4.7 Given a troubleshooting scenario involving a network with a particular physical topology (For example: bus, star, mesh or ring) and including a network diagram, identify the network area affected and the cause of the stated failure. *(Chapters 3 and 19)*

4.8 Given a network troubleshooting scenario involving an infrastructure (For example: wired or wireless) problem, identify the cause of a stated problem (For example: bad media, interference, network hardware or environment). *(Chapters 3 and 19)*

4.9 Given a network problem scenario, select an appropriate course of action based on a logical troubleshooting strategy. This strategy can include the following steps:

1. Identify the symptoms and potential causes *(Chapter 19)*
2. Identify the affected area *(Chapter 19)*
3. Establish what has changed *(Chapter 19)*
4. Select the most probable cause *(Chapter 19)*
5. Implement an action plan and solution including potential effects *(Chapter 19)*
6. Test the result *(Chapter 19)*
7. Identify the results and effects of the solution *(Chapter 19)*
8. Document the solution and process *(Chapter 19)*

PART ONE

An Introduction to Networking

CHAPTER 1

SOME RAW BASICS OF NETWORKING

Before I dive headfirst into the technologies of networking, it is probably a good idea to lay some basic groundwork. I'm going to be throwing around a lot of terms in this book that are fundamental to understanding the field of networking. In this chapter, in addition to some basic terminology, I'll be covering some concepts and taking a brief look at some hardware components used by networking professionals.

Some of the CompTIA exam goals that will be covered in this chapter include:

1.1 Recognize the following logical or physical network topologies given a diagram, schematic or description: Star, Bus, Mesh, Ring.

1.3 Specify characteristics (For example: speed, length, topology, and cable type) of cable standards.

1.4 Recognize media connectors and describe their uses.

1.6 Identify the purposes, features and functions of key network components.

GETTING DOWN TO THE BASICS

This is a book designed to prepare a person for professional certification as a network specialist. If you are just starting down this path and are seeing this material for the first time, or if you just need a little brushing up on the fundamentals, this chapter is for you. If you are already a working professional, and have been on the trail for a few years, you can skip all the basics and dive right into the fun stuff. If you happen to fall into that category, you might want to skip over to Chapter Two. On the other hand, a little review never hurt anyone.

WHY ARE WE BOTHERING WITH A NETWORK?

The simplest and most basic questions that need to be addressed are "What is a network?" and "What do I need with one?" The answer to the first question is actually pretty easy. Any time you create a connection between two computers that enables them to communicate, you have a network on its most rudimentary level. On a more advanced level, networks can and do span the globe. The Internet itself is nothing more than a very elaborate, albeit loosely configured, network.

As to why a person or organization needs a network—the answers to that can vary considerably. There are several situations that make a network appealing. And networks don't appeal only to business and larger organizations either. It has become increasingly common for families to accumulate multiple computers so that family members aren't always arguing over whose turn it is to play *The Sims*. Now that each family member has his or her own computer, you're all arguing over whose turn it is to use the Internet connection. Sound familiar? (I know it does for me!) This brings us to the many advantages of setting up a network.

COMMUNICATIONS

The Internet is only one of many forms of communication we all need to be able to share. Access to electronic mail and fax services ranks pretty high up there as well. We might as well face the facts; the days of jotting messages down on scraps of paper are reaching an end. Email has eliminated the necessity of delivering message by sneakernet, and in doing so it has enabled us to deliver the same message to as many people as we want as long as we know their email address.

Most companies sponsor some form of Intranet as well. Similar to the Internet, and structured in pretty much the same way, an Intranet provides the company an electronic company lounge, bulletin board, and conference room all rolled into one (**Figure 1.1**). Many companies even provide for electronic "classified ads" for their employees to use.

In theory, this technology is supposed to allow for the "paperless office." Cutting-edge technology means we will waste far less time sitting through endless meetings, and organizing our daily work will become infinitely easier.

That's the theory, anyway. However, we all know that paper production is the highest it has ever been. There's no sign that the weekly pep talks will ever go online, so we still have our meetings. As for our work? Perhaps that's one area in which we've seen some return on our investment in technology. The theory, however, is sound.

SHARING FILES

The primary reason most organizations maintain so many computers is so that all their precious information can be accurately maintained and instantly accessed. Of course, how often is it the case that just a single individual needs to access an information resource? Customer data files, employee information, and research and development are just a few resources that need to be kept available to a number of different people (see **Figure 1.2**).

Unfortunately, the practice of keeping multiple copies of the same file isn't very efficient, and more importantly, it isn't safe. Which version of the file is the most recent, and thereby the most accurate? A customer database spread out across multiple computers would wreak incredible havoc. Different records might have different addresses or phone numbers. Security is, at best, feeble. It is all too easy for a disgruntled employee to copy sensitive company data to floppy diskettes before making a departure.

If the database is maintained in a central location and access is shared out to those that need it, everybody sees the same data. If your network is set up for even a small degree of security, you can dictate who can and who can't see that data. (I'll be discussing security in Chapter Fifteen, *Working with Network Security.*) Who-

Figure 1.1 For the most part, networked computers eliminate the need for telepathy in the business environment. For instance, employees working in various parts of a building can be "invited" to the meeting on the top floor without the need for sending a runner.

ever does access a record will be seeing the most updated version. When a record is opened by one user, nobody else can get in. The other users are locked out of the record until the one who is using it finally closes it.

Figure 1.2   Frisbee®-net works for some folks, but most of us prefer the convenience of modern technology.

Group projects are made much easier when networked as well. A master copy of a document can be maintained in a central location while an editable copy is shared out to those working on the project. Editing marks and comments can be embedded in the document where they can be seen and commented on by all those involved. Coordination and efficiency are greatly improved.

SHARING PERIPHERALS

Wouldn't you just love it if your company put a printer on everybody's desk? Especially one of those slick new color lasers like the marketing department just got. You might love it, but would the boss? More importantly, would the accountants whose job it is to keep track of company finances like it?

What companies generally do is scatter a few printers here and there throughout the facility and share them out to the employees who need access. That is a much more efficient use of company resources and it gives people a chance to get up and stretch their legs once and a while.

The key phrase here is "those who need access." You might not want everybody to access the same printers. Color printers cost a lot more for each page of print than do laser printers. You might prefer to restrict use of the color printers to specific individuals and point everybody else at a monochrome printer. In some cases, you might have a security issue that makes you want to restrict printing altogether. The beauty of networking is that you can do this.

SECURITY

Several times in this chapter I've mentioned (or alluded to) security. A key concern of any network administrator is that of keeping the information on the network safe and secure. Sometimes it's easy to assume that just because a company is small, or that a computer only belongs to an individual, that security is not an issue. However, you can't deny the fact that attacks on your network come from individuals. Once an individual is inside your network, he or she has an excellent head start in piling on more and more damage.

Also, just because a company is small doesn't mean its information isn't just as valuable—to the owners of the company, anyway. How much damage can be done if a competitor gets hold of your bid specifications before you're even ready to release them? How about that new invention you have yet to secure a patent on?

> **EXAM NOTE:** Know the difference between physical security and network security. You can have all the network security you want, but if all your data is on removable hard disks that just anybody can walk out with—you have no security. Just ask the Pentagon.

A properly implemented network may not ensure that unauthorized people never get at your information. There have been plenty of recent examples to demonstrate that if hackers are good enough, and have the right incentive, they can find their way into your network. But a good security plan, properly implemented, can make it so hard that only the most dedicated hackers will even want to try.

SOFTWARE MANAGEMENT

A lot of people (and far too many books) overlook the importance of software management as a network function. However, a well-designed network makes the task of rolling out new applications and maintaining licensing information infinitely easier. Installing new programs on a number of users' computers is a lot easier if the particular program can be installed over the network onto the machines simultaneously. This reduces downtime for the computers and legwork for the individuals assigned to perform the rollout. A company-wide software installation that might take weeks by hand can be done in a day or two over the network.

Recently, a lot more emphasis has been placed on documenting companies' software licenses, and rightly so. Most Network Operating Systems (NOSs) provide some form of software license management in the form of a database. Maintaining software licenses is made much easier this way. As you roll out the applications over the network, you can record the licenses used in the license manager. Should your organization ever be audited for software licensing, you will have absolutely nothing to worry about.

SOME BASIC NETWORKING HARDWARE

Hopefully, it isn't going to come as much of a surprise that two devices on a network don't communicate telepathically. They actually need a little help from other devices. Now I'm going to give you a quick tour through some of the more commonly used networking devices. Most of these devices will be covered in more detail in later chapters, but I'd like to introduce them here so they will be familiar to you as I discuss them along the line.

TRANSCEIVERS

Each device on the network needs to be able to send and receive data. That much should be pretty obvious. A generic term for any device that interfaces another device to the network is a *transceiver*. The most familiar transceiver to most of us is the *network interface card* (NIC) (**Figure 1.3**). Any computer on the network needs one of these little toys. For most of us, it comes as a separate expansion card that will need to be installed and configured. Some computers have an NIC built onto the motherboard. You have to make sure that your NIC supports the hardware protocols and topology of your network.

It isn't just computers that use NICs, either. Most printer manufacturers provide some form of network interface device for their products as well. On some of the high-end products, a network interface is built in. For others, a separate device needs to be purchased. Sometimes these are installed inside the printer, making it a network device. Other times, it is an external device to which the printer attaches. Some of Hewlett Packard's JetDirect devices are examples of the later (**Figure 1.4**).

REPEATERS

Network signals move, for the most part, over physical media. The nature of the media dictates that the signal can only go so far before it becomes unusable. Each form of medium has its own distinct characteristics in this respect, and I'll discuss those limitations in Chapter Three.

Repeaters are relatively inexpensive devices that allow you to work with distances beyond those limitations. Repeaters come in two forms. On the simplest

Figure 1.3 The Network Interface Card is one of the most common devices you'll deal with as a network administrator.

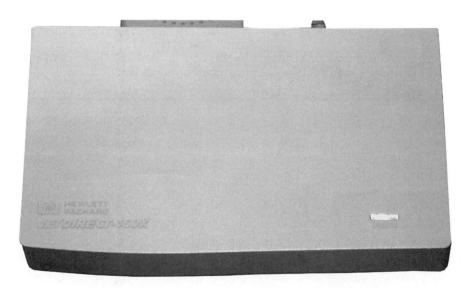

Figure 1.4 HP's JetDirect is a good example of an external transceiver that interfaces a printer to the network.

level, you can purchase a box into which a network cable is plugged. You plug a second cable into the output port and keep on moving. The repeater works by taking the incoming signal, cleaning up any noise, interference, or distortion it may have picked up along the way, amplifying the signal to its original strength, and sending it on its way. The second form of repeater is a kind of hub, and that is covered in the next section.

HUBS

The hub is the central point for a typical star network using Ethernet. The simplest hubs aren't very complex devices. They consist of a box with a collection of interfaces that network cables can plug into. Any signal that comes into any port is transmitted out all ports—including the one the signal came in on. Hubs do nothing to process information.

Hubs can be either *active* or *passive*. A passive hub is the simplest and least expensive. Any incoming signal simply comes into the hub by way of one port and then moves on along through all ports. Active hubs clean up and amplify the signal before they send it on its way. They function as a kind of repeater and are the second form to which I alluded in that discussion.

SWITCHES

On the surface, switches don't look that much different than hubs. Physically, they're not. Electronically, however, they are much more sophisticated devices. As I mentioned earlier, a hub simply broadcasts every packet it hears out of every available port. Switches can examine the contents of the data being transmitted, and based on certain information contained in each packet, send that packet out the port that hosts the device for which the packet is intended. As you might imagine, that extra little service can greatly reduce extraneous network traffic.

BRIDGES

The network bridge doesn't get used as often in networking as it used to, but when a bridge is needed, nothing else will work. An ideal network would consist of only a single computer platform (i.e., PC or Macintosh), a single topology (Ethernet or Token Ring), or a single NOS (Windows 2000 Server or NetWare). Unfortunately, this isn't always the case. The engineering and marketing departments might be equipped with Macs, while the rest of the company is set up with PCs. There might be one or two classrooms still on a Token Ring network, but for the most part, the school is Ethernet. And there are many reasons why a network might be a mix of NOSs.

A bridge allows the network administrator to interconnect two disparate segments so transparently that the end user never knows there's a difference. While its function is complex enough to merit a separate discussion later on (see Chapter Six, The Data Link Layer) it is enough for now to simply say that the device opens the data packages created by one protocol and repackages them for the receiving protocol.

ROUTERS

Until now, all the devices I've discussed become part of a single network once they are installed. However, there comes a time when you will need to get two different networks to talk to each other. Organizations that have offices in different cities need to link those offices together. Large corporations frequently organize their IT infrastructure into smaller networks for reasons of security and manageability and then interconnect those small networks. The Internet is nothing more than that: a vast empire of linked networks.

The *router* is the key to making this happen. Routers have multiple ports the same way switches and hubs have. Unlike the other devices, however, the router will most likely have several different types of ports. Some will be serial ports, others will have the port native to the internal network, and then there will usually be some way of hooking the router to the telecommunications system. I'll discuss those in more detail in Chapter Seven, The Network Layer.

It isn't the different ports that make the router special, though. It's the fact that each one of these ports can be configured to a unique network address and data can be sent back and forth over the various ports based on what network that information is intended for. Thus, two different networks are connected.

BROUTER

Many bridges have configurable interfaces. Therefore, they perform the functions of both bridges and routers. The term coined for these devices is *brouter*. To accomplish this dual functionality, each interface needs to be configurable not just for a separate network address, but for different protocols as well. As it turns out, most high-end routers possess this split personality these days, and the term isn't bandied about as much. Still, it is a technically correct and occasionally used term.

CSU/DSU

In order to connect most conventional networks to a communications carrier, a device known as a *channel service unit/data service unit* (CSU/DSU) is used. From the network engineer's standpoint, this is a device that is usually provided and maintained by your service provider and therefore will receive only a brief mention.

The CSU is responsible for data and circuit protection as well as for performing diagnostics on the line when needed. It transmits and receives the signals from the communications line and filters interference as well. The DSU acts essentially like a digital modem. It provides the data link to the digital line. Its responsibilities include error management and signal regeneration.

> **EXAM NOTE:** It is critical that you be able to describe the function of each piece of equipment discussed in this section. Later on in the book, I'll be discussing in which of the OSI layers these devices function. You'll want to know that as well.

THE BASIC CONCEPTS OF NETWORKING

Earlier in this chapter, I defined a network as being, on its simplest level, any two computers that can talk to each other. Getting those computers to talk is what this book is all about. There are a few fundamental issues that need to be embedded in your psyche, and some words that need to be a basic part of your vocabulary, before I even begin delving into the technology. So let's get those out of the way right now.

To begin with, you'll need to know what is involved in interconnecting multiple computers. In addition to understanding how they connect, you'll need to understand how information moves from one machine to another. Also, different types of computers speak different languages and follow different rules. You need to get them to agree on how they're going to communicate once you've got them hooked up.

Network structure can be broken down into four basic components. These are the *media*, the *topology*, the *protocols*, and the *standards*. On the physical side, I will be discussing at great length the types of *media* over which signals will be transmitted and the network *topology*, which is the physical or logical structure. I'll explain that distinction in a bit. The software end of networking can be broken down into protocols and standards. *Protocols* define the language of the network as well as the rules that it will follow. The *standards* are the rules that software and hardware engineers must follow when designing their products. Without standards, this would be a very messy industry indeed!

MEDIA

While all of the following material will be discussed in great detail in the following chapters, there are a few basic concepts and terms that I'll need to be able to throw around; therefore, I'll introduce these here, but I'm going to keep it very simple.

> **EXAM NOTE:** Be able to distinguish between bounded and unbounded media types.

BUZZ WORDS

Twisted-Pair: Wire that consists of multiple strands of wire. Strands are separated into pairs that are twisted together to eliminate crosstalk.

Crosstalk: The migration of signal from one wire to another in adjacent conductors.

Media can be broken down into *bounded* and *unbounded* types. Unbounded media includes various technologies, such as radio waves, light pulses, and microwave, that allow signals to travel through the air. The bounded media are those that directly and physically interconnect devices, and consist of copper and/or fiber-optic connectors. The most common form of copper cabling in use today is one of the several types of *twisted-pair* (see **Figure 1.5**) cable currently available on the market. The term is derived from the basic design of the cable. Twisted-pair cable consists of eight strands of wire separated into four pairs. Each pair is twisted together. The reason for the twists is to reduce *crosstalk*. Crosstalk is a phenomenon that occurs any time two or more signal conductors share the same physical space, even if they are independently insulated. Some of the signal from one wire leaks over into the other wire and vice versa. Twisting the conductors reduces this tendency. The greater the twist in a given length of wire, the greater the reduction in crosstalk.

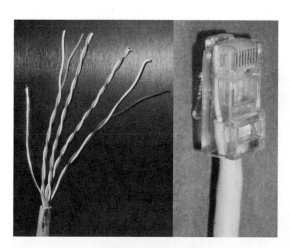

Figure 1.5 The copper cable most commonly used by network engineers is the twisted pair. It is clearly distinguishable by the RJ-45 connector, which resembles a telephone connector.

Generally, a connector called the *RJ-45* terminates twisted-pair cable. The RJ-45 is an 8-pronged clip that looks similar to the one on the end of your telephone cord. The one on the telephone cord is called an RJ-11. RJ stands for *registered jack* and is used in the communications industry to indicate that a particular connector was approved for use under the regulations set forth by *Federal Standard 1037C.*

Another form of copper cabling that is still covered under the Network+ exam, although you don't see it as much in the real world these days, is *coaxial cabling.* The term coaxial refers to the fact that the signal and the ground share the same axis. Your cable TV uses coaxial cabling, although it doesn't use the same grade of cable.

Coaxial cable terminates in a BNC connector. While some sources insist BNC stands for either *British Naval connector* or *banana nut connector,* it actually stands for *Bayonet Neill-Concelman.* Other little parts used exclusively by coaxial media include *T-connectors* and *coaxial terminators.* T-connectors merge two separate coaxial cables into a single output (see **Figure 1.6**). Coaxial terminators are resistors that must be installed on either end of any network wired with coaxial cable. I'll show how all of these are useful in Chapter Three, The Highways and Byways of the Network.

Fiber optics is another stranded medium that is used rather extensively in modern networks. Unlike the bounded media that I've discussed so far, fiber optics doesn't use strands of copper to conduct the signal. Instead, pulses of light

Figure 1.6 The BNC shown in this T-connector is the connector most commonly associated with coaxial cable.

travel over strands of optically clear glass or plastic. This strategy has the advantages of higher speed potentials and greater security. It's faster because pulses of light can be modulated faster than pulses of electric current, along with other reasons I will discuss further in Chapter Three. It is more secure because, in order to tap a signal traveling over fiber optics, a hacker would actually have to cut into the cable. In order to do this he would need to bring that particular segment of the network down. If you had not voluntarily brought it down for some reason, cutting the cable is going to bring it crashing down. People have a tendency to notice that sort of thing.

Unbounded media do not make use of physical conductors to carry the signal. Instead, the transceivers take advantage of the characteristics of different forms of energy to carry the encoded signal. These forms include infrared light, laser beams, radio waves, and microwave transmissions.

NETWORK TOPOLOGIES

The network topology, as I've mentioned, is the way that the network is laid out. Fundamentally, there are really only four topologies to discuss. In practice, however, you will find that many networks are *hybrids* that incorporate two or even all four of the redundant basic topologies.

The big four are the bus network, the ring network, the star network and the mesh network. These topologies differ not only in their outward physical appearance, but also in how they carry their signals. The Institute of Electrical and Electronic Engineers (IEEE, commonly referred to as I-triple-E) got together in February of 1980 and defined the conventional network topologies. It also set up committees to keep these standards, as well as some of the hardware protocols, which I'll discuss a little later, up to date. This became known as the 802 Project simply because it was initiated in the second month of 1980.

BUS NETWORKS

The bus network has undoubtedly been around longer than any other type. The attraction of the bus network is its simplicity. They're a piece of cake to set up. The disadvantage is that they're very difficult to manage. Remember that string of Christmas tree lights you had as a kid? The one where, when one bulb went, the whole

BUZZ WORD ————

Topology: Physical or logical configuration. For example, the topology of a network shows the pattern in which the computers are interconnected. Common network topologies are the star, bus, and ring.

THE IEEE 802 SUBCOMMITTEES

The IEEE 802 standards came about in 1980 as a result of the 802 Project. In that historical meeting IEEE established the committees that would define networking as we know it. In order to pass the Network+ exam, it is essential that you be able to list of these committees as well as the technologies they oversee. You will see questions that require you to know what committee works on what standards.

Most of the books I've read suggest that the 802 Project was a one-time event and afterwards all these committees went off on their merry way to do their own thing. This couldn't be more incorrect. The 802 Group meets on a regular basis, and new committees continue to be added, while those committees in charge of obsolete technologies are put on hiatus, or, if they are really obsolete, disbanded.

802.0 SEC

802.1 High Level Interface (HILI) Working Group (Frequently called the Internetworking Standards)

802.2 Logical Link Control (LLC) Working Group

802.3 CSMA/CD Working Group (Frequently called the Ethernet Standards)

802.4 Token Bus Working Group (currently on permanent hiatus)

802.5 Token Ring Working Group (currently on permanent hiatus)

---

string went down? That's the way a bus network is. If, for example, one workstation is accidentally disconnected from the network, the whole network goes down.

Bus networks still show up from time to time, however, and you need to know how to deal with them. Since a bus is so easy to install, it might be a reasonable choice for a small office or home network with only a few computers. So a few basic concepts need to be discussed.

BUZZ WORD

Bus: In general terms, a bus is simply the path data takes to move from one location to another. In network topology, it refers to a layout that connects all devices in line with one another.

Both ends of the network have to be terminated. This is done with small resistors that have been encapsulated into BNC-terminated cylinders that can be hooked onto the end of a coaxial patch cord or one end of a T-connector. Lose the

802.6 Metropolitan Area Network (MAN) Working Group (currently on permanent hiatus)

802.7 Broadband Technical Adv. Group (BBTAG)

802.8 Fiber Optics Technical Adv. Group (FOTAG) (permanently disbanded)

802.9 Integrated Services LAN (ISLAN) Working Group (currently on permanent hiatus)

802.10 Standard for Interoperable LAN Security (SILS) Working Group

801.11 Wireless LAN (WLAN) Working Group

802.12 Demand Priority Working Group (currently on permanent hiatus)

802.14 Cable-TV Based Broadband Communication Network Working Group (permanently disbanded)

802.15 Wireless Personal Area Network (WPAN) Working Group

802.16 Broadband Wireless Access (BBWA) Working Group

802.17 RPRSG Resilient Packet Ring Study Group (RPRSG)

On another note, the committees currently listed as *on permanent hiatus* continue to exist and are assigned chairpersons to maintain and oversee the groups. These groups all published standards and continue to oversee those standards. Should any of these technologies return to the spotlight, IEEE will be ready to roll. Those listed as *permanently disbanded* are no longer considered functional and in fact never published standards.

termination, and you lose the network. In **Figure 1.7**, therefore, the devices on either end of the network would have to have terminating resistors plugged into the outbound port of their T-connectors. If the resistor is knocked off, your network goes down.

The bus topology is far from dead, however. In addition to tiny office and home networks, it also might be considered a useful method for interconnecting segments on a larger network.

RING NETWORKS

The ring network is a topology that is enjoying a resurrection (see **Figure 1.8**). It used to be very popular as the foundation for a technology called *Token Ring*, which has fallen from favor despite efforts by IBM to keep it alive. But don't ignore the

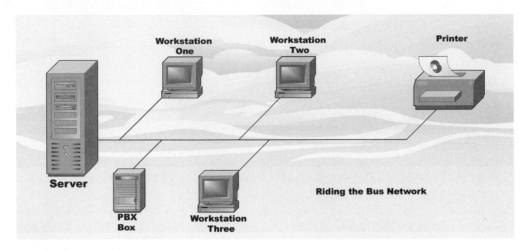

Figure 1.7 The bus network is pretty much a dying technology. It isn't very popular for a couple of reasons. For one, it uses coaxial cable. Not only is this cable more difficult to work with, it's also more expensive, and it's limited to a maximum bandwidth of 10Mb/s. The combined factors of inconvenience, high cost, and low speed have resulted in the medium being practically abandoned.

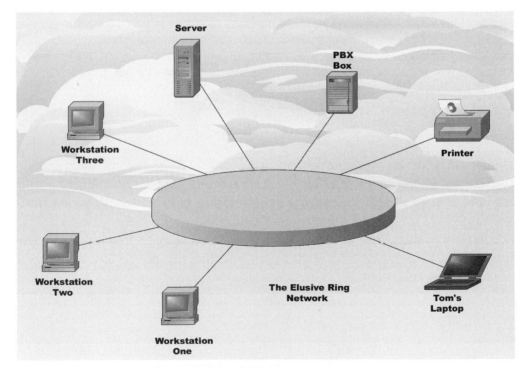

Figure 1.8 Conceptual diagram of a ring network

IS IT A RING OR IS IT A STAR?

While the ring network is conceptually a circle of computers and other devices endlessly circling data around and around, on a structural level it looks more like the star topology that I'll discuss next. The *multistation access unit* (MAU) used by Token Ring looks, feels, smells, and tastes just like a standard hub with only a few minor cosmetic differences. Internally, however, the device is wired in such a way that it keeps the structure of the ring intact. You run a patch cable from the device to the MAU just as you would to a hub. The MAU keeps the data moving in a ring-around-the-rosey fashion.

ring topology. An emerging technology, the *Fiber Distributed Data Interface* (FDDI), takes the concepts of the ring network as well as token passing to the next level (these different technologies will be discussed in detail later in the book). Another very good reason for being familiar with the ring network is that you will be asked about it on the Network+ Exam.

Token Ring networks are logical rings and not physical ones. In actual implementation, the network is interconnected by *multistation access units* (MAU) devices. They look, feel, smell, and taste just like typical hubs in most respects. A cable runs from the computer to the MAU, just like it would to a hub. Internally, however, the MAU is wired in a ring. The circuitry of an MAU can detect when a computer goes offline and redirect the signal around the port that went down. Also, MAUs have two additional ports on the back: a *ring-in* and a *ring-out*. These aren't for hooking up telephones; they are the input and output connectors for interconnecting MAUs. They allow the network to be expanded without losing the logic of the ring.

STAR NETWORKS

The star network is the topology you're going to run into most frequently in the real world. **Figure 1.9** shows a star network on its simplest level. Several computers or other devices interconnect to one another over a hub. Simple but elegant. What makes the star such a beautiful concept is that it is modular. Networks can be made as big and complex as you want—or can afford—simply by piling on more network segments and hooking them up with the right gear.

Most administrators prefer a star for its ease of administration as well. It lends itself very well to centralized network administration. Servers, hubs, routers, and such can be located in a single server closet where everything can be tweaked, administered, or nursed back to health in one place. Or, for security purposes,

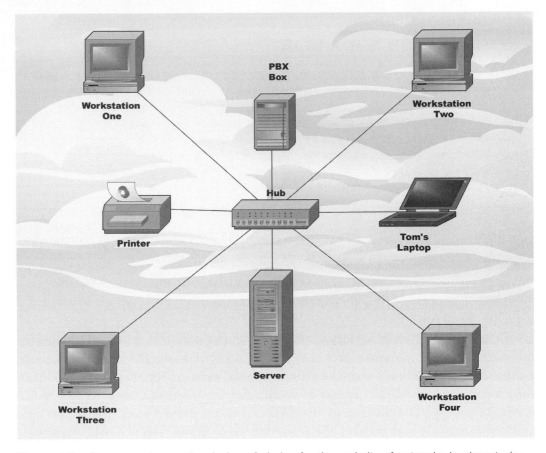

Figure 1.9 Star networks are the design of choice for the majority of networks in place today.

several similar server closets can be scattered across the site. This greatly eases the administration burden of larger networks. For the most part, troubleshooting is simplified as well.

If there is any disadvantage at all, it is that star networks require a very complex cabling scheme. Each workstation or other networked device needs its own "umbilical cord" to connect it to the network. This may be a simple patch cord going to a jack on the wall or a dedicated cable running all the way to the hub or switch to which it is attached. Furthermore, all of the hubs, switches, routers, and other devices need to be interconnected. As the network administrator, it's your job to keep track of it all! Do yourself a favor and start maintaining a good set of network documentation from the outset. I'll be covering those principles in Chapter Eighteen, Network Documentation and Scheduled Maintenance.

MESH NETWORKS

Logically, the mesh is a network in which every single device directly connects with every other device on the network (**Figure 1.10**). As you might imagine, this architecture is rarely (if ever) implemented throughout the network. The mesh can be either a full mesh or a partial mesh. The full mesh is where everybody talks to everybody. In the partial mesh, there are a few nodes that connect to all others, but the majority of connections interact with only a few. The mesh is used predominately to interconnect the backbones of most networks and not the individual nodes.

HYBRID NETWORKS

As networks get larger and more complex, sometimes maintaining a single topology isn't as easy as it sounds. At times, it's downright impossible. Therefore, be prepared to see networks that consist of a mixture of different topologies. Some common mixes of the past were to have a few star networks hooked together over a bus. As

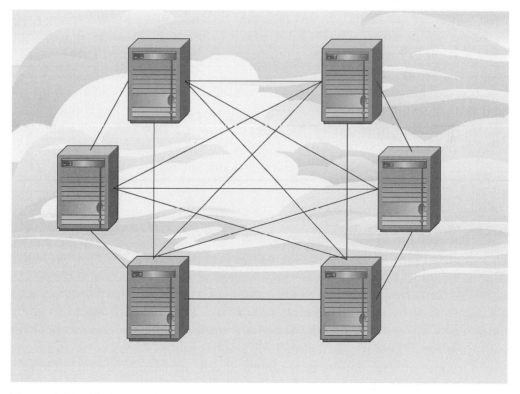

Figure 1.10   Mesh networks are complex and difficult to both configure and maintain.

you might imagine, this was called the *star-bus* network. Another common mix, especially with school districts, was the *ring-bus.* Individual classrooms were hooked up in a Token Ring network, and then the classrooms were linked over a bus. With FDDI being a ring-structured network, I think we might see a resurgence of this particular hybrid.

> **EXAM NOTE:** Know your network topologies inside and out. You might get those thrown at you several times in several different ways.

THE HARDWARE PROTOCOLS

Earlier in the chapter, I said there were both hardware and software protocols. Software protocols define methods by which applications running on the network—or even the protocols themselves—exchange data among themselves over a network. Hardware protocols define how the devices themselves put data onto the network.

Sometimes even professionals get so tied up in their discussions that they confuse the topology with the protocol. When they discuss whether they have a Token Ring network or an Ethernet network, they're actually discussing the protocols the network follows. While it's true that it's a bit problematic to try to imagine a Token Ring network on a star configuration, it's important to stop short of discounting mixing Token Ring with a bus network. They actually did define a token bus and assigned it to the 802.4 Committee. Nobody ever did anything with it and the committee has been in hibernation for years, but it was defined. These days, the hardware protocols in use are primarily *Carrier Sense, Multiple Access/ Collision Detection* (CSMA/CD), and *Fiber Distributed Data Interface* (FDDI). Token Ring isn't used much these days, but since it is covered on the exam, I'll provide a look at that protocol as well.

CSMA/CD

The Ethernet in use today isn't really Ethernet. But I'll get to that. The technology got its roots back in 1972 at Xerox Corporation when David Boggs and Robert Metcalfe figured out a way for more than one device to send signals across the same wire without getting in each other's way. Together with Intel and Digital Equipment Corporation, they developed a proprietary networking protocol they called Ethernet. These standards (the DIX Standards, for Digital, Intel, and Xerox) defined a network that used coaxial cable and sent signals across that cable using CSMA/CD as a media access method at a speed of 10Mb/s.

> **EXAM NOTE:** You'll want to be able to describe CMSA/CD pretty thoroughly before you go in to take your exam. They have several different ways of having you describe this technology.

Ethernet, as it currently exists, has changed quite a bit since then. IEEE expanded on the DIX specifications and gave us the 802.3 standards of CMSA/CD. (Since everybody else incorrectly calls the 802.3 standards Ethernet, I might as well go ahead and use that term from here on out as well.) It provided specifications for moving data across both twisted-pair cable and coaxial cable, and it also defined the terminators used today. Later revisions of Ethernet include Fast Ethernet, which is a 100Mb/s system, and Gigabit Ethernet, a 1000Mb/s standard.

I mentioned earlier that 802.3 defined CSMA/CD. It's easier to understand what that means if you take the acronym apart. CS stands for Carrier Sense. Devices that wish to access the wire "listen" to the media and "sense" when it is safe to transmit. When it seems to be safe, the device throws a frame of data onto the wire. A frame consists of the data being sent by the transmitting device (or just as likely, a small portion of that data) along with certain control information added into header and trailer fields that are tacked onto that data. MA stands for Multiple Access, which is the goal of the protocol. CD is good old Collision Detection. The developers of the protocol realized that two devices would attempt to access the wire at the same time. The result of an event like this would be for the electrical signals of each device to blend in with each other, making both signals useless. These are called *collisions*. The protocol is designed to detect collisions and force the devices to resend their data.

There have actually been four frame structures defined for Ethernet. Only two are in common use today. These are the 802.2 and the 802.3 frames. The 802.2 frame (or Ethernet II, as it is sometimes called) was the first structure developed to move over an Ethernet network. It is one of the simpler frames in use. It consists of an 8-byte preamble, 6 bytes each for destination and source addresses, a 2-byte field that identifies the frame type, the payload (which can range from 46 bytes to 1,500 bytes), and finally, a frame check sequence field that holds error correction data. (See **Figure 1.11**.)

The 802.3 frame is structurally very similar and is the one used by default in most operating systems. In 802.3, the frame *type* field is replaced with a frame *length* field (see **Figure 1.12**). In order to prevent two devices from exchanging unlike frame types (hence corrupting the data), the first two bytes of an 802.3 frame consists of all 1s. This makes no sense to the 802.2 devices, and the two won't communicate.

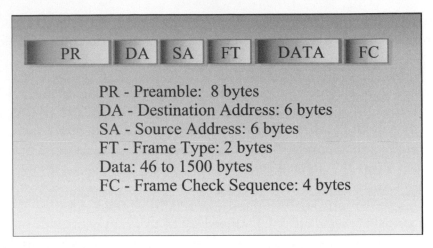

Figure 1.11 The basic structure of an Ethernet 802.2 frame.

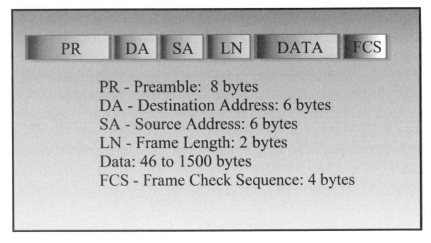

Figure 1.12 The basic structure of an Ethernet 802.3 frame.

CSMA/CD is what is known as *contention-based* access. Another word you might see to describe this access method is *probabilistic*. Devices are contending with each other for time on the wire. And, as happens on any busy freeway, there are going to be collisions. But for the most part, the data is probably going to get there (hence the term "probabilistic"). If a collision occurs, the data is simply sent again. For the most part, it works pretty well. However, as networks grow in size, the frequency of collisions increases. All that resending of data can bring a network down to a crawl. Therefore, network administrators are constantly looking for ways to isolate traffic. I'll be looking at some of these methods in later chapters.

Ethernet networks can be set up in either a bus network or a star network. However, primarily because of the speed limitations of the bus network, most contemporary Ethernet networks are set up in a star. The equipment for setting up a simple hub-centric network has gotten to be so inexpensive that even a family's household budget won't be too stretched by going in that direction.

FDDI

Fiber Distributed Data Interface represents the next step in evolution for a token-passing protocol. It uses a token-passing deterministic approach to media access the same way Token Ring did. FDDI differs, however, in its use of a dual-ring topology. Data travels in one direction along a primary ring. Should that ring fail, a secondary ring exists as a backup. While FDDI was designed to use fiber optics as the transmission medium, a similar technology known as the *Copper Distributed Data Interface* (CDDI) uses copper wire.

That secondary ring is actually an option, not a requirement, however. Stations on an FDDI network can be either *dual-attached* or *single-attached* stations. A dual-attached station is connected to both rings, while a single-attached station is connected only to the primary ring.

Dual-attached stations will be connected to the network via at least one A port, where they attach to the primary ring, and one B port, where they attach to the secondary ring. They may or may not also have one or more M ports installed. The M port is the port that a single-station unit uses to attach to the network. It hooks up only to the primary ring.

TOKEN RING

Token Ring was the brainchild of IBM. In contrast to Ethernet, the goal of Token Ring is to prevent collisions from happening. It did so by sending a chunk of data called the token around the network. The only time a computer could transmit was when it had the token. While there are some minor differences that are not even worth discussing, standards presented by the IEEE 802.5 committee differ little from those of IBM.

The big word I used for Ethernet was probabilistic. The Token Ring method of media access is said to be a *deterministic* approach. As I said earlier, a small packet of data—the token—passes from computer to computer. In order for a computer to transmit data, it must have possession of the token. So where does that token come from? On a Token Ring network, the first computer to come on during the day becomes the *active monitor*. This is the computer that generates the first token

25

and any subsequent tokens that might need to be created further on down the line, should the original token be lost or discarded. At any given time, however, there will be only a single token on any subnet.

The token itself is three bytes wide and consists of a *start delimiter,* an *access control byte,* and an *end delimiter* (see **Figure 1.13**). Each of these is one byte wide. The start delimiter simply notifies the receiving station that it is receiving the token. The access control byte actually performs four different functions. The most significant three bits comprise the *priority field,* while the least significant three bits make up the *reservation field.* In between these two fields are the *token bit* and the *monitor bit.* The purpose of the monitor bit is to let the active monitor know if the token has gotten lost and is simply circling the network over and over again without ever picking up any data. This would be a bad thing.

Data itself moves on *data-command frames.* The information carried by this frame dictates its overall size, and that, in turn, is dictated by the token holding time allocated by the network. Data-command fields are divided up into nine segments (see **Figure 1.14**). As with the token itself, there are start and end delimiters and an access control byte. These are identical to those contained by the token. In addition, there is a *frame control byte,* which dictates whether the frame is carrying data or control information, the *destination* and *source addresses,* a *frame check sequence,* which acts as an error control mechanism, and a *frame status field.* This latter simply terminates the frame. And then, of course, there is the data or control information itself. No point in having a frame if you're not sending something.

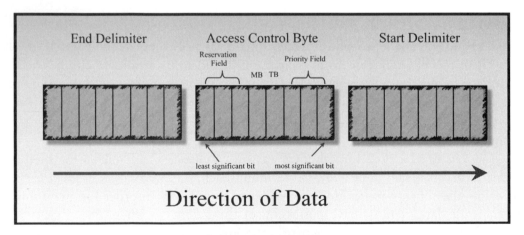

Figure 1.13   The token used by a Token Ring network is actually only three bytes long.

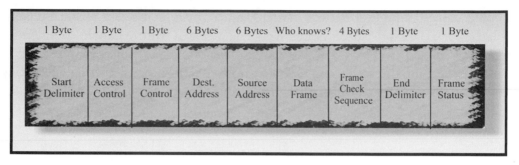

1 Byte	1 Byte	1 Byte	6 Bytes	6 Bytes	Who knows?	4 Bytes	1 Byte	1 Byte
Start Delimiter	Access Control	Frame Control	Dest. Address	Source Address	Data Frame	Frame Check Sequence	End Delimiter	Frame Status

Figure 1.14 The actual data frame carried on a Token Ring network can be divided into nine precisely defined segments.

Token Ring has several built-in mechanisms for detecting and correcting certain errors. One thing that's already been mentioned is a perpetually busy token. This can happen when a computer on the network fails unexpectedly. One of the other tasks of the active monitor is to pick up on the endlessly circling token, take it off the network, and generate a fresh token.

There is also another function that can be initiated by any computer on a Token Ring network called *beaconing*. Any computer that fails to receive the token can send a *beacon frame* to both its nearest upstream neighbor and its nearest downstream neighbor, which in turn send one to their neighbors, and so on and so on. As this process suggests, a device will be queried by its neighbors even after having initiated the previous query. This beacon frame is basically asking, "Are you hogging the token?" During this beaconing process, each device is communicating with each of its adjacent neighbors.

In reality, data moves only in one direction along the ring. The idea is that if each device sends directed query to each of its neighbors, eventually there will be two different devices getting a negative response from the same address. If the MAU determines that a computer has been taken off the network, it can bypass that station and reconfigure the network.

With all it had going for it, you'd almost have to think that Token Ring would have been the protocol of choice for any sensible network administrator. Unfortunately, all these little tricks the protocol had been taught extracted a price in performance. In the days of 10Mb/s Ethernet, there was the 4Mb/s Token Ring. Token Ring made the jump to 16Mb/s, but was almost instantly leapfrogged by Ethernet as it moved to 100Mb/s. The High Speed Token Ring Alliance was established and responded with a 100Mb/s Token Ring, but it was too little, too late. The Gigabit Ethernet was already available.

Will Token Ring ever return? Perhaps, but right now it seems rather unlikely. By late 1999, the High Speed Token Ring Alliance was whittled down to just three members. Shortly after that, IBM, the originator of Token Ring, began pulling in its sails. Some of the IBM plants have already begun pulling their Token Ring networks and replacing them with high-speed Ethernet. Offhand, I'd have to say that wasn't a good sign.

NETWORKING STANDARDS

In the very early days of developing networking technologies, the companies involved realized that unless there were certain rules and processes that everybody agreed upon and followed, chaos would result. As a result, several organizations either stepped up to the plate, or were created, that assumed the role of creating standards for the industry. Throughout this book I will be referring to different organizations and the role they play in keeping the networking industry as orderly as it is. But I would like to introduce a few of the key players right now.

The *Institute of Electrical and Electronic Engineers* (IEEE) has played a crucial role in setting the standards that companies follow when developing their products or new technologies. IEEE established and continues to oversee the different committees that study and ratify different networking standards.

The *Electronic Industries Alliance/Telecommunications Industries Association* (EIA/TIA) is involved in cabling standards as well. They were the ones who decided what order the different colored strands of wire in twisted-pair cabling should run. They also defined the colors to be used.

The *Industry Standards Organization* (ISO) is involved in many fields other than computing. Still, the role it has played in our industry cannot be overlooked. It was ISO that developed the basic network model called the *Open Systems Interconnect* (OSI, see Chapter Four, Welcome to OSI) that is used today. It also standardized many of the cables used every day.

The *American National Standards Institute* (ANSI) was involved early on in standardizing character sets and control code.

A group you don't hear a lot about is the one that keeps the Internet running, stable, and as secure as it can be. That is the *Internet Engineering Task Force* (IETF). IETF maintains teams of engineers that monitor the Internet backbone for problems. And when a major security issue occurs, such as a globally active virus, it has teams to track down and isolate the virus and to track down and prosecute the individual that propagated it.

While there are literally hundreds of others, the last one I'll discuss here is the *Internet Network Information Center* (InterNIC). This may well be one of the most powerful organizations to be discussed here. It assigns domain names and IP addresses for use on the Internet. It also retains the right to revoke a domain name if it is found to infringe on another company or individual's rights.

As I said earlier, this only represents a smattering of all the different organizations involved. However, these are the ones you are likely to encounter on a regular basis. Be thankful they exist. Without them, this would be a very chaotic industry.

CHAPTER SUMMARY

By the time you're finished with this chapter you should have a pretty good grasp of much of the basic vocabulary I'll be using throughout the book. But don't get too excited. Each chapter is going to throw many more new terms and concepts your way. You'll also know what I'm talking about when I discuss the different topologies and when and how they are used. The basic hardware used in a network got introduced in this chapter as well, although there is plenty more to be discussed in later chapters as well.

BRAIN DRAIN

1. In your own words, describe a bus network in detail, including its advantages, disadvantages, and limitations.

2. List at least five reasons for wanting to set up a network.

3. Why would I describe Token Ring as being logically a ring, but physically a star?

4. Describe how a device would get onto the network using CSMA/CD.

5. Discuss why segmenting a network using switches is superior to using hubs.

THE 64K$ QUESTIONS

1. Which device would be used to connect our Cleveland office with our Chicago office? Each office is on its own LAN.

   a. A switch

   b. An active hub

    c. A router

    d. A repeater

2. CSMA/CD stands for _____.

    a. Carrier Sense, Multiple Access/Concentrated Data

    b. Carrier Signal, Multiple Access/Collision Detection

    c. Carrier Sense, Multiple Access/Collision Distribution

    d. Carrier Sense, Multiple Access/Collision Detection

3. The most commonly used network technology that uses CSMA/CD is _____.

    a. Ethernet

    b. Token Ring

    c. FDDI

    d. ATSM

4. Which of the following devices keeps all devices downstream of each of its ports on a separate collision domain, but on the same broadcast domain?

    a. A hub

    b. A switch

    c. A router

    d. A brouter

5. BNC Stands for _____.

    a. Bayonet Nut Connector

    b. British Naval Connector

    c. Bayonet Neil Connector

    e. Bayonet Neil-Concelman

6. Which of the following represents a device on an FDDI network? (Choose all that apply).

    a. Active monitor

    b. Dual-attached station

    c. Browse master

    d. Single-attached station

7. What technology is used by Token Ring to detect which station on the network has gone down?

    a. CSMA/CD

    b. Beaconing

   c. Token bouncing

   d. Signal reflections

8. On a Token Ring network, which computer will be selected as the active monitor?

   a. The server

   b. The machine with the fastest CPU

   c. The machine with the most RAM

   d. The first station to come onto the network

9. Which Ethernet frame is most commonly used today?

   a. 802.2

   b. 802.3

   c. SNAP

   d. Ethernet II

10. Which device listed below can be used to interconnect two or more different networks?

   a. A hub

   b. A repeater

   c. A switch

   d. A router

11. You have four servers that you wish to configure into a single cluster. Which network topology is most suitable for this purpose?

   a. Ring

   b. Star

   c. Mesh

   d. Hybrid

12. Which of the following is an example of unbounded media?

   a. Unshielded twisted pair

   b. Coaxial

   c. Fiber optics

   d. Laser

13. Which of the following types of cable is going to use a Registered Jack for a terminal?

   b. Unshielded twisted pair

    b. Coaxial

    c. Fiber optics

    d. Laser

14. Which of the following types of cable is going to use a BNC for a terminal?

    a. Unshielded twisted pair

    b. Coaxial

    c. Fiber optics

    d. Laser

15. Why are the pairs of wires in twisted pair cabling twisted?

    a. To reduce EMI.

    b. To reduce crosstalk.

    c. To keep matching signal carriers together

    d. As an encoding mechanism.

16. RG-58 is a form of _____ cable.

    a. Unshielded twisted pair

    b. Coaxial

    c. Fiber optics

    d. Laser

17. Which committee is responsible for the 802 standards?

    a. JEDEC

    b. IANA

    c. ISO

    d. IEEE

18. Ethernet is a standard supervised by the _____ committee.

    a. 802.3

    b. 802.5

    c. 802.10

    d. 802.11

19. A segment on your network is still made up of token ring. If you want to attach it to your Ethernet network, what kind of device will you use?

    a. A switch

    b. A bridge

    c. A hub

    d. A MAU

20. What is the other hardware protocol that makes use of a ring topology?

    a. CSMA/CD

    b. CSMA/CA

    c. FDDI

    d. Ethernet

TRICKY TERMINOLOGY

Bounded media: Material that moves data and that is directly connected to the devices, such as copper cable or fiber optics.

Bridge: A device that interconnects two different networks using two different hardware protocols or two different computing platforms.

Brouter: A hybrid device that combines the functions of both a router and a bridge.

Bus: In general terms, a bus is simply the path data takes to move from one location to another. In network topology, it refers to a layout that connects all devices in line with one another.

Hub: An unintelligent device that distributes data across a subnet. What goes in one port goes out all ports, including the one from whence it came.

Hybrid: A network that consists of two or more different topologies. For example, a star/bus network is relatively common.

Mesh: A network in which all devices directly interconnect with all other devices. Also sometimes called a "mess" network.

Network: Any two or more devices connected either directly or indirectly and configured to communicate with one another.

Repeater: A device that takes a signal, cleans it up, amplifies it back to its original strength, and then sends it along its way.

Ring: A topology that keeps data moving in a logical circle around the network.

Router: A device that interconnects two autonomous networks.

Segment: A cluster of devices on the network that exist in the same collision domain. Also, a single length of cable connecting one device to another.

Star: A topology in which a central device interconnects all other devices on a segment of the network.

Subnet: A smaller network that exists within a larger network.

Switch: An intelligent device that distributes data between subnets. Packet filtering keeps unwanted data from cluttering up segments where it is not intended to go.

Topology: Physical or logical configuration. For example, the topology of a network shows the pattern in which the computers are interconnected. Common network topologies are the star, bus, and ring.

Transceiver: Any device that can both transmit and receive

Unbounded media: Typical wireless media, such as radio waves, infrared, laser, or microwave transmissions.

ACRONYM ALERT

BNC: Bayonet Neil-Concelman. A connector used in coaxial cable that attaches in a simple twist-and-lock motion.

CSMA/CD: Carrier Sense, Multiple Access/Collision Detection. The media access method used by Ethernet.

CSU/DSU: Channel Service Unit/Data Service Unit. This is the device that interconnects a network to a communications carrier.

FDDI: Fiber Distributed Data Interface. A newer token passing technology that makes use of one or two rings and supports fiber-optics media.

IEEE: The Institute of Electrical and Electronic Engineers. An organization deeply involved in the development and ratification of standards throughout the electronics industry.

NIC: Network Interface Card

RJ-45: Registered Jack number 45. An 8-conductor connector used with twisted-pair cable that looks very similar to a standard telephone jack, only larger.

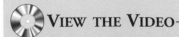 **VIEW THE VIDEO**

A video clip on Types of Networks is available on the accompanying CD.

CHAPTER 2

CLIENTS AND SERVERS— WHO'S THE BOSS?

In Chapter One, I discussed a number of different types of networks. There is the bus network, the star network, the ring, and the mesh. Now I'm going to introduce a couple of new terms into the mix and then try to clear up any confusion that ensues. The network topologies discussed in Chapter One were based on the physical structure of the network. Once the physical network is built, the network can be further broken down into logical structures. The two most commonly used logical structures are the *peer-to-peer* (P2P) network (sometimes called the workgroup), and the *client-server* network. Later in the book I'll discuss some additional logical network structures, but for the purposes of this chapter, I'll limit our discussion to these two types. While the Network+ exam expects you to be able to describe either type, the majority of questions you're going to see deal with the client-server end. That's why it gets its own chapter, and the workgroup has to settle for a brief mention here and there.

In this chapter, I'm going to cover the following objectives for the Network+ exam:

> **BUZZ WORDS**
>
> **Peer-to-peer:** A network in which there is no single controlling device. All devices act as both client and server, depending on circumstances.
>
> **Client-server:** A network in which one or more master computers keeps a database of users and/or doles out files on an as-needed basis.

3.1 Identify the basic capabilities (For example: client support, interoperability, authentication, file and print services, application support and security) of server operating systems to access network resources.

3.2 Identify the basic capabilities needed for client workstations to connect to and use network resources.

4.4 Given a troubleshooting scenario involving a client accessing remote network services, identify the cause of the problem (For example: file services, print services, authentication failure, protocol configuration, physical connectivity and SOHO (Small Office / Home Office) router).

4.5 Given a troubleshooting scenario between a client and a server environment, identify the cause of a stated problem.

Are We Peer-to-Peer, or Are We Client-Server?

The difference between peer-to-peer and client-server is made far too complicated in most of the articles I've read. In reality, it's quite simple. If you have a peer-to-peer network, there is no single machine that controls the network. In the client-server model, there is. How hard is that? The question is what do I mean by "control the network"?

> **Exam Note:** Be able to describe in detail the differences between P2P networking and a client-server based network. Questions can come in many forms.

Working in Peer-to-Peer

In a business environment, when you speak of your "peers," in general you are referring to those people on your level. In other words, you're talking about your equals. It's the same way in the world of networking. A peer-to-peer network is a network of computers that perform basically the same functions. There is no "master" that they look up to. If a user working at one station needs files from another station, the user's machine that is accessing the files becomes the *client* and the computer that houses the information becomes the *server*. Assuming that each computer in a P2P network contains shared resources, at any given time any computer on the network can be working as either a client or a server.

If it's really that simple, why don't most people just set up all of their networks in P2P and be done with it? On a small network, where security is not much of an issue, they might do just that. As a network increases in size or as security takes on greater importance, this option becomes less desirable. Since every computer is playing two parts, security and resource administration become a little problematic (see **Figure 2.1**). As soon as a user logs on to a machine on a P2P network, she

Figure 2.1 In a peer-to-peer network, everybody's the general. Then again, everybody's the grunt as well.

becomes the administrator. Therefore, she can set permissions on files, create passwords, share or unshare resources, and so on and so forth. The next user to log onto the machine may take exception to the changes the first user made and undo everything she did. She will come in the next morning and not be able to access a file she created.

Here's another scenario that needs to be considered. You have one file that contains all of your customer records. One person accesses that file, changes it, and saves it to his or her own local hard drive. Since the original file was never overwritten, it remains unchanged. Now another person does the same thing and then another and then another. Now there are four different versions of the file, on four different hard drives, not counting the original version, which is unchanged on a fifth hard drive. Which one is the accurate version? None of them! Data integrity becomes a major issue.

In addition, the only security available in a peer-to-peer network is to set a password on the resource you want protected. This is called *share-level security*. Each and every protected file, folder, or printer will have its own password, assigned by the person who originally set the permissions. Imagine if you will, how many passwords a person would have to memorize if there were 250 users on a P2P network assigning separate passwords to every file created!

Therefore, you can probably get away with using a peer-to-peer approach on very small networks, when there is not a lot of information being shared among users and security is not an issue. Somebody creating a home network so she can hook her computer up to her husband's computer can easily get by with this level of network, as long as the electronic checkbook or other critical files stay on one computer and only one computer. Smaller offices can survive on P2P as long as there is some organized methodology for managing information and one person is in charge of setting passwords.

MANAGING THE CLIENT-SERVER NETWORK

Most networks require a much higher level of security than afforded by peer-to-peer. I'm not sure a company the size of Anheuser-Busch would be terribly excited about having multiple copies of its financial records floating around the company. More importantly, I'm willing to bet that it wants to have a certain degree of control over who can see those records.

When an organization reaches the point where security and data integrity are of greater concern than avoiding the cost of a separate server, the client-server network becomes the only alternative (see **Figure 2.2**). This network has one or more computers that become dedicated servers, running specialized software called the *network operating system* (NOS). A good NOS provides many more services than those provided by OSs designed for stand-alone machines.

In order for a user to access to the network he or she must be assigned a user account with a *user ID* and (usually) a password that confirms the identity of the person attempting to log on. Once the user has successfully logged on, the NOS continues to play a role. Any time that user attempts to access a resource on the network, the NOS uses the combination of user ID and password to determine whether or not that person has been given access to that resource. These are the user's *permissions*. In addition to permissions, a user can be granted *privileges*. Privileges are the actions a user is allowed to perform on the network. For example, you might give a user the right to create new accounts.

> **BUZZ WORDS**
>
> **Permissions:** Access rights a user has been given to network resources.
>
> **Privileges:** The rights a user has been given to perform certain functions on the network, such as to add or administer user accounts.

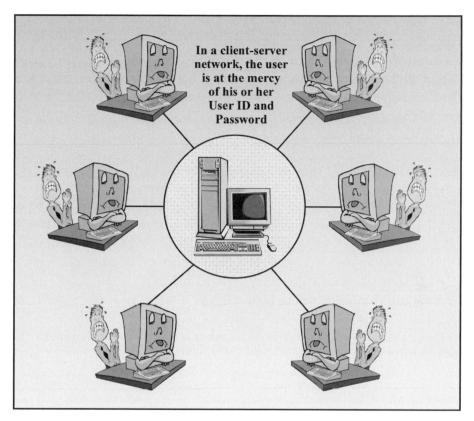

Figure 2.2   In the client-server environment, one or more machines is in charge.

The beauty of this setup is two-fold. First, each user only needs to know one password to access everything on the network to which he or she has been given permission. Second, a single individual or group of individuals can be responsible for managing security. Generally, these people are called *administrators*. However, depending on the NOS selected, this person might be called the Supervisor (Novell) or even the Superuser (Unix). I'll be using the term administrator throughout this book.

The administrator can centrally control all aspects of the network from a single location. New user accounts or links to remote networks can be created, as long as the administrator has the appropriate permissions on the remote network.

> **BUZZ WORD**
>
> **Administrator:** The user and/or account that has full and complete privileges to do anything and everything on the network.

> **EXAM NOTE:** Depending on the NOS in use, the administrator account can be called a number of different things. In Microsoft terminology, it is simply the administrator. That same account in Unix or Linux is the Superuser, while in Novell, it is called the Supervisor. Know them all for the exam.

NETWORK MODELS

I discussed earlier the differences between peer-to-peer and client-server networks. In the client-server realm, for many years, there has been a sharp division between two different models of client-server structure. Microsoft has espoused the *domain* model, whereas Novell has perpetually sung the virtues of a network based on *directory services.* With its release of Windows 2000 Server, Microsoft straddled the fence. While keeping the concept of the domain alive, it embraced *Active Directory,* its implementation of a directory services model.

Having a good understanding of these two models, how they work, and the difference between them will make it easier to understand the differences between the various network operating systems. So what, then, is the difference? The next few pages should make that quite clear.

THE DOMAIN MODEL

The domain model originally espoused by Microsoft is based on the idea that a network would consist of a group of devices under the control of a single administrative unit. In this particular case the administrative unit in question is not necessarily a person. The administrative unit that controls a Microsoft domain is the *Security Accounts Manager* (SAM). SAM is a database located in the registry of an NT domain controller that contains the information for all resources on the network. This includes the user accounts. It is through the user accounts that a person is either permitted or denied access to any given resource.

In an NT domain, there is a single "master" computer called the *primary domain controller* (PDC) that maintains the original copy of the SAM. Additional servers known as *backup domain controllers* (BDC) can be installed on the network to take some of the load off of the PDC. Logon and access authentication can be handled by either the PDC or a BDC. However, changes to the SAM can only be made on the PDC. Periodically, the PDC will synchronize with the BDCs on the network and, if changes have been made to the SAM, it will refresh the copy stored on each of the BDCs.

If your network began to get too large or too cumbersome for a single server to manage, the administrator could create additional domains. In order to get these domains to talk to one another, the administrators of each domain could set up *trusts* between their domains. A trust is a virtual link between two domains that allows one domain to perform authentication and provide resources to another domain.

In a trust, there is the *trusted domain* and the *trusting domain.* The trusted domain is the one that contains information in its SAM or a resource within its confines that a user on the trusting domain requires. I think the best way to define a trust is to give an example of one in action.

Let us create an imaginary company with offices in New York City and in Los Angeles.

> ## BUZZ WORDS
>
> **Domain:** All network resources, including devices, software, and users, that fall under a single administrative unit of the network.
>
> **Trust:** A virtual link between two domains that allows one domain to perform authentication and provide resources to another domain.
>
> **Trusted domain:** The domain that contains the security database that is providing authentication and/or resource access to another domain.
>
> **Trusting domain:** A domain that is requesting authentication services or access to the resources from another domain.

I'll call my company MyComp, Inc. In the New York office, the domain name is MYCOMPNY and in LA it is MYCOMPLA. Convenient, wouldn't you say? Rebecca works in the MYCOMPLA domain but will be on loan to NY for several weeks. When she goes out to NY and tries to log onto the network, she is denied access. Why is that?

While she has an account in MYCOMPLA, she does not have one in MYCOMPNY. An easy solution would be to create an account for her in MYCOMPNY and be done with it. A couple of things might make that an undesirable solution, however. For one, there is the matter of security. How can you make sure that she is given all of the same network privileges she has in LA, but no more? Second, a 32-bit number randomly assigned by the OS internally marks each user account in the SAM. NT uses this number and not the user ID to keep track of each account. Having multiple accounts open for the same individual could be considered by many as a security risk. On top of all that, in order for her to access all of her files in the LA office, you'll have to make sure her new account has the same permissions.

However, if you set up a trust between MYCOMPNY and MYCOMPLA, none of this will be an issue. With MYCOMPNY as the trusting domain and MYCOMPLA as the trusted domain, Rebecca can log on to a machine on the NY network and gain access, using all of the parameters of her existing account. Why? It happens through the magic of *pass-through authentication.* When she logs on in NY, NY's domain controllers reject her logon attempt. She does not have a valid account. However, because there is a trust established between NY and LA, the logon request is handed off to the LA domain before any action is taken. The LA domain controllers have her account information. Her credentials match up and she is allowed access (see **Figure 2.3**).

In NT, trusts are one-way. By that, I mean simply this. Just because you have a trust set up between NY and LA doesn't mean a user from NY can now go to LA and automatically log on. In my first example, LA was the trusted domain and NY the trusted. For an NY user to log on in LA, you need to have an additional trust established where NY is trusted and LA is trusting.

Figure 2.3 Pass-through authentication between trusts allows for users to transparently log on to a domain on which they have no established account.

NT trusts are also *nontransitive.* In Windows 2000 Server, they are *transitive.* In the event that there are multiple domains set up on the network, a trust works only from point A to point B. If there is a trust set up between Domain A and Domain B, Domain A now trusts Domain B. Now you set up a trust between Domain B and Domain C. In NT, should a trust between Domain A and Domain C be required, you will have to establish it separately. That is what I mean

by nontransitive. In W2K Server, since the trusts are transitive, if Domain A trusts Domain B, then as soon as the trust between Domain B and Domain C is established, Domain A automatically trusts Domain C (see **Figure 2.4**).

Domain structures fall under four different categories. There is the *single domain,* the *single-master domain,* the *multiple-master domain,* and the *complete trust domain.* Properly selecting the domain type for a particular network can make for a more secure network, in addition to making it easier to administer.

The single domain model is the easiest to implement. There is one domain with one PDC. One administrator (or group of administrators) handles the entire structure. This is probably the best setup for small to midsize networks.

Once in a while, you come across a situation where the single domain isn't appropriate, either for security reasons or for geographic considerations. The single-master domain allows for several different *resource domains* to allow the administration of different aspects of the network, while all user management still falls under the auspices of a single PDC. One example of a network that might use a single-master model is one in which security is an issue.

For example, you might have a large database set up on a server running Oracle. Bill, your network administrator, is the best there is when it comes to managing a network in general, but he doesn't know his feet from his fingers when it comes to Oracle. Linda, on the other hand, is an expert Oracle administrator but only knows enough to be dangerous when it comes to network infrastructure. The perfect solution to your dilemma is to set up a single-master domain.

Bill handles the overall network. All user accounts and general administration issues are under his control. This is your master domain and contains the SAM for all user accounts. You set up a separate domain on which your Oracle server will run. Linda is in charge of that. Through the use of trusts, you can control who has permissions to do what when it comes to the Oracle database, but Linda won't be bothered with the ins and outs of day-to-day administration.

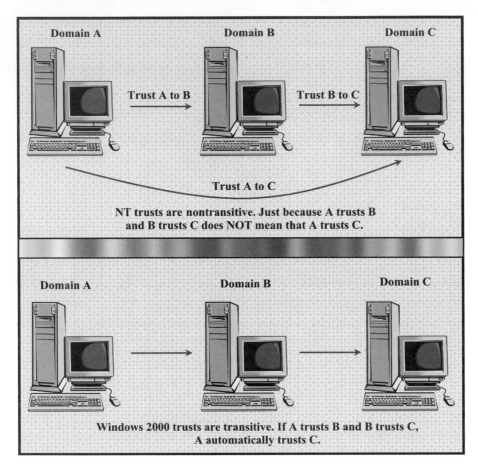

Figure 2.4 Trusts are handled differently between Windows NT and Windows 2000 domains.

Multiple-master domains become important when the network becomes too large for a single domain controller to host the entire database. Since the SAM is housed in the registry of the domain controllers, and since the registry of NT can only be so large, there is a finite limit to the number of user or group accounts a single database can hold. The theoretical limit is around 40,000 accounts. In practice, it is far less.

With a multiple-master domain, there are two or more separate domains in charge of logon authentication. These domains can be set up geographically, administratively, or any other way the administrators desire. Each domain is a separate administrative unit and can be managed by separate groups if desired. Setting up trusts provides pass-through authentication where needed.

The complete trust domain is a multiple-master domain in which every domain has a trust established with every other domain. While this might be useful in a limited number of situations, most administrators would consider it both a security risk and an administrative nightmare.

Windows 2000 Server versions have eliminated the limitation of a single PDC on the network. All domain controllers are simply domain controllers. This has a lot to do with the implementation of Active Directory into the NOS, which I will be discussing later in the chapter.

DIRECTORY SERVICES

The domain model does provide for security as well as scalability, but for the average user you could never really call it friendly. As networks grew larger and larger, users were finding it increasingly difficult to locate resources on the network. The *International Telecommunications Union* (ITU) addressed that problem in 1987 when it first proposed something it called the X.500 *Directory Access Protocol* (DAP, or sometimes X.500). In its proposal, it defined methods for generating a directory to the network to which users would have access. Novell was among the first to jump on the bandwagon when NetWare 4.0 included directory services as it foundation.

Other companies weren't exactly lining up for their turn to use this protocol. They complained that it was too complex. In response to these concerns, the *Lightweight Directory Access Protocol* (LDAP) was released. Since LDAP is based on TCP/IP, it is simpler to implement and has been more readily accepted.

> **EXAM NOTE:** Be prepared to identify the different components of Directory Services as described in this section. It is a key component to the Novell portion of the exam.

The directory structure is based on the concept of a tree. It starts with a root. The root generally consists of a country (such as the U.S.) followed by an organization (such as Delmar). The root branches out into *organizational units* (OU). Novell refers to the OUs as *container objects*. Into the OUs you can either add other OUs or you can add directory entries, or as Novell calls them, the *leaf objects*. The complete path to any given entry in the directory tree is called the *distinguished name* (DN).

Logically speaking, this is basically the same way the structure of your hard drive is made up, as you can see in **Figure 2.5**. You have a root directory, into which you can add as many directories as you wish. Into the directories, you can add either subdirectories or files.

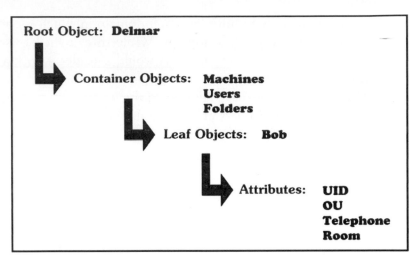

Figure 2.5 The structure of a directory tree isn't that much different than the file system of your hard drive.

In order to control security and network access, the objects can be assigned attributes. At a minimum, each object must include an *objectclass* field and if the entry represents a user, a UID field that holds the user ID. Any given entry can have more than one objectclass field if need be. Other fields can define where in the structure of the network the object exists. This may include country unit and OU. Specific information can also be included, such as a user's email address, telephone number, and title.

Access to resources is controlled by the directory entry that defines that resource. Access is allowed through a *bind* operation that provides authentication. LDAP provides for three basic forms of authentication—anonymous, simple, and secure.

An anonymous bind allows a user with no established identity within the network to gain access to resources that allow it. An example of this would be the FTP server that provides anonymous access. Anybody who can gain access to the network can gain access to the resources. As you might imagine, this isn't exactly the most secure access.

A little more security is provided by the simple bind. A resource is password encoded and to gain access, the user must provide that password along with a request for access. This isn't a lot different from the share-level access used by Microsoft.

The tightest security is provided by a secure bind, as its name implies. A resource is associated with an *access control list* (ACL). When users attempt to access that resource, their credentials are compared to the entries in the ACL. If their information is found, they are permitted access. If anything fails to match up, they are denied.

As I mentioned earlier, up through and including the days of NT 4.0, Microsoft embraced the domain model of networking. That is not to say that it didn't provide

ACTIVE DIRECTORY VERSUS DIRECTORY SERVICES

I've seen a lot of loose talk running around on the Internet accusing Microsoft of "stealing" Novell's Directory Services and incorporating it into its NOS. Active Directory is simply Microsoft's implementation of LDAP, which is a protocol available to all comers. Microsoft incorporated TCP/IP into its NOS architecture long before Novell accepted it as a default. To say that Microsoft stole Active Directory from Novell is like saying Novell stole TCP/IP from Microsoft. Neither company can be accused of "stealing" an industry-standard protocol and using it as part of its basic architecture.

directory services. Directory services were definitely a part of the NT structure. They just weren't something that was very useful to the general user. In networks consisting of multiple domains a user to would either have to be told the direct path to any given object outside of his or her own domain, or be psychic.

Starting with Windows 2000, Microsoft incorporated *Active Directory* (AD) into all of its operating systems. AD is an LDAP-based implementation of directory services that places the directory of the entire network at the user's fingertips.

AD takes DNS and makes it visible to the user in a way that is easy to understand. The user can browse the network for any class of object, such as printers, and AD will display a list showing each object within that class, along with its attributes. Then, if the user wants to access a particular object in the class, and the network security structure permits that access, the user can simply double-click on the object in Explorer. DNS will resolve the object's name to an IP address and create a connection.

From an administrator's standpoint AD can be a boon as well. The amount of information that can be associated with an object is immense. A user account can have virtually an entire personnel folder attached to it if necessary. **Figure 2.6** illustrates just how much information is readily available to the administrator for any given object.

NETWORK OPERATING SYSTEMS—THE SERVER

The first thing I should do is make sure that the difference between a network operating system and a network-aware operating system is clear. If you want your computer to be able to access the network, either as a client, or, in a P2P network,

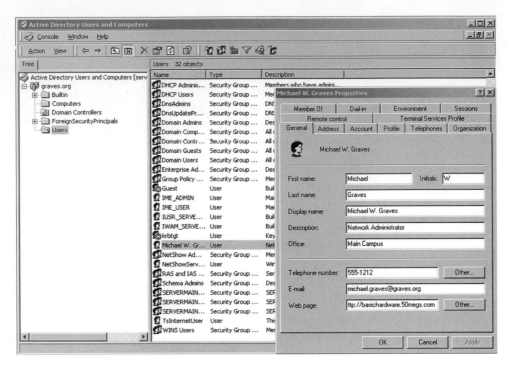

Figure 2.6 Active Directory allows the administrator to access massive amounts of information about any given user or object on the network.

even as a server, it is essential that the operating system of your computer be aware of the network and to be able to work with the network as if it were just another component in the computer.

At its most basic, network awareness is simply a function of an OS that enables the computers to communicate over the network. An NOS goes far beyond simple com-

munications and incorporates features such as security and internetwork communications as built-in functions. But if you're setting up a peer-to-peer network, then nearly any OS available could be considered an NOS. Microsoft has included network capabilities in every operating system it has distributed since the days of Windows 3.11 for Workgroups. Linux users and Macintosh users can also easily interconnect their computers with no additional software. Therefore, on the simplest level, these all fall under the category of an NOS.

The client-server model needs something a little more complex. A dedicated server with a specialized NOS installed onto it becomes a necessity. Over the years, a number of different companies have taken a stab at the NOS market. Only a few of those have survived the competition. These days, I can limit my discussion to four leading NOSs. There are others, of course. For the most part, however, those are specialized applications used in specific environments and therefore not covered on the Network+ exam. Those covered are, in alphabetical order, Linux, Microsoft, Novell, and Unix.

Which one is best? Thankfully, the answer to that question does not fall within the scope of this book. Each one needs to perform basically the same functions. The differences are something I will look at later in this chapter. As far as which one an individual organization goes with, it may come down simply to whether or not there is already somebody lined up to administer the network. In that case, the company installs the NOS that the administrator is most familiar with. On more complex networks, there might be other factors that have to be taken into consideration. And on any given network, there may be multiple NOSs installed. A detailed comparison of all of the available options is far beyond the scope of Network+. Therefore, I will be providing only the briefest overview in this chapter. Since this is a vendor-neutral exam, I'll give them to you in alphabetical order.

LINUX

Linux is an OS that is only briefly covered on the exam. What the exam is most interested in having you know is a few of the concepts behind Linux. A few years back, a man by the name of Linus Torvalds began work on an operating system that was to become the foundation of a worldwide grassroots effort to provide a free operating system to anyone who wanted to use it. The OS is based on a uniform kernel, over which any number of different option packages can be installed. On its most basic level, Linux can be a stand-alone workstation with P2P support, or it can act as a client to virtually any other NOS out there. However, as you search the Web, you'll find that implementations of Linux have been written that provide many levels of NOS support as well. You can take a machine and turn it into anything from a member server to a full-blown enterprise server, depending on the packages you install.

These days there are literally thousands of professional programmers who volunteer their services writing code for the OS. The OS and any patches, fixes, or option packages must be made available at no charge and the source code provided. That allows for anyone who is able to add features or improve the OS. Linux buffs call this open sourcing at no charge *copyleft* (and you thought my puns were bad). The movement does allow companies to put the OS together with different collections of options and then provide a package including documentation for a reasonable charge. For many people, the convenience of having everything collected onto a single CD and then getting a set of books showing them what to do is worth shelling out a few bucks.

In Linux (as in Unix), the primary user on the network who has full privileges and responsibilities is known as the *Superuser.* This is the person who, in a Windows network, would be known as the administrator. Linux supports symmetric multi-processing, cluster services (the ability to make more than one server look like a single machine to the network), and much more. All this, and it can be downloaded off of the Internet for free!

With all that going for it, you would think that Linux would be a hands-down favorite. Unfortunately, a few things keep that from happening. For one thing, earlier versions have all been afflicted with a command-line driven interface that requires a solid understanding of both the hardware end of the system as well as the OS itself. Therefore, while it is very powerful, it can be a little intimidating to learn. Second, even minor changes, such as adding a new module or even a new device driver, required that the entire operating system be recompiled, and that can take hours. Most network administrators are a little hesitant to bring their server down for that long at a time for any reason.

Recent releases of Linux have reduced the OS's dependence on recompiling with every little change. The addition of a very friendly user interface makes the software a lot easier for the novice to use. As a result, Linux has begun to take its place among the top NOSs.

Linux servers can act as the central core to a network of Windows workstations as well. A piece of software called Samba, when properly configured, allows a Unix or Linux server to play the role of a file server to Windows clients. Samba is an implementation of the Common Internet File System (CIFS) file-sharing protocol that Windows uses. The protocol is useful only for file sharing, however. It does not handle user authentication. Curiously, Samba got its name because CIFS is the next step in evolution for the early Server Message Block protocol used by DOS and early Windows versions. The acronym SMB sounded kind of like Samba when you tried to say it as a word, and the name stuck.

MICROSOFT

The biggest percentage of networks out there in the real world that you will encounter will be based on one form of Microsoft software or the other. In a way, that's actually a bit of an anomaly. Microsoft makes a very good NOS, but there aren't many people around willing to say it is the best. Its products certainly aren't cheap, but then again, they're not the most expensive options either. I think the key to its success has been its point-and-click interface. It is easier to learn.

Starting with NT Version 3.1, there has been a steady outpouring of NOS offerings from Microsoft over the years. Fortunately, in terms of both the real world and the exam, there are only a few you need to be concerned with.

- *NT 4.0 Server*: NT uses a domain-based networking model in which a domain has a single *primary domain controller* (PDC) that governs the entire network. Allowing trusts between domains provides a scalable model for networking that allows virtually unlimited expansion of a network. *Backup domain controllers* provide a certain level of load balancing. Out of the box, NT 4.0 provided support for asymmetric multiprocessing on up to four processors, and custom packages were available that supported up to thirty-two processors.

- *NT 4.0 Enterprise Edition*: This is a beefed-up version of 4.0. This version supports cluster services (on a limited basis), which can be used either to provide a greater level of fault tolerance on the network or to enable load balancing.

- *NT 4.0 Terminal Server*: This version of NT 4.0 puts all applications and data for the entire network onto the servers. The network doesn't require a powerful PC on each desktop, because the PCs are not responsible for doing a whole lot of the work. Of course, that does mean that pretty potent servers are in order. The advent of cheap desktop PCs has caused this type of architecture to lose popularity to a great extent.

- *2000 Server (W2K)*: Take two cups of NT 4.0 and two cups of Windows 98. Add water and stir. You get Windows 2000 Server. (I bet Microsoft *wishes* it was that easy!) A new service called *Active Directory* greatly enhances network operability as well as security. Adding Plug 'n Play to the OS makes building and/or upgrading servers substantially easier.

- *2000 Advanced Server*: Enterprise Edition gets a hefty dose of steroids and is taught to play Plug 'n Play.

- *2000 Data Center*: At last! Microsoft has an NOS that competes on the level of Unix. This is by far the most potent offering Microsoft has yet to achieve.

In fact, it is so potent that you aren't allowed to buy it. Not by itself anyway. This particular version ships only on preconfigured servers from a select few companies. Be prepared to belly up to the bar for a pretty hefty tab as well.

In the early Microsoft server products, NetBEUI was the protocol of choice. This was fine for small networks but was easily outgrown. Starting with NT 4.0, TCP/IP became the default protocol.

NOVELL

For a while it looked like Novell was a fading giant. Once the undisputed leader in the networking industry with its NetWare products, it was losing market share to Microsoft hand over fist. While it made no claims to compete on Unix's level, it did produce a product that was able to provide many of the same features as Unix as well as vast network scalability and flexibility for a reasonable price. What shot it down was its strict adherence to a command-line interface. Power and performance were considered to be of greater importance than a pretty interface. It didn't bother Novell that someone actually had to *learn* something in order to use the product. Imagine that. So Microsoft comes along with a paint-by-numbers OS and takes away Novell's market share. Still, Novell hung in there. A faithful following that preferred power over pretty kept NetWare moving out the door, and, to a certain extent, Novell bent to the winds of the inevitable. They bolstered their revenues by selling Directory Services (discussed later in this section) support for NT. Despite the company's travails, NetWare has always been a very robust operating system that is capable of keeping up with even the largest of networking environments.

Early on, Novell developed its own networking protocol called *Internet Packet Exchange/Sequenced Packet Exchange* (IPX/SPX). IPX is an incredibly capable protocol, but its methods of addressing are not very conducive to sewing large numbers of networks together. In addition, its broadcast-based methods of network management and maintenance make for less-than-efficient usage of available bandwidth. Therefore, it was sidestepped as the protocol of choice for the Internet. IPX packets had to be encapsulated before they could be sent over the Internet. This added more overhead to both the sending and receiving machines. In yet another example of bending with the wind, Novell made TCP/IP the default protocol starting with version 5.0.

One of the biggest challenges of administering a large network is keeping track of where everything and everybody is located. To simplify this task, Novell developed *Novell Directory Services* (NDS). On its most basic level, this is a method by which the entire network—every single computer, user, printer, or other device—is represented in a tree structure, similar to the way you view what is on your computer in Windows Explorer.

A Novell server is actually a more protected device than is any machine in the Microsoft environment. The person in charge of a Novell network, the *supervisor,* manipulates the server over the network from one of the workstations. Programs and services are added to the server by means of *NetWare Loadable Modules* (NLM).

UNIX

Unix is by far the most powerful of the quartet of NOSs I will discuss. It is also by far the most difficult to learn and the most difficult to administer. It is the core for many of the mainframe computers on the market and is the NOS of choice for organizations putting together huge enterprise networks that can never go down.

It started out way back in the 1970s in AT&T Bell Laboratories and over the years has moved from one company to another. Eventually it fell into the hands of The Open Group, who currently oversees development of the OS. Various incarnations include SCO Unix, Sun Solaris, Digital Unix, Hewlett Packard's HP-UX, and many others. Regardless of the originating company, the command structure is pretty much the same.

One of the things that make Unix so difficult is that a company can modify the code to fit its needs. The source code is available to developers for that very reason. However, this means that there are minor variations among the different versions of the NOS on the market. In order to ease the pain involved in learning this complex operating system, a graphical interface called *X-Windows* emerged in the late 1980s. However, no one chose to set any standards for what the interface should look like. So a system manufactured by Sun Microsystems looks different than one made by Hewlett Packard. This began to change when The Open Group began to push for standardization on a motif it called *Common Desktop Environment* (CDE).

The biggest advantage of Unix is that it makes much more powerful computers possible by enabling them to use large numbers of microprocessors. There are versions of Unix that support as few as one single processor, while other versions support up to thirty-two. Many computers can be grouped together to form a cluster that is both fault tolerant and load balancing.

NETWORK CLIENTS

In order to get any device onto the network there is a specific piece of software that must be loaded called the *client*. Don't confuse the user with the client. The user is a carbon-based life form that sits at the controls requesting data (or playing games). The client is a silicon-based or binary nonlife form that follows the instructions of the carbon-based life form. In other words, by definition, a client can either be any piece of equipment requesting services from another network appliance, or it can be a piece of software running on that equipment that handles those requests. For the purposes of this discussion, I'll be talking about the software-based client.

Network clients perform two critical functions for a network device. First of all, they provide an interface for the user and the user's applications for network services. The other function is that of being the network *redirector*. Without a redirector, you don't have access to the network.

The redirector works like this. Any time you make a request for either data or instructions on your computer, the first place the computer looks for that information is to itself. However, if, as a user, you are requesting data from another machine on the network, the computer discovers that it can't retrieve the information from any local source. It has to go remote. The redirector takes that request and "redirects" it to the appropriate location (see **Figure 2.7**).

Network clients have to be specific to the OS of both the host system and the network in use. To be more specific, a DOS-based machine needs one type of client software if it is being hooked up to a Microsoft network and another if it is being hung off a NetWare server. They aren't interchangeable, and neither will work in a

BUZZ WORDS

Client: Any device or piece of software requesting the services of another device or piece of software.

Redirector: An application process that distinguishes whether a requested resource is local or remote. It then initiates a local procedure call for localized services and a remote procedure call for those that reside outside the local system.

Local procedure call: A request for services that can be performed by or resources that reside on the machine from which the request was made.

Remote procedure call: A request for services that can be performed by or resources that reside on a machine other than that from which the request was made.

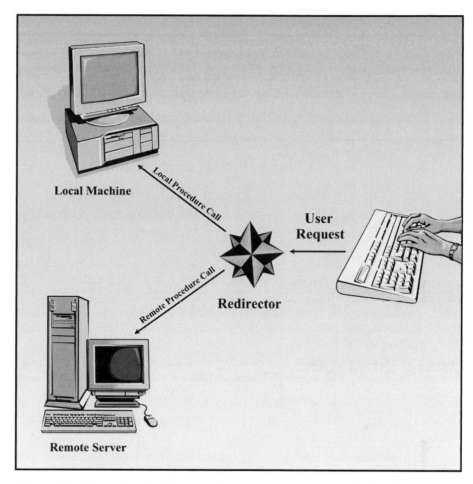

Figure 2.7 The redirector figures out where a service request is intended to go and sends that request off in the right direction.

Windows environment. The Windows machine needs Windows-specific network clients for the appropriate NOS.

Clients will also appear in 16-bit or 32-bit form. As with any other industry, always make sure you use the right tool for the job. For example, if you have any legacy machines still running under MS-DOS—and yes, there are still some of those out there—then you must use a 16-bit client. Most operating systems offer a certain number of built-in clients from which to select. Those that aren't offered can be added in most situations.

Table 2.1   Built-in Clients for Microsoft Operating Systems

Operating System	NOS Supported	Available Client
Windows 98	*Banyan VINES*	*Banyan DOS/WIN 3.1 Client*
	Microsoft	*Client for Microsoft Networks*
		Client for Novell Networks
		Microsoft Family Logon
	Novell	*Novell NetWare (Workstation Shell 3x)*
		Novell NetWare (Workstation Shell 4.0 and above
Windows 2000	*Microsoft*	*Client For Microsoft Networks*
	Novell	*Client Services for Novell*

CHAPTER SUMMARY

The concept of a network revolves around the client/server relationship. Even in a peer-to-peer network, there are clients and there are servers. The relationships simply aren't as well defined as in a client-server network.

The major players in the server market are Linux, Novell, Microsoft, and Unix. Each of these companies provides different levels of server software targeted at everything from a home network to a worldwide enterprise. Selecting the right server application will have a dramatic impact on the success of your network and how scalable it will be.

The server is only half the equation, though. Without clients, there is no need for servers. The client software is what provides network access to the device on which it is installed. Each OS will require the installation of a client specific to that OS.

As far as network structure is concerned, over the years there has been a bit of a chasm between the domain-based networks and the directory services-based networks. Domains are based on organizational structure, but aren't very user friendly. Directory services allow easier access to network resources, but can be a bit complex to manage. Microsoft bridged that chasm with Active Directory. They keep the concept of the domain alive and well, but incorporate a very user-friendly directory services interface.

BRAIN DRAIN

1. In your own words, describe the differences between a peer-to-peer network and a client-server network.
2. Explain the concept of a redirector and how it works.
3. Define as best you can the concept of a domain.
4. Write a short paragraph explaining why a directory services network model might provide advantages over a domain model.
5. What do I mean by pass-through authentication and how does it work?

THE 64K$ QUESTIONS

1. A client is _____.
   a. An end user logging onto the network
   b. An end user requesting services on the network
   c. A device providing services on the network
   d. An application or device requesting services on a network
2. A server is _____.
   a. That big computer in the closet that nobody is allowed to touch
   b. A device that handles logon authentication
   c. A person responsible for managing a network
   d. Any device or piece of software that processes requests for services and/or information by clients and subsequently provides services that another device or piece of software requires.
3. In order to access a file across the network Tammy must type in a separate password, even though she has already logged onto the network. Her regular password does not give her access. This file has been secured with _____.
   a. NTFS permissions
   b. User Level permissions
   c. Share level permissions
   d. Kerberos authentication
4. In Microsoft's first NOS release, the protocol of choice was _____.
   a. NetBEUI
   b. TCP/IP

    c. IPX/SPX

    d. The Network Access Protocol

5. For many years, the default protocol for the NetWare NOS was _____.

    a. NetBEUI

    b. TCP/IP

    c. IPX/SPX

    d. The Network Access Protocol

6. On an NT 4.0-based network, there can only be one _____.

    a. Domain

    b. Backup

    c. Primary Domain Controller

    d. Member Server

7. In an NT 4.0 network, trusts are said to be _____.

    a. Transitive

    b. Nontransitive

    c. Reciprocal

    d. Nonreciprocal

8. Susan is logging onto the Philadelphia domain in her corporation's network. She is actually a member of the New Orleans domain. She logs on successfully. The Philadelphia domain is acting as a _____.

    a. Trusting domain

    b. Trusted domain

    c. Reciprocal domain

    d. Authentication domain

9. An employee recently quit and you deleted that employee's account on the network. Now a customer is claiming that the employee made promises in an exchange of emails, and those promises were never kept. You re-create that employee's account but still cannot access those emails. Why?

    a. The employee deleted the emails.

    b. You did not re-create the employee's password correctly.

    c. The Exchange Server account uses different security procedures than the NOS.

    d. The NOS uses a unique number assigned to each account to identify that account. Re-creating the account generated a new number.

10. Your network consists of several different domains. Each of these domains provides logon authentication services. Your network is an example of a
    a. Single domain
    b. Single-master domain
    c. Multiple-master domain
    d. Complete trust domain

11. Which of the following is an example of a client?
    a. Tammy Sue
    b. Outlook Express
    c. NT 4.0 Enterprise Edition
    d. www.mwgraves.com

12. Which of the following is an example of a server?
    a. Administrator
    b. Outlook Express
    c. NT 4.0 Enterprise Edition
    d. www.mwgraves.com

13. On your network, everyone who creates a file is responsible for assigning passwords. What kind of network are you likely to be on? (Choose all that apply.)
    a. A domain
    b. A workgroup
    c. Client/server
    d. Peer-to-peer

14. Microsoft's implementation of LDAP is called the _____.
    a. Primary Domain Controller
    b. LSASS
    c. Directory Services
    d. Active Directory

15. On a client/server network users are very likely to be assigned _____..
    a. A token
    b. A designated computer where they can log on
    c. A specific supervisor
    d. A unique set of credentials

16. Microsoft NOSs generally store security information in the _____.
    a. Organizational unit
    b. Container object
    c. SAM
    d. Accounts Manager

17. Microsoft's implementation of LDAP is called the _____.
    a. Primary Domain Controller
    b. LSASS
    c. Directory Services
    d. Active Directory

18. The first NOS to implement a domain network model was _____.
    a. NT 3.5
    b. Novell 4.11
    c. NT 4.0
    d. Novel 5.0

19. If Judy is normally a member of EDNACOMP.COM and EDNACOMP.COM has a trust set up with DYNACORE.COM, what process allows her to log onto her EDNACOMP account from a DYNACORE location?
    a. The Trust Authority
    b. Passthrough Authentication
    c. The Local Security Authority
    d. As long as the two networks are connected through a router, it doesn't matter.

20. Which NOS modeled itself after the Unix operating system?
    a. Novell
    b. Microsoft
    c. Linux
    d. None of them. Unix is unique.

TRICKY TERMINOLOGY

Administrator: The user and/or account that has full and complete privileges to do anything and everything on the network.

Client-server: A network in which one or more master computers keep a database of users and/or dole out files on an as-needed basis.

Client: Any device or piece of software requesting the services of another device or piece of software.

Copyleft: A coined term that decribes the lack of a copyright applied to open-source software.

Domain: All network resources, including devices, software, and users, that fall under a single administrative unit of the network.

Local procedure call: A request for services that can be performed by or resources that reside on the machine from which the request was made.

Nontransitive: Trusts begin at Point A and end at Point B. They will not automatically pass through to Point C.

Pass-through authentication: The procedure by which one domain hands off the responsibility for logon authentication to another domain.

Peer-to-peer: A network in which there is no single controlling device. All devices act as both client and server, depending on circumstances.

Permissions: Access rights a user has been given to network resources.

Privileges: The rights a user has been given to perform certain functions on the network, such as to add or administer user accounts.

Redirector: An application process that distinguishes whether a requested resource is local or remote. It then initiates a local procedure call for localized services and a remote procedure call for those that reside outside the local system.

Remote procedure call: A request for services that can be performed by or resources that reside on a machine other than that from which the request was made.

Server: Any device or piece of software that processes requests for services and/or information by clients and subsequently provides services that another device or piece of software requires.

Supervisor: The administrator account in a Novell network.

Superuser: The administrator account for a Unix or Linux system.

Transitive: Trust relationships can pass from one domain to another, through a third domain, simply on the basis of trusts that already exist.

Trust: A virtual link between two domains that allows one domain to perform authentication and provide resources to another domain.

Trusted domain: The domain that contains the security database that is providing authentication and/or resource access to another domain.

Trusting domain: A domain that is requesting authentication services or access to the resources from another domain.

Acronym Alert

ACL: Access Control List. The security database used by Directory Services.

BDC: Backup Domain Controller

DAP: Directory Access Protocol. A early incarnation of directory access based on the OSI model.

DN: Distinguished Name. The complete network path to any object on a network using Directory Services.

ITU: The International Telecommunications Union. An organization that deals primarily with communications protocols.

LDAP: The Lightweight Directory Access Protocol. A more recent directory access protocol based on TCP/IP.

NDS: Novell Directory Services

NLM: NetWare Loadable Module

NOS: Network Operating System

OU: Organizational Unit. One of the container objects used in Novell's Directory Services model.

P2P: Peer-to-Peer

PDC: Primary Domain Controller

SAM: Security Accounts Manager

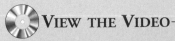 VIEW THE VIDEO

A video clip on Network Computing Models is available on the accompanying CD.

CHAPTER 3

THE HIGHWAYS AND BYWAYS OF THE NETWORK

Those of us working on a network don't have magical computers, nor do computers have psychic powers. Our systems do not telepathically transmit data back and forth between themselves and the other devices on the network. Something called the network media does that for us. For most of us, the media consists of the wires that run from the back of our computer into the bowels of the building. These wires eventually emerge somewhere in the vicinity of the server. If you can physically reach out and touch the cable that moves your data, you're using *bounded media*.

Of course, not all of us are hooked up to the network by wires or cables. More and more homes and offices are taking advantage of wireless technology to interconnect their networks. There are no physical cables carrying our data, and therefore, to the untrained eye, it may appear that our computers are telepathic. These wireless methods of data transmission are examples of *unbounded media*.

Whether you're using bounded or unbounded media depends rather heavily on several considerations. Site conditions and restrictions may favor one form over the other, or, in some cases, prevent you from using a specific form of media. I'll be discussing the advantages and disadvantages of different types of media as I move through this chapter, and examining situations where particular types may be more or less suitable under certain installation situations. In many cases, it is simply a matter of how thick the boss's wallet happens to be.

Before I get too heavily into discussing this subject, there are a few terms I should define. Throughout this chapter (and the rest of the book, for that matter) whenever I refer to cable, I'll be talking about physical bounded media. I don't care if it's made out of copper and carries electrical signals or made out of glass and carries pulses of light. If you can touch it, feel it, smell it, and taste it—it's cable.

EXAM NOTE: You're going to want to be able to identify each of the connectors used by network devices. Go over the diagrams carefully.

The connector is the clip, plug, or snap on the end of the cable that interconnects it to another device. Connectors come in many forms. Every cable has to have one, unless for some reason it is being hardwired into the device. It's very unlikely that, as a network professional, you'd be doing much of that kind of work.

Anything else you need to know, I think I can discuss along the way. Before I get too heavily into my discussion of media, however, perhaps I should start with a quick look at how signals actually get sent over the medium.

Exam Objectives that will be covered in this chapter include:

1.3 Specify characteristics (For example: speed, length, topology, and cable type) of cable standards.

1.4 Recognize media connectors and describe their uses.

1.5 Recognize different media types and describe their uses.

1.7 Specify the general characteristics (For example: carrier speed, frequency, transmission type and topology) of the following wireless technologies: 802.11 (Frequency hopping spread spectrum), 802.11x (Direct sequence spread spectrum), Infrared, Bluetooth.

1.8 Identify factors which affect the range and speed of wireless service (For example: interference, antenna type and environmental factors).

3.3 Identify the appropriate tool for a given wiring task (For example: wire crimper, media tester/certifier, punch down tool or tone generator)..

4.7 Given a troubleshooting scenario involving a network with a particular physical topology (For example: bus, star, mesh or ring) and including a network diagram, identify the network area affected and the cause of the stated failure.

4.8 Given a network troubleshooting scenario involving an infrastructure (For example: wired or wireless) problem, identify the cause of a stated problem. (For example: bad media, interference, network hardware or environment).

MOVING DATA OVER THE MEDIUM

Since copper cable is still the predominant form of cable in use today, I might as well start there. When you are using an electrical signal to move data, data is being carried over an electrical current. The strength of the current is measured in voltage and generally remains constant. This is the *carrier wave.*

Your computer, on the other hand, deals with digital signals. Zeros and ones or on and off are the only concepts your computer understands. Modifying the electrical current so network devices can use that current to move data is the process of *encoding*. Electrical current exhibits two different characteristics that design engineers can modify for the purposes of encoding. These characteristics are *frequency* and *amplitude*. I'll revisit these concepts a little later in this chapter.

Once the data is encoded, the next step is getting the different devices on the network to decide which one gets to talk when. In this respect, not all devices are created equal. Nor do they have to be. As long as devices can agree on a method of communication, the network will be all right.

REVIEWING BINARY

Computers really only know two numbers—0 and 1. This is Base 2 or binary counting. Counting in binary can be interesting. It goes something like this: 1, 10, 11, 100, 101, 111, 1000, 1001, 1010, 1011, 1100, and so forth. We humans know ten numbers—0 through 9. This is Base 10 or decimal counting. All computer code consists of a complex language based on binary. To the computer or programmer, a single 0 or 1 is known as a bit. Programmers have developed different languages to translate binary into useful commands.

EXAM NOTE: Be able to convert a decimal value to binary and back again. Also be familiar with hexadecimal notation and be able to do conversions between hex and binary and hex and decimal.

However, programmers don't deal much with individual bits. The basic unit of data used by most programmers is the byte. A byte consists of eight individual bits. As you can see in **Figure 3.1**, there is a most significant bit and a least significant bit. In addition, each bit is assigned a relative value. The number of values a byte can represent can be determined by taking the number of positions the switch can occupy (2) and multiplying that number by itself eight times. 2 x 2 x 2 x 2 x 2 x 2 x 2 x 2 (two to the eighth power) = 256. Therefore, from an 8-bit byte, 256 different combinations can be achieved.

BIT 8	BIT 7	BIT 6	BIT 5	BIT 4	BIT 3	BIT 2	BIT 1
128	64	32	16	8	4	2	1
Most Significant Bit							Least Significant Bit

Figure 3.1   Relative bit values of a byte.

WHAT'S WITH THIS BINARY AND HEXADECIMAL?

At first, it may seem a bit unfair to have to learn all of this binary to decimal and hexadecimal to binary and so on and so forth. However, be aware that your TCP/IP address is nothing more than a decimal alliteration of a 32-bit binary value. The newest release of TCP/IP, IR6, utilizes a 128-bit address that is listed in hexadecimal notation. Most of the error messages you receive when something goes wrong will deliver an address, usually in hexadecimal, that will help you figure out what driver or application was active when things went awry. Therefore, binary and hexadecimal can be your friends.

Depending on the protocol in use, data may stream over the wire with the most significant bit first or with the least significant bit first. As you might imagine, it's a pretty good idea to keep that straight. Inverting the order of bits would have catastrophic effects on your data. However, since the protocols take care of those issues for you, the only reason it becomes significant to network engineers is when they are using a utility called a *packet sniffer* to capture packets of data off the medium and analyze the contents.

HEXADECIMAL

Dealing with binary by itself can be a little cumbersome. If you had eight bytes of data you wanted to communicate to another technician, you might find yourself writing something along the lines of "0110 1111, 1100 0000, 0001 1010, 1110 0000, 1011 0001, 0000 0001, 1001 0001, 1111 0000." Now, memorize that, walk down the hall to the next office, and recite it to your coworker.

Needless to say, there must to be a better way. That way is called *hexadecimal*. Hexadecimal is a way of counting in Base 16. Now you were just getting the hang of Base 2, and here I am throwing Base 16 at you. But don't worry, it isn't that difficult.

A byte consists of eight bits. If you divide a byte into two nibbles, there will be two four-bit chunks to deal with. Hexadecimal provides a single character that represents each possible combination of four bits. Two raised to the fourth is sixteen, so if we want to come up with a character set based on Base16, there must be a total of sixteen symbols. The numerical symbols 0-9 cover the first ten, and the remainder are represented as the alphabetic symbols A-F. Therefore, in Base16, you count 0, 1, 2, 3, 4, 5, 6, 7, 8, 9, A, B, C, D, E, and F. In order to indicate that a particular value is hexadecimal notation, it is customary to place a lower-case *h* at the end of the value. For example 0FFFh suggests that the value 0FFF is being represented in hex.

There are several different places where the computer provides information in hex, so having a good understanding of the concept is important. **Table 3.1** translates numerical values into hex.

When you're processing data inside the computer, it exists in digital form. Zeros

and ones can be interpreted as all or none. There is no in-between. From an electrical standpoint, that means that a switch is either open or closed, or that current is either present on the wire or not present on the wire. When you send data out over the medium, however, you're very likely going to be using some form of analog signaling. An analog signal is one that exhibits a continuous nature rather than a pulsed or discrete nature. Analog signals can occur as electrical signals, radio waves, or microwaves. Analog signals will vary in both frequency and amplitude (strength). Therefore, one of the tasks of your transceiver is to take that digital data and convert it into an analog signal before it sends it out over the wire—and on the receiving end, it must be able to take the analog signal and convert it back to digital.

DO YOU WANT YOUR DATA IN TUNE OR WITH THE BEAT?

One of the problems that network engineers have to deal with is that an electrical current moves over the wire at a specific voltage. If you were to look at the visual representation of current on an oscilloscope, this voltage would be represented as a sine wave. This sine wave is a constant and relatively regular sweep of intensity—or amplitude as it is called—moving up and down. Amplitude is one of the attributes used to encode data. An example of a sine wave can be seen in **Figure 3.2**. One thing to remember is that there are actually two wave signals at work here. There is the carrier wave—which never changes in either amplitude or frequency—and then there is the signal wave. It is this signal wave that I'll be looking at over the next few pages.

In order for one device to send data to another over an electrical signal, it will use either frequency modulation (FM) or amplitude modulation (AM) to encode the data. With FM, the strength of the signal remains constant. In order to interpret the difference between a 0 and a 1 in binary, the frequency of the signal changes. **Figure 3.3** illustrates a typical signal utilizing frequency modulation.

Table 3.1   The Hexadecimal Chart

Dec	Hex	Dec	Hex	Dec	Hex	Dec	Hex	Dec	Hex	Dec	Hex	Dec	Hex	Dec	Hex
0	0	32	20	64	40	96	60	128	80	160	a0	192	c0	224	e0
1	1	33	21	65	41	97	61	129	81	161	a1	193	c1	225	e1
2	2	34	22	66	42	98	62	130	82	162	a2	194	c2	226	e2
3	3	35	23	67	43	99	63	131	83	163	a3	195	c3	227	e3
4	4	36	24	68	44	100	64	132	84	164	a4	196	c4	228	e4
5	5	37	25	69	45	101	65	133	85	165	a5	197	c5	229	e5
6	6	38	26	70	46	102	66	134	86	166	a6	198	c6	230	e6
7	7	39	27	71	47	103	67	135	87	167	a7	199	c7	231	e7
8	8	40	28	72	48	104	68	136	88	168	a8	200	c8	232	e8
9	9	41	29	73	49	105	69	137	89	169	a9	201	c9	233	e9
10	a	42	2a	74	4a	106	6a	138	8a	170	aa	202	ca	234	ea
11	b	43	2b	75	4b	107	6b	139	8b	171	ab	203	cb	235	eb
12	c	44	2c	76	4c	108	6c	140	8c	172	ac	204	cc	236	ec
13	d	45	2d	77	4d	109	6d	141	8d	173	ad	205	cd	237	ed
14	e	46	2e	78	4e	110	6e	142	8e	174	ae	206	ce	238	ee
15	f	47	2f	79	4f	111	6f	143	8f	175	af	207	cf	239	ef
16	10	48	30	80	50	112	70	144	90	176	b0	208	d0	240	f0
17	11	49	31	81	51	113	71	145	91	177	b1	209	d1	241	f1
18	12	50	32	82	52	114	72	146	92	178	b2	210	d2	242	f2
19	13	51	33	83	53	115	73	147	93	179	b3	211	d3	243	f3
20	14	52	34	84	54	116	74	148	94	180	b4	212	d4	244	f4
21	15	53	35	85	55	117	75	149	95	181	b5	213	d5	245	f5
22	16	54	36	86	56	118	76	150	96	182	b6	214	d6	246	f6
23	17	55	37	87	57	119	77	151	97	183	b7	215	d7	247	f7
24	18	56	38	88	58	120	78	152	98	184	b8	216	d8	248	f8
25	19	57	39	89	59	121	79	153	99	185	b9	217	d9	249	f9
26	1a	58	3a	90	5a	122	7a	154	9a	186	ba	218	da	250	fa
27	1b	59	3b	91	5b	123	7b	155	9b	187	bb	219	db	251	fb
28	1c	60	3c	92	5c	124	7c	156	9c	188	bc	220	dc	252	fc
29	1d	61	3d	93	5d	125	7d	157	9d	189	bd	221	dd	253	fd
30	1e	62	3e	94	5e	126	7e	158	9e	190	be	222	de	254	fe
31	1f	63	3f	95	5f	127	7f	159	9f	191	bf	223	df	255	ff

Hexadecimal Conversion Table. Note that all leading 0s are dropped.

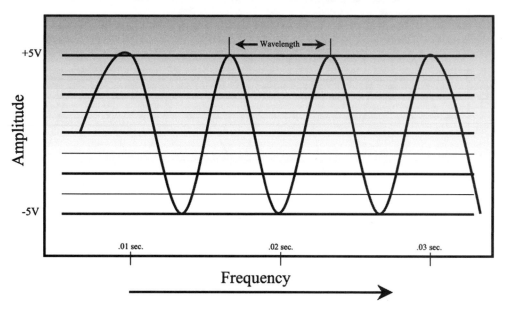

Figure 3.2 A typical sine wave representation

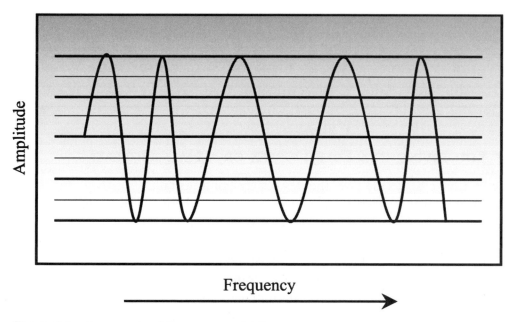

Figure 3.3 An example of frequency modulation

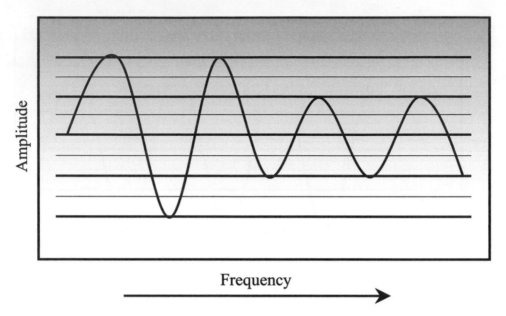

Figure 3.4 An example of amplitude modulation

AM works in the opposite manner. It keeps the frequency of the signal the same. Variations in value show up as variations in signal strength. **Figure 3.4** represents amplitude modulation.

This may sound complicated, but if you think about the way music works, it would be a lot easier. The bass drum is carrying the signal. If you're using FM, the drum never gets any louder or softer. It simply beats fast for 1s and slow for 0s. With AM, the drumbeat maintains a steady rhythm, but beats really loud for 1s and really soft for 0s.

ARE YOU LIVING IN A FULL DUPLEX OR A HALF DUPLEX?

Now you have to decide how the devices are going to talk. Can they both talk at once, or does one device have to shut up and listen whenever the other one has the floor? There are three different methods of determining communication. There is simplex, half duplex, and full duplex.

Simplex is the easiest method to understand, but the least frequently employed. A simplex transmission between two devices means that one device is always talking and the other is always listening. Communications only go in one direction.

Half duplex is more commonly seen on conventional network interface cards. With half duplex either device is capable of sending or receiving data, but only one device can talk at a time. While one device has the wire, the other shuts up. However, both devices have an equal shot at time on the wire. Communications can move in either direction.

Full duplex allows both devices to be either sending or receiving data at the same time. A telephone is an example of a full duplex device. Both parties can send and receive at the same time. The difference here is that, while people might get lost in a conversation trying to do this, transceivers maintain separate transmit and receive buffers for maintaining data integrity.

> **BUZZ WORDS**
>
> **Crosstalk:** The tendency of an electrical current to "leak" from one conductor to another when they are run alongside one another.
>
> **Twisted pair:** A form of cable that consists of multiple strands of wire. The strands are separated into pairs and each of these pairs is twisted together.
>
> **Coaxial:** A conductor that has both the signal conductor and the ground running along the same axis.

EXAM NOTE: Be able to describe full duplex, half duplex, and simplex operation in detail. Also, as this book unfolds, take note of different devices that make use of these techniques and which ones use which modes.

BOUNDED MEDIA

Now that you have a basic understanding of the form signals can take, I will start looking at the pathways that the data will follow. I'll start by examining the more common forms of bounded media. At this point in time—although this is rapidly changing—most of the networks you run into are going to make use of bounded media. They are hooked up by way of copper wire or fiber-optic cables. Copper wire probably doesn't need a lot of explanation. We use it every day of our lives in hundreds of ways. Not all of us have been exposed to fiber optics, however. Fiber-optic cables consist of very long strands of optically clear glass or plastic that carry pulses of light instead of electrical signals.

For years, copper cable has been the medium of choice for network engineers. It's cheap, readily available, and easy to work with. However, changing technology is making fiber optics more and more appealing. Since it moves data along a stream of light, much faster data transmission rates are possible. Also, improvements in manufacturing technology have made it easier to work with. Therefore, the industry is beginning to see fiber being used in more and more situations.

Copper cable for the network will be twisted-pair cabling in virtually any modern network you see. *Twisted-pair cabling* is made by taking either four or eight strands of wire and separating them by pairs. One of the problems with running two wires parallel to one another is that some of the signal from one wire will leak over into the other. This is called *crosstalk*. In order to prevent data from being corrupted, or completely lost, crosstalk must be minimized, if not eliminated all together. One way of minimizing crosstalk is by twisting the pairs of wire together. Oddly enough, this is why it is called twisted pair.

Coaxial cable runs the signal down a single wire in the middle. This is called the core. A metal shielding serves two purposes. First off, it acts as the ground. Second, it acts as a barrier for radio and television waves or other forms of electrical interference that might otherwise corrupt the signal. Since the ground and signal follow the same axis, the wire is called coaxial. There are a few older networks out there that still use coaxial cable. Some proprietary systems still use coaxial cable for interconnecting certain infrastructure devices on their network.

TWISTED PAIR

Twisted-pair cable can come as either *unshielded twisted pair* (UTP) or *shielded twisted pair* (STP). UTP was, until recently, the most common medium used on most networks. Shielded twisted pair borrows a page from coaxial cabling in that it adds a layer of metal foil or braiding underneath the outside layer of insulation. This shielding acts to block radio frequency interference. The twisted-pair cabling used by most networks consists of four pairs of 22- to 24-gauge strands of wire. The insulation around each of the strands is color-coded with some of the wires being solid colors and others being white with a colored stripe. On a single segment, twisted-pair cable is limited to a maximum run of 100 meters. This distance can be greatly affected by the presences of EMF or RFI.

- Pair 1 = Orange - White/Orange striped
- Pair 2 = Green - White/Green striped
- Pair 3 = Blue - White/Blue striped
- Pair 4 = Brown - White/Brown striped

The type of connector used on twisted-pair network cable is the *RJ-45 connector*. Telephone lines use RJ-11 connectors. We've all seen the little plastic clip on the end of our telephone wire, so we know what the RJ-11 looks like. The RJ-45 looks just like it, only bigger. It has a total of eight conductors instead of four or six.

Table 3.2 EIA/TIA 568A and 568B standards for twisted-pair cabling

Pin No.	Signal Carried	568B	568A
1	Transmit (+)	White/Orange	White/Green
2	Transmit (-)	Orange	Green
3	Receive (+)	White/Green	White/Orange
4	Not Used	Blue	Blue
5	Not Used	White/Blue	White/Blue
6	Receive (-)	Green	Orange
7	Not Used	White/Brown	White/Brown
8	Not Used	Brown	Brown

As you'll notice, the only way the two standards differ is in the colors used for voltage-carrying wires.

If we just let anybody and everybody make their cables using those colored wires any way they wanted, there would be chaos. Nobody's patch cables would work with anybody else's. Therefore an organization called the Electronic Industry Association (EIA) got together with the Telecommunications Industry Association (TIA) and ratified color-coding standards to assure that uniform wiring was used from installation to installation. There were two different standards adopted for twisted-pair wiring: EIA/TIA 568A and 568B. The most commonly used color-coding standard is 568B. Those wiring configurations are shown in **Table 3.2**.

You'll notice that the pairs of wires don't just run directly together. The pairs of wire that actually carry signal split at each end. There's a reason for that, and it isn't simply to annoy network engineers. Separating the wires carrying positive voltage from one another and those carrying negative voltage from one another further reduces crosstalk and electrical interference.

A handy little accessory every self-respecting network engineer needs to carry around is the *crossover cable*. This is a patch cable in which the transmit voltage switches sides with the receive voltage from one end to the other. Using a crossover cable, two computers can be directly connected to one another over the NICs. If

---

BUZZ WORD

Crossover cable: A twisted-pair cable that has the transmit and receive signals reversed from the conventional wiring standard. This allows two devices to talk directly to one another without the need for a hub or switch in the path.

73

Table 3.3 Wiring Diagram for Crossover Cable

Pin No. End 1	Signal Transmitted (device)	569A Color Coding	568B Color Coding	Pin No. End 2	Signal Received (device)
1	Transmit (+)	White/Green	White/Orange	3	Receive (+)
2	Transmit (−)	Green	Orange	6	Receive (−)
3	Receive (+)	White/Orange	White/Green	1	Transmit (+)
4	Not Used	Blue	Blue	4	Not Used
5	Not Used	White/Blue	White/Blue		Not Used
6	Receive (−)	Orange	Green	2	Transmit (−)
7	Not Used	White/Brown	White/Brown	7	Not Used
8	Not Used	Brown	Brown	8	Not Used

If you need to directly interconnect two devices, you'll need a crossover cable. The above wiring pinout shows you how to make your own.

you ever get involved in configuring routers, you'll need one of these little toys as well. They can also be used to interconnect two hubs or switches.

Crossover cables are sold in most decent computer stores and electronic super marts. They're not terribly expensive, and they'll pay for themselves the first time you ever really need one out on site. However, you can also save yourself a few sheckles if you simply make your own. All you need is a piece of twisted-pair cabling of the appropriate category and length, a couple of RJ-45 connectors, and a crimping tool. Then follow the wiring pinouts shown in **Table 3.3**.

A couple of times during this discussion, I have used the term *category* in relation to twisted-pair wiring. Over the years, twisted-pair cable has appeared in several different forms. These forms are designated by category. Different categories are capable of maintaining different speeds, and in a couple of cases, physical differences exist as well. For the last several years, category 5, or CAT5 as it is commonly called, has been the cable of choice. The emergence of faster standards has resulted in a couple of new offerings as well.

The transmission speeds that the cable can support are affected in two ways. The first method has nothing to do with the materials used to make the cable. Higher speeds are achieved by increasing the number of twists in a given length of wire. We mentioned earlier that the reason the wire is twisted to begin with is to reduce crosstalk. The more twists there are, the more crosstalk is reduced. The more crosstalk is reduced, the faster data can move across the wire. For example, CAT3 cable is

Table 3.4 Twisted-Pair Categories

Type	Frequency Supported	Usage
1	Voice only, no data	Telephone only
2	4MHz	Localtalk/ISDN
3	16MHz	Ethernet
4	20MHz	Token Ring
5	100MHz	Fast Ethernet
5e	100MHz	100 Baset and Gigabit Ethernet
6	350MHz	Gigabit Ethernet/Asynchronous Transfer Mode (ATM) to 622MB/sec
7	550MHz	Gigabit Ethernet/ATM to 2.4GB/sec

Categories of twisted-pair cabling, past, present, and future

capable of carrying a 10Mb/s signal. It has four twists per foot. CAT5 is good for 100Mb/s and has four twists per inch.

Proposed standards for twisted pair wiring include CAT6 and CAT7. Some of these proposed designs increase speed by changing the materials used. For example, category 7 adds a separate layer of shielding around each individual pair of wires. **Table 3.4** compares the most common twisted-pair cable types, and **Figure 3.5** gives a close up of how the cable is put together.

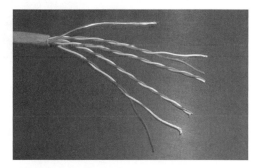

Figure 3.5 Twisted-pair cable is made up of eight individual wires, twisted into pairs. Notice also the strand of filaments that runs the length of the cable. That is there for strength.

COAXIAL CABLING

Coaxial cable (coax) isn't used nearly as often in the networking environment as it used to be. In fact, I'm going to go out on a limb and say that, with the exception of certain proprietary systems, it is never used any more as the primary medium in new installations. However, we're still going to discuss it for two reasons. First, there are still some older networks in place that make use of this medium. Second, it's covered on the exam. If the first reason isn't good enough for you, the second one sure ought to be.

WILL THE REAL BNC PLEASE STAND UP?

Over the years, in different texts and articles, the acronym BNC has been defined as standing for either British Naval Connector or Bayonet Nut Connector. Actually, it stands for neither. The real term is Bayonet Neill-Concelman. This term derives from the two engineers, Carl Concelman of Amphenol and Paul Neill of Bell Labs, each whom was involved in the development of a connector. Neill invented the N-connector and Concelman developed the C-connector. Amphenol went on develop a connector that incorporated features of each. This became the BNC connector we know and love today.

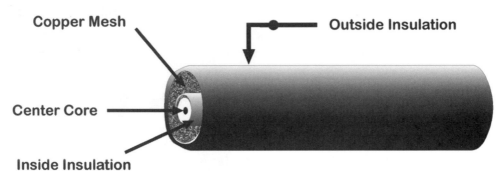

Figure 3.6   Cross-section of a coaxial cable.

In this day and age, you know what coax is, even if you think you don't. If you've ever hooked up a VCR to your television, you've used coax. However, be aware that coax used in video applications and that used in computer networks are not the same. Coaxial cable gets its name from the fact that the data signal travels along the same axis as the ground. If you look at **Figure 3.6**, you'll see that coax consists of a center core, an inside insulator, a mesh or foil shielding (or ground), and an outside insulator.

The form of coax most commonly used in networking is RG58U. This is a 50-ohm cable that meets all standards for Ethernet. You'll also see it called *thinnet*. It is capable of carrying an Ethernet signal for a distance of 185 meters without help. RG59 is what you use in television installations and is a 75-ohm cable. As you might imagine, they are not interchangeable. Don't use television cable for computer networks. Conversely, you probably won't appreciate the results if you use RG58U to hook up your antenna.

Another coaxial cable used in networks is RG-8, or *thicknet*. RG-8 is about as big around as a finger and can be a pain in the neck to deal with. However, it can carry a signal for up to 500 meters. In a coax environment, that makes it the ideal medium for running a backbone cable between distant points.

The connector that RG-58U cable hooks up to is called a *bayonet Neill-Concelman* (BNC) connector. The BNC connector is a bayonet assembly, as illustrated in **Figure 3.7**.

RG-8 is connected to the network by way of a device called a *vampire clamp*. The rather

Figure 3.7 A BNC connector.

macabre name of this device comes from the fact that it consists of two halves that are drawn together around the cable by tightening some screws. Sharp teeth sink in through the insulation and make contact with the conductor. On the outside of the clamp, a 15-pin D-shell connector, called an AUI connector, hooks up to the patch cable.

A third device unique to coax is the *T-connector*. Coax was frequently used in the bus topology that was covered in Chapter One. When computers are wired in a bus configuration, the cables run from one computer to the next, hooking them up in a long chain. In order to do this, there is a little plug that goes into the back of an NIC. That's the T-connector. The incoming coax plugs into one side of the T and the outgoing plugs into the other.

Another terminating connector used with coaxial cable is the F-connector. This differs from the BNC in that it is threaded rather than being a bayonet mount connector. F-connectors are 3/8" in diameter with 32 threads per inch and are typically used in video installations. Early F-connectors were designed with Very High Frequency (VHF) television in mind, with an optimum frequency range of around 175-250MHz. While they can be (and are) used at much higher frequencies, performance of signals beyond this range suffers. To counter this, High Quality (HQ) F-connectors are frequently used with UHF and High Definition television.

Coax was far and away the most common medium used for setting up bus networks. A problem inherent to the bus network is that there is a definite beginning and end to the network. Electrical signals don't like ends. When they reach the end of the wire, they don't simply fly off into space. They need their conductor, which is the wire. So when the signals reach the end of the wire, they simply turn around and go back the other way. Unless something stops this from happening, you won't have a network, you'll have wires filled with random electrical noise. So on each end of a bus network, you need to plug in a *terminating resistor* or terminator. (I prefer the first name. The second sounds too much like a second-rate sci-fi movie to me.)

Fiber-Optic Cable

More and more networks are beginning to discover the advantages of fiber optics. It allows for faster and more secure networks. While there is a 100Mb/s standard for fiber, typically it is used in networks that support gigabit speeds and up. However, once you start using fiber, you need to start developing a whole new vocabulary. You don't have a network card; you have an optical transmitter and an optical receiver. Together, these are your *optical transceiver.*

Two forms of fiber in use are *single-mode* and *multimode fiber.* Single mode allows very little reflection of the light beam as it travels along the fiber. With less reflection of the light, there is less signal scatter and the cable is capable of both higher throughput rates and much longer distances. It makes use of an extremely thin fiber, typically less than 10 microns in diameter. This is the form of cable used by most carriers to move data great distances. However, making fibers that thin and then producing the final product is complex and somewhat expensive. As a result, single mode is too expensive to be using in conventional networks.

Multimode fiber uses a much thicker glass fiber (around 100 microns in diameter) and assumes that a certain amount of reflection of the beam is going to take place. To prevent signal loss, a cladding is wrapped around the fiber. While it does reduce the length of cable that can be used before the signal becomes unusable, manufacturing costs are significantly less.

The cable is quite a bit different from coax as well. For one thing it is made of either glass or optically clear plastic instead of copper. That means it can only bend so far before it breaks. Also, there is the little problem that light can only travel in one direction at a time. Therefore, there are two choices. You can use a single cable, and your transceivers will have to work in half duplex mode all the time. Or, if you want a device that is capable of full duplex operation, you're going to need two cables. Incoming and outbound signals won't be able to share the same strand of fiber. Most cabling designed for network implementation uses the dual-strand method. It has both strands bundled into a single cable. **Figure 3.8** shows a cross

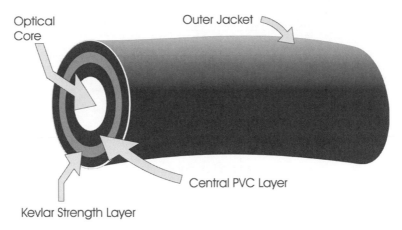

Figure 3.8 Fiber-optic cable consists of a glass core, protected by Kevlar and PVC.

section of a single-stranded cable. Keep in mind that it is very likely that the cable you use will have two strands.

As I mentioned earlier, fiber optics has some advantages over copper. For one thing, much faster data transmission rates are possible. It is already being used to carry data in the range of several gigabits per second, and that is only beginning to tap its potential. Fiber optics can also carry a signal for much greater distances before attenuation begins to degrade the signal.

Because it is not an electrical signal, it is immune to most of the forms of electrical interference that hamper copper-based digital systems. Neither Radio Frequency Interference (RFI) nor Electromagnetic Interference (EMI) has any effect on it. It could care less if you lay it directly along a high-voltage power line. The photons moving along the fiber optics aren't in the least affected by crosstalk. Since it is made of glass, it does not corrode. As a result, it is less affected by the elements. It is, however, much more susceptible to being physically broken by rough usage.

Fiber optics is also the best medium to use in an installation requiring a high degree of security. It is virtually impossible to tap into the medium without bringing the network down. With copper, there are devices that can tap into the cable and intercept the electronic signal without interrupting it. In order to do this with fiber, you have to intercept the beam of light. This means actually breaking the cable to put a device on-line, which brings the network down. This sort of event doesn't go unnoticed.

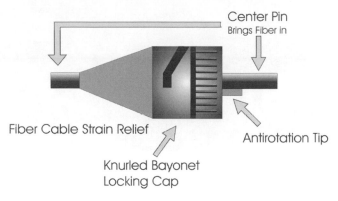

Figure 3.9   Diagram of an ST fiber-optic connector.

If there is any downside to the use of fiber optics at all, it is cost. Both the medium itself and the devices used to propagate, transmit, and receive the signals are all more expensive than traditional copper cable. It is also somewhat more difficult to install. This results in a higher cost for the initial installation.

The optical transmitter is the device that generates the signal for transmission. Depending on the type of device, it uses either a *light emitting diode* (LED) or a *laser diode* (LD) to generate pulses of light. The LED is good for short to moderate distances, while the LD is used in devices that need to pump the data over long distances of cable. It is the job of the LED or LD to translate the digital stream into pulses of light that go out over the cable. The section in Chapter Five about fiber optics will cover just how this works in more detail.

The connectors used for interfacing fiber-optic cable to the device resemble their copper counterparts in many respects. Internally, however, they are much different. They are moving photons instead of electrons, and a precise interface is required for the link to occur.

One of the more common connectors used is the *straight tip* (ST) connector (see **Figure 3.9**). This connector bayonets onto the device. It is available in either single-mode or multimode configurations. You must, of course, use the correct connector with the fiber-optic cable you are using. The two types are not interchangeable.

A connector that has been used in the past, and that you still might see from time to time, is the *Subminiature Assembly* (SMA) connector shown in **Figure 3.10**. These connectors require rather precise assembly and are not for those who suffer from Coordination Deficiency Syndrome. A center conduit that brings the fiber into the device slides into a round center pin. This pin mounts into a threaded cap

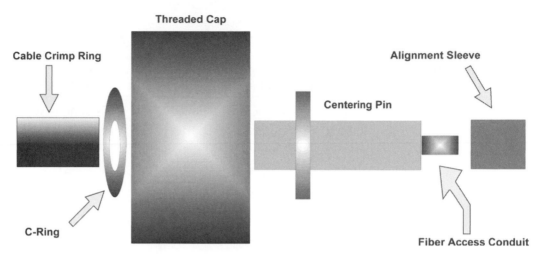

Figure 3.10 The parts and pieces that make up the SMA connector.

and a C-ring holds it in place. A fiber crimping ring locks the cable in place on the outside of the connector and an alignment sleeve makes sure the cable is securely and properly inserted into the device. It actually is not as complicated as it sounds, but still, it takes some practice.

The SC connector uses a push-pull mechanism for mating. The basic SC connector is built around a plug assembly containing a ferrule. A connector housing that aligns the ferrules brings the fiber core into proper alignment. Connectors are keyed in such a way to prevents misalignment. Several plugs can be joined together to form a multi-position connector. The advantage of this is in the creation of bi-directional connectors. One fiber can carry information in one direction, while the other fiber can carry information in the other direction.

See **Table 3.5** for a summary of bounded media and their characteristics.

UNBOUNDED MEDIA

Wireless networking has been with us for a while. However, certain limitations in speed, security, cost, and transmission distances have kept it from being more popular than it is. Its coverage on the exam is also somewhat limited. Therefore, I will limit this section to a brief overview of the different forms of wireless networking that are available and when you might want to use which one.

Table 3.5 Summary of Commonly Used Bounded Media

	Media Descriptor	Frequency	Bandwidth	Max. Segment Length	Typical Use
Twisted Pair	Cat1	1MHz	1Mb/s	N/A	Telephone wire
	Cat2	5MHz	4Mb/s	100M	ISDN/Token Ring
	Cat3	10Mhx	10Mb/s	100M	10BaseT
	Cat4	20MHz	16Mb/s	100M	Token Ring
	Cat5	100MHz	100Mb/s	100M	100BaseT
	Cat5e	100MHz	1000Mb/s	100M	100BaseT/ 1000BaseT
	Cat6*	350MHz	1000Mb/s	100M	1000BaseT
	Cat7*	500MHz	1000Mb/s+	Not yet defined	Not typically used in the United States
Coaxial	RG58	~4000MHz	10Mb/s	180M	10BaseT
	RG8	~4000MHz	10Mb/s	500M	10BaseT Backbone
Fiber Optics	Single mode	N/A	>10Gb/s	40000M	FDDI, ATM
	Multimode	N/A	>200Mb/s		
	2000M	FDDI			

A useful summary of everything I've covered about bounded media.

Note: *Cat6 and Cat7 are not yet ratified and specifications may change.

Be aware, however, that this is rapidly changing. Wireless technology is definitely in our future, as is evidenced by the integration of computer technology and cellular phones. In addition, the number of products on the market for wireless home networking seems to be increasing almost daily. They're becoming much less expensive and significantly easier for the novice to install. Still, before you rush out and spend several hundred bucks just so you can get rid of a bunch of ugly wires, there are some things you need to consider first. That's what this section is all about.

Wireless networking can, at best, be described as being in its infancy. Typical transmission speeds range from a low of less than 1Mb/s to a high of around

11Mb/s. Some recently emerging technologies threaten to push those speeds into the 100Mb/s range. As of this writing, several companies are already shipping products that function at 54Mb/s.

The different wireless technologies I will discuss fall into three categories of signal transmission—*optical, radio,* and *microwave.* Each has its advantages and disadvantages. Optical transmission is the most commonly used to interconnect two devices one to the other, so I'll start there.

OPTICAL NETWORKING

Optical networking gets its name from the fact that data is transmitted by pulses of light. This is done using one of two different methods. The first and most frequently used method uses *infrared* light waves. You see the technology behind it in use all the time, whether you happen to be aware of it or not. Every time someone asks you to turn the TV down and you reach for the remote, you're using a form of infrared networking. To be sure, you are not dealing with computers in the conventional sense. Still, there are two devices interacting with one another by way of pulses of infrared light.

The second method resembles fiber optics in that it uses a *laser beam* to send data. The similarity breaks down in one key respect, however. There is no cable interconnecting the devices. The beam shoots through the air and is picked up by the receiving device.

Even though it may seem that wireless networking has only recently become the newest and latest technology fad, the technology has been around for a while. IEEE defined the standards for wireless networking in Section 802.11 of the OSI standards (to be discussed later in the chapter) back in 1997.

COMMUNICATING OVER INFRARED

As I mentioned earlier, infrared networking works in a manner extremely similar to that of a typical remote control. The transmitting device takes the stream of 0s and 1s from the computer and encodes them into pulses of infrared light. The hard part is getting it from one device to another. Since this is a beam of light carrying that precious data, there are all kinds of things that might go wrong. Therefore, depending on the environment, there are a few different transmission methods from which to choose. Each has its own advantages and disadvantages.

Line-of-sight networking is primarily used for interconnecting two devices. Each communicating device needs to have an unobstructed path between itself and its partner (see **Figure 3.11**). You need to be able to stand in the position

Figure 3.11 Line-of-sight transmission requires that the communicating devices have an unobstructed view of each other.

of one transceiver and look over and see the other (which is, by the way, why it is called line of sight). This works well for linking your notebook to your PC or a wireless printer to any computer similarly equipped.

Reflective networks might work well for networking multiple devices in a smaller environment. Every device needs to be able to act as either a transmitter or a receiver. Since you never really know at any given point in time which role a device will play, you will also make use of a central access point. Some companies call this a transmission redirector while others simply call it an access hub. Each device needs to have a direct and unobstructed path between itself and the access point over which the beam can travel. Then the access point relays the data.

Scatter infrared networking bounces the signal off of reflective surfaces and therefore can "go around corners" without the added cost of a central access point, as you can see in **Figure 3.12**. It does require that the environment be friendly to reflected light. Porous stone walls painted a matte black probably won't be your best choice for decorator schemes (whether you're employing wireless networking or not!). You want nice smooth walls painted in light colors.

Another thing that hinders scatter infrared is sharp pulses of reflected light. For example, if your office happens to be on street level, on a sunny day reflections of sunlight off of the bumpers and windshields of the cars can interfere with the signal. This forces data to be resent, slowing the network's throughput down significantly. Since scatter infrared is already one of the slower technologies in use today, you can really do without that.

Broadband optical telepoint isn't something you're likely to see in your average small office/home office (SOHO) environment. It is the fastest of infrared technologies and has no trouble moving multimedia and streaming video. Since it is a

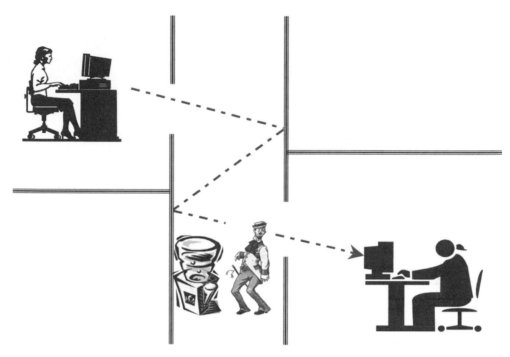

Figure 3.12 Even the boss blocking the door while he gets a drink won't interfere with a properly designed scatter infrared network.

broadband technology, multiple signals can be carried at once, each carried on a different frequency of light wave representing a separate channel.

MOVING DATA ON LASER BEAMS

Transmitting data over infrared isn't without its limitations. One of the key disadvantages of infrared is speed. While progress is being made in that direction, it is still one of the slower technologies currently in use. The distance limitations of infrared frequently become a factor as well.

Communication over laser helps to overcome both of these problems. Laser connections can prove to be a little more difficult to install at the outset and the cost of deploying a laser system reflects that. Not only is the hardware more expensive, but the costs associated with getting it up and running are higher as well. However, since it can provide very fast transmission rates and much greater distances between stations, there are situations that specifically call for laser. Also, despite its initial outlay, laser technology can provide much more efficient and cost-effective means for interconnecting offices, compared to leasing out a high-speed telecommunications line. All those monthly service charges and fees go away. This is, of course, assuming a line of sight can be maintained. It's a real bummer to pour all of that money into new technology, only to have a new high-rise sprout up between your two offices.

The technology involved in converting and transmitting data by way of optical means is very similar to that used by fiber optics. The key difference is that you don't have a contained system over which data is sent. The most common conventional laser systems provide speeds of either 155Mb/s or 622Mb/s. Distances of up to 4km (two and a half miles for the non-metric-oriented readers out there) are supported, although this can be affected by a number of factors. Inclement weather (such as a dust storm), atmospheric conditions (i.e., pollution), and physical obstructions (a flock of pigeons flying across the beam) all can affect the signal. Another thing that affects distance is the speed of the signal being transmitted. A 622Mb/s transmission would only go about half as far as a 155Mb/s signal.

Some technologies, such as LightPointe Teledata Communications' Lightstation Multilink Series, use multiple beams to minimize the distance-limiting factors listed above. Therefore, if a bird should interrupt one beam, another beam will pick up the slack. In either case, most networking protocols have error-correction mechanisms that will cause the offending or lost packets to be resent.

The laser interconnect is protocol transparent. This means that, whatever networking protocols you might be using, the signal can be sent and received, unlike with some other media that only work with certain protocols (more on this little complication in Chapter Fourteen, Working with Remote Access). Therefore, a 10BaseT network can move over the beam just as easily as a 622Mb/s ATM. If you're new to networking and don't know what 10BaseT and ATM are, they will be discussed in more detail in later chapters.

NETWORKING OVER THE RADIO

Beginners frequently don't think of good old-fashioned radio as being very high tech, and it is rarely associated with computers. For most people, our only exposure to radio transmissions is the output of Q99 Acid Rock pouring from the car speakers as we navigate the freeway on the way to work. Even that is going by the wayside, as we all add 12-disk CD changers to our cars. Emerging technology, in fact is making radio transmissions the medium of choice for the SOHO environment.

Radio waves fall into three categories: *short wave, very high frequency* (VHF), and *ultrahigh frequency* (UHF). In the U.S., the Federal Communications Commission (FCC) oversees usage of these frequencies. With a few exceptions, if you want to use radio waves, you must first be licensed to operate your equipment, and, second, you need to be assigned your frequency. The exceptions are certain frequency ranges that do not fall under the FCC's watchful eye (except, of course, in how you put the frequencies to use). These are the public bands, and they fall within the ranges of 902 to 928MHz and 5.72 to 5.85GHz. However, since anyone can use them, two factors impact on their usefulness.

First of all, you are severely limited in the amount of power you use to broadcast. The purpose of doing this is to limit the distance over which transmissions can be sent. That way one signal doesn't get so saturated with usage that it becomes useless to everyone else.

Second, you do not have exclusive control of the frequency and if somebody else jumps in, that signal gets mixed with yours. If you're familiar with citizen's band radio, you know all about this. When you're simply exchanging pleasantries with the trucker on I-89 about the smokies on the prowl, there will always be somebody that joins in your conversation with his or her contributions. On a voice channel, that's no big deal. However, when that signal is your precious data, this is a problem. For one thing, you don't want your data getting corrupted by unwanted signals, and maybe even more important, you probably don't want just anybody picking your data out of the air.

Networking over radio is generally done with either *single frequency* or *spread spectrum*. Single-frequency transmission is just what it sounds like. You are assigned a single frequency by the FCC, or perhaps your device is configured for a public access frequency, and that frequency is what you use to transmit your data. If security is not a huge issue, this technology works pretty well and offers slightly higher transmission speeds than spread spectrum. When you use spread spectrum, you are assigned several frequencies and you "hop" from one to the other. This makes it a little more difficult for someone to intercept your transmissions.

SINGLE-FREQUENCY TRANSMISSIONS

As I stated in the last paragraph, the concept is simple. You have one frequency. Your data is converted from digital to analog radio waves and transmitted over the air. Implementation of a single-frequency radio network will be one of two types:

- *Low Power, Single Frequency* (LPSF): You are permitted an extremely limited broadcast power. The effective operating range between devices ranges from 20 and 25 meters. Speeds (depending on choice of equipment) range from as low as 1Mb/s to a maximum of about 10Mb/s. These networks are useful for small offices where it is impractical to run wiring for any reason.
- *High Power, Single Frequency* (HPSF): This technology is useful for setting up low-speed wide-area network (WAN) links where conventional bounded media are not feasible. The broadcast equipment is permitted to operate at

a higher power, allowing for line-of-sight telecommunications. In some cases, a controlled atmospheric bounce can extend the range of the network beyond the horizon. Speed limitations are similar to that of LPSF.

Whichever single-frequency model you choose, you are going to be looking at some limitations. Unlike the optical technologies I discussed earlier, radio waves are virtually impervious to conditions such as smoke, smog, or birds. However, anything that generates EMI can degrade or interrupt the signal. And almost anything electrical generates EMI. A lightning strike, radio and television transmitters, electrical substations, and almost anything else you can think of may inadvertently generate signals that overlap yours. Another key issue is that the signals you are transmitting are also easily picked out of the air and intercepted. Therefore, security can become a very real issue.

SPREAD-SPECTRUM RADIO

Spread-spectrum transmission addresses the issue of security. The transceiver is programmed with a range of frequencies. Because the broadcast signal is continually bouncing from one frequency to another, intercepting the signal is more of a challenge. It isn't impossible. Anybody with the cash can pick up equipment over the Internet that make it possible. However, it does mean that you're safe from all but the most dedicated of hackers. This security unfortunately does not come without its associated costs. The equipment required for spread spectrum is substantially more expensive and the speeds are abysmally low. How low depends on which of the two primary spread-spectrum technologies you choose to implement. In order to make sure the transmitting station and the intended recipient get all the data that was sent, and receive it intact, some form of synchronization of frequency hopping has to take place. There are basically two choices.

Direct-sequence transmission is the faster of the two methods. Both the sending and the receiving device employ a predefined sequence of radio frequencies along with a predefined timing sequence. They use those sequences to jump from one frequency to the other and never vary from the sequence. As you might imagine, this is the less secure of the two methods. While it will keep out the casual eavesdropper, a dedicated hacker will have no problem cracking the frequencies in use, the hop sequence, or the timing sequence.

Frequency hopping uses a far more complicated timing scheme for switching from frequency to frequency. Also, there can be alternating patterns in the hop sequence. This makes it far more difficult to hack, since both the timing and the sequence change. This is a far more secure method of sending data; however, it comes at the cost of speed. Frequency-hopping networks are measured in kilobits per second and not megabits per second.

NETWORKING OVER MICROWAVES

Sorry. I'm not going to teach you how to program your microwave oven over the network from your PC, although it probably won't be long before we can do that. However, the same energy that bakes your potato or heats up your bowl of clam chowder can also be used to send data. And it can send that data across extremely long distances. As with the laser link I discussed earlier, microwave transmission requires that the sender and the receiver have a direct line-of-sight communications link. And unlike radio, you can't bounce the signal off the atmosphere.

Microwave networking comes in two flavors, *terrestrial microwave* and *satellite microwave*. As the names suggest, terrestrial microwave is ground-based, while satellite microwave bounces the signal off of a satellite orbiting in space.

Terrestrial microwave technology makes use of parabolic antennae connected to specialized transceivers. As I said earlier, each of these dishes must have a direct line of sight with its partner, so the height of the mirror directly affects distance of transmission. If a mountain happened to choose to sit in the spot between you and your remote office, then the simple solution is to put a relay station on top of the mountain. Terrestrial microwave can be an ideal replacement for bounded WAN media. It is capable of transmission speeds of several gigabits per second and once it is in place, you are no longer at the mercy of questionable service providers and inept ISPs, or the weather and wayward pigeons.

If you ever saw the movie based on Michael Crichton's novel *Congo*, you saw satellite microwave in use. All you need in order to set up a satellite link is to have the FCC assign you a frequency and install the right equipment; that means piles of paperwork and tons of permits. There is an impressive array of satellites in orbit that are capable of bouncing your signal. Therefore, there are precious few (if any) places on the surface of the planet from which you won't be able to receive the signal.

The one minor inconvenience of this technology is that the distances involved will generate something called a propagation delay. This is the amount of time that elapses from the time you send your signal out, it travels 50,000 miles to the nearest satellite, gets processed and sent back over the 50,000-mile return trip to your intended recipient, who replies and sends that signal on the same path back. This results in delays of up to several seconds.

Whichever method you choose, you're going to spend a pretty good chunk of change on the hardware you need, an assigned frequency, and the licensed operators necessary to keep the system up and running. This is not "basic" networking technology, and your average network engineer is going to give you a blank, or possibly horrified, look if you ask him or her to troubleshoot a downed link.

CHAPTER SUMMARY

In this chapter, I introduced some key concepts to understanding network technology. I discussed the difference between a digital and an analog signal, and looked at how those signals get moved over the medium. In addition, you learned that not all networking media can be seen, touched, smelled, or tasted. In addition to the bounded media types, there are also the unbounded types—or wireless media, as they're affectionately called. It's important to understand these concepts, because in later chapters, I'll be assuming this is familiar territory as I get into discussions about more advanced topics.

BRAIN DRAIN

1. Describe in your own words the difference between bounded and unbounded media.

2. Describe in as much detail as possible how Frequency-Hopping Spread-Spectrum networking works.

3. How many transmission modes can you think of for sending encoded data over an electrical signal running on copper wire?

4. If you are setting up a 100Mb/s backbone connection between two buildings 1,000 feet apart and need the connection to be as secure as possible, what medium will you use and why?

THE 64K$ QUESTIONS

1. Which of the following would be considered unbounded media?
   a. Coaxial cable
   b. Scatter infrared
   c. Microwave
   d. Multimode fiber optics

2. The address A2 00 B1 11 is an example of _____.
   a. Binary notation
   b. Decimal notation

    c. Hexadecimal notation

    d. A MAC address

3. IEEE 802.11 standards describe _____.

    a. Cabling

    b. Wireless networking

    c. Transceiver design specifications

    d. EMF resistance requirements

4. Vampire clamps are used to connect _____.

    a. Fiber-optic cabling

    b. Thinnet cabling

    c. Thicknet cabling

    d. Twisted-pair cabling

5. Which wireless technology makes use of frequency-hopping spread spectrum?

    a. Radio

    b. Infrared

    c. Laser

    d. Microwave

6. In the hexadecimal value A200h, the *h* represents the value _____.

    a. 12

    b. 14

    c. 16

    d. It doesn't represent a value. It simply indicates hexadecimal notation.

7. Data encoded and moved over an electrical current is said to be a(n) _____signal.

    a. Physical

    b. Analog

    c. Digital

    d. Crosstalk

8. For continuous full duplex operation over fiber optics, a circuit would require two separate cables.

    a. True

    b. False

9. An ST connector is used to _____.

   a. Interconnect coaxial segments

   b. Terminate twisted-pair cable

   c. Connect fiber optics to a transceiver

   d. Link two hubs together

10. Which of the following offers global communications?

   a. Spread spectrum

   b. Gigabit Ethernet

   c. Laser

   d. Satellite microwave

11. What was one of the biggest limitations of coaxial cable?

   a. Coax allowed much shorter cable runs than twisted pair.

   b. It was much more expensive.

   c. Installation costs were prohibitive.

   d. Networks were limited to 10MB/s throughput.

12. When measuring the strength of a carrier signal, you are measuring _____.

   a. Amplitude

   b. Amperage

   c. Frequency

   d. Voltage

13. A carrier signal that encodes data by assigning each value a different number of beats per second on the carrier is called _____.

   a. Pulse modulation

   b. Frequency modulation

   c. Amplitude modulation

   d. Beat modulation

14. You have two devices set up. One is a data collector/transmitter installed in a remote wilderness location that simply sends information to you. You cannot send back to it. What form of communications is this?

   a. Duplex

   b. Half duplex

    c. Directional

    d. Simplex

15. CAT5 twisted pair can send signals farther than CAT3 cable.

    a. True

    b. False

16. Which of the following media is the most difficult to tap into without the user knowing it's been done?

    a. UTP

    b. Coax

    c. Radio

    d. Fiber optics

17. The electrical phenomenon that causes the signal from one wire to bleed into another wire running parallel to it is called _____.

    a. EMI

    b. ESD

    c. Crosstalk

    d. Crossover

18. The proper terminal for CAT5 cable is an RJ-ll connector.

    a. True

    b. False

19. The organization that define the wiring diagrams for twisted pair patch cords is _____.

    a. CompTIA

    b. EIA/TIA

    c. IEEE

    d. Icomp

20. How many of the wires in a typical Ethernet cable actually carry data signals?

    a. 1

    b. 2

    c. 4

    d. 8

Tricky Terminology

Amplitude: The relative strength of an electrical signal.

Coaxial: A conductor that has both the signal conductor and the ground running along the same axis.

Crossover cable: A twisted-pair cable that has the transmit and receive signals reversed from the conventional wiring standard. This allows two devices to talk directly to one another without the need for a hub or switch in the path.

Crosstalk: The tendency of an electrical current to "leak" from one conductor to another when they are run alongside one another.

Frequency: How many times in a specifically defined timer interval an event occurs. Usually measured in hertz.

Full duplex: The ability to send and receive data in either direction, both directions at the same time.

Half duplex: The ability to send and receive data in either direction, but in only one direction at a time.

Hexadecimal: A Base 16 counting method that makes use of the 10 numeric characters plus six alphabetical characters as well.

Simplex: The ability to send data in only one direction, but not the other way.

Sniffer: A device or piece of software that is used to capture data packets off the network for analysis.

Spread spectrum: A radio networking technology that makes use of multiple assigned radio frequencies.

Terminating resistor: Small device that absorbs the electrical signal at the end of the conductor to prevent it from rebounding in the opposite direction.

Twisted pair: A form of cable that consists of multiple strands of wire. The strands are separated into pairs and each of these pairs is twisted together.

Acronym Alert

AM: Amplitude Modulation. A method of sending signals over an analog medium that encodes data by changing the relative strength of the signal without affecting the frequency.

EMI: Electromagnetic Interference. A form of unwanted electrical modification that occurs because of the magnetic energy of some form.

FCC: Federal Communications Commission

FM: Frequency Modulation. A method of sending signals over an analog medium that encodes data by changing the frequency of the signal without affecting the relative strength.

LD: Laser Diode. A small electrical device that emits pulses of laser light.

LED: Light Emitting Diode. Small electrical device that emits conventional light waves (usually in the visible spectrum).

RFI: Radio Frequency Interference. Similar to EMI, except that it specifically defines wavelengths in the Radio/Television area of the Electromagnetic Spectrum.

SMA: Subminiature Assembly. One of several forms of connector used with fiber-optic cabling.

SOHO: Small Office, Home Office

ST: Straight Tip. One of several forms of connector used with fiber-optic cabling.

UHF: Ultrahigh Frequency

VHF: Very High Frequency

PART TWO

THE WORLD OF OSI

CHAPTER 4

WELCOME TO OSI

Imagine for a moment, if you will, a world in which every manufacturer of computer hardware and every producer of system software or operating systems approached the networking of computers using their own proprietary method. Wouldn't that be fun? Once you started with one brand of network card, you'd be stuck with that brand. All systems in your network would have to run the same operating system, and, in many cases, the same applications. If some new technology came out that you just couldn't live without, you'd have to scrap the whole system and start again.

Well that obviously isn't the case. While there are a few compatibility issues that raise their heads now and again, for the most part, our world is getting to be pretty well networked across dozens of platforms and hundreds of brands of computers and types of computer hardware. The reason we can do this is because of *protocols*. Protocols are small, compact programs that take data from one source and translate that data into a form that a completely different system can recognize and use.

The reason protocols work so well today is that in the early days of networking, it became abundantly evident that some standards were going to have to be agreed upon and applied. The International Standards Organization (ISO) described its proposed architectural network structure in 1987 in a paper entitled ISO TR/9007, *Information Processing Systems—Concepts and Terminology for the Conceptual Schema and the Information Base*. These concepts were further refined in 1989 in ISO 7498-2, *Information Processing Systems: Open Systems Interconnection A Formal Description Technique Based on the Temporal Ordering of Observational Behavior*. Thus was born the *Open Systems Interconnect* model, or more simply, OSI.

BUZZ WORD ————————

Protocol: A set of predefined rules and formats used to allow two unlike devices or applications to communicate. Protocols also act as a translator for devices that use unlike command sets.

The theory was that the latter paper would be the definitive guide around which all network drivers, protocols, applications, and hardware would be designed. The authors of the paper defined seven specific layers—the OSI layers—that separate and define specific functions that must be performed in the process of interdevice communication. Each layer performs only its own function and communicates only with its counterpart on the other side from one end of the communications link to the other.

I say "theory" because, while for several years the industry was loyal to OSI in both theory and application, for the most part, it has simply become an educational model. For example, very few companies take the top three layers, Application, Presentation, and Session, very seriously any more. For the most part, they can be considered historical artifacts. However, for the purposes of completeness, detailed discussions of their intended functions are included in this book.

Many manufacturers complained that the standards were too loosely defined and they chose to take their own paths. These days, there is so much proprietary technology in use that it would be difficult to consider OSI a true standard. However, even the proprietary technologies (most of Cisco's technologies are excellent examples of this) work around OSI in order to assure that their devices communicate with other manufacturers' devices. Therefore, we don't have the OSI Standards; we have the OSI Model.

I will be introducing relatively few concepts in this chapter that are CompTIA Exam Objectives. But the ones that are covered are key items that receive intense scrutiny on the exam. Many of these will receive additional and more detailed coverage later in the book. Objectives introduced here include:

1.2 Specify the main features of 802.2 (Logical Link Control), 802.3 (Ethernet), 802.5 (token ring), 802.11 (wireless), and FDDI (Fiber Distributed Data Interface) networking technologies.

2.2 Identify the seven layers of the OSI (Open Systems Interconnect) model and their functions.

2.3 Identify the OSI (Open Systems Interconnect) layers at which the following network components operate: Hubs, Switches, Bridges, Routers, NICs (Network Interface Card), WAPs (Wireless Access Point).

THE SEVEN LAYERS OF OSI

Okay, so I have explained how ISO defined seven different layers in its architecture. The accepted custom to is to number the layers from one at the bottom to seven at the top. You frequently see layers five, six, and seven referred to as the "top layers" or the "upper layers." The layers defined by OSI, starting at the bottom and working up are:

- Layer One – Physical
- Layer Two – Data Link
- Layer Three – Network
- Layer Four – Transport
- Layer Five – Session
- Layer Six – Presentation
- Layer Seven – Application

You're going to need to memorize these layers for the exam and be able to spout them off as easily as you do your own name. Most people do better if they use a phrase or *mnemonic* to make the process of memorization easier. I happen to like, from Layer Seven to Layer One, *Apple Pie Seems To Need Dill Pickles*. Since you didn't grow up in my family, that phrase probably won't make as much sense to you as it does me. Going from Layer One to Layer Seven, I use *People Don't Need To See Private Auctions*. Make up your own, if it will be easier to remember.

> **EXAM NOTE:** If you want to have any chance at all of passing the exam, know the OSI Model inside and out and backwards and forwards. You'll need to know what pieces of hardware work at each layer, what protocols and utilities function at each layer, and how each layer interacts. Do not underestimate the importance of knowing this material.

As I mentioned in the previous section, each of these layers is responsible for its own tasks and only its own tasks. If the Transport Layer fails to perform its job as expected, the Session Layer won't fill in for it and fix the problem. The Session Layer will simply take the data it's been handed and perform its magic and move it on down the line. And once again, from one end of the communications chain to the other, between systems, each layer only communicates with itself.

To understand what I mean by this, I should probably explain that your data is sent out over the media in chunks. For example, if you are copying a 20MB file from the server to your workstation, that file doesn't come to you in a steady stream of data 20MB long. If that were the case, every time somebody transferred a file, the network would become unusable to all other users on the network. That would be

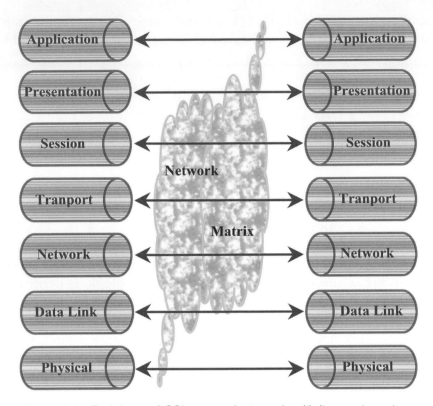

Figure 4.1 Each layer of OSI communicates only with its counterpart layer on the other computer.

ungainly and frustrating. Instead, the data is sent out in smaller sections called *frames.* The creation and destruction of those frames is a primary task that has been defined by the OSI model.

What the Application Layer of the transmitting computer does to the data is undone by the Application Layer of the receiving computer. Likewise, the information added by the Transport Layer of the computer sending the data is seen and processed only by the Transport Layer of the intended recipient (see **Figure 4.1**). I will show you how that works as this chapter unfolds, and examine each layer in more detail in subsequent chapters.

So why does there need to be a layered model? Why can't you just say, "This is how networking is done. It's my way or the highway!"

There are several reasons why a layered architecture is useful. One of these reasons is something you should be appreciating greatly right now. And that is breaking the architecture down into separate layers makes the concepts easier to understand, and thereby easier to learn.

Another reason is that a layered structure allows the development of new technologies or concepts to occur without continually requiring the restructure of networking in general. For example, as I will discuss later, routers operate primarily at the network layer. If a company develops a new routing protocol that requires that a function of the network layer be manipulated in some way, it is only making modifications within the network layer. The remaining layers remain unaffected. That makes it much easier to develop new protocols and/or applications.

Finally, troubleshooting problems is easier if you fully understand each layer, its functions, and what devices operate at that layer. For example, if you are certain that your trouble originates at the Network Layer, you can concentrate your efforts on devices and protocols that operate within that layer.

MOVEMENT OF DATA BETWEEN LAYERS

You have seen already that each layer is communicating with its counterpart on the other side of the link. These two communicating layers are known as *peer entities*. While different, adjacent layers on the same machine don't communicate with one another in the classical sense, they still need to interact with one another. Each layer is dependent on the services performed by the one above it or below it, depending on the direction of data flow. Movement of data between layers on the same machine is done through *service access points* (SAP).

Within any given layer, there is going to be some service, application, or piece of hardware that is performing a function during a communications session. Any hardware or software that exists and functions within a specific layer is known as an *entity*. The hardware or software that is actually doing some work during a particular session is known as the *active element*.
During any given session, it is likely that several different active elements will be at work, making the transfer of data between computers happen. The active elements at work are performing some sort of service that is necessary to the adjacent layer. The specific function to be performed is known as the *service primitive*. The layer makes use of *parameters* to define certain data and control information.

When it comes time for one active element to move data to another active element in a neighboring layer, it needs to

BUZZ WORDS

Peer entity: Any two devices, protocols, or services that operate on the same layer that can communicate with one another.

Service access point: A predefined address that is used to transfer data between OSI layers.

Service primitive: A specific function or activity that is performed by any specific layer entity.

103

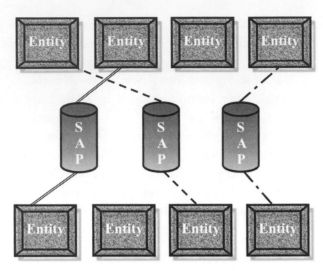

Figure 4.2 Service access points are logical addresses between active elements within the OSI layers.

know how to find the other entity. The service access point is an address in memory that acts as a conduit between the two entities. Each active element needs to have its own address, or SAP. **Figure 4.2** illustrates how this principal works.

PROTOCOL DATA UNITS

As data moves between layers, it changes form. The way it works could almost remind you of a scary movie from the 1960s. But it's not quite that bad. It does tend to confuse beginners, however, when they see terms like *message, packet, segment,* or *frame* being thrown around, seemingly indiscriminately, as if they're all one and the same.

They're not. As the data moves through the layers, it is broken down into smaller pieces, and different types of information are added at each step of the way, until the network has something it can send across the wire in very short bursts. Each layer has a specific function to perform, and in each layer the slice of data being worked on has a specific format. This is known as the *protocol data unit* (PDU). Starting at the top layer, the Application Layer, and working down, the data gets broken down from that 20MB file I was discussing into raw bits of binary data. The data is moved across the wire in specifically timed bursts that contain a certain number of bits.

The part that can be a little confusing to the beginner is that the actual breaking down of the data doesn't begin until the data reaches the Transport Layer. There-

Table 4.1 PDUs and Their Layers

Layer Number	Layer Name	PDU
Seven	Application	Message
Six	Presentation	Message
Five	Session	Message
Four	Transport	Segment
Three	Network	Packet
Two	Data Link	Frame
One	Physical	Bits

With the exception of the top three layers, where data is always referred to as a message, there is a protocol data unit specific to each layer.

fore, the top three layers are all dealing with a steady stream of data. **Table 4.1** lists the PDUs as they are defined at each layer.

Another term you'll see used frequently is *Service Data Unit.* Don't get overly confused. The service data unit is simply the PDU arriving from the adjacent layer. Also, it is generally accepted that the cluster of bits moving along the wire that makes up a singular data chunk is referred to as a frame, or sometimes (popularly, but not necessarily accurately) as a packet.

EXAM NOTE: Know the protocol data units as they relate to each of the OSI layers. These become the source of several different types of question.

THE LAYERS DEFINED

While I will be going into each of the layers in detail in subsequent chapters in this book, it is almost impossible to continue without at least a basic idea of what each layer is and what it does. Therefore, I'm going to take the next few pages to provide a very simplified overview of the layers. Here I will simply discuss the primary responsibilities and functions for each layer, and, where relevant, point out what pieces of hardware work at any given level. Since I have not yet discussed protocols, network services, or applications, I'll defer that to the chapters specific to each layer.

To put the process into a nutshell, the network is taking a continuous stream of data, breaking it into smaller pieces, and sending it out across the wire in packets of data. As the data moves through the seven OSI layers, each layer performs its magic, adding its own layer-specific information to the packet before handing it off to the next layer. By the time it is ready to go out over the wire, the piece of data that originated from an application that you are running has a whole lot of information that has been added to the front of the packet. These pieces of information are called *headers*. In addition, there will be a smaller amount of control data added to the end of the packet. This is the packet's *trailer*. The process of creating packets, from beginning to end, is the process of *encapsulation*.

> **EXAM NOTE:** Read the next few sections carefully. You will need to be able to describe the process of encapsulation in detail.

THE APPLICATION LAYER

Beginning students frequently confuse the Application Layer with the applications running on the computer. This is not the case. While there are a few applications specific to this layer, the actual purpose of the layer is to act as an interface between the networking infrastructure and the applications that the end user actually sees.

As I mentioned, there are applications designed specifically to run in this layer. Examples of these would be email applications, FTP applications, and Telnet. These programs are small utilities that provide some form of user-friendly interface to the services they actually perform. On a more generic level, the more common applications running on the system, such as word processors, spreadsheets, and so forth, make use of the Application Layer as the gateway to the network. It is this layer that provides the interface to network services.

In terms of network services actually provided by this layer, in addition to the network access described above, it also makes sure that data is streaming to the upper levels at an acceptable rate. This is a process known as *flow control*. Also, in the event that an error is detected by one of the upper layers, the application layer can initiate certain error recovery procedures. It can do nothing to actually detect these errors, but if an upper layer indicates that an error state exists, the application layer can initiate the response necessary to fix the problem. See **Table 4.2** for a summary of Application Layer protocols.

Table 4.2 Application Layer Protocols

Protocol	What it does
Network Terminal Protocol (Telnet)	Provides text communication for remote login and communication across the network
File Transfer Protocol (FTP)	Used to download and upload files across the network
Simple Mail Transfer Protocol (SMTP)	Delivers electronic mail messages across the network
Post Office Protocol, Version 3 (POP-3)	Allows users to pick up email across the network from a central server
Domain Name Service (DNS)	Maps IP addresses to Internet domain names
Hyper Text Transfer Protocol (HTTP)	The protocol used by the World Wide Web to exchange text, pictures, sounds, and other multimedia information via a graphical user interface (GUI)
Routing Information Protocol (RIP)	Used by network devices to exchange routing information
AppleShare (Apple)	Allows Apple (Macintosh) clients to access data from remote locations, or request services from server applications

Protocols running in the Application Layer are easily recognized by many people. It should be noted that these protocols perform functions in the Presentation and Session layers as well.

THE PRESENTATION LAYER

Not all computers talk and act the same way. As I discussed earlier, that's the whole reason behind having protocols. It is the Presentation Layer that comes up with the "happy medium" that allows two unlike computers or two unlike applications to communicate.

A primary function of the Presentation Layer is to translate the data from one format to another. It does so by taking any format known to it and converting it to a common format known by all other applications, services, hardware, or platforms that use the OSI standards as a base. You'll sometimes see the phrase "getting the data ready for the network" used in relationship to this process. And that's a good description of what the layer does.

That's not all it does, however. Not all computers use the same character sets or file formats. Sometimes you make use of data encryption and sometimes you don't.

These forms of conversion are also the responsibility of the Presentation Layer. For example, if you make use of MP3 files a lot or JPEG or TIFF or any other popular compression format when you send the data over the wire, it is the Presentation Layer that is handling the format conversion, and if necessary, data translation. Data encryption and decryption are all performed at this layer as well. As a result of all of these functions combined, the Presentation Layer is sometimes known as the network translator.

There are no major networking protocols unique to the Presentation Layer. Application Layer protocols function in the Presentation Layer by selecting modes of compression and/or encryption.

THE SESSION LAYER

For two computers to talk to one another, a communications link has to first be established, then it must be maintained for a sufficient amount of time for the data to be moved. It's like when you call a friend on the telephone to invite her over to watch the playoffs. You dial your friend's number, it rings a few times, and she answers. You talk for a while and when you're done, you hang up. That entire transaction would be a *session*. Computers use a very similar process in order to move data across the wire.

It is the responsibility of the Session Layer to establish and maintain a communications link between computers while data is being transmitted. In doing so, it will establish a duration for the session, a transmission speed acceptable to both devices, and then who gets to talk first. It is then up to the Session Layer to break down the link and clean up when the session is completed.

The Session Layer will not only maintain the link; it will also keep track of data coming in so that only packets relevant to that particular transmission can become a part of the data transfer. What I mean by this is simply that when you log onto the Internet, you know it is possible to download more than one file at a time. That is true of more conventional network communications as well. If you're copying *business.xls* from the server to your machine at the same time that Sally in Marketing is copying *proposal.doc* from your computer to hers, something needs to keep track of what packets of data go to what applications as well as what packets are coming from or intended for what device. That something is the Session Layer (see **Figure 4.3**).

Also, it is not uncommon for a session to be inadvertently or

Figure 4.3 Coming out of the Application Layer, and proceeding through the Presentation and Session Layers, the data passes through as a message. Later on, when the Transport Layer segments the data, header information provided by the Presentation and Session Layers will be applied to each segment.

intentionally broken off before data transmission is complete. The Session Layer puts checkpoints in the data stream as specific intervals. If a session is broken and then reestablished, the Session Layer can use these checkpoints to move only data that hasn't yet been transmitted. It does not need to resend data that is already there. See **Table 4.3** for a summary of Session Layer protocols.

Table 4.3 Session Layer Protocols

Protocol	What it does
Network File System (NFS)	Developed by Sun Microsystems and used with TCP/IP and Unix workstations. NFS provides transparent access to resources stored on remote locations.
Structured Query Language (SQL)	Developed by IBM to provide users with a simpler way to define their information requirements between local and remote systems.
Remote Procedure Call (RPC)	A broad client-server redirection tool used for disparate service environments. It allows procedures to be created on a client and subsequently be performed on a remote device, such as a server.
X Window	A thin-client protocol used for accessing the services of the host (usually Unix) server, allowing them to operate as though they were locally attached monitors.
Network Basic Input/Output Services (NetBIOS)	A protocol that provides session-layer interoperability with other NetBIOS-enabled operating systems such as LAN Manager and Microsoft Windows NT.
User Datagram Protocol (UDP)	Provides very little functionality beyond IP. Its job is to provide fast (albeit unreliable) data delivery.
NetWare Core Protocol (NCP)	A protocol that services requests from applications such as the NetWare shell. NCP supports file and print services, management of network and host names, and accounting and security functions.
AppleTalk Session Protocol (ASP)	Provides session layer services by establishing, maintaining, and releasing connections between Apple clients and any server app that supports ASP.
AppleTalk Data Stream Protocol (ADSP)	A session layer protocol that runs at both the Transport and Session Layer. It allows communications to take place in a sequence of multiple transactions.

Session Layer protocols are generally transparent to the end user. Without them, however, you cannot initialize and maintain a virtual connection between clients.

THE TRANSPORT LAYER

Once a session has been established and two devices are talking, it becomes important that the data moves across the wire smoothly. You know you can't move that entire 20MB file in one big chunk because you would hog the network, and most likely, the data would have a 100 percent chance of becoming corrupted in transit. Once you detected an error, that entire 20MB file would have to be sent again.

The Transport Layer begins the process of breaking the data into smaller pieces called *segments* (see **Figure 4.4**). Prior to the Transport Layer receiving the data, it has been moving through the system in a continuous stream called a *message*. Once the remaining layers perform their magic on these segments, the 20MB file is going across the wire in pieces. I've seen some references use the analogy of a train in this regard. Each chunk of data represents an individual car on the train. It's a good image, but it doesn't really give an accurate impression of what is going on. It's more like delivery vans. Train cars are all hooked together and follow the same route. Delivery vans take the shortest path to get where they're going, and if an accident along the way blocks one road, the vans can take different routes. That's what happens with networks.

Because it is up to the Transport Layer to make sure data gets where it is going, it is at this layer that one of several different forms of error detection will occur. Note that I said detection and not correction. The Transport Layer only figures out that something went wrong. It doesn't do anything at all to fix the problem. If a piece of data from the other end of the link arrives intact, it sends out a packet called the *ACK,* or acknowledgment packet. If it determines that the data is corrupt, it sends out a *NACK,* or no-acknowledgment packet. The transmitting machine keeps

BUZZ WORDS

Message: The format of data, or PDU, processed by the Application, Presentation, and Session Layers and sent downward to the Transport Layer.

Segment: The format of data, or PDU, processed by the Transport Layer and sent downward to the Network Layer.

Flow control: Maintaining a mutually acceptable data transfer speed between two devices on the network, making sure that all data arrives intact.

Packet: The format of data, or PDU, processed by the Network Layer and sent downward to the

Figure 4.4 It isn't until the Transport Layer that data is broken into smaller pieces for transport. Along with information provided by the Presentation and Session Layers, the Transport Layer adds information needed for reliable end-to-end movement of data.

track of packets already sent and if it doesn't receive an ACK in a certain amount of time, known as the *time to live* (TTL), it will automatically resend that frame. (Remember, once the data is on the wire, we're back to calling it a frame.)

The final significant service of the Transport Layer is that of *flow control.* Not all devices are capable of sending and receiving at the same speed. While it is the Session Layer that negotiates initial transmission speed, the Transport Layer can make adjustments along the way. See **Table 4.4** for a summary of Transport Layer protocols.

Table 4.4 Transport Layer Protocols

Protocol	What it does
Transmission Control Protocol (TCP)	The main Transport Layer protocol that provides reliable, full-duplex, connection-oriented transport service to upper-layer protocols. In addition it provides certain addressing services at the Network Layer.
User Datagram Protocol (UDP)	I first discussed this protocol while examining the Session Layer. UDP is also involved at the Transport Layer as a connectionless transport service.
NWLink	Microsoft's implementation of IPX/SPX
Sequenced Packet Exchange (SPX)	A Transport Layer protocol that provides reliable, connection-oriented communication sessions between hosts on a network.
Name Binding Protocol (NBP)	Apple's Transport Layer protocol that matches a logical device name with its associated address.
AppleTalk Transaction Protocol (ATP)	Apple's connectionless protocol that functions at the Transport Layer. ATP acknowledges packet delivery and initiates retransmission if a packet remains unacknowledged for too long.
Zone Information Protocol (ZIP)	Apple protocol that allows devices to be organized into logical groups called zones. This helps reduce the apparent complexity of an internetwork.
Sequenced Packet Protocol (SPP)	Xerox protocol that provides reliable, connection-based, flow-controlled packet transmission on behalf of client processes.
Packet Exchange Protocol (PEP)	Xerox protocol that is a request-response protocol designed to have greater reliability than simple datagram service.

Transport Layer protocols are responsible for assuring that data gets from Point A to Point B

Note: This list represents only a fraction of all Transport Layer protocols. If I were to include all proprietary protocols, this list would include over one hundred different protocols. Therefore, I only included the most common.

Figure 4.5 The Network Layer takes the segment handed down by the Transport Layer and adds logical addressing information into the Network Layer header. This becomes a packet.

THE NETWORK LAYER

The problem with all I've discussed so far is that I've intrinsically assumed that each machine involved in a session automatically knows precisely what path it needs to use to send data no matter how many simultaneous sessions are involved. Each packet of data on the wire needs to know where it is going and where it came from. As I will discuss in greater detail later on down the road, devices can have both logical addresses and physical addresses. A physical address is one that is burned in at the factory and won't change, regardless of where that device might move throughout its life. A logical address is one assigned by the network or network administrator. This may change several times over the life of the device. An example of a logical address is the TCP/IP address bound to an NIC or modem.

The primary job of the Network Layer is to translate the actual physical address of the device into it logical address and vice versa. It does this by taking the segment sent to it by the Transport Layer and adding addressing information into the header (see **Figure 4.5**). The PDU generated by the Network Layer once this information has been added is called a *packet*. This information will include both the sending and receiving computers' logical address information as well as their physical addresses.

The Network Layer also allows for certain types of devices to keep track of line conditions around the network and determine the best route over which data should be sent. This feature is most frequently seen in routers. The final service that the Network Layer is capable of performing is to take a packet that is too large for an intermediate device, such as a router, and break it down into smaller pieces.See **Table 4.5** for a summary of Network Layer protocols.

THE DATA LINK LAYER

The Data Link Layer is a bit different from other layers in that it has been subdivided. Within this layer reside two sublayers called *Logic Link Control* (LLC) and *Media Access Control* (MAC). LLC monitors the wire for errors that occur in

Table 4.5 Network Layer Protocols

Protocol	What it does
Internetwork Packet Exchange (IPX)	A Network Layer protocol that identifies stations and the networks they reside on and can be used to route packets from one network to another on an IPX internetwork.
Routing Information Protocol (RIP)	A distance-vector Network Layer protocol. RIP is a routing protocol.
Datagram Delivery Protocol (DDP)	AppleTalk's Network Layer protocol that provides connection-less or datagram service.
Routing Table Maintenance Protocol (RTMP)	A distance-vector routing protocol, similar to RIP, which functions at the Network Layer.
Internet Protocol (IP) address	A Network Layer protocol that uses the logical network and the packet-switching method and the dynamic method for route selection. It also provides error control for connection services. IP is a connectionless, datagram protocol.
Address Resolution Protocol (ARP)	A protocol that is responsible for mapping node names to IP addresses. ARP also resolves logical addresses to physical device addresses.
Reverse Address Resolution Protocol (RARP)	A protocol that is responsible for mapping IP addresses to node names. RARP also resolves physical device addresses to logical addresses.
Internet Control Message Protocol (ICMP)	A protocol used with IP to augment error handling and control procedures. ICMP provides error control and Network Layer flow control.
Open Shortest Path First (OSPF)	A protocol that is responsible for route discovery. OSPF provides load balancing and routing based on current quality of service.

Network Layer protocols allow users on different networks to communicate, but they also are responsible for selecting the appropriate route.

Note: As with the Transport Layer protocols, trying to include all of the proprietary protocols that work at the Network Layer would be unwieldy. Therefore, once again only the ones most commonly seen are included.

transmission and defines those service access points that I discussed earlier in the chapter. MAC does just what its name infers. It defines different methods by which your computer can put data out onto the network cable.

Within LLC, the service access points that I discussed earlier are defined. This layer is also responsible for monitoring the data for errors that occur in the process of transmission. Another task of LLC is to make sure that frame transmission between computers is kept synchronized.

Figure 4.6 Data Link takes the packet sent by the Network Layer and adds physical addressing information into the Data Link header. This becomes a datagram, or a frame.

The primary responsibility of MAC is to define the methods by which data will move over the wire. Therefore, it is at this layer that the network topologies that I discussed in Chapter One, Some Raw Basics of Networking, are defined. It takes the packets created by the Network Layer and breaks them down into a stream of individual bits with a defined beginning and end. Information regarding the physical address of both the sending computer and the intended recipient is added (see **Figure 4.6**).

The methods by which the NIC can access the wire are also defined at this layer. Therefore, when I discuss topics such as Ethernet, Token Ring and the other methods getting the data onto the wire and how the signal is moved, I'm talking about events that occur at this layer. See **Table 4.6** for a summary of Data Link Layer protocols.

Table 4.6   Data Link Protocols

Protocol	What it does
802.3 Ethernet	10Mb CSMA/CD
802.3u Fast Ethernet	100Mb CSMA/CD
802.3.z Gigabit Ethernet	1000Mb CSMA/CD
802.5 Token Ring	4/14Mb Token Passing
802.11 Wireless Signaling	Radio and Infrared
802.12 Demand Priority	100Mb Prioritized
Integrated Services Digital Network (ISDN)	128Kb to 1.52Mb over standard telephone lines
Fiber Distributed Data Interface (FDDI)	100Mb+ Over fiber optics
X.25	Packet Switching

Data Link protocols define different methods of allowing a device to access the network medium.

Figure 4.7 Once the data has passed through the Data Link Layer, encapsulation is complete. The Physical Layer simply converts the data into signals and sends it out over the medium in a series of bits.

THE PHYSICAL LAYER

Of all the layers, this is probably the easiest one for the beginner to understand. The Physical Layer defines the electrical and mechanical aspects of the network. The different types of cables used are all defined at this layer. The voltages used for different signaling types are defined here. Things you might not otherwise think of are the responsibility of this layer, things like the size and shape of the connectors used. The Physical Layer defines diameter, gauge, and impedance of the cables themselves as well.

The networking function provided by this layer is to take the stream of bits sent to it by the Data Link Layer and convert it into electronic, radio, or optical impulses (see **Figure 4.7**). This becomes the actual signal that moves between the computers.

PUTTING IT ALL TOGETHER

Now I'll follow a stream of data through the process and see what happens as it goes. Starting with the application running on the sending computer, I'll move a file over to another computer on the network. Once I, as a user, elect to save a file to a remote computer, a piece of software running on my computer, called a *redirector*, determines that the intended destination is not actually on the local computer, but rather a remote device. When the network client is installed, so is the network redirector. The redirector sends the data down along the remaining layers, eventually to be transmitted across the network. This all happens at the Application Layer.

At the Presentation Layer, the data is translated to the appropriate format and if any compression is being used, the data is compressed. If I am using any encryption, the data will be appropriately jumbled for transmission.

While all this has been going on, the Session Layer has been having a conversation with the destination computer, deciding on a mutually acceptable speed of transmission and figuring out how long the

BUZZ WORD

Redirector: A process or service running on a computer that determines that a particular request is not local and puts the request out on the network for resolution.

session needs to stay open to move this data. They decide that it would be best if the receiving computer talked first, because it needs to be able to tell the sending computer that it is ready to receive data.

The Transport Layer picks up the stream of data and starts slicing it into little pieces. It performs a mathematical calculation on the data and puts the results of that calculation into a field in the trailer called the Frame Check Sequence (FCS). If the Session Layer has decided that it is simply going to blow the data out onto the wire and not worry about whether it gets there, this step will be skipped. There are some protocols that do this by default, and most broadcast messages don't worry about error correction.

Once the Network Layer gets its hands on the segment created by the Transport Layer, it adds any logical addresses used by the computer. This is where the IP address of both sending and receiving computers is added. Also, if there are intermediate devices along the way, such as a router or two, information about the intermediate systems will be incorporated. Those devices, in turn, as they receive the packets, will examine the address of the final destination and determine the fastest way to get that particular packet to its final home. As line conditions change, so can intermediate routes. So if a packet is going from the home office in New York to the West Coast office in LA, some packets get there through Chicago and others go by way of Omaha.

The Network Layer passes its packet off to the Data Link Layer, which adds the physical addresses of known devices (this obviously wouldn't include intermediate devices). It also looks at the physical topology of the network and decides what kind of frame it is supposed to create. Finally, it uses the media access method specific to the network to place it onto the wire.

It is up to the Physical Layer to actually put the data onto the wire. This layer will convert the digital signals to analog electrical signals, or to light pulses or radio waves, whatever the network foundation is based upon. It sends these signals out over the media to the other end. **Figure 4.8** illustrates this concept.

The Physical Layer takes the signals off the media and turns them back into bits, and then packages the bits into frames and hands them off to the Data Link Layer. Data Link examines the MAC address to see if the data is intended for that particular computer or not. If not, the frame is discarded. If the data is meant for the device, the Data Link strips off the Data Link header and moves the frames on up to the Network Layer, where logical addresses are examined. If for any reason the logical address of the packet doesn't match that of the recipient device, the data will be discarded at this point. If accepted, the Network Layer header will be stripped

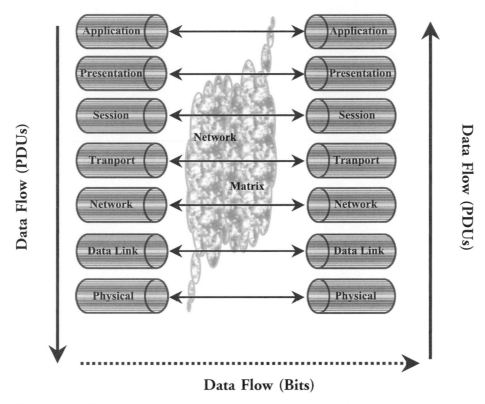

Figure 4.8 Data flows in an orderly fashion through the sending computer, from Layer 7 down to Layer 1. On the receiving end, it moves from 1 to 7. Each layer on the receiving end undoes what its counterpart did on the transmitting end.

off and the frames will move on up to Transport, where the data will be reassembled and the Transport header will be removed.

The Session Layer determines which communications link owns the data. For example, if multiple files are downloading, each file will be assigned to a specific session. The Session Layer makes sure the right files go to the right place. Once the communications link has been determined, the Session Layer will give the data to the Presentation Layer, where it will be unencrypted, if necessary, and translated back to the language of the particular platform and application.

Presentation gives the data to the Application Layer, which sends the data to the correct application. As you can see, it isn't a complicated process to understand. It's making it work that is a challenge. **Figure 4.9** shows one side of the operation. See **Table 4.7** for an overview of the OSI Layers.

Table 4.7 The OSI Layers at a Glance

Layer	Description	Service Provided	Level Protocols	Level Functions	Hardware devices that run at this Layer
Layer 7 – The Application Layer	Provides an interface between user applications and network services. Provides network access and upper-level error recovery. Data moves to Layer 6 as a Message.	Telnet, FTP over TCP, TFTP, NFS, NMP, SMTP over STCP	DNS, FTP, TFTP, BOOTP, SNMP, RLOGIN, SMTP, MIME, NFS, FINGER, TELNET, NCP, APPC, AFP, SMB	Interface with Applications, Gateways	No specific device
Layer 6 – The Presentation Layer	Provides data compression, translation, and encryption. Data moves to Layer 5 as a Message.	Telnet, FTP over TCP, TFTP, NFS, SNMP, SMTP over TCP	NCP	Gateways	No specific device
Layer 5 – The Session Layer	Establishes and maintains a communications link between devices for the transfer of data. Synchronizes Data Flow. Data moves to Layer Four 4 as a Message.	Telnet, FTP over TCP, TFTP, NFS, SNMP, SMTP over TCP	NetBIOS, Named Pipes, RPC	Gateways	No specific device
Layer 4 – The Transport Layer	Breaks data coming from Layer 5 into smaller chunks called Segments. Adds information in a trailer that can be used for detection of errors. Data Moves to Layer 3 as a Segment.	TCP, SPX, UDP TCP, ARP, RARP, SPX, NWLink. NetBIOS/ NetBEUI. ATP	Gateways, some Brouter functions, advanced cable testers	Gateways and Advanced	Cable Testers

Layer					
Layer 3 – The Network Layer	Resolves NetBIOS names and logical address into physical addresses. Determines the best route for data to travel over the network. Reassembles data into smaller packages when needed. Data moves to Layer 2 as either a Packet or Datagram.	Name and address resolution. Route Discovery.	IPX, IP, ICMP, ARP, RARP, RIP, OSPF, EGP, IGMP, NetBEUI, DLC, and DecNET	Routers and Brouters, Frame Relay devices, ATM switches, advanced cable tester	Routers, Brouters, advanced cable tester
Layer 2 – The Data Link Layer	Prepares the data for transmission over the medium. Packages data into Frames. Manages physical addressing. Sends Data to Layer 1 as Frames.	Ethernet, Token Ring, LLC (802.2). Manages link control and defines SAP's. Links system to NIC.	HDLC	Intelligent switches, brouters. Bridges, ISDN router and NIC	Switches, bridges, NIC, Brouter
Layer 1 – The Physical Layer	Transmits data over a physical medium. Defines cables, cards, and physical aspects. Sends data out over the wire as bits.	Ethernet (CSMA/CD), Token Ring and other communications services.	None	Repeaters, hubs and multiplexers	NIC, device interfaces, hubs, repeaters, media

An overview of the OSI layers.

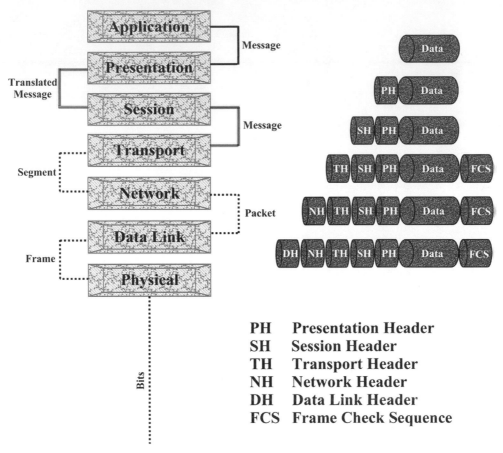

PH   Presentation Header
SH   Session Header
TH   Transport Header
NH   Network Header
DH   Data Link Header
FCS   Frame Check Sequence

Figure 4.9   Particular functions needed by other layers are performed at each layer. On the receiving end, these services are confirmed and the control information is stripped from the packet.

WHERE DO THE 802 STANDARDS FIT IN?

It doesn't take much imagination to recognize that there is a lot going on in Layers 1 and 2. In fact, I think it would be safe to say that more technology advances originate in these layers than any others. Any time you develop a new way of moving data, either faster or more efficiently, it is either the medium itself that is changing or how the data is moved over the medium. Imagine what a chaotic world networking would be if everybody who was involved in design and development didn't play by the same rules!

In order to assure that uniformity and compatibility exist between different technologies and different products, IEEE met in February of 1980 and established several different committees to oversee the design and development of new protocols, standards, and technologies. In honor of the month and year in which these committees were established, they are now called the 802 committees and the standards ratified by these committees are the 802 standards. The following list encompasses the different committees and their oversight responsibilities. This list includes all committees, past and present, including those that have been disbanded.

- 802.1: LAN/MAN Bridging and Management. Covers different internetworking standards as well as the Spanning Tree Algorithm
- 802.2: Logic Link Control. As its name suggests, this committee oversees the standards used by the LLC sublayer of the Data Link Layer.
- 802.3: CSMA/CD Access Method. Sometimes simply called Ethernet. This committee keeps up with the different advances in Ethernet technology
- 802.4: Token Passing Bus Access Method. A bus network that used a token passing method of media access. This committee is no longer active.
- 802.5: Token Ring Access Method. A ring network that uses a token passing method of media access.
- 802.6: DQDB Access Method. *Distributed Queue Dual Bus* access to media.
- 802.7: Broadband LAN. A technology for building LANs using broadband technology instead of baseband technology.
- 802.8: The Fiber Optics Technical Advisory Group. Oversees development of fiber-optics solutions.
- 802.9: Isosynchronous LANs. Frequently referred to as Integrated Voice/ Data communications.
- 802.10: Integrated Services. Also known as Security. Administers development of methods by which access to the network and the transmission of data can be made secure.
- 802.11: Wireless Networking. Defines various methods of moving data without wires.
- 802.12: Demand Priority Access. Allows access to network media based on message priority.
- 802.14: Standard Protocol for Cable TV-based Broadband Communications.
- 802.15: Working Group for Personal Area Networks. Very short-range wireless networks.

- 802.16: Broadband Wireless Access Standards.
- 802.17: Resilient Packet Ring Working Group. Uses fiber-optic ring networks and packet data transmission.

EXAM NOTE: While the Network+ Exam does not require complete knowledge of all the activities of any given working group, it does expect you to be able to recognize the responsibilities of each group. You should be able to list off the committee number and title for each of the working committees.

Each of these groups has produced standards and the documentation for those standards. While it is beyond the scope of this book to go into detail as to what each standard set encompasses, if you are interested in pursuing any of these standards further, you can access them at IEEE's Web site at standards.ieee.org. Six months after a standard has been released, the document defining that standard will be available for free download. Should you require that information prior to the six-month holding period, IEEE will make it available to you for a nominal charge.

CHAPTER SUMMARY

After reading this chapter, you should have a good overall view of the OSI layers and their responsibilities. But hang tight, because it only gets better from here. Over the next few chapters, I'm going to visit each of these layers in detail and show you how they really do their thing. Another key collection of details presented in this chapter is the IEEE 802 committees. Knowing the information introduced in this chapter is a great step in beginning your understanding of how the process of networking takes place.

BRAIN DRAIN

1. Develop your own analogy that best describes what a protocol is and what its functions include.
2. Think of as many reasons as you can as to why a layered model for describing networking standards is favored over a homogenous model.
3. Why would understanding the OSI layers give you a head start in troubleshooting network issues?
4. Describe in as much detail as possible how a message is moved from one computer to another across the OSI layers.

THE 64K$ QUESTIONS

1. Which of the following constitute logical reasons for creating a layered architecture in networking? (Choose all correct)

   a. When a feature is either added or modified in one layer, it has no impact on another layer.

   b. Different companies were instrumental in developing the layers and own intellectual rights.

   c. New technologies are more quickly developed, approved, and ratified.

   d. It makes the concepts easier to learn.

2. What is the format of the chunk of data moving between layers called?

   a. SAP

   b. Frame

   c. Packet

   d. PDU

3. Which OSI layer is responsible for logical addressing?

   a. The Application Layer

   b. The Presentation Layer

   c. The Session Layer

   d. The Transport Layer

   e. The Network Layer

   f. The Data Link Layer

   g. The Physical Layer

4. Which OSI Layer is known as the "translator?"

   a. The Application Layer

   b. The Presentation Layer

   c. The Session Layer

   d. The Transport Layer

   e. The Network Layer

   f. The Data Link Layer

   g. The Physical Layer

5. Which OSI layer determines what method is used to get data onto the wire without interfering with other devices?

   a. The Application Layer

   b. The Presentation Layer

    c. The Session Layer

    d. The Transport Layer

    e. The Network Layer

    f. The Data Link Layer

    g. The Physical Layer

6. Which layer sets up a logical communications link between two hosts and makes sure that link stays alive throughout the exchange of data?

    a. The Application Layer

    b. The Presentation Layer

    c. The Session Layer

    d. The Transport Layer

    e. The Network Layer

    f. The Data Link Layer

    g. The Physical Layer

7. Which layer handles physical addressing?

    a. The Application Layer

    b. The Presentation Layer

    c. The Session Layer

    d. The Transport Layer

    e. The Network Layer

    f. The Data Link Layer

    g. The Physical Layer

8. Which IEEE 802 committee is responsible for Ethernet standards?

    a. 802.2

    b. 802.3

    c. 802.4

    d. 802.5

9. Which IEEE 802 committee is responsible for Token Ring standards?

    a. 802.2

    b. 802.3

    c. 802.4

    d. 802.5

10. Which IEEE 802 committee is responsible for network security standards?
    a. 802.9
    b. 802.10
    c. 802.11
    d. 802.12

11. In a situation where Computer A is transmitting data to Computer B, the Network Layer on Computer A will be adding information that will be used by the _____ Layer on Computer B.
    a. Transport
    b. Session
    c. Physical
    d. Network

12. Which layer uses a Service Access Point to transmit its information to the next adjacent layer?
    a. The Application Layer
    b. The Transport Layer
    c. The Physical Layer
    d. They all do.

13. Which OSI layer breaks a long message down into smaller chunks for transmission?
    a. The Presentation Layer
    b. The Transport Layer
    c. The Session Layer
    d. The Data Link Layer

14. If the Transport Layer detects that a session has timed out, it will generate a SYNC packet to recreate the session.
    a. True
    b. False

15. Each adjacent layer watches out for its neighbors to make sure that data is properly transferred.
    a. True
    b. False

16. Which layer is responsible for providing FTP services to a client?

    a. The Application Layer

    b. The Presentation Layer

    c. The Session Layer

    d. The Network Layer

17. Every NIC in the world has a unique MAC address assigned to it. Which layer keeps track of the MAC?

    a. The Physical Layer

    b. The Data Link Layer

    c. The Network Layer

    d. The Transport Layer

18. The Address Resolution Protocol is a _____ Layer protocol.

    a. Transport

    b. Network

    c. Data Link

    d. Physical

19. Demand Priority is a _____ Layer protocol.

    a. Transport

    b. Network

    c. Data Link

    d. Physical

20. Gigabit Ethernet is under the oversight of the _____ committee.

    a. 802.2

    b. 802.3

    c. 802.5

    d. 802.11

TRICKY TERMINOLOGY

Encapsulation: The process of dividing a stream of data into smaller pieces for transmission and then adding layer-specific information to each segment as it passes from layer to layer.

Flow control: Maintaining a mutually acceptable data transfer speed between two devices on the network, making sure that all data arrives intact.

Header: Information placed at the beginning of a segment/packet/frame by the layer protocol or device processing the data.

Message: The format of data, or PDU, processed by the Application, Presentation, and Session Layers and sent downward to the Transport Layer.

Packet: The format of data, or PDU, processed by the Network Layer and sent downward to the Data Link Layer by the transmitting computer, or up to the Transport Layer by the receiving computer.

Peer entity: Any two devices, protocols, or services that operate on the same layer that can communicate with one another.

Protocol: A set of predefined rules and formats used to allow two unlike devices or applications to communicate.

Redirector: A process or service running on a computer that determines that a particular request is not local and puts the request out on the network for resolution.

Segment: The format of data, or PDU, processed by the Transport Layer and sent downward to the Network Layer.

Service access point: A predefined address that is used to transfer data between OSI layers.

Service primitive: A specific function or activity that is performed by any specific layer entity.

Trailer: Information placed at the end of a segment/packet/frame by the layer protocol or device processing the data.

ACRONYM ALERT

IEEE: The Institute of Electrical and Electronic Engineers. One of several organizational bodies devoted to the development and ratification of international standards in various industries.

ISO: Industry Standards Organization. One of several organizational bodies devoted to the development and ratification of international standards in various industries.

LLC: Logic Link Control. One of the sublayers of the Data Link Layer.

MAC: Media Access Control. One of the sublayers of the Data Link Layer.

OSI: Open Standards Interconnect. The seven-layer model of networking defined by ISO.

PDU: Protocol Data Unit. The format of data as it moves between OSI layers

SAP: Service Access Point

VIEW THE VIDEO

A video clip on Encapsulation/Deencapsulation and Data within the PDU are available on the accompanying CD.

CHAPTER 5

UNDERSTANDING THE PHYSICAL LAYER

While it may be true that the Physical Layer is the easiest for the beginning student to understand in terms of function, it may well be the most difficult to understand in terms of how it does what it does. It is the responsibility of this layer to take a stream of binary information, turn it into a completely different form of energy, and move it across space to its final destination. The computer receiving the data has to make sense of a bunch of electrical signals, radio waves, or flashes of light, somehow understanding that it's really digital data, and then turning it back into something the computer can decipher. Tell me that's easy!

One of the primary functions of the Physical Layer is to define and control the network media. However, that was covered in detail in Chapter Three, The Highways and Byways of the Network. Just be aware that all of that information is a part of understanding the Physical Layer. In this chapter, I will give you a closer look at the actual signaling technologies used to move data across space and at how the network makes sure that the receiving computer actually interprets the data it receives the same way the transmitting computer intended it to. Then I'll look at a few of the most commonly used transmission methods.

This chapter is targeted for the advanced networking student and not exclusively Network+ exam candidates. Therefore, only the following Exam Objectives are introduced or covered in this chapter:

1.3 Specify the characteristics (For example: speed, length, topology, and cable type) of cable standards.

1.4 Recognize media connectors and describe their uses.

1.6 Identify the purposes, features and functions of key network components.

1.7 Specify the general characteristics (For example: carrier speed, frequency, transmission type and topology) of the following wireless technologies: 802.11 (Frequency hopping spread spectrum), 802.11x (Direct sequence spread spectrum), Infrared, Bluetooth.

1.8 Identify factors which affect the range and speed of wireless service (For example: interference, antenna type and environmental factors).

2.2 Identify the seven layers of the OSI (Open Systems Interconnect) model and their functions.

2.3 Identify the OSI (Open Systems Interconnect) layers at which the following network components operate: Hubs, Switches, Bridges, Routers, NICs (Network Interface Card), WAPs (Wireless Access Point).

THE FUNCTIONS OF THE PHYSICAL LAYER

As I discussed in Chapter Four, Introducing the OSI Model, another primary function of the Physical Layer is to turn the data into some form of signal that can move across the medium of choice—and then move it across that medium. First it gets the signal ready for transmission, then it can worry about the physical medium itself.

Essentially, the Physical Layer is broken down into three components. The *Physical Signaling* (PLS) component is responsible for bit encoding and decoding, timing, and synchronization. The *Physical Medium Attachment* (PMA) section defines properties of transceivers. Finally, the *Medium Dependant Interface* (MDI) describes the cables and connectors that will be used by the different platforms.

BOUNDED PHYSICAL SIGNALING

Physical Signaling is the portion of the Physical Layer that takes the binary data handed to it by the Data Link Layer and turns it into a stream of signals that can be transmitted across the medium. How it goes about doing this will depend entirely upon the medium in use. The Data Link Layer defines the medium for Physical Signaling before handing the segments off to the Physical Layer. The transmission medium defines how the signals are converted. Obviously you're going to have to manipulate electrical signals in a completely different manner than you will light, microwave, or radio. In most cases, there is more than one way to feed an elephant. In the following sections, I'll take a look at methods used for each type of media, both past and present.

MOVING DATA OVER COPPER

Taking digital data, turning it into an electrical signal, and then sending it over a piece of copper wire is actually a pretty complex procedure. To begin with, the network needs to take a series of 0s and 1s and turn it into some form of signal that can be sent over an electrical current. Just as importantly, it needs to make sure the data actually arrives in the same order that it was transmitted, with no alterations of content.

In order to accomplish this, the network needs some form of data encoding. This will take the digital data and turn it into an analog signal. Second, the network needs to synchronize the transceivers on either end to make sure that they're both on the same page. It wouldn't do for one device to transmit a series of twenty 0s and have the receiving device interpret the string as nineteen or twenty-one 0s. Not only would it corrupt that particular string of data, but all the data that followed in the same packet would also be corrupted. Therefore, bit timing and synchronization are key elements of the Physical Signaling component of the Physical Layer.

DATA ENCODING

In Chapter Three, I discussed the characteristics of an electrical signal that enable you to encode data and transmit it over wire. Here, I will take a look at some of the encoding techniques used to make that happen. There are three basic forms of signal coding I will examine.

The first of these is *Return to Zero* (RTZ), or sometimes called *pulse signaling* (see **Figure 5.1**). Using this technique there is either a signal on the wire or there isn't. A lack of a signal represents a 0, while the presence of signal is interpreted as a 1. This technique worked okay in the early days of computing when signals weren't quite as fast as they are today, but is rarely, if ever, used in modern equipment.

In *Non-Return to Zero* (NRZ) encoding, a 1 is represented by a high voltage level and a 0 is represented by a low voltage level. The time duration for the voltage pulse of any

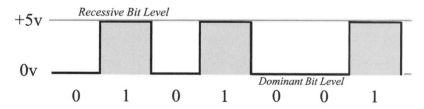

Figure 5.1 Return to Zero encoding makes use of the simple presence or absence of a signal on the wire to encode data.

HOW MANY BITS FIT ON A CABLE?

Many people getting into networking technology for the first time envision the data moving across the copper wire in single file, like first-graders moving down the hall to the cafeteria. To a certain extent, this is a valid image. Where the image breaks down is in how much of the piece of wire is occupied by a single bit. The truth of the matter is, electrical currents travel along wire at about 80 percent of the speed of light.

Let's take a look at just what that means. With a 10Mb/s signal, just the basic time available it takes to transmit a single bit is about a tenth of a microsecond. Doesn't sound like much does it? But when we're talking about something traveling at pretty close to 150,000 miles per second, a single bit is occupying about 70 feet of cable. That's approximately one-fourth of the length of cable you can have on a 10BaseT segment.

It gets worse. Data doesn't travel in single bits; it travels in frames. The size of frame varies from protocol to protocol. However, if you send the smallest frame currently in use, and if that frame were capable of residing on a single segment (which it isn't), you would need a length of cable 6 miles long to house the frame. What that really means is that the frame owns the segment for quite a number of milliseconds. Since Ethernet uses baseband technology, that one signal owns the entire wire. No other machine can transmit data until that frame is off the wire.

---

single bit is identical. This is called the *unit interval* (UI). The UI is equal to the reciprocal of the data rate. For example, one UI for a 622 Mbit/s data rate is $1/(622 * 10^6 \text{ bit/s}) = 1.6$ ns per bit.

For a while, a variation of RTZ, called *Alternate Mark Inversion* (AMI), was the signal of choice in devices such as repeaters. With AMI, the voltage of a 1 bit can be either positive or negative. All zeros were encoded as a 0-volt signal. However, in a long string of zeros, the lack of transitions made it difficult, if not impossible, for a clock signal to be maintained. Some devices still use an improvement of AMI called *High Density Bipolar Order Three Encoding* (HDB3). HDB3 takes a long string of 0s and breaks the string down into an encoded string where no more than four 0s will

BUZZ WORDS

Bit timing: A method used by transceivers to accurately extract encoded data from an analog signal using clock cycles as a basis.

Bit stuffing: Adding nondata information to a frame in order to bring it up to a minimum size.

be transmitted in succession. After the fourth 0 a *violation bit* will be inserted into the string. You'll sometimes see this technique referred to as *bit stuffing.* This violation bit will be transmitted using the same polarity as the last 1 to be transmitted. In order to assure that it will not be interpreted as a 1, any binary 1 that is meant to be interpreted as a 1 will be preceded by a *balancing pulse,* consisting of a signal using the opposite polarity of the last 1 (see **Figure 5.2**).

The final bit encoding method I'll discuss is known as *Manchester Encoding.* Manchester Encoding makes use of both the rising and falling end of the voltage signals to encode data. The center of each cycle in the waveform is the center of the bit. Binary data is encoded as a transition from center. A movement downward from center would be interpreted as a 1, while an upward movement would be read as a 0. In order to maintain proper clocking, a coinciding signal called the *Digital Phase Locked Loop* (DPLL) is present on the carrier. **Figure 5.3** illustrates the overall process. Manchester Encoding is how Ethernet signals are transmitted.

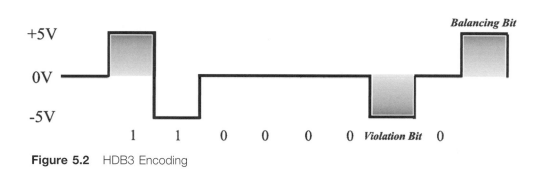

Figure 5.2   HDB3 Encoding

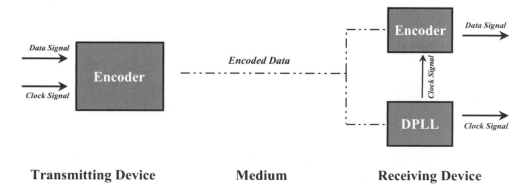

Figure 5.3   Diagram of a DPLL circuit

> **EXAM NOTE:** Be able to describe the differences between RTZ and NRZ Encoding and how they differ from Manchester Encoding.

BIT TIMING AND SYNCHRONIZATION

Bit timing can be done in one of two methods, and both methods of timing see quite a bit of use. There is *asynchronous communication* and *synchronous communication*. Each method has a slightly different method of timing the signal, and each one has a different method of determining if an error has occurred in transmission. As a result, each method of timing is suitable for different types of communication.

Asynchronous Communication   With asynchronous communication, the network is not really sending data out in frames the way I have been discussing. Data moves across the wire a single byte at a time. The only form of error detection possible is *parity* checking.

With parity checking enabled, a byte of data will be nine bits long and not eight bits. The ninth bit is the parity bit. A network can use even parity or it can use odd parity. Both mean the same thing, only opposite. With odd parity checking enabled, the sending device will count the number of 1s in the byte of data. If there is an even number of ones, the device will set the parity bit to 1. If there are an odd number of 1s, it will set the parity bit to 0. This assures that all bytes of data, including the parity bit, will have an odd number of 1s at the receiving end. The receiving device counts the number of 1s in the byte, including the parity bit. If it detects an even number of 1s, the byte is assumed to be corrupt and is discarded.

The only synchronization of the signal is the presence of a *start bit* and one or two *stop bits* that are transmitted along with each byte of data. The start bit is always a 0 and the stop bits are always 1s. Both devices obviously have to be set to agree on the number of stop bits.

As far as a clock signal goes, none is sent. Each device uses its own oscillator to perform timing checks to measure bit duration. In order to assure that each device is operating at speeds that are close enough to the other for government work, the oscillators actually tick off cycles that are sixteen to thirty-two times faster than the actual transmission rate of the data. As a result, minor differences between the two oscillators go unnoticed.

Printers and modems are the devices that primarily use asynchronous communication.

> **BUZZ WORD**
>
> **Parity:** An error detection mechanism that simply counts the number of 1s in a byte and indicates in a unique bit whether there is an even number of 1s or an odd number.

Most (but not all) networking protocols and devices use synchronous communication.

Synchronous Communication   I provided an introduction to this form of communication when I discussed Manchester Encoding earlier in the chapter. With synchronous communication, the transmitting device will generate a clock signal that it sends along with the stream of data. The receiving device will send the signal through a DPLL circuit to extract the clock signal and use it to synchronize its own clock.

With synchronous communication, data will move across the wire using the frames that I discussed earlier. Therefore a more sophisticated method of error detection and recovery is in order. Using a simple parity bit for a stream of data that could include 2400 bytes of data along with a fairly substantial amount of control information, in the form of headers and trailers, attached to the data itself, would be about as effective as having an ejection seat in a helicopter. A computer might be able to figure out that there is a problem, but its method of dealing with the problem wouldn't be all that appealing. You don't want entire packets of data discarded without some method of insuring that they will be resent. Instead, synchronous communication protocols make use of either *checksum* or *cyclical redundancy check* (CRC) to figure out if an error has occurred.

Checksum is the simplest of these two methods, but unfortunately, it also is the least effective. Checksum simply counts the number of 1s in the frame and inserts the total into a trailer at the end of the segment. While this may seem all fine and good, it is not at all inconceivable for a frame to lose a few 1s along the way due to electrical anomalies, having them turn into 0s. Likewise, 0s can suddenly transform into 1s. If we have 8 bytes of data in the frame, and each loses a 1 to a 0, and 8 more bytes that have a 0 transformed into a 1, the checksum is accurate, but there may be up to sixteen bytes of data that are corrupt!

CRC treats the entire frame as if it were a single very large binary number. It takes this number and performs a rather complex mathematical calculation on it, storing the results of that calculation in the trailer. On the receiving end, the reverse of that calculation is performed on all of the data in the frame ahead of the trailer.

BUZZ WORDS

Checksum: A method of error detection that simply keeps track of the number of 1s in the packet. If the receiving devices calculate a different checksum than that stored in the trailer, the packet will be rejected and a *NACK* returned to the sender.

CRC: *Cyclical Redundancy Check.* A more accurate form of error detection that performs a mathematical calculation on the packet, treating the binary data as if it were a very large number. The receiving computer performs the same calculation. If the results match, the packet is accepted. If not, it is rejected and a *NACK* sent back.

If the answer it gets is the same as the one stored in the trailer, the frame is accepted and an *acknowledgment* (ACK) frame is sent. If not, a *nonacknowledgment* (NACK) frame is generated and sent to the transmitting device. The frame is dropped.

EXAM NOTE: Being able to differentiate between asynchronous communication and synchronous communication is very important.

MOVING DATA OVER FIBER

Many of the emerging technologies that support faster bandwidths are leaving the limitations of copper behind and taking advantage of the characteristics of light to move data. Fiber optics carries several advantages over conventional copper cabling. As I pointed out in Chapter Four, not only is fiber faster, but it can move data much greater distances over a single segment. Since its central component is glass, it doesn't rust or corrode. While the copper wires I discussed in Chapter Three give ranges of up to 500 meters, fiber optics starts at 2 km and moves up from there.

EXAM NOTE: The key advantages of fiber are speed, distance, security, and immunity from interference. The key disadvantages are cost and difficulty of installation.

THE TYPES OF FIBER

In the world of fiber optics, there seems to be a myriad of different options available. It would be a good idea to be familiar with the most common types. There are two generic categories of fiber optics commonly used—*loose-tube* and *tight-buffered* cable.

Loose-tube cable houses several strands of fiber in a single cable and takes several steps to make sure that the delicate strands of glass don't get damaged over long runs of cable or due to rough handling. Each strand of fiber is housed in a tube filled with a gel compound. These tubes follow along the same axis as a steel wire to give the whole thing tensile strength. A tough jacket surrounds the fiber tubes and is packed with an interstitial filling to further buffer the tubes from stress. Around the jacket is a steel mesh covering, and over the mesh the outer jacket is applied. Designers have gone out of their way to make sure the product is durable.

Tight-buffered fiber consists of a single strand of fiber buffered with an additional layer of protective coating and placed directly into the cable construction. The majority of manufacturers standardize on a working diameter of 900um for this outer coating. Wrapped with Kevlar for added protection, the fibers are then protected within a variety of sheaths. These cables generally exhibit greater flexibility than

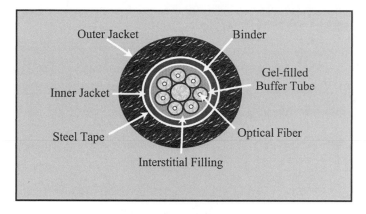

Loose-Tube Fiber-Optic Cable

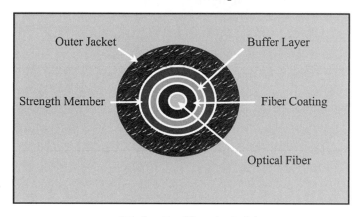

Tight-Buffered Cable

Figure 5.4 Loose-Tube versus Tight-Buffered Fiber-Optic Cable

loose-tube construction, and with the proper sheath they can be used in indoor installations. The tight-buffered constructed cable is the cable of choice for interior and sometimes indoor/outdoor installations. The 900um buffered coating allows for the direct interconnection of the fiber using the appropriate connectors. See **Figure 5.4** for a visual comparison of the two types.

SIGNALING OVER LIGHT

As I discussed in Chapter Three, the optical transmitter is the device that generates the signal for transmission over fiber optics, and it uses either a *light emitting diode* (LED) or a *laser diode* (LD) to generate pulses of light. The LED or LD translates the digital stream into pulses of light that go out over the cable in one of three ways.

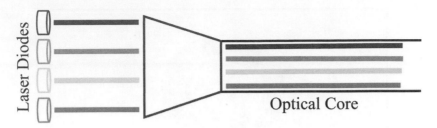

Figure 5.5 A fiber-optic cable using wavelength division multiplexing sends different signals over different colors of light.

The simplest of the three is a simple light-on/light-off logic. A pulse of light signifies a binary 1, and lack of light represents a binary 0. The speed of data transmission is a direct corollary of the pulse rate of the LED or LD used. The slower devices are several hundred megahertz (usually LEDs), whereas there are now LDs capable of frequencies of several gigahertz.

More recent technologies promise even higher bandwidths. *Pulse-width modulation* is a method by which data is sent in consists of a steady stream of light pulses, with extremely short separations between them. Zeros and 1s are differentiated by how long the pulse lasts. One pulse width represents a 0 and another represents a 1. *Pulse-rate modulation* keeps the width of each pulse the same and distinguishes between 0s and 1s by way of the rate at which the pulses are transmitted. In other words, instead of altering the duration of the pulse, the duration of the time between pulses in manipulated.

There are two kinds of fiber for those signals to travel along, as well. Single-mode fiber allows only a single optical signal to be carried over the strand of fiber. Since there is only one signal on the cable, faster rates are possible, and a thinner strand of fiber can be used. Multimode cable is a much thicker strand of fiber. Several different light beams can move across the cable using *wavelength division multiplexing*. This is the term for a technology that works by sending specific signals over light of specific wavelengths (see **Figure 5.5**). However, in doing this, the different beams tend to disperse as they travel the cable. This phenomenon is called *modal dispersion*. As a result, only shorter runs are possible. You must, of course, use the correct connector with the fiber-optic cable you are using. The two types are not interchangeable.

UNBOUNDED PHYSICAL SIGNALING

So far, the aspects of the Physical Layer that I have been discussing all deal with bounded media. So how does it work with wireless networking? Of course, the answer to that is that it depends on the type of wireless signal you're using. As I discussed in Chapter Three, there are three types of wireless media—optical, radio, and microwave. Each type of carrier has its own little idiosyncrasies. (Don't we all?)

> **BUZZ WORD**
>
> **Spread spectrum:** The transmission of data by spreading it across several different radio frequencies.

Conveniently, bounded optical transmissions (fiber optics) and unbounded optical transmissions (infrared and laser) are similar in the manner in which they generate signals. The differences that do exist are beyond the scope of this book. Therefore, you can simply check back into the last section and say "ditto" for the unbounded optical signaling section. Radio and microwave transmission will be my key focus here.

NETWORKING OVER RADIO

The original underlying technology for wireless networking was the radio wave. As early as 1971, radio waves were used to interconnect computers—and the PC hadn't even been invented yet! The University of Hawaii linked seven computers across four islands in the first radio-based network. They called it ALOHNET. IEEE gave the responsibilities for developing this technology to the 802.11 committee.

The original 802.11 standard worked across the 2.4GHz range. Top speeds were 1Mb/s and 2Mb/s. As you can see, these networks weren't exactly speed demons. 802.11a introduced access to the 5GHz band and defined methods for higher speeds of data transmission. Speeds of 5Mb/s, 11Mb/s, and 54Mb/s were introduced. 802.11b took the existing 2.4GHz specifications and extended them to allow for higher speeds across that bandwidth.

There are three base technologies for transmitting over radio. They are *low-power single frequency (LPSF) transmission, high-power single frequency (HPSF),* and two varieties of *spread spectrum—direct sequence spread spectrum* (DSSS) and *frequency hopping spread spectrum* (FHSS).

Since we covered these different methods in Chapter Three, The Highways and Byways of the Network, it won't be necessary to rehash old material. A few minor additions concerning signaling are in order, however.

SINGLE-FREQUENCY TRANSMISSION

At this point in time, LPSF is targeted primarily at the *small office/home office (*SOHO) environment. Most of the product shipping today is based on the *Shared Wireless Access Protocol* (SWAP). Since these products operate in a frequency range that is not restricted by the FCC, they are only allowed to operate with enough power to transmit to a distance of approximately 50 meters. HPSF is generally used for longer distances. For the most part, any two devices that have a theoretical line of sight can communicate. If conditions are favorable, distances can be extended ever further by bouncing the signal off the ionosphere. To use HPSF, one must be licensed by the FCC and the radio frequency will be a restricted frequency assigned by the FCC.

SPREAD-SPECTRUM RADIO

As I mentioned in Chapter Three, the use of spread spectrum adds a degree of security to a network by making use of multiple radio frequencies and bouncing the signal from one frequency to another. Direct Sequence Spread Spectrum is the fastest, but least secure of the frequency-hopping methods. In order to assume a semblance of security the sending and receiving units employ a *chipping code*. Frequency modulation of the transmission is encoded into a sequence of patterns, or *chips*, that represents a 0 and another sequence that represents a 1. A chip would be a single modulation of the frequency. The sequence for a 0 is simply an inverse of that of a 1 (see **Figure 5.6**)

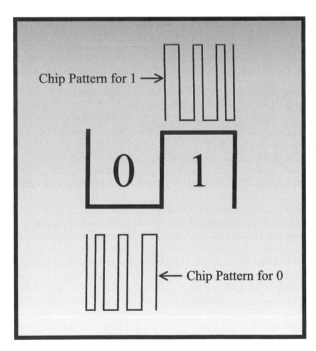

Figure 5.6 Chipping code allows a degree of security for devices that employ DSSS transmission.

Frequency hopping spread spectrum uses a far more complicated timing scheme for switching from frequency to frequency. Also, there can be alternating patterns in the hop sequence. This makes it far more difficult to hack, since both the timing and the sequence change. This is a far more secure method of sending data, however it comes at the cost of speed.

The method for shifting frequencies is called *Gaussian frequency shift keying* (GFSK). Two devices using GFSK agree on a pattern of frequency shifts as well as a scheme for altering the pattern at certain intervals. Somebody trying to break into the signal might be able to lock onto one frequency and, in fact, might be able to determine the frequency shifts. But by the time he or she has accomplished that, the pattern changes. This allows for very good security.

NETWORKING OVER MICROWAVES

No, we haven't come up with a scheme forcing everybody in the world to interconnect their microwave ovens. However, the same technology that bakes your potato or heats up your frozen burrito can also be used to send data. Microwave transmissions are not only fast, they're capable of covering very long distances. See **Figure 5.7** for one way to increase distances.

One of the recent improvements to microwave technology is a technology called the *Multipoint Microwave Distribution System* (MMDS). This allows for broadband

Figure 5.7 Microwave transmissions are line of sight. However, a relay point mutually visible to both locations can significantly extend your reach.

communications over microwave. Each carrier is given a channel that is 6MHz wide and the frequencies are assigned by the FCC. This allows a single transponder to carry a large number of different signals.

CHAPTER SUMMARY

As I have mentioned before, understanding the Physical Layer also includes a comprehension of all of the material presented in Chapter Three, The Highways and Byways of the Network. In this chapter, I discussed how the different signaling methods used by networking protocols are encoded to transfer data.

As is most likely very obvious, sending data over an electrical signal moving across a copper wire involves completely different issues from encoding that data into pulses of light. I examined several methods of signaling, involving both bounded and unbounded media types.

Many people wonder why it is so critical to understand a concept over which they have little, if any, control. However, later in the book, when I discuss troubleshooting the network, you will discover that an understanding of these concepts carries you a long way.

BRAIN DRAIN

1. List as many functions of the Physical Layer as you can think of.

2. Discuss the differences between RTZ and AMI signaling.

3. Explain in your own words the differences between synchronous and asynchronous communication.

4. Explain in your own words the differences between "bit timing" and synchronization.

THE 64K$ QUESTIONS

1. Which of the three subcomponents of the Physical Layer is responsible for bit encoding and decoding?
   a. PLS
   b. PMA
   c. MDI

2. Which of the three subcomponents of the Physical Layer describes the cables used by different platforms?

   a. PLS

   b. PMA

   c. MDI

3. Which of the three subcomponents of the Physical Layer defines the properties of transceivers?

   a. PLS

   b. PMA

   c. MDI

4. Return to Zero is a signaling method used when _____.

   a. Moving data over copper wire

   b. Moving data over fiber optics

   c. Moving data over radio waves

   d. Moving data over laser pulses

5. Which of the following are characteristics of asynchronous communication?

   a. A trailer containing either CRC or Checksum information is added to the packet.

   b. Parity information is used for error checking.

   c. A virtual connection is defined and configured before data is transferred.

   d. The transmitting device throws data out onto the medium and hopes that it gets there.

6. Which of the following are characteristics of synchronous communication?

   a. A trailer containing either CRC or Checksum information is added to the packet.

   b. Parity information is used for error checking.

   c. A virtual connection is defined and configured before data is transferred.

   d. The transmitting device throws data out onto the medium and hopes that it gets there.

7. CRC is the preferred error correction mechanism because _____.

   a. It requires less overhead

   b. It is more accurate

   c. It is more universally accepted by most protocols

   d. It isn't the preferred method. Checksum is.

8. Spread spectrum is a transmission method used by _____.

   a. Signaling over copper

   b. Signaling over fiber optics

   c. Signaling over microwave

   d. Signaling over radio waves

9. MMDS is a technology that allows _____.

   a. Multiple carrier signals to be carried over a single fiber-optic line.

   b. Several microwave frequencies to carry a single carrier.

   c. Several microwave carriers to be managed by a single transponder.

   d. Multimedia information to be moved over radio.

10. Gaussian frequency shift keying does what?

    a. It synchronizes the frequency and pattern of radio frequencies used by Spread-Spectrum transmissions.

    b. It encrypts the patterns of bits sent out over optical signals.

    c. It prevents a long series of 1s in a broadcast from disrupting the clock frequencies used by the tranceivers.

    d. It overrides error correction of encapsulated protocols.

11. Which of the following is a function of the Physical Layer. (Check all that apply.)

    a. Defining the physical cables used by the network

    b. Determining an encoding mechanism

    c. Deciding which access control method the network will use to get data onto the wire

    d. All of the above

12. One of the following is a copper-based medium. Which one is it?

    a. 802.11b

    b. FDDI

    c. ATM

    d. CDDI

13. The data encoding mechanism called Return to Zero is also sometimes called _____.

    a. Pulse signaling

    b. HDB3

    c. CSMA/CD

    d. Manchester Encoding

14. With Asynchronous Communication, the transmitting computer waits for an ACK packet from the receiving computer before sending more data.

    a. True

    b. False

15. Which of the following communications methods uses parity checking to detect the presence of an error?

    a. Synchronous

    b. Asynchronous

    c. Duplex

    d. Simplex

16. DPLL is a form of _____ signal.

    a. Error checking

    b. Carrier

    c. Timing

    d. Acknowledgement

17. The package of data sent in a typical asynchronous event is _____ long.

    a. 8 bytes

    b. 11 bytes

    c. 2460 bytes

    d. Asynchronous communications sends only one byte at a time. It just adds extra bits.

18. The form of error correction most commonly used by today's protocols for sending large amounts of data is _____.

    a. Even parity

    b. Odd parity

    c. Checksum

    d. Cyclical redundancy check

19. Checksum monitors errors in a data transmission by _____.

    a. Adding up all the 1s in a packet and storing the value in the trailer.

    b. Treating the entire packet as a huge mathematical number and performing a calculation on that number.

c. Counting the number of 1s in the packet and storing a 1 in the trailer if there is an even number of 1s or a 0 if there is an odd number of 1s.

d. Counting the number of 1s in the packet and storing a 0 in the trailer if there is an even number of 1s or a 1 if there is an odd number of 1s.

20. Tight-buffered cable is another form of _____ cable.

a. Twisted pair

b. Coaxial

c. Single-stranded copper

d. Fiber optics

TRICKY TERMINOLOGY

Bit stuffing: Adding nondata information to a frame in order to bring it up to a minimum size.

Bit timing: A method used by transceivers to accurately extract encoded data from an analog signal using clock cycles as a basis.

Checksum: A method of error detection that simply keeps track of the number of 1s in the packet. If the receiving devices calculates a different checksum than that stored in the trailer, the packet will be rejected and a *NACK* returned to the sender.

Chipping code: A pattern of several changes in the signal carrier to represent a single bit. These changes can be either frequency, amplitude, or pulse modulated.

Parity: An error detection mechanism that simply counts the number of 1s in a byte and indicates in a unique bit whether there is an even number of 1s or an odd number.

Spread spectrum: The transmission of data by spreading it across several different radio frequencies.

ACRONYM ALERT

AMI: Alternate Mark Inversion. A modification of RTZ.

DPLL: Digital Phase Locked Loop. A clock signal carried in an electrical transmission of data.

DSSS: Direct Sequence Spread Spectrum. One of the frequency-hopping methods used in radio-based wireless networking.

FHSS: Frequency Hopping Spread Spectrum. One of the frequency-hopping methods used in radio-based wireless networking.

GFSK: Gaussian Frequency Shift Keying. A scheme for determining shift patterns and frequency in spread-spectrum radio networking.

HDB3: A modification of AMI that prevents more than four 0s from occurring in sequence.

HPSF: High-Power Single Frequency. A radio wave-based networking technology using high-powered, assigned radio frequencies.

LD: Laser Diode

LED: Light Emitting Diode

LPSF: Low-Power Single Frequency. A radio wave-based networking technology using weak, publicly available radio frequencies.

MDI: The Media Dependent Interface component of the Physical Layer

MMDS: Multipoint Microwave Distribution System. A technology for sending broadband signals over microwave.

NRZ: Non-Return to Zero. An analog signaling scheme in which zeros and ones are each represented by a different voltage.

PLS: The Physical Signaling component of the Physical Layer

PMA: The Physical Medium Attachment component of the Physical Layer

RTZ: Return to Zero. A pulse signaling method used when moving data over copper wire.

SOHO: Small Office/Home Office. A generic term for offices used either by a single individual or a small group.

SWAP: Shared Wireless Access Protocol. A protocol that uses the same technology as cordless telephones to interconnect network devices.

CHAPTER 6

THE DATA LINK LAYER

As you continue up the stack to the next layer, you come to Data Link, or sometimes more simply, Layer 2. This is the one layer of the OSI Model to be split into two sublayers. These sublayers are known as *Media Access Control* (MAC) and *Logical Link Control* (LLC). There are key functions that occur at the Data Link Layers, and a good understanding of this layer goes a long way in providing a good understanding of networking in general. As mentioned in Chapter Four, Welcome to OSI, the primary functions of this layer include the following:

- Physical addressing
- Network topology
- Error notification
- Access to the physical medium
- Flow control

The sublayers of Data Link have specific functions to perform. LLC defines the rules that govern the establishment and maintenance of logical connections between communication devices. (Note that this does not duplicate or replace the functions of the Session Layer that we will discuss later in the book.) LLC is responsible for the logical addressing that goes on in Data Link. MAC determines how data will eventually get its turn at the physical medium and also deals with physical addressing.

Two devices that perform their magic at this layer are bridges and Layer 2 switches. I specify Layer 2 for the switches, because there are some switches with more advanced functionality that work in Layer 3 as well. I'll be looking at those in the next chapter, Chapter Seven, The Network Layer.

Protocols that function within the Data Link Layer include:

- High Level Data Link Protocol (HDLC)
- Point-to-Point Protocol (PPP)

- Link Control Protocol (LCP)
- Network Control Protocol (NCP)

Exam objectives that will be either introduced or covered in this chapter include:

1.2 Specify the main features of 802.2 (Logical Link Control), 802.3 (Ethernet), 802.5 (token ring), 802.11 (wireless), and FDDI (Fiber Distributed Data Interface) networking technologies.

1.3 Specify the characteristics (For example: speed, length, topology, and cable type) of cable standards.

1.6 Identify the purposes, features and functions of key network components.

2.2 Identify the seven layers of the OSI (Open Systems Interconnect) model and their functions.

2.3 Identify the OSI (Open Systems Interconnect) layers at which the following network components operate: Hubs, Switches, Bridges, Routers, NICs (Network Interface Card), WAPs (Wireless Access Point).

> **BUZZ WORDS**
>
> **Flat addressing model:** A method of addressing in which there is only one level of address for every node on the network. All addresses get thrown into the same pool and a network device has to dive in to find a specific address.
>
> **Hierarchical address model:** A method of addressing in which there are multiple levels of addressing, such as a network address and a host address. A network device can find the network it is looking for and let that network figure out which host is supposed to get the data.

ADDRESSING FUNCTIONS OF THE DATA LINK LAYER

I mentioned in Chapter Four that there are two types of addressing going on in a network communications session. To review, these are physical addresses and logical addresses. To break this down a little into even greater detail, physical addresses fall into a *flat addressing model,* while logical addresses fall into a *hierarchical addressing model.* This is sort of like the different ways people store books. Under a flat addressing model, there is one huge box into which all books go. Now you have to paw through the box until you find what you're looking for (see **Figure 6.1**). A hierarchical scheme breaks everything down into categories, putting the art books in one section and the computer books in another. This makes a quick search easier.

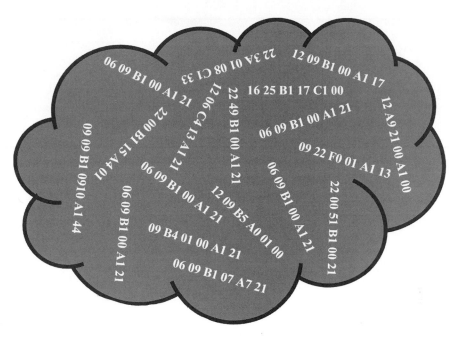

Figure 6.1 Flat addressing throws all the available addresses into a single pool. If you want to communicate with a device—go find it!

> **EXAM NOTE:** Be sure you can distinguish between flat addressing models and hierarchical addressing models. There is more than one way this can show up on the exam.

PHYSICAL ADDRESSING IN DATA LINK

To quickly review, network devices make use of two different addressing schemas. Logical addressing is configured by a user or network administrator to any given device and can be changed as needs change. I'll be looking at this in greater detail in Chapter Seven. In addition to logical addresses, all networkable devices also have a fixed physical address. This is an address that is burned in at the factory and goes with the device wherever it goes. This address is commonly referred to as the MAC address, in deference to the sublayer that makes the most use of this address. As the name implies, the MAC sublayer in the Data Link Layer handles this form of addressing.

The IEEE Registration Authority strictly administers MAC addressing assignments. This is a good thing, because having two devices with the same physical address on the network can cause no end of nightmares. While this is theoretically not supposed to happen, manufacturers make mistakes, too.

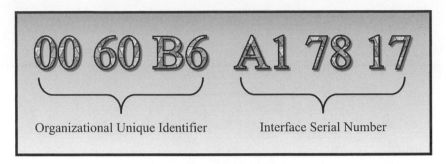

Figure 6.2   The structure of a MAC address.

The MAC address is a forty-eight-bit address, expressed as twelve hexadecimal digits. This address consists of two twenty-four-bit segments of twelve digits each. See **Figure 6.2** for an example. The first segment is a twenty-four-bit *Organizational Unique Identifier* (OUI) assigned by IEEE. The manufacturer cannot change this. The remaining twenty-four bits consist of a manufacturer-assigned *interface serial number.*

Notice that I called it an interface serial number and not just a device serial number. Many devices such as routers, switches, and bridges have multiple addressable ports. Each addressable port must have a unique MAC address. Therefore a router with twenty-four assignable ports will have twenty-four MAC addresses.

LOGICAL ADDRESSING IN DATA LINK

Data Link's relationship to the network isn't purely physical. There is something logical going on as well. It is at the LLC sublayer that Service Access Points (SAPs) are generated. These SAPs have a critical role in getting data where it needs to be once it reaches the destination computer.

Just because the data has found the correct computer doesn't mean the job is done. There also needs to be some way to get that data to correctly move from one OSI layer to the next, eventually reaching the correct application. As I defined in Chapter Four, the SAPs act to move data from one layer to the next. The two types of SAP are *Destination Service Access Point* (DSAP) and *Source Service Access Point* (SSAP). Each networking protocol in use needs one of each of these. The DSAP is the receiving station's logical link to the protocol, while the SSAP is the transmitting station's link. SAPs are defined in unique headers that identify the logical port assigned to the protocol. These values are defined by OSI and not simply assigned arbitrarily by the programmer.

Why does the network need unique SAPs for each protocol if the SAPs act as the data path between OSI layers? The answer to that is simple. In the event that multiple files are being moved simultaneously, then the network needs to keep the data segregated; otherwise data corruption will occur.

ENCAPSULATION IN THE DATA LINK LAYER

In Chapter Four, Welcome to OSI, I introduced the concept of encapsulation. If you recall, this is where a stream of data is broken down into manageable chunks and information from each of the OSI layers is added to that piece of data. The final step in the process is accomplished by the Data Link Layer.

Once the Data Link protocol or device has performed its functions on the data, it will encode information about what it has done and add that to the packet it received from the Network Layer. This appended piece of data becomes a frame.

The Data Link header adds information that tells the receiving computer where one frame begins and where it ends. A field called the *starting delimiter* is added into the header; the *ending delimiter* is added to the trailer. Other fields include source and destination MAC addresses, frame type, sequence number, and other types of control information, including whether this is an ACK or NACK frame. Each media access method relies on a specific type of packet, and where relevant, will be discussed in its own section.

DEFINING NETWORK TOPOLOGIES AND IMPLEMENTATION

A term that frequently confuses beginning (and sometimes even advanced) students of networking technology is the word *topology*. Strictly speaking, the topology of the network is the physical method by which the devices are interconnected. Therefore, the common topologies are as follows:

- Bus
- Ring
- Star
- Mesh
- Hybrid

These were discussed in detail in Chapter One, and I won't bother to rehash it here. The confusion that occasionally arises is when people see the terms "Ethernet topology," "Token Ring topology," or something else along these lines. These are not topologies, but rather media access methods.

Most of the LAN technology network engineers deal with today uses baseband signaling. This means that only one signal can be on the wire at a time. Media access methods deal with the problems of making sure every device has an equal opportunity to get its data onto the wire. The different access methods I will discuss include:

- Token Ring
- CSMA/CD
- CSMA/CA
- FDDI
- Demand Priority

EXAM NOTE: The different physical network topologies are covered very heavily on the exam. Be able to explain them all, complete with advantages and limitations, before you try to take the exam.

CSMA/CD

As a networking technology, Ethernet goes a long way back. I reviewed the history of Ethernet in Chapter One, Some Raw Basics of Networking. However, the original Ethernet standards only defined a 10Mb/s data stream moving over coaxial cable. Subsequent Ethernet standards have all been a result of work overseen by the 802.3 committee. Since Ethernet is actually a registered trademark of Xerox Corporation, technically speaking, I should be referring to CSMA/CD networks, rather than Ethernet networks. It would appear, however, that the term Ethernet has succumbed to being a generic term.

While the phrase may seem a bit intimidating at first, CSMA/CD isn't really all that difficult to understand once you break it down into its separate components. But first you have to keep in mind that we're dealing with baseband technology here. Only one signal can be on the wire at a time.

Carrier sense simply means that the computer gets its turn on the wire by listening to the carrier signal for a moment of silence. It's the same thing you do when you're trying to merge onto a busy highway from the on-ramp. You wait for an empty spot and jump in. Multiple access simply indicates that the goal is to allow multiple devices to access the wire, even though only one can have it at a time. To continue the highway analogy, it's like having an express lane over which only one car can be on any single segment of the freeway at any given time. If another car tries to access that ramp anywhere on the freeway while another is already there, there will be a collision. Collision detection is the acknowledgment that collisions are going to occur on a regular basis. If that red convertible jumps into the lane ahead of you just as you're moving in, you're going to have a collision. If a piece of data jumps onto the wire at exactly the same instant as another, there will be a collision.

A collision on a network isn't quite so messy as one on the freeway, however. The

BUZZ WORD

Probabilistic: Any approach that is likely to achieve the desired results, but is not guaranteed to achieve them.

data is simply discarded. The offending computers send out a *backoff algorithm,* telling both computers to wait a randomly generated amount of time before sending again. That way, they're not quite as likely to collide with each other again. They may collide with another computer, but at least they won't be exchanging phone numbers and insurance information with each other again.

The way the backoff algorithm works is that on the first collision between two devices, those two devices generate a random number between one and two. This unfortunately means that there is a fifty-fifty chance they will both generate the same number and collide again. If this happens, they generate a number between one and four. On the third occurrence, the range becomes one and eight, then one and sixteen, and finally one and thirty-two. After this, if there is yet another collision, they throw up their cables in despair and each machine creates a new session with the device with which it was originally trying to communicate.

This method of accessing the media is known as *contention-based* access. A term you might see on the exam to describe this access method is *probabilistic.* Any device is free to transmit any time it has data. If a collision occurs, the device simply sends the data again. For the most part, the system works pretty well. However, as networks grow in size, the network administrator needs to find a way of reducing collisions. One way to do this is by segmenting the network using a device called a *switch.*

A switch looks a lot like a hub. On the back panel, anywhere from a few to a great many connectors provide access to the switch. You can treat a switch just like a hub and hook individual computers into each connector, or you can interconnect hubs and/or other switches, off of which a number of computers or other devices can be hung. The switch can intelligently filter information. Information intended for any given port is blocked from transmission over the other ports.

If you're hanging hubs off the switch's ports, all of the computers connected to a given hub form an independent collision domain. Data meant for another computer in the same collision domain stays within that domain. It does not pass over other ports to other domains. Thus, overall traffic on the network is reduced. When traffic is reduced, collisions are reduced.

EXAM NOTE: Make sure you can describe the functional differences between a switch and a hub. You are likely going to be asked what device is the most appropriate for a given scenario.

Data is sent over Ethernet in frames, just like every other access method. The frame consists of nine sections (see **Figure 6.3**).

The first section is the *preamble*. This signals the beginning of a new frame and provides data used by the receiving devices for synchronization and timing purposes. It alerts all attached devices that there is incoming data.

Next is the *destination address*. This indicates what device originally sent the data. It is followed by the *source address*. This is, of course, the device intended to receive the data. Next is a field indicating *frame type*. The two types of frame used by Ethernet are 802.2 frames and 802.3 frames. The latter is by far the most universally used.

Now comes the *payload*. This is the actual data being carried by the frame. It can be either user data or protocol-specific information. This field varies in size from a minimum size of forty-six bytes to a maximum of 1500 bytes. After the data comes the *Frame Check Sequence* (FCS). This field contains the results of the error checking algorithm being used. Because the only algorithm currently in use is *cyclical redundancy check* (CRC), you will also see this field referred to as the *CRC footer*. This carries the code used for error detection and correction.

> **BUZZ WORD**
>
> **Payload:** The actual information carried in the frame that is the reason for the frame being transmitted to begin with. This may include user or application data or protocol-specific information.

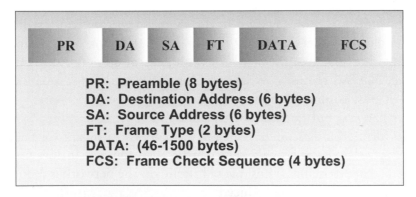

PR: Preamble (8 bytes)
DA: Destination Address (6 bytes)
SA: Source Address (6 bytes)
FT: Frame Type (2 bytes)
DATA: (46-1500 bytes)
FCS: Frame Check Sequence (4 bytes)

Figure 6.3 Structure of an Ethernet frame.

Ethernet networks can be set up in either a bus network or a star network. However, as I mentioned earlier, because of media limitations and the management issues I looked at in the last section, nearly all contemporary Ethernet networks are variations on the star network these days. The basic equipment to set up an Ethernet network includes an NIC for each computer on the network, sufficient cabling of the right lengths, and one or more hubs to interconnect the computers. I highly recommend that, if you are setting up a new network from scratch, you run at the very least CAT5e twisted-pair cabling. If it is available in your area, some companies are already shipping CAT6 (even though the standards have not been ratified as of this writing). You might want to consider installing CAT6 if it's available, even if you are going the inexpensive route and installing only a 10Mb/s network. Needs change over time, and a few bucks spent up front can save several hundred dollars later on down the road, and prevent the necessity of ripping out all the old cable and installing new.

There are several Ethernet standards to choose from, ranging from 10Mb/s to the newer Gigabit Ethernet. The standards go by some rather arcane names, but once you understand the structure of the names, the standards are actually pretty easy to understand (see **Figure 6.4**).

Some of the more commonly seen Ethernet types include:

- 10BaseT   10Mb/s, Baseband, Twisted pair
- 10Base2   10Mb/s, Baseband, Thinnet (2 = 200 meters, which is rounded up from the actual 185 meters RG-58 cable will support)
- 10Base5   10Mb/s, Baseband, Thicknet (5 = 500 meters)
- 100BaseT   100Mb/s, Baseband, Twisted pair using two pairs

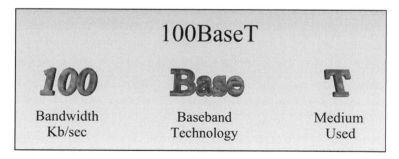

Figure 6.4 Understanding the names of Ethernet standards doesn't have to be that hard.

157

- 100BaseT4   100Mb/s, Baseband, Twisted pair using four pairs
- 100BaseTX   100Mb/s, Baseband, Twisted pair using two data-grade pairs
- 100BaseFL   100Mb/s, Baseband, Fiber-optic cable
- 100BaseFB   100Mb/s, Baseband, Fiber-optic backbone
- 1000BaseT   1000Mb/s, Baseband, Twisted pair
- 1000BaseCX 1000Mb/s, Baseband, Balanced copper over coax
- 1000BaseLX 1000Mb/s, Baseband, Long wave light over fiber
- 1000BaseSX 1000Mb/s, Baseband, Shortwave light over fiber

EXAM NOTE: Know your Ethernet types backwards and forwards. You are most likely going to be asked to define at least one of them, and it probably won't be one of the easier ones.

Anyone planning to set up a home network or a small office/home office (SOHO) network is likely to be looking at Ethernet as the basis for that network. The equipment is the most reasonably priced and most widely supported of all the hardware protocols. Any of the major office-supply chains and/or consumer electronics chains carries two or more lines of each of the main components you'll need for setting up a network. You can even purchase bundled kits that include two or more NICs, a hub, and some cable.

DEMAND PRIORITY

If there's any fault to be found with CSMA/CD at all it lies in the fact that it is a probabilistic access method. Running simultaneous signals over the wire, such as voice over data, or multimedia, would theoretically be more efficient with a deterministic media access protocol. In 1995, the IEEE 802.12 Committee answered the call with a network standard called *demand priority*. The first incarnation of this standard appeared as Hewlett Packard's 100VG-AnyLAN, the VG referring to *virtual graphic*.

The way demand priority works is this. Media access rules for demand priority are implemented in the hub. The hub, or hubs, control device access to the network. Any device at any time can receive a frame. However, each device has to "ask permission" to transmit. There is neither cooperation nor contention between nodes on the network. The hub provides access control.

When a device has data to transmit, it sends the hub a signal that is basically demanding access to the network. A node can send a hub two types of transmit requests—normal priority and high priority. It's up to the hub to decide when the device will actually be able to send its data. When the hub decides it is time for the node to transmit, the hub sends the node a signal giving it permission to send.

The hub itself cycles through each of the requesting nodes, in port order, allowing each to transmit *one* packet. This process of cycling is sometimes called the *round-robin algorithm*. One of the things that speeds up demand priority a bit is that the hub bypasses all ports not generating a request to send. As it moves through a cycle, a hub will respond first to a device issuing a high priority request before servicing any nodes with normal priority requests. Because the hub pays no attention to nodes that don't need to transmit, they are skipped and do not take time in the hub's round-robin algorithm.

> **BUZZ WORD**
>
> **Round-robin algorithm:** A media access method in which a centralized device, such as an intelligent hub, scans each interface, searching for a device that wants to send data. It skips devices that do not need to transmit. If two or more devices need to transmit on the same cycle a priority method is used to determine who gets to go first.

Now go back a paragraph or two. Remember that I mentioned that there are two types of transmit demands. There is normal priority and high priority. This feature wasn't put into the standard just so the boss could get his information on the network before everybody else. Certain types of data have different needs. Priorities are based on data type. This feature is designed to support multimedia video streams or other time-critical applications that require low transmit latency.

Of course, the network needs to stop the boss's videocast over the network from preventing the real work from being done as well. In order to avoid high priority transmissions from hogging the network and blocking normal priority nodes, the hub maintains a *priority promotion timer* for each node. This timer starts when a node submits a normal priority transmit request. If the timer expires and the device still hasn't had its turn on the network, its request will be upgraded to high priority.

As with any network, there has to be some provision for expansion. It would be a very small network indeed, if only a single hub could control access for an entire network. In a VG-AnyLAN network with multiple hubs, *child* hubs are nodes to an associated *parent* hub. If any one of the subordinate devices of a child hub needs to transmit data, it will signal a request to transmit to its parent hub. The parent hub will then allow the child hub's nodes and/or hubs to transmit their packets (see **Figure 6.5**).

So how is this better than CSMA/CD? Well, the demand priority scheme is designed to improve on the CSMA/CD access method used by 10Mb/s Ethernet and 100Mb/s fast Ethernet. On either of the Ethernet standards, the rated speed is

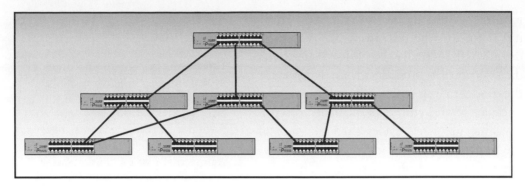

Figure 6.5 Demand priority allows for network expansion by cascading hubs. Each child hub is at the mercy of its parent hub.

a maximum speed shared by all devices on a segment. On a collision-based network, there is no predictable time between the point when a packet becomes available to transmit and the time that it actually gains access to the wire. Collisions further exacerbate the issue with the necessity of resending the packets that collided. On a VG network, it is easy to predict the maximum time any given packet will wait for access, whether it be a normal or high priority request. Actual utilization of the wire is far more efficient.

A final advantage of the demand priority protocol is that it can support both 802.3 Ethernet frames and 802.5 Token Ring frames. This allows for an easier migration of hybrid networks as well as simple Token Ring.

Unfortunately, while all of the above suggests that demand priority is a far superior access method to CSMA/CD, it has really never caught on much in the LAN environment. The cost and limited availability of demand priority products accounts for much of the resistance. 802.12 repeaters need to be "intelligent devices." Therefore they cost more to develop and manufacture, which is passed onto the consumer in the form of substantially higher cost. This past year, HP discontinued support for the standard.

CSMA/CA

Anyone who uses Apple Computer Corporation's Localtalk protocol on his or her networks is using *Carrier Sense Multiple Access/ Collision Avoidance* (CSMA/CA) signaling. It is also used by wireless LAN protocols. Like its counterpart, CSMA/CD, this access method listens to the media's carrier, looking for a moment of silence before it attempts to transmit data. The key difference is that with CSMA/CA, the machine attempts to avoid any possible collisions by announcing its intent to broadcast prior to putting its data on the wire. This broadcast is in the form of a *request to send/clear to send* (RTS/CTS) packet. All other clients are then induced to wait for a number of time slots before trying to broadcast. The duration of these time slots varies with the type of medium used. This delay is known as the *contention window.* If another machine senses activity on the wire, it sets its *backoff timer* a randomly selected number of time slots. This backoff timer dictates how long the device waits before trying to send again.

IEEE's 802.11 committee, which now has oversight over CSMA/CA, does not dictate the number of time slots that must be set as minimum and maximum values for this random number. As the number of collisions between devices increases, the contention window range increases, just like in CSMA/CD. IEEE advises, however, that a minimum value of fifteen and a maximum value of 1023 be used.

With CSMA/CA, collisions do occur, but unlike CSMA/CD, there is no way of detecting them. Therefore, CSMA/CA makes use of an acknowledgment frame (ACK) that must be sent by the receiving device for every frame that arrives intact. If the transmitting device doesn't receive an ACK within a certain time frame, it sends the data again.

The key virtue of CSMA/CA is that very few collisions occur. This is of key importance in the wireless arena because wireless networking has no way of detecting the occurrence of a collision. The key drawback is the amount of traffic generated by the constant stream of RTS/CTS and ACK packets in addition to the data itself.

> **EXAM NOTE:** For the Network+ exam, all you really need to know about CSMA/CA is that is it the access method used primarily by wireless networks.

TOKEN PASSING

Token Ring had a fairly long and popular reign, but for the most part, it is becoming a bygone standard. In a way, that's too bad, because it had everything going for it—except speed. IBM began development of the Token Ring back in the early 1970s. It became one of the OSI committees in 1980. While there are some minor differences that are not even worth discussing, the IEEE 802.5 standard and IBM's Token Ring are pretty much the same thing.

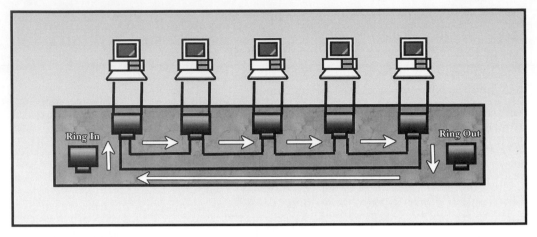

Figure 6.6 While the concept of Token Ring suggests data moving around in an endless circle, use of an MAU allows the network to be wired like a hub.

While the ideology of the Token Ring network is based on the concept of a ring network, actual implementation is achieved in a physical star. In place of a hub, a *multi-station access unit* (MAU) is used. This is a device that, while superficially very similar to

BUZZ WORD

Deterministic: Any approach that is guaranteed to achieve the desired results.

a hub, is wired internally to achieve a ring topology (see **Figure 6.6**). The one visible difference between a hub and an MAU is the presence of ring in and ring out jacks. This allows additional MAUs to be added to the network for purposes of expansion.

Unlike the probabilistic media access used by Ethernet, Token Ring uses a *deterministic* approach. A small packet of data—the token—passes from computer to computer. Only the computer that has possession of the token may transmit data at any give time. No token; no media access. Unlike Ethernet, where people can shoot onto the freeway anytime they want, Token Ring is a toll road. You have to pick up your token before you get on.

STRUCTURE OF THE TOKEN

The token that circulates the network is a twenty-four-bit piece of data divided into three octets. The first octet is the *starting delimiter*. This simply notifies receiving devices that there is incoming data. Following the starting delimiter is another octet called the *access control byte.* This lets the receiving device know if the following data is a token or a frame. After this is the *ending delimiter,* which signifies that this is the final byte of this particular piece of information (see **Figure 6.7**). The token carries no data of its own.

Figure 6.7 The token is a twenty-four-bit ticket to the network.

STRUCTURE OF THE TOKEN RING FRAME

A Token Ring frame consists of several sections. There is a physical header, a routing information field, a header, the information field, and finally, the physical trailer (see **Figure 6.8**).

The Physical Header The physical header consists of five components. The first of these is called the *starting delimiter.* This is a single byte that begins every frame or token. It is responsible for alerting the receiving hardware adapter that there is an incoming frame or token. The starting delimiter cannot be distinguished as a valid byte of information and will be ignored by most devices other than an interface card.

The starting delimiter is followed by the *access control byte.* This byte allows the adapter to discern between a frame and a token. It also is the byte that is used by the beaconing process to correct for lost or perpetually busy tokens.

Next comes the *frame control byte.* Token Ring frames can be LLC frames or MAC frames. If it is an LLC frame, the value of this byte will be 0100 0000. A MAC frame will be 0000 0000.

Next comes a six-byte *destination address.* This tells each station on the ring whether or not it is supposed to copy this frame. The first bit of byte number one identifies the address as being either an individual address or a group address. If that bit is a 0, it is an individual address. A 1 indicates a group address. If it is an individual address, then only the intended station will copy the frame. A group address suggests multiple recipients.

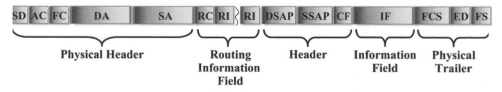

Figure 6.8 The actual frame itself is a bit more complicated.

Following the destination address is a six-byte *source address.* As with the destination address, the first bit of byte one contains critical information. If the bit value is 0, there is no routing information contained in the frame. A 1 in this position announces the presence of routing information.

The Routing Information Field   This section is only present when routing information is required. Token Ring's approach to creating larger and more complex networks is to interconnect multiple rings. The routing information field provides information used to move data from one ring to another. Its presence is indicated in the first bit of the source address (as I mentioned above). This section is broken down into fields as well. First off is the *routing control field.* This field is two bytes long and provides the devices along the way with three critical pieces of information. It indicates whether or not the frame is a directly routed frame, a frame that should follow all routes on the network, or a frame that must be kept within specific rings. Next, the routing control field indicates the length of the overall *Routing Information Field.* After this come the route designations. This consists of one or more two-byte fields directing the frame to specific routes.

The Header   This is the portion of the Token Ring frame that provides the service access points described earlier in this chapter. There are one-byte fields that define the DSAP and the SSAP. Following that is a field of one or more bytes that is called the *control field.* The control field can hold many different types of information. It can carry commands or responses to commands. It will hold sequence information if a conversation consists of multiple frames.

The Information Field   This is the part of the frame that actually carries the data being moved. Depending on the transaction that is occurring, this could be user data or it can be information being moved by upper-layer protocols. This field varies in length. In the 4Mb/s networks, data packets can range from one to 4,442 bytes. In 16Mb/s they can be from one to 17,946 bytes.

The Physical Trailer   This field consists of three sections. The first is the *frame check sequence.* This is the part of the frame that contains the error correction information provided by CRC. It is a four-byte field and the CRC is calculated on the entire frame, from the beginning up to, but not including, the first bit of the frame check sequence.

Following the frame check sequence is the *ending delimiter.* Like the starting delimiter, this is a one-byte field that cannot be distinguished as data. It simply tells the receiving device that the end of the frame is near.

Finally there is the *frame status.* It is a single byte that is added to the frame. The destination device fills in this part of the frame and sends it along the ring back to the source computer. This field tells the source device one of three things:

- The frame was successfully copied.

- The destination device could not be found.

- The destination device was found but for some reason did not copy the frame.

> **BUZZ WORD**
>
> **Beaconing:** A process Token Ring uses to find out what station has dropped from the network. Each device sends a beacon frame to both its upstream neighbor and its downstream neighbor. Once the culprit has been found, the MAU can bypass that station internally.

TOKEN RING AT WORK

On a Token Ring network, the first computer to come on during a networking session becomes the token generator. In the event that a token is lost or discarded, it is up to the token generator to figure out that this has happened and then generate a new token. The way it figures out that a problem has occurred is through a process called *beaconing*.

When a computer has gone an inordinately long time without its chance at the token, it sends a broadcast signal down the wire known as the *beacon*. It is basically a message alerting other machines to announce themselves. Each machine that receives the beaconing message responds to both its nearest upstream neighbor and its nearest downstream neighbor until, all of a sudden, there's a computer that doesn't respond. The MAU will bypass the offending port, the active monitor will generate a new token and send it down the wire, and all will be well again.

As a protocol, Token Ring had a lot going for it. In terms of error correction and detection and fail-safe fallbacks, it was among the best. However, it had some key limitations. You had your choice of a 4Mb/s or a 16Mb/s ring. In the days of 10Base2 and 10BaseT, the 16Mb/s implementation offered an improvement in speed. However, with the release of 100Mb networks, Token Ring's appeal began to fade. The higher cost of components didn't justify the advantages.

As a standard, however, Token Ring apparently refuses to die. The *High Speed Token Ring Alliance*, consisting of IBM, Madge Networks, Olicom, 3Com, and several others, has set out to define 100Mb and Gigabit standards for Token Ring. Standards for 100Mb were proposed in 1997 and in July of 1999 the first products began to ship.

Unfortunately for supporters of Token Ring technology, this may be a classic case of "too little, too late." Token Ring vendors are shipping 100Mb product at a time when Gigabit Ethernet is becoming the de facto standard. Gigabit Token Ring standards (as of this writing) are still in the works, but only by certain holdout manufacturers. IEEE, as an organization, has put the 802.5 committee into hibernation.

Therefore, it would be premature to say that Token Ring is dead. There are a variety of companies in the marketplace still shipping product.

> **EXAM NOTE:** The key concepts to look for on the exam are how MAUs work, what the Active Monitor does, and how the process of beaconing works. Token Ring may be a fading technology, but the Network+ exam still emphasizes it fairly heavily.

10-GIGABYTE ETHERNET

The 802.3ae committtee's newest standards are the 10-gigabyte Ethernet (10GE) standards. The 10GE standards use the Ethernet media protocols defined by 802.3 and continue to transmit data in a standard Ethernet frame, but faster. However, 10GE also provides the ability to merge voice and data which is carried over fiber. So the CSMA/CD protocol is no longer needed.

10GE also uses different data-encoding methods than Ethernet over copper. Two common encoding methods are 8B/10B and 64B/66B. These are really pretty straightforward.

- **8B/10B:** You may recall that only 8 bits are needed for 256 characters. With 8B/10B, 10 bits are used to encode 256 data characters, and offer a total of 1,024 combinations. The other bits are used to encode specialized control characters (K characters), such as start and end characters for each packet, synch characters, and other characters used exclusively to manage data flow. User data is packaged into D characters. 8B/10B transmissions are *run length limited* (RLL) coded. This assures that there will be no more than five consecutive 0s or 1s, preventing the receiver clock from losing synchronization with the transmitter clock. The downside to 8B/10B is that it experiences a 25 percent overhead for control data.

- **64B/66B:** This encoding mechanism takes 8 bytes of data and scrambles it. Next, the transmitter adds two extra bits as synchronization bits, with the result that a 66-bit block of data is transmitted. While 802.3ae provides for control frames to be used by 64B/66B, these frames aren't required. The advantage to this method is that there is only a 3 percent overhead lost to data control bits.

As an optical standard, the 10GE naming scheme also differs. When I discussed Ethernet over copper, I talked about the 10BaseT, 100BaseT, and so forth. The

10GE standard uses a similar format, but has a two-letter suffix. The notations used follow a pattern of 10Gbase(X)(Y). X and the Y in that notation each represent a different specification. X represents the wavelength of light used and will be represented by the letters S, L, or E, listed with each of their values:

- S = 850nm
- L = 1300nm
- E = 1550nm

Y refers to the type of coding used by the protocol. The values here will be represented by the letters X, R, and W, which indicate the following:

- X = 8B/10B coding
- R = 64B/66B coding
- W = 64B/66B coding encapsulated for transmission over SONET

The 802.3 recognized this protocol would be useful on either the LAN or the WAN, so it identified two separate Layer 2 interfacing schemas—the LAN PHY and the WAN PHY. How convenient.

The two basic 10GE standards targeted for the LAN PHY are 10GBase-X and 10GBase-R. The one standard target at the WAN PHY is 10GBase-W.

10GBase-X uses the 8B/10B coding, as the suffix tells you. It actually provides for an aggregate bandwidth of 12.5Gb/s. It divides this bandwidth into four separate channels of 3.125Gb/channel. 10GBase-R provides a single 10Gb/s channel. Its actual raw bandwidth is 10.3124Gb/s. 10GBase-W takes a 64B/66B data packet and encapsulates it for transmission over another protocol called SONET (to be discussed in greater detail in Chapter Fourteen, "Working with Remote Access"). The result of the encapsulation is a 9.294Gb/s bandwidth. **Table 6.1** compares the 10GE standards that I have discussed here.

Table 6.1 10GE Coding and Transmission Rates

	PHY	LAN	WAN
Protocol	10GBase-X	10GBase-R	10GBase-W
Data Encoding	8B/10B	64B/66B	64B/66B
Data Rate	10Gb/s	10Gb/s	9.294Gb/s
Line Rate	4 x 3.125	10.3124	9.95328
A comparison of 10GE standards			

FDDI

Fiber Distributed Data Interface takes up where Token Ring left off. Like Token Ring, it uses a token-passing deterministic approach to media access. FDDI, however, uses a dual-ring topology. A primary ring sends data in one direction, while a secondary ring provides for an alternate path in the event of a failure in the first ring. It was designed to use fiber optics as the transmission medium, which is where it gets its name. There are, however, implementations of FDDI that use copper cable as well. The latter is known as the *Copper Distributed Data Interface* (CDDI).

Stations on an FDDI network can be either *dual-attached* or *single-attached* stations. A dual-attached station is connected to both rings, while a single-attached station is connected only to the primary ring. An example of an FDDI network with both types of nodes can be seen in **Figure 6.9.**

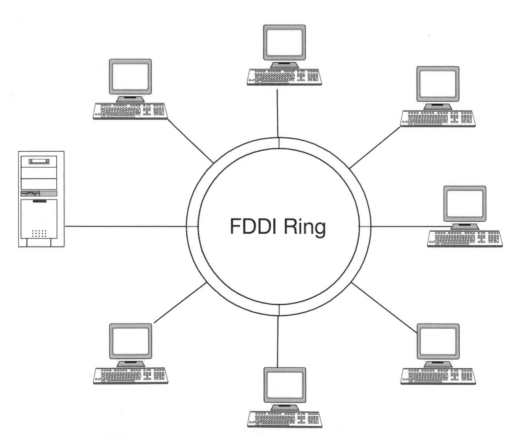

Figure 6.9 Logical diagram of an FDDI network.

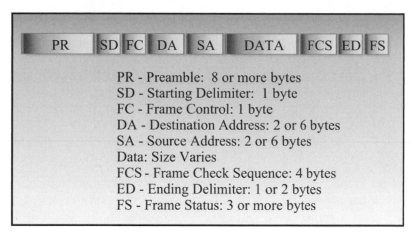

PR - Preamble: 8 or more bytes
SD - Starting Delimiter: 1 byte
FC - Frame Control: 1 byte
DA - Destination Address: 2 or 6 bytes
SA - Source Address: 2 or 6 bytes
Data: Size Varies
FCS - Frame Check Sequence: 4 bytes
ED - Ending Delimiter: 1 or 2 bytes
FS - Frame Status: 3 or more bytes

Figure 6.10   Structure of the FDDI Frame

A dual-attached station will be connected to the network via at least one A port, where it attaches to the primary ring, and one B port, where it attaches to the secondary ring. It may or may not also have one or more M ports installed. The M port is the port that a single-station unit uses to attach to the network. These hook up only to the primary ring.

When using fiber optics as a medium, very large networks over great distances are possible. There is a maximum distance of 2KM (nearly a mile) permissible between stations. While currently implementations of FDDI are 100Mb/s and Gigabit, the potential is there for much higher speeds.

Since FDDI is a reincarnated version of Token Ring, it shouldn't come as a surprise that the token that is passed has an identical structure to that used by 802.5. The actual data frame is slightly different in that it is more compact. All of the information contained in the 802.5 frame physical header is contained in a field called the *preamble.* The other fields in the FDDI frame are similar to their like-named counterparts on the 802.5 frame, although they may vary in size. **Figure 6.10** illustrates all of the fields in the FDDI frame along with their relative sizes.

ERROR DETECTION AND DATA LINK

Now that I have provided a basic explanation of how the network card uses different ways to figure out how to get onto the wire, let me approach the subject of how it figures out what to do when something goes wrong, or better yet, how it even knows something did go wrong. This is where the various error-correction algorithms come

ERROR CORRECTION VERSUS ERROR DETECTION

It is critical to understand that there is a significant difference between error detection and error correction. Error detection simply is a process of figuring out something went wrong. When you look in your checkbook ledger and see a balance of $1,000.00, but go to the ATM to withdraw some cash and get a message telling you that you're overdrawn, you've just been exposed to error detection.

When you go to the bank branch and discover they charged your account twice for your car payment check, you get huffy and demand that they back off the second charge immediately. Or perhaps they point out that you forgot to record your mortgage check and you contritely correct your ledger. Either way, you performed an error-correction function.

Error detection on the network is primarily the responsibility of Data Link. Correction, for the most part, is done by the Transport Layer and will be discussed in Chapter Eight, The Transport Layer.

into play. Before I go into these various error-detection and correction methods, it is necessary to understand exactly what constitutes an error. Errors can occur because of:

- Lost frames
- Incorrect checksum
- Offending frame size
- Buffer overflow
- Interference

These different types of errors occur at different points in the transmission and have their own specific ways of being dealt with. Sometimes errors need to be detected and corrected by the transmitting computer, and others are the responsibility of the receiving computer.

LOST FRAMES

Lost frames are exactly what they sound like. A frame is sent, but never arrives. Obviously, this is something that the transmitting computer needs to know, but consider this: how is the receiving computer supposed to know a lost frame was sent in the first place? It can't tell the transmitting computer it didn't get a frame that it didn't even know was coming!

The solution is for the receiving computer to tell the transmitting computer about every frame it receives. It does so in the form of the ACK packets I discussed in Chapter Four, Welcome to OSI. If a frame is lost, the intended recipient will never send an ACK. It is up to the transmitting computer to keep track of all the frames it sends. There is a little built-in timer to every packet called a *time to live* (TTL). If the TTL expires before the transmitting computer receives the ACK, the frame will be resent. In the event that the ACK arrives at the sending computer after a frame has been retransmitted, the recipient will simply discard the duplicate frame.

INCORRECT CHECKSUM OR CRC

As I discussed the various media access methods earlier in the chapter, I examined the structure of the different packets that were created by each method. One field that was present in each of these frames was something called a *frame check sequence* (FCS). This is where error-correction information is stored. The two methods of error correction used by synchronous communication are *checksum* and *cyclical redundancy check* (CRC).

Checksum is the simplest of these error-correction methods. It simply counts the number of 1s in the entire frame, excluding the FCS. It then stores the total as a binary number in the FCS. **Figure 6.11** illustrates a frame using checksum. On the receiving end, the same count is performed and the result of that calculation is compared to the contents of the FCS. If the results match, the frame is passed on as good. If not, Data Link can't do a thing about it, except mark it as bad. It will be up to the Transport Layer to issue a NACK.

The problem inherent with the checksum design is that it is entirely feasible for a frame to be altered along the way by noise, voltage fluctuations, and a myriad of other problems. 1s can drop to 0s and vice versa. If a packet were to lose eight

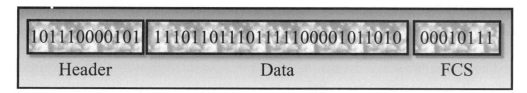

Figure 6.11 While the diagram above is extremely simplified, it shows a packet with a header, a data payload, and an FCS. There are twenty-three 1s in the payload and header. The FCS contains the binary value for the number twenty-three.

1s to 0s and eight 0s to 1s, checksum would still return a correct value, yet the packet could contain up to sixteen corrupted bytes. This is probably something you don't want.

CRC uses a significantly more powerful algorithm. It treats the contents of the header and payload information as if it were a single very large binary number. It looks at that number and performs a mathematical calculation on it, storing the value in the FCS. The receiving computer performs the same calculation. If the values match, the frame is good. If not it is discarded. Once again, it will be up to the Transport Layer to fix the problem.

EXAM NOTE: Make sure you know the difference between Checksum and CRC.

OFFENDING FRAME SIZE

Some protocols are very picky about the size of the frames that are transmitted. There is a limited range of acceptable lengths. Frames can't be smaller than the minimum length, nor can they be larger than the maximum. The ones that are too small are called *runts,* and those that are too large are called *giants.* I hope the extremely technical jargon doesn't throw you off.

Data link can prevent errors from the get-go by repackaging the frames so that they fit into an acceptable range for these protocols. A frame that is too small can be combined with another frame and the two sent together with a single set of header information and a single footer. If the receiving computer receives too much data for a single frame, it can break it down.

If for any reason the runt or giant frame is transmitted anyway, Data Link will discard it. The result will be a lost frame, which I discussed earlier.

BUFFER OVERFLOW

As data flows into the recipient computer, it is stored in a memory location known as the *buffer.* This buffer is only so large (depending on OS, NIC driver, and a number of other parameters). If data is moving in too fast for the recipient to handle, the buffer fills up. Once the buffer fills, any other incoming frames will be lost.

The lost frames will be treated in the manner discussed above, and the Transport Layer will get a nasty message from Data Link telling it to slow the other device down. This is the process of flow control and will be discussed in more detail in Chapter Eight, The Transport Layer.

INTERFERENCE

Interference that corrupts data can come in a number of forms. RFI or EMF can corrupt the signal as it moves across the wire. Voltage fluctuations can affect electronically based transmissions, and atmospheric conditions can have negative effects on wireless transmissions. The results of this interference can be invalid CRC or checksum values, lost frames, or completely unintelligible frames. How these utterly scrambled frames will be dealt with depends on how the receiving computer interprets the problem. If the receiving computer recognizes that the signal coming in was supposed to be a packet, and can extract enough information from the header, but the rest of the frame is messed up beyond all recognition, it can issue a NACK and have the other computer resend the data. If the receiving computer hasn't a clue what it just now received, the packet will be discarded and treated by the sending computer as a lost frame.

ERROR CORRECTION IN DATA LINK

Okay, now I've explained how the communicating devices figure out that an error occurred. Now what can they do to fix the problem? There are actually several methods of resolving these problems. And none of them is under the control of Data Link. It is up to the Transport Layer to fix any problems. All Data Link can do is notify the Transport Layer of the error. Therefore, error correction will be discussed in detail in Chapter Eight.

FLOW CONTROL IN THE DATA LINK LAYER

The concept of flow control is very simple. If one device is transmitting data faster than another is capable of receiving that data, some information is sure to be lost. Flow control is a method by which a device can hold up its hand, so to speak, and tell the other device to either stop or slow down.

For the most part, flow control is managed by the Transport Layer and will be discussed in more detail in Chapter Eight. However, there are certain Data Link protocols that make use of link level flow control. The *High Level Data Link Control* (HDLC) Protocol is one of these.

Flow control methods in Data Link include *X-on/X-off*, *Stop and wait*, and *sliding window*. Stop and wait and sliding window are discussed in detail in Chapter Eight and therefore will be described only briefly in this section.

X-on/X-off is a flow control method under the control of the recipient device. As data is moving into this device, its buffers fill. Once the buffers receive as much data as they can hold until it has been processed, the recipient device will issue an X-off command. Once it has cleared its buffers, it issues an X-on and the flow of data can be resumed.

Stop and wait is a more simplified method of flow control. The transmitting device sends a frame. When the receiving device has received and processed the frame, it will send an ACK and the transmitting device can then send the next frame. This is a very effective, but relatively inefficient, method.

Sliding window allows a number of frames to be sent in a burst by the transmitting device. The receiving device will then process those frames and send ACKs or NACKs back for all of the frames at once. The window begins with some mutually acceptable number of frames, usually predetermined by the size of the buffer on the receiving device. If that rate is too fast, the number of NACKs will suggest to the transmitting device how many frames the receiving device is capable of handling. It will adjust the window accordingly.

> **Buzz Word**
>
> **X-on/X-off:** A flow control method in which the transmitting device will continue to send data until the recipient tells it to stop. When the recipient is once again ready to receive data, it will send a message to the transmitting device that it is okay to resume.

Data Link Protocols

Some networking protocols exist within the Data Link sublayers that are critical to understand. These include PPP, HDLC, LCP, and NCP. Each of these protocols is used for different purposes and is capable of performing its own unique functions. However, as you will see, they are very similar in structure and function.

HDLC

The High Level Data Link Protocol (HDLC) is very likely the most heavily implemented Layer 2 protocol of them all. In fact, you will see that some of the subsequent protocols that I will discuss rely very much on the principles of HDLC. The two operational functions of HDLC are link management and the transfer of data.

HDLC can operate in one of three different communication modes. *Normal Response Mode* (NRM) takes on the approach of a master-slave relationship. Connections can be either point-to-point or multipoint. In other words, the devices are either talking one-on-one, or several devices are involved in the link. In either situation, only one device can be master. All others (or the other device in a point-to-point connection) are slaves. Slaves may only transmit data under the instruction of the master.

Asynchronous Response Mode (ARM) gives a little more latitude to the slave stations. The network still has a master-slave relationship, but in certain connection types, such as point-to-point or full duplex, the slave station does not have to wait for permission to transmit data.

> **BUZZ WORDS**
>
> **Point-to-point:** A communications link in which two devices set up a logical connection in order to communicate one to the other.
>
> **Multipoint:** A communications link in which several devices set up a logical connection in order to communicate among themselves.

Asynchronous Balanced Mode (ABM) can be used on connections that are both point-to-point and full duplex. In this mode, all stations are peers and at any given point in time any station may be a master or a slave. This protocol is used for most packet switching protocols, including X.25.

There are three classes of frames used by HDLC. *Unnumbered frames* are primarily used for link management functions. They set up the logical link between stations and instruct the secondary station which of the communication modes will be used.

Information frames are used to carry the actual data transferred in a session. In HDLC, information frames are a bit more flexible than data frames in other formats. In a full duplex transfer of information, link control information can be bundled along with actual data into the same information frame. *Supervisory frames* are used for error detection and correction and flow control. They are also used to send and receive sequence and acknowledgment numbers.

PPP

Point-to-point protocol (PPP) emulates HDLC in many respects. However, as its name infers, it is a protocol written specifically to establish and maintain point-to-point connections. It is actually broken down into two subcomponents, *Link Control Protocol* (LCP) and *Network Control Protocol* (NCP).

In order to establish a point-to-point connection, PPP calls on the services of LCP. LCP goes through a four-step procedure in order to establish a connection. First, it establishes the connection between devices and the two devices exchange information about their capabilities. Through this exchange of data, a mutually acceptable configuration is established. Next, LCP will test the quality of the link it has created. If physical conditions actually support the capabilities of the devices as configured, step three is to call on NCP to create the link. The final responsibility of LCP is to tear down the connection when it is no longer needed or present. This can occur because the data transfer is complete, because the session has exceeded a predetermined time to live, or because one or the other stations has stopped responding.

NCP is the PPP component that communicates with the Network Layer. It is through NCP that Data Link information necessary for configuring a network connection is provided to the Network Layer.

CHAPTER SUMMARY

As you can see, the Data Link Layer is a very busy layer. It handles some critical network functions, such as being able to identify the physical addresses of devices on the network and then figuring out how to get the data onto that network. The work of IEEE was instrumental in defining how the latter was to be done.

Because of the two different responsibilities of this layer, it has been subdivided into two sublayers: logical link control and media access control. Different network topologies have different methods by which they access the media. LLC is the sublayer that defines these methods. The MAC sublayer is responsible for physical addressing.

Much of the information contained in this chapter about the different media access methods, such as CSMA/CD, Token Ring, and FDDI, will be critical to your passing the Network+ exam. Go over this information again and again until you are absolutely certain you understand it.

Also, make sure you have a decent understanding of the Data Link protocols. If you have a decent grasp of HDLC, you should be able to understand the others with no difficulty.

BRAIN DRAIN

1. In your own words, list and describe the various functions of the Data Link Layer.

2. Describe how a flat addressing model differs from a hierarchical model.

3. Write out an example of a typical MAC address and define what the two components of this address are.

4. Describe in detail how a device uses CSMA/CD to get data onto the network.

5. Describe the process of beaconing, as used by Token Ring.

THE 64K$ QUESTIONS

1. Which of the following are Layer 2 devices? (Choose all that apply.)
   a. Switch
   b. Hub
   c. Bridge
   d. Router

2. A MAC address would fall under which addressing model?
   a. Hierarchical
   b. Topical
   c. Flat
   d. Dimensional

3. Data Link uses which of the following to move data between layers on the same machine?
   a. MAC address
   b. IP address
   c. Ports
   d. APs

4. An Ethernet frame has a minimum payload of _____ bytes and a maximum of _____ bytes.
   a. 46 and 1500
   b. 0 and 16K
   c. 1500 and 64K
   d. There are no minimum or maximum values.

5. Demand Priority uses the _____ algorithm to determine media access for devices on the network.
   a. CSMA/CD
   b. CSMA/CA
   c. Round-robin
   d. Close-knit

6. FDDI and CDDI differ in that _____.
   a. FDDI is only supported by Ethernet
   b. CDDI uses a copper-based medium

    c. FDDI and CDDI are similar technologies proposed by two competing companies.

    d. They differ only in packet size.

7. Error detection is accomplished through _____.

    a. Calculation of either the checksum or CRC values and comparing those values to data included in the frame check sequence

    b. Transmitting a NACK to indicate that the frame is corrupt

    c. The use of a parity bit

    d. Time-outs that indicate that the frame never arrived.

    e. All of the above

8. Error notification is accomplished through _____.

    a. Calculation of either checksum or CRC values and comparing those values to data included in the frame check sequence

    b. Transmitting a NACK to indicate that the frame is corrupt

    c. The use of a parity bit

    d. Time-outs that indicate that the frame never arrived

    e. All of the above

9. Which flow control method allows for several frames to be transmitted before an ACK is required?

    a. Stop and wait

    b. ARQ

    c. X-on/X-off

    d. Sliding window

10. Under HDLC, which frame type is used to send flow control information?

    a. Unnumbered frames

    b. Information frames

    c. Supervisory frames

    d. 802.3 frames

11. Which of the following are responsibilities of the LLC sub-layer of Data Link?

    a. Physical addressing

    b. Network topology

c. Error notification

d. Access to the physical medium

e. Flow control

12. Which of the following are responsibilities of the MAC sub-layer of Data Link?

a. Physical addressing

b. Network topology

c. Error notification

d. Access to the physical medium

e. Flow control

13. Two devices that work almost exclusively at the Data Link Layer are _____ and _____. (Select two.)

a. Hubs

b. Repeaters

c. Bridges

d. Routers

e. Switches

14. One of the following is **not** a Data Link protocol. Which one is it?

a. High Level Data Link Protocol (HDLC)

b. Address Resolution Protocol (ARP)

c. Point to Point Protocol (PPP)

d. Link Control Protocol (LCP)

e. Network Control Protocol (NCP)

15. What kind of address would Data Link be responsible for managing?

a. The hard-coded address on a NIC

b. The network address configured by the administrator

c. The port address used by the applications

d. The email address used by the user

16. MAC addresses are 32 bits long.

a. True

b. False

17. MAC addresses are divided into _____ and _____. (Select two.)
    a. Service access identifiers
    b. Organizational unit numbers
    c. Physical unit identifiers
    d. Interface serial numbers

18. Data Link creates a node called the _____ that is used to move data from one layer to the next.
    a. Pointer node
    b. Service address
    c. Interstitial access identifier
    d. Service access point

19. The term *baseband technology* refers to the fact that _____.
    a. Only one device can occupy the medium at a time
    b. A token must be used to transport data
    c. An electrical carrier current is used to encode data
    d. The medium provides a baseline throughput which all devices must share

20. The difference between a switch and a hub is that _____.
    a. The hub can filter traffic based on the MAC address
    b. The switch can filter traffic based on the MAC address
    c. The hub can filter traffic based on the IP address
    d. The switch can filter traffic based on the IP address

TRICKY TERMINOLOGY

Backoff timer: A logical mechanism that tells a device how long it must wait to retransmit after a collision occurs.

Beaconing: A process Token Ring uses to find out what station has dropped from the network. Each devices sends a beacon frame to both its upstream neighbor and its downstream neighbor. Once the culprit has been found, the MAU can bypass that station internally.

Contention window: The number of time slots a device will wait after a collision occurs. This is the value used to set the backoff timer.

Deterministic: Any approach that is guaranteed to achieve the desired results.

Flat addressing model: A method of addressing in which there is only one level of address for every node on the network. All addresses get thrown into the same pool and a network device has to dive in to find a specific address.

Hierarchical address model: A method of addressing in which there are multiple levels of addressing, such as a network address and a host address. A network device can find the network it's looking for and let that network figure out which host is supposed to get the data.

Multipoint: A communications link in which several devices set up a logical connection in order to communicate among themselves.

Payload: The actual information carried in the frame that is the reason for the frame being transmitted to begin with. This may include user or application data or protocol specific information.

Point-to-point: A communications link in which two devices set up a logical connection in order to communicate one to the other.

Probabilistic: Any approach that is likely to achieve the desired results, but is not guaranteed to achieve them.

Round-robin algorithm: A media access method in which a centralized device, such as an intelligent hub, scans each interface, searching for a device that wants to send data. It skips devices that do not need to transmit. If two or more devices need to transmit on the same cycle a priority method is used to determine who gets to go first.

X-on/X-off: A flow control method in which the transmitting device will continue to send data until the recipient tells it to stop. Once the recipient is once again ready to receive data, it will send a message to the transmitting device that it is okay to resume.

ACRONYM ALERT

ABM: Asynchronous Balanced Mode. An HDLC communications mode in which there is no specific master/slave relationship.

ARM: Asynchronous Response Mode. An HDLC communications mode that allows the "slave" device to transmit with permission from the "master" under certain circumstances.

CDDI: Copper Distributed Data Interface. A dual-ring network topology that uses two redundant rings of copper cabling, capable of sending data in opposite directions.

CRC: Cyclical Redundancy Check. The error correction algorithm most commonly used in networking protocols today. It performs a mathematical calculation on the stream of data and stores the results as a numerical value.

CSMA/CA: Carrier Sense, Multiple Access/Collision Avoidance. The media access method frequently used by wireless networking.

CSMA/CD: Carrier Sense, Multiple Access/Collision Detection. The media access method used by Ethernet.

DSAP: Destination Service Access Point. The address a layer uses to send data to the next layer in the flow.

FCS: Frame Check Sequence. A field in the trailer of a frame that holds error correction data.

FDDI: Fiber Distributed Data Interface. A dual-ring network topology that uses two redundant rings of fiber-optic cabling, capable of sending data in opposite directions.

HDLC: High Level Data Link Control. A networking protocol that works at the Data Link Layer.

LCP: Link Control Protocol. One of the subordinate protocols of PPP.

LLC: Logical Link Control. One of the sublayers of Data Link.

MAC: Media Access Control. One of the sublayers of Data Link.

MAU: Multistation Access Unit. A device used on the Token Ring network that interconnects hosts in a physical star, but maintains the logical configuration of a ring.

NCP: Network Control Protocol. One of the subordinate protocols of PPP.

NRM: Normal Response Mode. A communications mode of HDLC in which one or more devices are involved in the exchange of data, but only one machine controls the session.

OUI: Organizational Unique Identifier. Half of a MAC address that has been assigned to the manufacturer by the IEEE Registration Authority.

PPP: Point-to-Point Protocol. A networking protocol that works at the Data Link Layer.

RTS/CTS: Ready to Send/Clear to Send. A type of packet that indicates a device using CSMA/CA is about to transmit data.

SAP: Service Access Point. A logical address that moves data between OSI layers on the same machine.

SSAP: Source Service Access Point. The address from which a layer will receive data from an adjacent layer.

TTL: Time to Live. A built-in countdown timer put into packets. If the transmitting device counts down to zero before receiving an ACK, it will automatically resend the packet.

CHAPTER 7

THE NETWORK LAYER

To be truly accurate, I should probably call this the "internetwork" layer, since it is through the functions of this layer that different networks find each other. Nearly all literature will simply refer to this layer as *Layer 3*. While a LAN does make use of the services of this layer, a *wide area network* (WAN), which consists of a collection of interconnected LANs, (*local area networks*, but you probably already knew that) cannot exist without them. It is up to the Network Layer to make sure data gets from the source to the destination. Over a WAN the route can tend to get very complicated. It's a jungle out there! It is up to the Network Layer to pick and choose routes based on a number of different factors. But that's not the only responsibility of this layer. Overall, the Network Layer does all of the following:

- Manages logical addressing of messages
- Routes messages between networks
- Determines the best path between source and destination devices residing on different networks
- Controls congestion on a subnet
- Translates logical addresses into physical addresses

The PDU of the Network Layer is a *packet.* In an outbound message, the Network Layer takes the segment it receives from the Transport Layer, stamps its information into a header field, and moves the packet on to the Data Link Layer. Conversely, on inbound messages, the Network Layer takes the incoming frame from Data Link, processes the data it finds in those same fields imprinted by the source device, and then strips the information off of the frame before moving it on to Transport.

There are various different devices that make use of Network Layer functions. The best known of these are the router and its close relative, the brouter. There are also devices known as *Layer 3 switches* that function at this level. ATM and frame relay switches all rely on Layer 3 functions. Another device that you might not immediately think of when discussing Layer 3 devices is the advanced cable tester. Some of its testing functions rely on the Network Layer.

Exam objectives that will be either introduced or covered in this chapter include:

1.6 Identify the purposes, features and functions of key network components.

2.2 Identify the seven layers of the OSI (Open Systems Interconnect) model and their functions.

2.3 Identify the OSI (Open Systems Interconnect) layers at which the following network components operate: Hubs, Switches, Bridges, Routers, NICs (Network Interface Card), WAPs (Wireless Access Point).

3.7 Given a connectivity scenario, determine the impact on network functionality of a particular security implementation (For example: port blocking/filtering, authentication and encryption).

ADDRESSING IN THE NETWORK LAYER

In the previous chapter, I discussed how the network could use physical addresses to identify a specific device on the network. However, very few networks rely exclusively on physical addresses for moving data. If you think about it logically, you would see just how cumbersome that would be. As I pointed out earlier, physical addressing is a flat-model addressing scheme. All addresses reside in a singular pool of addresses, and a device looking for the address of another device must wade through the entire pool to find the address it is looking for (see **Figure 7.1**).

That's a great concept in theory, but it won't really come home to you until you consider what that means in the real world. If you wanted to build routers that worked with physical addresses, the router would have to know every single address of every node on every subnet of the network. That's all fine and good if you only have a couple of dozen devices on your network, or maybe even a couple of hundred. But what if you have several thousand or several hundred thousand nodes? Routers build tables of addresses that match a specific address to a specific port on the router. It could care less where the intended recipient is actually located, or for that matter how many devices may be located between itself and the other device. All it knows is that to get from point A to point B, the data must go out a specific port.

The more entries you have in that routing table, the longer a packet sits in a buffer while the router figures out what to do with it. This time delay is known as *latency*. A packet is only given so much time to live on the network before it will

Figure 7.1 In a flat addressing model all addresses are thrown into a big pool, and any device that needs to find a single address has to jump right in and wade around in all of them.

be discarded. If the cumulative latencies of all the routers between here and there become larger than the time to live of the packets sent between two devices, those two devices can't communicate.

Now let's carry it a step farther. Since the Internet is based entirely upon the routing of messages, just how big do you think it could be if the routers along the Internet had to maintain tables that included the physical addresses of every single device on every single network in the entire world?

I rest my case.

Therefore networks use logical addressing instead of physical addressing for all routable protocols. Not all logical addresses look the same, so it is worth examining a couple of protocols to see just how they go about creating their logical addresses. The two I'll look at are IPX/SPX and TCP/IP.

LOGICAL ADDRESSING IN IPX/SPX

As with all logical addresses, the IPX address consists of two portions. There is a network address that consists of up to 32 bits. I say "up to 32 bits" because with the IPX protocol, leading 0s of a network address can be dropped, or *truncated.* The second portion of the IPX address is the 48-bit MAC address that I discussed in Chapter Five, The Data Link Layer. The protocols will add an additional *socket number* to identify the process or application for which the data is intended.

When a node on an IPX network first boots up, unless the NIC has been bound to a specific network, it doesn't know its IPX address. It uses a protocol known as a *Service Advertising Protocol* (SAP) to send a *Get Nearest Server* packet. All servers running the IPX protocol will respond with their IPX address. The first server to respond provides the workstation with the information it will use to fill in its network address. Since the host portion of the address is its MAC address, it already knows that. The node now has a complete IPX address.

LOGICAL ADDRESSING IN TCP/IP

This logical address consists of a 32-bit address that is broken down four octets (an octet being the eight bits that make up that particular byte). These octets appear to the end user in decimal form, as shown in **Figure 7.2**. The address is divided into two sections. One part of the IP address is the network address and the other half is the host address. When data is transmitted from one computer to the other, TCP/IP breaks the information down into packets before sending it across the wire. Each packet contains the sending computer's IP address as well as the intended recipient's address.

You'll notice in Figure 7.2 another component of the TCP/IP configuration called the subnet mask. This tells the computer which part of the address is the

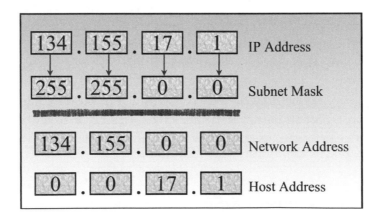

Figure 7.2 The relationship between an IP address and its subnet mask is very closely knit. One does not work without the other.

network address and which part is the host address. The part of the subnet mask represented by the number 255 covers the network address.

There are five different classes of TCP/IP address, but networks use only three of them. The other two types of address are for specialized purposes. The three types commonly used in networks are Class A, Class B, and Class C addresses. These are the classes of *unicast address*. A unicast is a message targeted to a specific device. Class D addresses are used for *multicast addresses*. A multicast is a message targeted at a group of devices running a similar protocol.

> **BUZZ WORDS**
>
> **Unicast:** A data transmission directed at a single host.
>
> **Multicast:** A data transmission directed at selected multiple hosts.
>
> **Broadcast:** A data transmission directed at all hosts on the network.

> **EXAM NOTE:** Know the different classes of IP address and their associated subnet masks. This information is required knowledge for a number of different type of questions and scenarios. Also, be able to distinguish between a unicast, a multicast, and a broadcast message.

In a Class A address, only the first octet is used for a network address. In addition, the first bit of the octet must always be a zero. If you recall your binary, you should realize that with only eight bits allocated to the network address, there are only 256 possibilities for creating network numbers. However, since the first bit of the octet *must* be a 0, the options are further limited to only 128 possibilities. On the other hand, that leaves 24 bits for host addresses. That means there are a small number of networks that can have up to 16,777,214 (16,777,216 minus two—a host address can't be either all 0s or all 1s). In reality, there are not even 128 possibilities. Neither a network address or a host address can be all 0s. An address of all 0s represents the wire itself. So now there are only 127 possible Class A networks. In addition, all addresses starting with 127 are designated as loop-back addresses used for diagnostic purposes only, and IP addresses starting with 10 are reserved for private networks. Therefore only 124 Class A networks were ever available for assignment.

Class B addresses use the first two octets for the network address and the last two for a host address. All Class B addresses must start with 10 as their first two bits. As a result you can have a little over 49,000 networks, each of which can have over 65,000 hosts, and the network address will always start in the range of 128 to 191. As with Class A addresses, a certain range of Class B addresses is reserved for use in private networks. All addresses between 172.16.0.0 and 172.31.255.255 are set aside for private use. They will not be assigned to any one person or organization. All addresses starting with 128 are reserved for experimental purposes.

In Class C addresses, the first three octets identify the network and the last octet identifies host addresses. Therefore, there are over fourteen million possible networks of only 254 users on each network. The first three bits must start with 110, therefore the range of possible address as will go from 192 to 223. The range of addresses reserved for private use is 192.168.0.0 to 192.168.255.255.

BUZZ WORDS

Cluster addressing: The ability to identify the topological location of a host by its IP address.

Source routing: The ability of the host to maintain its own routing tables and make route selections before transmitting data.

Class D addresses are considered multicast addresses. The first four bits will start with 1110, which gives us a range of addresses from 224.0.0.1 to 239.255.255.254. These addresses are used by groups of hosts or routers that share a common characteristic. In other words, all devices configured to the same routing protocol and that see one another will respond to packets sent to address 224.0.0.2. This address class does not break down to a specific network or host. All devices on a physical link running a similar routing protocol will pick up a packet with a multicast address.

Class E addresses are considered "experimental" addresses. They're reserved for some future use that will probably never come to pass, in that the newer version of TCP/IP is moving to IPv6, or IP, Version 6.

The 128-bit addresses of IPv6 can theoretically provide the global networking community with a total of approximately 340,282,366,920,938,463, 463,374,607,431,768,211,456 addresses. These addresses are presented in hexadecimal form consisting of eight 16-bit segments. **Figure 7.3** illustrates an IPv6 address.

There are a couple of advantages to IPv6, aside from the vast number of available addresses. One is the fact that the new version will support *cluster addressing*. Cluster addresses will identify the topological region in which a device is located.

20A1:1701:0:0:200:F8FF:FE21:67CF
An IPv6 address consists of eight 16-bit fields, separated by colons.

20A1:1701:: 200:F8FF:FE21:67CF
However, multiple fields consisting of all zeros can be represented by a double colon.

Figure 7.3 IPv6 addresses are a bit more complex than IPv4 addresses.

Second, it will provide built-in support for a more advanced form of routing called *source routing*. With source routing, each host on the network maintains a table of routes and constantly updates the condition of those routes. The transmitting device selects the route over which it will transmit. The beauty of this approach is that it takes the responsibility of routing away from being a distributed network issue and makes it a local and centralized issue. In theory, this substantially reduces the overhead of intermediate routers and hence their inherent latency.

ADDRESS RESOLUTION

Okay, so I've now explained how to identify an individual host on the network in two different ways. In Chapter Six, The Data Link Layer, I looked at the physical, or MAC, address. Now I've discussed how different protocols make use of different logical addresses to identify that same host. MAC addresses are used in the lowest layer of communications in order to move the message from NIC to NIC. The logical address is usually configured in the protocol stack software, and is used to convey the message from logical endpoint to logical endpoint. Some protocols do not implement a Network Layer and move data using only the MAC address, and others make use of the logical address. Either way, you have to find a way of making sure that various devices on the network know that 192.168.1.1 and 00 10 4B 9C 27 01 are one and the same.

In IPX/SPX, this is a nonissue, because the node number in the logical address and the MAC address is the same. No resolution is required. In TCP/IP, this is done through the *Address Resolution Protocol* (ARP). A device that needs to resolve an IP address into a MAC address will send an *ARP request* to the IP address it is trying to resolve. The *ARP reply* sent by the recipient will contain both the MAC address and IP address of that host.

ROUTING AND THE NETWORK LAYER

Routing is one of the most complex functions handled by the Network Layer. It is up to Layer 3 to find routes for data to follow as it moves from host to host. Different protocols have different ways of handling routing functions, and there are quite a few different protocols in this big wide world. The two protocols you're most likely to have to deal with in your world are going to be IPX/SPX and TCP/IP. Therefore, that is where I'll concentrate my discussion.

191

ROUTING IN **IP/IPX**

Routing in the IPX environment is intended to be basically simple. Of course, if you ask the Cisco CCNA or CCNP candidates if they think it's simple, you might get a different answer. However, IPX routing protocols use a dynamic structure that induces the router to learn routing tables by way of those SAP packets that are running around the network.

ROUTING IN **TCP/IP**

As I pointed out earlier, an IP address consists of two portions: the network portion and the host portion. All IP addresses on any given device are also associated with something called a *subnet mask.* The subnet mask identifies what part of an address is network and what part is host. A subnet mask can be either the default subnet mask for the specific class of the address or it can be a custom subnet mask. I'll discuss custom subnet masking in detail in Chapter Thirteen, IP Addressing.

A default subnet mask associates all bits in the IP address that are part of the network address with 1s. If you recall, in a Class A address, the first octet identified the network. Therefore, the first octet of a default Class A subnet mask would be all 1s. In decimal form, that would be represented as the number 255. All other numbers would be 0. So the default subnet mask of a Class A address is 255.0.0.0. **Table 7.1**

BUZZ WORD

Subnet mask: An entry into the TCP/IP configuration, formatted similarly to an IP address. This is a 32-bit value that defines which portion of the address is network and which portion is host.

Table 7.1 IP Address Classes

Class	First Bits	Range	Subnet
A	0xxx	001-126	255.0.0.0
B	10xx	128-191	255.255.0.0
C	110x	192.223	255.255.255.0
D	111x	224-239	N/A
E	1111	240-254	N/A

IP address classes and their default subnet masks.

Note: Class D and E addresses do not make use of subnet masks.

shows the various classes of IP address, along with their ranges and default subnet mask.

On the most basic level, a device can only see other devices that are on its network. In other words, a computer configured to IP address 192.168.100.16 and a default subnet mask could communicate

with any device in an address range of 192.168.100.1 through 192.168.100.254. To review, you can't use either 0 or 255 in the last octet because neither a host address nor a network address can contain all 0s or all 1s. Any device outside of that range would be on a different network and not visible to the computer.

However, an optional configuration parameter for TCP/IP is the *default gateway,* or sometimes more simply, just the gateway. This is the address that gets you out of your local network to somewhere else. Whenever a gateway is configured, any frame that cannot be successfully resolved is forwarded to the gateway. It then becomes the responsibility of the gateway to decide what to do with that frame.

EXAM NOTE: Be able to fully describe the function of a gateway. Note that on the exam you may see it as either "gateway" or "default gateway."

Routers are frequently used as default gateways. A router is a device with multiple ports, and each port can be configured to a different IP address. So if you want to connect your 192.168.100.xxx network to the 129.115.xxx.xxx network, simply install a router. Configure one of the ports with an address in the 192.168.100.xxx range and another to the 129.115.xxx.xxx range. On the workstations, in the advanced TCP/IP settings, you configure the gateway to be the same address you configured for the router port connected to the local network. When one of those workstations tries to resolve an IP address and sees that it is not part of the local network, but that there is a default gateway, it will simply forward the packet to the gateway and let the gateway worry about it from there.

The router maintains a list of tables for each port that tells it what networks are downstream. When it receives a packet from any port, it compares the network portion of the IP address to those in its tables. If it finds an entry in any table for any port, it will forward that packet out of that port and let the next device worry about what to do with it. Its job is finished. If it cannot find a corresponding entry in its tables, it will simply discard the packet. Eventually the time to live of the packet will expire and the session will time out.

ROUTE DETERMINATION AT THE NETWORK LAYER

As I mentioned earlier, routers build tables for each of their ports that tells them out of which port to forward a message. These tables can be built either statically or dynamically. A static routing table requires no special help in building and maintaining except for a lot of spare time on the administrator's hands. Routers that build dynamic tables use one of the routing protocols to communicate with other routers and borrow information from those other routers to build the tables.

Administrators who choose to use static routing will be manually entering the routing tables for each port on each router in their network. This information tells the router what network addresses lay downstream of any given port. An administrator who uses static routing has complete control over the pathways data will take in its travels over the network. This can be good, because it is a bit more secure than dynamic routing, and because as long as the administrator is completely familiar with the topology of his or her network, the fastest routes will always be used.

The downside is that whenever a router is changed in any way, for example, if the router's IP addresses are changed or the router is completely removed from the network, then the routing tables of all routers impacted by that change must be manually reconfigured. Missing even a single entry can result in certain hosts losing connectivity with certain others. And then the troubleshooting nightmare begins.

Dynamic routing makes use of one or more *routing protocols* to automatically provide the information a router needs to build the routing tables. I'll get into the specific protocols later in this chapter. First, however, I think it would be a good idea if I explained a bit more about these routing tables and how they work.

ROUTING TABLES

Routing tables can take on a number of different forms, but at their heart they must contain a minimum of two fields. One of these is the *IP Address Prefix* and the other is *Next Hop*. The IP address prefix specifies a network address (possibly subnetted) and the next hop defines the specific IP address of a router interface (or possibly a direct host) that is directly connected to the host router by way of a serial link, Ethernet connection, or any other supported medium.

BUZZ WORDS

Static: Any variable that must be manually configured and/or updated.

Dynamic: Any variable that allows itself to be configured or edited on the fly by a device or protocol.

Hop: An intermediate stop, dictated by the chosen path of the router, that data must make as it travels from its source to its destination.

A couple of alternative fields that you will see in most routing tables are a *gateway address* and the *routing mask* (sometimes called the *netmask* in Microsoft applications). Most routing tables also include a field that defines the *metric* of a specific route.

The gateway address consists of the specific IP address of an interface the router will use for all packets it can't find a specific home for. For example, a packet comes through. The router examines the network address and compares it to the IP address prefixes in its table. Nothing matches. So rather than simply discard the packet, the router sends it out the default gateway.

A router uses the routing mask along with the destination address to determine when a specific route is to be used. By default, a host route has a mask of 255.255.255.255 and a default route has a mask of 0.0.0.0. A subnet or network route will fall somewhere between these extremes.

Wherever there are 1s in the mask, the destination IP must exactly match. A mask of 255.255.255.255 indicates that each octet in the address consists of all 1s. What this means to the router is that only an exact match of the destination address uses this route. A packet comes in with a destination IP of 192.168.0.2. A mask of 255.255.255.255 indicates that in order for the packet to be forwarded, there must be an entry in the routing tables for 192.168.0.2. A mask of 255.255.255.0 would allow any packet with a destination IP that had 192.168.0 in the first three octets. Any number in the final octet would be considered acceptable. A mask of 0.0.0.0 means that any packet containing any destination IP can use the route.

The metric field indicates the relative *cost* to the network of using that interface or route. In this case cost isn't measured in dollars and cents, but rather in time. An interface connected to a Gigabit Ethernet connection would have a significantly lower cost than one hooked up to 10BaseT. **Figure 7.4** illustrates a typical routing table using all four of these fields.

Routing tables in UNIX and Linux have some additional fields that should be noted. In addition to the fields mentioned above, they also include a *Flag* field, a *Ref* field, and a *Use* field. The Flag field shows the status of a particular entry in a routing table. The various flags used in this field include:

- D – Entry was created dynamically
- G – Destination indicated is a gateway
- H – Destination indicated is a host
- R – Route will be reinstated after time-out

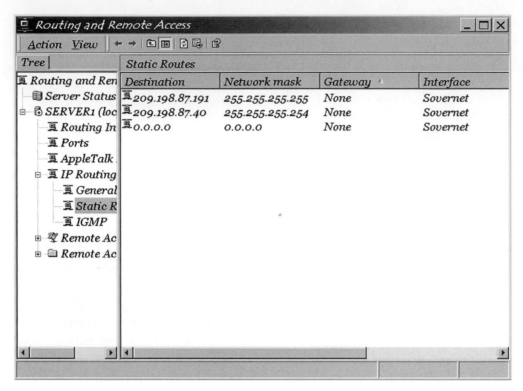

Figure 7.4   An example of a Microsoft routing table

- U – This route is useable
- M – Entry has been modified dynamically

The Ref column simply indicates how many times a specific MAC address is referenced in a routing table. The Use column shows how many packets have passed through a particular interface.

ROUTING PROTOCOLS

I once saw it written that "real network administrators use static routing." That's like saying "real dogs eat cats." Not only is the statement a deviation from truth, but it also enters the realm of ludicrous—and it might even offend some folks. In some cases, dynamic routing is the only way to go. With dynamic routing, you will configure your device to use one of the several *routing protocols* available. Over time, your routing tables will be built for you. Better still, in the event that there are changes to a specific route, those changes will be detected and the routing tables edited accordingly.

Routing protocols work by sending out periodic broadcast packets to the other routers on the network. Routing protocols come in several variations on two different flavors. There are interior routing protocols and there are exterior routing protocols. The interior routing protocols (sometimes called interior gateway protocols) are designed to work within a singular organization. Exterior routing protocols (or exterior gateway protocols) provide the services that allow multiple disparate organizations to interlink between one another (see **Figure 7.5**).

INTERIOR ROUTING PROTOCOLS

Interior routing protocols fall under one of two categories: *distance vector* protocols or *link state* protocols. Distance vector protocols are the simplest and arguably the most primitive. With distance vector, each router knows only the information related to devices directly attached to an interface. The router maintains a table of what addresses lie downstream of the next *hop* on a specific interface. In its simplest

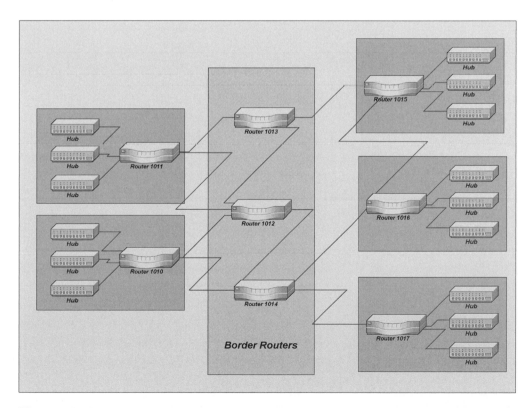

Figure 7.5 Interior routers and border routers (routers that interconnect two geographically isolated networks) are the same types of devices. They simply are configured to use different protocols.

form, in order to decide which route to choose, distance vector simply counts the number of hops involved. The number of hops to any given destination is stored as the *metric*.

In Figure 7.5, in order for Router 1011 to communicate with Router 1015, it could send the data either through Router 1012, which would involve a total of four hops, or it could go through Router 1013, which would only involve two hops. Therefore, it chooses to send the signal through Router 1013. However, there are a few tricks that distance vector protocols can be taught to make them a bit more efficient.

EXAM NOTE: Know the difference between link state and distance vector protocols, and be able to identify which specific protocols are of which type.

One commonly used distance vector protocol is the *Routing Information Protocol* (RIP). RIP has several features built in to provide a certain degree of network stability. Examine **Figure 7.6** very closely. There are several ways to move data from Router 1011 to Router 1015. Normally, to move data from Router 1011 to Router 1015, the protocols would select a path from 1011 to 1013 to 1015, because that is the fewest

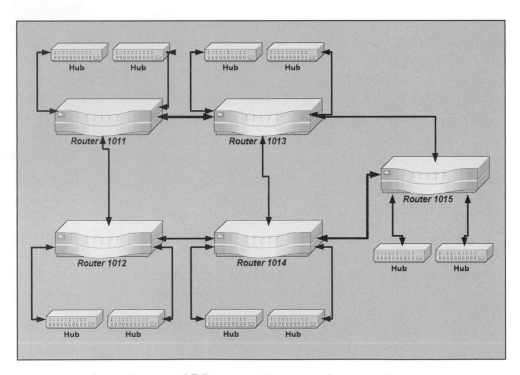

Figure 7.6 Certain features of RIP prevent infinite loops from occurring when a router on a complex network goes down.

number of hops. Alternatively, if Router 1013 goes down or is pulled from the network, the routing tables are already in place to reroute data from 1011 to 1013, then on to 1014 and finally to 1015. However, consider this. Unless you figure out a way to tell it otherwise, Router 1013 could actually figure out that it can get to 1015 by going back through 1011 and following the entire circuit back again.

This normally wouldn't be a problem, because that would involve the most hops you could have on this network. Since distance vector chooses the least number of hops, this will never happen, right?

What if Router 1015 goes down? Router 1013 would see that it couldn't send the packets through the interface directly connected to it, but it sees an alternative route through Router 1011 that it thinks can reach Router 1015. This, of course, results in the packets becoming caught in a perpetual loop. Two features built into RIP keep this from being a fatal problem.

First of all, RIP has a fixed maximum of fifteen hops. This doesn't help in this particular instance because there are fewer than fifteen hops whichever way the signal goes. However, there is also a built-in timer of 180 seconds. If a particular route remains silent for longer than this period, other routers that make use of that router set its hop count to sixteen. That route is taken out of the tables. Then the routers will advertise their new routing tables for 120 seconds. Therefore, in the event that loop does occur, it isn't a fatal problem.

Still, it's better to prevent problems than it is to be perpetually solving the same ones over and over again. RIP accomplishes this through a technique called *poison loop*. It detects the reverse loop and advertises that loop as having a hop count of sixteen. That puts that interface over the limit and it will never be used.

To prevent these entries from occurring, a technique called *split horizon* is used. Split horizon prevents a router from advertising any loop over the same router interface from which that loop was originally learned. Not only does this help inhibit (but not prevent) loops from occurring, it also prevents two routers from perpetually bouncing information back and forth between one another.

> **EXAM NOTE:** The concepts of poison loop and split horizon frequently appear on the exam. Be able to define either concept.

RIP Version 1 (RIPv1) was a little on the feeble side. It was very susceptible to hacking. It made no use of authentication passwords, cryptographic keys, or any other security measures. Therefore, a router configured to RIP was easily *spoofed*. Spoofing is a process of where hackers basically tell a device they are something they're not and then acquiring the routing tables. Since the routing tables include all internal as well as external addresses, once they have that, they're halfway into the network.

RIP Version 2 (RIPv2) added a few features to make it a bit more secure. For one thing, it added clear text authentication. While clear text is pretty easy to hack, it is arguably better than no authentication at all. It also added the ability to use network masking.

Another problem with distance vector protocols is that they do not lend themselves well to extremely large networks. There is no built-in scalability, and a fixed limit of fifteen hops. For small to midsized organizations this might be sufficient. To work on a larger scale requires something with a little more horsepower. Because of security and scalability issues, distance vector protocols are losing ground to link state protocols.

Link state protocols constantly monitor the condition of each link to which they are connected and then advertise those conditions to neighboring routers. These conditions include relative link speed, latency, and status of all routers on the network. The routing tables they produce as a result of this information provide a logical map of the network that the protocol uses to figure out which route will take the least amount of time to traverse.

Why is this better than simply counting the number of hops? The answer to that question is a bit more complicated than you might imagine. For example, you might have a large network that was split equally between 100BaseT and Gigabit Ethernet. There might be several ways to get from a specific host to a specific destination. There might be a way to get there in only three hops using 100BaseT, and another way to get there using four hops over Gigabit Ethernet. A distance vector protocol would automatically select the 100BaseT link, even though data would obviously travel over the Gigabit link at a significantly faster rate. A link state protocol will choose the faster of the two routes.

An interior routing protocol that uses link state technology is *Open Shortest Path First* (OSPF). Every router that uses OSPF maintains its own independent database of its assigned routing area. The data maintained includes information regarding other networks within its administrative region, the routers that operate on these networks, and the metric cost for each router's interface to its available networks. As you might imagine, there is a bit more overhead involved here in memory and processing requirements.

In OSPF, any time anything changes that affects the routing of data, the first router to detect the change alters its routing tables and advertises the change. Each router within a specific administrative region then rebuilds its routing maps accordingly. New routes are configured based on the cost of the network paths for a specific destination using the metrics. The router could care less about number of hops that are required to get from one point to the next.

The central key to how OSPF works is something called the *administrative routing area*. OSPF messages are only exchanged within a specific area. Routers that operate within an administrative area exchange detailed information from their databases with one another, but will provide only basic information with routers from other areas. Organizations that require multiple areas need to set up an independent area known as the *backbone area* in order to exchange information between the multiple areas. The only way for the independent routing areas to exchange information is through the backbone area. As such, OSPF constitutes a two-tier hierarchy any time multiple areas are involved.

EXTERIOR ROUTING PROTOCOLS

As I mentioned earlier, exterior routing protocols are designed to interconnect two or more separate and autonomous networks together over an intermediate transport system. The two most common exterior routing protocols are the *Exterior Gateway Protocol* (EGP) and the *Border Gateway Protocol* (BGP).

EGP was the first exterior routing protocol to be released. It was first described in 1984 and was the protocol that tied ARPANet together. Routers running EGP automatically detect their set of neighbors. This would be all other routers to which they are directly connected and can exchange routing tables. However, EGP does not make use of metrics. Therefore, its routing decisions are based on second-hand information it receives from its neighbors.

When a router running EGP first comes on-line, it must perform a function known as *neighbor acquisition*. The neighbor acquisition message contains two critical fields. One is the *hello interval* field. This establishes the interval over which it will poll its neighbors to make sure they're still up and running (more on that later). The second field is the *poll interval* field. It determines how often the router will check for router updates from its neighbors.

The router uses the *polling* message to find out what other routers are accessible beyond the immediate neighbors. Periodically, the EGP router will send out *neighbor reachability* messages. These messages indicate that the list of neighbors in the database is still accurate and each of the neighbors is still up and running. If a router does not respond to one of these messages, the routers sending the message will remove that router from the routing tables and initiate a rebuild. The routing tables themselves are exchanged after *routing update* messages move back and forth between the routers.

Back in the fledgling days of the Internet, EGP was an acceptable solution. However, because of its inability to make intelligent routing decisions concerning the best and fastest path for data to take, it imposed some rather severe restrictions. As a result, it is giving way to the more recently released BGP.

BGP takes up where EGP fell short. It allows for very sophisticated algorithms to constantly update router tables to indicate the fastest route between autonomous networks. It then enables the individual network to worry about what to do with the data once it arrives. BGP routers only advertise the routes that they themselves actually use and each router can independently decide on routes. That way an extremely large network (the Internet, for example) is more efficiently served as the best route is decided at each step along the way.

The Internet Group Management Protocol (IGMP) allows routers to advertise their multicast group membership to adjacent routers. You can include IGMP in your router configuration to assure that multicast transmissions do not run into a brick wall at the first router interface they encounter.

CHAPTER SUMMARY

In this chapter I covered some critical information about what goes on at OSI's infamous Layer 3, the Network Layer. A key ingredient to the entire chapter is understanding how logical addressing is handled and why it is preferable to physical addressing when it comes to moving data across larger network infrastructures. Then I looked at how those logical addresses are translated into the physical address of the host systems.

Since one of the key functions of the Network Layer is in the routing of messages, a lot of emphasis is placed on this subject. It is important to know how different protocols make sure data gets where it is supposed to go. Therefore I took a close look at some of the routing protocols used and the techniques they used to perform their magic.

BRAIN DRAIN

1. List as many functions of the Network Layer as you can.

2. Discuss the differences between an IP address and an IPX address.

3. What are the minimum fields necessary to build a routing table, and what additional fields can be added by some protocols?

4. Explain why a link state protocol is more efficient on large networks than a distance vector protocol.

5. Explain how a router using EGP begins the process of building its routing tables.

THE 64K$ QUESTIONS

1. The first two bits of any Class B IP address must be _____.
   a. 01

    b. 00

    c. 10

    d. 11

2. Which of the following is **not** a function of the Network Layer? (Choose all that apply.)

    a. Establishing and maintaining a communications session

    b. Determining the best route

    c. Interpreting and managing logical addresses

    d. Maintaining proper voltages on the wire

3. What is the maximum number of hosts in a Class B network that has not been subnetted?

    a. 254

    b. 16,536

    c. 65,534

    d. 16,534

4. The IPX/SPX protocol derives its host address from _____.

    a. A value assigned by the administrator

    b. The MAC address of the interface

    c. Its nearest server

    d. A host server

5. What role does the MAC address play in routing protocols?

    a. It identifies the specific target machine to the router.

    b. The routing protocol passes the MAC address to receiving devices as a Layer 3 trailer.

    c. It plays no role whatsoever.

    d. It plays Hendrick, the mad Gravedigger.

6. A Class C network can have up to _____ hosts.

    a. 65,534

    b. 16,382

    c. 16,777,216

    d. 254

7. The Default subnet mask for a Class B address is _____.

    a. 255.255.255.240

    b. 255.255.255.0

    c. 255.255.0.0

    d. 255.0.0.0

8. Subnet masks work because they _____.

    a. Hide the network portion of the IP address behind a string of 0s

    b. Hide the host portion behind a string of 1s

    c. Prevent unwanted bits from slipping through the mask

    d. Hide the network portion of the IP address behind a string of 1s and the host portion behind a string of 0s

9. The first thing a router running EGP does when it is first turned on is _____.

    a. Broadcast its own IP addresses

    b. Run a neighbor acquisition algorithm

    c. Scan its ports for preconfigured addresses

    d. Block all ports from incoming packets until its tables have been completed

10. Which type of routing protocol uses only the number of hops to decide the best route for data to take?

    a. EGP

    b. BGP

    c. Link state

    d. Distance vector

11. The protocol data unit used by the network layer is called a _____.

    a. Segment

    b. Parcel

    c. Capsule

    d. Packet

12. Layer 3 switches differ from the switches discussed in Chapter Six in that the L3 switch can _____. (Choose all that apply.)

    a. Filter packets based on a NetBIOS name

    b. Filter packets based on an IP address

    c. Forward packets to a different network

    d. Filter packets based on protocol

13. The delay caused by a router taking time to figure out what to do with an individual packet is called _____.

    a. Latency

    c. Translation decay

    d. Network noise

    c. Chatter

14. IPX/SXP allows up to _____ bits for a network address.

    a. 16

    b. 32

    c. 48

    d. 64

15. PX/SXP allows up to _____ bits for a host address.

    a. 16

    b. 32

    c. 48

    d. 64

16. In a subnet mask, the number 255 covers octets that are used exclusively to identify the network.

    a. True

    b. False

17. Class D addresses are used for what purpose?

    a. Very large networks

    b. They're reserved for experimental purposes.

    c. Broadcast addresses

    d. Multicast addresses

18. Your ISP assigned you a block of Class A addresses to use on your network. Which of the following might possibly be one of those addresses? Ignore the fact that most of these addresses are already taken.

    a. 10.16.35.11

    b. 116.25.43.7

    c. 26.56.78.109

    d. 176.45.114.7

19. Ipv6 allows for a _____ IP address.
    a. 64
    b. 96
    c. 128
    d. 256

20. A metric of 10 indicates a faster hop than one with a metric of 1.
    a. True
    b. False

TRICKY TERMINOLOGY

Broadcast: A data transmission directed at all hosts on the network.

Cluster addressing: The ability to identify the topological location of a host by its IP address.

Default gateway: The address to which a host will dump any packet whose address it cannot resolve.

Dynamic: Any variable that allows itself to be configured or edited on the fly by a device or protocol.

Hop: An intermediate stop, dictated by the chosen path of the router, that data must make as it travels from its source to its destination.

Metric: A value placed in a routing table that defines the relative cost, in time, of taking that particular hop.

Multicast: A data transmission directed at selected multiple hosts.

Source routing: The ability of the host to maintain its own routing tables and make route selections before transmitting data.

Static: Any variable that must be manually configured and/or updated.

Subnet mask: An entry into the TCP/IP configuration, formatted similarly to an IP address. This is a 32-bit value that defines which portion of the address is network and which portion is host.

Unicast: A data transmission directed at a single host.

ACRONYM ALERT

ARP: Address Resolution Protocol. A protocol that can determine the MAC address of any host by sending a query to the IP address.

BGP: Border Gateway Protocol. A routing protocol that takes up where the Exterior Gateway Protocol left off. Advanced algorithms allow for more sophisticated routing decisions.

EGP: Exterior Gateway Protocol. The first of the border gateway protocols to be released.

IPv6: Internet Protocol, Version 6. The latest release of IP that supports 128-bit addresses and several advanced features.

OSPF: Open Shortest Path First. An interior gateway protocol that uses a link state method of route determination.

RIP: Routing Information Protocol. One of the earlier interior gateway protocols.

SAP: Service Addressing Protocol. A protocol used by network operating systems to identify services offered by a particular device.

CHAPTER 8

THE TRANSPORT LAYER

In this chapter, you finally get to see how the networking protocols actually go about breaking the data into chunks from the steady stream sent by the application. The responsibilities of the Transport Layer are as follows:

- Handle end-to-end addressing
- Repackage long messages (when necessary) into smaller segments for transmission
- At the receiving end, rebuild packets into the original message
- Monitor flow control of data
- Handle end-to-end error detection and recovery
- At the receiving end, send receipt acknowledgments for frames that arrive intact
- Request retransmission of frames that are deemed to be unusable
- Handle congestion control on the network

As you can see, there is a lot going on at this layer on a software level. Certain pieces of hardware also perform their functions at this level. These include brouters, advanced cable testers, and gateways. The PDU of the Transport Layer is the segment.

There are a few exam objectives covered in this chapter as well as some advanced networking theory. Exam objectives include:

2.2 Identify the seven layers of the OSI (Open Systems Interconnect) model and their functions.

2.3 Identify the OSI (Open Systems Interconnect) layers at which the following network components operate: Hubs, Switches, Bridges, Routers, NICs (Network Interface Card), WAPs (Wireless Access Point).

2.11 Define the function of TCP / UDP (Transmission Control Protocol/ User Datagram Protocol) ports.

2.12 Identify the well-known ports associated with commonly used services and protocols.

3.7 Given a connectivity scenario, determine the impact on network functionality of a particular security implementation (For example: port blocking/filtering, authentication and encryption).

BUZZ WORDS

Port: A logical address added to each segment of data transmitted that indicates what application or protocol is expecting the data.

Ephemeral port: A port created by a client application that identifies the place where all incoming data intended for that application will go.

Well-known port: A port used by common applications and processes through which data specific to that application or process will be sent.

ADDRESSING IN THE TRANSPORT LAYER

You'd almost think that I would be finished with addressing issues once I left the Network Layer. After all, once I've discussed the issues of both logical and physical addressing, what more is there?

Well, there is still a bit more about logical addressing you need to understand. You know how data finds its way across the network to the target device. But once it gets there, that device still has to figure out precisely what application or protocol requested or is intended to receive the data. For that the network uses *ports*.

In order to direct data to the correct application, the Transport Layer inserts 16-bit port numbers into each segment that it creates. A port is a logical address that points to a specific protocol or application.

Port numbers come in one of two different forms. There are the *well-known ports* and the *ephemeral ports*. The well-known ports are ports 0 through 1023 (see **Table 8.1**). These are assigned and administered by an organization called the Internet Assigned Numbers Authority (IANA). Ephemeral ports are addresses used by the client software to establish a connection with a server (or other host). The segment will contain two port addresses. The first of these is the *source port*. The source port is the ephemeral port created by the application and tells the server to which logical address it should send its replies. The *destination port* will usually be one of the well-known ports and indicates to the server what application or protocol should process the data.

Table 8.1 Commonly Used Well-Known Ports

Port	Protocol
20	FTP, File Transfer Protocol, data
21	FTP, File Transfer Protocol, control
23	Telnet
25	SMTP, Simple Mail Transfer Protocol
80	HTTP, HyperText Transfer Protocol
109	POP, Post Office Protocol, version 2
110	POP, Post Office Protocol, version 3
666	Doom, Id Software

While this list hardly represents *all* the well-known ports, these are the most common ones featured on the exam and encountered by engineers.

Note: Okay, so Doom probably isn't one you'll be tested on. But it's pretty critical to know, don't you think?

EXAM NOTE: For the exam it is necessary to know the well-known ports for some of the key TCP/IP protocols. These are listed in Table 8.1.

Ephemeral ports can also be used as both source and destination ports in some cases. Sometimes programmers use these ports in custom applications. An example of this would be a game designed to be played over the Internet. A game server would be assigned one ephemeral port while all clients would be transmitting data through another.

You should be aware that there are registered ephemeral ports as well. If you find yourself involved in writing network-aware applications, you should check with IANA before arbitrarily selecting a port that your application can bind to.

PACKAGING DATA IN THE TRANSPORT LAYER

One of the key functions of the Transport Layer is to break the stream of data being transmitted down into manageable chunks. Then, on the receiving end, it has to be able to put those pieces of data back together in the right order. At the Transport Layer, these data units are called segments.

PORTS VERSUS SOCKETS

Some older applications (and even a few current ones) make use of the concept of sockets instead of ports. Winsock is an example of one of these applications. Sockets require a bit more overhead and do not function exclusively at the Transport Level. A socket consists of a predefined combination of a port and an IP address. Most server products are designed to support either sockets or ports, depending on the needs of the client application. But you may have to configure your server software to provide that support in the event that you require that service.

Since a great number of applications still use sockets, it's a good idea to be able to troubleshoot some of the more common problems. Some common socket errors that can occur include:

Socket error 10004 – Interrupted function call

Socket error 10013 – Permission denied

Socket error 10014 – Invalid address

Socket error 10022 – Invalid argument

Socket error 10024 – Too many open files

Socket error 10035 – Resource temporarily unavailable

Socket error 10036 – Operation currently in progress

Socket error 10037 – This operation already in progress

Socket error 10038 – Attempted operation on non-socket

Socket error 10039 – Destination address required

Socket error 10040 – Excessive message length

Socket error 10041 – Incorrect protocol for socket

Socket error 10042 – Invalid protocol option

Socket error 10043 – Protocol not supported

Socket error 10044 – Socket type not supported

Socket error 10045 – Operation not supported

Socket error 10046 – Protocol family not supported

Socket error 10047 – Address family not supported by protocol family

Socket error 10048 – Address already in use

Socket error 10049 – Cannot assign requested address

Socket error 10050 – Network unavailable

Socket error 10051 – Network is unreachable

Socket error 10052 – Network lost connection during reset

Socket error 10053 – Connection aborted by software call

Socket error 10054 – Connection reset by peer

Socket error 10055 – Buffer overflow

Socket error 10056 – Socket is already connected

Socket error 10057 – Socket is not connected

Socket error 10058 – Cannot send after socket shutdown

Socket error 10060 – Connection timed out

Socket error 10061 – Connection refused

Socket error 10064 – Host is down

Socket error 10065 – No route to host

Socket error 10067 – Too many processes

Socket error 10091 – Network subsystem is unavailable

Socket error 10092 – WINSOCK.DLL version out of range

Socket error 10093 – Successful WSAStartup not yet performed

Socket error 10094 – Graceful shutdown in progress

Socket error 11001 – Host not found

Socket error 11002 – Nonauthoritative host not found

Socket error 11003 – Nonrecoverable error

Socket error 11004 – Valid name, Invalid data type requested

Also, it is very likely—especially on a busy server—that there will be several different sessions open at the same time. Therefore, the server has to keep track of which segments of data go with which open sessions. If one user is downloading a patch for an operating system and another is downloading a game, it certainly would not do for the streams of data to become intermixed.

> **Exam Note:** Be able to define the process of encapsulation in detail. The process begins at the Transport Layer, and as the data moves down through the lower layers, additional header and trailer information specific to those layers is added. This is encapsulation.

Buzz Word

Segment: The PDU of the Transport Layer. The term can also be used to define a specific length of cable, or the network devices that all share a singular collision domain.

Connectionless service: A networking service that establishes no virtual link between transmitting devices and makes use of no error control.

Connection-oriented service: A networking service that does establish a virtual link between transmitting devices and incorporates end-to-end error control.

As you might imagine, keeping track of all of this information can involve quite a bit of overhead on the part of the server. Not all transfers of data require this degree of care and feeding. Therefore, programmers have the option of transmitting data using either connection-oriented or connectionless services.

A connectionless service simply throws the data out there and hopes that it gets where it's going. The User Datagram Protocol (UDP) is an example of a connectionless service. In a connectionless transmission, the only information added to each segment is source and destination ports, a length field to indicate how long the segment is, and a frame check field into which either checksum or CRC data is added for error correction. There is no virtual connection established (hence the name), and sequencing information is not added to each frame.

The secure transmission of data requires a bit more attention than that. The network needs to make sure frames arrive in the correct order, and if they don't, it needs to be able to resequence them. The network also needs to establish a virtual connection for each open session and make sure it keeps track of what data goes to what session. For this type of data transmission the network will use a connection-oriented protocol, such as the File Transport Protocol (FTP) or Transmission Control Protocol (TCP).

Sometimes there is a smaller file that needs to be moved and it really isn't necessary to maintain that much overhead for such a tiny little file. In this case, an application may choose the *Trivial File Transport Protocol* (TFTP). This protocol is a connectionless protocol that does not make use of error correction and/or ACKS and NACKS. An example of a place where this protocol is used is when Cisco routers upload copies of their configuration files to a server.

The Transport Layer takes care of session management issues through a process called multiplexing/demultiplexing. As it strips pieces of data from the message for transmission, it adds Transport Layer-specific header information to each segment. This information includes the source and destination ports for the data just like in the connectionless services. Two other fields that are added to the header include a 32-bit sequence number and a 32-bit acknowledgment number. Another field that I will discuss later in the chapter defines the window size. This field determines how many bytes of data the receiving computer can handle in any given frame. **Figure 8.1** shows the structure of a TCP frame.

- 16-bit Source Port Number – Identifies a unique connection to a source application.

- 16-bit Destination Port Number – Identifies a unique connection to a destination application.

- 32-bit Sequence Number – Identifies the byte in the data stream represented by the first byte of data following the TCP header.

- 32-bit Acknowledgment Number – This number identifies the number of the next byte in the sequence that the receiver should get in the transmission.

- 4-bit Header Length – Indicates the size of the entire TCP header to the receiver.

BUZZ WORDS

Window size: The amount of data a given host is capable of absorbing before its buffers overflow.

Demultiplexing: The separation and resequencing of multiple messages coming off of a single communications link.

Multiplexing: The combining of multiple signals from different sources to be transferred over a single communications link.

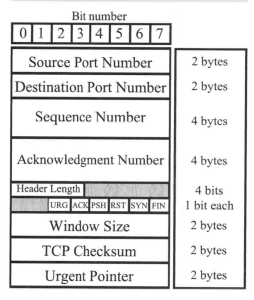

Figure 8.1 Structure of a TCP packet. A TCP packet can be broken down into several fields. See the text for a detailed description.

URG – 0 or 1. When set to 1, this bit indicates that the urgent pointer field is valid and should be considered.

ACK – 0 or 1. When set to 1, this bit indicates that the acknowledgment number field is valid and being used.

PSH – 0 or 1. When set to 1, this bit tells the receiver to pass all data received at this point immediately to the receiving application.

RST – 0 or 1. When set to 1, this bit indicates an error condition has been detected and notifies the receiver to reset the connection.

SYN – 0 or 1. When set to 1, this bit synchronizes the sequence numbers in order to establish a connection.

FIN – 0 or 1. When set to 1, this bit indicates that the transmission is completed.

16-bit Window Size – This field represents the number of bytes starting with the byte specified in the acknowledgment number field that the receiver is next willing to accept. Typically, this is limited to 65,535 bytes.

16-bit TCP Checksum – Validation of this checksum ensures that the TCP header has not been modified in transit. If this checksum is invalid, the receiver generates a NACK. Note that this field is placed in a TCP/IP packet in addition to the Frame Sequence check placed in the trailer by the Data Link Layer.

16-bit Urgent Pointer – This pointer is added to the sequence number field of the segment to yield the sequence number of the transmission of urgent data. Data marked Urgent precludes any other data which is being sent.

Options Field – Varies in content.

> **Buzz Word**
>
> **Payload:** The part of a frame that actually consists of user or application data, separate from header and trailer information.

After the header comes the data itself, or the payload as it is most often called. This can vary in size and is dependent on the type of data being sent and the protocol in use. While the example used above is a TCP frame, any connection-oriented protocol will build a frame structure very similar.

> **Exam Note:** While it is not necessary to completely memorize the structure of a frame, it is important to know the differences between a connection-oriented service segment and a connectionless segment. Be able to identify a connection-oriented segment by the presence of sequence number and acknowledgment numbers.

Once this little package has been nicely assembled, it will be passed on to the Network Layer where the tasks I discussed in Chapter Seven, The Network Layer, are performed. The Transport Layer has finished with the packaging of data.

THE CONCEPTS OF FLOW CONTROL

Another key task of the Transport Layer is to make sure data moves as quickly as it can without overtaxing any device involved in the connection. There are different methods for dealing with the issue of *flow control.*

The simplest method, and the one that requires the least overhead, is to simply do nothing. This is called *buffer overflow.* The recipient device is storing all incoming data in a memory buffer. When the buffer overflows, any frames that can't be buffered will simply be discarded. Since no ACK will be returned, the discarded frames will eventually be resent. The problem inherent in this approach is that the potential for large numbers of resends will result in increased network congestion.

Equally simple (and equally inefficient) are the *stop-and-wait* protocols. With stop and wait, one frame gets sent and the transmitting computer does nothing else until it receives the acknowledgment, good or bad.

> **EXAM NOTE:** Know the different methods of flow control inside and out. This is an item that is frequently presented more than once on any given exam.

Another method is *static window* flow control. Remember the field in the header that indicated window size? This is one of the areas in which that field comes into play. A fixed number of frames will be sent consecutively without waiting for ACKs or NACKs from the intended recipient. This value is set during an initial handshaking process in which the receiving device announces its buffer size. Once the frames are sent, the transmitting device sits back and waits for the replies to come in. If, for example, the window value is set to 8, eight frames will be sent and then the transmitting device will wait for eight replies. If it gets six ACKs and two NACKs, or simply six replies of any sort, it will close the session and initiate a new session based on a smaller window size. Crude, but effective.

> **BUZZ WORDS**
>
> **Flow control:** Managing the transfer of data between two hosts on the network.
>
> **Stop-and-wait:** A flow control method that requires that the transmitting device wait for the acknowledgment of each packet transmitted before it can send the next packet.

A more elegant and even more effective scheme is the *sliding window*. With sliding window, when the receiving device becomes bogged down with data coming in too quickly, it can send out a hold packet, telling the transmitting device to stop sending data until otherwise notified. Once the buffer is cleared, the receiving device will send a resume packet and transmission will continue.

One form of sliding window is the *selectively repeat* variety of protocol. Each packet received by the target device is acknowledged. Good packets get an ACK and bad packets get a NACK and then go to that place where all bad packets go. They are discarded into digital oblivion (see **Figure 8.2**).

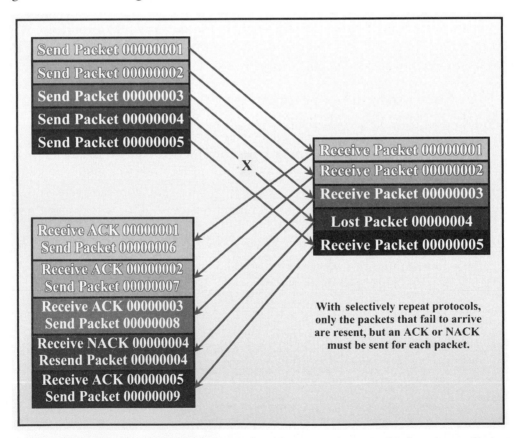

With selectively repeat protocols, only the packets that fail to arrive are resent, but an ACK or NACK must be sent for each packet.

Figure 8.2   With selectively repeat protocols, only bad packets need to be retransmitted.

A variation on the sliding window that significantly reduces network congestion is called go back n. Go back n uses a sliding window method, but sends a cumulative ACK packet for the number of frames supported by the window. This ACK is sent for the highest number packet that was received correctly and in order. Out of order packets are discarded. A time to live timer is set for the oldest packet in the windowing sequence. In the event of a transmission failure, the receiving device will request a retransmission of this packet and each one that followed it (see **Figure 8.3**).

> **BUZZ WORDS** ————————
>
> **Go back n:** A flow control method that requires that all packets arrive in sequence. If one packet is rejected, then all subsequently received packets must be retransmitting by the sending device along with the offending packet.

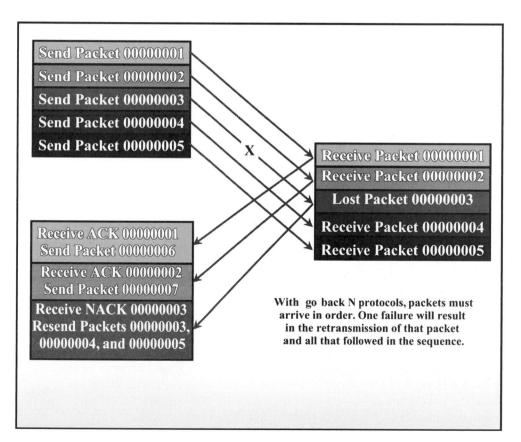

Figure 8.3 With go back n protocols, data must arrive in the correct order. One bad packet will result in the retransmission of that packet and the packets that followed it.

ERROR CONTROL IN THE TRANSPORT LAYER

In Chapter Six, The Data Link Layer, I discussed how the use of checksum and CRC could detect data corruption and packet loss, and then do something to fix it. As long as Data Link is doing its thing correctly, why then does a network have error correction at the Transport Layer?

To simplify that answer, it is simply that both layers are doing the same thing, only different. Data Link is concerned with bit-level error correction. Its job is to make sure the data arrives complete and intact. The task of error control in the Transport Layer is to provide end-to-end error control. It is interested only in packet level errors. It doesn't look for errors on a bit level.

While initially this may seem to be a bit redundant (and it is), it is a necessary redundancy. For certain, the CRC applied by Data Link would detect any corruption, but this algorithm is applied at the Data Link Layer. What happens if an error occurs in the encapsulation process between layers? Data Link won't know these are errors and will calculate its CRC accordingly. The errors will not be detected, which obviously means they won't be corrected.

It is possible for bit-level errors to be detected by the Transport Layer. However, in most reliable transport methods, errors at the bit level are detected by the receiving host at the Data Link level.

UNDERSTANDING ERROR CONTROL

You saw the concept of error detection and correction brought up in Chapter Six, The Data Link Layer, and now you are seeing it again here. This is because Data Link deals exclusively with bit-level error correction. It takes a packet the receiving computer already has in its possession and determines if an error occurred in transmission and whether the data is intact or corrupt. However, there need to be additional controls in place to make sure the system knows that all packets are arriving. This is called *end-to-end* error control and is the responsibility of the Transport Layer. Transport couldn't care less whether the data in the payload is good or bad. That's Data Link's job. Transport only cares if it is getting every packet that it is supposed to, and whether or not they're arriving in the right order. It is the Transport Layer that detects the absence of packets or the corruption of packets that occurred on the transmission end before they arrived at the Data Link Layer.

Packet level errors can include packet loss, packet corruption, and packet duplication. All of these are bad because they all result in the data being corrupted. Therefore, in order to assure that none of them occurs, the network uses a combination of three processes to avoid them. These processes are a *three-way handshake,* the *sequence numbers* I discussed earlier, and a predefined *timeout* for each packet.

It all starts with the three-way handshake. In this process, the client computer makes a request for a virtual connection by issuing a synchronization (SYN) packet to the device from which it is requesting services. In this instance I will simply refer to the devices as client and server. This is the first step.

The server responds with an SYN/ACK packet, which will establish a randomly selected initial sequence number. Most likely it will also include additional protocol-specific data needed for other Transport Layer mechanisms such as flow control. That is step number two in the process. In the final step, the client acknowledges the SYN/ACK and the transfer of data begins (see **Figure 8.4**).

Packet corruption at the Transport Layer is detected because Transport uses its own independent checksum or CRC field. The client performs the same

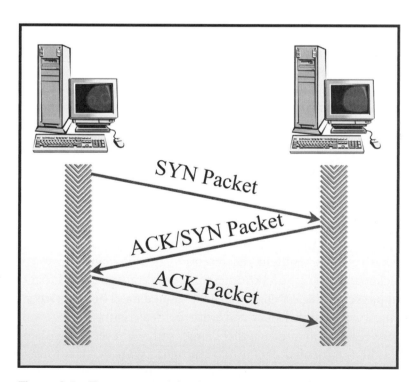

Figure 8.4 The concept of the three-way handshake.

algorithm on that data as did the server, and if the resultant values match then the packet may or may not be declared to be good. If not, a NACK is generated and sent back to the server.

The one reason the packet may still be rejected would be if the network was using

a go back n method of flow control. If a previous packet in the go back n sequence has already been rejected, then all subsequent packets will be rejected in the next phase of Transport Layer error correction.

That next phase is the sequence number check. Some protocols are not sensitive to whether or not packets arrive in sequence. The Transport Layer uses the sequence number to reassemble out-of-order packets into the correct sequence. If the protocol is sequence sensitive, then if packets arrive out of order, they are discarded and NACKs are sent. This is where the go back n flow control method is used.

This is all fine and good for the packets that arrive. But how does the client send a NACK for data it never received? Does it telepathically know that there was a packet that the server sent that never arrived?

In a way, yes, it does, because the acknowledgment number in the Transport Layer header indicates the sequence number of the next packet that should arrive. If that packet never arrives, a NACK can be generated.

If, for any reason, the client does not have a way of knowing that a packet was supposed to arrive—for example, if a cluster of multiple packets are lost and the whole sequence is out of whack—then the server has a fallback method of detecting lost packets. This is the timeout process.

Protocols such as TCP use a timer process to figure out how long it should take a packet to make its way to the destination and then for the ACK or NACK to make the subsequent return trip. This is called the *round trip time* (RTT). If the round trip time for any packet is exceeded, then the server will automatically retransmit that packet. This assures the arrival of all packets.

This can, of course, result in the reception of duplicate packets. Perhaps the offending packet arrives just as its counterpart was retransmitted. If that occurs, then two identical packets will exist containing the same data. This is just as much a form of data corruption as garbled data and must be dealt with.

During the reassembly process, the Transport Layer uses the sequence numbers to reassemble the fragmented data into a contiguous stream of information. In the event that it finds two packets with the same sequence number, the client will discard the second packet. It will send no response from the Transport Layer to the server regarding the duplicate packet.

CONGESTION CONTROL AT THE TRANSPORT LAYER

BUZZ WORD

Congestion control: Managing the overall flow of data between all hosts on the network.

The first thing that you need to understand is that there is a difference between flow control (discussed earlier in the chapter) and *congestion control.* Flow control is the handling of data streaming from host to host. Congestion control is the management of data moving between all hosts on a network segment.

So how can the Transport Layer of a single device handle congestion problems for the entire network? Obviously, it can't. What it can do, however, is maximize the efficiency of bandwidth used for its own transmissions. With all devices monitoring their own bandwidth usage, network congestion is effectively controlled.

The things that result in increased congestion include excessive retransmission of data, long delays in queuing times by any given device on the network (which results in the perpetual retransmission of data), and at the simplest level, simply having too many devices on the network for the available bandwidth. If congestion gets excessively high, it can bring the network down.

EXAM NOTE: Please be aware that there is a big difference between flow control and congestion control. Flow control is the management of data movement from device to device. Congestion control is the management of the amount of data moving over the entire network across any given time frame.

There's not a lot the Transport Layer can do about the last item in that list. There are mechanisms in place to deal with excessive data retransmission. This method is crude, but very effective. When excessive transmission becomes an issue the connection between the two devices is reset. If you recall, one of the flags in the header was the RST field. The Transport Layer sets this field to 1 in an SYN packet and upon receipt of this packet the receiving device must close the current connection, and if necessary, reestablish a new one.

CHAPTER SUMMARY

By the time you've finished with this chapter, you should have a pretty good grasp on several things. One of the first things I examined was the addressing scheme that the Transport Layer uses in order to assure that data gets to the appropriate application or process once it has arrived at the correct device.

Next, I covered how the Transport Layer actually begins the process of encapsulation in order to send data over the wire. I took a close look at Transport Layer header information and how these headers differ between a connection-oriented service, such as UDP, and a connectionless service such as TCP.

A critical issue covered in this chapter was the Transport Layer's varying methods of handling flow control between devices on the network. By examining these different methods, you actually got a first-hand look at the purpose of much of the information included in the Layer 4 header.

You should also be able to intelligently discuss the difference between bit-level and end-to-end error control mechanisms. The Transport Layer does implement error control, but as I pointed out, it is only concerned with the safe arrival of packets. It doesn't care whether those packets are usable or not. That, as you now know, is the job of the Data Link Layer.

Finally, I compared and contrasted the concepts of error control versus congestion control. While there really isn't a lot the network administrator can do on a case-by-case level, knowing the symptoms and causes of congestion can help the administrator understand when it is time to upgrade the bandwidth of a particular segment.

Overall, you saw that the Transport Layer is responsible for the end-to-end transmission of data. One end is the process or application running on the sending device, and the other end is the process or application running on the receiving device. Transport neither knows nor cares about the logical or physical host addresses of the devices themselves nor how the data moved from one end of the network to the other. It relies on the lower layers for those services.

Brain Drain

1. List as many of the functions of the Transport Layer as you can.
2. Define in your own words the purpose of a port number in the networking protocols.
3. Discuss the differences between connection-oriented and connectionless services.
4. Describe in your own words why CRC is a better error detection method than checksum.
5. Describe in detail how sliding window flow control works.

THE 64K$ QUESTIONS

1. A port number is _____.
    a. A logical address of a host
    b. A physical address of a host
    c. A logical address of a process or application
    d. A physical address of a process or application

2. Ports 0 through 1023 are called the
    a. Destination ports
    b. Source ports
    c. Ephemeral ports
    d. Well-known ports

3. The process of breaking data down into smaller pieces and then adding information from other layers before sending over the wire is _____.
    a. Segmentation
    b. Packetization
    c. Encapsulation
    d. Dissection

4. UDP is _____.
    a. Connectionless
    b. Connection-oriented

5. TCP is _____.
    a. Connectionless
    b. Connection-oriented

6. The form of flow control that can adjust the number of packets transmitted before the ACKs must begin to flow is called _____.
    a. Sliding window
    b. Static window
    c. Go back n
    d. Selectively repeat

7. Error Control in the Transport Layer effectively identifies and corrects bit-level errors.
    a. True
    b. False

8. What process establishes the parameters used by the hosts in a communications link necessary for error control?

   a. Synchronization

   b. The three-step handshake

   c. Establishment of a virtual private network

   d. Host damping

9. The first step in the Transport Layer's error control mechanism is _____.

   a. The server sends a SYN packet

   b. The client sends a SYN packet

   c. The server sends an ACK/SYN packet

   d. The client sends an ACK/SYN packet

10. A device that is sending too many retransmissions will _____.

    a. Be quenched

    b. Be reset by the server

    c. Renegotiate the session

    d. Be dropped from the network

11. The Transport Layer is **not** responsible for which of the following?

    a. Handling end-to-end addressing

    b. Adding a CRC trailer to the end of the packet

    c. Repackaging long messages into smaller segments for transmission

    d. Rebuilding packets into the original message at the receiving end

    e. Monitoring flow control of data

12. The protocol data unit used by the Transport Layer is called a _____.

    a. Segment

    b. Parcel

    c. Capsule

    d. Packet

13. The Transport Layer makes its contribution to network address by _____.

    a. Adding the host address

    b. Providing service access points

    c. Resolving MAC addresses

    d. Inserting port numbers for applications

14. FTP uses port _____.
    a. 21
    b. 25
    c. 80
    d. 110

15. How is a socket different from a port?
    a. A socket embeds the MAC address of the intended recipient.
    b. A port embeds the MAC address of the intended recipient.
    c. A socket embeds the IP address of the intended recipient.
    d. A port embeds the IP address of the intended recipient.

16. The User Datagram protocol is a connectionless protocol.
    a. True
    b. False

17. The Transport Layer makes use of a _____ to identify what application is to receive the data.
    a. A 16-bit port
    b. A 4-bit header
    c. A 32-bit port
    d. A sequence number

18. Which of the following protocols is connection oriented?
    a. UDP
    b. TCP
    c. PING
    d. All of them are.

19. The Transport Layer takes care of network congestion in what way?
    a. It recognizes duplicate packets and drops them before they are transmitted.
    b. Transport layer protocols use far less overhead.
    c. All packets are compressed before transmission.
    d. It cleans up its own mess before sending it out to the world.

20. If the Transport Layer detects an error so severe as to require closing a session, it will communicate directly with the Session Layer to order the closure.
    a. True
    b. False

TRICKY TERMINOLOGY

Congestion control: Managing the overall flow of data between all hosts on the network.

Connectionless service: A networking service that establishes no virtual link between transmitting devices and makes use of no error control.

Connection-oriented service: A networking service that does establish a virtual link between transmitting devices and incorporates end-to-end error control.

Demultiplexing: The separation and resequencing of multiple messages coming off of a single communications link.

Ephemeral port: A port created by a client application that identifies the place where all incoming data intended for that application will go.

Flow control: Managing the transfer of data between two hosts on the network.

Go back n: A flow control method that requires that all packets arrive in sequence. If one packet is rejected, then all subsequently received packets must be retransmitted by the sending device along with the offending packet.

Multiplexing: The combining of multiple signals from different sources to be transferred over a single communications link.

Payload: The part of a frame that actually consists of user or application data, separate from header and trailer information.

Port: A logical address added to each segment of data transmitted that indicates what application or protocol is expecting the data.

Segment: In reference to the Transport Layer, it is the PDU of the Transport Layer. The term can also be used to define a specific length of cable or the network devices that all share a singular collision domain.

Selectively repeat: A flow control method that allows only offending packets to be retransmitted.

Sliding window: A flow control method that allows two transmitting devices to adjust the number of packets that can be sent before waiting for ACKs as line conditions and congestion states change over time.

Static window: A flow control method that allows a fixed number of packets to be sent. The transmitting device will then wait for ACKs for each of those packets to return before sending any more data.

Stop-and-wait: A flow control method that requires that the transmitting device wait for the acknowledgment of each packet transmitted before it can sent the next packet.

Well-known port: A port used by common applications and processes through which data specific to that application or process will be sent.

Window size: The amount of data a given host is capable of absorbing before its buffers overflow.

ACRONYM ALERT

ACK: Acknowledgment. Thank you, it arrived safe and sound.

FTP: File Transfer Protocol. Protocol used for transferring critical data.

IANA: Internet Assigned Numbers Authority. The organization responsible for TCP/IP address and port number assignments.

NACK: No Acknowledgment. It arrived, but there's something wrong. Can you retransmit?

RST: Reset. Field or packet that initiates the breakdown of a session.

RTT: Round Trip Time. The amount of time it takes a packet to go from host to host, and for the resultant ACK or NACK to return.

SYN: Synchronization. Field or packet type that establishes transmission speeds.

TCP: Transmission Control Protocol

TFTP: Trivial File Transfer Protocol. Protocol used for transferring files that are smaller or not necessarily critical.

UDP: User Datagram Protocol. Connectionless protocol that simply throws data onto the network and hopes that it gets there.

CHAPTER 9

THE SESSION LAYER

So far in this book you have seen a lot on information on how the data gets broken down into little bitty pieces and packaged for shipping in order to assure that each little piece gets where it needs to be intact. One group of people who can appreciate the importance of that is the crew that broke down the London Bridge and moved it to Lake Havasu, Arizona, in the latter part of the twentieth century.

During many of my discussions, I kept bringing up concepts of virtual connections, handshaking, and other issues related to the communication link between two devices. It is the Session Layer that is responsible for building and maintaining these virtual links, and once the data is successfully transferred, it is up to the Session Layer to break everything down and clean up after itself. Therefore, you can consider the Session Layer to have three responsibilities:

- Establish a connection
- Provide dialogue management and synchronization
- Release the connection

In this chapter, I will discuss in detail how the system goes about doing this. In the process, I cover a few of the CompTIA exam objectives. However, there won't be as many in this chapter as there have been in others. As I said in Chapter Four, Welcome to OSI, the top three layers of OSI are rarely addressed by modern software and hardware. They are primarily historical artifacts. Therefore, the advanced networking theory in this chapter will be of value to some, but not much revolving around the exam is here. Those that you will see include:

2.2 Identify the seven layers of the OSI (Open Systems Interconnect) model and their functions.

2.3 Identify the OSI (Open Systems Interconnect) layers at which the following network components operate: Hubs, Switches, Bridges, Routers, NICs (Network Interface Card), WAPs (Wireless Access Point).

3.7 Given a connectivity scenario, determine the impact on network functionality of a particular security implementation (For example: port blocking/filtering, authentication and encryption).

Exam Note: As with all of the layers, it is critical that you understand each of the Session Layer's responsibilities.

ESTABLISHING A CONNECTION

The initial setup of a communications link between two different hosts is more complicated than you might realize at first. In order for two devices to communicate, they must first establish a *session*. A session can be defined as a virtual connection between two devices for the purpose of transferring data. Many times, data is transferred over a series of sessions in order to keep network congestion at a minimum. Any time multiple sessions are used by devices, it is considered to be a *dialogue.*

Consider that not only do two different devices have to agree on protocols and speeds, the different processes or applications that are actually doing the communicating have to figure out how to talk to one another. The process or application is called the *process entity,* or usually more simply, just the entity. During the connection, the Session Layer will be making use of small packages of data known as *service protocol data units* (SPDU) in order to request specific services or activities.

But before the network goes to all that trouble, it needs to make sure that the user attempting to access this data has all the necessary rights and privileges. This is done through a process called *logon authentication.*

BUZZ WORDS

Session: A virtual connection created between two devices for the purpose of transmitting data.

Dialogue: A series of independent sessions between two devices that are used for a complex process or the transfer of a large quantity of data.

Process entity: The protocol or application on a host that is actually requesting or transmitting data during a network session.

Logon authentication: In this process, a user's logon ID and password are transferred to the host providing the requested service. These pieces of identification are compared to a security database, and if confirmed, the user is allowed in.

The actual steps involved in establishing a session, in the order that they are performed, include the following:

- Verify the user's logon name and password
- Establish a connection ID number
- Agree upon which services are required and for what duration
- Determine which device begins the conversation
- Coordinate the acknowledgment numbering and retransmission procedures

INITIATING A LINK

When a client application or process decides that it requires a service that exists on a remote device, it is up to the Session Layer to establish a link with that remote device. For this, the Session Layer will rely heavily upon services provided by the lower layers in the OSI model. The first thing the Session Layer will do is to issue a *T-connect request* to the Network Layer.

The Transport Layer will then identify the services that will be required for the particular session and the protocol that will be used. The Transport Layer now asks the Network Layer to send all this information to the other device and then waits for confirmation. This information will be handed back to the Session Layer and used for all subsequent processes. **Figure 9.1** illustrates the procedures used to initialize a new session.

Then the real fun begins.

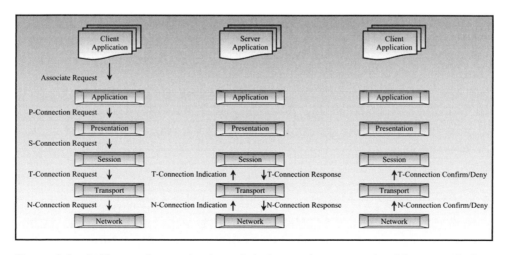

Figure 9.1 Setting up the session is a relatively complex process involving several of the OSI layers.

LOGON AUTHENTICATION

In any connection-oriented protocol, logon authentication is required of the session before any session building can begin. After all, there isn't a lot of point in generating the network traffic required to build a session if the user isn't going to be allowed access once the connection is made. This is not necessarily required in a connectionless transfer of information.

> **EXAM NOTE:** Know the process of logon authentication backwards and forwards for the exam.

BUZZ WORDS

Credentials: User information required by a system in order to permit access by that user to network resources. At a minimum this would include the user name and password.

Connection ID: A randomly generated number that the server application assigns to each session to assure that data is kept together and in sequence.

Once users log on to the network for the first time, their *credentials* stay in cache. These credentials consist essentially of their user names and passwords. As far as end users are concerned, once they're logged on, that's the last time they have to use this information. And for them, it is. The system, however, makes use of that information every time they attempt to access any network resource.

The process of establishing a session begins the second a user attempts to access any network resource. This might be done by sending a print job to a network printer, double-clicking on a file in Network Neighborhood, or any number of other ways.

Once the client host has located the resource, if there are password restrictions on the resource, the device housing that resource will forward a logon authentication request to the server. The security database will be checked, and if all the information is correct, the user will be allowed access to that particular resource. **Figure 9.2** illustrates the process of logon authentication at work.

In a client/server model, this authentication must be confirmed by the security database of the server application running on the network. In a peer-to-peer network, it may be as simple as comparing the password to that assigned to the resource, if any.

THE CONNECTION ID

Now that the network has established that it is permissible for the session to transpire, it is going to have to give the session a name. On a busy network, it is highly unlikely that this is going to be the only transfer of data that is occurring over

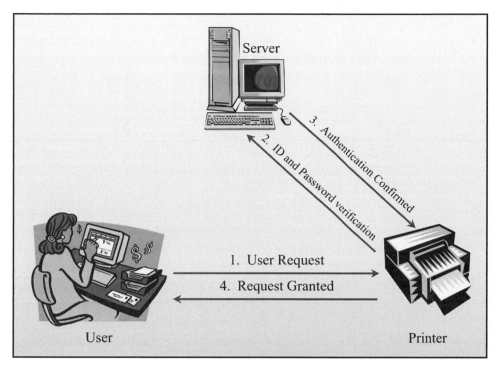

Figure 9.2 An example of logon authentication at work.

the next several milliseconds. In fact, it is very likely that any given host will have multiple sessions open simultaneously. It is critical that only the data frames relevant to this specific transfer of data be accepted by this particular session. This is the purpose of the connection ID. For each session that is established, the network will create a source connection ID and a destination connection ID.

> **BUZZ WORD**
>
> **Handshaking:** The process two devices go through in order to agree on protocols used, connection speeds, and a number of other issues.

This number will then be provided to the lower layer entities in order to make sure this information is added to the appropriate fields in their headers.

> **EXAM NOTE:** Be aware that TCP/IP makes very little use of the connection ID once the connection has been established.

Not all protocols are as dependent on the connection ID as others. IPX incorporates the connection ID into the header of every packet it sends. TCP does not make much use of the Session Layer. Some TCP/IP functions make use of a connection ID in the handshaking process, but rely on sequence numbers to keep packets from different sessions in order. Since each session begins with a unique and randomly generated number, the flow of information is kept separate in that fashion.

THE DURATION OF THE CONNECTION AND SERVICES REQUIRED

For the most part, a network session is open ended. Once the two computers have agreed on certain parameters, they will continue to exchange data until that data has been completely transferred from device to device. Still, the communicating devices will establish a duration for the session. In the event that one of the devices drops the connection for any reason, the other device will not just leave the virtual link hanging open. When the time to live expires, the still-connected device can either reestablish the connection or close it.

The devices will also negotiate what services are being requested and those that will be required. In Chapter Four, I introduced the concept of the service primitive, which is a specific function or activity that is performed by any specific layer entity. Many are protocol-specific. A process or application will obviously call on those services it requires. The services provided by the Session Layer include:

- Kernel
- Activity management
- Half-duplex
- Duplex
- Negotiated release
- Expedited data
- Typed data
- Capability data
- Minor synchronization
- Major synchronization
- Resynchronization
- Exceptions

Any given session will make use of one or more of these services. Some of these services provide information used by the lower layers in the transfer of data. Others provide services to the applications. The service primitives that are specific to the Session Layer include:

- Activity-Discard
- Activity-End
- Activity-Interrupt
- Activity-Resume
- Activity-Start
- Capability-Data
- Connect
- Control-Give
- Data
- Expedited-Data

- P-Abort
- P-Exception-Report
- Release
- Resynchronize
- Sync-Major
- Sync-Minor

- Token-Give
- Token-Please
- Typed-Data
- U-Abort
- U-Exception-Report

In order to request a specific service or action, the Session Layer issues an SPDU appropriate to the service requested. **Table 9.1** lists the typical service primitives, along with the SPDUs specific to that primitive.

For the purposes of Network+ it is not necessary to understand the function of each service, but rather to be aware of their existence within the structure of the Session Layer.

THE FINAL STEPS OF INITIALIZING A SESSION

The hard part of setting up a session is now done. The last two steps are relatively painless and easy to explain. Those steps are to determine which entity begins the conversation and to coordinate the acknowledgment numbering and retransmission procedures.

Deciding who talks first is simply a matter of what type of service is being provided. The client may be requesting access to a resource on the server, or the server may be synchronizing data on the client. There is no fast rule as to which machine should begin the dialogue once the session is established. That will be decided in the handshaking process.

It is also the Session Layer that negotiates the methods of acknowledgment numbering and procedures for the retransmission of data when necessary. Connection-oriented protocols require that acknowledgments be sent for each packet received. The flow control methods discussed in Chapter Eight, The Transport Layer, make use of different procedures. If you recall, sliding window sent out several packets before waiting for the ACKs to come home to roost. Stop and wait sends a packet and waits for the reply. It is the Session Layer that negotiates which method will be used.

> **BUZZ WORD** ——————
>
> **Acknowledgment number:** A sequence of numbers, beginning with a randomly generated number, that identifies each packet in a transmission and the order in which it goes.

Table 9.1   Session Layer Service Primitives and SPDUs

Service	SPDU
Activity-Discard	Activity Discard
Activity-Discard	Activity Discard Ack
Activity-Interrupt	Activity Interrupt
Activity-Interrupt	Activity Interrupt Ack
Activity-Resume	Activity Resume
Activity-Start	Activity Start
Capability-Data	Capability Data
Capability-Data	Capability Data Ack
Connect	Connect
Connect	Accept
Connect	Refuse
Control-Give	Give Tokens Confirm
Control-Give	Give Tokens Ack
Data	Data Transfer
Expedited-Data	Expedited Data
P-Abort	
P-Exception-Report	Exception Report
Release	Finish
Release	Disconnect
Release	Not Finished
Resynchronize	Resynchronize
Resynchronize	Resynchronize Ack
Sync-Major	Major Sync Point
Sync-Major	Major Sync Point Ack
Sync-Minor	Minor Sync Point
Sync-Minor	Minor Sync Point Ack
Token-Give	Give Tokens
Token-Please	Please Tokens
Typed-Data	Typed Data
U-Abort	Abort
U-Exception-Report	Exception Data

The session layer depends heavily upon the services of lower-layer protocols. It is the Service Primitives that request these services.

DIALOGUE MANAGEMENT AND SYNCHRONIZATION

A key ingredient in a decent conversation between two entities, whether they are carbon-based or silicon-based, is to set certain rules as they pertain to conversations. People consider it rude when you break into their conversations without permission. Computers consider it unacceptable. Likewise, there has to be agreement on fundamental concepts, such as the principle that when one entity stops communicating, it is alright for the other to begin. This is the concept of synchronization.

> **BUZZ WORD**
>
> **Dialogue:** The two-way transfer of data between devices, including control data used to maintain the session.

DIALOGUE CONTROL

When discussing the process of initializing a session I pointed out that a pre-defined duration for a connection would be established along with the services that would be provided. Among these service primitives were included the communications process that would be used, including full-duplex and half-duplex communication.

If full duplex is the selected mode of transmission, then either device can send data any time it is required. If half duplex (or simplex) is the default procedure, the process of communication will be controlled by a token. The types of tokens available are listed on the following page.

- Data token – Permits the transmission of data
- Synchronize minor token – A fine-tuning of the session's flow control is required, or a checkpoint is being issued.
- Major activity token – The entire session is out of synch and needs to be realigned or reset.
- Release token – All finished. Let's go home.
- Disconnect token – The data transfer is complete and the session can be broken down.
- Abort token – Some catastrophic failure has occurred and the session is to be ended immediately.

The data token is pretty self-explanatory. When a device has the token, it may transmit. Synchronize minor and major activity tokens are worth taking a closer look at. Start by checking out **Figure 9.3**.

239

Figure 9.3 Without some form of dialogue control, getting two unlike devices to have any meaningful communication would be impossible.

During the transmission of data during a session, the Session Layer periodically places checkpoints in the data stream. This is so that in the event of a session failure, certain protocols can reestablish a connection and pick up where they left off. A synchronize minor token is used in this procedure so that the receiving device won't confuse the checkpoint with actual data, thereby corrupting a message. Once a minor synchronization has occurred, it is assumed that all data received by the target device to this point is accepted. A reset session would not need to retransmit that data.

Sessions themselves can be broken down into a series of *activities*. An activity would be considered to be the largest subset of any given session. An example of an activity would be a user authentication. Once a session is under way, activities can be started, ended, interrupted, resumed, or simply discarded.

A few points to consider are these. When an activity is first initiated, a numbering sequence will be initiated. This corresponds to the connection ID I discussed earlier. Should the session be interrupted or reset, this numbering sequence can be used to reestablish a new session, and the communicating machines can simply begin where they left off.

If a session is currently under way, but there are no activities in progress, there are

> **BUZZ WORD**
>
> **Activity:** The most basic transfer of information that occurs in the course of a session.

a few options that may be considered activity management. The devices may initiate a *capabilities exchange*. This procedure makes sure a faster device doesn't leave the slower one in the dust.

One device can initiate a new activity with an *activity begin* sequence. Or either device can send an *abort* request or a *release* request, both of which put an end to the session. The difference is that a release request suggests a graceful end to a session, while an abort sequence suggests that an unexpected event occurred and that the current session had to be ended immediately.

SYNCHRONIZATION METHODS AT THE SESSION LAYER

Some of the procedures of session synchronization were discussed in the section of dialogue control because they occur as a result of events that occur during that process. Here, I will look at those events in a little more detail.

The four types of synchronization that can occur are:

- Initial synchronization
- Major synchronization
- Minor synchronization
- Resynchronization

Initial synchronization occurs when the connection ID and starting sequence number for the packets (to be assembled in the lower layers) are first generated. As the session proceeds, the sequence numbers are automatically incremented. Should there be a new activity established or a resynchronization be required, these numbers will be reset.

A *major synchronization* reestablishes everything and starts the activity over from scratch. For a major synchronization to occur, one device must request it, the other device must confirm it, and until the event has been completed no further data can be transmitted between the two devices.

A *minor synchronization* simply fine-tunes an existing session (usually between activities). As I mentioned earlier, when a minor synchronization event occurs, it assumes that all data received during the session prior to the event is accepted. Data can continue to move between devices, and no confirmation is required by either device.

Resynchronization can define one of several events. A *restart* will begin a new session, but take advantage of the checkpoints inserted in the data to resume transmission of data from one of the previously inserted checkpoints. This checkpoint may be the last one inserted by the last minor synchronization event, or the session may be forced to go back to the last major resynchronization event. A *set* command can be used to return to a specified checkpoint.

Either device can issue an *abandon* request. This will force the current session to be dropped and a new one to be initiated. This results in new connection IDs and starting sequence numbers. All data received up to that point during the session being abandoned will be discarded.

RELEASING THE CONNECTION

The final responsibility of the Session Layer is to disconnect a communications link and remove any temporary files that have been created during the session. Disconnections basically fall under two categories, the *expected* and the *unexpected*.

Expected disconnections occur because either the duration of the session has expired or the transfer of data is completed. In either of these circumstances, one of the devices will issue an Activity-End service primitive. Different variations that are possible include either a *finish* or a *not-finished* protocol data unit. Either of these would be accompanied by a Disconnect or an Abort token. The session will be closed, and, in the event that all data has been transferred to the client application, any temporary files will be cleaned up.

A not-finished SPDU assumes that another attempt will be made to transfer that data. Therefore, the temporary files that contain the data successfully transmitted will remain intact. Once a reconnection has been made, the checkpoint procedure will be used to resume the transfer where it left off.

An unexpected release doesn't have the luxury of preparing a graceful end. Therefore, all files created by the session remain. Generally any attempt to reconnect will have to be initiated by the client application.

CHAPTER SUMMARY

Now that you've gotten this far, you realize that the Session Layer is a much busier layer than many people give it credit for. This layer not only has the job of getting two completely different devices to talk to one another, it also has to keep them organized, coordinated, and synchronized. It is very much like the tasks that a coach for Little League baseball faces.

Simply establishing a connection requires several steps. The network first had to initiate a link with the other device. Next, it had to make sure it was alright for the client application requesting the services to actually receive them. After all, one of the chief concerns of the network is security. You don't want just anybody accessing critical company information or resources.

Once logon authentication was verified, the network began the process of hand-shaking. What kinds of services are really needed during this connection, how long are the machines going to talk, and who gets to talk first? Now, in order to assure that all the devices are understanding one another properly, the network must establish some rules for making sure the information that is sent and received is the same. The network will use sequence numbering and acknowledgments for that purpose.

While the data is being transferred, it is essential that both devices be properly synchronized. Therefore, throughout the session, the network is constantly asking, "Did you get that? Is it okay?" And once in a while, it needs to be able to say, "Slow down, you move too fast. Try to make the session last."

Once the data is moved, the network can finally "hang up the phone," so to speak. Even this process requires specific procedures. In the real world, you don't just slam the phone down in the boss's ear (if you want to keep your job, that is). You go through a series of wind-down statements, such as, "Well, that about wraps it up," and, "Hey, it was nice talking with you," and finally, "Goodbye, Mr. Rogers." Then you hang up. Under normal circumstances, computers try to do the same thing. They issue an SPDU indicating that it is time to close and then finally issue a Disconnect SPDU. And the Session Layer is finished.

BRAIN DRAIN

1. List as many functions of the Session Layer as you can.
2. Describe in detail the process of logon authentication.
3. Discuss the differences between a session and a dialogue.
4. Describe the process of releasing a connection, along with the conditions under which a release will occur.

THE 64K$ QUESTIONS

1. What is an individual service provided by the Session Layer called?
   a. A session entity
   b. A session service
   c. A primitive
   d. An SPDU

2. Session Layer service requests are passed from one device to another by way of _____.

   a. A session entity

   b. A session service

   c. A primitive

   d. An SPDU

3. All communications sessions require logon authentication to occur before data transfer can take place.

   a. True

   b. False

4. Which of the networking protocols does not make very much use of Connection IDs?

   a. TCP/IP

   b. NetBEUI

   c. AppleTalk

   d. IPX/SP

5. Which of the following Session Layer activities will result in a new Connection ID and acknowledgment numbering sequence?

   a. Synchronize minor

   b. Synchronize major

   c. Connection release

   d. Resynchronize

6. The purpose of checkpoints is to _____.

   a. Provide error correction

   b. Provide error detection

   c. Allow the retransmission of data to resume where it left off

   d. To provide a disconnection point for the session

7. What two events lead to an expected disconnect?

   a. A server reset

   b. The session duration has expired

   c. A negotiated release

   d. A system crash

8. A session, by definition, consists of a series of _____.
   a. Activities
   b. Events
   c. Dialogues
   d. Handshakes

9. In a half-duplex session, communications are controlled by the exchange of _____.
   a. SYNC packets
   b. Control headers
   c. Tokens
   d. Data payload

10. The Session Layer creates acknowledgment numbers using _____.
    a. The port number of the application requesting the services
    b. Sequential numbers, starting with the acknowledgment number of the last packet sent in the previous session
    c. A random number
    d. An algorithm similar to CRC

11. The Session Layer is responsible for _____.
    a. Adding a MAC address to the packet
    b. Breaking the user data down into smaller packages for transmission
    c. Deciding on the format of the data for transmission
    d. Providing dialogue management and synchronization

12. In order for a network session to be successful, the two communicating devices must own the physical connection until all data is transferred.
    a. True
    b. False

13. If a device has multiple connections set up with other devices it is said to be involved in a _____.
    a. Conference
    b. Dialogue
    c. Multi-session transfer
    d. Chat

14. A process or application that initiates a session with a remote computer is known as what?

    a. An entity

    b. A server

    c. A client

    d. An initiator

15. When the Session Layer needs to open communications with another device it initiates a request to the _____ Layer.

    a. Transport

    b. Network

    c. Data Link

    d. Physical

16. Even though the Session Layer is responsible for establishing and maintaining a session, logon authentication is actually a responsibility of the Network Layer.

    a. True

    b. False

17. The Connection ID consists of _____.

    a. The MAC address of the initiating computer

    b. The MAC address of the initiating computer plus a number from a consecutive sequence

    c. The IP address of the initiating computer plus a number from a consecutive sequence

    d. A randomly generated number

18. Which of the following protocols has little use for Connection IDs?

    a. NetBEUI

    b. IPX/SPX

    c. TCP/IP

    d. AppleTalk

19. The Acknowledgement Number consists of _____.

    a. The next number in a sequential list of numbers that begins with a randomly generated number

    b. The MAC address of the initiating computer

    c. The MAC address of the initiating computer plus a number from a consecutive sequence

    d The IP address of the initiating computer plus a number from a consecutive sequence

20. If a session has gotten so completely out of whack that it needs to be completely restarted, what will the Session Layer do?

    a. Close the application that initiated the session.

    b. Initiate a minor synchronization.

    c. Initiate a major synchronization.

    d. It can't do anything. Such an event will lock up the computer.

TRICKY TERMINOLOGY

Acknowledgment number: A sequence of numbers, beginning with a randomly generated number, that identifies each packet in a transmission and the order in which it goes.

Activity: The most basic transfer of information that occurs in the course of a session.

Connection ID: A randomly generated number that the server application assigns to each session to assure that data is kept together and in sequence.

Credentials: Users' logon IDs and passwords, along with the permissions they have been assigned.

Dialogue: The two-way transfer of data between devices, including control data used to maintain the session.

Handshaking: The process two devices go through in order to agree on protocols used, connection speeds, and a number of other issues.

Logon authentication: In this process, a user's logon ID and password are transferred to the host providing the requested service. It is compared to a security database, and if confirmed, the user is allowed in.

Process entity: The protocol or application on a host that is actually requesting or transmitting data during a network session.

Session: A virtual connection created between two devices for the purpose of transmitting data.

ACRONYM ALERT

SPDU: Service Protocol Data Unit. A small package of data used between OSI layers to request a specific service or activity.

CHAPTER 10

THE APPLICATION AND PRESENTATION LAYERS

The top two layers of the OSI model don't provide as much to talk about in terms of technical detail. Therefore, I will bundle the two layers into a single chapter. That is not to say, however, that the work these layers do is not important. As you will see, there are some pretty important functions going on at this level. A large number of protocols reside at these layers, and in terms of the TCP/IP and IPX protocols, I will reserve a detailed discussion for the appropriate chapters. The one piece of hardware (or in many cases, software) that functions in these layers is a gateway. Networking protocols that span the Application and Presentation Layers include:

- Network Terminal Protocol (Telnet): Provides text communication for remote login and communication across the network.
- File Transfer Protocol (FTP): Used to download and upload files across the network.
- Simple Mail Transfer Protocol (SMTP): Delivers electronic mail messages across the network.
- Post Office Protocol, Version 3 (POP-3): Allows users to pick up email across the network from a central server.
- Domain Name Service (DNS): Maps IP addresses to Internet domain names.
- HyperText Transfer Protocol (HTTP): The protocol used by the World Wide Web to exchange text, pictures, sounds, and other multimedia information via a graphical user interface (GUI).

- Routing Information Protocol (RIP): Used by network devices to exchange routing information.
- AppleShare (Apple): Allows Apple (Macintosh) clients to access data from a remote location or request services from server applications.

As with the Session Layer, the data flowing through these layers is referred to as a message. At this point in the data flow, the transmitting machine either has not yet segmented the data, or the receiving machine has already pieced it back together. Since I've been discussing the OSI model from the bottom to the top, I will continue in that fashion and begin this chapter with the Presentation Layer.

As with the Session Layer, there aren't many exam objectives covered in this chapter. But there is a substantial amount of advanced networking theory. The exam objectives I'll cover include:

2.2 Identify the seven layers of the OSI (Open Systems Interconnect) model and their functions.

2.3 Identify the OSI (Open Systems Interconnect) layers at which the following network components operate: Hubs, Switches, Bridges, Routers, NICs (Network Interface Card), WAPs (Wireless Access Point).

3.7 Given a connectivity scenario, determine the impact on network functionality of a particular security implementation (For example: port blocking/filtering, authentication and encryption).

THE PRESENTATION LAYER

The Presentation Layer is sometimes referred to as the "network translator." The primary responsibility of this layer is to place the data coming from the transmitting device into a bit pattern that the receiving device can comprehend. This is often referred to as the *data format*. Don't confuse data format with file format. While it is true that different file formats incorporate different data formats, the same file format going over two different networks may assume different data formats as well.

This is because other functions of the Presentation Layer include data compression, encryption, and the choice of charac-

> **BUZZ WORDS**
>
> **Data format:** The structure that data will assume as it is moved over the wire.
>
> **File format:** The structure data assumes while stored on the system.

OSI AND THE REST OF THE WORLD

Throughout this book, I've been treating OSI as though it were gospel. It should be noted that not all companies and organizations are all that attached to OSI. I mentioned previously that Cisco tends to walk its own path, but that it always provides a back door of support for non-Cisco technology by supporting OSI standard protocols. An example of a protocol that isn't 100 percent OSI is TCP/IP. As I will discuss in detail in Chapter Eleven, An Introduction to TCP/IP, the developers of this protocol follow a four-layer model. The Application, Session, and Presentation Layers are all incorporated into a single layer.

ter set used by the communicating devices. These factors all impact the bit pattern sent over the wire by the transmitting computer, and the receiving device must be in full agreement on all factors that went into creating this bit pattern. If not, the pattern cannot be interpreted correctly.

Therefore, to summarize, the Presentation Layer is going to be responsible for data encoding and data conversion. While the lower layers were responsible for making sure that data moved from point A to point B in an orderly fashion, the Presentation Layer is concerned with preserving the integrity of the payload as it makes its trip. To accomplish this, the Presentation Layer handles the following:

- File format
- Compression scheme
- Encryption scheme
- Character set

Likewise, there are certain functions of networking specific to the Presentation Layer. These functions are going to be discussed in detail in the next section. One thing you'll notice is that the concept of *syntax* will be mentioned a lot. Quite simply put, syntax refers to the bit order and structure of data, whether it resides on a host machine or is traveling over the medium. There will be a more detailed discussion of syntax later in this chapter.

EXAM NOTE: It's already been mentioned that you should be able to list all the responsibilities of each of the OSI layers. You should be able to list the function of each layer as well.

Functions of the Presentation Layer

As with the Session Layer, certain functions are either called by other layers or are used by the Presentation Layer to request services of adjacent layers. These functions include:

- Requesting the establishment of a session
- Negotiating and renegotiating syntax
- Transferring data
- Translating syntax including data encoding or encryption, formatting, and special-purpose transformations
- Requesting the termination of a session

In order to perform these functions, the Presentation Layer uses certain service primitives, similar to those I discussed in Chapter Nine, The Session Layer. Once again, it is not necessary to memorize all of these services, but since they are frequently referred to in the literature, it's a good idea to be familiar with the concepts. The service primitives are listed below.

- P-Activity-Discard
- P-Activity-End
- P-Activity-Interrupt
- P-Activity-Resume
- P-Activity-Start
- P-Alter-Context
- P-Capability-Data
- P-Connect
- P-Control-Give
- P-Data
- P-Expedited-Data
- P-P-Abort
- P-P-Exception-Report
- P-Release
- P-Resynchronize
- P-Sync-Major
- P-Sync-Minor
- P-Token-Give
- P-Token-Please
- P-Typed-Data
- P-U-Abort
- P-U-Exception-Report

In order to agree on specific transfer syntax, the Presentation Layer will issue a P-Connect primitive. Later on in the chapter, I will discuss the differences between the abstract and transfer syntaxes as well as the presentation context and the defined context set. P-Connect will establish an initial context set as well as a default context set.

During the transfer of data, either device can issue a P-Alter-Context request. This command will effectively renegotiate a new context set. If, for any reason, the two devices get out of synch with one another, either can issue a P-Resynchronize or a P-Abort. The P-Resynchronize attempts to get the existing session back on the right track, while P-Abort basically says, "To heck with this. I quit!"

Once the transfer of data is complete, the Presentation Layer can issue a P-Release. This notifies the Session Layer that all data has been transferred and that the session can be ended and broken down. The Presentation Layer has finished its assigned tasks.

FILE FORMAT AND COMPRESSION

The choice of file format is one of the first things that must be decided. It also dictates the compression scheme that will be used, so I'll discuss them together. Each type of data that a device can transmit can be transmitted in one of several different file formats. The fact of the matter is, something that appears to a human to be completely identical can have many different computer representations. For example, many of the images I created for this book existed in several formats before they finally reached the printed page.

The network diagrams were originally produced in Microsoft Visio. Visio uses a proprietary file format internally. However, in order to manipulate them and add additional elements, I moved the files over to PhotoDraw. The file format that maintained the highest quality that both programs could understand was a *bitmap* (.bmp) file. Once the image was finished in PhotoDraw, I found that I could "tweak" the images quite nicely in Adobe Photoshop. The final images were generally in the 5MB to 12MB range.

In order to get quick approval on any given image, I converted the image to a file format created by the *Joint Photographic Experts Group*, or JPEG file (.jpg). This compressed the images to a fraction of their original size, although with a rather drastic loss of quality. In the final phase of production, the final images were sent out as a *Tagged Image File Format* or TIFF file (.tif).

The fact that each of these files was of a different size is the best evidence I can offer that the packaging of data was different at each step along the way. Yet, regardless of what file format in which the image happened to exist at any moment in time, that picture of a star network was always the same picture of a star network.

The concept I'm discussing here has a name, and that name is syntax. You may recall that a few pages ago, I mentioned that a discussion of syntax was to follow.

Well, this is it. Here, I'm referring to the difference between *abstract syntax* and *transfer syntax.* Abstract syntax refers to the message type. Are you transferring a document, an image, or a sound clip? Each one of these is a unique form of message. And each one of these messages can be stored as one of several different file formats, or packages. The choice of file format used to move the data is the transfer syntax (see **Figure 10.1**).

BUZZ WORDS

Abstract syntax: The type of data that is to be moved or stored. For example, a music or video clip is one form of abstract syntax, while a text document is another.

Transfer syntax: The form that data will assume as it moves over the wire.

Since a large amount of data transfer involves multiple message types, that means that there will be multiple abstract syntaxes involved. For example, in a multimedia presentation going out over the wire, there will be audio, video, plain text, and protocol data, all of which are required to reassemble the presentation properly at the receiving end. In order to transfer such complex data, the Presentation Layer negotiates the specific transfer syntax for each abstract syntax involved. The complete package is called the *presentation context* and the collection of abstract and transfer syntaxes is the *defined context set.*

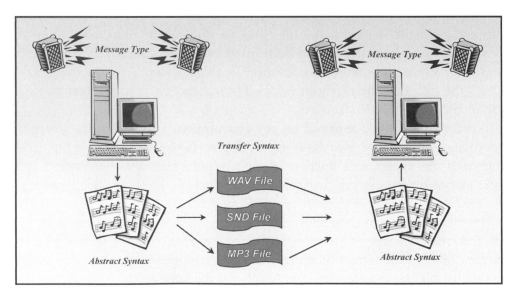

Figure 10.1 To the user, it's just music. However, moving that music from one computer to another involves several complex decisions.

In most cases, choice of a file format is made by the user, and that choice should be made carefully, considering all the ramifications. Different file formats were designed because the designers were trying to incorporate certain features. Features can include quality, initial file size, and degree of compression.

It is beyond the scope of this book to go into each of the file formats imposed by different message types, but in order to provide an intelligent discussion of the factors involved, I will describe some of the file formats used in the storage and transfer of images.

When images are first digitized they may appear in one of several formats. Photoshop generates a proprietary image with a .psd extension. These files are capable of storing data in multiple layers and each layer can be manipulated independently. The file format does not compress data either, so as you might imagine, file sizes can be quite large.

File compression is a major issue to consider. There are two types of compression, *lossy* and *lossless.* Lossless compression is preferred because, as its name implies, use of a lossless method results in no loss of quality. Lossy methods "throw away" a few pixels here and there in order to save space. Lossless methods include .tif and .bmp files. The most popular lossy methods are .gif and .jpg files.

EXAM NOTE: Be able to differentiate between lossy and lossless compression algorithms.

Figure 10.2 is a photograph I made with my digital camera while on vacation. (Don't laugh. I'm a network engineer and writer, not a photographer!) While stored in the camera, it occupied 820KB. When Photoshop imported the image from the camera, with no image manipulation whatsoever, it blossomed out to 2.5MB when converted to Photoshop's *.psd* format. Once I resized the image to 400dpi and a 7.5" x 10" size, I was working with a 35MB file! As a .tif file, it dropped down to 34.5MB. What a difference! A bitmap wasn't much better, coming in at just a hair under 34MB.

However, as a .gif, selecting the highest quality option, I brought that file down to 4.1MB and as a .jpg it was only 565KB. On the computer monitor, you couldn't

Figure 10.2 This library in Maine has nothing to do with networking. We're just using it to compare file sizes of different image formats and as an excuse to get one of my personal shots into the book.

tell the difference between them. Printed out on a 2400dpi color printer, the differences were obvious.

> **EXAM NOTE:** Be able to describe the difference between file format and data format.

Which one should I use? Obviously, the decision will be based on whether image size or image quality is the most critical factor. If the image is part of a Web page, then it will only be viewed on a computer monitor most if not all of the time. How quickly the image will load is the most significant issue, and that is solely based on image size. To reproduce the image on paper, image quality is more critical. However, not everyone uses the same applications to process his or her images, and not all image formats are compatible with all applications. So I chose my file format based on compatibility issues. You find a file format that both the sender and the receiver are capable of using.

Transfer syntax is negotiated by the communicating devices and is not under the control of the end user. Transfer syntax will be a mutually recognizable data package that either the transmitting device or the receiving device can translate into something useful to the local system. Compression at a file level is called *source encoding*. Using source encoding, you're not really transmitting an identical copy of the data, but rather an approximation of it.

> **BUZZ WORD**
>
> **Source encoding:** A file compression scheme that introduces compression onto the file itself, regardless of whether or not that file will be transmitted.

Not all data compression is done at the file level, however. Several different compression algorithms allow data to be compressed as it is sent over the wire. There are several methods for doing this. With the *Finite Set of Symbols* approach, a large set of data that is frequently accessed can be stored on both ends of the communications link. That "set of symbols" is assigned an arbitrary value, and any time you wish to refer to that data specifically, you use that symbol, rather than sending the entire data set. Libraries use this approach with ISBN numbers. They don't refer to title, author, and publisher every time they reference a certain book. Each book is assigned a unique number. While this is an admittedly simplified explanation, I think it clearly gets the idea across.

Another commonly used approach is called *run length encoding*. Data frequently consists of long strings of identical characters. A mathematical expression is used to indicate how many identical characters there are in a string, and the expression is transmitted, rather than the string itself.

DATA ENCRYPTION

Decisions concerning encryption aren't always based on a speed versus quality calculation. Sometimes data security is the main issue. For example, when you log on to your bank's server to do some on-line banking, you kind of like to think that nobody else is seeing everything that is going on and snagging your personal information. Once someone has your user name and password, he or she has your money. Chances are extremely good that person won't be using that information to pay your bills for you.

Therefore, certain protocols employ different schemes of *data encryption*. Data encryption occurs when one device scrambles the bit order of data before transmitting it, but the device on the other end has a key for putting the data back together in the correct bit sequence. While data encryption can also occur at the Network and Physical Layers in certain proprietary implementations, for the most part, it is the responsibility of the Presentation Layer.

> **EXAM NOTE:** While it won't be necessary on the exam to precisely define the algorithms used by DES to provide secure encryption, you will be expected to be able to identify the different encryption types and their limitations.

The three most commonly recognized encryption methods are *substitution cipher, transposition cipher,* and the *Data Encryption Standard* (DES). Substitution cipher and transposition cipher both work by simply reordering the sequence of characters before they move over the wire and then putting them back into the correct order at the other end.

Substitution cipher is simply substituting one letter (or ASCII character, as it were) for another. The simplest example I can give for substitution cipher is your computer keyboard. (For the purposes of simplicity, I will use only the alphabetic characters in this example.) Starting on your bottom row of keys and working right to left, bottom to top, substitute the letters of the alphabet for the order in which the keys are arranged (see **Figure 10.3**). Therefore, A B C D E F G H I J K L M N O P Q R S T U V W X Y Z, when encrypted could possibly become M N B V C X Z L K J H G F D S A P O I U Y T R E W Q. In which case, MY NAME, encrypted would be FW DMFC. For a dedicated hacker, this is a pretty easy code to break.

Transposition cipher works in a similar manner, except that is takes the characters that really exist in the text and reorders them. MY NAME could be NEM YAM. Or it could be YM EMAN, or any other transposition of characters the encoding scheme might use. As with substitution cipher, it is pretty easy to hack.

DES is the most secure of the encryption methods. In the original implementation, a 64-bit *key* is used. Or, to be more accurate, a 56-bit key is used, with 8 bits of parity for error correction while transmitting the key. This key determines the bit order (or *subkey*) into which data will be rearranged. The encryption software breaks the data down into 64-bit chunks, and the algorithm rearranges the block of data into the new bit order. What makes the process so powerful is the enormous number of subkeys that a 56-bit key can generate. To be precise, there are 72,057,594,037,927,936 of them.

To make the scheme even more difficult to break, a function called an *Exclusive Or-Gate* (EXOR) can be placed in the digital bit stream at various points along the way. The EXOR performs a mathematical calculation, effectively changing the 56-bit key that is being used.

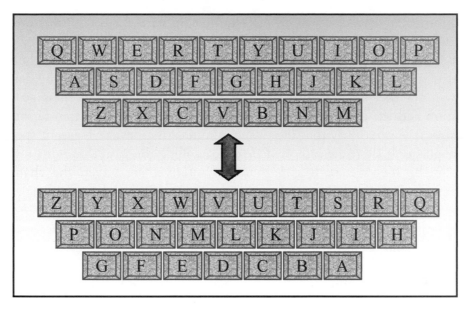

Figure 10.3 Substitution cipher is simply a matter of exchanging one character for another throughout the sequence. In this illustration, I'm only using the alphabetic keys. In an actual implementation, all keys would be used, and the substitutions would not be so orderly.

For DES to work, the systems must have a way of exchanging encryption keys. This is done at the beginning of the session. The EXOR occurs between sessions, which has the same effect of transferring a new key.

THE APPLICATION LAYER

The first rule to remember here is that the Application Layer is not the application that the user is running (usually). There are some exceptions to this that I'll take a look at, but for the most part, the Application Layer simply provides the door through which applications get their data onto the network. The purpose of the Application Layer is simply to take the user's data and convert it into a message that the lower layers are able to process.

The next rule to remember is that the applications running on the systems do not communicate directly with one another. If this was the case, only identical applications could exchange data. But as everyone knows, some people use Outlook for email, some use Outlook Express, and some use Lotus Notes. It isn't the application itself sending or receiving data, but rather a process running on that application.

When the technology of networking was in its infancy, long before the development of a standardized model, it was clear to everyone working in the field that there was a rather large chasm between the development of a message by an application and the process of turning it into electrical signals for transfer over the wire. Also, it is very likely that the two communicating devices may not speak the same language. If there are intermediate devices along the path that must intercept and relay the message, such as a router or intermediate server, the chances of programming language disparity becomes even more likely.

The Application Layer provides the services necessary for complete end-to-end communications between the source application and destination application.

When an end user either transmits data or requests another device to transmit data back, the application running on that user's machine will have to make several service requests. The application running on the other end that is responsible for responding to that request will somehow have to be notified that its services are required. Once all that has transpired, the network now has to find a form in which the data can be recognized by both systems.

In those dark ages of networking that I mentioned earlier, the most commonly used language of networking was 7-bit ASCII. This was something that pretty much every platform in existence could translate. It wasn't pretty, but it got the job done. These days, Application Layer protocols have been developed for moving just about every type of data imaginable.

Once the network has a mutually acceptable language, it now needs to establish a mutually acceptable set of rules for exchanging data. For both the purpose of data translation and the setting of rules, the network will make heavy use of protocols. The discussion of the Application Layer essentially becomes a discussion of protocols. For the purposes of Network+, there are specific protocols that need to be covered, and I have elected to cover these protocols in their specific chapters. For example, TCP/IP Protocols will be discussed in Chapter Thirteen, Using TCP/IP on the Network.

However, a brief description of the categories of Application Layer processes might be in order. These processes fall under the category of either a *Common Application-Specific Element* (CASE) or a *Specific Application-Specific Element* (SASE).

SASEs would be processes that would be called specifically by the programmer only when needed. Because these are application-specific processes and not used in every case, they are beyond the scope of this text and won't be covered.

IS IT AN APPLICATION OR IS IT A PROCESS?

Many people get confused when trying to understand the difference between a process and an application. It really isn't that difficult. An application is a program you run on a device in order to perform a certain task. As simple as that may sound, performing what appears to you to be a simple task may require the application to be able to perform a number of different functions. These individual functions are called *processes.*

A word processor is an example of an application. It exists solely for me, so that I can write this book. However, in the process of writing the book, a large number of different processes come into play. Formatting of characters, page formatting, pagination, and hundreds of other things users take for granted are accomplished automatically, compliments of the electronic magic of the computer.

When two applications communicate, it is not the entire application that talks, but rather the process or processes that require the exchange of information. You can see this concept at work if you run Windows 2000 or XP. Pressing Ctrl>Alt>Delete will bring up the Windows Security screen. At the bottom is a button called Task Manager. The middle tab of that screen is the Processes tab. With only one application running, take a look at all the different processes running. Some are specific to the OS and others relate to the application that you're running. Each one represents a string of code currently running on the system that either the OS or the application needs in order to function.

CASE processes are those whose services are likely to be required regardless of the type of communication in which the devices are engaged. Some examples of CASE are *association control* (ACSE); *reliable transfer* (RTSE); *remote operations* (ROSE); and *commitment, concurrency, and recovery* (CCR).

ACSE is the process by which two devices are able to establish and then subsequently terminate a logical connection between two communicating applications. As I mentioned before, two applications don't talk directly; two processes running on applications talk. ACSE is the Application Layer process that provides that link.

RTSE assures that the data moved from one device to another gets there safely and intact. This process relies heavily on services provided by the lower layers in order to perform its job completely.

ROSE is a process required by every network communications link. The whole concept of network computing is to manipulate data or programs that reside on another machine. In order to accomplish this, you must be able to execute *remote procedure calls* (RPC). ROSE is the process through which RPCs are generated.

CCR is the process by which a transaction is either finished or it never happened. (It was also an excellent rock band from the seventies.) You don't want your bank transaction to be half-finished now, do you? If there is a system failure between the time you punch in a request to withdraw money and the time the machine spits your money out, you would be really bummed to find out that there was no way to prove you didn't actually receive your cash. CCR is one of the processes that prevent this from happening.

CHAPTER SUMMARY

As you can see, not all of networking is concerned with traffic management and directional control. The whole reason you have a network is so that people (or devices) can communicate effectively. For that, you need to be able to generate messages, and those messages must be created in a manner that will be understood by the recipient of that message, and, in many cases, *only* the intended recipient and not any unexpected eavesdroppers.

The Presentation Layer provides all the tools needed for data compression and data formatting. It also gives you the ability to encrypt and subsequently decipher messages you don't want the outside world to hear.

The Application Layer is your program's key to the network. Any application that is network-aware has the ability to make remote procedure calls or do file system searches on devices on the other side of the world. It is through the services of the Application Layer that this is accomplished. Some of these services are used all the time, while others are incorporated into the applications, to be used as needed.

BRAIN DRAIN

1. List as many functions of the Presentation Layer as you can.
2. Discuss the difference between substitution cipher and transposition cipher in encryption.
3. Define in your own terms the difference between abstract syntax and transfer syntax.

4. How is the Application Layer different from the applications running on the system?

5. In as much detail as you can, describe how an application differs from a process.

THE 64K$ QUESTIONS

1. The arrangement of bits in a message as they are sent out over the wire is an example of _____.

    a. File format

    b. Data format

    c. Abstract syntax

    e. Transfer syntax

2. A JPEG file is an example of _____.

    a. Source encoding

    b. Transfer syntax

    c. Lossless compression

    d. Lossy compression

3. A data compression method that uses a mathematical expression to represent a long string of characters is _____.

    a. Source compression

    b. Run length encoding

    c. Manchester Encoding

    d. A finite set of symbols

4. An encryption method that takes the existing characters in a message and simply scrambles them into a different order is _____.

    a. Substitution cipher

    b. Transposition cipher

    c. Run length encoding

    d. DES encryption

5. A process in the Application Layer that is one frequently called on to perform is an example of a _____ process.

    a. CASE

    b. SASE

    c. Thread

    d. Common

6. SASE in a networking context stands for _____.

    a. Self-Addressed Stamped Envelope

    b. Specific Application-Specific Element

    c. Standard Algorithm for Strong Encryption

    d. Standards Association for Strong Encryption

7. A process is _____.

    a. An application running on a computer

    b. An exchange of packets between the transmitting device and the receiving device

    c. The hashing of data during encryption

    d. A thread of code from an application currently being run

8. The first version of DES encryption used a _____ -bit key.

    a. 56

    b. 64

    c. 112

    d. 128

9. Which of the following is **not** a compression scheme generated by the application creating the data?

    a. .jpg

    b. .mpeg

    c. .rll

    d. .gif

10. Which of the following are lossless compression methods? (Choose all that apply.)

    a. .tif

    b. .jpg

    c. .gif

    d. .psd

11. _____ is an example of an Application Layer protocol.

    a. SNMP

    b. Telnet

    c. JPEG

    d. ARP

12. _____ is an example of a Presentation Layer protocol.

    a. SNMP

    b. Telnet

    c. JPEG

    d. ARP

13. The reason it is possible to resume a broken session between computers is that the Presentation Layer places bookmarks into each packet.

    a. True

    b. False

14. The Presentation Layer is responsible for _____.

    a. Assuring that both communicating devices are using the same protocols

    b. Breaking data down into smaller chunks

    c. Preserving the integrity of the data payload

    d. Maintaining network security

15. When a user chooses to send a file over the network to another device, it is the responsibility of the _____ Layer to determine whether or not compression is used.

    a. Application

    b. Presentation

    d. Session

    e. Data Link

16. When data transfer is complete, the _____ Layer will issue a P-Release token.

    a. Application

    b. Presentation

    d. Session

    e. Data Link

17. One of the following is not a compressed image. Which one is it?

    a. .jpg

    b. .gif

    c. .pic

    d. .tif

18. _____ is a good example of presentation context.

    a. Compression level

    b. Encryption key

    c. Character set

    d. Communications protocol

19. Which of the following file formats uses lossy compression?

    a. PSD

    b. TIF

    c. JPG

    d. None of the above

20. Data encryption is a function of the Presentation Layer.

    a. True

    b. False

TRICKY TERMINOLOGY

Abstract syntax: The type of data that is to be moved or stored. For instance, a music or video clip is one form of abstract syntax, while a text document is another.

Data format: The structure that your data will assume as it is moved over the wire.

Defined context set: The complete set of transfer syntaxes used in the transfer of data along with the abstract syntaxes to which they are associated.

File format: The structure your data assumes while stored on the system.

Presentation context: The collection of syntaxes that will be used to move data during a session.

Source encoding: A file compression scheme that introduces compression onto the file itself, regardless of whether or not that file will be transmitted.

Transfer syntax: The form that data will assume as it moves over the wire.

ACRONYM ALERT

ACSE: Association Control Specific Element. The Application Layer process that keeps track of the logical connection between two communicating applications.

CASE: Common Application-Specific Element. An Application Layer process that is required of most, if not all, transfers of data.

CCR: Commitment, Concurrency, and Recovery. An Application Layer process that makes sure that once a transaction begins, it is either completed or discarded if not complete.

DES: Data Encryption Standards. A secure set of methods by which data can be securely encoded on one side and decoded on the other.

JPEG: Joint Photographic Experts Group. An organization that developed compression techniques for digital graphic images.

ROSE: Remote Operation Specific Element. The Application Layer process that provides for remote procedure calls when necessary.

RPC: Remote Procedure Call. The request for services that a system will present when it requires support of nonlocal resources.

RTSE: Reliable Transfer Specific Element. The Application Layer process that makes sure the data that arrives is the same data that was sent.

SASE: Specific Application-Specific Element. An Application Layer process that is used only in certain circumstances and will be called by the program or protocol when needed.

PART THREE

THE NETWORKING PROTOCOLS

CHAPTER 11

AN INTRODUCTION TO TCP/IP

In this chapter, I'll begin taking a look at the various networking protocols. As you may have deduced from the chapter title, I will begin with the *Transmission Control Protocol/Internet Protocol* (TCP/IP). As you will learn, this isn't actually a single protocol, but rather a growing collection of protocols and utilities. TCP is the oldest of the protocols in this suite, whereas IP came along several years later.

In so much as this particular protocol is likely to take up a large portion of your professional life for the next several years, I will be devoting two chapters to this particular subject. This chapter will cover the origins of the protocol along with its structure. I will introduce the major TCP/IP protocols and utilities, but I won't go into much detail on the utilities until Chapter Twelve, Using TCP/IP on the Network.

This particular chapter is rich in exam material. Readers interested in passing the Network+ exam should pay particular attention to the material contained within. Exam objectives covered in this chapter include:

2.4 Differentiate between network protocols in terms of routing, addressing schemes, interoperability and naming conventions.

2.5 Identify the components and structure of IP (Internet Protocol) addresses (IPv4, IPv6) and the required setting for connections across the Internet.

2.6 Identify classful IP (Internet Protocol) ranges and their subnet masks (For example: Class A, B and C).

2.7 Identify the purpose of subnetting..

2.8 Identify the differences between private and public network addressing schemes.

2.9 Identify and differentiate between the following IP (Internet Protocol) addressing methods: Static, Dynamic, Self-assigned.

2.10 Define the purpose, function and use of protocols used in the TCP/IP (Transmission Control Protocol/Internet Protocol) suite.

2.13 Identify the purpose of network services and protocols.

TCP/IP'S ILLUSTRIOUS BACKGROUND

TCP got its start in the early sixties when Leonard Kleinrock published a paper called *Information Flow in Large Communication Nets*. As you shall see in Chapter Twenty, Navigating the Internet, that paper got the ball rolling for a government agency known as the *Defense Advanced Research Projects Agency* (DARPA).

EXAM NOTE: While it may not seem like much of a technical issue to you, be prepared to identify what DARPA and ARPANet are.

In 1974, using Kleinrock's paper as a springboard, Vincent Cerf and Robert Kahn copublished a paper entitled *A Protocol for Packet Network Intercommunication*. In this paper, they defined methods by which large files could be broken down into smaller chunks and sent out over an electrical signal. (Having just spent the last several chapters going over this entire process, by now you should have a pretty good idea about what they had in mind.) In those days, there was absolutely no attempt by any computer manufacturer to maintain any sense of compatibility with one another. Therefore, the concept was based around the idea that in most circumstances, the two communicating devices would be unable to communicate directly. Thus was born the Transmission Control Protocol (TCP).

The Internet Protocol (IP) came along a few years later. Its official date of birth should probably be listed as 1981, although it had been around in a couple of incarnations prior to that. It was in September 1981 that RFC 791, *Internet Protocol: DARPA Internet Program Protocol Specification*, was released. It was actually the offshoot of something known as the Host Access Protocol that DARPA had used to patch together its first endeavor in internetworking, the ARPANet.

IP is the protocol that allows two devices to communicate with one another when they reside on completely different networks. TCP could do an end-to-end transfer of data between two devices that were directly linked. However, once data had to "turn the corner," so to speak, the packets were lost. IP solves that problem.

TCP/IP protocols go through a strict regimen of development. They all begin life as a *Request for Comment* (RFC). Any individuals or organizations that have a new protocol they want to introduce, or a revision of an old one, submits an RFC to *The Internet Engineering Task Force* (IETF). This becomes a draft. Before any RFC will ever be released as a protocol or utility, it will undergo a battery of reviews and tests in an experimental environment. Once it has been deemed acceptable, another RFC will be issued that strictly defines this new protocol or utility.

Old RFCs never die. If a protocol undergoes a modification, the most recent RFC obsoletes all previous RFCs. This provides a mechanism by which the evolution of any particular protocol can be traced. RFCs may be reviewed on IETF's Web site at www.ietf.org.

TCP/IP vs. OSI

I spent several chapters talking about the OSI model and how it was developed as a layered model. TCP/IP was developed as a layered model as well. However, instead of seven layers, TCP/IP incorporates only four layers. These layers are:

- Process/Application
- Host to Host
- Internet
- Network Access

EXAM NOTE: The TCP/IP layers don't get hit as heavily as OSI on the exam, but they are covered, and you need to be prepared to answer questions surrounding this topic.

Before you get overly upset about having to learn a whole new set of layers just because two organizations couldn't see eye to eye, let me assure you of something. The layers of TCP/IP correspond very nicely to the layers of OSI. The Process/Application Layer maps to the top three OSI layers. Host to Host maps directly to the Transport Layer. The Internet Layer of TCP/IP maps directly to the Network Layer while the Network Access Layer of TCP/IP spans the Data Link and Physical Layers of OSI. **Figure 11.1** illustrates the relationship between TCP/IP and OSI. Later on in the chapter, I'll show you how the TCP/IP protocols and utilities fit into these layers.

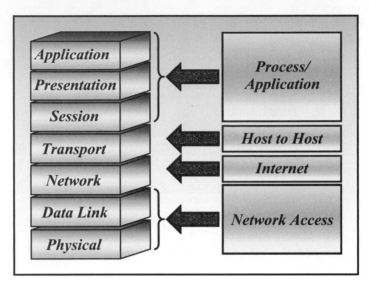

Figure 11.1 The layers of TCP/IP as they correspond to OSI.

THE BASICS OF IP ADDRESSING

IP can find hosts across multiple networks by way of a logical address that is assigned to each host. In the first several revisions of the protocol, this has always been a 32-bit address. (Later in the chapter, I will take a look at IPv6, which makes use of a 128-bit address.) Our 32-bit number actually consists of four bytes of data. Each byte is represented by its decimal value (see **Figure 11.2**). That's a good thing, because most of us would have a very difficult time trying to remember an address that consisted of a series of thirty-two 0s and 1s. Now here's where it gets confusing to many beginners. This decimal value is a one- to three-digit number, because it has been translated into decimal. However, because each of these numbers repre-sents the eight bits of a single byte, they are called *octets*. A typical IP address prior to IPv6 consists of four octets.

This address is broken down into two portions. The first part of this 32-bit value represents the network address on which the host resides. Instead of having to lo-cate the physical address of any given de-vice during a communication session, all IP really has to do is find the network on

> **BUZZ WORD**
>
> **Octet:** Any collection of eight bits. In the context of TCP/IP, it represents one of the four sections of an IP address, which will be represented by one to three decimal characters.

274

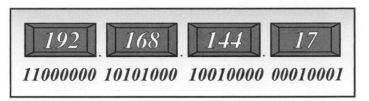

Figure 11.2 An IP address is a cluster of numbers that looks like the ones on top. But they represent a binary value that looks like the one on the bottom.

which that device resides. Once a packet has been delivered to the appropriate network, that network can find the device by way of the host portion of the address.

So how does any given device know how to tell which part of an IP address is network and which part is host? Another value assigned to any device running TCP/IP is the *subnet mask*. A subnet mask "hides" the network address behind 1s. But before that can make any sense, I have to give you a closer look at the structure of an IP address.

> **BUZZ WORD**
>
> **Subnet mask:** An entry into the TCP/IP configuration, formatted similarly to an IP address. This is a 32-bit value that defines which portion of the address is network and which portion is host.

As I said before, the numbers you see in an IP address are the decimal alliteration of a binary number. However, humans don't speak binary, only programmers do. To make it easier for the average person to remember an IP address long enough to write it down, that series of bits gets converted into a decimal number. Likewise, the subnet mask is a series of 1s that represents which part of the actual IP address is network and a series of 0s that represents which part is host. **Figure 11.3** illustrates the relationship between the IP address and the subnet mask.

There are actually five different *classes* of IP address defined. These are Class A, Class B, Class C, Class D, and Class E. The first three classes of IP address, Classes A, B, and C, represent network classes that network administrators can use in configuring networks. Class D is the home of multicast addresses, and Class E addresses are experimental addresses. Each class of address gives us a different number of networks and a different number of hosts, dependent on how many bits of that 32-bit address have been assigned to the network address and how many have been assigned to the host address.

EXAM NOTE: Learn all you can about the different classes of IP address. This will show up in a number of different ways on the exam.

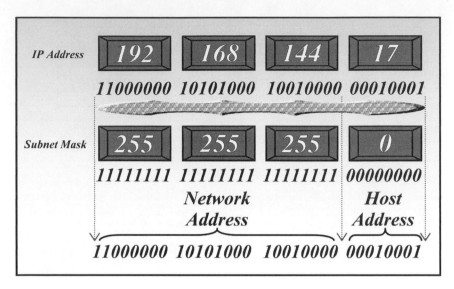

IP Address

192 168 144 17

11000000 10101000 10010000 00010001

Subnet Mask

255 255 255 0

11111111 11111111 11111111 00000000

Network Address   *Host Address*

11000000 10101000 10010000 00010001

Figure 11.3 The subnet mask uses 1s to isolate the network portion of the IP address from the host portion.

In a Class A address, the first octet represents the network address and the second represents the host portion. A Class B address is divided down the middle, two octets for network and two for host. The Class C address provides three for network and one for host. Other characteristics of the individual classes will be covered in more detail in the next section of this chapter, but for now, I mention them to make a point.

The number of bits available for either host or network address determines how many hosts or networks a particular class of address supports. In a Class B address, 16 bits are assigned to the network portion and 16 bits are assigned to the host portion. So how many networks and how many hosts can be configured in a Class B address?

This can be determined by a simple formula: $2^x-2=y$, where X equals the number of bits available for hosts or networks and Y equals the number of hosts or networks available.

For example, in class B addresses, there are 16 bits available for both host and network. $2^{16} = 65,536$. Subtract two and you're left with 65,534. Therefore, in a Class B address, there are a total of 65,534 possible networks with up to 65,534 hosts on each network.

This is further complicated by the fact that the network portion of a Class B address must start with 10. As a result of the required 0, there are actually only 49, 149 total addresses available.

EXAM NOTE: Know this formula. You will be asked to calculate how many hosts or networks are possible in a given scenario.

Of course, by now, you might be asking, "Why did you subtract two? Why isn't it just 2^x?" The answer to that question lies in two simple rules of IP addressing. The first is that you can have no network or host address that consists of all 0s. The second is that you can have no network or host address that consists of all 1s. An address of all 0s is the address of the network itself, or as many call it, the address of the wire. An address of all 1s is a broadcast to all hosts on the network. Therefore, you must subtract those two possibilities from your values.

ADDRESS CLASSES

I mentioned earlier that each class of address provides for a different number of networks and addresses. However, there are some other details about each class that you're going to need to understand if you expect to understand TCP/IP. For one thing, there are those other two address classes I didn't mention. Second, there are the usual bureaucratic mazes you need to negotiate. In other words, there are certain rules concerning IP addressing that are strictly enforced.

CLASS A ADDRESSES

In Chapter Seven, The Data Link Layer, I introduced the different classes of IP address. But to briefly review: In the Class A address, the first octet represents the network address while the last three octets represent hosts. As a result, there are a relatively small number of possible networks, but each network supports a vast number of hosts.

Of this small number of network address, not all were cleared by Internic for distribution. For example, 127.0.0.1 will always be the loop-back address to your specific interface. Also, all IP addresses starting with 10 are reserved for private networks. As you shall see, those responsible for administering IP addresses did remember that there was a public out there along with all the corporations and organizations. Therefore only 125 Class A networks were ever available for assignment. As you might imagine, those were assigned to extremely large organizations early on.

The default Class A subnet mask is 255.0.0.0 (see **Figure 11.4**).

EXAM NOTE: Be able to associate the proper default subnet masks to the address classes to which they belong.

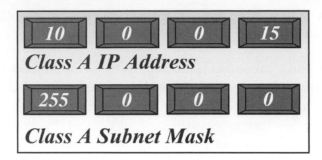

Figure 11.4 A default Class A IP address and its associated subnet mask.

Figure 11.5 A default Class B IP address and its associated subnet mask.

CLASS B ADDRESSES

Class B addresses use the first two octets for the network address and the last two for a host address. As a result you could almost believe that you would have 65,534 networks, each of which could have over 65,534 hosts. However, you would believe wrong. All Class B addresses must start with 10 as their first two bits. Losing that second bit limits you to a total of 49,149 network addresses, with 65,534 possible hosts on each.

Another result of that required 0 is that the network address will always start in the range of 128 to 191. All addresses starting with 128 are reserved for experimental purposes. As with Class A addresses, a certain range of Class B addresses was reserved for use in private networks. All addresses between 172.16.0.0 and 172.31.255.255 are set aside for private use. They will not be assigned to any one person or organization.

A Class B default subnet mask is 255.255.0.0 (see **Figure 11.5**).

Figure 11.6   A default Class C IP address and its associated subnet mask.

CLASS C ADDRESSES

The first three octets identify the network and the last octet identifies host addresses. The first three bits must start with 110; therefore, there are 14,626,333 possible networks of only 254 users on each network. The range of possible addresses goes from 192 to 223. As with all the other address classes, there was a range assigned for private usage. This range is 192.168.0.0 to 192.168.255.255.

A Class C default subnet mask is 255.255.255.0 (see **Figure 11.6**).

CLASS D, CLASS E, AND BROADCAST ADDRESSES

Class D addresses are used by applications and protocols for the purpose of multicast addressing. The first four bits are 1110 and Class D addresses range from 224.0.0.1 to 239.255.255.254. Class D addresses require no subnet mask and are dynamically allocated by the application or protocol that is using the address.

Class E addresses begin with the bits 11110, giving them a range of 240.0.0.1 to 255.255.255.254. For the most part, Class E addresses are considered either reserved or for experimental use only. Since Class E addresses are not useable by the public they don't draw a lot of attention. However, you should be aware that they account for 268,435,456, or a little over six percent, of total IP addresses available in IPv4.

> **EXAM NOTE:** One little tip about the starting bits of the different address classes is this: The first bit of a Class A address is a leading 0. Then that 0 moves one position to the right with each subsequent class.

One address that falls under no category but gets a lot of airplay is 255.255.255.255. It's not technically a Class E address, because it is a binary value of all 1s. This is a general broadcast to "all hosts."

THE TCP/IP PROTOCOL SUITE

Throughout this book, I've mentioned several times that protocols exist as suites. In other words, no single protocol stands alone. It has many friends to keep it company. TCP/IP is one of the larger suites and there are many protocols that make up the entire set. There are, in fact, far more protocols than can be readily discussed in an introduction to TCP/IP. Therefore, for the purposes of this discussion I will limit my discussion to the following protocols:

- FTP/TFTP
- HTTP/HTTPS
- Telnet
- SMTP/POP
- SNMP
- IMAP4
- NFS
- TCP

- UDP
- DNS
- IP
- BootP
- DHCP
- ICMP
- ARP/RARP

The list above is not sorted according to importance or frequency of use. Instead, I have chosen to discuss the protocols as they relate to the relative TCP/IP layer in which they reside. All TCP/IP protocols reside in the Process/Application, Host to Host, or Internet Layers of TCP/IP. I won't discuss any of the protocols residing in the Network Access Layer, since those protocols were discussed in Chapter Five, The Physical Layer, and Chapter Six, The Data Link Layer.

> **EXAM NOTE:** Be prepared to describe the purpose and function of each of the TCP/IP protocols that follow. This is an area that is heavily covered on the exam.

PROCESS/APPLICATION PROTOCOLS

The Process/Application protocols are generally those that provide some level of direct support to the end user. That is not to say that the other layers do not help the user accomplish whatever it is he or she is doing. These are simply the protocols with which the user can directly interact. They include:

- FTP/TFTP
- HTTP/HTTPS
- Telnet
- SMTP/POP

- IMAP4
- SNMP
- NFS

Most of the Process/Application protocols are associated with some form of front-end utility or application with which the user interfaces. Then the protocol does the work.

FTP AND TFTP

The *File Transport Protocol* (FTP) and the *Trivial File Transport Protocol* (TFTP) are actually two separate protocols. However, their functions are so similar that it easier to understand them if I discuss them together and simply emphasize the differences between them. FTP is a connection-oriented protocol designed for the purpose of transferring files over a network (see **Figure 11.7**). TFTP is also designed for this same purpose; however, it is a connectionless protocol and is primarily targeted at

Figure 11.7 FTP is a command line utility that requires a good knowledge of the available commands to be useful.

moving smaller files. Sometimes a file is so small that it fits into a single packet. In this case, the overhead required by maintaining a connection is unnecessary.

FTP is a venerable old protocol that has undergone many evolutionary forms over the years. It began life at MIT as a method for moving data between hosts in a direct link connection. As technology advanced, so did FTP. While there were RFCs that existed earlier related to the protocol, I think it is safe to say that it officially became known as FTP in RFC 172. It officially became a protocol in 1973 as described in RFC 454.

> **EXAM NOTE:** Know the default ports of each of the TCP/IP protocols discussed in this chapter.

FTP is a command-line protocol that supports a limited number of commands. In order to use it, you must have ports 20 and 21 open on your machine. Port 20 handles the transfer of data, while control information is exchanged over port 21. For FTP to work, there must be an FTP client and an FTP server. Technically speaking, no special software is required for either role. Simply having TCP/IP installed as a protocol provides the services. However, setting up a dedicated FTP server with controlled access requires something a bit more sophisticated. Likewise, unless you intimately know the structure of the device with which you're communicating, an FTP client might be in order as well. However, as long as connections can be made, FTP supports a number of commands. While I won't be covering all the commands FTP supports, the key ones are briefly described in the following list. The command is in bold-face and additional syntax follows in italics.

- **ftp** *dest.host.address* or **ftp** *xxx.xxx.xxx.xxx* – Establishes a connection between your machine and the host with which you wish to communicate. As the syntax suggests, the address can be either a domain name (as long as DNS services are available) or an IP address. When a connection is established you will be prompted for a user name and password.
- **quit** – Closes the FTP client as well as the FTP session.
- **close** – Closes an FTP session but does not close the client.
- **get** *file.name* – Initiates a download of the selected file. In order to use this command you must know the entire path to the file on the remote machine.
- **put** *file.name* – Uploads the selected file from your system to the remote system. Note that you must be logged into the desired directory on the remote machine.
- **mkdir** *dirname* – Creates a directory of that name on the remote machine.
- **cd** *dirname* – Changes to the selected directory on the remote machine.

- **dir** *selected/direct* – Lists the contents of the selected directory.
- **ls** – Lists the contents of the current directory on the remote machine.
- **bye** – Closes the FTP session and application.
- **ascii** – Sets the data transfer mode to ASCII. Transfers 7-bit characters and is used to transfer ASCII text files. This is the default mode.
- **binary** – Sets the data transfer mode to binary. Transfers 8-bit characters. Since this is the most accurate method, this should be selected whenever moving any file other than an ASCII text file.

Unlike FTP, TFTP does not have a command line interface on most conventional operating systems. You will, however, see it used by Cisco products to move configuration settings to a remote server.

HTTP AND HTTPS

The *HyperText Transfer Protocol* (HTTP) could effectively be called the protocol of the Internet. HTTP was designed for distributing and collecting *hypermedia* over a network. However, it should be noted that files other than hypermedia are supported as well. Just about any resource located on the World Wide Web can be managed by HTTP. HTTP moves its data over port 80.

So what is hypermedia, anyway? Any form of communication that allows a dynamic link to another location qualifies as hypermedia. Any time you include a link to an email address or Web site in the email you send to your boss, you've created hypermedia. All Web pages are hypermedia whether they include additional links or not. They must be accessed from outside sources and they must provide a facility for exiting or going back to the previous location.

An HTTP transaction works in client-server mode. A device requesting access to a resource on the network makes a request. Once the server is found, it either fulfills or denies that request. In either case, once a request has been made and acknowledgment sent by the server, the session is ended.

EXAM NOTE: Be able to describe the differences between HTTP and HTPPS, including how HTTPS provides additional layers of security.

HTTPS is the *Secure HyperText Transfer Protocol.* Connections implementing HTTPS will set up communications using

BUZZ WORD —————

Hypermedia: Any resource on the network or local system that can automatically redirect the user to another resource simply by clicking on a link.

a protocol known as *Secure Socket Layers* (SSL). SSL provides a mechanism for encrypting HTTPS transmissions. For HTTPS to function properly, there must be a secured server providing the services. In general, the transition from HTTP to HTTPS is transparent to the user, save for one major difference. The user will have to log on to the secure server as a separate procedure from logging onto the Internet.

NETWORK NEWS TRANSFER PROTOCOL

The Network News Transfer Protocol (NNTP) allows for the distribution, retrieval, and posting of news articles with a relable stream-based transmission over the Internet. News articles are stored in a central database and distributed selectively. This allows subscribers to select only those items they wish to read. It also allows service providers to provide articles only to paying subscribers.

NNTP is designed so that subscribers can either search the database for information on an as-needed basis, or they can received periodic email broadcasts of "issues," similar to a subscription to the morning paper. The protocol provides indexing, cross-referencing, and expiration services for all information stored.

TELNET

Telnet is a protocol that provides the facilities for performing a remote logon to a remote device over the Internet. Once logon has been established, each communicating device becomes a *Network Virtual Terminal* (NVT). User data does not actually move from device to device in a Telnet connection. The user is manipulating the selected device remotely and the data is staying put. What *is* moving is keyboard and display information. There are a number of terminal emulation modes that Telnet supports, and both devices must be in agreement. Once you make a connection to the remote device and your logon has been accepted, you will be logged onto the network as though you were on the LAN (see **Figure 11.8**). Telnet requires access to port 23.

SMTP AND POP

Simple Mail Transfer Protocol (SMTP) and the *Post Office Protocol* (POP) are the two protocols for sending and receiving email messages. Without these protocols, our lives wouldn't be the same. SMTP is used for sending messages out over port 25. POP is used for distributing messages and requires the services of port 110. The version of POP currently in use is POP3. Should you have an older application that supports the older POP2, that protocol operates on port 109.

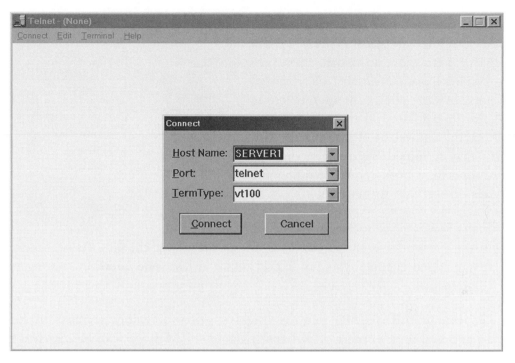

Figure 11.8 Bringing up a Telnet session for the first time gives you a screen like this. Once you're on, it will be no different than a normal session on the remote device.

In an SMTP exchange, the mail is treated nearly as it would by conventional postal services. There is a package of data that the sender wants to get into the possession of the recipient. Therefore, there must be a mailing address and a return address. However, there is a pretty significant difference between how a network treats mail and how the Post Office treats it. When you first transmit an email, your system sends out the addresses of the intended recipients along with your address. Once you are validated as a user, the server will then request the contents of the message.

Once the message has been sent, it is up to the POP protocol to make sure it gets into the right hands (or device, as it were). Currently, most networks use version three of this protocol, or more simply, POP3. POP allows the client to retrieve its messages from the POP server. POP servers can be either local or remote. An example of a local POP server would be either a Microsoft Exchange server or a Lotus Notes server. If you use Internet email, you use a remote POP server located at your ISP's location.

IMAP4

The *Internet Message Access Protocol, Version 4* (IMAP4) is a more up-to-date email protocol that supports a number of advanced features. IMAP4 allows the user to create and maintain folders on the remote server that are the equivalent of mailboxes. With POP, that is something that can only be done on a local host. IMAP4 requires the services of port 220 to function.

> **BUZZ WORDS**
>
> **Manager:** In TCP/IP terminology, this is an application or utility that initiates requests for information to be gathered.
>
> **Agent:** In TCP/IP terminology, this is an application or utility that fulfills requests by gathering the information requested by a manager application.

EXAM NOTE: The inclusion of IMAP in the Network+ exam objectives is one of the newer changes. As with other newly added changes, you can expect to see at least one question relating to this protocol.

On top of this, IMAP4 permits users to perform remote searches in their messages based on a number of different parameters. Messages can be searched on the basis of the text they contain, certain attributes of the message (such as whether or not the message had been read or the priority of the message), and a number of other different possibilities.

Like POP, IMAP is a protocol for retrieving messages. Transmitting a message under IMAP4 still requires the services of SMTP.

SNMP

Properly used, the *Simple Network Management Protocol* (SNMP) can be a boon to network engineers. To use SNMP, you'll need a *manager* and an *agent.* The manager provides an interface through which the network administrator can perform his or her magic. The agent is the object on the network being managed. An agent can be a device, a piece of software, or simply a statistic the administrator is gathering. Generally, however, there will be a specific target device or process that is being manipulated or observed. SNMP relies on ports 161 and 162 in order to function.

Managers and agents both must have the SNMP protocol installed and implemented in its entirety. There is not one set of specifications for a manager application and another for an agent. The differences in how they behave are rather important though.

A computer running a manager application or utility becomes a *network management station.* Once an administrator has defined the task at hand the responsibility of the manager is to send queries to the various agents, then subsequently monitor and store their responses. Managers can also be configured to send queries and monitor responses over an extended period of time.

The job of the agent is to collect the information requested by the manager and make it available when requested by the manager. However, for certain types of queries, the agent doesn't wait around for the manager to ask for its input. A typical agent can be configured to send updates and critical alerts whenever they become available.

The way the SNMP protocol works is that an administrator identifies the target information to be collected, along with the agents that should do the collecting. This information is either stored in a file until requested by the management software, or acted upon immediately, if the agent has been configured to send updates and/or alerts. The manager collects the information it gathers into a *management information base* (MIB). When a network administrator wants a report, it is a simple matter of opening the SNMP manager and making the appropriate queries.

The beauty of SNMP is that it is simple, just like its name claims. It requires very little code to implement, and therefore, every current server application has at least a rudimentary network management implementation. More advanced and very sophisticated SNMP platforms are available from several vendors, including Hewlett Packard, Microsoft, and IBM, among others.

NFS

The *Network File System* (NFS) is one of those protocols that everybody uses and nobody thinks about. Sun Microsystems first developed this protocol back in the early 1980s to simplify remote access to files over a network. This protocol solves a critical problem. How does your local machine keep track of where individual files are located on a remote machine?

Your machine does this on its own local hard drives through the file allocation tables stored on the drives. On CD-ROM drives, files are located through the table of contents. However, the network may consist of hundreds or even thousands of different machines that contain accessible files. Your machine needs some method of locating and accessing these files. In addition, the network needs to make sure that multiple users cannot have the same file open at once. Were this to happen, data corruption would be almost inevitable. Tracking and maintaining permissions is another primary task of NFS.

THE HOST-TO-HOST PROTOCOLS

The Host to Host protocols are the ones that make sure your data gets where it is supposed to be, and that it gets there in the same condition as you sent it. Keep in mind that the TCP/IP Host to Host Layer performs all of the same functions as OSI's Transport Layer. Therefore, you can assume that the protocols of this layer are responsible for transport functions.

The three main protocols that I will discuss in this section are TCP, the *User Datagram Protocol* (UDP), and *Domain Name System* (DNS). Each of these protocols takes a different approach to getting data from one host to another on a network.

TCP

The *Transmission Control Protocol* is the grand master of all the TCP/IP protocols. TCP started it all. It is the protocol that orchestrates the movement of data across the wire. In early implementations, it was simply a host-to-host data transfer mechanism. However, the concept of internetworking came into the picture, and the protocol could no longer stand alone.

As a protocol, TCP is connection-oriented. It requires a virtual connection and relies on the acknowledgement of each packet sent in order to insure reliability of transmission. In order to accomplish this function, TCP has the following responsibilities:

- Logical connection maintenance
- Data transfer
- Multiplexing
- Flow control
- Reliability

I'm not going to rehash how each of these functions is accomplished in this chapter. This was discussed in detail in Chapter Eight, The Transport Layer. But for the purposes of the exam, please be aware of these responsibilities.

UDP

The *User Datagram Protocol* (UDP) is a simplified, scaled-down version of TCP. UDP is a connectionless protocol. It maintains no virtual link between hosts and does not make use of acknowledgments. The data either gets there or it doesn't. Flow control and error recovery are not a part of this protocol. If these services are required, they must be provided by the application itself.

It may not sound like UDP is all that desirable of a protocol. However, that is not the case. Certain functions that send data in small packages don't need the additional overhead imposed by a connection-oriented protocol. Likewise, the network doesn't want acknowledgments of every broadcast propagated by every device on the network cluttering up bandwidth. Therefore, many other protocols make use of UDP's services to perform their own functions. These include SNMP, TFTP, DNS, NFS, and several others.

DNS

The Internet has made everyone at least partially cognizant of the *Domain Name System* (DNS). An Internet address such as http://www.delmar.com doesn't bother anyone in the least. It is how people find the Web sites they're looking for. However, to your computer system, DNS isn't just a fancy name for a Web site. It is a way of locating resources outside of your own physical network and making them available.

> **BUZZ WORD**
>
> **Fully qualified domain name:** An identification of an internet location that completely describes the path to that location, including the root domain, the top-level domain, and all subdomains.

EXAM NOTE: Be prepared to completely dissect a fully qualified domain name and identify the level of each component and its relative importance.

DNS performs this feat by translating domain names into IP addresses. A DNS server maintains a huge database of these translations, and when a client wants to locate a resource, the DNS server looks it up and provides the client with an IP address for its communications.

To understand how this all works, you must first understand the structure of a domain name. Domain names are built on a *hierarchical model.* There is a base level from which all domain names begin, and then they develop from that base point. That base point is a simple dot. This points to the DNS root of the domain name in question. Let's take that Web site I gave you earlier as an example, http://www.delmar.com. This is an example of a *fully qualified domain name.*

This domain name begins with the dot between "delmar" and "com". This dot represents the *root domain*, and the root domain is under the watchful eye of IANA. This dot points the server to one of the several established *top-level domains.* Top-level domains will fall under one of three categories:

- Country code domains: These provide the basic information for top-level domains of individual countries, such as *.us, .uk, .jp*, and so forth.

- Generic domains: The current list of generic top-level domains includes *.aero, .biz, .com, .coop, .edu, .gov, .info, .int, .mil, .museum, .name, .net, .org,* and *.pro.*

- Infrastructure domain: *.arpa.* This is the *Address and Routing Parameter Area* domain and is used exclusively by IANA and those who administer the technical end of the Internet.

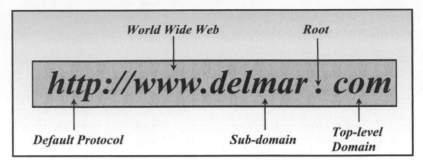

Figure 11.9 The structure of a fully qualified domain name.

So, in the http://www.delmar.com domain name, the *.com* indicates the top-level domain. For every top-level domain, there will be a primary root server that maintains a database of every registered domain name in its class. The word "delmar" points DNS to the correct subdomain. This is the working territory of the organization that registered the domain to begin with. It points DNS to the server that hosts Delmar's Web site. WWW indicates that the domain is part of the *World Wide Web,* and http:// identifies the protocol to be used to connect (see **Figure 11.9**).

Now that I have provided a basic explanation of how a domain name is structured, let's take a look at how your computer locates a resource on the Web when you do a search.

First off, understand that you are not actually looking specifically for an organization's domain when you perform a search. You are looking for a resource that resides within their domain. The domain itself may consist of several Web servers, one or more FTP servers, and their internal infrastructure as well. Not only would you not want to suck their entire domain into your computer, they wouldn't let you even if you did. When you browse to a company's Web site, you browse to its index page. This is a singe resource that points you to other resources that it has made available. The specific address of this resource is the *universal resource locator* (URL).

So, what happens when you type in a URL for the first time? First, your computer checks to see if you are searching for a resource that resides locally. Obviously, in this case it won't be. Since your computer doesn't recognize the domain name, it looks for some help in resolving that name. It finds that help in DNS. You computer issues a query to a DNS server. This query can be one of two types. A *recursive* query tells the DNS server to check its own resources first and return the information to the client. If a server supports recursive queries, the server can forward the request to other DNS servers or to a *root server.*

An *iterative* or *nonrecursive* query comes into play whenever the DNS server that was contacted does not support recursive queries. An iterative query tells the DNS server to return whatever information it has along with its list of other servers that the client might be able to query.

> **EXAM NOTE:** Be prepared to either define recursive and iterative queries, or possibly to point out the differences between the two types of query.

If your network supports its own DNS server, then the IP address of that server will be configured into the advanced settings of your TCP/IP. Your system will send the request to that address for resolution. If you are on an Internet connection, the DNS server will most likely reside at your ISP's site. In this case, the addresses of DNS servers will be dynamically assigned to your machine by the *Dynamic Host Configuration Protocol* (DHCP) that I will discuss later in this chapter.

> **BUZZ WORDS**
>
> **Root server:** One of several collections of servers scattered around the world that maintains the databases of all domains that reside in any given top-level domain.
>
> **Recursive query:** A request for information that can be forwarded to other locations for fulfillment.
>
> **Iterative query:** A request that must be fulfilled on the local server, providing whatever information it has, if any.

The DNS server checks its database for the URL you've requested. If it finds that URL in its database, it simply replies with an IP address and your computer can now attempt to connect directly with the server that hosts that particular resource. If the resource is not found in the DNS database, the next step depends on whether the query is recursive or iterative. The DNS server will respond to the iterative query with a list of other servers the client might check. This may include DNS servers configured in the server's TCP/IP settings or the root servers (see **Figure 11.10**). All DNS servers have as the foundation of their database the location of all root servers.

If a recursive query is requested, the DNS server will first check any other DNS servers that have been configured into its TCP/IP settings. If the server doesn't find the URL, it will forward the request to the appropriate root server. In either case, when the request comes back to the DNS server, it will forward the results of that query to the client. In addition, it will add the information it obtained to its own database. The next time anyone asks for that same URL, it will be available in the server's local DNS database.

INTERNET LAYER PROTOCOLS

A big part of establishing complete communication between devices involves logical addressing. All of TCP/IP revolves around the IP address. Therefore, every one of

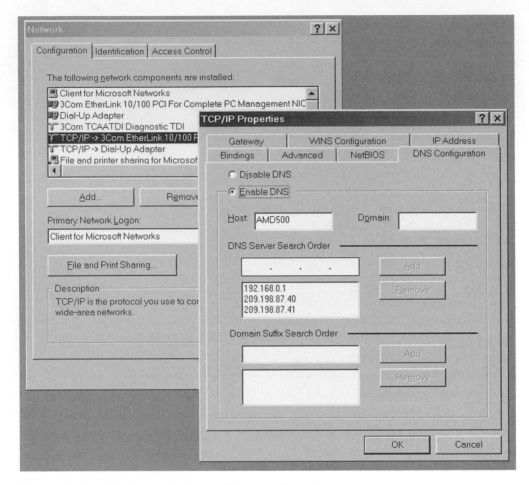

Figure 11.10   Configuring DNS on a Windows 98 machine.

the TCP/IP protocols relies heavily upon the services provided by other protocols that operate at the Internet Layer of TCP/IP.

There are a number of different protocols that operate at this layer. Many of them are used for task-specific purposes. Therefore, for the purposes of this discussion, I will limit myself to the primary protocols of the Internet Layer. This will include:

- The *Internet Protocol* (IP)
- The *Bootstrap Protocol* (BootP)
- The *Dynamic Host Configuration Protocol* (DHCP)
- The *Internet Control Message Protocol* (ICMP)

- The *Address Resolution Protocol* (ARP)
- The *Reverse Address Resolution Protocol* (RARP)

IP

As a protocol, IP is nearly as old and venerable as TCP. It was developed in response to DARPA's desire to interconnect two different networks of computers and not just a few computers onto a single network. Over the years, several different versions of IP have evolved. As of this writing, the Internet community is trying to migrate an IP Version 4 (IPv4) world into one revolving around IP Version 6 (IPv6).

So what happened to Version 5? It seems that Version 5 was assigned to an experimental protocol that was to support real-time streaming of data. This protocol, officially known as the *Internet Streaming Protocol* (ST), never got off the ground.

IP is the protocol that allows the process of routing. Without IP all anyone could manage to build would be local area networks. IP allows data to cross between networks. In order to do this, it needs to be able to perform two main functions. First of all, it must be able to send data over a connectionless link. Since this link will be connectionless, the best you can hope for in terms of reliability is what the designers of TCP/IP refer to as *best-effort delivery*.

The second task of IP is to provide for fragmentation of data for transmission over the medium, and subsequent reassembly of that data when it is received. In order to do this it may have to deal with devices that support a different *maximum transmission unit* (MTU) size. Simply put, the MTU is the largest number of bits packed into a single frame that a particular device can support.

There are six basic services that IP provides in order to support these tasks. These services include:

- Addressing – IP headers contain addresses, which identify the sending and receiving devices.
- Routing – IPv4 makes use of 32-bit addresses, while IPv6 uses 128-bit addresses. Intermediate devices can use these addresses to select a path through the network for any given packet.
- Fragmentation – While the job of segmenting a message is handled by the Host to Host Layer (or Transport Layer in OSI), IP packets may be further divided into smaller packets. This permits a large packet to travel across a network that is only capable of smaller packets than were originally transmitted. IP fragments and reassembles packets transparently.
- Options – IP allows for several optional features. These features include source routing, route recording, and additional security implementations.

- Packet timeouts – When IP puts a packet onto the network, it includes a *Time To Live* (TTL) field. Each device that handles the packet reduces that TTL appropriately. Should TTL reach zero, the packet will be discarded. This prevents lost packets wandering through the digital world for an eternity, thus flooding the network.

- Type of service – Packets can be given a different priority level by defining what kind of service they are supporting. In the event that multiple packets are waiting in cache on a server or router for processing, higher priority packets take precedence.

Earlier in the chapter, I provided a detailed discussion on IP addressing. This is the most significant of IP's features. A good understanding of IP addressing will be essential in fully understanding TCP/IP.

BootP

In early networks, it was common to see networks based on *thin clients* that relied exclusively on their server for all services, including providing an operating system and all necessary applications. These thin clients consisted of stripped-down computer systems with no disk drives and only sufficient memory to run the client application. The inherent problem with this process was that there was no local OS to boot the system, and, once it was booted, since there was no OS, an IP address could not be locally administered.

The *Bootstrap Protocol* addresses these issues. A NIC equipped with a chip called *boot PROM* could obtain its IP address, pointers to the OS, and much more information from the BootP server. The boot PROM is a programmable read-only memory chip that stores the basic information needed by the computer to send packets out over the wire. The way it works is simple but elegant. When a normal machine begins its boot process, the BIOS on the computer runs a program called the *bootstrap loader.* This program goes out and finds the master boot record of the bootable disk. Since a thin client has no disk, bootstrap loader is pointed to the boot PROM.

The NIC issues a *boot request* packet to the broadcast address of 255.255.255.255 on port 67. For its own address it will use 0.0.0.0. Once the request is sent, one of two things will happen.

If there is a BootP server on the local network, that server will reply with a *bootreply* packet on port 68 that contains a set of fields, which contain information that will be bound to the NIC. **Table 11.1** lists the fields of a BootP packet and the information they provide.

Table 11.1 Contents of the BootP Reply Packet

Field	Function	Type
BOOTP_NET_IP	IP address	IP address
BOOTP_NET_NETMASK	Subnet Mask	IP address
BOOTP_NET_GATEWAY	IP Address of Default Gateway	IP address
BOOTP_NET_SERVER	IP Address of responding BootP server	IP address
BOOTP_NET_DNS_SERVER	IP Address of DNS Server	List of IP addresses
BOOTP_NET_TIME_SERVER	IP Address of Time Servers	List of IP addresses
BOOTP_NET_LOG_SERVER	IP Address of Logging Servers	List of IP addresses
BOOTP_NET_LPR_SERVER	IP Address of LPR Servers	List of IP addreses
BOOTP_NET_TIME_OFFSET	Time offset between local subnet and UTC Server	Unsigned interrupt
BOOTP_NET_HOSTNAME	NetBIOS name for local host	String
BOOTP_NET_SERVER_NAME	NetBIOS name for BootP server	String
BOOTP_NET_BOOTFILE_NAME	File name for bootable file	String
BOOTP_NET_DOMAINNAME	DNS domain name	String
BOOTP_NET_SERVER_ADDR	MAC address of BootP server	Unsigned char[6]

An abbreviated list of the most common fields of a BootP Reply Packet.

After processing the bootreply packet, the client will then issue a directed transmission to the BootP server, requesting the boot file that was included in the bootreply packet. The client now has everything it needs to boot.

In the event that there was no BootP server on the local network, it is essential that the router that intercepts the bootrequest packet be equipped with a *BootP Relay Agent*. This relay agent will forward the request to the appropriate entity. If there is no relay agent installed, the bootrequest packet will be discarded and the client will not be able to boot.

DHCP

One of the biggest problems facing network administrators is keeping track of all those IP addresses and who has what address. The *Dynamic Host Configuration Protocol* (DHCP) was designed to alleviate most, if not all, of those problems. DHCP is an extension of BootP and allows for dynamic configuration of network clients.

> **EXAM NOTE:** Be prepared to describe in detail how DCHP works before going in to take the exam. This is a favorite topic on the exam.

DHCP works in a similar manner to BootP, with a few enhancements and one notable limitation. The enhancements are that DHCP allows the administrator to put all the available IP addresses into a pool and dole them out for a limited time. This time is known as the *DHCP lease.* Leases can be for as long or as short as the administrator wishes them to be. When a very short lease, such as one hour, is assigned to an IP address, that address essentially becomes available again once that person logs off of his or her machine. It can then be handed out to the next person who wishes to log on. This is useful when there are a limited number of addresses available and you don't want them tied up for any extended period. ISPs frequently use this technique. Longer leases are useful when there are plenty of addresses to go around.

Once that lease has been configured, the client machine can keep the IP address for that amount of time. When the lease reaches 50 percent of its maturity, the client will begin sending messages to the DHCP server that issued the original address to renew the lease or reassign a new address. At approximately 75 percent of maturity, the client begins broadcasting to all hosts, looking for any DHCP server that will give it a new IP address.

Other advantages of DHCP are the number of options that can be configured

> **BUZZ WORD**
>
> **Lease:** In TCP/IP, this is the amount of time a client that has received its IP address over DHCP can keep that address.

by an administrator. Nearly every parameter of a client TCP/IP configuration can be handed out by DHCP. In the event that something changes, such as the static address of a DNS server or a router interface, those changes can be placed into the DHCP options and then everybody's leases get set to one minute. The next time a person restarts a machine the new configuration will automatically take effect. If you have a network of 2500 users, which do you think might be easier: the DHCP method or trotting around to 2500 different machines manually changing their configurations?

The limitation, if you want to consider it that, is that DHCP does not allow for the distribution of a boot file. Machines configured for DHCP can obtain configuration information remotely, but to boot remotely, they will still need a BootP server. Both DHCP and BootP use ports 67 and 68 for their operation.

APIPA

Automatic Private IP Addressing (APIPA) comes with newer versions of Windows. With this protocol, computers configured with DHCP, but without an available DHCP server, are automatically assigned an Internet Protocol (IP) address. This is useful for those folks who don't have a DHCP server running on their network.

If a system boots using DHCP and doesn't find a server, a private address is automatically assigned from the Internet Assigned Numbers Authority (IANA). These addresses are in the range of 169.254.0.0–169.254.255.255 for Automatic Private IP Addressing. Now, the computer can communicate with any other computers on the local network also configured by APIPA. This also works for computers with a static IP address manually configured in the Automatic IP Addressing address range with a subnet mask of 255.255.0.0.

ICMP

The *Internet Control Message Protocol* (ICMP) is a protocol that was first announced in RFC 792 and is one of TCP/IP's best troubleshooting aids. ICMP delivers *out-of-band* messages that are directly related to network performance and/or malfunction. By out of band, I mean that these messages are delivered separately from any packets of data being sent between machines. These messages can report the following conditions:

- Announce network errors – This includes such conditions as a host or entire portion of the network being unreachable. A TCP or UDP packet directed at a port number with no receiver attached is also reported via ICMP.

- Announce network congestion – When any intermediate device, such as a router or server, begins receiving data faster than it can process it, it will generate ICMP Source Quench messages. This results in the transmitting device or devices slowing their transmission rate.

- Assist troubleshooting – ICMP supports an Echo Request/Echo Reply function. An echo request packet is sent on a there-and-back mission. If it gets where it's going, the receiving computer sends an echo reply. Ping, a common network management tool, is based on this feature. Ping will transmit a series of packets, measuring average round-trip times and computing loss percentages.

- Announce timeouts – You've already seen that if a packet's TTL field drops to 0, the router that decrements the value to 0 will discard the packet. Some routing protocols generate an ICMP packet letting the transmitting device know this occurred. Trace Route is a tool that maps network routes by sending packets with small TTL values and watching the ICMP timeout announcements.

EXAM NOTE: While a detailed understanding of all of ICMP's capabilities is not required to pass the exam, you should be able to recognize that the Ping utility makes use of the protocol. You also need to be able to define what the error messages mean.

It is a good idea to understand some of the more common ICMP messages. *Destination unreachable* lets you know that the host you were trying to reach could not be found. Of course, that could mean a number of things. Was the network not found or just the host? Or perhaps both were found, but the port specified in the packet could not be found. By using a *packet sniffer*, such as Microsoft's Network Monitor, you can capture and analyze the destination unreachable packet. The second field in the packet contains a code that indicates the failure condition. These codes are listed in **Table 11.2**.

Another common ICMP message is the *timeout* message. This means that your packet did not arrive at its destination in the allotted time. This can be caused by one of two reasons, and as with the destination unreachable message, the code field can tell you why. In this case, there are only two possibilities. A code of 0 tells you that the total transit time is longer than the time to live defined in the packet header. Code 1 tells you that the amount of time required for the reassembly of fragmented packets exceeded the TTL.

A message less frequently seen is the *parameter problem* message. This indicates that the device processing the packet found an error in one of the packet's header

Table 11.2 Destination Unreachable Error Codes

Code	Description
1	Network unreachable
2	Host unreachable
3	Protocol unreachable
4	Port unreachable
5	Packet size too large, fragmentation needed
6	Source route failure
7	Destination host unknown
8	Source host isolated
9	Communication with destination network prohibited
10	Communication with destination host prohibited
11	Network unreachable for type of service
12	Host unreachable for type of service

Destination unreachable messages received by ICMP may or may not also include an error code explaining why the transmission failed.

fields. If the packet must be discarded because of this error, then the parameter problem message will be sent to the originating machine.

Echo and *echo reply* are messages you will see when you use the *Packet Internet Groper* (Ping) utility. Ping sends an echo request and the target machine hopefully responds with an echo reply. If not, you'll likely get a destination unreachable message, as described above.

ARP AND RARP

The *Address Resolution Protocol* and the *Reverse Address Resolution Protocol* are two very closely related protocols, and so I will discuss them together. ARP is a protocol that can either be used from a command line or called on by another protocol or utility when its services are needed. RARP was used almost exclusively for obtaining an IP address at boot time. For the most part, BootP has superceded it for most of its services. These protocols were defined in RFC 903 in 1984.

ARP resolves an IP address to a MAC address (see **Figure 11.11**). Therefore, it assumes that the IP address is already known. ARP sends a packet with that IP as

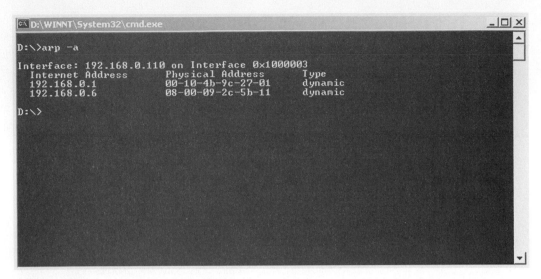

Figure 11.11 The ARP utility will allow you to find out the MAC address of any machine using its IP address.

the destination address and waits for the reply. The device that owns that IP address will respond with its IP address and MAC address. ARP will then maintain that information in the ARP cache.

RARP requires the services of a central server. A machine sends out a broadcast packet containing its MAC address and a RARP server responds by assigning an IP address. As I mentioned earlier, BootP has supplanted RARP for this purpose.

ADDRESS TRANSLATION IN TCP/IP

As you learned from the previous discussions, TCP/IP provides a number of utilities for address translation. DNS is used to resolve domain names to IP addresses, and ARP is used to resolve MAC addresses to IP addresses. RARP, BootP, or DHCP can be used to assign IP addresses to known MAC addresses.

There are three other methods of address translation that can be used as well. These are WINS, the HOSTS file, and the LMHOSTS file. For the most part, these all represent older technology. However, because many networks still contain older legacy devices that require their services, a good understanding of all three is required.

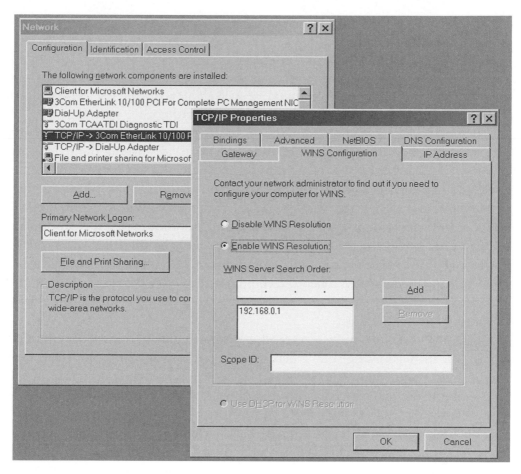

Figure 11.12 Configuring WINS on a Windows 98 machine.

WINS

The *Windows Internet Name Service* is a protocol developed by Microsoft that resolves NetBIOS names to IP addresses. It works by providing a dynamically mapped distributed database of computer names and their corresponding IP address.

As you already know, each computer on the network must have a unique name, its NetBIOS name. You configure that when you first put a computer on the network, either by adding it yourself or letting the OS do it for you (see **Figure 11.12**). With WINS working, you can browse to a computer by its name rather by IP address.

> **EXAM NOTE:** WINS may be a protocol that is waning in popularity as far as the real world is concerned. However, it is still something that gets covered on practically every Network+ exam ever administered.

For WINS to function, there must be a WINS server on the network. The address to this server is configured in the TCP/IP settings.

When a request is made for a resource by its NetBIOS name, the NetBIOS name must first be converted to an IP address. The device making the request will query the WINS server. If that name is in the database, the server responds with an IP address, and then the device can direct its request to the appropriate interface.

As mentioned earlier, the WINS database is dynamic. When a computer first comes onto the network, it sends out a broadcast that indicates that it is now up and running. That broadcast includes the IP address and the NetBIOS name of the computer. The WINS server examines that packet, extracts the information it needs and adds it to the database. When the computer shuts down, it sends out another broadcast telling everybody on the network it is doing so. WINS will then delete that entry from the database.

This is one of the reasons why a graceful shutdown of a machine is so important. If John over in Accounting simply gets irritated with his machine and turns it off without shutting down, the shutdown announcement is obviously not made. WINS does not know the machine has been shut down and will continue to direct traffic to that IP address.

A network configured to use DHCP exclusively does not necessarily need the additional overhead imposed by WINS. DHCP can perform these same functions, and one of the options you can check in your network configuration is to use DHCP for WINS resolution. However, in a hybrid network of newer and older machines, WINS can still be quite useful.

HOSTS AND LMHOSTS FILES

The *HOSTS* and the *LMHOSTS* files are files that exist on Windows-based computers that statically resolve addresses. In the event that there are devices on the network that cannot respond to NetBIOS name query broadcasts, these files can be used to provide address resolution. Both files provide mappings of IP address to host name.

> **EXAM NOTE:** Be able to describe the differences between HOSTS and LMHOSTS files.

So, exactly what is the difference between the two? An LMHOSTS file specifies the NetBIOS computer name and IP address mappings, whereas a HOSTS file specifies the DNS name and IP address. On a local computer, the HOSTS file can be used by Windows Sockets applications to find TCP/IP host names. HOSTS is used as a local DNS equivalent to resolve host names to IP addresses.

The LMHOSTS file is used by NetBIOS over TCP/IP to find NetBIOS computer names. It is used to list known IP addresses mapped with corresponding computer names. LMHOSTS is sometimes used for name resolution in earlier versions of Windows on networks where a WINS server was not available. The LMHOSTS file can be considered to be a local WINS equivalent. Having an LMHOSTS file on a machine is useful as a method of allowing the local host to map to certain critical network locations when a WINS server can't be found.

CHAPTER SUMMARY

In this chapter you got your first taste of the complexities of TCP/IP. The history of the protocol goes back a long way and it has taken years to stitch it all together. Its development is now under the watchful eye of IETF. The history of any given TCP/IP protocol or utility can be traced through a series of RFCs.

IP addresses are used to identify the address of the specific device as well as the address of the network on which it resides. The specific class of address along with its subnet mask defines the part of an address that is network and the part that identifies the host. There are three address classes, Class A, Class B, and Class C, that are used for unicast transmissions.

The developers of TCP/IP used a layered model, just as ISO did with the OSI model. However, unlike OSI, which has seven layers, TCP/IP has only four. It is critical that you understand how the TCP/IP layers correspond to the OSI layers.

The TCP/IP suite probably consists of more protocols than any other protocol suite. You won't get very far in this industry unless you have a very good grasp of the basic protocols. There are protocols that function at every layer of the TCP/IP suite.

Since there are addressing schemes other than TCP/IP it is essential that there be ways of mapping an IP address to a domain name, a NetBIOS name, or a MAC address. This chapter covered several different methods of address resolution provided by TCP/IP.

BRAIN DRAIN

1. Discuss the differences between the TCP protocol and the IP protocol and how they relate to one another.

2. Draw your own diagram that illustrates the relationship between the TCP/IP layers and the OSI layers.

3. Explain how the subnet mask differentiates between the host portion of an IP address and the network portion.

4. Define the five different address classes, describing how to differentiate among them.

5. How do the Process/Application protocols differ from the other protocols in the TCP/IP suite?

THE 64K$ QUESTIONS

1. The government agency that first got involved in the networking of computers was _____.
   a. INAC
   b. DARPA
   c. ARPA
   d. DOD

2. The TCP/IP layer that best maps to OSI's Transport Layer is _____.
   a. Process/Application
   b. Host to Host
   c. Internet
   d. Network Access

3. The TCP/IP layer that best maps to OSI's Network Layer is _____.
   a. Process/Application
   b. Host to Host
   c. Internet
   d. Network Access

4. Which of the following represents a Class A address?
   a. 17.2.3.5
   b. 145.16.5.6

    c. 192.168.0.1

    d. 255.255.255.255

5. Which of the following represents a Class C address?

    a. 17.2.3.5

    b. 145.16.5.6

    c. 192.168.0.1

    d. 255.255.255.255

6. Which of the following represents a broadcast address?

    a. 17.2.3.5

    b. 145.16.5.6

    c. 192.168.0.1

    d. 255.255.255.255

7. Which protocol is used to transmit an email message from your computer to the outside world?

    a. POP

    b. IMAP4

    c. SMTP

    d. SNMP

8. Which protocol provides end-to-end services for the reliable transmission of data?

    a. TCP

    b. IP

    c. UDP

    d. TFTP

9. Which protocol provides addressing functions to allow data to pass between networks?

    a. TCP

    b. IP

    c. ICMP

    d. NFS

10. If you have an older Windows machine and you need to configure it to connect to a machine that does not support NetBIOS broadcasts, which static file can you edit to include address resolution for that device?

    a. WINS

   b. HOSTS

   c. LMHOSTS

   d. HOSTS.INF

11. The first networking protocol to be defined was _____.

   a. TCP/IP

   b. IP

   c. TCP

   d. TP

12. A huge barrier that had to be overcome by the early network designers was that _____.

   a. The only medium available for transmitting data was the telephone wire

   b. Data security

   c. No two computer manufacturers used the same programming language

   d. FCC regulations prohibited sending data over telephone wires

13. The Internet Protocol wouldn't be released until _____.

   a. 1979

   b. 1981

   c. 1990

   d. 1991

14. TCP/IP was rigidly designed around the OSI model.

   a. True

   b. False

15. A typical IPv4 address consists of _____ octets divided by dots.

   a. 2

   b. 4

   c. 8

   d. TCP/IP doesn't use octets.

16. What function of an IP configuration defines which numbers in the IP address identify the network?

   a. The gateway

   b. DNS

   c. The first octet

   d. The subnet mask

17. There are _____ classes of IP address.

    a. 3

    b. 4

    c. 5

    d. 6

18. A Class B address can have up to _____ hosts.

    a. 32,768

    b. 65,536

    c. 65,534

    d. Over 16 million

19. A network address that consisted of all 0s is _____.

    a. Impossible

    b. The address of the wire

    c. A broadcast address

    d. The address of the Internet

20. A network address that consisted of all 1s is _____.

    a. Impossible

    b. The address of the wire

    c. A broadcast address

    d. The address of the Internet

TRICKY TERMINOLOGY

Agent: In TCP/IP terminology, this is an application or utility that fulfills requests by gathering the information requested by a manager application.

Fully qualified domain name: An identification of an Internet location that completely describes the path to that location, including the root domain, the top-level domain, and all subdomains.

Hypermedia: Any resource on the network or local system that can automatically redirect the user to another resource simply by clicking on a link.

Iterative query: A request that must be fulfilled on the local server, providing whatever information it has, if any.

Lease: In TCP/IP, this is the amount of time a client that has received its IP address over DHCP can keep that address.

Manager: In TCP/IP terminology, this is an application or utility that initiates requests for information to be gathered.

Octet: Any collection of eight bits. In the context of TCP/IP, it represents one of the four sections of an IP address, which will be represented by one to three decimal characters.

Recursive query: A request for information that can be forwarded to other locations for fulfillment.

Root server: One of several collections of servers scattered around the world that maintains the databases of all domains that reside in any given top-level domain.

Subnet mask: An entry into the TCP/IP configuration, formatted similarly to an IP address. This is a 32-bit value that defines which portion of the address is network and which portion is host.

ACRONYM ALERT

ARP: Address Resolution Protocol

BootP: Bootstrap Protocol

DARPA: Defense Advanced Research Projects Agency. The government agency that first began the research that would eventually lead to the Internet.

DHCP: Dynamic Host Configuration Protocol

DNS: Domain Name System

HTTP: HyperText Transport Protocol

HTTPS: Secure HyperText Transport Protocol

ICMP: Internet Control Message Protocol

IETF: The Internet Engineering Task Force. An organization charged with technological development of the Internet.

IMAP4: Internet Message Access Protocol

IP: Internet Protocol

MTU: Maximum Transmission Unit. The largest size a packet can be in order to be used by a specific protocol.

NFS: Network File System

PING: Packet Internet Groper

POP: Post Office Protocol

RARP: Reverse Address Resolution Protocol

RFC: Request for Comment. The method by which TCP/IP protocols and utilities are introduced and subsequently defined.

SMTP: Simple Mail Transport Protocol

SNMP: Simple Network Management Protocol

ST: Internet Streaming Protocol

TCP/IP: Transmission Control Protocol/Internet Protocol. The protocol suite of the Internet.

TCP: Transmission Control Protocol

UDP: User Datagram Protocol

WINS: Windows Internet Name Service

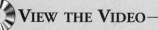 VIEW THE VIDEO

A video clip on Name Resolution is available on the accompanying CD.

CHAPTER 12

USING TCP/IP ON THE NETWORK

Now that you've got a handle on what TCP/IP is all about, it's time to put it to work on the network. It's pretty amazing the number of places where you use the protocol or one of its utilities without even thinking about it. The first thing I'll discuss is how to configure a machine to use TCP/IP. I'll also examine some of the advanced settings available. After that I'll look at some of the TCP/IP utilities and show you how to put them to work.

One of the most complex subjects that this chapter covers is that of subnetting. Admittedly, it isn't one of the easiest things to understand. However, it isn't as complicated as many beginning students make it out to be.

As with Chapter Eleven, An Introduction to TCP/IP, there is a lot of material in this chapter that will show up on the exam. Go over it thoroughly before you attempt to take the test. Topics covered in this chapter include:

1.6 Identify the purposes, features and functions of key network components.

2.4 Differentiate between network protocols in terms of routing, addressing schemes, interoperability and naming conventions.

2.10 Define the purpose, function and use of protocols used in the TCP/IP (Transmission Control Protocol/Internet Protocol) suite.

4.1 Given a troubleshooting scenario, select the appropriate network utility.

4.2 Given output from a network diagnostic utility (For example: those utilities listed in objective 4.1), identify the utility and interpret the output.

4.6 Given a scenario, determine the impact of modifying, adding or removing network services (For example: DHCP (Dynamic Host Configuration Protocol), DNS (Domain Name Service) and WINS (Windows Internet Name Service)) for network resources and users.

CONFIGURING A DEVICE FOR TCP/IP

There are many devices out there and many ways in which they are configured. Some devices, such as routers, require that you Telnet in from another device and configure them remotely. Fortunately, the majority of the network administrator's job is done from the keyboard. In this chapter, I'll concern myself with configuring a typical user's workstation and leave the more esoteric devices to their user's manuals.

The methods by which protocols are configured don't change much from one version of OS to another within the same brand, so the following examples will be based on a Windows 98 box.

You start by opening the Network Properties dialogue box. There are two ways to do that. You can right-click on Network Neighborhood and select Properties or you can open Control Panel and double-click on the Network applet. Either way gets to the screen you see in **Figure 12.1**. TCP/IP will be listed for each adapter on which it is bound. Select the adapter you wish to configure, as shown in the figure. Click on Properties.

That brings up the TCP/IP Properties screen shown in **Figure 12.2**. There are several tabs at the top that bring you to different properties you can configure. The default opening screen is for basic IP properties. You have two choices. You can either click on Obtain an IP address automatically, or you can select Specify an IP address. If you choose to use automatic IP configuration, you will be configuring your machine to be a DHCP client. That will only work if there is a DHCP server on the network.

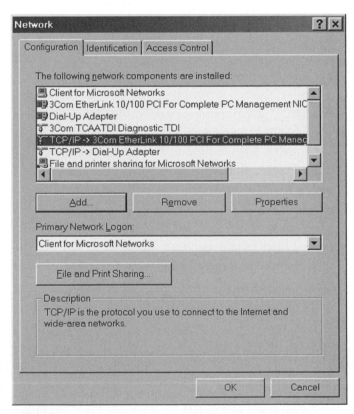

Figure 12.1 The Network Properties screen.

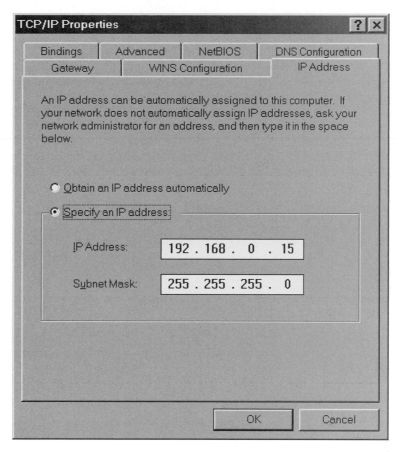

Figure 12.2 The TCP/IP Properties screen.

If you are assigning a static IP address, there are at a minimum two components of the address you'll need to configure. Those are the IP address itself and a subnet mask.

In Chapter Eleven, An Introduction to TCP/IP, I examined a number of the more important protocols of the TCP/IP suite. The tabs at the top of the TCP/IP Properties screen will allow you to configure your machine to make use of those protocols and point it to whatever servers provide the services.

The most common setting beyond the basic that needs to be configured is the Gateway. This is the address of the device that acts as your doorway to the world outside your own network. Usually it represents the internal port of a router. **Figure 12.3** shows the Gateway configuration screen.

You can point your computer to as many gateways as you have set up on your network. Perhaps you have one router that interfaces with satellite offices in your organization and another that provides Internet service. Keep in mind that the gateways will be queried in the order in which they're configured on the machine. Therefore, to maximize performance, the gateway that is hit the most frequently should be the first on the list. To configure a gateway, simply type in the address and click Add.

> **BUZZ WORD**
>
> **Gateway:** The default address to which all packets with unknown network addresses will be forwarded.

WINS and DNS servers are configured in exactly the same way as a gateway. As with the gateway, you can configure multiple WINS or DNS servers. All of the same rules apply.

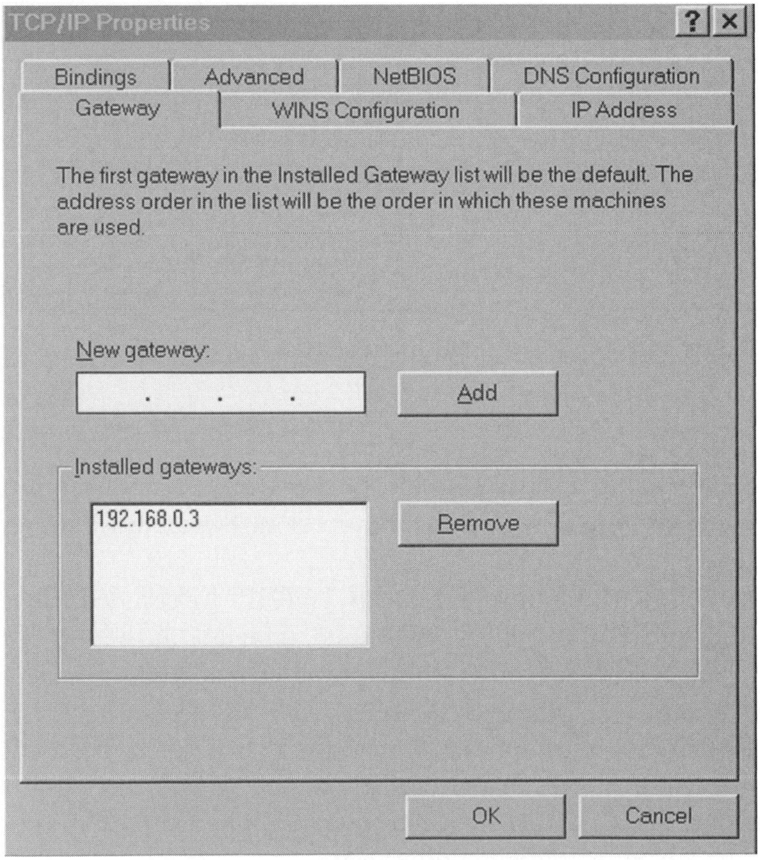

TCP/IP Properties

| Bindings | Advanced | NetBIOS | DNS Configuration |
| Gateway | WINS Configuration | IP Address |

The first gateway in the Installed Gateway list will be the default. The address order in the list will be the order in which these machines are used.

New gateway:

. . .   Add

Installed gateways:

192.168.0.3   Remove

OK   Cancel

Figure 12.3 Configuring a default gateway on a client.

EXAM NOTE: For the exam, you need to know not only the basic TCP/IP components that make up a configuration. You need to have an understanding of the advanced settings as well.

The Bindings Tab (**Figure 12.4**) allows you to dictate which of the networking components will use the TCP/IP properties. It is very rare that you would need to change anything on this screen. The majority of the time, on a TCP/IP network all components need to be able to access the protocol. An exception to this might be a network client that accesses a server not configured with TCP/IP. For example, if there was still a Novell server on your network that was earlier than Version 5, it might be using only the IPX/SPX protocol. You could deselect that client with no ill effects.

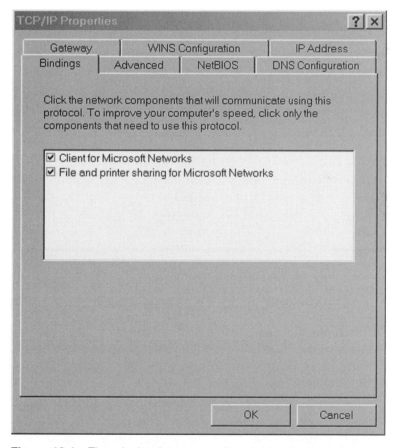

Figure 12.4 There isn't a lot you usually need to change in the Bindings tab. But if something isn't checked, that might be a good indication as to why it isn't working.

However, there is no real performance gain achieved by doing so. Follow the old adage, "If it ain't broke—don't fix it!"

The NetBIOS tab may or may not let you select whether or not you want to run NetBIOS data over TCP/IP. It does this by encapsulating the NetBIOS packets into a TCP/IP packet, so that intermediate devices, such as routers, don't know the difference. This is another screen you're better off not playing with.

SUBNETTING IN TCP/IP

Over and over again, I've harped on the idea that for a TCP/IP configuration to be correct and usable, it must include both the IP address and a subnet mask. As you recall, the subnet mask identifies to the OS which part of the IP address represents the network address and which part represents the host address. It does so by placing all the bits of the network address behind a series of 1s and all bits representing the host behind 0s.

> **EXAM NOTE:** Know your subnetting inside and out. You are likely to be given a scenario in which you are assigned to subnet a network with a specific number of networks and hosts. Understanding the next few pages will be critical to answering these questions correctly.

A default subnet mask means that you will have only a single network. However, as a network gets larger, congestion becomes an issue and one of the best ways to tame it is to break your big network down into several small ones. This is the process of *subnetting*. Another reason for subnetting might have to do with security. Perhaps there are certain parts of the network that you don't *want* everybody having access to. Surely, the proper use of permissions goes a long way in securing resources. But keeping the casual hacker from even knowing the resources are there is even better.

TCP/IP allows a large block of addresses with a single network address component to be broken down into several smaller blocks of addresses, each on their own network. Subnetting works by stealing bits from the host portion of the address and giving them to the network side. Since the network hides behind 1s and the hosts hide behind 0s, this is a simple matter of turning some of those 0s into 1s.

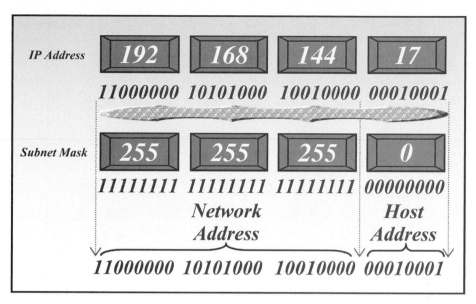

Figure 12.5 A default subnet mask at work.

Before I get involved in the details on how to do this, perhaps now would be a good time to review the subnet mask and its relationship to the host address. **Figure 12.5** is a familiar face from Chapter Eleven, but it will serve useful here as well. However, I've changed it to represent a Class B address.

Now let's look at what would happen if you were to take the first 4 bits of the host portion of the subnet mask and convert them to 1s. This creates a custom subnet mask. In the default subnet mask, the first octet that represents the host portion is all 0s, and if translated to binary, would still be 0. That was easy, wasn't it? When you borrow 4 bits from that first octet and give them to the network side, you now have an octet that reads 1111 0000. In decimal, this converts to 240. Therefore, in the IP Address configuration screen of your Network Applet, you type in a subnet mask of 255.255.240.0 instead of 255.255.0.0, as shown in **Figure 12.6**.

Okay, that was easy, but what have you accomplished? As you see in Figure 12.5, the network portion of the address now extends into the third octet. What you've done is given yourself those extra networks you need. Naturally, each network is going to have fewer hosts, and this is something you shall have to take into consideration when subnetting. But there is a very simple formula for calculating how many new networks you have and how many hosts each of those networks can contain. The formula for both is the same, $2^x - 2 = Y$. When calculating the number

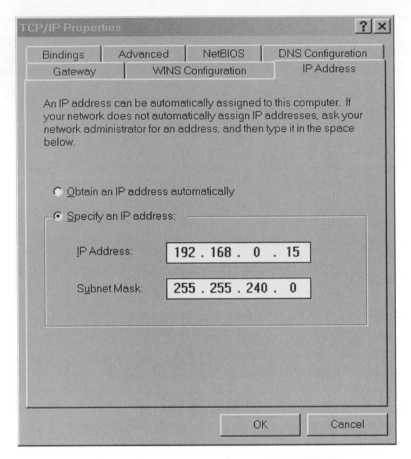

Figure 12.6 Configuring a custom subnet mask in TCP/IP.

of networks you've created, X equals the number of bits you borrowed from the host portion. When calculating the number of hosts left available, X represents the total number of bits remaining hidden behind 0s—or the host portion.

So, you borrowed 4 bits from the host. Before you did anything, your Class B address had 16 bits for each host and network portion. You gave up 4 from the host, so there are 12 bits left.

According to the formula, you now have $2^4 - 2$ networks available. A handy-dandy scientific calculator will tell you that you've created fourteen subnets. Since there are 12 bits remaining in the host portion, you have 4094 hosts in each subnet.

Why did you subtract two from each of these numbers? If you recall from the last chapter, neither a host address nor a network address can consist of all 0s or all 1s. Therefore, those are not legitimate addresses and cannot be used. They are not available.

Table 12.1   Custom Subnet Mask Values

# bits borrowed	Decimal Value
1	128
2	192
3	224
4	240
5	248
6	252
7	254
8	255

The number of bits borrowed from the host portion of the IP address determines how many new subnets you can create.

In a subnet mask, all 1s in the network portion must be contiguous, as must all the 0s in the host portion. Therefore, there are a limited number of custom subnets you can use. **Table 12.1** goes over the possible custom subnet numbers.

There is a reason I didn't include the number of networks and clients made available by each value. In a Class A or Class B address, you might be subnetting into the second, or even third (in the case of a Class A address) octet of the host portion. Therefore all of the different possibilities get pretty convoluted.

EXAM NOTE: You might want to commit Table 12.1 to memory. It will greatly ease the task of subnetting. In the real world, everyone uses calculators for this purpose. During the exam, that is not allowed.

The next thing you need to consider is where the addresses from one network end and those from the next begin. As you might imagine, that too is done with a simple formula. Using *only* the host octet from which you borrowed the bits for the network side, count the bits remaining for the host portion of the address. That number becomes X and the formula is to raise two to the X power. For example, when you borrow 4 bits, you have 4 bits remaining in the donor octet. Therefore to get the starting subnet address, you calculate the value 2^4. This becomes the starting subnet address and subsequently becomes the interval over which subnets begin and end. Now, remember the rule that says that an address of all 0s is the address of the wire and an address of all 1s is a broadcast address? That rule applies to subnets as well. Keep that in mind as I go over the example.

In the example above, you borrowed 4 bits from the first octet. That means you have 4 bits remaining. $2^4 = 16$. Therefore, the first subnet would begin with 145.168.16.1 and end with 145.168.31.254. The address of the network itself is 145.158.16.0 and a broadcast intended for just that subnet would be addressed to 145.168.31.255.

The next subnet begins at 145.168.32.1 and ends at 145.168.17.254. The address of the wire is 145.168.32.0 and the broadcast address is 145.168.32.255. **Table 12.2** breaks the example down into its entire range of networks and their associated network and broadcast addresses. Keep incrementing like this until you run out of addresses. The thing to keep in mind is that since you have subnetted,

Table 12.2 An Example of Class B Subnetting

Original Network Address: 145.168.0.0
Custom Subnet Mask: 255.255.240.0

Network Address	Starting Address	Ending Address	Broadcast Address
145.168.16.0	145.168.16.1	145.168.31.254	145.168.31.255
145.168.32.0	145.168.32.1	145.168.47.254	145.168.47.255
145.168.48.0	145.168.48.1	145.168.63.254	145.168.63.255
145.168.64.0	145.168.64.1	145.168.79.254	145.168.79.255
145.168.80.0	145.168.80.1	145.168.95.254	145.168.95.255
145.168.96.0	145.168.96.1	145.168.111.254	145.168.111.255
145.168.112.0	145.168.112.1	145.168.127.254	145.168.127.255
145.168.128.0	145.168.128.1	145.168.143.254	145.168.143.255
145.168.144.0	145.168.144.1	145.168.159.254	145.168.159.255
145.168.160.0	145.168.160.1	145.168.175.254	145.168.175.255
145.168.176.0	145.168.176.1	145.168.191.254	145.168.191.255
145.168.192.0	145.168.192.1	145.168.207.254	145.168.207.255
145.168.208.0	145.168.208.1	145.168.223.254	145.168.223.255
145.168.224.0	145.168.224.1	145.168.239.254	145.168.239.255
145.168.240.0	145.168.240.1	145.168.255.254	145.168.255.255

Borrowing four bits from the host portion of a Class B address created all of the above subnets.

you have to make sure you put the right IP address on the device you are configuring. You have now created a number of different autonomous networks from a single block of addresses.

Of course, if you're observant, you see that there are only fifteen networks outlined in Table 12.2. According to the formula, you're supposed to get sixteen. The sixteenth network is the "missing" network at 145.168.0.0. Most devices won't recognize this as a legitimate network address. There are some exceptions. For example, Cisco's routers will make use of that range.

CLASSLESS INTERDOMAIN ROUTING

On the other end of the spectrum from subnetting is *classless interdomain routing* (CIDR), sometimes also referred to as classless IP addressing and sometimes as supernetting. Whatever you want to call it (CIDR is the correct term), it boils down to the same thing. You're borrowing bits from the network portion of a subnet mask to force multiple blocks of addresses onto a single network.

> **EXAM NOTE:** As with subnetting, it is expected on the exam that you be able to supernet a network from smaller blocks of addresses. Don't sell this section short.

CIDR came about as a result of two different but related issues. The depletion of IPv4 addresses has been a problem for a while. More recently the extended use of Class C addresses on the Internet has resulted in a problem IBM and others call the *router table explosion* issue.

The depletion of addresses makes it increasingly difficult for midsized to large organizations to get a sufficiently large block of assigned addresses. Some companies approach this issue simply by getting as many addresses as they need for public exposure and using a combination of a private addressing scheme and a technique called *Network Address Translation* (NAT) to hide those addresses from the public. (I'll be discussing Network Address Translation in detail in Chapter Fifteen, Working with Network Security.)

If, for any reason, private addressing is not an option, and the organization requires a large block of assigned addresses, it can be a problem. Any network larger than 254 hosts would require a Class B address,

> **BUZZ WORD**
>
> **Supernetting:** The use of Classless Interdomain Routing to combine multiple blocks of contiguous IP addresses into a single network.

and anything with more than 65,534 addresses will require a Class A address. Address depletion has made it virtually impossible to get one of these addresses. Therefore, an organization might find itself in possession of several contiguous blocks of Class C addresses.

That company then has two choices. It can either build up its network as a collection of smaller networks of 254 (or fewer) hosts on each network, or it can use CIDR to combine them into one large block.

The router table explosion problem is a direct result of the extended use of Class C addresses on the Internet. To give you an example, if a company was to put a network of 2500 users onto a single block of Class B addresses, that would require one entry into the router tables of each backbone router. Doing the same thing with blocks of Class C addresses requires sixteen entries into each table. That's just one company. Now consider 1000 different companies with networks subnetted in this manner. How many router table entries will you need in order to get all of them to talk to one another? I don't want to think about it. It makes my brain hurt! Since CIDR moves each block of addresses on a single network into a single entry, it drastically reduces this problem.

Here's how it works. As with subnetting, you are going to borrow bits from the other half of the subnet mask. Only in this case, the host portion of the address is borrowing from the network portion.

As you know, on a typical Class C network the default subnet mask is 255.255.255.0. In order to borrow 4 bits from the network address and give them to the host portion for use, you would use a subnet mask of 255.255.240.0. As long as the blocks of Class C addresses are contiguous (or at least fall within the range of addresses our subnet mask covers), they will now all be members of the same network.

How do you know if your addresses fall in the range covered by the mask? There are a few simple rules to follow. To combine two Class C networks, the third octet of the first address must be evenly divisible by two. If you're trying to combine eight Class C networks, the third octet needs to be evenly divisible by eight. For example, 198.168.15.0 and 198.168.16.0 could not be supernetted. The value in the third octet of the first block is not divisible by two. However, you could combine 198.168.18.0 and 198.168.19.0. Let's look at an example.

You have a network address of 192.168.16.0, which will give you a range of addresses from 192.168.16.1 to 192.168.16.254. You also have a network address of 192.168.32.0, with a range of addresses from 192.168.32.1 to 192.168.32.254. **Figure 12.7** shows what these addresses will look like in binary.

Note the arrow going down the image about a third of the way from the right. These are bits that are common to both network addresses and the selected subnet

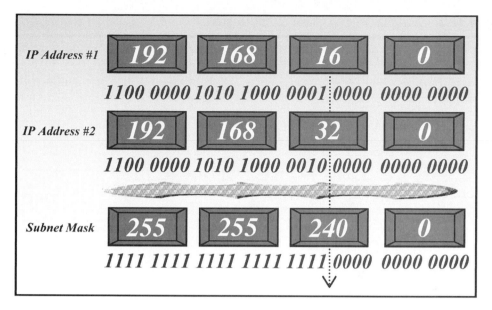

Figure 12.7   Binary translation of two Class C addresses with a custom subnet mask.

mask. The first address is divisible by sixteen and you need to be able to group
together sixteen Class C addresses to span
the range from the first network address to
the second.

Now if the addresses were contiguous,
you wouldn't need to borrow all 4 bits.

BUZZ WORD

CIDR block: A network address
that includes the number of 1s
used in the subnet mask as part of
its format.

And in fact, if you were working with public addresses instead of private, the use
of contiguous address blocks would be essential. You cannot include somebody else's
network addresses in your range.

Not only does the network now consist of a larger number of hosts than a
conventional Class C network would be able to support, but it also will take up only
a single entry into the router tables.

Many OSs allow supernetted addresses to be configured as *CIDR blocks*. You
simply specify the number of 1s in the subnet mask after the network address. For
example, in the example table, you borrowed 4 bits from the network address,
leaving a total of twenty 1s in the custom subnet mask. The network address is
effectively 192.168.16.0 /20. The network address you've now created is known as
the *IP Prefix*. **Table 12.3** lists the possible CIDR blocks for a Class C address and
how they will affect the network.

Table 12.3 Using CIDR with Class C Addresses

CIDR Block	Supernet Mask	Number of Class Cs	Number of Hosts
/14	255.252.0.0	1024	262144
/15	255.254.0.0	512	131072
/16	255.255.0.0	256	65536
/17	255.255.128.0	128	32768
/18	255.255.192.0	64	16384
/19	255.255.224.0	32	8192
/20	255.255.240.0	16	4096
/21	255.255.248.0	8	2048
/22	255.255.252.0	4	1024
/23	255.255.254.0	2	512
/24	255.255.255.0	1	254
/25	255.255.255.128	1/2	126
/26	255.255.255.192	1/4	62

Classless Interdomain Routing (CIDR) allows a network engineer to combine multiple address blocks into a single larger network.

THE TCP/IP UTILITIES

One of the beauties of using TCP/IP as your default protocol lies in the number of elegant little utilities that are part of the suite. These handy little programs provide an immense amount of troubleshooting capability without spending any extra money. In addition to the ones that are part of the suite, there are huge numbers of utilities available for download on the Web that are not officially part of the suite. It is a good idea to really know your way around the TCP/IP utilities. The ones I will be discussing in this section include:

- Ping
- Trace Route
- Netstat
- Route
- Nbtstat
- Ipconfig

- Nslookup
- Dig
- Ifconfig

EXAM NOTE: The Network+ exam is likely to have several questions asking you to identify which utility would be best used in a specific set of circumstances. Know them all.

PING

The *Packet Internet Groper* (Ping) is one of those utilities you must understand well. It

BUZZ WORD

Ping: *Packet Internet Groper.* A utility that sends packets to a target host and uses the ICMP protocol to generate messages concerning the connectivity of the target. Not only is Ping an acronym, it has been universally adopted as a term that can be either a noun or a verb. As a noun it represents the packets sent when pinging another host. As a verb, it represents the process of pinging another host.

works on the basis of the ICMP protocol I discussed in Chapter Eleven and can tell you whether or not a particular host on the network is reachable. It works by sending out a series of ECHO packets. The intended host, upon receiving the packets, will return an ECHO REPLY. If the ECHO REPLY returns successfully, Ping will calculate the total time elapsed for the round trip. The information will be returned in a screen similar to the one in **Figure 12.8**.

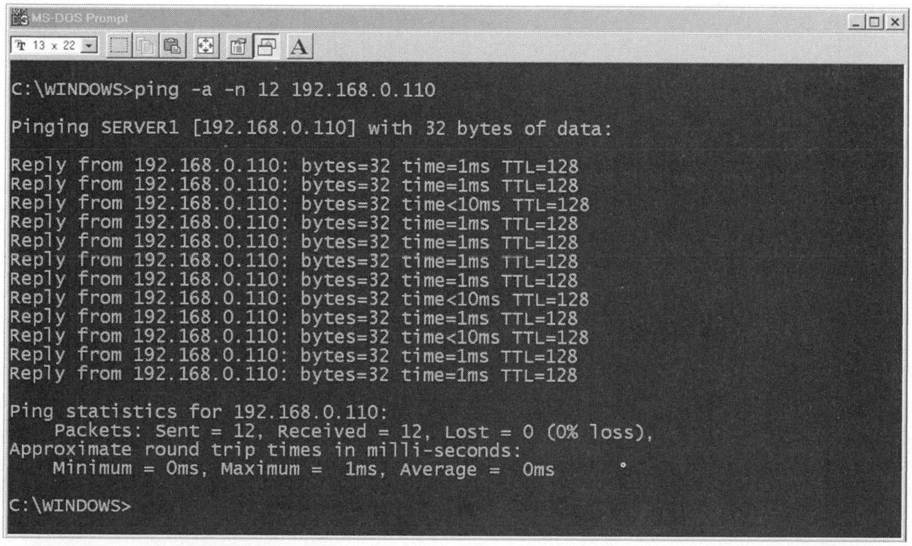

```
MS-DOS Prompt

C:\WINDOWS>ping -a -n 12 192.168.0.110

Pinging SERVER1 [192.168.0.110] with 32 bytes of data:

Reply from 192.168.0.110: bytes=32 time=1ms TTL=128
Reply from 192.168.0.110: bytes=32 time=1ms TTL=128
Reply from 192.168.0.110: bytes=32 time<10ms TTL=128
Reply from 192.168.0.110: bytes=32 time=1ms TTL=128
Reply from 192.168.0.110: bytes=32 time=1ms TTL=128
Reply from 192.168.0.110: bytes=32 time=1ms TTL=128
Reply from 192.168.0.110: bytes=32 time=1ms TTL=128
Reply from 192.168.0.110: bytes=32 time<10ms TTL=128
Reply from 192.168.0.110: bytes=32 time=1ms TTL=128
Reply from 192.168.0.110: bytes=32 time<10ms TTL=128
Reply from 192.168.0.110: bytes=32 time=1ms TTL=128
Reply from 192.168.0.110: bytes=32 time=1ms TTL=128

Ping statistics for 192.168.0.110:
    Packets: Sent = 12, Received = 12, Lost = 0 (0% loss),
Approximate round trip times in milli-seconds:
    Minimum = 0ms, Maximum = 1ms, Average = 0ms

C:\WINDOWS>
```

Figure 12.8 Ping at work.

The syntax for a ping command is as follows:

```
ping —{trigger} host
```

Some of the triggers that are useful in Ping include:

-t – Sends a continuous ping to the targeted host until stopped by the user. Ctrl>Break will display statistics and then allow you to continue, while Ctrl>C stops the ping.

-a – Resolves a host name to an IP address.

-n {count} – Sends the number of ECHO packets defined in the count. For example, ping —n 16 192.168.0.110 will send a total of 16 ECHO packets to the specified IP address.

-l {size} – Sends a buffer size to the target host.

-f – Sets the Don't Fragment field in the ECHO packet.

-i {TTL} – Sets the time to live for the packet.

-r {count} – Records the route for up to the number of hops specified in the count.

-s {count} – Puts a timestamp on the number of hops specified in the count.

-w {timeout} – Specifies a timeout in milliseconds that the sending device will wait for a reply.

In the event that a host is not reachable, ICMP will generate a message that explains the event. Those messages are described in Chapter Eleven.

TRACE ROUTE

Trace Route is a command-prompt that will prompt each intermediate device from source to destination to respond with its IP address and the TTL of each hop along the way. Type tracert {host}, where host is the IP address or domain name of the device you want to trace, from the command prompt. It works by deliberately exceeding the TTL of any given host. **Figure 12.9** shows Trace Route at work.

When you send a trace route request, the utility will send out a packet with an

> **BUZZ WORD**
>
> **Trace Route:** The utility used by TCP/IP to generate a report of all intermediate devices between a source and a destination.

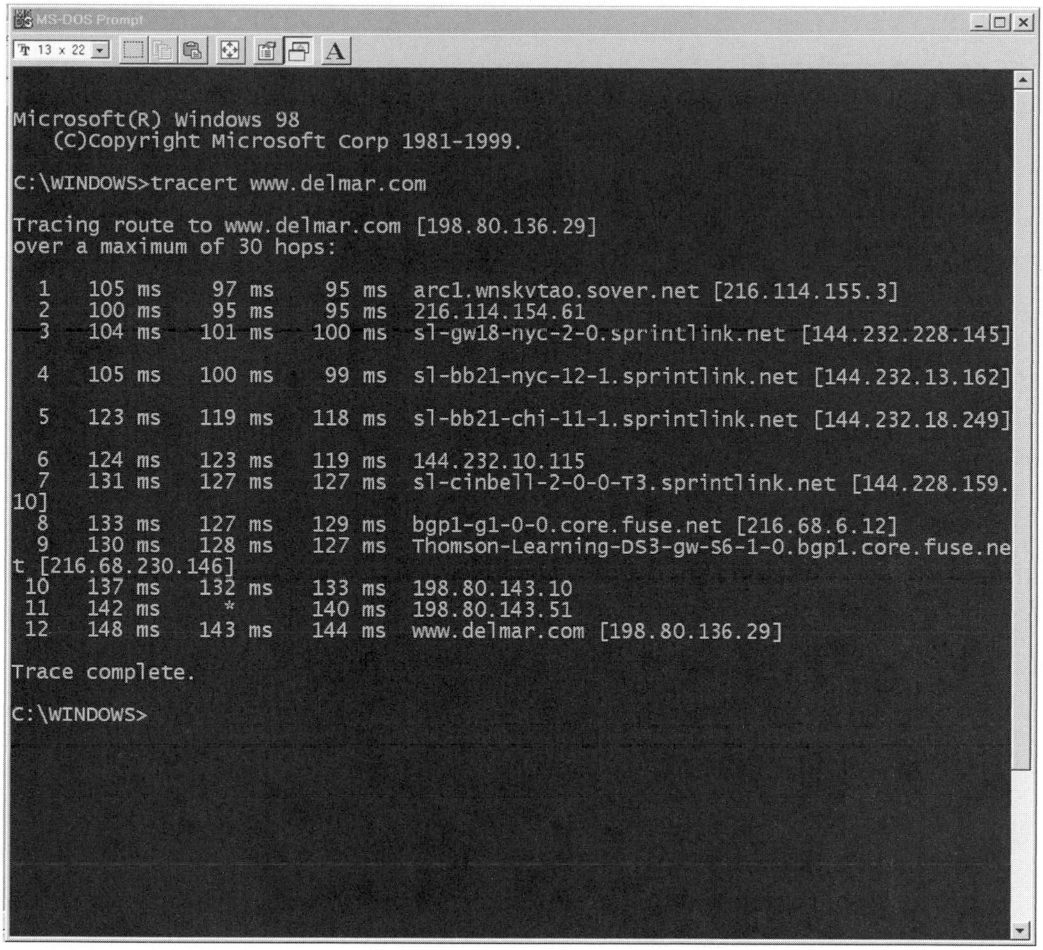

```
MS-DOS Prompt                                                    _ □ ×

13 x 22

Microsoft(R) Windows 98
   (C)Copyright Microsoft Corp 1981-1999.

C:\WINDOWS>tracert www.delmar.com

Tracing route to www.delmar.com [198.80.136.29]
over a maximum of 30 hops:

   1    105 ms     97 ms     95 ms  arc1.wnskvtao.sover.net [216.114.155.3]
   2    100 ms     95 ms     95 ms  216.114.154.61
   3    104 ms    101 ms    100 ms  sl-gw18-nyc-2-0.sprintlink.net [144.232.228.145]

   4    105 ms    100 ms     99 ms  sl-bb21-nyc-12-1.sprintlink.net [144.232.13.162]

   5    123 ms    119 ms    118 ms  sl-bb21-chi-11-1.sprintlink.net [144.232.18.249]

   6    124 ms    123 ms    119 ms  144.232.10.115
   7    131 ms    127 ms    127 ms  sl-cinbell-2-0-0-T3.sprintlink.net [144.228.159.
10]
   8    133 ms    127 ms    129 ms  bgp1-g1-0-0.core.fuse.net [216.68.6.12]
   9    130 ms    128 ms    127 ms  Thomson-Learning-DS3-gw-S6-1-0.bgp1.core.fuse.ne
t [216.68.230.146]
  10    137 ms    132 ms    133 ms  198.80.143.10
  11    142 ms       *      140 ms  198.80.143.51
  12    148 ms    143 ms    144 ms  www.delmar.com [198.80.136.29]

Trace complete.

C:\WINDOWS>
```

Figure 12.9 Trace Route at work.

unreasonably high TTL. When the first device receives that packet, and the TTL is exceeded, that device responds with its IP address and the amount of time it took for the packet to expire. However, the source computer doesn't discard the packet in this case. It resends it along with another TTL that is even higher. Now the first intermediate device will process the packet and send it on its way, but the next device will timeout. This process repeats itself until the final destination is reached. The administrator now has a complete path, from source to destination, along with IP addresses and how long each device will take to process a packet.

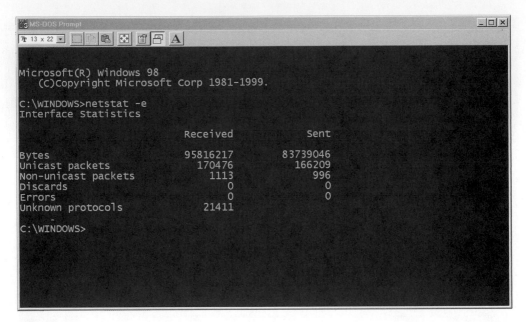

Figure 12.10 Netstat in action.

NETSTAT

The Netstat utility is another command-line program that retrieves various network statistics on any given interface. From the command line, type `netstat –{trigger}` and you will receive a report similar to the one in **Figure 12.10**. The various triggers include:

- `-a` – Displays information for all connections and active ports.

- `-e` – Displays all Ethernet statistics.

- `-n` – Displays addresses and ports in numeric format.

- `-p {protocol}` – Displays information specific to the protocol specified.

- `-r` – Displays the routing table.

- `-s` – Displays per-protocol statistics. Unless otherwise specified, the protocols reported will include TCP, IP, and UDP. May be combined with the `–p` trigger to specify other protocols in the TCP/IP suite.

- `{Interval}` – May be used in conjunction with above triggers to repeat the request at the specified interval. To stop displaying information, press Ctrl>C.

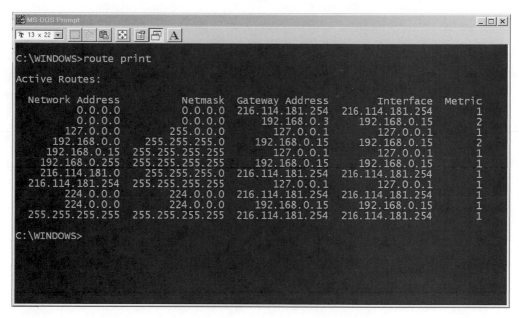

Figure 12.11 Using the `route` command to display local routing tables.

ROUTE

The `route` command allows the user to view or add static entries to the local routing table. These entries can include routes to networks or routes to hosts. Entries can also be introduced in numeric fashion or by name, if DNS is available.

When inputting a static entry using the `route` command, the user would need to

know the format of the routing tables used by the OS. By typing `route print` at the command prompt, the existing routing table will be displayed, as shown in **Figure 12.11**. When generating your own tables, type in your entries accordingly.

Uses of the `route` command are as follows:

`route print` – Displays current local routing tables.

`route add` – Adds a static entry to local routing tables.

`route delete` – Deletes an entry from the local routing tables.

`route change` – Modifies an existing route.

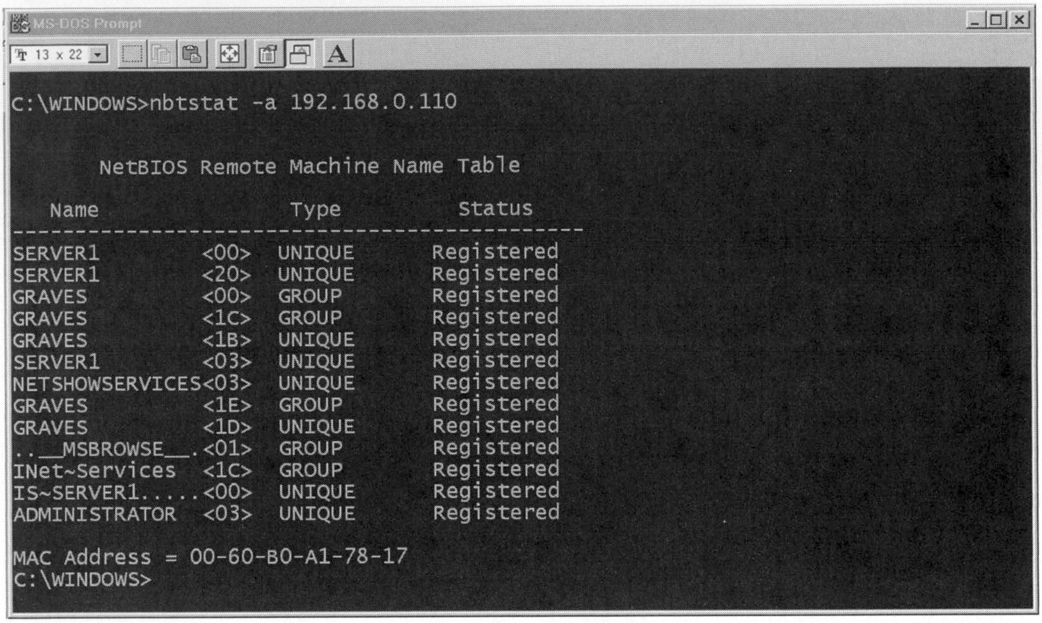
MS-DOS Prompt
13 x 22
C:\WINDOWS>nbtstat -a 192.168.0.110
NetBIOS Remote Machine Name Table
Name Type Status
SERVER1 <00> UNIQUE Registered
SERVER1 <20> UNIQUE Registered
GRAVES <00> GROUP Registered
GRAVES <1C> GROUP Registered
GRAVES <1B> UNIQUE Registered
SERVER1 <03> UNIQUE Registered
NETSHOWSERVICES<03> UNIQUE Registered
GRAVES <1E> GROUP Registered
GRAVES <1D> UNIQUE Registered
..__MSBROWSE__.<01> GROUP Registered
INet~Services <1C> GROUP Registered
IS~SERVER1.....<00> UNIQUE Registered
ADMINISTRATOR <03> UNIQUE Registered
MAC Address = 00-60-B0-A1-78-17
C:\WINDOWS>

Figure 12.12 A typical Nbtstat report.

NBTSTAT

Nbtstat will display statistics for all connections that relate to running NetBIOS over TCP/IP. These connections include computers with current connections to an interface as well as open ports. The utility will also indicate whether a specific connection is unique or part of a group. **Figure 12.12** shows the connections to my system as currently connected to my home network's server.

> **BUZZ WORD**
>
> **Nbtstat:** The TCP/IP utility that displays information for all NetBIOS over TCP/IP connections.

From this list you can see that my AMD machine currently has three connections, my workgroup has two connections, and I, as a user, am logged on once.

The Nbtstat triggers are as follows:

- `-a {remotehost}` – Lists the name table of the remote device named in remotehost.
- `-A {Ipaddress}` – Lists the name table of the remote device with that specific IP address.
- `-c` – Lists the remote name cache along with IP addresses.
- `-n` – Lists local NetBIOS names.

-R – Dumps and reloads the remote cache table.

-s – Lists open sessions, along with destination IP address.

-s – Lists open sessions, along with destination host name.

BUZZ WORD

Ipconfig: The TCP/IP utility that displays all TCP/IP configuration information for any given interface or for all interfaces on a system.

IPCONFIG

Ipconfig is undoubtedly the most widely used of the TCP/IP utilities. This utility can return statistics on every connection configured to use TCP/IP. If a device is configured to use DHCP, a user can use Ipconfig to release an IP address and subsequently renew it.

Ipconfig displays information for all local TCP/IP connections, whether they be a NIC or a modem. As with the other utilities I've discussed, there are a number of triggers associated with Ipconfig. The triggers vary a bit between Windows 98 and the subsequent Microsoft OSs. Therefore, I will list the triggers for both. Those for WIN98 are as follows:

/all – Displays detailed report of all adapters on system.

/batch {filename} – Writes report to the file specified by filename.

/renew_all – Renews the IP configuration for all adapters on the system.

/release_all – Releases the IP configuration for all adapters on the system.

/renew N – Renews the IP configuration for only the adapter specified in N.

/release N – Releases the IP configuration for only the adapter specified in N.

The command line parameters for Windows 2000 are a bit different and there are more of them as well. They are as follows:

/all – Shows complete configuration for all interfaces on system.

/release {adapter} – Releases IP configuration for adapter specified.

/renew {adapter} – Renews IP configuration for adapter specified.

/flushdns – Dumps the contents of the current DNS Resolver cache.

/registerdns – Refreshes all DHCP leases and reregisters DNS names.

/displaydns – Displays contents of the DNS Resolver cache.

/showclassid – Displays the DHCP classes allowed by the adapter.

/setclassid – Modifies the DHCP class.

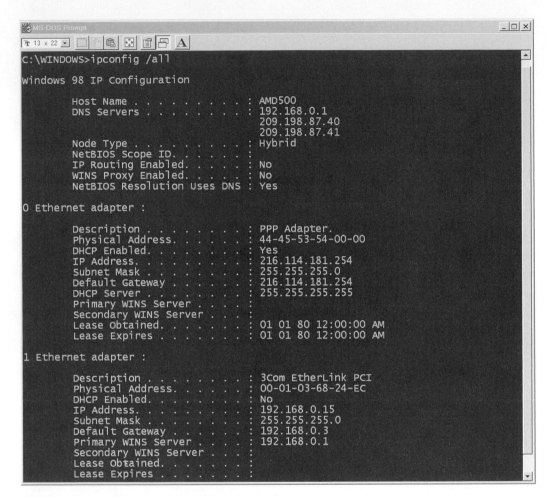

Figure 12.13   The command-line version of Ipconfig

Windows 98 offers a graphical version of Ipconfig that will display this information as well. To access this utility, click Start, then Run, and type winipcfg in the Run field. **Figure 12.13** shows the command-line version of Ipconfig while **Figure 12.14** shows Winipcfg.

NSLOOKUP

When you install TCP/IP, its utility, Nslookup, is also installed. It's a command-line tool used to extract information about DNS servers. Nslookup returns the domain name and IP address of any DNS server on the network. For it to function properly, it is necessary for Nslookup to directly transmit to a DNS server. If there is no DNS

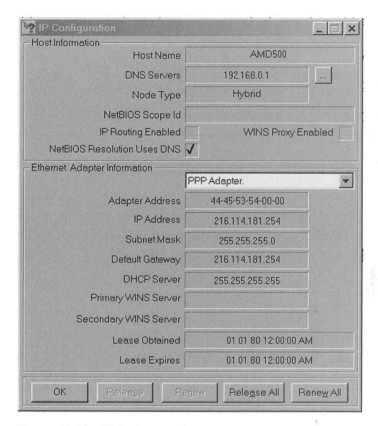

Figure 12.14   Winipcfg at work

server configured, the command will error out. Typing Nslookup at the command prompt, with no triggers, will result in a reply such as this:

```
default server: mwgraves.com
address: 10.15.65.1
```

As with all other commands, there are a number of different triggers that will customize the information produced by this command. This is one of those utilities with enough options to fill an entire chapter. So I'll just mention a few.

- `all` – Print options, current server and host
- `[no]debug` – Print debugging information
- `[no]defname` – Append domain name to each query
- `[no]recurse` – Ask for recursive answer to query

- [no]search – Use domain search list
- domain={name} – Set default domain name to
- root={name} – Set root server to NAME
- retry={x} – Set number of retries to X
- timeout={x} – Set initial time-out interval to X seconds

Dig

Linux users often don't notice the Dig utility. This little gem mines the DNS databases and spits out all the information it can find about a specific URL. It performs a similar function as the Nslookup. As with the Windows Nslookup equivalent, there are some options.

- ; <<>> DiG 2.2 <<>> www.mwgraves.comANY
- ;; res options: init recurs defnam dnsrch ;; got answer:
- ;; ->>HEADER<<- opcode: QUERY, status: NOERROR, id: 6
- ;; flags: qr aa rd ra; Ques: 1, Ans: 1, Auth: 2, Addit: 0
- ;; QUESTIONS:
- ;; www.mwgraves.com, type = ANY, class = IN
- ;; ANSWERS:
- www.mwgraves.com. 14400 CNAME mwgraves.com.
- ;; AUTHORITY RECORDS:
- mwgraves.com. 14400 NS ns1.e3-kracken.com.
- mwgraves.com. 14400 NS ns2.e3-kracken.com.
- ;; Total query time: 70 msec
- ;; FROM: rpm.completeweb.net to SERVER: default – 216.226.128.3
- ;; WHEN: Sat Feb 19 19:52:05 2005 ;; MSG SIZE sent: 34 rcvd: 95

Ifconfig

While Ipconfig is the TCP/IP utility used in the Windows world, Linux and Unix users haven't been left completely out of the loop. With Ifconfig, these users gain a more robust utility with a lot more flexibility in configuration viewing and changes.

Without arguments, Ifconfig displays the current configuration for a network interface. Used with a single interface argument, Ifconfig displays that particular interface's current configuration. Ifconfig can be used at boot time to define IP configurations for each interface on a machine. After that, it can be used at any time to display the settings.

CHAPTER SUMMARY

In the previous chapter, you learned something about the theory behind TCP/IP. In this chapter, you learned how to put it to work. TCP/IP allows big networks to be chopped up into smaller ones through the process of subnetting. And it allows smaller networks to be combined into larger ones through supernetting.

TCP/IP also provides a generous collection of troubleshooting aids in the form of small utilities that are part of the suite. Make sure you have a very good handle on what utility does what before you go in to take your exam.

BRAIN DRAIN

1. Write out on a sheet of paper as many items as you can think of that can be configured into your TCP/IP settings in the Windows Network Applet.

2. Describe conditions that would suggest that it was time to incorporate CIDR onto your network.

3. You have network address of 142.15.0.0. You want to subnet it down into a minimum of twelve networks. What is your subnet mask? Also list each new network address along with its range of host addresses and its broadcast address.

4. List as many of the common TCP/IP utilities as you can, and explain what they do.

5. Explain why, on a network running DHCP, Ipconfig can help a Network Administrator roll out a network configuration change more rapidly.

THE 64K$ QUESTIONS

1. Which of the following two are required of all TCP/IP configurations?
   a. An IP address
   b. A DHCP server address

    c. A subnet mask

    d. A DNS server address

2. Which of the following will forward a packet with a network address unknown to your system?

    a. DNS

    b. DHCP

    c. Gateway

    d. WINS

3. You have a network address of 147.15.0.0 and you want to subnet it into a minimum of twelve networks. What custom subnet mask will do that for you?

    a. 255.240.0.0

    b. 255.255.240.0

    c. 255.248.0.0

    d. 255.255.248.0

4. You want to take a total of four blocks of Class C addresses and combine them into a single network. Which of the following subnet masks will accomplish that?

    a. 255.255.252.0

    b. 255.255.240.0

    c. 255.255.255.252

    d. 255.255.255.240

5. Which of the following utilities will tell you how many hops exist between point A and point B and how long it will take to get there from here?

    a. Ping

    b. Nbtstat

    c. Tracert

    d. Netstat

6. You want to know how many people are currently connected to your computer over the network. Which utility should you use?

    a. Ping

    b. Nbtstat

    c. Tracert

    d. Netstat

7. A user on your network running Windows 98 is not connecting to the DNS server this morning. You're running DHCP on your network and use it to hand out DNS, WINS, and Gateway information. Last night you changed the address of the DNS server. What is the most likely method of getting your user back up and running?

   a. Run Tracert, locate the new IP address, and type it into the network configuration.

   b. From the command prompt, type IPCONFIG /RELEASE_ALL, then type IPCONFIG /RENEW_ALL

   c. Type IPCONFIG /RENEW_DNS

   d. Type IPCONFIG/FLUSHDNS

8. How can you display the local routing tables for a host?

   a. Type IPCONFIG /ROUTE

   b. Type ROUTE PRINT

   c. Type ROUTE ENTER

   d. Type ROUTE DISPLAY

9. Which of the following Ping triggers will keep sending packets until the user manually stops it?

   a. /EXT

   b. /S

   c. /T

   d. /E

10. What protocol does Ping rely on for its services?

    a. RARP

    b. ICMP

    c. SNMP

    d. SMTP

11. The first Microsoft OS to use TCP/IP as the default networking protocol was _____.

    a. WIN3.11 for Workgroups

    b. MS-DOS

    c. WIN95

    d. WIN2K

12. A protocol that can automatically configure devices on the network to use TCP/IP is called _____.

    a. ICMP

    b. SNMP

    c. DARP

    d. DHCP

13. If Device A with a statically assigned IP address tries to get onto the network and Device B is already using that address, what will happen?

    a. Device A will get onto the network, but won't be able to use Browse functions.

    b. Device B will get kicked off.

    c. Device A will be denied access.

    d. It won't matter as long as each device has a different NetBIOS name.

14. A device is trying to transmit information to another device that is not on the local network. This is possible as long as a _____ has been configured.

    a. Subnet mask

    b. DNS server

    c. Gateway

    d. Layer 3 switch

15. What is the correct formula for finding out how many networks can be created using a custom subnet mask?

    a. 2^x

    b. $2^x + 2$

    c. $2^x - 2$

    d. $2^x - 1$

16. You have just subnetted your Class B network, using a subnet mask of 255.255.252.0. How many networks will you now have available?

    a. 6

    b. 8

    c. 14

    d. 30

    e. 32

17. The proper term for combining two smaller network into a single larger network using custom subnet masks is _____.

    a. Reverse subnetting

    b. Ultranetting

    c. Classless interdomain routing

    d. Common interface domain routing

18. It is only possible to supernet using Cisco routers.

    a. True

    b. False

19. One way of adding security to a network hooked up to the Internet would be to make use of _____.

    a. NAT

    b. SDS

    c. NAD

    d. ADR

20. You want to find out what gateway address was added to your NIC by DHCP. What utility would you use to do that?

    a. Ping

    b. Ipconfig

    c. Arp

    d. Netstat

TRICKY TERMINOLOGY

CIDR Block: A network address that includes the number of 1s used in the subnet mask as part of its format.

Gateway: The default address to which all packets with unknown network addresses will be forwarded.

Ipconfig: The TCP/IP utility that displays all TCP/IP configuration information for any given interface or for all interfaces on a system.

Nbtstat: The TCP/IP utility that displays information for all NetBIOS over TCP/IP connections.

Netstat: The TCP/IP utility that displays TCP/IP statistics for a specific interface on the system.

Ping: Not only is Ping an acronym, it has been universally adopted as a term that can be either a noun or a verb. As a noun, it represents the packets sent when pinging another host. As a verb, it represents the process of pinging another host.

Subnet: To break a larger network down into smaller networks.

Supernetting: The use of Classless Interdomain Routing to combine multiple blocks of contiguous IP addresses into a single network.

Trace Route: The utility used by TCP/IP to generate a report of all intermediate devices between a source and a destination.

Acronym Alert

CIDR: Classless Interdomain Routing. A technology that allows multiple smaller network addresses to be bundled into a single network.

NAT: Network Address Translation. A technology that hides a private addressing scheme from the public view.

PING: Packet Internet Groper. A TCP/IP utility that sends ECHO packets and waits for the reply.

CHAPTER 13

THE OTHER PROTOCOLS

Since TCP/IP has become, for the most part, the *de facto* standard for modern networking, I spent a substantial amount of time discussing that particular suite. It isn't, however, the only protocol on the block. There are still quite a few networks out there using protocols other than TCP/IP. Among these protocols are *Internetwork Packet Exchange/Sequenced Packet Exchange* (IPX/SPX), *NetBEUI,* and *AppleTalk.* Your training will not be complete without a decent understanding of each of these protocols. However, there's not a huge amount in this chapter that will appear on the exam. Some exam objectives that will be covered in this chapter include:

2.1 Identify a MAC (Media Access Control) address and its parts.

2.4 Differentiate between network protocols in terms of routing, addressing schemes, interoperability and naming conventions.

2.13 Identify the purpose of network services and protocols (For example: DNS (Domain Name Service), NAT (Network Address Translation), ICS (Internet Connection Sharing), WINS (Windows Internet Name Service), SNMP (Simple Network Management Protocol), NFS (Network File System), Zeroconf (Zero configuration), SMB (Server Message Block), AFP (Apple File Protocol), LPD (Line Printer Daemon) and Samba).

IPX/SPX

Xerox Corporation developed IPX/SPX in the early 1980s. Novell made the protocol popular when the company made it the default networking protocol for the NetWare line of server products. This protocol is designed to provide transport services for data over the network. IPX is a connectionless protocol that is used when the overhead of a reliable service is not required. SPX provides reliable connection-oriented services.

For many years, IPX/SPX was the default protocol for all NetWare servers. It wasn't until Version 5.0 that TCP/IP became their default. Therefore, while IPX/SPX may be experiencing a downward turn in popularity, it is still alive and well.

EXAM NOTE: While the Network+ Exam heavily favors TCP/IP in the choice of exam questions, IPX/SPX comes in a close second. Make sure you understand this protocol as well as you can.

ADDRESSING IN **IPX/SPX**

An IPX/SPX address consists of three separate components: a *network number*, a *node address*, and a *socket number*. **Figure 13.1** shows an IPX/SPX address broken down into its components. While this doesn't superficially appear to be that much different from TCP/IP, how these values are derived makes a big difference.

The network number is a 32-bit value assigned by an administrator and bound to a specific network. Only network interfaces bound to that specific network number would be able to communicate without the services of an intermediate device such as a router or a multi-homed server.

EXAM NOTE: Be able to break down an IPX/SPX address from beginning to end. Be aware that leading 0s will be truncated.

The node address is derived from the 48-bit MAC address of the interface. Since all MAC addresses are unique, this requires no specific configuration by a network administrator. Together, the network number and node address form the *station address.*

Now here is where it gets a bit confusing. The term *socket* in IPX/SPX is used somewhat differently than it is in either the TCP/IP or Windows environments, although for similar functions. In IPX/SPX the socket address is a 16-bit number assigned by the NOS to a process or dialogue operating on a

---

BUZZ WORDS

Network number: A number used by IPX/SPX and AppleTalk to identify the network on which a device resides. In IPX/SPX it is a 32-bit number; in AppleTalk it is a 16-bit number.

Node address: A unique number assigned to an individual host on the network. In IPX/SPX, this number is derived from the MAC address of the interface.

Socket number: A 16-bit number assigned to a specific process or function that is accessing the network in IPX/SPX.

Station address: In IPX/SPX, this is the combination of the network number and node address. A socket number is added to create the complete IPX/SPX address.

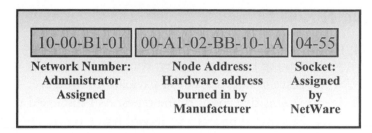

Figure 13.1 Breakdown of an IPX/SPX address.

Table 13.1 Reserved IPX/SPX Sockets

Socket number	Description
0001h	Routing Information Packet (RIP)
0002h	Echo Protocol Packet
0003h	Error Handler Packet
0020h-003Fh	Experimental
0001h-0BB8h	Used by Xerox
247h	Novell Virtual Terminal Server
451h	NetWare Core Protocol
452h	Service Advertising Protocol
453h	Routing Information Protocol
455h	NetBIOS
456h	Diagnostics
4000h-6000h	Ephemeral sockets; used for interaction with file servers and other network communications
8000-90B2	Third-party assigned sockets

specific node. When a process needs network access, it will request a socket number. Once that number is assigned, any packet containing that socket number will be passed on to that process. Certain socket numbers are reserved for NetWare processes. These are shown in **Table 13.1**.

Socket numbers are used with a specific node address. Therefore, IPX/SPX can multiplex the same socket number over several communications sessions.

CONFIGURING **IPX/SPX**

IPX/SPX is a protocol designed to be independent of the hardware protocol used. It doesn't care if you are using Ethernet, Token Ring, or FDDI. The way that works is that the IPX/SPX packet is inserted as the payload for whatever frame type the network uses. It is rather sensitive about frame types. As I discussed in Chapter Six, The Data Link Layer, Ethernet supports a variety of frame types. Your IPX configuration must be configured to use the correct frame type.

In Token Ring, 802.5 Token Ring and Token Ring Snap packets are recognized. IPX/SPX recognizes four different types of Ethernet frame. They include:

- 802.3 (Raw)
- 802.2
- Ethernet II
- Ethernet Snap

Each device on the network must be configured to use the same frame type. Otherwise they cannot communicate. Most NICs these days support an auto-detect feature that prevents this from being much of a problem.

> **EXAM NOTE:** Make sure you know the four different types of Ethernet frame as well as the two different Token Ring frame types.

Figure 13.2 shows how this is configured on a Windows machine. Other configuration settings you see here include *Force Even Length Packets*, *Maximum Connections*, *Maximum Sockets*, *Network Address*, and *Source Routing*.

The IPX packet itself consists of a 30-byte header. The payload can range from 0 to 1470 bytes, although some earlier Ethernet standards limited payload to 546 bytes. You may occasionally encounter older routers with this 546-byte limitation. If you enable the Force Even Length Packets option, packets will be padded with null bits in order to maintain equal length. This is usually not a good idea unless there is a particular device on your network that requires it.

The Maximum Connections setting determines how many different sessions can be open on your system at one time, while Maximum Sockets assigns a value to the number of processes on your system that can be assigned socket numbers. If you fill in a value here that is lower than the default, it can mess up your configuration to the point that your machine can't log onto the network. Should you get an error message that indicates there is a problem loading the protocol, or if, after adding a value to these fields, you cannot log on to a Novell network, it is probably because of this. The defaults are sixteen connections and thirty-two sockets.

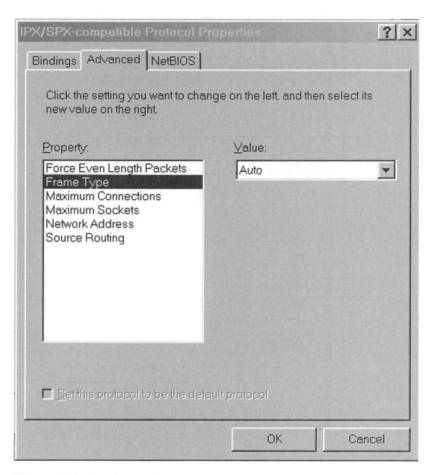

Figure 13.2 Configuring IPX packets on a Windows-based computer.

The Network Address is where you fill in the 32-bit network number for the network on which the device is to participate. The default value is all 0s. To set up multiple subnets in an IPX network, simply give each subnet a different network number and make sure the devices are configured with the correct number.

If source routing is enabled, the device will place its own routing information into the IPX header that indicates the route that the packet should take as it crosses the network. The technique is used primarily in Token Ring and FDDI networks. However, there are Ethernet technologies that support source routing as well.

THE IPX PACKET STRUCTURE

As stated earlier, the IPX/SPX packet consists of a 30-byte header followed by the payload. In most cases, the IPX/SPX packet will be encapsulated into the frame

345

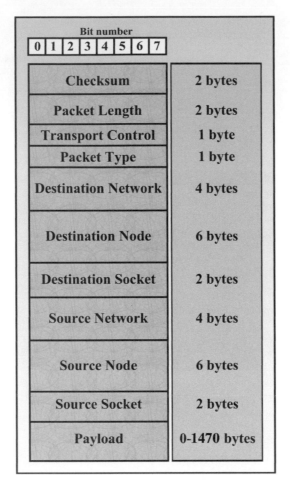

Figure 13.3 Structure of the IPX packet.

created by the hardware protocols. These are the frame types I discussed earlier in the chapter. See **Figure 13.3** for the structure of the IPX packet.

The IPX/SPX header fields are shown in **Table 13.2.**

ROUTING IN IPX/SPX

When a workstation wants to transmit data it is pretty safe to assume that one of two situations will exist. The device to which it wants to transmit is either on the local network or on a remote network. If the network numbers of both transmitting and receiving devices are the same, no routing is necessary.

Table 13.2 Contents of IPX/SPX Packet

Field	Field Length	Field Description
Checksum	2 bytes	Used for error detection and correction
Packet Length	2 bytes	Indicates overall packet size, including payload
Transport Control	1 byte	Keeps track of the number of routers a packet passes through. Each router increments this field before passing it on and the sixteenth router will discard the packet. This number can be configured on routers using the *NetWare Link Services Protocol* (NLSP).
Packet Type	1 byte	Indicates whether packet is IPX, SPX, SAP, RIP, or a NetBIOS broadcast
Destination Network	4 bytes	Network number of target network
Destination Node	6 bytes	MAC address of target device
Destination Socket Number	2 bytes	Socket number of target process
Source Network	4 bytes	Network number of source network
Source Node	6 bytes	MAC address of transmitting device
Source Socket Number	2 bytes	Socket number of transmitting process
Payload	0 to 1470 bytes	Actual data being transmitted, if any

If the network addresses differ, the transmitting device needs to find a suitable router. It broadcasts a RIP packet (see Chapter Seven, The Network Layer) that includes both the source and destination network numbers. If there are multiple routers on the network with access to that destination, all will reply with their own network number and their node address as well. The one with the shortest number of hops to the destination wins. The router information goes into the MAC header of the hardware protocol. The destination information goes into the IPX header.

A router receiving an IPX/SPX packet will perform the following actions. First, it will check the Transport Control field in the IPX header. If that value becomes sixteen when incremented, it discards the packet, unless it is an NLSP packet. NLSP can be configured to support up to 127 hops. Next, it checks the Packet Type field. If the packet type is NetBIOS and the Transport Control field was incremented to eight, the packet is discarded. IPX/SPX limits the propagation of NetBIOS packets to a maximum of eight hops. If the packet survives to this point, the Transport Control field is incremented. The router compares the Destination Network number to its routing tables and transmits the packet through the appropriate interface.

PROS AND CONS OF IPX/SPX

As a protocol, IPX/SPX is rather elegant. It requires very little overhead on the part of the workstation because there is far less address translation going on. Configuring it on a single network is a piece of cake, although it becomes a bit more complex on multilevel networks. Because it requires less address translation, on a network with no routers it is a faster protocol.

IPX/SPX came up short in the battle of the protocols for two reasons—scalability and network overhead. Theoretically, scalability should not have been an issue. A limitation of sixteen hops allows for extremely large networks, and the 127 hops supported by NLSP actually exceed the capabilities of TCP/IP. The problem arises in internetworking.

On a global basis, there was never any governing body assigned to the task of managing network numbers. Network administrators frequently just picked them out of their hat. Practically every IPX network I've ever seen that consisted of a single network address used the default address. On a body of networks such as the Internet, this would be a disaster. Therefore, while an organization can internetwork itself just about any way it wants, trying to interconnect the world without a complete retrofit would be pretty much impossible.

Also, while the protocol requires less overhead on the part of the individual workstation, it imposes a heavier burden on the network as a whole. It relies heavily on broadcasts to keep individual devices updated as to network conditions. Workstations broadcast to find routers, routers broadcast to find other routers, and servers broadcast advertisements of the services they offer. In addition, there is a heavy flow of data between routers and servers, constantly updating tables and confirming the integrity of routes. Therefore, overall, even though IPX/SPX was designed for enterprise level networks, it really functions best in small to midsize networks.

NETBEUI

IBM originally developed the NetBIOS Enhanced User Interface (NetBEUI) protocol in 1985 for their LAN Manager server application. It really became popular when Microsoft adopted it as the default protocol for NT 3.51. It was modeled heavily after the Logical Link Control, Type 2 (LLC2) defined by OSI.

EXAM NOTE: The key thing to remember about NetBEUI as far as Network+ is concerned is that the protocol is not routable. The reason for this is that there is no Layer 3 addressing support built into the protocol.

As a result of this, the protocol operates mostly within the Data Link Layer of the OSI model. There is also a certain degree of NetBEUI support at the Transport Layer. Since there is no Network Layer addressing at all, LLC2 is not routable. And NetBEUI is nothing more than LLC2 on steroids. In order to break a network down into segments, the only option is to use a bridge or switch. Interconnecting two different networks using NetBEUI alone is not possible.

However, on a smaller network that does not require routing, NetBEUI has some distinct advantages. For one, it is the fastest of all protocols currently in use. (Although, starting with Windows XP, Microsoft has discontinued use of the protocol.)

Early versions of NetBEUI had a limitation of 254 sessions that could be open on a single interface. On a workstation this is no problem, but it did seriously impact the number of connections to a server. Starting with Version 3.0, which shipped with NT 4.0, this limitation was eliminated.

WINDOWS XP AND NETBEUI

For many years, Microsoft has been a strong proponent of the NetBEUI protocol. It has been one of the protocols that installed by default whenever networking was installed on every Microsoft OS since Windows 3.1 for Workgroups. This ended with the release of Windows XP. There is no native OS support for NetBEUI in XP. However, Microsoft was not so cruel as to completely abandon the protocol. Since XP does support installable file systems, NetBEUI can be added. On the XP CD-ROM in the retail version, you will find it in the VALUEADD directory. First browse to the Valueadd\MSFT\Net\NetBEUI folder on the CD-ROM. Copy nbf.sys to your %systemroot%\system32\drivers directory. Then copy netnbf.inf to your %systemroot%\inf directory. The %systemroot% directory is usually your WINNT directory. The \inf subdirectory is hidden, so you will have to go into your folder options and enable the option to view hidden files and folders. Now when you go to add a new protocol, NetBEUI will be listed.

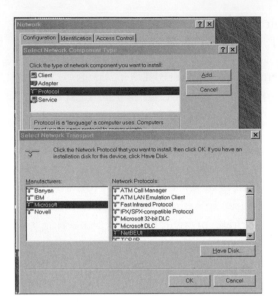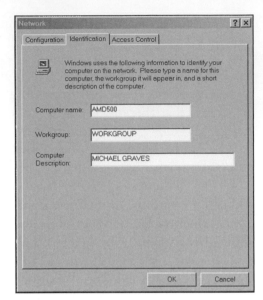

Figure 13.4 Configuring a Windows machine to use NetBEUI.

Configuring a computer to use NetBEUI couldn't be easier. All you have to do is to make sure that each computer has a unique NetBIOS name on the network and that each is assigned to the same workgroup, as shown in **Figure 13.4**.

Make sure File and Print Sharing is enabled and that's all there is to it. For smaller offices or home networks this could well be the protocol of choice—unless you have machines with the Windows XP (or later) operating system installed.

APPLETALK

The last networking protocol I'll discuss in this chapter is the AppleTalk Protocol. As you might imagine, Apple Computer Corporation developed the protocol for its systems. The protocol greatly resembles TCP/IP in its layered architecture, but uses a unique addressing function. As with TCP/IP, there is a relatively large collection of related protocols that go along with the suite.

Data is moved over the network in *datagrams*. The various protocols of AppleTalk make use of specific datagram structures. Since this is not an issue covered by the exam and is of relatively little use in

BUZZ WORD

Datagram: The format of the data fragment used by AppleTalk to send information over the network.

the field, you will not need to concern yourself with the different AppleTalk datagram structures.

ADDRESSING IN APPLETALK

One of the core protocols of AppleTalk is the *Name Binding Protocol* (NBP). AppleTalk locates an individual host on the network by its *node ID*. It assigns node IDs dynamically, so that a single host might have a different ID every time it logs on. Each device on an AppleTalk network needs to have a unique NBP name, sometimes called the *entity name*. When NBP assigns a node ID, it binds it to that entity name.

The *Datagram Delivery Protocol* (DDP) provides point-to-point delivery functions for AppleTalk. As with IPX/SPX, AppleTalk keeps track of networks by way of network number. However, the AppleTalk network number is only a 16-bit field. Therefore, AppleTalk only supports network numbers from 0 through 65,534. 65,535 is reserved. A network number of 0 specifies all nodes on the local network.

EXAM NOTE: The key features to remember about AppleTalk are the different protocols supported. Be able to identify which of the AppleTalk protocols provide what types of services.

A DDP packet can contain either a short header or a long header. Data intended for the local network requires only the short header, which includes fields that define the source and destination sockets; the frame type; and length. If the datagram needs to be routed, a long header must be used. The long header includes fields that define source and destination networks, the hop count, and a checksum field. With AppleTalk, if the hop count exceeds sixteen, the datagram will be discarded.

Routers that support AppleTalk make use of the *Routing Table Maintenance Protocol* (RTMP). This protocol dynamically builds routing tables by exchanging known network numbers and accessibility between routers.

The *AppleTalk Echo Protocol* (AEP) is Apple's answer to ICMP. It provides the background services for Echo, Echo Response, and messaging.

As with TCP/IP, AppleTalk provides for both reliable, connection-oriented transfer of data as well as best-effort connectionless services. The *AppleTalk Transaction Protocol* (ATP) and the *AppleTalk Data Streaming Protocol* (ADSP) both provide connection-oriented services.

With ATP, any request for an ATP transaction must fit into a single datagram. ATP responses can use up to eight datagrams. It is used for transferring smaller amounts of data. Acknowledgments and flow control are maintained through tokens exchanged by devices. Each transaction is assigned a transaction ID and a starting sequence number for datagrams, in addition to other fields that provide flow control and status reports.

ADSP is the preferred protocol for transferring larger amounts of data. It is a full duplex protocol that does not depend on individual transactions for the transfer of data. It guarantees that all data will arrive intact and in the correct sequence. For connectionless services, AppleTalk relies on DDP.

In AppleTalk, individual sessions are maintained by the *AppleTalk Session Protocol* (ASP). When a session is first initiated, ASP assigns it a unique session number. Then, in order to maintain the session, it will periodically send out *keep-alive* frames. When a session is completed, it closes everything down and cleans up after itself. Now, if only it could teach my son to do that.

AppleTalk over IP

To get an idea about how AppleTalk gets transmitted over an IP network, it is necessary to understand a bit more about how the protocol deals with routers. This involves learning a few more terms specific to how Apple deals with routers. In previous discussions about routers, I simply took the approach that routers were like cigars. Sometimes a router is simply a router. With Apple there are several types of routers. These include the following:

- Seed routers
- Non-seed routers
- Soft-seed routers
- Half routers

An administrator statically configures *seed routers*. They retain their configuration when first fired up on the network, even if that configuration conflicts with an existing router. A *non-seed router* is configured to dynamically obtain its configuration from other routers already configured on the network. It's the *soft-seed router* that has an identity problem. This device is statically configured, but it reconfigures itself using information provided by neighboring routers when it is fired up on a network containing a previously existing router with the same configuration.

So what, then, is a *half router*? Is it half a router and half an inkjet printer? While that would be amusing, it wouldn't be accurate. The half router is nothing more than a router configured to talk to an AppleTalk network on one port to a network using some other protocol on other ports.

By now, you're most likely wondering how all this relates to sending AppleTalk over an IP network. By default, AppleTalk and IP are about as different as apples and peas. The packets are created differently and data is transmitted differently. In order to send AppleTalk data over a TCP/IP interface, it must first be encapsulated into IP packets.

A number of utilities accomplish this, and different Apple protocols use different utilities to perform the encapsulation. TCP and IP can be transmitted with IPTalk, and data sent via the Apple Filing Protocol (AFP) can use MacServerIP. The list goes on and on. Fortunately, this problem is less common because TCP/IP has become a default protocol for the MAC OS.

THE OTHER PROTOCOLS AND OSI

As I discussed TCP/IP in the previous chapters, I associated the different protocols of that stack to the appropriate OSI layers as I came to them. When it comes to the protocols discussed in this chapter, there are so few of them that I decided they would be easier to understand if I grouped them together. **Table 13.3** summarizes the various protocols of NetBEUI, IPX/SPX, and Appletalk as they relate to OSI.

Table 13.3 The "other" networking protocols, as they relate to OSI.

OSI Layer	NetBEUI	Appletalk	IPX/SPX
Application		AFP	NCP, SAP, RIP
Presentation			
Session	NetBIOS	ZIP, ASP, ADSP	NetBIOS
Transport	NetBEUI	ATP, NBP	SPX
Network		DDP	IPX, RIP
Data Link	NetBEUI	LLAP, ELAP	
Physical	No networking protocols are specific to this layer.		

CHAPTER SUMMARY

For many, the information in this chapter is for reference only. A growing number of networks are using TCP/IP as their exclusive networking protocol, and administrators of those networks will never make use of the other protocols. You won't, however, pass the Network+ exam without this information.

The three protocols covered in this chapter are IPX/SPX, NetBEUI, and AppleTalk. The bulk of your exam material will come from the IPX/SPX section, but don't slack off on the other two. There are a good number of questions covering both NetBEUI and AppleTalk in CompTIA's database of questions.

BRAIN DRAIN

1. Describe in detail a complete IPX/SPX address.

2. How does the IPX/SPX address differ from a TCP/IP address?

3. Explain why NetBEUI would not be the protocol of choice in a larger network.

4. Compare and contrast addressing between AppleTalk and IPX/SPX.

5. Compare and contrast the AppleTalk Suite to what you learned about TCP/IP.

THE 64K$ QUESTIONS

1. IPX/SPX stands for _____.
   a. Internet Packet Exchange/Sequenced Packet Exchange
   b. Internet Packet Exchange/Serial Packet Exchange
   c. Internetwork Packet Exchange/Sequenced Packet Exchange
   d. Internetwork Packet Exchange/Serial Packet Exchange

2. The host portion of an IPX address is derived from _____.
   a. The MAC address of the interface
   b. A number dynamically assigned by the server
   c. A number statically assigned by an administrator
   d. The serial number of the NIC

3. IPX/SPX uses _____ to identify a process for which data is intended.

   a. Ports

   b. Sockets

   c. Transaction IDs

   d. Sequence numbers

4. How many hops over the network can an IPX packet survive?

   a. 8

   b. 16

   c. 127

   d. There is no limit.

5. How many hops can an NLFC packet survive?

   a. 8

   b. 16

   c. 127

   d. There is no limit.

6. NetBEUI isn't routable because _____.

   a. It has no Layer 3 services

   b. It supports a maximum of 254 devices on a network

   c. Routers do not support the NetBEUI protocol

   d. NetBIOS information cannot be fragmented

7. AppleTalk moves information in _____.

   a. Packets

   b. Frames

   c. Segments

   d. Datagrams

8. An AppleTalk network number is _____ bits long.

   a. 16

   b. 32

   c. 64

   d. 128

9. Which AppleTalk protocol handles routing functions?

    a. DDP

    b. ATP

    c. RIP

    d. RTMP

10. Which of the following are connection-oriented protocols?

    a. DDP

    b. ATP

    c. RTMP

    d. ADSP

11. _____ was the company that invented IPX/SPX.

    a. Novell

    b. Microsoft

    c. DEC

    d. Xerox

12. What was the biggest limitation to IPX/SPX that prevented it from being used on the Internet?

    a. It only offers a16-bit network address.

    b. It makes heavy use of broadcast messages to advertise services.

    c. It was a connection-oriented service.

    d. There was no built-in mechanism for blocking broadcasts across networks.

13. The node address in IPX/SPX is directly obtained from the MAC address.

    a. True

    b. False

14. The address that identifies a specific computer on an IPX network is called the _____ address.

    a. Station

    b. Host

    c. Persona

    d. Node ID

15. IPX identified the application that was to receive incoming data by way of its _____ address.

    a. Station

    b. Host

    c. Port

    d. Socket

16. The reason NetBEUI couldn't be routed was that _____.

    a. It makes no use of subnet masks

    b. It is a Data Link Layer protocol

    c. It uses a singular network address

    d. You can't fool me. NetBEUI is routable.

17. The parcel of data sent over the network by Appletalk is called a _____.

    a. Datagram

    b. Parcel

    c. Segment

    d. Packet

18. The address that identifies a specific computer on an Appletalk network is called the _____ address.

    a. Station

    b. Host

    c. Persona

    d. Node ID

19. The AppleTalk protocol that resolves individual host addresses is _____.

    a. The AppleTalk Routing Protocol

    b. The Name Binding Protocol

    c. The Node Maintenance Protocol

    d. The Station Routing Protocol

20. Appletalk is a connectionless protocol.

    a. True

    b. False

TRICKY TERMINOLOGY

Datagram: The format of the data fragment used by AppleTalk to send information over the network.

Entity name: A user-friendly host name used by NBP for identifying hosts on the network.

Network number: A number used by IPX/SPX and AppleTalk to identify the network on which a device resides. In IPX/SPX it is a 32-bit number; in AppleTalk it is a 16-bit number.

Node address: A unique number assigned to an individual host on the network. In IPX/SPX, this number is derived from the MAC address of the interface.

Node ID: A number assigned by the AppleTalk protocol that identifies a specific host on the network.

Socket number: A 16-bit number assigned to a specific process or function that is accessing the network in IPX/SPX.

Station address: In IPX/SPX, this is the combination of the network number and node address. A socket number is added to create the complete IPX/SPX address.

ACRONYM ALERT

ADSP: AppleTalk Data Streaming Protocol. A connection-oriented protocol used by AppleTalk for sending large groups of data. It does not require the maintenance of transactions in order to function.

AEP: AppleTalk Echo Protocol. AppleTalk's answer to ICMP.

ASP: AppleTalk Session Protocol. The AppleTalk protocol that establishes, maintains, and breaks down logical connections between devices.

ATP: AppleTalk Transaction Protocol. A connection-oriented protocol used by AppleTalk for sending small pieces of data.

DDP: Datagram Delivery Protocol. The AppleTalk protocol that provides end-to-end support services.

IPX/SPX: Internetwork Packet Exchange/Sequenced Packet Exchange

LLC2: Logical Link Control, Type 2

NBP: Name Binding Protocol. The AppleTalk protocol that handles name resolution.

NetBEUI: NetBIOS Enhanced User Interface

NLSP: NetWare Link Services Protocol

RTMP: Routing Table Maintenance Protocol. The AppleTalk protocol that dynamically maintains routing table information.

PART FOUR

Putting It All to Work

CHAPTER 14

WORKING WITH REMOTE ACCESS

Setting up a Local Area Network (LAN) isn't all that complicated. A little basic knowledge and a few essential pieces of equipment and it's a fairly simple procedure. If it wasn't, how could there be so many home networks out there?

Setting up a Wide Area Network (WAN) requires a bit more knowledge. A key segment of that knowledge revolves around the different methods of gaining remote access. Remote access is a funny thing. Sometimes that term is used to describe giving a user access to the network from an outside location. Other times, it refers to intranetwork communications.

Regardless of the reasoning behind the connection, network administrators still have to consider the fact that they are going to be making use of third-party services. This third party will be some form of telecommunications company (telco), and you will have no control over its infrastructure.

This chapter will deal primarily with the different services that are available for data communication. Toward the end I will take a look at the different methods operating systems have of allowing users remote access to the network, including *Dial-up Networking* (DUN) and *Remote Access Services* (RAS). By the time you've finished this chapter you will have been introduced to the following exam objectives:

1.6 Identify the purposes, features and functions of key network components.

1.7 Specify the general characteristics (For example: carrier speed, frequency, transmission type and topology) of the following wireless

---

BUZZ WORD ————————

Telco: A generic term for any provider of telecommunications services.

technologies: 802.11 (Frequency hopping spread spectrum), 802.11x (Direct sequence spread spectrum), Infrared, Bluetooth.

2.14 Identify the basic characteristics (For example: speed, capacity and media) of WAN (Wide Area Networks) technologies.

2.15 Identify the basic characteristics of Internet access technologies.

2.16 Define the function of remote access protocols and services.

2.17 Identify the security protocols and describe their purpose and function.

2.18 Identify authentication protocols (For example: CHAP (Challenge Handshake Authentication Protocol), MS-CHAP (Microsoft Challenge Handshake Authentication Protocol), PAP (Password Authentication Protocol), RADIUS (Remote Authentication Dial-In User Service), Kerberos and EAP (Extensible Authentication Protocol)).

3.4 Given a remote connectivity scenario comprised of a protocol, an authentication scheme, and physical connectivity, configure the connection. Includes connection to the following servers: UNIX/Linux/MAC OS X Server, Netware, Windows, Appleshare IP (Internet Protocol).

THE PROTOCOLS

Making a remote connection is no different than any other network connection. You need to have the proper protocols installed or it won't work. I need to cover a few protocols specific to remote access that facilitate the connection and/or to provide security for the connection. The simplest of these is the *Point-to-Point Protocol* (PPP). For more security, you can set up a *Virtual Private Network* (VPN) and use the *Point-to-Point Tunneling Protocol* (PPTP).

Sometimes networks that use a thin-client architecture may use either Microsoft's *Remote Desktop Protocol* (RDP) or the Citrix *Independent Computing Architecture* (ICA) protocol for remote services. Both of these protocols provide a rather unique service and deserve a closer look as well.

PPP

PPP is a protocol that replaced an earlier one called the *Serial Line IP* (SLIP) as the standard protocol for dial-up connections or ISDN connections. It is a layered protocol that allows the transfer of IP packets over the connection. The three layers are the *Link Control Protocol* (LCP); the *Network Control Protocols* (NCP), of which there are several; and finally, the *IP Control Protocol* (IPCP).

EXAM NOTE: Know the dial-up networking protocols and which one is used for which type of connection. This is a frequent question on the exam.

LCP provides the end-to-end services. It handles the tasks of establishing the connection, exchanging configuration information, and monitoring the connection while it exists. The NCPs transport the data being sent by specific networking protocol suites, such as TCP/IP or IPX/SPX. IPCP allows for IP packets to be transmitted over a PPP connection.

There are several services provided by PPP. These include:

- Address notification
- Authentication
- Link monitoring
- Support of multiple protocols

Address notification allows a server to dynamically provide a remote client with TCP/IP configuration that exists only for that specific connection. Once the connection is released, so is the IP configuration.

Authentication is provided through one of two authentication protocols. The *Password Authentication Protocol* (PAP) is the simplest. It is also the least secure, in that it transmits passwords and data in plain text. PAP uses a two-way handshake. The machine attempting to log on will transmit its credentials (in plain text). That information is compared to the security database on the machine being logged on to, and if the information matches, access is granted.

PAP has a few weak points. The most significant of these has already been mentioned; that is that it transmits user credentials in plain text. In addition, it allows users to try over and over again until they get it right. This allows hackers to break into a network by using password guessing techniques or something called *dictionary attacks*. The latter is when a server is assaulted with a database of possible user IDs and passwords until one works.

A more secure protocol used by *Virtual Private Networks* (VPN) is the *Challenge-Handshake Authentication Protocol* (CHAP).

BUZZ WORDS

Dictionary attack: An attempt by a hacker to break into a network by barraging the server with a database of user IDs and passwords.

CHAP uses a three-way handshake instead of a two-way handshake. When CHAP is first configured on a client the server provides it with a string of code known as the *secret*. The server keeps a database of the secrets it has assigned. This secret is used to verify the client during the authentication process and is linked to the User ID and password. Once a link has been estab-

BUZZ WORDS

Retry counter: A value maintained by an RAS server that increments with each attempt to log on. When configured with a specific value, once that value is reached, the account will be locked out.

lished, the server doesn't simply trust the logon credentials it receives from the client. It waits for the client to return the secret string of code assigned by the server. The number of times a client can respond to the challenge is limited by means of a *retry counter*. This is something that is configured on the server. The challenge is repeated several times during the session to assure that an intruder has not tapped into the session.

CHAP still sends its information in plain text. Therefore in this respect, it is no more secure that PAP. It is the three-way handshake and the authentication secret that provides a bit more security.

PPTP

PPP provides adequate services for such activities as browsing the Internet. But if security requirements are a bit more stringent, PPP simply doesn't cut it. For employees who do a great deal of their work at home, it might be necessary to be able to access the office network. If long-distance charges are an issue, it will be preferable to make that connection over the Internet. In that case you don't want to jeopardize office security.

PPTP provides the answer. It works by incorporating one of several encryption standards (to be discussed in detail in Chapter Fifteen, Working with Network Security). The encrypted data is encapsulated into upper-level protocol packets for transmission. On the receiving end, the data is stripped from the packets, unencrypted, and reassembled. The upper-level protocols supported by PPTN include IP, IPX, and NetBEUI. Whatever protocol is selected for transmission over the Internet, the packets created by these upper-level protocols are buried in IP packets from transmission.

Later in the chapter, I'll be pointing out the virtues of using a virtual private network (VPN). To create one of these, you will be invoking PPTP. A more recent protocol being supported that is built on the foundation of PPTP is *Layer 2*

Tunneling Protocol (L2TP). This protocol takes advantages of the best features and concepts of PPTP and operates at the Data Link Layer. The process of tunneling consists of encrypting an entire packet generated by any other networking protocol and subsequently encapsulating into its own packet structure.

PPPoE

Security is one of the key issues faced by cable modem and DSL users. Both of these connections make use of an Ethernet connection. Point-to-Point Protocol (PPP) is no good because it uses completely different access methods. However, Point-to-Point Protocol over Ethernet (PPPoE) encapsulates PPP packets into Ethernet for transport between the user's interface and the ISP. PPPoE uses the ARP protocol to determine the Ethernet MAC address of the remote device in order to establish a session.

Most cable modem companies use PPPoE because it supports the protocol layers and authentication methods used in PPP along with the Ethernet interface. While it can be used by DSL connections as well (and sometimes is), other protocols are more suitable.

RDP AND ICA

Networks based on thin clients have completely different requirements from the standard client-server network. A thin client, if you recall from Chapter One, has very little processing power and memory resources of its own. In many cases there is no local storage at all. The client makes use of the BootP protocol to boot to a server, where all applications are run and all data is stored and maintained. What the user sees are actually just screen shots passed over the network showing the user what is going on at the server level. User input, such as keystrokes and mouse movements, pass to the server, where the application is executed. Video information is sent back from the server to the client to show the user what transpired.

EXAM NOTE: RDP and ICA have only recently been added to the exam objectives. Therefore, there is a very good chance of seeing these protocols somewhere on the exam.

RDP was the original protocol used by Microsoft's NT 4.0 Terminal Server and the Terminal Services of the various Windows 2000 Server editions. A server using

RDP can set up two channels for each user. User input moves over one channel, return graphics over the other. The protocol supports up to 64,000 simultaneous channels and can do multipoint transmissions as well.

ICA is a nearly identical protocol developed by Citrix for its thin-client server applications. It is a little more robust in that it can encapsulate other protocols and is backwardly compatible to older 16-bit clients for DOS and Windows 3.1, whereas the only 16-bit client RDP supports is one for Windows 3.11 for Workgroups. It will also publish available applications to clients on the network. With RDP, each client is configured with a group of applications it can use on the server.

This is only the briefest overview of these two protocols, simply because thin-client networks are a fading technology. Today's systems are so much cheaper and more robust, high-speed networks are far more commonplace. Since thin-client networks are also somewhat more difficult to manage, many organizations have simply gone the way of a conventional client-server network and run applications on the local system.

REMOTE CONNECTION OPTIONS

The absolute key ingredient to performance on a remote connection is the choice of service. The old cliché states that a chain is no stronger than its weakest link. Likewise, a network connection is no faster than its slowest link. When two devices that normally use Gigabit Ethernet on their local networks are forced to exchange data over a 56K modem, I don't care what world your computer was made on, that data moves slowly!

The thing to remember is that not all of the services mentioned in this chapter are available in all areas. In fact, a couple of services are going to be described that I doubt you can still find anywhere. The Network+ exam just hasn't figured that out yet.

CIRCUIT SWITCHING VS. PACKET SWITCHING

I've spent a rather large amount of time pointing out that when data moves over the network, it gets broken down into packets and sent along its way. In a LAN, you have control over the entire process. You own all the transceivers and any intermediate devices, and therefore, you control the routes.

In a WAN, you have to make use of services provided by a third party. And as I said earlier, you have no control over the third-party infrastructure. Still, your data is going to move across the wire (or light beams) in packets. That won't change.

The different services available will come in one of two basic forms. There is *circuit switching*, and there is *packet switching*.

> **EXAM NOTE:** The Network+ folks have a couple of fairly oblique approaches to testing your knowledge of which services are packet switching and which ones are circuit switching. Make sure you can describe the differences clearly.

Circuit switching is the type of service that you use when you pick up your telephone. When you dial a number, the telco's switches will figure out a path from point A to point B based on current line conditions that will give the optimum link. Throughout the duration of the connection, that circuit will be yours. Your entire telephone network relies on banks of switches installed at the various substations along the way. These switches are constantly monitoring traffic along each backbone and at any given station will have a choice of routes over which signals can be sent. Once a choice of circuits has been made, the two end-points have exclusive use of that circuit until the connection has ended. However, if a user in New York routinely transmits data to an office in LA, on some connections, the data might go through Chicago, and on others, it might get to LA by way of Omaha. But each connection uses a defined path, and all packets will arrive in order.

Packet switching gets a bit more complicated. The telco's switches will analyze the route for each packet. So on any given communications link some packets go by way of Chicago and others by way of Omaha. To complicate matters even further, on any given circuit, the packets from hundreds or even thousands of different communications links are all mixed together. You are relying on the different protocols and OSI layers I've spent the last few hundred pages discussing to make sure the right packets get where they belong and that they get put together in the correct order when they arrive.

BUZZ WORDS

Circuit switching: A telecommunications technology that selects the best route for data to take, based on current network conditions, and then creates a virtual circuit over which all data from that session will flow.

Packet switching: A telecommunications technology that selects the best route for each packet of data to take based on current network conditions. There is no single path used throughout the session and packets may not arrive in sequence.

CIRCUIT SWITCHING OPTIONS

Circuit switching is primarily the domain of voice communication. This is because in voice communication, having the packets arrive in sequence is critical to the quality of the connection. In some cases, you also need to rely on circuit switching techniques for the transfer of your data. There aren't really that many telecommunications options available today that make use of circuit switching. The two that I will discuss are the *Public Switched Telephone Network* (PSTN) and the *Integrated Services Digital Network* (ISDN).

PSTN

Ah, yes! The good old *public switched telephone network* is still alive and well, despite deathly slow transfer rates and marginal reliability. Why? Because it's there—wherever you go. In the small Vermont village where I live, it is currently the only link available to the Internet that the average nine-to-fiver can afford. There is no cable service and we're much too distant from any of the telephone company's main offices for them to consider DSL.

> **EXAM NOTE:** PSTN may be a dying entity in the commercial market, but it is still a favorite topic on the Network+ Exam.

Sometimes you'll see this same service described as POTS. This refers to *plain old telephone service.* That's cute, but in this book, I'll stick to PSTN.

Either way you look at it, you're moving data over a wire designed to move voice signals. In the old days, voice signals were transferred using an analog electrical current. Since computers all use a digital signal, a device called a *modulator-demodulator* (modem) is used as the transceiver. Exactly how a modem does its job is beyond the scope of this book, but if you're interested, you can find a complete description of the process in my book *PC Hardware Maintenance and Repair,* also published by Delmar.

Now here's the odd part. The majority of telephone circuits have gone digital. Voice signals are moved on a 64K signal, sampling the voice approximately 8000 times per second and delivering each sample as an 8-bit value. However, because the majority of telephones in use are still analog, the connection from the telephone companies (telco) office to the end user is converted back to analog. This last link is referred to as the *last mile.*

Therefore, your digital data moves from digital to analog so it can move from your computer, across that last mile, and finally to the telco. The telco converts it to a digital signal and shoots it over a high-capacity interface, along with a few

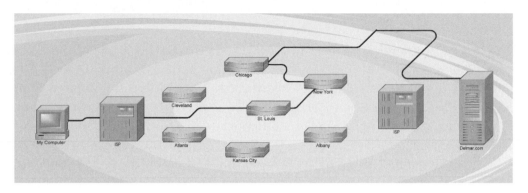

Figure 14.1 Signals over a PSTN take a rather convoluted route to get from point A to point B.

million other calls. It then gets converted back to analog to be sent to the other modem, where it will be converted back to digital (see **Figure 14.1**).

Of course, there is still the question of why, if the telco is using a 64K channel, we only have 56K modems. What happened to the other 8K?

In the U.S., data is transmitted over telephone wires using a technique called *robbed-bit signaling* (RBS). If you recall, the now-digitized voice circuits make use of around 8000 6-bit samples per second. For every six of these samples, 1 bit is reserved for use by the telephone company. As far as data transfer is concerned, that 8-bit sample is now useless for moving data. So let's do the math.

On a 64K line (65,536Kb/s) there are a total of 8192 8-bit samples going over the line. If you lose one in six, that means every second you are transmitting a maximum of 6826.666666~ samples per second. This gives a total bandwidth of 54613.3333~ bits per second that is the theoretical maximum that can be transmitted. So your 56K modem isn't really 56K after all.

On top of that, data being transmitted cannot make use of this maximum speed if it must go through an analog-to-digital conversion cycle, as all modems must do. Therefore, when uploading from your computer, you are limited to a 33.6Kb/s speed (upgraded to 48K in V.92 standards). Since most servers are on one of the forms of digital technology that I will discuss later in the chapter, the download is frequently unaffected. However, if you connect to a server that does use analog modems as its transceivers, that same limitation will affect downloads.

Frequently, people ask why the telephone companies don't simply increase the bandwidth allotted to each signal. While that may sound fine and dandy on the outset, to accomplish this would require completely gutting just about everything in the system, except perhaps for the wire itself, and starting from scratch.

RADIUS

The Remote Authentication Dial-In User Service (RADIUS) is one of the class of protocols known as Authentication, Authorization and Accounting (AAA). These are used in applications requiring network access from different, and often unpredictable, locations. These protocols offer secure access to the home network for road warriors, such as traveling sales folks or other professionals who spend more time out of the office than in it.

When you connect to an ISP using a modem, DSL, cable or wireless connection, the first thing you do is to enter your username and password. RADIUS transmits this over the PPP, to a RADIUS server, which verifies authenticity of that information. This is generally done using one of the other protocols I've already discussed such as PAP or CHAP. Once the user's credentials are accepted, the server then authorizes access.

ISDN

For some people, the speed of a modem is simply too slow. Yet some of the faster technologies that I will discuss in the next few sections are too expensive to be justifiable. In cases such as these, ISDN might be the key. This is a service that, on its most basic level, provides noticeably faster throughput in both directions.

EXAM NOTE: ISDN is a topic that is heavily covered on the exam. You might want to go over this section a couple of times.

Unlike a telephone line, an ISDN signal is digital from end to end. This eliminates the analog-to-digital conversion that robs some of our bandwidth. In addition, bit robbing is not used, so the entire bandwidth is available.

There are two forms of ISDN available—*Basic Rate ISDN* (BRI) and *Primary Rate ISDN* (PRI). In the majority of areas I've surveyed, however, I've found that only BRI is offered as an option.

Basic Rate ISDN (BRI) provides the user with two 64K channels for carrying data (although some service providers drop that to 56K due to the type of switches they use). These are the *B-channels*. These carry nothing but user information. This can include digital data, digitized voice communications, and so forth. A third channel, the *D-channel*, is a 16K connection that carries the transmission control signals.

Primary Rate ISDN (PRI) provides even higher speeds. Up to twenty-three channels can be combined to provide the user with up to 1536K of throughput. In Europe, ISDN services can provide for up to thirty B-channels for 1920K.) The D-channel is a 64K channel. **Table 14.1** lists some of the more common options.

Table 14.1   Summary of ISDN Services

ISDN Service	Structure	Maximum Speed
H0	6B, 1D	384K
H10	23B, 1D	1472K
H11	24B, 1D	1536
H12	30B, 1D	1920K

Note: H11 and H12 services are only available in Europe

ISDN services take different forms between the U.S. and European markets.

How you interconnect your system to the ISDN line will be determined by where you live. In the U.S., the signal is going to enter the building by way of a *U interface.* The U interface only supports a single device, and that device is going to be the *Network Termination-1* (NT1). All the NT1 really does is convert the incoming two-wire circuit to a four-wire *S/T Interface.* The S/T interface provides access to more than one device. It is possible to get S/T interfaces that support up to seven different devices. It is also possible that your provider might install equipment that has the NT1 and S/T interface designed into the device, making it impossible to add other devices.

> **BUZZ WORDS**
>
> **U interface:** The device that accepts an incoming ISDN signal and brings it into the building.
>
> **S/T interface:** A device that allows access to the ISDN signal by multiple other devices.

The signal must also pass through a *Network Termination-2* (NT2) interface. It's unlikely that you'll have to deal with that interface directly because it is built into the ISDN equipment and is not a separate device. From here, the circuit can now be interconnected with the user's equipment. It sounds pretty complicated, but since much of this can be integrated into the equipment supplied by your provider, it need not be intimidating. **Figure 14.2** shows a block diagram of a complete ISDN circuit.

This equipment will fall under one of two categories. Devices that are designed around ISDN are *Terminal Equipment-1* (TE1) devices. Those devices that were originally designed to interface with conventional telephone lines are designated *Terminal Equipment-2* (TE2). In order to interconnect TE2 devices, you're going to need a *Terminal Adapter* (TA). A TA brings the ISDN into your building and provides either RJ45 ports or standard serial ports for interconnecting to your computer. An ISDN modem is a prime example of a TA.

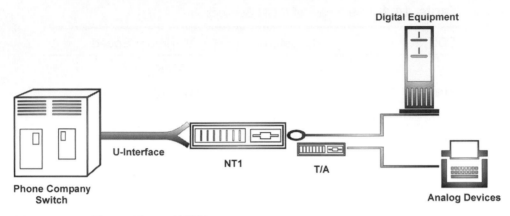

Figure 14.2   The makings of ISDN.

CAUTION: While the TA provides an RJ45 connection, you must pay attention to the type of TA installed. Plugging an analog device into a digital circuit will kill that device. If a TA is designed for analog circuits, it will have a port labeled either *A/B* or *POTS* (an acronym for plain old telephone service). Along those same lines (figuratively speaking), it is essential that, in an office environment, you know if a digital telephone system is in place. If you plug the analog modem in your laptop into a digital line, you'll be shopping for a new modem that afternoon. The one you plugged into a digital line will be fried.

BUZZ WORD

Channel aggregation protocol: A protocol that binds two or more signals of lower bandwidth into a single signal of higher bandwidth.

By using a *channel aggregation protocol,* the two incoming channels can be combined into a single 128K connection. The two protocols most commonly used are *Bonding* (Bandwidth on Demand) and *Multilink-PPP*. The latter is the more recently introduced protocol and is supposedly superior in its error handling capabilities.

It isn't necessary to combine the two channels if your requirements are not purely data transmission. The signals can be separated, allowing voice over one channel and data over the other.

PACKET SWITCHING TECHNOLOGIES

The majority of telecommunication is done by way of packet-switching technologies. In fact, the technology is moving in that direction as far as voice communications are concerned as well. Several different protocols have been developed that provide high quality voice links over packet-switched networks. These include Cellular Digital Packet Data (CDPD), General Packet Radio Service (GPRS), and Bluetooth, among others. These technologies are beyond the scope of Network+ and will not be discussed here. I include them as a point of reference, should you desire to pursue the further study of these technologies.

> **BUZZ WORD** ————————
>
> **Fractional T1:** A telco service that allows users to select how much bandwidth they need, without having to pay for the services of an entire T1 line.

In order to make use of the higher speeds made possible by packet-switching technologies, you need faster carriers as well. Therefore, in this section I will also discuss some of the high-speed carriers available for your WAN. Please understand that there is a difference between the protocols and the selection of carrier. The different technologies I will discuss in this section are as follows:

- T1/E1 and T3/E3
- Frame Relay
- FDDI
- ATM
- Sonet/SDH
- OCx

These discussions will be somewhat limited, because as a network engineer, you will have little or no control over the infrastructure and need not concern yourself with the intricacies of each technology. However, an overview of each one will help you make an informed decision as to which technology you should use in your specific environment. And chances are, it'll be on the test.

T-LINES AND E-LINES

AT&T gave the world *Digital Trunk Lines* (T1) back in 1962 as an answer to two different problems. First off, increasing use of long-distance services was putting a strain on the existing lines, and second, the analog signals being used degraded quickly over distance. By converting the signals from analog to digital, few repeaters were needed. By multiplexing twenty-four different signals onto a single carrier, more calls could be carried on a single twisted pair.

> **EXAM NOTE:** Know the makeup of the various T and E connections well. You may be asked to describe all of them.

T1 combines the twenty-four digitized channels and sends them over the wire in frames, just like conventional networking technology. Each frame consists of one 8-bit voice sample for each of the twenty-four channels plus a single framing bit. If you do your math correctly, you will see that this results in a 193-bit frame. If you recall from our discussion of PSTN, digital telephone signaling samples the voice 8000 times per second. The reason for this sample rate is simple. Take the highest frequency you wish to reproduce in your digital signal, and set your sample rate to twice that frequency. AT&T engineers set the highest frequency for voice reproduction at 4000Hz. Thus, they needed a sample rate of 8000/sec.

An effective throughput of 1.544 Mb/s is given by 8000 frames of 193 bits. This is your basic T1 line. Service providers will provide you with an entire T1 line of your own, should you require it, or you can lease just a portion of the available channels. The latter is known as *fractional T1*.

Typical fractional T1 services are two channels (128 Kbps), four channels (256 Kbps), six channels (384 Kbps), eight channels (512 Kbps), or twelve channels (768 Kbps). In order to provide a network interface for your T1 connection, you will need to install a *channel service unit/data service unit* (CSU/DSU). These can be either stand-alone devices or an interface card that installs in a router.

As the name implies, a CSU/DSU provides two functions. The CSU transmits and receives signals from the WAN interface. In addition it provides a barrier against any electrical interference that may come in from the carrier's outside lines. Once in a while, the telco may need to send a loopback signal through your T1 line as a part of some diagnostics procedure. You don't want that loopback signal interpreted as data, so the CSU intercepts these signals and echoes them.

The DSU takes those 193-bit frames off of the T1 line and converts them into a frame your computer can recognize. The different frame types supported include standard RS-232C serial format, the higher-speed RS-449, or any one of the conventional modem protocols, such as V.42 or V.90. Synchronization and timing of data signals are also the responsibility of the DSU.

Now that you've got a grasp of what the T1 line is all about, you can put that information to work and figure out the remainder of the T-lines and E-lines.

While AT&T had decided on twenty-four channels for a T1 line, the telcos in Europe had a different vision. They combined thirty-two channels into a single line called the E1 line. This thirty-two-channel line provides 2.048 Mb/s of bandwidth. With either T-lines or E-lines, telcos can bundle the lines themselves for even higher speeds. **Table 14.2** lists the various options.

Table 14.2 Overview of T1/E1 Options

Line Type	Description	Bandwidth
T1	24 channels	1.544Mb/s
E1	32 channels	2.048Mb/s
T1C	48 channels, or 2xT1	3.088Mb/s
T2	96 channels, or 4xT1	6.176Mb/s
E2	120 channels	8.448Mb/s
E3	512 channels, or 16xE1	32.768Mb/s
T3	672 channels, or 28xT1	44.736Mb/s
T3C	1344 channels, or 56xT1	89.472Mb/s
T4	4032 channels, or 168xT1	274.176Mb/s

The beauty of these lines, aside from their raw speed, is that they are protocol-independent. Data is converted into serial format and moved over the wire in a fixed format. At the other end, it's put back together. The T-line doesn't care if it is carrying voice or data, and it doesn't care what form the data takes.

FRAME RELAY

Frame Relay is a packet-switching technology that takes advantage of the speed of T1 lines. It was originally released in the early 1990s in a combined effort between AT&T and Sprint as a foundation for PR1 ISDN. It is not, however, limited to that architecture.

> **BUZZ WORD**
>
> **Frame Relay:** A packet-switching WAN protocol that makes use of Layer 2 networking services.

Based on the HDLC protocol (see Chapter Six, The Data Link Layer), data moves over the wire using HDLC frames. The key to Frame Relay's speed is that is provides no error correction mechanisms whatsoever. It counts on the networking protocol to provide those services. And since the vast majority of Frame Relay networks use TCP/IP as the protocol of choice, the error correction is built in, with the work being done by the transmitting and receiving devices. Intermediate devices neither know nor care if there are errors in the data they forward.

EXAM NOTE: Of all the packet switching services, Frame Relay is most likely to be the most heavily covered. Know this section well.

Since error correction is done at the end points of the link, an intermediate device simply reads the frame deep enough to extract addressing information. As soon as it has that, the frame is on its way to the next stop. As a result, there is extremely low latency in these intermediate devices.

With Frame Relay, you can choose to go with a *virtual circuit* or a *permanent virtual circuit* (PVC). With a virtual circuit, when a session is first established, the service provider's equipment will determine the best route and create a path from point A to point B. This is good for connect-on-demand services. A PVC is a leased line that establishes a dedicated circuit that is yours as long as you subscribe.

Either way, data moves over virtual circuits known as *Data Link Connection Identifiers* (DLCI). You don't need your own T1 line coming into your office. You tell the service provider what you want your *committed information rate* (CIR) to be. That is the throughput for which you will be charged.

However, all transmissions will occur at line speed. Should your bandwidth exceed your CIR, a bit in the frame called the *discharge eligibility* (DE) bit will be set to 1. If possible, these frames will be delivered. However, if congestion becomes a problem, DE-flagged frames are the first to be dropped. Many of the less-expensive Frame Relay services automatically set your CIR to 0. All of your frames go out as DE frames. When network congestion is low this isn't bad, because you take advantage of what bandwidth is available. Your connection can become intolerable when congestion becomes high, because the majority of your frames are being dropped. Since there is no error detection mechanism in Frame Relay, it will be up to the transmitting device to retransmit lost frames when those frames' TTL expires without having received ACKs.

In many areas, Frame Relay is the best choice for a high-speed connection between remote offices—or even fast access to the Internet. Since most Frame Relay services are based on the speed of a T1 line, speeds of up to 1.544 Mb/s are possible. Even higher speeds are possible if you specify a higher CIR (and that service is available in your area.)

FDDI

I discussed FDDI in detail in Chapter Six as a Data Link protocol, and therefore, the basic theory behind an FDDI connection will not be rehashed here. However, you should be aware that FDDI is available in some areas as a telecommunications service as well. An FDDI hookup will provide 100Mb/s throughput.

In order to obtain an FDDI hookup, first of all, it has to be available in your area. Second, a dedicated line will have to be run to your location. Not surprisingly, the cost of doing this will be your responsibility.

Once the installation is complete, your network has a dedicated link to that of your service provider. Once your connection has been established, you will be charged a monthly, semiannual, or annual rate for the service. You can expect this rate to be approximately five times that of conventional T1 service. However, you will benefit from approximately eight times the speed.

ATM

Asynchronous Transfer Mode (ATM) is most likely the widely deployed technology in use across the telecom backbone. ATM breaks your data down into small pieces of a fixed length called *cells*. Like T-lines, ATM is protocol-independent. Ethernet, Frame Relay, and some of the technologies I will discuss later in the chapter can all be run over ATM.

The cell consists of 53 bytes. The first 5 bytes make up a header containing control information. Following the header is a 48-byte payload. This payload can contain any type of data you want to transmit. If the signal is carrying a voice transmission, the payload will consist of six samples. If it carries data, then it will contain a 48-byte fragment of the original frame transmitted by the originating device.

ATM is a connection-oriented service. Therefore, for communications to occur, there must be a logical connection created between the devices.

ATM borrows a few points from OSI in its technology. It, too, uses a layered approach. In ATM's case, there are five layers. These are listed here:

- Application
- High-Level Protocols
- Adaptation Layer
- ATM Layer
- Physical Layer

The Physical Layer is identical to that of OSI's stack. It defines the connectors, the medium, and the bit timing of transmissions. The ATM Layer sets up and maintains the connections. It generates the header and provides flow control. The Adaptation Layer provides end-to-end services. It manages the sequencing of packets, provides error detection and correction services, and takes care of cell synchronization. The upper-layer protocols are those used by the devices on either end.

Naturally, those devices must be in agreement on the protocol they use. However, ATM provides services for all of the primary networking protocols. Finally, the Application Layer is similar to OSI's Application Layer. It simply provides network access and services to the application running on the system.

ATM provides for a scalable architecture. Its bandwidth provides speeds up to 622Mb/s and proposed standards will soon bump that beyond the gigabit range. On a LAN it can be used at the speed of a T1 line, yet it can be incorporated over the Internet backbone using its maximum rate.

SONET/SDH

The *Synchronous Optical Network* (SONET) and the *Synchronous Digital Hierarchy* (SDH) are very similar competing technologies. As the name implies, SONET relies on fiber optics to transmit data. It is a Physical Layer protocol and, therefore, transparent to upper-layer protocols. In other words, you can move any networking protocol I've discussed over SONET. It supports speeds of 155Mb/s and 2.5Gb/s.

However, since very few of the upper-level protocols were built around these speeds, it works by using a process called *time division multiplexing* (TDM) to mix signals of different speeds into a single transmission of a much higher speed (see **Figure 14.3**). Each channel can have its own independent bandwidth allotment, ranging from the 64K required for a voice transmission to whatever speed is required. Since each

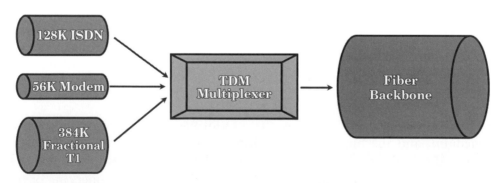

Figure 14.3 An example of TDM at work.

channel is capable of using any upper-layer protocol it requires, a single SONET connection will be carrying any number of protocols at any given time.

Another example of SONET's versatility is that it can be configured in either a dual-ring or a linear topology. The ring topology offers a very high degree of fault tolerance. There are two rings employed, similar to FDDI. The working ring handles all traffic. The *protection ring* is there in case the primary ring fails. In a SONET connection crossing a large geographical region, these two connections won't even follow the same route. Physically separating the two rings prevents a localized natural disaster from bringing the entire network down.

> **BUZZ WORDS**
>
> **Regional network:** The portion of the SONET network that provides services to users at varying bandwidths, and collates the signals into a single high-speed pipeline.
>
> **Local collector ring:** The network of end users with their different bandwidths that interconnect to a single regional network.

A SONET network will be divided into three separate regions. The *local collector ring* provides access to the ring to the individual subscribers. The SONET *regional network* would best be defined as the services provided by a single service provider. It is the regional network that brings all of the disparate signals together and then sends them out on to the pipeline as a single signal. Finally, the *broadband backbone* moves the data over the pipeline. **Figure 14.4** illustrates the concept of SONET hierarchy.

UNDERSTANDING OCX

One of the features introduced by SONET, which has been subsequently utilized in ATM as well, is the use of *optical carrier levels* (OCx) to define throughput. These numbers are presented in a format such as OC-1, OC-3, and so forth. OC-1 represents the base rate of 51.84Mb/s, and all other values are multiples of that rate. For example OC-3 is 3 x 51.84, or 155.52Mb/s. **Table 14.3** lists the currently active OCx levels.

MAKING THE CONNECTION

Now that you have a handle on how data is going to get from point A to point B, I can take a look at the most commonly used methods of remote network access. For this to work, you need to have a client service and a server service. On the client

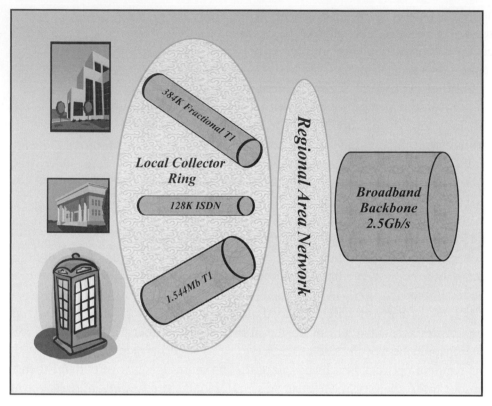

Figure 14.4   A breakdown of SONET.

Table 14.3   Optical Carrier Levels

Carrier Level	Throughput
OC-1	51.84 Mb/s
OC-3	155.52 Mb/s
OC-12	622.08 Mb/s
OC-24	1.244 Gb/s
OC-48	2.488 Gb/s
OC-192	10 Gb/s
OC-256	13.271 Gb/s
OC-768	40 Gb/s

end, I'll examine the most commonly used service today, which is dial-up networking (DUN). On the server end, I'll take a look at Remote Access Services (RAS).

DIAL-UP NETWORKING

DUN is a simple means of providing access to a network over a telephone line using a basic modem. While DUN is used most of the time for hooking someone up to the Internet, it can also be used to connect a home computer to an office network or a notebook to the network wherever you are in the world (if you can afford to pay the phone bills, that is).

For this to work, both your computer and the server must be equipped with modems. The user must have an account on the network and know the logon ID and password in order to gain access to the network.

To set up DUN on a Windows 98 computer, you would find DUN by double-clicking on the My Computer icon. In Windows 2000 and XP, you're looking for Network and Dial-up Connections under Settings in the Start menu. I'll look at setting up a connection in Windows 2000.

When you first open Network and Dial-up Connections, you will get a screen similar to the one in **Figure 14.5**.

From here, you have the options of either setting up a new connection or configuring an existing connection. Your purpose here is to set up a new one. So double-click on New Connection. This opens the Network Connection Wizard and you get the screen shown in **Figure 14.6**.

In Windows 98 or ME you'll only have the options of setting up a dial-up connection. As you see in Figure 14.6, in Windows 2000, you have several options. You can set up a direct-dial connection, a connection that goes over the Internet, a connection to an ISP, or a direct connection between two computers. Whichever one you select will determine the protocols that are installed. A simple dial-up connection between two computers or to an ISP will install PPP. If you select the option to create a connection over the Internet, PPTP will be installed as well. I'll take a closer look at both of those protocols later in this chapter.

The rest of the process is simply answering the questions that are presented. You'll need to know the telephone number to dial and a user ID and password. It is designed to be simple enough for the average end user to be able to install without difficulty.

VIRTUAL PRIVATE NETWORKS

Setting up a VPN is necessary whenever you want to log onto the network remotely, using the Internet as a platform. The advantage to the VPN is that the person

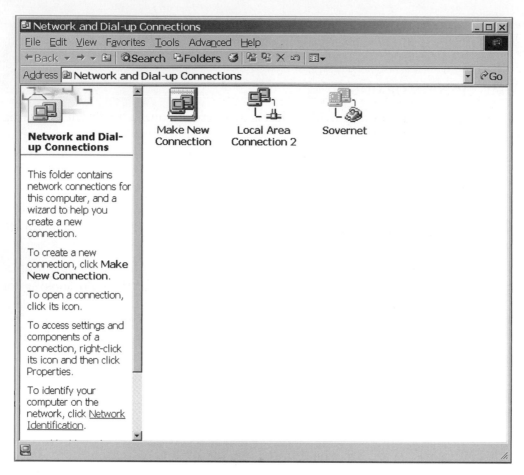

Figure 14.5 Network and Dial-up Connections in Windows 2000.

initiating the connection can generally connect to the Internet using a local number. If a direct connection requires the use of long-distance services, costs can mount up rather quickly.

The thing that makes a VPN different from conventional DUN connections is that with DUN, your data will be exposed to the outside world while traveling through Internet routers and links. DUN uses PPP, which offers very little security. Passwords are transmitted in plain text and are easily intercepted. When you connect to the network over a VPN, you use the PPTN protocol. Data is encrypted before it is transmitted, keeping your connection secure.

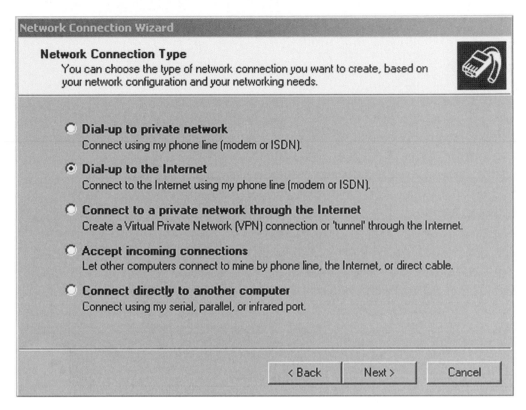

Network Connection Wizard

Network Connection Type
You can choose the type of network connection you want to create, based on your network configuration and your networking needs.

○ **Dial-up to private network**
Connect using my phone line (modem or ISDN).

⊙ **Dial-up to the Internet**
Connect to the Internet using my phone line (modem or ISDN).

○ **Connect to a private network through the Internet**
Create a Virtual Private Network (VPN) connection or 'tunnel' through the Internet.

○ **Accept incoming connections**
Let other computers connect to mine by phone line, the Internet, or direct cable.

○ **Connect directly to another computer**
Connect using my serial, parallel, or infrared port.

[< Back] [Next >] [Cancel]

Figure 14.6   The Network Connection Wizard.

LINE PRINTER REMOTE

The Line Printer Remote (LPR) protocol is a popular protocol used to print across the network to remote printers. To use it, your computer must be using software that can send jobs with the LPR protocol. Novell and Microsoft print servers are configured to receive such print jobs by default, since most networks take advantage of network printing. However, LPR printing isn't limited to the LAN. By installing LPR Client software, you can print to any LPR capable printer anywhere on the Internet. All you need is either the printer's host name or IP address, if it is so equipped.

Home users can even print documents onto the printers at work using a protocol called the Line Printer Daemon. Print jobs are first spooled onto their system and then transmitted as files to a print sever on the network. There the print job is queued with the rest of the print jobs. When Linda gets to work the next day, there is her document, printed out and ready to go.

REMOTE ACCESS SERVICES

Now you need a server set up to accept your call and log you onto the network. While there are other methods of doing this, the most commonly used is to set up RAS on the server. RAS allows the administrator to control who is accessing the network from the outside from a centralized location.

I'll be looking at Windows 2000 Advanced Server in the following setup. To set up RAS, you go to the Start menu, select Programs and open the Administrative Tools menu. Select Routing and Remote Access. The first thing you need to do is select the server that will be used to provide the services. Once you do that, you will be prompted to run the Routing and Remote Access Server Setup Wizard. Run the Wizard and click Next. You'll get the screen shown in **Figure 14.7**.

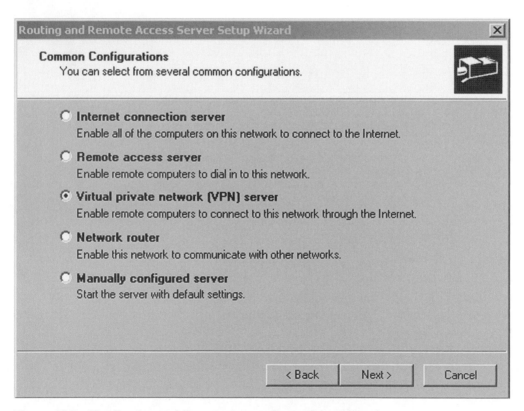

Figure 14.7 The Routing and Remote Access Server Setup Wizard.

The options are to set up an Internet Connection Server, a Remote Access Server, a Virtual Private Network Server, a Network Router, or a Manually Configured Server. Since this is a section on RAS, guess which one you'll select.

When you select RAS and click Next, you'll be prompted to select the protocols you wish installed. Here's the key. It doesn't matter what protocols you have running on your internal network. If your user has an older Macintosh computer, you might need to install AppleTalk. On a larger network, it's probably a good idea to simply install them all. It won't take up that much overhead.

The next thing you'll see is an option to allow Macintosh users to log on using the guest account. The box is unchecked by default. If you check that box, you will be allowing anyone who knows the telephone number to your server to log on to your network. As far as security holes go, this one is about the size of the Grand Canyon. If security is evenly remotely (no pun intended) an issue on your network you will *not* select that box. You will force the user to provide their credentials.

Now you'll be asked how IP addresses are to be assigned. The choices are Automatically and From a Specified Range of Addresses. If you select Automatically, one of two things will happen. If DHCP is installed on your network, then RAS will defer to the DHCP server to provide the addresses. If DHCP is not being used, the RAS server will act as a DHCP server, but only to RAS clients.

On the following screen you are asked if you want to collect information about RAS connections from multiple RAS servers. If your network has multiple RAS servers and you need to audit remote access, then install this service. If you only have one RAS server, auditing can be done on that server and you won't need this service. The default is to not install the service.

After that, you are given the screen that tells you you're about to finish setting up your server. If you selected the option to automatically dole out IP address to clients logging in remotely, then you will be informed that you must configure the DHCP Relay Agent with the IP address of your DHCP server. It will then start the services.

RDP

The Remote Desktop Protocol (RDP) was developed by Microsoft for use on Windows NT 4.0 Terminal Server and its subsequent versions. With it, network administrators can set up remote users to work on a thin-client network using an NOS, such as Terminal Server or Citrix. These types of networks offload all the processing and most of the memory and storage requirements onto the server and simply send screenshots back and forth between the server and the clients.

RDP is considered to be a multi-channel protocol, in that it sets up distinct sessions between multiple users. This allows the server to be processing several users at the same time, with each one thinking nobody else is home. RDP works over a variety of different network topologies as well. It doesn't care if the user is hooked up over a DUN connection, via ISDN, or over the LAN. RDP data is encapsulated into TCP packets, so any interface that supports TCP/IP can be used for an RDP connection.

Chapter Summary

This chapter provided the foundation for a more detailed study in data telecommunications. It was not intended to be a detailed primer on the subject. That would require a book unto itself. However, enough information was provided to accomplish two things. First off, it covers the information likely to be presented on the Network+ exam, which is the core purpose of this book.

Second, it provides an outline of where to begin, should WAN technology be an area of interest for you. Several different technologies were introduced and the more common protocols introduced.

Brain Drain

1. List as many protocols as you can that are specific to remote communications.
2. How does PPP differ from PPTP?
3. Why is CHAP a better protocol to use than PAP if security is an issue?
4. In as much detail as you can, describe the differences between circuit-switching technology and packet-switching technology.
5. Explain the concept of the VPN.

The 64K$ Questions

1. The protocol most commonly used by Microsoft operating systems in establishing a VPN is _____.
   a. PPP
   b. ADP

    c. PPTP

    d. LDAP

2. PPP is a layered protocol, consisting of _____ layers.

    a. 3

    b. 4

    c. 5

    d. 7

3. If, during a lengthy transmission of data, some of your data during that transmission arrives out of order and must be resequenced, you are using a _____ connection.

    a. Circuit balanced

    b. Packet balanced

    c. Circuit switching

    d. Packet switching

4. The connection used by a conventional modem uses _____ and is a _____ technology.

    a. PSTN and packet switching

    b. ISDN and packet switching

    c. PSTN and circuit switching

    d. ISDN and circuit switching

5. BRI ISDN provides the user with _____.

    a. Twenty-three 64K A channels and one 64K B channel

    b. Two 64K A channels and one 16K B channel

    c. Twenty-three 64K D channels and one 64K B channel

    d. Two 64K D channels and one 64K D channel

    e. None of the above

6. A T3 line is the equivalent of _____.

    a. Three T1 lines

    b. Sixteen T1 lines

    c. Twenty-eight T1 lines

    d. Ninety-six T1 lines

7. Frame Relay is based on a _____ protocol.

   a. Layer 1

   b. Layer 2

   c. Layer 3

   d. Layer 4

8. ATM currently provides a maximum bandwidth of _____.

   a. 46Mb/s

   b. 144Mb/s

   c. 622Mb/s

   d. 2.1Gb/s

9. A Windows 2000 workstation connecting to the Internet over a conventional modem is most likely using _____. (Pick two.)

   a. RAS

   b. DUN

   c. PPTP

   d. PPP

10. A remote computer connected to a network over the Internet will be using _____. (Pick two.)

    a. VPN

    b. RPD

    c. PPP

    d. PPTP

11. One of the early protocols used for setting up a VPN was _____.

    a. PPP

    b. DUN

    c. PPTP

    d. RDP

12. Which of the following were used as protocols on thin-client networks? (Select two.)

    a. PPTP

    b. RDP

    c. ANCR

    d. ICA

13. A limitation of PPP was _____.

    a. Since it was designed around packet-switching technology, it couldn't be used on DSL connections

    b. It transmitted logon credentials in plain text

    c. It was exclusively an IPX protocol

    d. It couldn't be used to link Apple computers with PCs

14. A protocol used by VPNs to keep the logon process secure was called _____.

    a. LSASS

    b. RDP

    c. ICAN

    d. CHAP

15. The reason thin-client networks use so little bandwidth is _____.

    a. All packets sent over the wire use a heavy-duty compression algorithm

    b. All applications run on the client computer and only send processed data back to the server

    c. All applications and data use MS-DOS based code so there is far less overhead

    d. All processing and storage is done on the server side. Only screenshots are passed on to the client computer

16. ISDN is a perfect example of circuit switching technology.

    a. True

    b. False

17. BRI offers a maximum bandwidth of _____.

    a. 64Kb/s

    b. 128Kb/s

    c. 384Kb/s

    d. 1.44Mb/s

18. If you wanted the fastest connection possible, and cost was no object, which of the following services would be the best option?

    a. DSL

    b. ISDN

    c. ATM

    d. Frame Relay

19. POTS is another term often used for _____.

    a. Frame Relay

    b. DUN

    c. iDSL

    d. Fiber Optics

20. You are in an area where the best combination of performance and price seems to be Frame Relay. Which option should you choose for maximum security?

    a. A PVC

    b. CIR

    c. A virtual circuit

    d. Closed Circuit Networking

TRICKY TERMINOLOGY

Cell: The 53-byte fragment of data transmitted over an ATM connection. Frames generated by upper-level protocols will be broken down into multiple ATM cells.

Channel aggregation protocol: A protocol that binds two or more signals of lower bandwidth into a single signal of higher bandwidth.

Circuit switching: A telecommunications technology that selects the best route for data to take, based on current network conditions, and then creates a virtual circuit over which all data from that session will flow.

Dictionary attack: An attempt by a hacker to break into a network by barraging the server with a database of user IDs and passwords.

Fractional T1: A telco service that allows users to select how much bandwidth they need, without having to pay for the services of an entire T1 line.

Frame Relay: A packet-switching WAN protocol that makes use of Layer 2 networking services.

Local collector ring: The network of end users with their different bandwidths that interconnect to a single regional network.

Packet switching: A telecommunications technology that selects the best route for each packet of data to take, based on current network conditions. There is no single path used throughout the session and packets may not arrive in sequence.

Protection ring: A secondary circuit used by SONET to provide a backup path for data in the event that the primary ring fails.

Regional network: The portion of the SONET network that provides services to users at varying bandwidths and collates the signals into a single high-speed pipeline.

Retry counter: A value maintained by a RAS server that increments with each attempt to log on. When configured with a specific value, once that value is reached, the account will be locked out.

S/T interface: A device that allows access to the ISDN signal by multiple other devices.

Telco: A generic term for any provider of telecommunications services.

U interface: The device that accepts an incoming ISDN signal and brings it into the building.

ACRONYM ALERT

ATM: Asynchronous Transfer Mode. A high-speed telecommunications protocol that breaks down upper-level protocol packets into 53-byte cells and transmits them over a high-speed link.

BRI: Basic Rate ISDN. An ISDN service that provides two 64K B channels and one 16K D channel.

CDPD: Cellular Digital Packet Data. A packet-switching technology used to send voice communications.

CHAP: Challenge Handshake Authentication Protocol. A password authentication protocol that makes use of a three-way handshake to provide authentication.

CIR: Committed Information Rate. The minimum bandwidth guaranteed to a Frame Relay subscriber. Depending on network conditions, subscribers may actually enjoy the benefits of even higher bandwidths than those for which they subscribed.

DLCI: Data Link Communication Identifier. A specific circuit assigned to a Frame Relay subscriber. It may consist of either a virtual circuit or a permanent virtual circuit, depending on the level of service selected by the subscriber.

DUN: Dial-Up Networking: A method for interconnecting a remote user to a network using a modem and a conventional telephone or an ISDN line.

GPRS: General Packet Radio Service. A packet-switching technology used to send voice communications.

ICA: Citrix's thin-client protocol.

IPCP: IP Control Protocol. One of the lower level protocols of PPP.

ISDN: Integrated Services Digital Network

L2TP: Layer 2 Tunneling Protocol. A more recent implementation of PPTP that works exclusively at the Data Link Layer.

LCP: Link Control Protocol. One of the lower level protocols of PPP.

NCP: Network Control Protocol. One of the lower level protocols of PPP.

NT1: Network Termination-1. The interface of an incoming ISDN line that converts the incoming two-wire circuit to a four-wire ISDN circuit.

OCx: Optical Carrier Level. A method of defining the different levels of transmission speed over high-speed networks. The *x* represents the specific level.

PAP: Password Authentication Protocol. A nonsecure protocol for providing user credentials between hosts on a network. It is nonsecure in that passwords are transmitted in plain text.

POTS: Plain Old Telephone Service

PPP: Point-to-Point Protocol. The default protocol of dial-up networking.

PPTP: Point-to-Point Tunneling Protocol. A protocol that allows the encapsulation of encrypted packets for secure transmission over the Internet.

PRI: Primary Rate ISDN. An ISDN service that provides twenty-three 64K B channels and one 64K D channel.

PSTN: Public Switched Telephone Network

PVC: Permanent Virtual Circuit. A dedicated circuit assigned to a subscriber of Frame Relay services.

RAS: Remote Access Services. A method of authenticating and controlling access to the network by remote users.

RBS: Robbed Bit Signaling. A technology used in voice communications in which a bit is "borrowed" from every eighth byte of data going over the wire for use by the telco.

RDP: Remote Desktop Protocol. Microsoft's thin-client protocol.

SDH: Synchronous Digital Hierarchy. A high-speed telecommunications technology, very similar to SONET, that combines multiple signals of different speeds into a single high-speed signal that moves over a fiber-optics backbone.

SLIP: Serial Line IP. An early protocol used to transmit IP packets over a serial connection.

SONET: Synchronous Optical Network. A high-speed telecommunications technology that combines multiple signals of different speeds into a single high-speed signal that moves over a fiber-optics backbone.

T1: Digital Trunk Line. A circuit that combines up to twenty-four signals into one.

TDM: Time Division Multiplexing. The technology used by SONET and SDH to combine different signals of different speeds into a single high-speed transmission.

VPN: Virtual Private Network. A secure connection between two devices over the Internet.

VIEW THE VIDEO

A video clip on WAN Standards is available on the accompanying CD.

WORKING WITH NETWORK SECURITY

In this chapter I'm going to cover in a bit more detail a subject I've been harping on throughout this book—network security. One of the biggest issues organizations face these days when it comes to networks is the safety of information and intellectual property. These are at constant risk from many factors ranging from viruses to misappropriation.

Security risks come from both within and without. It is one thing to totally isolate your network from the outside world in an effort to keep all those hackers out there from getting in. Unfortunately that won't protect you from the hackers that work for you.

Security is also a physical thing as well as a logical thing, as the Pentagon recently found out. Okay, so you've secured your network so tightly that only after a retinal scan and thumbprint ID will someone be allowed in. Have you prevented someone from simply stealing the hard drives and running off with them? These and many more are the issues I'll be covering in this chapter. Perhaps I can be forgiven if I provide more information than CompTIA really requires in this section. After all, it is an important subject. The things that do concern CompTIA in this chapter include:

1.7 Specify the general characteristics (For example: carrier speed, frequency, transmission type and topology) of the following wireless technologies: 802.11 (Frequency hopping spread spectrum), 802.11x (Direct sequence spread spectrum), Infrared, Bluetooth.

2.16 Define the function of remote access protocols and services.

2.17 Identify the security protocols and describe their purpose and function.

 3.5 Identify the purpose, benefits and characteristics of using a firewall..

 3.6 Identify the purpose, benefits and characteristics of using a proxy service.

 3.7 Given a connectivity scenario, determine the impact on network functionality of a particular security implementation (For example: port blocking / filtering, authentication and encryption).

 3.8 Identify the main characteristics of VLANs (Virtual Local Area Networks).

Just What Are We Protecting Ourselves From?

Practically any time I get into a conversation with another IT professional about network security, the first thing that person wants to talk about is how a firewall has made the network secure. (If you don't know what a firewall is just yet, don't worry. I'm getting there.) That's a good start, I always suggest. But what are you doing about the other risks to your network?

This fixation on firewalls suggests to me that a very good job has been done in educating the public about the dangers from Internet intrusion, but little has been done in any other direction. Data on a network faces risks that come from many different directions, and those risks are increasing every day. Common ways data can be compromised include the following:

- Being accessed and/or destroyed from the outside by hackers
- Being accessed and/or destroyed from the inside by hackers or disgruntled employees
- Getting physically stolen, through printing, transmission through an unauthorized modem, or theft of hardware
- Getting lost or damaged due to equipment failure
- Being damaged or destroyed by a virus intrusion

For your security plan to be complete you need to address all of these concerns. Then, for continued security, you need to be constantly reeducating yourself on the new ways people come up with to make your life miserable. The simple fact of the matter is, there are people (using the term loosely) running around out there who live for that very purpose.

SOME BASIC CONCEPTS OF SECURITY

As I said earlier, threats to your network come from multiple directions. You need to protect your systems from attacks from the outside as well as attacks from the inside. And attacks from the inside are not necessarily logical threats. Securing the equipment is a good idea for two reasons. First off, there may be valuable data on local hard drives that someone may put to use. Second, while computer hardware may be dropping in price, that doesn't mean you want to always be replacing it because a couple of bad eggs have found out how easy you've made it to simply walk out of the office with desktop computers under their trench coats. (Before you scoff too much at that notion, you should probably know that I once had a client who experienced that very problem.)

PROTECTION FROM THE INSIDE

I might as well start here because this is an issue *all* networks face (see **Figure 15.1**). There are still a few networks out there that have no access from the outside. Unless there is some form of access from the inside, you don't have a network.

The issue here is that you have a collection of devices that, by the nature of the network, have been made available to anyone and everyone who can log on. As a network administrator, it is your job to make sure that all the employees have access to all the information and equipment they need to do their jobs—and no more. There are several different ways to go about this.

The first thing is to make efficient use of the security features the NOS provides. No member of any organization

Figure 15.1 It's easy to assume that all your defenses should be concentrated on the outside world. Unfortunately, though, a large percentage of data theft comes from within.

should be assigned more privileges or permissions on the network than his or her job requires. That applies to everyone from the groundskeeper to the CEO.

There are those that argue that the CEO should have the right to do anything he or she pleases on the network. And I suppose as long as that person is a qualified network engineer, there might be some validity to that argument. Conversely, there are tasks that can be done on the network that should be performed only by a person trained to perform those tasks. If top management doesn't know how to do those tasks, then that is one set of controls they should keep their hands away from. Also, as we've seen in recent years, even CEOs have a shorter lifespan in some companies than people used to expect. As of this writing, the CEO of one major corporation was fired after being at the helm for less than six months. What say the network administrators who work there just let that person walk out with all of the company data? That way he can take it to his next job and use it to his advantage. After all, he's the CEO!

How you implement and maintain password policy can have a significant impact on internal security. This is an issue that I will discuss in detail later in this chapter. So for now, suffice it to say that password policy may well be one of the more significant decisions you make.

SECURING YOUR NETWORK FROM THE OUTSIDE

While there are a relatively few networks that have no access to the outside world, this is becoming exceedingly rare. Internet access and email have both become a way of life for the working person. To gain either of these requires a conduit to the outside. Also, any time you set up a connection between remote locations, you're opening a potential hole. Someone who wants to get into your network badly enough can find a way. Your job is to make it as difficult as possible (see **Figure 15.2**).

Some of the tools at your disposal can make this job a bit easier. Many routers allow the administrator to create *access lists* that permit or deny packets going in or out. Firewalls are also an essential tool. Even the cheaper ones keep the average hacker from exploring your system, while the best ones are difficult to break through even by a dedicated professional. I'll take a closer look at both access lists and firewalls later in this chapter.

For the telecommuter, how you configure RAS can have an impact as well. Improperly configured, all a person has to do to gain access to your network is steal someone's notebook computer. If you've done your job right, as you shall see, that would only be the first step.

Figure 15.2 Some networks just seem more prone to attack than others. Still, any network administrator should be able to build a good security perimeter.

PHYSICAL SECURITY

Even after your internal and external logical barriers are in place, your data may still be at risk. Not long ago, an incident made news when two hard disk drives disappeared from Los Alamos Laboratories in New Mexico. These drives happened to contain extremely top-secret information, including the blueprints to some of our nuclear arsenal. These drives were missing for about a month before they "conveniently" reappeared behind a copy machine. We will probably never know how much information was extracted from those drives and into whose hands that information fell.

In addition to that, it was discovered that computers donated to schools and charitable organizations by the Pentagon were sometimes arriving at their destination with the data on the hard drives still intact. In a knee-jerk reaction, upon discovering this was the case, the Pentagon ordered all hard drives physically destroyed before allowing donated equipment to leave government premises. However, in this case, cooler heads prevailed, and that order was rescinded. Now the hard drives are wiped clean with a special utility that completely obliterates any data that once existed. Still, in the case of a hard drive that once contained highly classified information—that drive will be destroyed.

The point here is that if your equipment can be stolen, or if your organization occasionally donates retired equipment to charitable organizations, then you need to consider what information is at risk. As I alluded to earlier, I once worked with a client who was having a problem with computer systems leaving the office. The client used those small-footprint desktops that are only about three inches high. Shortly before Christmas one year, the machines were walking out of the office one after the other. We literally had to chain the computers to the desks to stop it.

SECURITY CONSIDERATIONS

Now before I get started, I need to discuss a couple of other issues. First off, how much security does a particular network need? You are not going to apply the same standards to a home network that you are at the National Security Agency. Next, you need to consider how much and what kind of access your network has from the outside. Last, what is the likelihood that someone would even *want* to hack into your network, and even if someone did, how valuable is any information that might be found?

HOW MUCH SECURITY IS NEEDED?

Obviously, these are questions that only the owners of networks can answer. It is not your job to second-guess them or to question their motives. You wouldn't think that a bookstore would be likely to spend as much money securing its network as would a bank. On the other hand, until you know all of the facts, it isn't your job to decide. I happen to know of one book dealer in particular who has an extensive security setup. This particular dealer specializes in extremely rare volumes and antiquities, and doesn't want anyone knowing anything about the collection until the information is ready to be released. Security risks can be broken down into three levels, as described below:

Low risk: The information contained on a low-risk system would cause no interruption to the flow of business should it be lost. Data on the system either needs not be restored or is easily restored in the event of loss. Misappropriation of that data would have no legal ramifications or financial impact on the organization, nor would anyone's health or safety be compromised.

Medium risk: Loss of that data would result in a noticeable interruption in the flow of business. Data can be restored, albeit with a certain amount of effort. Possible, but not certain, legal ramifications and/or financial impact would result from the misuse of this information.

High risk: Loss of this data could bring the company to a standstill until restored. Restoration is a complicated process. Misappropriation of the data could result in extreme legal ramifications and/or financial impact. Misuse of the data could result in compromising the safety or health of individuals.

EXAM NOTE: The "levels" of security are relatively new to the Network+ exam. Therefore, it is a good bet that more than a few people are going to be asked to identify the characteristics of each level.

The flip side to that coin is that you may have to convince clients that they really need more security than they currently have. I once demonstrated the gaping holes in the network of a nonprofit organization by logging onto its network and printing out case histories for several of its clients and hand-delivering them the next day. How did I get in?

Obviously, they assumed that since I had access to their network as a service provider, I had left myself a back door. And this is an issue for any organization who contracts its technology services out to a third party to consider. In this case, however, I got into the network in a way anyone else might have been able to accomplish. One of the workers had left a sheet of paper taped to his desk with his user name and password. Elsewhere in the office, I noticed another little note that said SERVER=xxx-xxx-xxxx. Except instead of all those x's there was a telephone number.

PERMITTING ACCESS FROM THE OUTSIDE

There was a time, albeit long ago, that this was not an issue for many companies. They had a LAN and that was it. However, expanding corporations and emerging technologies made it necessary to gain Internet access, provide links between offices around the world, and then give everybody their daily dose of email. Add to that the telecommuter, and you have a hole in network security about the size of Carlsbad Caverns that must be filled.

A report issued in 2001 by the FBI in conjunction with the Computer Security Institute (CSI) stated that 85 percent of all network intrusions came in through the Internet. ("The Computer Crime and Security Survey, 2001", March, 2001.) If your only access to the outside is through an Internet connection to your ISP, a firewall on your gateway is a good first step. WAN and RAS connections open up an entire new set of problems. You now have two or more possible entrances to your network that must be secured. In the case of the RAS connections, you want to make sure your users are all who they say they are.

The entrance ways to our networks can be protected by either those firewalls or access lists that I mentioned earlier. Since both will be discussed in greater detail later in the chapter, I will defer those two subjects to the appropriate time.

To secure a RAS connection, you have a couple of options. First off, make sure each user is aware of the sensitivity of the issue. I am always harping to my clients that a little time and money spent on proper training can save a lot of time and money later on cleaning up after a major security breach. Make sure that they know to keep user IDs and passwords safe, secure, and secret.

There are also things you can do from your end as well. In the RAS configuration you have a couple of dial-in options (see **Figure 15.3**). The first, and the default, is to allow a direct dial-up connection to occur. The users dial, the server answers and logs them in. The users work—or steal, if you have hackers with stolen user IDs and passwords—to their hearts' content.

Another option is to have the server disconnect and dial the computer back at whatever number it dialed from. This is not a security feature as much as it is a convenience feature. It keeps your hackers from paying the long-distance phone bills while they download your data.

It is the third setting that was put there for security reasons. The user dials in and the RAS server dials back at a number that the administrator specifies. If you have users who for any reason must work from home, have the server dial them back on a specified number. For additional security, make it a dedicated line with an unpublished number.

Relevant to this issue, I should discuss the use of modems in the network environment. A modem is a device easily installed by even novice computer users. It is very easy for an employee to install a modem on an office machine. The user doesn't even need to have access to the inside of the computer. External modems can be hung off either the serial port or a USB port.

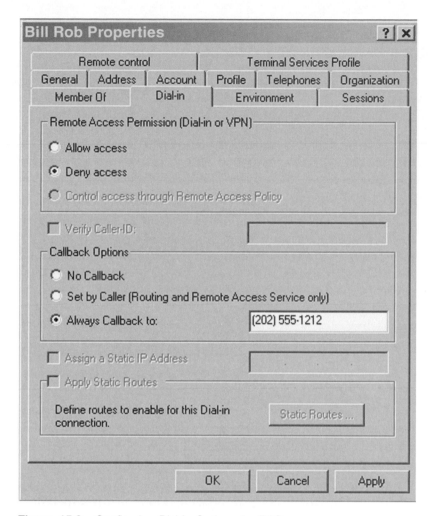

Figure 15.3 Configuring Dial-in Options for RAS.

Users may not be doing this for malicious reasons, but rather so they can get some work done at home. Still, this imposes a serious security risk to your network. Not only does it provide them a means by which they can export company data out of the network, it gives outside hackers another interface through which they can penetrate. And a modem is a much easier interface to hack than that of a router.

Educate your users to this risk. If an employee legitimately needs outside access, provide him or her with a RAS connection so that you can control it.

SECURITY HOLES IN THE NOS

In 2001, Microsoft was taking a beating from some of its detractors because of some well-published holes in its operating systems. Then in 2003, practically the entire global Internet was brought down by a worm that attacked a known SQL security flaw. The anti-Microsoft coalition was once again out in force. These detractors weren't so quick to publish the fact that within weeks—and in some cases within mere days—of having discovered the holes, Microsoft had found a way to close them up and provided patches on its Downloads site free of charge. The event of 2003 attacked an issue for which Microsoft had published a patch several months earlier!

Microsoft is not alone in having the occasional security glitch. All NOS manufacturers have had to retrofit virtually every version of NOS ever released— or plug the holes, as they say. It is the responsibility of network administrators to keep their various operating systems up to date, applying necessary patches as they are released.

SECURITY IN THE NOS

Putting a tight lid on your network begins with your selection of an NOS. Fortunately, these days it is pretty safe to say that all of the commercially available NOSs provide fairly tight security. Most NOSs offer security features that are fairly consistent with each other. Therefore, rather than discuss each brand in turn, I will address the security features unique to an NOS in general. These features include:

- Share level versus user level security
- User authentication
- File system security
- Securing printing devices
- Directory services

There are two additional NOS features that are not universally used by all vendors. These are *IP Security* (IPSEC) and *Kerberos.* These are both key security implementations and deserve note.

SHARE LEVEL SECURITY VS. USER LEVEL

These are issues that used to be unique to Windows operating systems. They started to go away with NT 4.0, and with Windows 2000 and later, they are officially gone. However, considering the millions of Windows 9x workstations still in use, you need to have an understanding of what they mean and the impact they have on your network.

> **EXAM NOTE:** Share level and user level security may seem like mundane topics to us sophisticated network engineers. However, it is a favorite topic of the designers of the exam, and they have lots of ways of testing your knowledge of this subject. Don't slack on it.

SHARE LEVEL SECURITY

Share level security is most often identified with a workgroup rather than a domain model of a network. In share level security, as the name implies, what security is available is implemented on the resource that is being shared out. In addition, it is the owner, creator, or manager of the resource that is responsible for setting security. Unfortunately, in the case of share level security, the manager of any resource not already secured is whoever happens to be logged on at the time.

When a share is created on a Windows 9x computer, a screen like that in **Figure 15.4** appears. The share name that you type into that field is what users on the network will see. The permissions they have to that share are the ones you select by clicking on one of the checkboxes.

Read-only is just that. Users with read-only rights can open the file, but they cannot make changes to it. If they do edit a read-only file, they must save it under a different name. If the directory has been shared out as read-only, they must save it to a different directory as well.

Full allows users to do anything they darn well please with the file. They can edit it, rename it, or even delete it if they choose. With either Read-only or Full permissions, passwords are optional. Depends on Password requires that you type in a separate password for each level of permission.

Windows 2000 and later differs slightly in the permissions offered. In addition to Read-only and Full, we also have Change. Change permissions allow people to read a file, edit and change a file, or even delete a file if they choose. The reason that this differs from full permission is that, despite outward appearance, it is still more restrictive than full permissions.

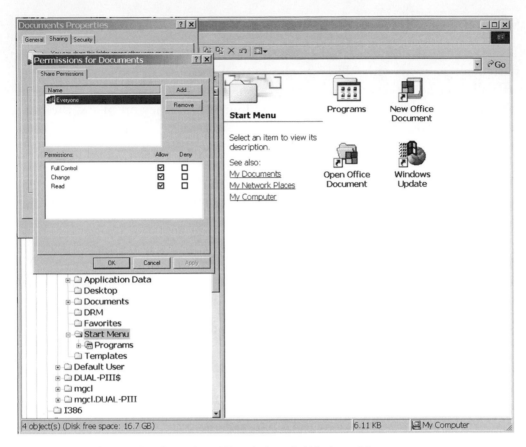

Figure 15.4 Configuring Share Level Permissions in Windows 98.

Full permissions allow a person to assign permissions to a file. Change permissions do not. Full permissions allow someone to take ownership of a file, while Change permissions do not.

This becomes an issue, because, by default, the creator of a file has full permissions. Administrators also have full permissions to files. As an administrator, I might assign a coworker to build me a database that contains critical company information. As the creator of that database, that employee has full permissions to the files. In a secure network, this is not a good idea. I may want that person to be able to add and modify data contained in the database, but I sure don't want him or her deciding who can and can't use that information.

Therefore, I use my administrative privileges to take ownership of that database, and then restrict the creator's rights to Change. He or she can now do everything with the database that the job requires, except set permissions and log on to the server and reclaim ownership of the file.

From a network administrator's point of view, there are some glaring problems with using share level permissions. To start with, just because people have the ability to, do you really want them determining who can and who can't use the data on your network? If one employee gets involved in a dispute with another, one of them might just decide to put a password on the customer database, just because it happens to reside on his or her machine. Now that person can pick and choose who gets that password.

Also consider the number of passwords an average user would have to know if you have twenty-five computers on a network with five shared resources on each computer—and each resource is set to Depends on Password. You'd need an encyclopedia to keep track.

USER LEVEL SECURITY

That is why client-server networks all make use of user level security. User level security is based on the concept that each user who is granted access to the network is given a user ID and a password. I've certainly talked about these enough in this book. The user ID and password act as the key to any resource on the network.

This works because the server maintains a database of all user and group accounts along with associated permissions and privileges. In Windows, the rights assigned to a user are not associated with a user ID or even account name. Each account and each group has a unique 32-bit number assigned to that account. This is called the *security identification* (SID) number. Information relating to all SIDs is maintained in the Windows NT or Windows 2000 registry as the *Security Accounts Management* (SAM) database. Entering a proper user ID and password opens an account associated with that number.

In Novell, the user is an object on the network and permissions are assigned as properties to that object. When access to a resource is requested, Directory Services checks the user ID (UID) and/or group ID (GID) against the object properties. Once verified, the user is granted the appropriate access.

The user must provide those credentials just to log on. But it doesn't stop there. Once users are logged on, every time they try to access a network resource that information is sent once again and compared to the permission list assigned to those credentials. If users have permission to use that resource, then access will be granted. If not, they will get a message informing them that they have been denied access.

USER AUTHENTICATION

The process of logon authentication is something that I have already discussed in detail in this book. Therefore this section is devoted to the security implications.

Logon can be either *interactive* or *noninteractive*. An interactive logon is one that prompts the user to enter data. An example of this would be the Windows *secure attention sequence* (SAS). To log onto a Windows NT 4.0 (or later) machine, the user must first press Ctrl>Alt>Delete to bring up the logon screens. This feature prevents the presence of a program known as a *Trojan horse* (to be discussed later in this chapter) from being used to collect user data.

Once users have entered this sequence they are given a screen prompting them for their user IDs and passwords. If users are on a computer that is a member of a domain, they will also have the option of either logging onto the domain or onto the local machine.

Once they provide their credentials, the *Local Security Authority* (LSA) examines that information and compares it to the local SAM if users are attempting to log on to the local machine or passes the request to a domain controller if logging onto the domain. If the information matches that stored in the SAM, users will be granted access to the network.

Authentication doesn't stop here, however. Once interactive authentication has taken place, users have access to network resources—but only those to which they've been granted permissions. Should users subsequently require access to resources on another machine, they will have to log on to a session on that machine as well. However, on these subsequent logons, the user takes no action. This time the process of noninteractive authentication will be used.

All of their credentials remain in cache. Any time users attempt to access other resources on the network, their credentials will be passed on to the machine hosting that resource. The *Security Support Provider Interface* (SSPI) will perform the authentication sequence transparently. Users with the appropriate permissions will be provided access.

File System Security

The choice of file system has a significant impact on security as well. Older computers that use FAT16 or FAT32 file systems have virtually no security imposed by the file system at all. The *Novell File System* (NFS) and Microsoft's *New Technology*

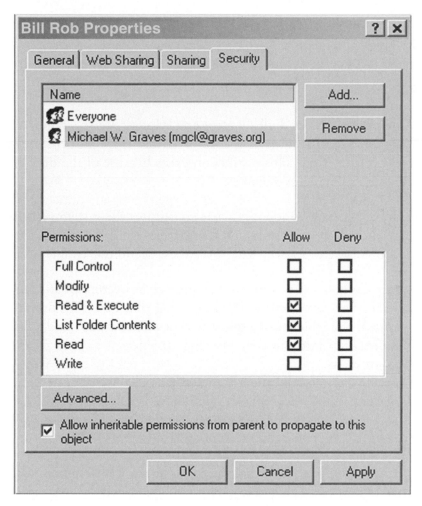

Figure 15.5 Setting File System Security in Windows 2000.

File System (NTFS) all provide security beyond that of user access. NTFS will be looked at in a little more detail because there are two different versions, 4.0 and 5.0, that offer different features (see **Figure 15.5**).

Novell and Windows differ slightly in the technology behind how these rights are enforced, as discussed earlier. They also differ slightly in the permission levels that are available. Windows rights include:

- Full Control
- Modify

411

- Read & Execute
- List Folder Contents
- Read
- Write

The differences between Full Control and Modify are the same as those discussed in the section on share level access. Note that there are separate listings for Read & Execute and Read. This distinction exists because of the different security issues facing data files and executables.

Exam Note: Be able to identify what constitutes file system security and what constitutes NOS security. To the newbie, it can be difficult to distinguish between the two. Read over these sections a couple of times.

List Folder Contents allows the user to display a directory of all files contained within a directory or subdirectory. By deselecting that box, the administrator can effectively conceal the existence of a folder from a user or group. And as I mentioned earlier, a key first step in completely securing an object is to prevent anyone from knowing it even exists.

Novell permissions are a bit more complex. They will be discussed in the section on Directory Services.

SECURING PRINTING DEVICES

Superficially, you wouldn't think that the ability to print a document would be any different than that of being able to read and modify. However, printing critical data out and carrying it out of the building in one's briefcase is an easy way to steal sensitive information. In many cases it is not essential for users to print information from a file in order to do their jobs. If they don't have a need to print, then it's a good idea to prevent them from printing (see **Figure 15.6**).

Unfortunately, there is no way that individual files can be marked for printing security. Therefore, it is the printers themselves that you need to secure. By delegating specific printers to specific users, you control the point of output for all of their print jobs.

Printers can be assigned permissions the same way you do any other object on the network. A user can be denied access to any and all printers if necessary. However, once printer access has been granted, data that can be accessed can be printed. It becomes an issue of physical security.

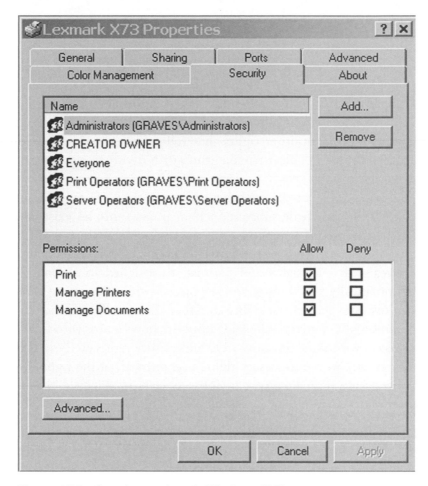

Figure 15.6 Securing a printer in Windows 2000.

DIRECTORY SERVICES

Novell's Directory Services provides for permissions specific to objects and containers, and there are attributes assigned to those objects and containers that specify how a certain individual or group can use them. It is one thing to be able to access an object and another to create or manage objects in Novell. Permissions specific to object management include:

- Browse
- Create
- Delete

- Inheritance Control
- Rename
- Supervisor

Browse rights are basically read-only rights. Another object (and remember that in NetWare, a user is considered an object) can see that the object exists, but unless assigned one of the other rights that follow, cannot do anything with it. Once again, to conceal an object from a group or individual, simply do not assign them browse rights.

Create allows an object to create other objects in the Directory Services tree. In addition, the object can create subcontainers or objects into an existing container.

Inheritance Rights are something introduced in NetWare 5.0. Prior to that, inheritance was not something the administrator could easily control. Simply defined, inheritance means that all rights and permissions assigned to a container or subcontainer automatically pass through to the objects within. Beginning with NetWare 5.0, the administrator gained the ability to either allow or block inheritance.

The Rename right is pretty self-explanatory. It allows a user with that permission to rename objects within the directory tree. Supervisory rights are Novell's version of Full Control. A user with Supervisory rights is granted all of the rights listed above.

Once objects are created, access to those objects is managed through the attributes assigned to them. These rights include:

- Compare
- Read
- Add and Delete Self
- Write
- Supervisor
- Inheritance Control

The Compare right allows a user to test the attributes of another object without necessarily seeing those rights. For example, in a database, a user that is only granted Compare rights could not ask the database to return a telephone number. That user could, however, provide a telephone number and ask if it was correct.

Read allows the user read permissions of an object, similar to those discussed earlier, but also allows the user to peruse the attributes of an object in the Directory Tree. Any user given Read permissions automatically is granted Compare permissions.

Add and Delete Self gives an object the right to include itself in any attribute of another object. If the user above with the telephone number that needs checking has Add and Delete Self permissions, he or she can simply add himself or herself to the permissions attached to the database. Obviously, this is not a permission you should be haphazardly tossing around.

The Write permission allows a user to modify the contents or attributes of another object. A user with Write permission can not only edit and save a file, but can also edit the attributes assigned to that file, as long as that file has not already been marked Read Only. Supervisory and Inheritance Control rights are the same as described above.

PASSWORD POLICY MANAGEMENT

Since the key to the network for any user is that person's password, the password should be considered to be as important, and kept as secure, as one's safe deposit box key. Allowing another to use your password not only compromises the network, it also can potentially compromise you.

A key example was a particular government worker (who shall remain unnamed) who allowed a coworker to use his password. Supposedly the coworker was under pressure to meet a virtually impossible deadline and needed access to information that his own credentials did not provide.

While logged on as the other user, the one who "borrowed" the password sent an incredibly offensive and very incriminating email to a female supervisor. I guess you don't have to try very hard to figure out which individual got the axe. At first, anyway. A rather nasty lawsuit resulted. Eventually, the truth emerged and the guilty party paid his dues. Unfortunately for many, truth does not always prevail.

Therefore, there are a few simple rules to follow when it comes to password management.

- Do not reveal your password to anyone.
- Change your password periodically.
- Do not use common names or words as your password.
- Make your password difficult to guess.
- Keep passwords a minimum length.
- Use a combination of letters and numbers, and/or upper and lower case.
- Do not write your password on a "hidden" surface and leave it lying around for another person to find.

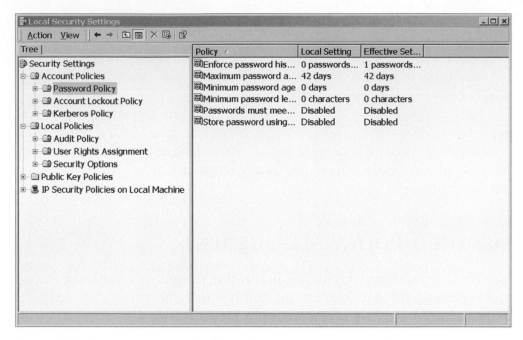

Figure 15.7 Setting a password policy in Windows 2000 Advanced Server

The NOS provides methods for the network administrator to enforce these rules as well (see **Figure 15.7**). You don't necessarily have to put your faith in the users.

I have already discussed why sharing your password can be a dangerous thing. It is for basically those same reasons one should occasionally change a password. Constantly using the same password throughout one's life can be potentially dangerous. Someone trying to gain access to your network can watch you log on. He or she might not get the password right the first time, but if the opportunity presents itself on more than one occasion, eventually your password will get figured out.

Also it is a very bad idea to use common names or words as a password. Someone trying to hack into the network can find user IDs easily enough. It's finding the password that's difficult. The first thing a hacker will do is to try the obvious passwords first. If no minimum length is enforced in the password policy, a user can simply select the Enter key as a password. Users frequently use their user IDs as their password. That way they only have to remember one thing. Don't do that. And don't use your name, your children's names, or your pets' names. And *don't* tape your password and user ID to your monitor.

Since you know the thing a hacker will try first is to guess your password, one of the best things you can do is make it as difficult as possible for someone to do this. To start with, you can enforce a rule that states passwords must be a minimum length, such

ON PASSWORD SECURITY

I was once doing some maintenance at a client's site. I needed to work on one of the client machines and then I needed to so some work on the server. I serviced the client machine first, and when I asked for the password, I was firmly rejected. In fact, I was asked to stand at a distance while the person logged on. I was not in the least offended. In fact, I was quite impressed and made note of this to the office manager.

Then, I went to work on the server. I didn't have to get anyone to log on for me. There on the monitor, on an 8½x11 sheet of paper, was the administrator password for the server! Needless to say, my bubble was popped. I called the office manager to the server room and pointed out that, first of all, the server was accessible to anyone who could get into the office. And second, anyone who had access to the administrator password had access to everything on the network, including sensitive company information. We agreed to change the password and distribute it only to those who absolutely required it. While on the server, I was tempted to change the user's password who wouldn't let me log on to her machine. But I didn't.

as six or eight characters. This precludes someone from using the Enter key or simple words like cat or dog. You can also enforce a policy that says passwords must be a combination of letters and numbers, such as *ent12er*. Now your user can just type enter and get in. He or she just has to remember how to spell it and where to put the 12.

Passwords are case-sensitive. Therefore, if your password is all lower case and you happen to have the Caps Lock key on when you type it in, you will be denied access. An administrator can put this fact to advantage in the password policy by requiring that passwords include a combination of capitalized and lower-case letters.

Earlier in the chapter I discussed the use of dictionary attacks in order to gain access to the network. As you recall, this is when the hacker "throws the dictionary" at the network until one of the words in the dictionary works. A network administrator can prevent this simply by configuring the password policy in the NOS to lock an account out after so many failed attempts. This can be set from 1 to 999 or Never. If you set it to some reasonable value, such as three or five, the user can make a couple of typos, discover Caps Lock is on, and so on without being locked out, but dictionary attacks are thwarted.

Here is where you need to find a happy medium. Minimum password length can be set to as many as fourteen characters. If you define a password policy that requires a password of that length that must be a combination of letters and numbers and must also contain both upper- and lower-case characters—and then set the lockout threshold to two failed attempts—you will spend most of your professional life resetting people's accounts.

DATA ENCRYPTION

I discussed the technology of data encryption briefly in Chapter 10, The Application and Presentation Layers. Here, I will take a look at when and where data encryption is used on the network and by the OS to provide high levels of security.

For the purposes of data transmission, protocols such as PPTP provide the encryption you will require. However, that does not protect you from data theft from within. Therefore, a plethora of third-party applications became available for encrypting the data on your hard disk. Beginning with Windows 2000, as a function of the NTFS 5.0 file system used by that NOS, data encryption became available to the end user.

NTFS 5.0, as part of its structure, includes the *Encrypting File System* (EFS). EFS provides encryption/decryption services within the operating system using a combination of DESX (an extension of the DES I discussed in Chapter 10) combined with a public key exchange (see **Figure 15.8**).

Unlike third-party applications that required the use of separate passwords to access data, EFS is transparent to the user. The user's private key is stored as part of his or her profile. A public key is maintained in the OS so that a *recovery agent* can access the encrypted files if necessary. The recovery agent is an individual (usually an administrator) whose permissions extend to that of accessing encryption keys.

> **EXAM NOTE:** You're going to want to be able to identify the functions of the public key and the private key in the process of encryption.

When a user chooses to encrypt a file or directory, his or her private key is used to generate the encryption algorithm. (For a more detailed explanation of how DES encryption works, see Chapter 10.) As EFS performs the task of encrypting data, it generates a log file that includes an encoded filename that links it to the actual file being encoded. This log keeps track of everything that happens to the user's file along the way. That way, if there is a system failure before the process is finished, DES can undo what it has done so far, starting from scratch if necessary.

A service called the *Base Cryptographic Provider* (BCP) generates a random 128-bit *File Encryption Key* (FEK). This number is associated with the public/private key pair and is included in the *Data Decryption Field* (DDF). In addition, BCP creates

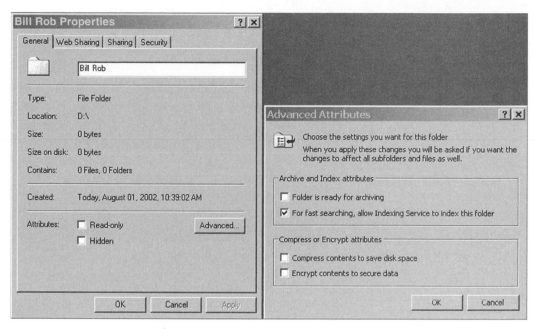

Figure 15.8 Using EFS in Windows 2000.

a *Data Recovery Field* (DRF) that includes the key pair for every recovery agent listed in the registry.

During the encryption process, the target file is backed up to a temporary file, where it will reside until the process is finished. EFS takes the DDF and DRF information and places it into a file header and adds it to the file as EFS attributes. It then applies the encryption algorithm to the backup file and marks it as encrypted. The original is copied to the backup location and the backup is copied to the original. The original file is destroyed and log file is deleted. The file is now encrypted.

All of this is done transparently. When the user who first encrypted a file opens it, that file takes slightly longer to open than a plain-text file. This makes sense, since EFS has to apply the keys, run the algorithm, and provide the file to the user in legible form. However, only that user can read the file. If multiple users use a system, anyone else who logs in cannot open these files. The keys are specific to the profile of an individual user. If Becky and Sam both use the same machine and employ encryption, when Becky is logged on she can't see Sam's files and vice versa. The critical element here is to not leave your computer system running and logged on when you're away from your desk. That kind of defeats the purpose, don't you think?

Now, what happens when Sam has a run-in with management and leaves without notice, refusing to give anyone his password? Can you get those files back?

419

Sure you can. That is the purpose of the recovery agent. Any authorized recovery agent registered in the system can log onto Sam's machine and open the files and/or disable encryption. Let me list some key points here:

- Make sure you have a recovery agent assigned.
- Be very careful who you assign as a recovery agent. He or she will be able to access any encrypted file on any system.
- Only use encryption when absolutely necessary. If you don't need it, enforce a strict policy preventing users from using it arbitrarily.

Just like everything else, EFS has some limitations, but as a security mechanism, it can do a powerful job of protecting sensitive data.

- It's part of the OS kernel, so no additional software need be installed.
- Encryption/decryption keys are never written to page files, so they can't be extracted from a temporary file left over after an unexpected system shutdown.
- If a file is moved from an unencrypted location to an encrypted folder, it will automatically be encrypted on the fly.
- It works in the background, using a user's existing credentials. No additional security or password is needed.

However, as I say, there are some minor issues with it that need to be considered. I hesitate to call them weaknesses, because as long as the administrator and user are both aware of these limitations they aren't really weaknesses.

- EFT only works on systems with NTFS 5.0. It is not backwardly compatible with NTFS 4.0, FAT32, or FAT16.
- System files cannot be encrypted.
- Third-party backup utilities frequently will not work with encrypted files.
- I'm assuming that stringent password policies are already in place. If a user's password is simply the Enter key, anyone has access to all of those encrypted files with a single keystroke.
- Antivirus software must be able to run with the master key incorporated. Files must be opened before they can be scanned.
- If encryption is done on a folder level, and an encrypted file is moved to an unencrypted folder, it will assume the attributes of the folder. Ergo, it will no longer be encrypted.

One other issue that might cause concern for some is that, without a trained recovery agent, files encrypted by a user who subsequently leaves the organization become inaccessible. In order to retrieve them, you would have to entrust your entire network (and its future security) to an outsider to come in and recover the files.

As long as the user and administrator use EFS responsibly, it provides a very high degree of security for locally stored information. Improperly used, it can either negate the benefits or actually create problems. For example, I have mentioned before that one should never delete a user account if that person leaves the organization. If encryption is used, this becomes more important than ever. The private keys are linked to the SID. While a registered recovery agent can still go in and retrieve the files—what happens if it is your recovery agent who leaves? It's probably a good idea to have more than one recovery agent in many organizations.

BUILDING YOUR BARRIERS

Once you've built a network and exposed it to the outside world, you have basically opened a gate for others to come marching through. It doesn't really matter if it's an Internet connection or a WAN interface between remote offices. It's still a gateway. Therefore, you want some method by which you can open that gate to desirable traffic and close it to anything else. Two methods frequently used are firewalls and proxy servers.

The term "firewall" is one that has been used for years by those who fight forest fires. It is some form of physical barrier—sometimes in the form of a controlled fire managed by the firefighters—that blocks the onslaught of an uncontrolled blaze. It stops that fire from spreading from one area to the next. Our virtual firewall prevents virtual fires from spreading from one area to another.

Closely related to firewalls are access lists configured on a router. There are those who consider a router configured with an access list to simply be another form of firewall. However, there are some minor differences worth examining.

Proxy servers are designed to provide secure but reliable and controllable access

> **BUZZ WORDS**
>
> **Firewall:** A device or piece of software that examines all traffic going in or out of a network and uses a preconfigured set of rules to determine whether or not that data is allowed to pass.
>
> **Access list:** A collection of statements mapped to a router interface that define conditions under which packets will be permitted to pass or denied access.

to the Internet. A properly designed proxy server not only keeps undesirable elements from the outside away from your network, but it also enhances performance for the users inside who need Internet access.

Firewalls

Firewalls can come in a variety of forms. Predominately, however, they are a dedicated piece of equipment installed at every port of entry to your network. This can include you, Internet connections or your WAN connections. Firewalls can also consist of a specialized piece of software that runs at the server and can perform the same functions. In this way, your firewall is operating as either a *circuit gateway* or an *application gateway.*

The key difference between the two is not really in their effectiveness. There are extremely good hardware firewalls and extremely good software firewalls. Unfortunately, there is the opposite spectrum for both devices as well.

Buzz Words

Proxy server: A device or piece of software that provides a singular point of entry for an Internet connection, masking IP addresses of internal users. It also caches Web pages for faster access.

Stateful inspection: A process by which a firewall can inspect the contents of a packet to determine whether or not it will be allowed to pass through the interface.

Exam Note: Be able to describe firewalls in detail—in both form and function.

The circuit gateway will direct all outbound traffic to the IP address of the gateway port. This device will substitute the IP address of the transmitting computer in the packet's header with the IP address of the gateway. It keeps track of all outbound traffic from that machine and intercepts all inbound traffic, filters it, and then passes it on. A circuit gateway operates at the Session Layer of OSI. Application gateways control traffic primarily on the basis of opening and closing ports.

Firewalls will generally take one or more, or even all three, of the following approaches to directing traffic in and out of your network:

- Packet filtering
- Stateful inspection
- Proxy service

Packet filtering works by examining the contents of the header of each packet coming through the interface. An administrator configures the firewall to either accept or reject packets based in information found in the header. Packets can be filtered on the basis of IP address, domain name, protocol, port, MAC address, or a number of other possibilities specific to the particular firewall in use. As such, a firewall needs to be able to operate on the Data Link, Network, and Transport Layers of the OSI model.

Stateful inspection is a more recently implemented and far more sophisticated method of filtering traffic. In addition to the more obvious header information examined by a firewall, a firewall capable of stateful inspection can examine the payload, looking for certain characteristics. What it looks for can be configured to be anything from specific strings to particular protocol information.

Proxy service works in a manner very similar to the proxy servers I will discuss later in this chapter. It intercepts packets coming from the outside world and then forwards them to the appropriate host. Conversely, all hosts forward outbound Internet traffic to the firewall, which then replaces the source IP of the host with its own IP. In essence, proxy service plays the part of a circuit gateway.

ACCESS LISTS

Not all exposure to the outside world is from the Internet, however. As I've mentioned, WAN connections can be a point of vulnerability as well. Most of the better routers, including 3Com, Bay Networks, and Cisco, all provide the capability of filtering traffic in a number of methods using an access list.

An access list is a group of statements defining conditions by which specific packets will either be permitted or denied access beyond the interface for which the access list is configured. When a packet is received, the access list is scanned from the first statement to the last, while the packet is examined for any potential matches to any of the statements.

Access lists can filter packets on the basis of IP address, protocol, or port. Also, access lists work only with the interface to which they've been bound and are configured to be either an inbound access list or an outbound access list.

PROXY SERVERS

Proxy servers can actually perform several valuable functions on the network. First off, they allow a large number of users to share a single point of access to the Internet. This is far more efficient and less expensive than providing a separate account for each user who needs access. From a security standpoint, proxy servers provide a circuit gateway behind which your actual network IP addresses can be hidden. And by caching recently accessed Web pages, they provide a degree of performance enhancement to the end users.

EXAM NOTE: Proxy servers are giving way to other methods for interconnecting your network to the Internet. However, it is still a topic that is covered on the exam. Know what they are and how they work.

As with firewalls, proxy servers can exist as an application running on a server or as a dedicated piece of hardware running a specialized application. In general, proxy servers will provide the gateway services to the Internet for all users. They also will usually incorporate some form of firewall protection. Unique to the proxy server is its ability to cache recently accessed pages.

Once a page has been permitted access and viewed by a user, that page is stored on the proxy server. The next person who accesses that page will see it load much more quickly because it's coming from a local server rather than over the slower Internet connection.

When a user makes a request for an Internet resource, that request is forwarded to the proxy server. Proxy checks the request against its filters to make sure the request will be permitted, and if so, does the DNS search, finds the web page, downloads it, and forwards it to the client. That page is maintained in cache.

THE SECURITY PROTOCOLS

Protocols are equally as important in the implementation of security as they are in any other aspect of networking. Both systems involved in a secure transmission need to know how the other end is going to be handling data. Security has been a huge factor in networking since day one. That shouldn't come as much of a surprise, considering it was a secret government defense agency that set up our first networks.

EXAM NOTE: Know your security protocols and which one is used where.

There are scores of security protocols that have been used in the past or are in current use. Fortunately, the industry in general seems to have settled on a few. The ones I will discuss in this chapter are:

- Secure Sockets Layer (SSL) and Transport Layer Security (TLS)
- Secure Multipurpose Internet Mail Extensions (SMIME)
- IP Security (IPSEC)
- Kerberos

Another protocol that should be added to that list is HTTPS. However, since I discussed that in Chapter Eleven, An Introduction to TCP/IP, there is no need to rehash it here. Please be aware, however, that HTTPS is considered to be a security protocol.

SSL AND TLS

SSL is an earlier protocol that provides a secured point-to-point connection between two devices across an intranet or the Internet. It is considered to be a *connection-security* protocol. It is not, however, exclusively a Transport Layer protocol. TLS is simply more recent implementation of SSL, putting more responsibility at the Transport Layer.

SSL works on several levels and requires the services of a couple of companion protocols to function. In order to work, SSL first requires that a secure connection be made, and that the credentials exchanged during the handshake operation be kept secure as well. The *SSL Handshake Protocol* allows the exchange of data during connection establishment to be transmitted in encrypted form. This information includes user ID and password, along with both public and private encryption keys (when necessary).

Once the connection is established, the *SSL Record Protocol* is responsible for encapsulating the information provided by the networking protocols. This information is subsequently encrypted and transmitted.

SMIME

One of the key security issues surrounding email is that the data must be warehoused before it ever reaches its final destination. Most of the security protocols are concerned with security during the transmission of data. Once it arrives, security becomes the responsibility of the receiving device.

Email is data that is transmitted by one device and received and stored by another. When the intended recipient finally gets around to checking his or her email, that data will be transmitted and received once again. SMIME makes sure that the information contained in the email is just as secure during the storage process as it is during transmission.

Although originally intended for email, SMIME has proven its worth in other areas as well. Another powerful security protocol built upon SMIME is *Electronic Data Interchange over the Internet* (EDI-INT). EDI-INT is a standard for transmitting documents over the Internet. This protocol provides for secure transfer and storage of data as well as support for electronic signatures.

IPSEC

The majority of the world has long since made the move to TCP/IP as the protocol of choice for nearly all of its internetworking needs. Unfortunately the one property of the protocol that draws us to it is also the one that makes it the least secure. Any device, anywhere in the world, can locate and communicate with any other device anywhere in the world as long as connectivity is there. The Internet provides connectivity to a huge percentage of computers in the world in one fashion or another.

IPSEC provides secured IP transmissions for any application designed to support the protocol. It operates on top of the L2TP protocol that I discussed in Chapter Fourteen, Working with Remote Access.

Once a connection has been made between two devices, the data is exchanged using one of two encryption methods. For compatibility purposes standard DES is supported (DES was discussed in Chapter Ten). As you might recall, DES uses a 56-bit key.

For more secure transmissions, *Triple-DES* is used. Triple-DES is an extension of DES that applies conventional DES encryption to the data three separate times, using three different keys. In order to ensure that only the intended recipient can decrypt the data, it contains a digital signature embedded in each packet.

Two things account for IPSEC's popularity. First of all, it is now part of the TCP/IP protocol suite. In IPv4, it must be implemented as an optional feature. In IPv6 it is a functional part of the suite. Second, because it works at the network layer, it is independent of protocols working at other layers. IPSEC can be used in conjunction with any of the other security protocols for even more greatly enhanced security.

SECURE SHELL

The Secure Shell protocol (SSH) answers the need for secure communications over an Internet connection. This protocol allows users to remotely control another computer, and to download sensitive files with a high degree of security. It does so by providing authentication services, data encryption, and data integrity to remote communications. Software solutions that implement SSH routinely use three different services to the client/server network:

- A secure command shell
- Secure file transfer
- Port forwarding

Together, these provide for a more secure and reliable VPN.

THE SECURE COMMAND SHELL

Today it's customary that operating systems offer some form of user-friendly environment for their complex and intricate command structure. The most familiar of these shells is the Windows desktop. With it, all a user has to do is blithely point the mouse at pretty little pictures and click away. For a vast number of users, this is as far into computing as they ever want to go.

The Secure Command Shell provides network administrators a remote shell from which they can launch applications, manage files and permissions, and perform a large number of other activities. The Secure Command Shell adds a level of security not previously enjoyed in remote system management.

SECURE FILE TRANSFER

Transferring large files in TCP/IP has long been the responsibility of FTP. The problem with FTP is that it is about as secure as a horse corral with no gate. All data moved by FTP is in plain text (unless encapsulated into packets generated by another protocol). The release of the *Secure File Transfer Protocol* (SFTP) eliminates the need for and overhead of secondary security protocols.

SFTP operates over the same port as SSH, so it doesn't require that other ports be opened on the system to use it. Also, all data transferred by SFTP is encrypted. This includes authentication information containing the users' credentials as well as user data. Now FTP servers are no longer a hole in the security of any given organization. Data can be shared with trusted customers over an intranet or an extranet without having to bury the server on the obscure side of the firewall.

PORT FORWARDING

Port forwarding is a powerful new tool that allows multiple applications to transmit data over a multiplexed channel using a single port. One of the biggest security issues faced by administrators is the number of ports that have to be left open over WAN or Internet connections in order for the users to be able to do their jobs properly. Once Port Forwarding is properly configured, several different applications can share a single port. The ports those applications normally use can be shut down on the firewall. That's a whole bunch of doors slammed on potential intruders.

SECURE COPY

The Secure Copy (SCP) protocol assures that data copied across SSH connections is kept safe. As with other SSH services, data moved with SCP is encrypted before transmission and decrypted on arrival. This prevents unauthorized intruders from using packet sniffers to intercept transmission and extract the contents of the packets. SCP is a command-line tool that is used to copy specific files.

WEP AND WPA

The growing popularity of wireless networking has revealed just how insecure such connections can be. From the start, steps were taken to protect user's data from being freely intercepted when transmitting over unbounded connections.

In 1999, the Wired Equivalency Protocol (WEP) was released in 1999. The concept was that it would provide the same degree of privacy over a wireless connection that someone physically connected to the LAN enjoyed. Unfortunately that was about as far from the truth as one could get. To begin with, WEP used relatively short encryption keys, and just a few keys were used for everybody. It wasn't long before there were tools all over the Internet for cracking the WEP, if you'll forgive a really bad pun.

An organization called the Wi-Fi Alliance put together their own protocol to address the weaknesses of WEP. (Wi-Fi refers to wireless networking using the 802.11b standards discussed in Chapter Four, Welcome to OSI.) Wi-Fi Protected Access (WPA) sewed a newly-developed protocol known as the Temporal Key Integrity Protocol (TKIP) into WEP.

TKIP makes use of dynamically-generated encryption keys to keep hackers guessing. Also the users' identities are verified with a challenge-response user authentication method based on that used by RADIUS. As of this writing, this is the security protocol of choice for wireless networking manufacturers.

KERBEROS

Kerberos is a protocol developed by the folks at MIT to provide authentication for what they defined as "slightly trusted" clients. By this, they mean that when a client makes a request, the server does not automatically assume that client is logged onto the network. It got its odd name from the legendary watchdog of Hades in Greek mythology.

Kerberos utilizes dedicated authentication servers to provide security. An authentication server can (and should) be independent from the servers providing the actual services. For every user and for every server on the network, Kerberos assigns a private encryption key based on conventional DES encryption.

When a user first logs onto the network, the authentication server will intervene. It will generate a *ticket* that authorizes that user for that specific session. The ticket includes the server's secret key along with a randomly generated session number. It is then time-stamped to expire within a certain period. This ticket is added to the client's credentials, which include user ID, password, session number, and the user's secret key.

> **EXAM NOTE:** Kerberos is another of the relative newcomers to the Network+ exam. As I've mentioned earlier, newer material is far more likely to show up on your exam.

As long as that ticket remains good, that user can access the resources granted. The added security is that, once the time stamp expires, the user's session will time out. For further network access, he or she will have to log on once again.

There are a few limitations of Kerberos. For one thing, the clock settings between client and authentication server must be within five minutes of each other. Some NOSs allow the server to update the time clock for clients when they log on. If Kerberos is to be implemented, using this feature might not be a bad idea. If your NOS doesn't support this feature, there are third-party add-on utilities that do.

Also, Kerberos won't protect a workstation that has been abandoned by its user for a coffee break. Anyone can still walk up and access the system using the logged on person's credentials. Also, if someone decides to share his or her password with others, it defeats the purpose. Still, properly used, Kerberos is a good enhancement to any network.

DEFENDING AGAINST VIRUSES

You can't work in this industry for any length of time at all without being aware of the constant barrage of insidious new viruses that are being released, practically every day. Despite a general awareness of the problem, many people aren't even aware of what a virus is and what it does.

The term "virus" is often used (incorrectly, I might add) to describe any malicious software out there. In fact, a virus is only one of many forms of malicious software you need to protect your systems from. The things to watch for are:

- Viruses
- Worms
- Trojan horses
- Logic bombs
- Trapdoors
- Embedded macros

BUZZ WORDS

Virus: A string of code embedded into a legitimate file that, when released, performs a mischievous or malignant function.

Logic bomb: A piece of code programmed to run at either a specific time or when a specific action is performed. Until then, it sits dormant.

Worm: An executable program that enters your system through another route and performs mischievous or malignant functions.

Each one of these types of software comes in a slightly different form. Their level of malevolence ranges from mischievous to disastrous.

> **EXAM NOTE:** CompTIA wants you to be well aware that not all malicious code comes your way as a virus. Be able to distinguish between the different types of programs described in this section.

Viruses are pieces of code that are inserted into an otherwise legitimate string of code, such as a piece of software or a file. Viruses can be embedded in software programs, image or video files, sound clips, or just about any other file type you want to imagine. Simply opening the file may activate the virus, or there might be a time/date stamp embedded in the code. When you open the file, the virus is copied to some location in your system. On the specified time and date, it runs as a self-executable. This is known as a *logic bomb.*

Viruses range from benign to destructive and are usually correctable once the major antivirus software manufacturers have found the virus's *signature.* The signature is a string of code unique to that virus. Since the code is by necessity quite small and will be the same on any system running the same OS, a simple scan of the system, comparing all known virus signatures with the code on your system will generally find the virus. Many viruses can be excised from the file in which they reside. In this case, the file is reported as *repaired.* If the file cannot be repaired, it will be moved to a different folder, where it will be reported as *quarantined.*

Worms perform the same malfunctions as viruses. They differ, however, in the fact that a worm is actually a complete program. Once a worm is transferred to your system it can do any one of a number of things. It can propagate itself through your email system by attaching itself to an email (usually generated by the author of the virus) and sending itself to everyone in your email database. Some worms have actually collected user passwords and sent them out over the Internet. Anyone who knew how to retrieve them had an entire collection of passwords to try when hacking. A worm set off the Internet attack of 2003 that I discussed earlier.

BUZZ WORD

Trojan horse: A malignant program designed to look like a conventional program that induces the user to perform certain functions.

Signature file: The data file used by antivirus software to compare known viruses to code embedded in your system. Without an up-to-date signature file, newer viruses can go unnoticed.

Like a worm, a Trojan horse is a complete program. However, the Trojan horse is designed to look, feel, and smell just like a regular program the user would want to run. The program induces the user to willingly perform some function, such as type in a password. Information thus collected can be stored in a file and subsequently transmitted to unauthorized persons. An early example of a Trojan horse was a program that emulated the logon screen of a popular NOS. Users would try to log on. When they failed, they would get someone else to try, until finally the administrator would attempt to log using the administrator ID and password. The program was collecting all of these passwords in a file, and they were later used to break into the network.

All of the above can be designed to perform different functions. They can be as benign as simply having your computer do something "amusing," or they can actually damage the boot sector of your hard drive, making your system unusable.

I mentioned logic bombs when discussing viruses. A logic bomb is any executable that is designed to run at a later date. This later time can be a specified time and date, as in the example used above, or a logic bomb can be set to activate when a certain function is performed. Logic bombs can arrive in your system as a virus, a worm, or a Trojan horse.

Another thing that malicious software can do is to open a *trap door*. This is a method of accessing a network or system without going through the usual routine of entering a user ID and password.

Operating systems themselves come with very little protection against malicious software. This is still the realm of the third-party manufacturer. Several different companies, including Symantec, McAfee, and Dr. Solomon, along with many others, write software specifically for the purpose of detecting and, where possible, eliminating malicious software from your system.

In order for these to be effective, you must regularly update your signature files. When a new virus or worm comes out, there is a very good chance that older signature files will not detect it. As soon a new virus has been detected and analyzed, the antivirus software manufacturers post new signature files that include the new species.

That is where they provide themselves with continual revenues. When you purchase antivirus software, you will receive the signature files that ship with the software, which will be seriously out of date. The process of installing the software will link you to the Website, where your signature files will be updated. Depending on the product and version that you purchased, you will most likely also receive a subscription, allowing you to download new signature files for a certain period of time. When that time elapses, you will need to pay to renew your subscription.

Chapter Summary

By this point you should be beginning to realize that administering a network is an ongoing thing. The protection of the data housed on a network is a key responsibility of any network administrator. If you establish a decent security policy early on, and strictly enforce that policy, your life can be a lot easier.

Security comes from both within and without. Your job isn't done simply because you slapped a firewall onto your Internet connection. You also need to protect any WAN connections and make sure your own employees aren't a threat.

Always keep in mind that it isn't just loss or theft of data that you need to worry about. You must endure an almost daily barrage of viruses and worms written and propagated by morons who think they're being clever. You need to protect your systems from malignant software as well. It's a nasty job, but somebody's gotta do it. Fortunately for us, it pays better than flipping burgers.

Brain Drain

1. How many ways can you think of in which your network is in danger?

2. You're establishing a security policy for your network and want it to be as complete as possible. What different things should you implement on your network?

3. Describe in as much detail as you can a good password policy.

4. Describe the process of user logon in as much detail as you can.

5. Describe the different ways a firewall can protect your network.

THE 64K$ QUESTIONS

1. Which of the following is not an issue of network security?

    a. Protecting the Internet connection from unwanted intrusion

    b. Detecting and blocking malicious software

    c. An employee printing out a list of customers to take home so he or she can work at home

    d. Keeping the hardware secure

    e. These are all security issues.

2. According to the FBI, over _____ of security breaches came in over an Internet connection in 2001.

    a. 65 percent

    b. 75 percent

    c. 85 percent

    d. 90 percent

3. If users are able to set their own password on a particular file, they are using

    a. System security

    b. File system security

    c. Share level security

    d. User level security

4. EFS is a form of _____.

    a. System security

    b. File system security

    c. Share level security

    d. User level security

5. Your network administrator recently installed a new firewall on your network. Now you can't upload a file to the FTP server. This is most likely because the firewall is using _____.

    a. IP filtering

    b. Packet filtering

    c. Source route filtering

    d. Stateful inspection

6. Inheritance Control is an example of a _____ permission.

    a. File system security

    b. User level

    c. Share level

    d. Directory services

7. Which of the following can be a part of password policy?

    a. A minimum length of sixteen characters

    b. A maximum length

    c. A combination of upper-case and lower-case letters

    d. A combination of letters and numbers

8. An application gateway is an example of _____.

    a. A proxy server

    b. A firewall

    c. A router's access list

    d. An antivirus software

9. The process of data filtering that can examine the contents of a packet's payload is _____.

    a. Packet filtering

    b. Header filtering

    c. Stateful inspection

    d. Payload filtering

10. A _____ is a complete program whose only purpose is to perform some malignant action on your computer.

    a. Virus

    b. Worm

    c. Logic bomb

    d. Trojan horse

11. It's a given that the CEO of your company should automatically be assigned administrative privileges to the network.

    a. True

    b. False

    c. Only if you'll lose your job if you don't.

12. One thing that no network attached to the Internet should ever be without is a _____.

    a. Virtual Private Network

    b. Layer 3 switch

    c. VLAN

    d. Firewall

13. What is one of the biggest holes in a network that needs to be patched?

    a. You need to secure RAS.

    b. You need to lock down the physical systems.

    c. You need to switch over to Linux operating systems.

    d. You need to train the users in security measures.

14. You have a TCP/IP network and want to tighten your security. Which of the following is a good option that is available on all IPv6 networks?

    a. IPSec

    b. Kerberos

    c. ISBAN

    d. NetLock

15. Windows network operating systems use the _____ to identify individual accounts.

    a. User ID

    b. Password

    c. Both a. and b.

    d. The SID

16. On a Windows network, the _____ compares a user's credentials to the security database before authenticating that user.

    a. SID

    b. SAM

    c. LSA

    d. Registry

17. Why is Full Control a more powerful permission that allowing Read, Write, and Execute permissions to the same user?

    a. It isn't.

    b. Full Control allows the user to add or modify other user accounts.

    c. Full Control allows the user to take ownership of files.

    d. Full Control assume administrative privileges.

18. A good password policy would require that users create passwords with a minimum of 15 characters.

    a. True

    b. False

19. What is the minimum password length imposed by Windows network operating systems by default?

    a. 1 character

    b. 4 characters

    c. 5 characters

    d. They don't require a password at all.

20. Which of the following components of a users credentials are case-sensitive in the Windows environment?

    a. The user ID

    b. The password

    c. Both the user ID and the password

    d. Neither the user ID nor the password

TRICKY TERMINOLOGY

Access list: A collection of statements mapped to a router interface that define conditions under which packets will be permitted to pass, or denied access.

Firewall: A device or piece of software that examines all traffic going in or out of a network and uses a preconfigured set of rules to determine whether or not that data is allowed to pass.

Interactive logon: An authentication procedure in which the user is prompted to enter his or her user ID and password.

Logic bomb: A piece of code programmed to run at either a specific time or when a specific action is performed. Until then, it sits dormant.

Noninteractive logon: Once a user is logged onto the network, subsequent access authentication is done in the background, transparent to the user.

Proxy server: A device or piece of software that provides a singular point of entry for an Internet connection, masking IP addresses of internal users. It also caches Web pages for faster access.

Signature file: The data file used by antivirus software to compare known viruses to code embedded in your system. Without an up-to-date signature file, newer viruses can go unnoticed.

Stateful inspection: A process by which a firewall can inspect the contents of a packet to determine whether or not it will be allowed to pass through the interface.

Trojan horse: A malignant program designed to look like a conventional program that induces the user to perform certain functions.

Virus: A string of code embedded into a legitimate file that, when released, performs a mischievous or malignant function.

Worm: A executable program that enters your system through another route and performs mischievous or malignant functions.

ACRONYM ALERT

BCP: Base Cryptographic Provider. A Windows service that generates user keys for encrypting data.

DDF: Data Decryption Field. A header field that is added to any file encrypted by EFS that allows the decryption of that file.

DRF: Data Recovery Field. A header field that is added to any file encrypted by EFS that allows a recovery agent to decrypt the data in the absence of the original user.

EFS: Encrypting File System. In NTFS 5.0, this is the portion of the file system that allows individual files and folders to be encrypted for local storage by the user.

FEK: File Encryption Key. The 128-bit value used by encrypting software to scramble the code.

GID: Group Identification. Identifies a group account, of which several users might be members.

IPSEC: IP Security. A security protocol for standard TCP/IP transmissions. While optional on IPv4, it is built into IPv6.

LSA: Local Security Authority. A Windows service that manages internal security on a local machine or server.

SSPI: Security Support Provider Interface. A Windows service that handles user authentication transparently after initial logon.

UID: User Identification. Identifies a specific user's account.

CHAPTER 16

DATA RECOVERY AND FAULT TOLERANCE

I spent the last chapter discussing different methods of securing your network. One of the risks that your data faces is loss through natural disaster or hardware failure. Servers do fail, and they generally do so at the time that will do the worst damage to your company. If you're lucky, all you have to do is replace a faulty part and you're ready to rock and roll.

Unfortunately, there are a number of different situations that can result in loss of data. These kinds of problems run the gamut from common hard drive failures to more esoteric problems, such as faulty memory causing data corruption. One of these days you will have to live through that inevitable day that your servers, instead of humming merrily in the background logging on users and doling out data, simply say either "Operating System Not Found" or "I/O Error Reading, Drive C:". If you plan ahead, there will be no need to panic. You will already have a plan of action that will have you back up and running in short order.

The first part of this chapter will review how data is stored on the hard drive. I'll examine various methods of getting a system back up and running in the event of failure. I'll also take a look at how you can recover the accidentally deleted file. Lost and inadvertently deleted files can frequently be restored with relative ease. Once in a great while, you might find yourself facing a catastrophic failure. This is one in which the only solution is a full system or drive array replacement. This might include an electrical event that takes out the servers, a fire that destroys the building, or any other disaster that completely destroys the data. A good disaster recovery plan, properly implemented, will make the process of rebuilding the system to the way it was before a whole lot easier, with a lot less downtime.

After that I'll examine the concept of fault tolerance. Modern technology even provides us with options that, when implemented, can make failed hardware—even a failed server—go unnoticed to users on the network. Not much in terms of the CompTIA exam resides in this chapter, but there are some items that may appear. These include:

3.1 Identify the basic capabilities (For example: client support, interoperability, authentication, file and print services, application support and security) of server operating systems to access network resources.

3.10 Identify the purpose, benefits and characteristics of using antivirus software.

3.11 Identify the purpose and characteristics of fault tolerance.

3.12 Identify the purpose and characteristics of disaster recovery.

DISK STRUCTURE AND DATA RECOVERY

I realize that this is not a book on computer hardware. However, an understanding of how data is stored on a disk drive is essential in the data recovery process. (It's also useful for passing the Network+ exam.) Therefore, a quick summary might be in order.

If you go into the CMOS setup of most computers, there will be a setting for identifying your hard disk drives. You'll almost always see the IDE drives set at AUTO. If you examine the options more closely, you will most likely also see options that read LARGE and LBA. There may also be others. These are the various modes your system supports for addressing hard drives. The SCSI adapter installed in the machine generally manages SCSI drives, but addressing rules are the same.

In reality, the basic routine in the BIOS that handles hard drive I/O operations knows only one set of rules. These rules are called the *CHS parameters*. CHS is an acronym for cylinders, heads, and sectors per track. CHS not only determines the storage capacity of the drive, it provides the road map that allows the file allocation tables to properly organize and subsequently retrieve information stored on the device (see **Figure 16.1**).

Figure 16.2 shows the internal mechanism of a hard drive. If you were able to look closely at the very tip of the actuator arm, you would see that there are *read/write* (R/W) heads associated with each platter surface. When the platter makes one complete rotation, the head tracks a complete circle along each platter surface. All of the circles combined make up a cylinder. The number of platter surfaces dictates how many heads are required.

BUZZ WORD

CHS parameters: A description of a hard disk drive's geometrical layout. It defines the location and number of all cylinders and read/write heads and how many sectors are contained in each track.

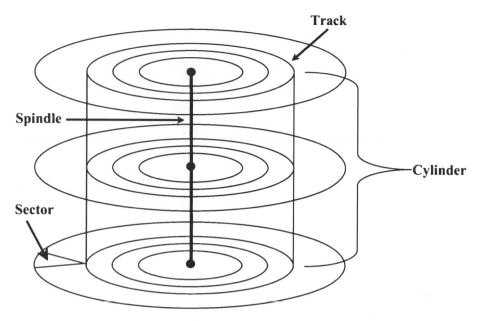

Figure 16.1 The CHS geometry of a hard drive dictates how much data can be stored on the drive and how the drive goes about finding that data when it's needed.

The limitation of the CHS parameters was that it was based on a BIOS call referred to as *Int13h*. Int13h only provided for a 24-bit address for information stored on the drive. Under this addressing scheme, you got:

- 10 bits for cylinder addressing: This allows for a maximum 1024 addressable cylinders

- 8 bits for head number: But at least you could have a total of 256 R/W heads!

- 6 bits for the number of sectors per track: This permitted 64 sectors per track, numbered from 0 to 63. Track 0 is reserved, so you only have 63 usable tracks.

If you pull out your trusty calculator and run the numbers, you will see that 1024 x 256 x 63 equals 16,515,072 sectors. A sector consists of 512 bytes. This means that the largest drive that Int13h is capable of reading without help is 8,455,716,864 bytes. The hard drive industry recognizes one million bytes as a megabyte; therefore, this is just a bit under 8.5GB. In the days of 20MB hard drives, it seemed inconceivable that anyone would ever exceed that limit.

That was then and this is now. I did a quick perusal of the Internet today and discovered that the smallest drive I could purchase new was 20GB. 80GB drives were the ones being most heavily pressed, and I could get a 120GB drive

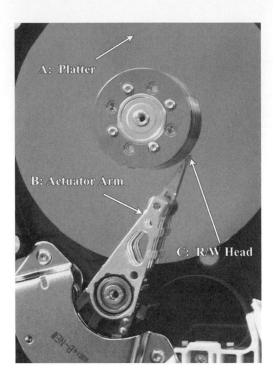

Figure 16.2 As the platter (A) spins inside the drive, the actuator arm (B) moves the heads (C) to the correct cylinder.

for about the cost of dinner and a movie. Someone obviously found a way around the CHS limitations.

The addressing schemes in use today worked around CHS limitations by including additional parameters in the Int13h call. These parameters, the *Int13 extensions*, provide translation methods that allow new technology to be introduced without rendering the older technology incompatible. One of the first to come out was called *Extended CHS* (ECHS). If you have a setting in your CMOS that says "LARGE", this is ECHS. This method assumes that nobody needs 256 heads in a hard drive. And since the most platters I was able to find on any drive, past or present, was sixteen, this would appear to be a pretty safe assumption. The manufacturers can, however, increase capacity by using a lot more cylinders. The older technologies had trouble reading tiny tracks. However, as technology improved, smaller tracks could be read. Smaller tracks mean that more of them could be crammed onto a drive.

ECHS translation method takes all cylinders beyond the 1024-cylinder limitation of CHS and internally divided the number by two. In other words, the manufacturer might make a drive with 2048 cylinders. Since Int13h couldn't read beyond the 1024th cylinder, those from 1025 through 2048 were renumbered. To compensate, ECHS then multiplied the number of heads physically present on the drive number by a factor ranging from two to sixteen (depending on the number of new ranges that needed to be mapped). If ECHS was using a factor of two, a drive that in reality had sixteen heads now logically has thirty-two. Therefore, in order to read track 1025 of head 1, it is reported to Int13h as Track 1, Head 17.

Now from the outset, it may not seem like you gain much. In reality, this allows you to "lie" to the BIOS. Read/write requests for cylinders beyond standard CHS limitations were generated by a separate command within the BIOS in order to prevent confusion as to what sector was actually being read, which could result in the drive returning incorrect data from the wrong sector. This method was somewhat clumsy and very short-lived. It was pretty much non-Microsoft OSs that supported it, such as Unix.

Drive manufacturers today use *logical block addressing* (LBA) for sector translation. LBA does not use standard CHS addressing, but rather numbers sectors sequentially, using a 28-bit address space. LBA translation algorithms subsequently translate those sectors into calls the BIOS can understand. The 28-bit address space of LBA allows for 268,435,456 sectors of 512 bytes, or roughly 137 gigabytes. This is how you get the bigger hard drives that are used in machines today. A recently released standard has extended that address space to 64 bits, allowing for drives of several terabytes.

PARTITIONS

Many times, rather than using a hard disk drive as a single large expanse of storage space, it is necessary to divide it up into smaller sections. When a drive is so divided, these smaller sections are referred to as partitions. There are any number of reasons why a single large partition is either not convenient, or not usable. For example, a machine running MS-DOS cannot see any partition larger than 2GB. Therefore, a DOS user would have no choice but to divide a larger hard drive into smaller partitions.

How a disk is partitioned will be determined by the operating system in use. The

> **BUZZ WORDS**
>
> **Partition:** A logical subdivision of a single hard disk drive. Partitions will be seen by the system as separate drives, or volumes.
>
> **Volume:** A logical drive generated when a hard disk is divided into multiple partitions.

file system used by the OS will determine the type of partition that can be used, which in turn determines the maximum size of the partitions. This is a function of how the OS deals with the *file allocation table* (FAT). The 16-bit file allocation table is generally referred to as FAT16. Other file allocation tables currently in use include FAT32, HPFS, and NTFS, although HPFS has pretty much gone by the wayside. These were all variations of 32-bit tables.

Table 16.1 Common File Systems and Partition Sizing

File System	Maximum Partition Size	File Name Limitations
FAT16	2GB	8.3
FAT32	2048GB	256 characters
HPFS	8GB	256 characters
NTFS 4.0	8GB (4GB max on boot partition)	255 characters
NTFS 5.0	16 exabytes	255 characters

As the Microsoft operating systems evolved, they began to support larger partitions and longer file names.

Hard drives very rarely read individual sectors. Most file systems rely on *file allocation units* (FAU) to make sure data is properly translated for the BIOS. FAUs are groups of sectors that the file system reads as though it were a single sector. An FAU is the minimum amount of hard drive space that a file will occupy, regardless of how small the file might be.

Exam Note: Be able to distinguish between a file allocation unit and a sector. The different file systems use different sized FAUs for any given partition size.

Think of the FAU as being a bottle that holds a certain amount of liquid. All the bottles have to be the same size. You can only put one liquid at a time in the bottle, so if there is a sixteen-ounce bottle of *novel.doc,* then only *novel.doc* fits into the bottle and that bottle can hold up to sixteen ounces of it. If you only have five ounces of *novel.doc,* you can't fill it the rest of the way to the top with *business.xls* because that would make both of the files unusable. However, if you get another five ounces of *novel.doc,* you can add it to that original bottle. But when the total amount of *novel.doc* exceeds sixteen ounces, you need to get a new bottle. This is what's happening on your hard drive, except instead of measuring in ounces, it is measuring in kilobytes.

The file system and partition size determine the size of our bottles. For example,

> **BUZZ WORD** —————
>
> **Disk slack:** Wasted disk space caused by inefficient storage of data by the file system.

a hard drive formatted in FAT16 with a 2GB partition uses sixty-four sectors per FAU. This means that even a fifty-byte file would occupy 32KB of space, while the remaining space would no longer be usable. This is known as *disk slack*. As **Table 16.2** demonstrates, the file system selected can have a dramatic effect on how much hard disk real estate small files can eat up. The 32-bit file system is much more efficient in sector usage. As you can see, the 2GB partition in FAT16 requires 32KB FAUs, whereas partitions up to 8GB in FAT32 or NTFS get by with 8KB FAUs.

To illustrate the effect the choice of a file system and the limitations of its partitioning structure can have on hard disk storage, consider this example. A single icon on the Windows desktop is a small bitmap of about 800 bytes, give or take. There are disks on the market that bundle thousands of these icons, providing users with dozens of creative new options for each program on their desktop. I once had a client with an older machine learn about disk slack the hard way.

This was a while back, and the drive was formatted to FAT16, partitioned to 2GB. Now, keep in mind that each file would occupy a single FAU, and these files are mostly 800 bytes or less. In this particular scenario, the FAU occupied by each file was 32KB. This particular individual had about 500MB left on the drive and had a CD containing 10,000 Windows icons. She wanted to copy all the icons onto her hard drive rather than have to pull out the CD every time she wanted to play. When she tried to calculate how much hard drive space this would require, she did the math based on file size, not knowing the effect of cluster size on hard disk usage.

She expected to use up a little over 8MB (10,000 x 800 = 8,000,000). Instead, each one of those pesky little icons sat down in 32K of space and wouldn't let anything else share. So instead of 10,000 x 800, she was actually looking at 10,000 x 32,000, or about 320MB. She was convinced that the CD had somehow corrupted the drive.

THE MASTER BOOT RECORD

All that hardware theory is fine and good, but what does any of it have to do with whether or not data can be retrieved from a hard drive if it goes down in

Table 16.2 Relationship between File System and Cluster Size

Partition Size	Sectors per File Allocation Unit	Total Size of Cluster
16-bit FAT		
0-15MB (12-bit)	8	4K
16-128MB	4	2K
129-256MB	8	4K
257-512MB	16	8K
512-1GB	32	16K
1GB-2GB	64	32K
2GB+	Not Possible	
FAT32		
0-260MB	4	2K
261-8GB	8	4K
8-16GB	16	8K
16-32GB	32	16K
32-2048GB	64	32K
NTFS 4.0		
0.5GB	1	0.5
0.5 to 1.0GB	2	1K
1.0 to 2.0GB	4	2K
2.0 to 4.0GB	8	4K
4.0 to 8.0GB	16	8K
NTFS 5.0		
0.5GB	1	0.5
0.5 to 1.0GB	2	1K
1.0 to 2.0GB	4	2K
2.0 to 4.0GB	8	4K
4.0 to 8.0GB	16	8K
8.0 to 16.0GB	32	16K
16.0 to 32.0GB	64	32K
32.0GB+	128	64K

Different file systems map the drive out in their own different ways.

flames? To fully answer that question, I need to go into a little more detail as to how the system deals with mass storage in general. The best place to start is on system boot, because if a computer won't boot, it won't do anything else either. And once again, this involves a little basic hardware theory.

When your system first boots, a program on the BIOS known as *Power On-Self Test* (POST) is the first thing to run. First

it checks the basic system components to make sure they're all working properly, then it performs the magic of Plug 'n Play, trying to detect new devices. The final thing POST does is run a routine called *Bootstrap Loader*. This tiny program goes out looking for a *boot sector*. The boot sector houses the all-important *master boot record* (MBR).

The MBR contains information that introduces the file system to system memory, maps out how the hard disk(s) are partitioned, and provides a pointer to the first line of code in the OS. Usually, this is the information stored on Cylinder 0, Track 0, and Sector 1 of the hard disk drive. Boot sectors can also be located on other devices, however, such as CD-ROMS, floppy diskettes, Zip drives, and a number of others.

FAT16 allows for only a single 512-byte sector to provide the system with all the information it needs in order to read a hard disk and find an operating system. Computers formatted to FAT32 and NTFS (either version) use the equivalent of two contiguous sectors.

The MBR manages to squeeze a lot of information into a mere 512 or 1024 bytes. The first few lines of code are executable code that identifies the file system. Directly following the executable are the partition tables. These define how each of the partitions on the drive is laid out. Following the partition tables, the MBR contains a pointer that tells the computer where the first line of the operating system kernel is located. All this information is critical to whether or not a computer is successful in completing the boot process. This also explains why computer viruses that infect the MBR can have such a devastating effect on the system. It has always been my humble, and perhaps semibiased, opinion that the only life form on this planet lower than a programmer who specializes in writing viruses is an amoeba. (Then again, if I expressed that opinion publicly, one might wonder what I have against an amoeba.)

GETTING AROUND THE LIMITATIONS OF THE MBR

Important Note: The master boot record, being only 512 or 1024 bytes long, only has sufficient room to define four primary partitions. Therefore, on any system containing more than four partitions, the additional partitions must be in the form of logical partitions. These are frequently referred to as logical DOS drives or logical volumes. While the MBR is only capable of handling up to four primary partitions, third-party utilities have been developed that offset additional partition tables to another part of the hard drive, allowing for additional primary partitions. One such utility, BootStar by Star Tools, can handle up to fifteen different primary partitions.

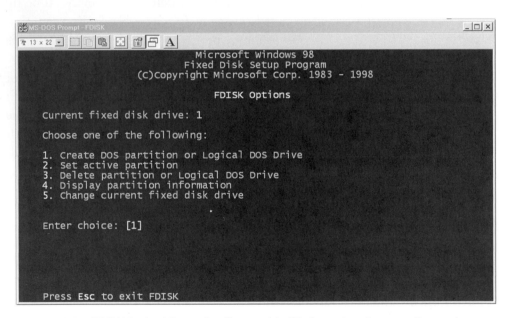

Figure 16.3 FDISK is the Microsoft utility used in Win9x and earlier operating systems.

When you first prepare a hard drive, using the FDISK utility (see **Figure 16.3**) or something similar, this is when the MBR is initially created. In order to run FDISK, you need to have a basic OS running in the background, so you'll be booting from a bootable floppy disk or CD-ROM. This is also true of the third-party utilities that perform similar functions.

It is this utility that generates the partition tables. It does not, however, create the pointers to the OS kernel. That is done when you install the operating system.

Since the OS has to write to the MBR, it is usually a good idea to disable any chip-level virus protection defined in the CMOS.

FDISK can also be executed on a system that has been in use for a while, but has had the MBR damaged in some way, such as by a virus attack. On a drive formatted to FAT16, FDISK /MBR typed at the command prompt might possibly rebuild the master boot record without overwriting data stored on the drive. It makes use of all master and logical partition parameters established when the drive was initially prepared. Many times, this is all that is required in order to salvage a hard drive on which the MBR has been damaged. My experience with that function of the FDISK utility has met with only moderate success in the past. But even moderate success is better than total failure. Note, however, that the command does nothing for a FAT32 or NTFS drive.

> **CAUTION:** While it is true that FDISK/MBR can successfully restore a corrupted MBR on a FAT16 drive it won't help on FAT32. It won't hurt anything, but it won't help. However, some disks use their own methods to handle larger drives. This is sometimes referred to as drive overlay software. Many hard drive manufacturers ship their drives with such software bundled with it. If drive overlay software is used, it is very likely that use of FDISK/MBR will do more damage than good. These utilities input their own executable code in the MBR and generally use a different format for partition tables. FDISK/MBR will replace the original MBR with one that will most likely render the disk unreadable.

When the operating system is installed, it will write into the MBR the location of the first lines of its primary file, or *kernel*. Obviously, the file itself would be too large to fit onto a single sector. This pointer will direct the boot process to a physical address on the hard drive and turn over the boot process to the operating system.

PARTITION TABLES

As I mentioned, partition tables are generated by FDISK when the drive is first prepared. Each primary partition created must have its own table in the MBR. The partition table contains some rather specific information that defines the structure of each partition. A key piece of the information provided concerns whether or not a particular partition is bootable. A single byte in the partition table's header determines this. This is the *partition state*. If partition state is set to 00h, it is a non-bootable partition. If it is set to 80h, it is active. This is a primary target for boot sector viruses.

449

Also indicated in the partition table is information concerning precisely what cylinder the partition starts on. A separate entry tells the system what head and sector initializes the partition. Following that will be entries that specify on what cylinder the partition ends, and another entry for the last head and sector of the cylinder. A full breakdown of a partition table looks something like this:

> **Buzz Word**
>
> **Partition table:** The portion of the MBR that defines the beginning and ending points of each logical division that was created on a hard drive.

- Byte 00: The boot indicator, which is always either 0x00 or 0x80. 0x80 indicates that the partition is active; 0x00 indicates that it is not active. This determines whether or not an OS can boot from this partition.

- Byte 01: The starting head number of the partition being defined.

- Bytes 02 and 03: Point to the starting sector and cylinder of the partition. The first 6 bits define the starting sector; the remaining 10 bits identify the starting cylinder number.

- Byte 04: The System ID. Identifies the file system being used on the partition. This is added by the `FORMAT` command when the partition is formatted with a particular file system.

- Byte 05: The ending head number of the partition being defined.

- Bytes 06 and 07: Point to the ending sector and cylinder of the partition. As with Bytes 02 and 03, the first 6 bits define the ending sector; the remaining 10 bits identify the ending cylinder number.

- Bytes 08 to 11: Indicate how many sectors there are between the end of the MBR and the first sector of the partition.

- Bytes 12 to 15: Define how many sectors there are in the partition.

FILE ALLOCATION TABLES

I've already talked about the file system and how it affects how data is stored on a drive at great length. And now I finally get down to how this can help you get back data that you've lost. It is precisely how the file systems handle data that makes it possible to get back those files you inadvertently deleted while making space on your hard drive. All file systems, from FAT to NTFS, use an entry system not terribly dissimilar to a database for keeping track of where everything stored on a drive is physically located. This is the *file allocation table* (FAT). Even NTFS has one, even though it is substantially more sophisticated and performs more functions than simple data mapping.

When you chop your hard disk up into partitions, each partition is treated as if it

> **BUZZ WORD**
>
> **Logical drive:** Another name for the volume created on a single hard drive when the disk was partitioned. To the end user, that partition appears as a separate disk drive.

was a separate disk drive or, as you will sometimes see it referenced, a *logical drive*. Logical drives are also called volumes. Each partition on a drive has its own volume boot record (VBR).

> **Exam Note:** Know the difference between an MBR and a VBR. They may try to trip you up on this one.

Similar to the MBR, the VBR contains information about the physical size and layout of the volume. In some OSs, the extended partitions can be made active. If you choose to do so, it will also contain the executable code necessary for the system to boot from that volume. The VBR is created by the operating system when you create the partition. Immediately following the VBR of the hard disk is the file allocation table.

Every operating system in use today follows a specific standard for organizing files on media. The most common system, in use by Microsoft operating systems, makes use of a directory tree. The volume has a root directory; on the C: drive this directory would be C:\. Beneath the root are directories, followed by subdirectories, and then, finally, come the files. The file allocation table maintains a record of the starting sector for every file on the drive. FAT16 maintained two copies of the FAT. More recent OSs may contain even more than that.

When a file is initially saved to disk, it will be assigned the minimum number of clusters needed to store the data it contains. FAT records the starting cluster of that file so that the next time that file is accessed, the OS will know where to locate it. Later on down the road, when the file is accessed and edited it may be too large to fit back onto the original clusters. Other files copied to the drive since may have occupied adjacent clusters. The computer will store what data it can on the original clusters and then find enough free clusters elsewhere on the drive to store the remainder of the data. As far as the end user is concerned, it is still a single file. The FAT, on the other hand, now contains multiple entries for that file. The more times a file is accessed, enlarged, and saved back to disk, the more different areas of hard drive it may occupy, which subsequently means additional entries to the file allocation tables. This is what leads to fragmentation of a hard drive.

With that in mind, let me get back to why it is possible to get back a file that you unintentionally deleted. When you decide to wipe a file from your drive, the data the file contains is actually not affected. The read/write heads don't go over the sectors erasing data. FAT merely stops allocating space to the file. That way, if those clusters are needed by another file, they are available for use. The operating system "deletes" the file by replacing the first character of the file name with the hexadecimal character E5. (For those who are interested, that character would be the å of the ASCII Character Set.) This is an invalid character for a file name to use, therefore the file logically ceases to exist.

At this point in time, however, nothing has happened to the actual data written to the drive. Unless other data is subsequently written to that physical location on the drive, the file can be recovered simply by replacing E5 with the correct character (or any other character that is valid in a file name, for that matter). This is what file recovery utilities such as Microft's Undelete and Norton's Disk Doctor do when they are able to recover files.

> **Exam Note:** Know what goes on in a file deletion process. Not only will you need it on the exam, it is also useful "real world" material.

Simpler utilities can only recover files on an "all-or-nothing" basis. If even one cluster is overwritten by another file, the original file is unreadable to that utility. Some of the more advanced utilities can partially recover a file even if part of it has been overwritten. They do their magic by reading the file allocation table and recovering what clusters they can, one at a time. Even if the starting cluster was used by another file since the deletion occurred, they may be able to retrieve the sectors that were not overwritten.

DISK EDITORS AND PARTIONING UTILITIES

Sometimes, a drive fails because of a corrupted MBR or FAT. These are areas of your hard drive that some of the more malicious viruses like to target. Assuming you could come up with an accurate map of the hard drive, you should be able to replace the information stored in the MBR. There are some very powerful (and very expensive) programs out there that, running from another disk, can scan the hard drive and collect that information. In this way, it might be possible to recover from a master boot record failure by manually rewriting that sector using a disk editor. A disk editor is a more powerful (and potentially more deadly) version of a text editor. It allows the user to view—and change the contents—of a disk drive one bit at a time. These programs can directly edit data on the drive that operating system file managers can't even see. These include the MBR and the FAT. As long as you know precisely what you are editing—and why—it is possible to rewrite a corrupted MBR to make it fully functional again or to repair a partition table.

Caution is the key word here. A misplaced byte of information in this file can render a computer system unbootable. As I mentioned earlier, the first few lines of code in the MBR consist of executables that define the file system. As such, this code describes the method by which the hard disk interacts with Int13h in the BIOS. An operating system such as Windows (any version after 3.xx) has its own way of dealing with hardware and will edit that code accordingly. Allowing software to directly access hardware in Windows can be disastrous. There are numerous Web sites that claim to have "safe" code for restoring master boot records. I say this: unless a person is truly familiar with how an operating system interacts with hardware and knows precisely how his or her hard drive is partitioned, it is a better idea to make use of one of several commercially available utilities that restore disks. Conversely, if you want to pick up a couple of used hard drives just to practice on, there's a lot of money to be made in data recovery.

Partitioning problems are easily addressed by one of several partitioning utilities. Two notable examples include PowerQuest's Partition Magic or Server Magic and Quarterdeck's Partition IT. Programs such as these allow the user to adjust, and in some cases repair, partition size on the fly without losing the data that is stored on those partitions. Let me warn you though. Even though these programs do a good job and work most of the time, they do have certain limitations. Do yourself a favor and carefully read the documentation that accompanies these programs. I know how easy it is to get into the habit of installing a new program and then figuring out how it works by poking around in it.

This is not something you want to do with disk partitioning utilities. Read through the documentation thoroughly, including any read-me files that may be included on the disk. Then, once you begin, make sure you finish the job. Do not let your computer power down during the process. If that happens while the program is still doing its job, your hard drive will be messed up beyond all recognition. Don't even *think* about using a disk partitioning utility until you have completely backed up the data on your drive.

UNFORMATTING UTILITIES

Have you ever formatted a drive by accident? It's actually pretty easy to do. Maybe you've got a Zip drive listed as F: and you want to format a disk. So you right-click on E:, which is your Oracle database, select "Format Drive" and when it asks you if you're sure you want to format this drive, you say, "Heck yeah, I'm sure. I'm the network administrator around here!" It's just as the message "Format Complete" appears that you realize the mistake you've made.

And that's when the fun begins. Under certain circumstances, even a formatted disk can be recovered. In the old days of DOS (starting with MS-DOS 5.0 and forward), there were variations on the Unformat command, as well as a myriad of third-party utilities, that could be run on a freshly formatted disk and restore it to functionality. Unformat disappeared from Windows 95 and later Microsoft OSs. However, that simply opened the door to the third-party applications that rushed in to replace it.

The key to success in recovering a formatted drive is that nothing else be put on the drive once the format has taken place. If any data has been written to the drive since the format occurred, it is unlikely that any data will be recovered.

One little problem, if you want to call it a problem (and I do), with some of these utilities is that primary directories off the root get renamed in many of these utilities. Instead of having a C:\WINDOWS directory, you find that you have a C:\DIR1 directory, or a C:\DIR2. All the other directories on your drive are similarly named DIR3, DIR4, and so on and so forth. It's up to you to figure out what these directories are and properly rename them yourself.

I've mentioned only a few of many utilities and suites on the market today that allow users to recover data they might have otherwise considered permanently lost. The key thing to remember is that as soon as the disaster occurs, until you have the recovery software in hand and are ready to attempt recovery, the affected machine needs to be left alone. Don't even power it up! Writing any new data over the affected areas can, and usually will, render the data unrecoverable. And many operating systems write all kinds of error logs (or try to, anyway) to the root directory when the system fails to boot.

INITIATING DISASTER RECOVERY

What I have discussed so far is all fine for a simple hard drive failure, but what about the ultimate disaster? Anything that renders a machine completely useless, such as a fire, theft of a system, or hard drive failure, means that you will need to rebuild your data onto a completely new machine or set of drives.

In that event, you have two options. There are data recovery services with specialized hardware and software than can do a bit-by-bit recovery of all data on any media that is left. This is a time-consuming and expensive process, and if the media is gone, as in the case of theft or fire, it doesn't help much. On the other hand, if the data is vital to operations and the media hasn't been destroyed, it may be worth it.

A more logical plan is to assume from day one that someday a disaster is going to happen, and be prepared with a plan of action to recover from it. That plan needs to include both preventative maintenance procedures and easy access to additional copies of all critical data. These copies need to be safely stored away from the site so that they can be retrieved if necessary. This portion of the chapter will deal with both preventative maintenance and preparing for a smooth rebound when the inevitable occurs.

HOLDING OFF DISASTER

The best way of preventing data loss is to make sure your hardware never fails. Naturally this can never be a 100 percent effective plan of action. However, there are several policies you can implement that prolong the life of hardware and reduce the chances and incidents of file corruption. Some of the simplest procedures are built right into your operating system. Frequent use of utilities such as ScanDisk can be useful in notifying a user of impending disaster. A hard drive technology that has been around for several years is *Self Monitoring, Analysis, and Reporting Technology* (SMART). As long as the SMART utilities have been installed, a SMART drive monitors conditions such as temperature, floating height of the heads, and other conditions to keep an eye on the drives' condition and predict impending failure. If you've got it, use it.

ScanDisk can tell you if new bad sectors are appearing on the hard drive with increasing regularity (see **Figure 16.4**). This is a good sign that the drive is sick and should probably be replaced. In most cases, ScanDisk has no problem moving the data from the bad cluster over to a good one elsewhere on the drive. ScanDisk then marks the sector it can't read as bad, preventing data from being stored on that particular cluster in the future. Because this is so easy, it is all too common for a user to go about his or her business, knowing that the data was saved, and ignore the fact that there must be a problem, or none of this would be happening. Then when disaster strikes, you are going to be glad you read the next section.

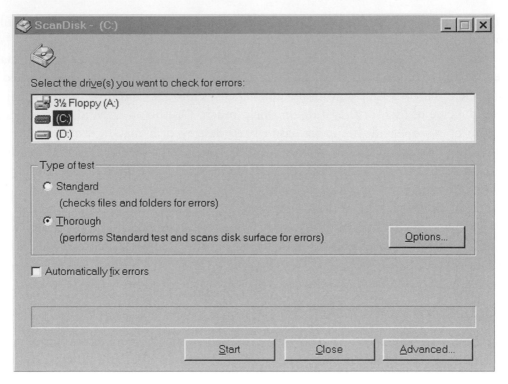

Figure 16.4 ScanDisk is a utility that should be run periodically. This utility can detect bad sectors on a hard drive and move the data to a safer location before you lose it.

PLANNING A GOOD BACKUP ROUTINE

In the movies, the good guy doesn't think twice about dropping into a burning building all by himself so he can save a couple of hostages held by a hundred heavily armed terrorists. Real-life cops rarely work that way. In a situation like that, they insist on having a backup or two. Or two hundred.

IT administrators need to be the same way. You don't want all of your critical data on machines that could very easily become part of that burning building without the safety net of a complete backup of the system, stored safely away (preferably far away), that you can easily access in the event of a system loss or failure.

Exam Note: Backup and Recovery processes are favorite topics in the security section of the exam. This is a section where you should pay close attention.

The first thing a user needs to decide is the method that will be used to back up data. If there is not a lot of vital data, simply copying individual files from the hard drive to another form of media might be all that is required. On the most rudimentary level, smaller files can be copied to floppy disks and stored. This is undoubtedly the least desirable. You can't restore an entire system from a scattered collection of individual files. To do a full recovery you need at least one copy of the complete system image.

BACKUP HARDWARE

Before you even begin to make those backups, you need something onto which you can copy all your precious data. As I mentioned, critical files can be copied onto floppy disks and stored, as long as those files are all under 1.44MB. But there are several reasons why very few people consider this to be a viable alternative.

For one thing, floppy disks are notoriously vulnerable to damage. Exposure to a strong magnetic field, excessive heat, or physical abuse can make the disk unreadable. Toss a floppy diskette into your shirt pocket, and there is a chance a piece of lint or other debris can get past the door and onto the surface of the media. This can damage the surface of the media to the point where it is no longer readable.

As I've already mentioned, file size is severely limited. How many of the important files on your hard drive are under 1.44MB? I don't know what other people's data sets consist of, but most of the images for this book are at least three times that size, and many are much larger than that.

You can squeeze a little more data onto the diskettes by using one of the many file compression utilities on the market. However, if you do use compression, make sure that the computer to which you're moving the file has some sort of software that can decompress the file.

For the most part, the majority of backup solutions are going to involve some form of tape drive (see **Figure 16.5**). Tape drives come in three primary formats.

The media you're most often going to see is *Digital Audiotape* (DAT). These drives cover an amazing range of sizes, from 1.2GB of storage to as much as 80GB. Some companies offer tape auto-loaders that automatically change tapes as the fill that can store over a terabyte of data. They are the fastest of the devices available, and their cost/performance ratio is sufficient to satisfy a fairly high percentage of consumers. They use a helical scan recording head, similar to that of a videocassette recorder. The tape must wrap itself around the head almost completely before read/write operations can begin. This puts a bit more strain on the tape than is really healthy, therefore the tapes should be replaced relatively frequently.

Figure 16.5 The tape drive is still the backup device of choice for most IT professionals.

EXAM NOTE: For the exam it is not necessary to know the technical details surrounding each of the tape technologies. Simply knowing what they are should suffice. However, this is one of those areas that will affect you more in the real world than it will on the exam. Have a good understanding of how the different types of drives differ.

Digital Linear Tape (DLT) uses similar technologies to DAT, but a different type of media. Instead of quarter-inch metal oxide tapes, DLT specifications call for half-inch metal particle tapes. Metal particle tapes are far less prone to shedding their coating and maintain a much higher signal-to-noise ratio. As a result, DLT is capable of a much higher native capacity (up to 160GB) and faster throughput. DLT autoloaders can store several terabytes of data. Also, since the DLT uses a straight path for the tape instead of the helical scan mechanism, tapes tend to last much longer. Needless to say, all this comes at a higher cost. DLTs are significantly more expensive than DATs.

For situations where speed and capacity are less critical issues, an older technology that refuses to die is the *Quarter Inch Cartridge* (QIC). Positioned at the lower end of the spectrum, these drives don't offer as much in capacity or in speed. Current drives are limited to about 13GB, so on a larger system you might find unattended full backups impossible. However, a much lower cost—both in terms of hardware and media—makes them very attractive to many users.

NOTE: A consortium of manufacturers called Quarter Inch Standards, Inc. is mounting a drive to resurrect the QIC as a leading technology. Newly proposed standards will compete with DAT in terms of native format storage and speed. It remains to be seen whether costs will continue to be lower than the other standards.

Recent versions of many of the third-party backup utilities are beginning to recognize CD-RWs as a viable medium. These can be very useful when the data being backed up will fit onto a single CD. (Yes, you could back up as much as you wanted using multiple CDs. Now go draw straws to see who has to hang around after work swapping out the disks, because they're not going to change themselves). DVD recorders are now beginning to flood the market as well. These allow for a little under 4.7GB of data to be copied and could well be viable alternatives for many individuals and small companies. Many manufacturers of software have started including the DVD as an accepted target device for data backups. One company, The Computer Upgrade Corporation even offers a device called the OmniLib DVD-1450A that can hold up to 24 DVD-R drives and back up over 13 terabytes of data.

For small amounts of data (in the 100-750MB range), or for performing manual backups, a very acceptable alternative is the Zip drive. The beauty of these devices is that they are nearly as fast as hard drives. Copying from hard drive to Zip is nearly as fast as copying from one hard drive to another. They work the same way as a floppy disk drive. The physical structure of a Zip disk is a lot sturdier, however, and the data store is somewhat safer from environmental hazards.

BACKUP SOFTWARE

What kind of software are you going to need to do your backups? That depends on your needs and the job at hand. For just a few files, you can get by using Windows Explorer to copy files from one drive to another. Nearly every OS comes with some form of backup utility, ranging from feeble to relatively powerful. Users of earlier versions of Microsoft Windows will find a backup utility included with their system tools in Accessories. The new backup utility in Windows 2000 actually provides for several more advanced functions, including unattended scheduled backups and support for tape carousels. This may be all that some companies (and most individuals) ever need.

However, for regularly scheduled unattended backups, there is no substitute for one of the better third-party solutions. Any time you can take the human factor away from the list of things that can go wrong, you've done yourself a favor. You've heard the saying, "To err is human; to really mess up requires a computer." This saying is usually only true when there is a human at the controls of the computer. Computers don't program themselves and they don't input the data. If your data is truly important to you, back up regularly and use good software.

BACKUP AND RECOVERY STRATEGIES

Effectively recovering from a system failure can be made a whole lot simpler if you've been assuming all along that the failure was going to occur and have planned accordingly. You have routinely and systematically made sure that company data has been copied and stored in a safe place. This is called the *backup strategy*. A decent backup strategy needs to take several things into account. If all is planned correctly, getting the system back up and running after a failure can result in fewer ulcers and/or gray hairs.

First off, figure out what you're going to need as far as hardware and software in order to perform the type of backup you desire. Also decide just what needs to be backed up. Is everything stored on the server, or are there other computers on the network with sensitive data? Next, determine how often the system needs to be backed up. A small network on which data changes infrequently can easily get by with a regularly scheduled *full backup*. Systems on which a large amount of data changes daily will almost certainly require daily backups.

Now that you've decided on how often and how much to back up, it is essential that a strict backup procedure be defined, along with the understanding of just who is responsible for doing backups. Having the best equipment in the world coupled with an efficient schedule accomplishes absolutely nothing if it is not correctly administered. Once you have decided who is responsible for doing the backups, emphasize the importance of this procedure. And make sure that you have a backup backup person. People go on vacation, they get sick, or they quit. It's pretty rough discovering that the only person who had a clue as to how to back up the system no longer works for the company. It's even worse if you find you have nobody who knows how to restore it.

Schedule the backups and make sure that the schedule is strictly followed. This is made much easier if third-party software is implemented to automate the process. Users of Microsoft NT 4.0 will find that

> **BUZZ WORD**
>
> **Backup strategy:** A complete plan of action detailing the hardware and software configuration used throughout an organization as well as the backup method and frequency that will be used.

the backup utility that ships with the NOS has no facility for scheduling an unattended backup. The administrator can write scripts using the AT command line to schedule backups, but this is certainly no match for a nicely designed program with a pretty interface and a technical support staff available when you need backup assistance for your backup software.

Once the backup is made, make sure any and all copies are readily available, yet secure. Some organizations maintain two copies of each set of a week's worth of backups. One is kept on-site for immediate retrieval, while the other is stored off-site, where it will be safe in the event of a physical disaster, such as fire or flood. If this is impractical, you should at the very least see to it that backup media is stored in a fireproof, and hopefully theft-proof, vault. And while this may sound like a no-brainer, label the tapes as you make them. I've visited far too many sites where the backup tapes were tossed into a shoebox and the only identification I could see was the brand of tape they were using.

"I've got my own system," one administrator once told me. "I know exactly which tape is which."

"Yeah?" I replied. "And what if you get run over by a bus on the way to work tomorrow morning? What are your coworkers over there going to do?" He just smiled and shrugged. Job security is a wonderful thing, isn't it?

Another thing I frequently quiz my clients on is whether or not they know how to effectively implement a recovery. It's one thing to sleep soundly, knowing your data is secure on tape or optical disk. It's quite another to come in to work one morning to a dead server and realize you haven't got the slightest idea how to perform a recovery. All you've ever done is back data up. Once in a while, do a practice recovery. Not only does this make sure you know what you're doing when the time comes, it also assures you that the system is working and lets you know what kind of time frame you are looking at to get the network back on-line.

DETERMINING A BACKUP TYPE

Okay, now you have figured out how much data you need to back up, you know how often you are going to back it up, and you have someone who is perfectly delighted to be the one chosen to stay late on Friday afternoon to do the job. Now you need to know just how long the backup is going to take and make sure there is enough time allotted to complete the job. Another consideration, and probably a more important one, is how quickly must the system be up and running in the event of failure. With some networks, the cost of a server being down is a little bit of an inconvenience. With others, it can be measured in thousands of dollars per hour. In the discussion that follows, please be aware that, using conventional backup/recovery methods, you must reinstall the NOS, reconfigure it, and install the backup software before you can apply the backup tapes to the system.

> **Exam Note:** For the exam, it is critical to know the differences between full, differential, and incremental backups. You *will* see it on the exam.

Most operating systems recognize three different types of backup—*full, incremental*, and *differential*. There are some pretty significant differences in how each of these backup types does its job. **Table 16.3** outlines these differences.

DETERMINING A BACKUP ROTATION

As I mentioned before, it's quite possible that, for a smaller organization or a single individual, the most effective backup routine might be regularly scheduled full backups. Many organizations maintain far too much data for this to be an option. Their backup strategies will usually involve a combination of multiple backup types. This works quite effectively as long as you rigorously maintain your backup rotation. The most common method is a simple weekly rotation. You pick one day out of the week in which you perform a full backup of the system and store the tapes away. For each day of the rest of the week, you'll perform either an incremental or a differential backup. Obviously, this is going to require more than one tape. The set of tapes you use for a given week is known as the *media set*.

Consider carefully your requirements before you decide whether to use incremental or differential. If a full backup followed by subsequent incremental backups throughout the week is selected, in the event of failure, every tape you made throughout the week will be needed in order to fully restore the system. First, the full backup would have to be restored. Once that is completed, each and every tape from the set of incremental backups will have to be restored—in the order they were created.

Table 16.3 Common Backup Types

Backup Type	Relative Backup Time	Relative Restore Time	Number of tapes/ disks required	Description
Full	Longest of all methods	Shortest of all methods	One set	Each file in the selected drive and/or directory is copied. The archive bit for the file is cleared, which marks the file as backed up. It doesn't matter when this file was last backed up.
Incremental	Shortest of all methods	Longest of all methods	One full set, plus four smaller sets	Only files that have been created or have changed since either the last full backup or the last incremental backup is copied. The archive bit is cleared.
Differential	Each day this method is used increases the amount of time required for backup.	Not quite as long as incremental, but somewhat longer than full.	One full set, plus four smaller sets	Any file that was created or has changed since the last full backup is copied. The archive bit is NOT cleared. It does not consider incremental backups.

Another method is to make one full backup each week, followed by daily differential backups. This method requires more time for each of the daily backups that follow the weekly full backup, but requires far less time to return the server to operation. You need only restore the full backup and follow that up with the most recent differential backup.

Something else that needs to be considered in a mission-critical environment is the likelihood of tape failure. A backup strategy isn't much good if, after the system goes down, the tape that the data was backed up to is no good either. As a result, several strategies of backup rotations that involve rotating the media itself have evolved.

The simplest of these methods is the Grandfather method. The schedule is broken down into four-week intervals with a separate media set for each week. If you plan on using this method, you have to juggle four sets of media, with each set containing a separate tape for each day of the week. Every month, one new set is purchased and one of the sets is retired, to be stored off-site until no longer needed. Once a year, you replace the entire collection with all new tapes and archive the final volume for that year.

One-Touch Disaster Recovery

Throughout this book, I've tried to avoid discussing anything proprietary to any specific manufacturer, unless it was to point out some glaring exception to normal standards. I'm going to make an exception here. There is one disaster recovery technique that has been recently released and that deserves attention. Just prior to their merger, Compaq Computer Corporation and Hewlett Packard, in cooperation with Veritas, Inc. (formerly Seagate Software), put their collective heads together and developed a method of getting a server back on its feet with an absolute minimum of downtime. They call this method *Intelligent Disaster Recovery Backup Solution* (IDR).

As I pointed out earlier, if you're restoring a downed server using conventional methods, there are several steps you must go through in order to get the machine back up and running. These steps must be performed in a precise order. Once the defective hardware has been replaced, it is necessary to reinstall the network operating system and configure all devices. Once you have a fully functioning machine it is time to install the backup software that was used to create the media set that you will be using to restore the system. Only after you've done all of this can you begin to restore the backup files. IDR puts the operating system, all configuration files, and all data onto a single bootable tape, allowing the system to be restored in a single operation.

IDR doesn't work on just any server. There are certain prerequisites that must be met. One of these involves the type of tape drive installed on the system. As of this writing, there are only a few choices in this respect. Compaq and HP (as of this writing, they're still being marketed under their separate names) each has three or four that will be suitable for the purpose. In some cases, new firmware is required to make the drive visible to the OS as a bootable device. By themselves, neither NT 4.0 nor Advanced Server 2000 support tape drives as bootable devices (although future Service Packs may address this issue). The BIOS of the computer needs to support this option as well. Therefore, the server's firmware may have to be updated as well.

At this point in time, the only backup software that can perform these tricks is Veritas Backup Exec, version 8.0 or later. And out of the package, one-touch backup isn't an option that can be installed. A separate installable option, called Intelligent Disaster Recovery, must be purchased along with the Backup Exec and installed prior to configuring the system. The software itself actually resides on the CD you receive when you purchase Backup Exec. In order to install the IDR option, you will need to contact Veritas. Upon receipt of payment, it will issue you a separate serial number that will allow you to enable the option.

Once the Backup Exec and the IDR option have been installed, the user is prompted to reboot the system. On startup, IDR notifies the user that an IDR-compatible device has been found and offers the option of creating a bootable backup. Needless to say, if you want all that money you've just spent to justify itself, this is the option you'll want to select. Insert a fresh tape into the drive and click YES to continue. Now sit back and wait while a complete backup is copied to the tape. A boot record will also be created, allowing the tape to be a bootable device. This can take anywhere from a few minutes to most of the rest of your life, depending on the amount of information on the drive being backed up.

Should you subsequently suffer a fatal system crash and find yourself rebuilding the server, the computer can be booted to the IDR tape and the entire restoration process is completely automatic. I built and configured one of these systems recently and performed some thoroughly unscientific, informal, but very informative tests. It consisted of an NT 4.0 box with a full complement of server applications, including the Veritas software with the IDR option. In order to simulate a medium-large data set, I simply copied the contents of fifteen CDs to the hard drive. (I told you it wasn't very scientific.) I then made a conventional backup set and a bootable IDR tape. Using conventional backup/recovery methods, this system required over four hours to rebuild from scratch. IDR had the server back up and running in an hour and ten minutes. If your network measures downtime in kilo-dollars per hour, this might be an option to consider.

INTERNET BACKUP STORAGE SOLUTIONS

All of the above strategies work great if you're able to access the backup tapes you've been making all these years. Certain physical disasters, such as fire or flood, are the kind of nightmare that haunts the sleep of any network administrator. It is one thing to have rigorously maintained an effective strategy. The server dies, and within a relatively short period of time, all is well again. It is another thing altogether to actually have that backed up material available when you need it.

The tragic events of 9/11 illustrated perfectly just how possible it is for disaster to occur. Most companies had their data, including backups, stored on-site. Along with the horrible loss of life, there was a tremendous loss of information.

For years, books and training manuals have preached the importance of keeping a recent backup stored off-site. Great idea, if you can make it work. But let's consider some of the reasons it might not be practical. First off, precisely where will this "off-site" backup be stored? Maybe our administrator can bring it home and store it in the closet. That might work well enough, unless of course the administrator has a tiff with management and quits abruptly, taking all that sensitive company data over to the competition.

One very plausible alternative is to have a safe deposit box at the bank. You can either assign an individual to deliver it on a daily basis or perhaps use a local courier service. Either way, you have a much safer storage routine. Until the person with the deposit box key leaves the company and makes one last visit to the bank on his way out the door.

A recently emerging solution to the dilemma of off-site storage is Internet-based storage. There are a number of companies that provide a fault-tolerant and secure site where data can be stored. You contract for a certain amount of storage and use it as you see fit.

Two things to consider before contracting for such a service is just how secure is the facility itself, and how the company bills for its service. Some of these outfits consist of a few servers and a T1 line coming in to the building. Data is stored in a collection of mass storage units hanging off the servers. A company like this is every bit as likely to suffer a loss as you are. Alternatively, there are companies that specialize in arrays of dual redundant server clusters linked to dual redundant mass storage. One such place has its facilities underground in a nuclear-hardened facility, so that you can even retrieve your data after a nuclear war. (Like you're going to care!)

The companies that provide these services vary greatly in how they bill their customers. That is why you should study carefully the fee structure of the companies you are considering. Some of them provide for a fixed "maximum" storage. If you contract for 20GB of storage, then you will be billed for 20GB each and every month, even if you only use a few megabytes. Others bill more like the utility companies. How much storage space you eat up is metered and you are charged only for what you actually use.

Whether or not a service of this nature is suitable for a particular organization depends on its telecommunications facilities. If we were still living in the days when a 33.6K modem was considered state of the art, this kind of service would never get off the ground. If you had to move several gigabytes worth of data over a line that slow, backups would be done annually, not daily.

These days, companies don't get by on modems. About the slowest connection a company is likely to use is ISDN. Companies using BRI service are not likely to attempt this trick, but those who take advantage of emerging Internet technologies such as Digital Subscriber Lines (DSL), or those with T1 or T3 coming into their building, might find the service very appealing. There's something to be said for being able to get to your data even if a nuclear war forces you to relocate to the other side of the planet.

NETWORK ATTACHED STORAGE VERSUS THE STORAGE AREA NETWORK

The random distribution of critical information across the network is one of the areas of data storage on the network that has long haunted the network. Certain critical applications are centrally located, such as the organization's database server. But then each employee creates and stores documents locally. So then each division within the organization has critical information that is most likely stored on one of its local servers. How is the network administrator to manage all of this data and more importantly, how can the administrator assure that it is being properly backed up?

Two competing technologies that offer solutions to both of these problems are *Network Attached Storage* (NAS) and *Storage Area Networks* (SAN). Typical network data storage solutions consist of installing an array of drives into one of the servers and then allotting space to users on an as-needed basis. It's nothing new for network administrators to limit users' disk usage: consider Unix, Linux, Novell, and Microsoft's Windows 2000 Server products. One of the things I pointed out while discussing those servers was just how much unnecessary overhead hard disk I/O operations impose on the system. NAS and SAN both offer solutions that take the load off the server. SAN even reduces congestion on the network.

NAS

With NAS, no changes need to be made to the network. The administrator simply adds another device that is really nothing more than a computer system with the bare essentials for supporting an array of disk drives. This device is one of several devices referred to as a *network appliance*. Its one function is to store data and dole it out to users on an as-needed basis. It consists of a *head unit* that contains the management software and controller circuitry and a *disk array*. In some appliances these two elements are combined into a single device.

The NAS appliance is treated like any other device on the network. On a TCP/IP network it must have its own IP address, and it simply becomes a host on the network. Client machines are mapped to that IP address for their storage requirements. Any machine that is part of the LAN or connected to the LAN over a WAN can access the NAS appliance. NAS has the following advantages:

- The head unit manages the file system. Therefore, it is OS independent. The NAS appliance is available as long as there is a volume on the appliance formatted to a file system appropriate to the OS.
- The NAS appliance imprints each file with critical information, such as file name, file owner, permissions assigned, creation data, and so forth.
- Backups can be performed on a file-by-file basis, rather than in blocks as with conventional tape backups.
- *Snapshots* of a volume can be used to recreate that volume, yet these snapshots take up a fraction of the space of the original volume.

SAN

A SAN takes the disk array and puts it on its own subnet. On that same subnet, the administrator can install a computer with a backup device, or a dedicated backup device that consists of a library of auto-changeable tapes. The SAN storage device is placed on its own dedicated port on a Fiber Channel switch or SCSI hub.

The SAN is similar to NAS in that a dedicated device stores all network information. While SAN has some advantages over NAS, its key disadvantages have kept it from completely killing NAS. The SAN's greatest advantage is the degree to which it reduces traffic on the part of the network on which the user resides. It also shares many of the NAS advantages of centralized storage and management.

The SAN has these disadvantages:

- With the SAN, the file system is under the control of the server.

- File sharing is OS dependent, and on a mixed network and all files might not all be visible to all clients.

- SAN backups must be done in disk blocks and do not offer the advantage of the snapshot.

FAULT TOLERANCE

Now that I've talked about what to do when things go wrong, why don't I point out a few ways of keeping that from happening? If your system never fails, you'll never have to worry about how good your backup strategy is. Admittedly, it's impossible to provide a one hundred percent guarantee of a fail-safe system. Computers are machines and machines fail. However, there are ways to drastically reduce the impact of system failure. Just as having backup data reduces the impact of data loss, having backup hardware can reduce system down time. Throughout the book, I've made mention of the concept of fault tolerance. I'll bring it all together in this section.

IMPLEMENTING FAULT TOLERANCE

The term fault tolerance simply is a phrase that acknowledges that systems are going to fail. A fault-tolerant system is one that does not completely stop functioning in the event of a single component failure. IBM, Hewlett Packard, Compaq, and many other companies provide servers that integrate a relatively high degree of hardware fault tolerance. Good fault tolerance can drastically reduce the amount of time a computer is physically down in the event of component failure.

RAID LEVELS

Conventional network operating systems support several levels of fault tolerance on a software level as well. A well-conceived implementation of *Redundant Array of Inexpensive Disks* (RAID) is an easy and relatively inexpensive way to keep a system up and running at all times. With a RAID implementation, data is stored across several hard disk drives, and not just on a single drive. Most RAID implementations incorporate some mechanism by which data from a failed drive can be recovered. There are several levels of RAID (outlined in **Table 16.4**) but not all are actually fault tolerant. This section will concentrate on those levels that do provide a measure of security.

Table 16.4 Levels of RAID

Level	Technique Used	Description	Tolerance
0	Disk striping without parity	Data is striped across multiple disks in blocks with no parity information stored	None
1	Mirroring or Duplexing	Data is copied directly to a second hard drive	Good
2	Disk Striping with Error Correction Code	Data is spread across multiple disks on a bit level with error correction rather than parity used. Now defunct.	Very High
3	Byte Level Striping with Dedicated Parity Disk	Data is striped across multiple disks in bytes, with a single disk being used to store the parity information.	Good
4	Block Striping with Dedicated Parity Disk	Data is striped across multiple disks in blocks of data, with a single disk being used to store the parity information.	Good
5	Block Striping with Distributed Parity	Data is striped across multiple disks in blocks of data, with parity being equally distributed among all disks.	Good
6	Block Striping with Dual Distributed Data	Data is striped across multiple disks in blocks of data, with two sets of parity blocks being equally distributed among all disks.	Very Good
7	Proprietary. Not used in the open market.		
10	Combines RAID 0 with RAID 1	See Text for a discussion of how RAID 10 differs from RAID 0/1.	Good
50	Combines RAID 1 with RAID 5	Two RAID 5 arrays are mirrored.	Extremely High

Different RAID levels provide different degrees of fault tolerance, ranging from none to extreme.

Exam Note: For the exam, be able to describe RAID levels 0, 1, and 5. In the real world, you'd better have a good grasp of levels 10 and 50 as well.

Of all the levels listed in Table 16.4, only three are actually in common use. RAID 0 provides no fault tolerance. It simply stripes the data across multiple drives, as shown in **Figure 16.6**. It's key reason for existing is that it provides for extremely good drive performance. For a machine designed exclusively for doling out data to large numbers of users, or one on which large files need to be opened quickly, this might be a viable choice. Just make sure you have a suitable backup strategy in place.

RAID 1 does provide a degree of fault tolerance in that the data is duplicated on two different drives. This duplication covers everything from the MBR to the last byte of data on the drive. With RAID 1 implemented, every bit of data written to Disk One is also written to Disk Two. If one disk fails, the other disk is available and the system does not go down.

RAID 1 can be implemented two ways. *Disk mirroring* involves putting two separate drives on the same controller. The other implementation of RAID 1 is *Disk duplexing*. This is identical to disk mirroring in every respect, except that each disk is on its own separate controller. The thought here is that, with mirroring, should the controller be the cause of failure, both drives would go down. By putting each drive on its own controller, failure of a single controller will not bring the system down. **Figure 16.6** and **Figure 16.7** illustrate the difference between mirroring and duplexing.

The other levels of RAID that will be discussed here all employ some level of disk striping. Disk striping is a method of storing

BUZZ WORDS

Disk mirroring: Exactly duplicating the data on a system on two different drives hanging off of a single controller.

Disk duplexing: Exactly duplicating the data on a system on two different drives, each hanging off of a separate controller.

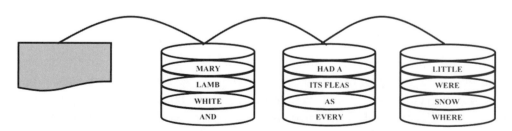

Figure 16.6   While RAID 0 provides no fault tolerance whatsoever, it is still used in cases where improved disk performance is a must.

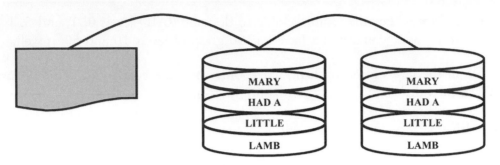

Figure 16.7   Disk mirroring simply duplicates the data on two separate disk drives.

data across multiple hard drives instead of placing it onto a single drive. There are two methods of disk striping—*bit striping* and *block striping*. Bit striping is when the data is distributed bit by bit across the drives. Block striping divides the data across the drives in larger chunks. The size of the block is something that can be adjusted on most hardware controllers.

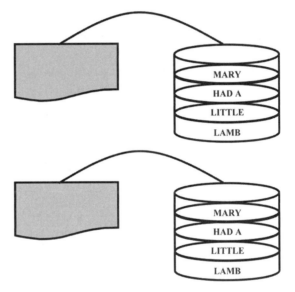

The RAID level most commonly used by network administrators is RAID 5. RAID 5 requires a minimum of three hard disks. The maximum number of drives you can use depends on whether you are using a hardware controller or the software

Figure 16.8   Disk duplexing is the same as mirroring, only each disk is on a separate controller.

RAID included in NT or Novell. Software raid can make use of up to thirty-two drives. Your hardware will dictate its own limitations.

RAID 5 resembles RAID 0, in that it spreads the data across the drives equally. It adds fault tolerance because for each block of data copied to the array, it generates a mathematical image of that data called a *parity block*. The parity information is also distributed evenly across the drives. If a single drive fails, the system continues as if nothing had happened. The parity information is used to rebuild all data in its entirety. As soon as the dead drive has been replaced, the array can be rebuilt. It should be noted, however, that while the faulty drive is still in place you have no fault tolerance. **Figure 16.9** shows you how RAID 5 works.

The RAID levels I've been discussing so far have all been what are called single RAID levels. In order to provide maximum security for your data, it is also possible to configure *nested RAID levels*. These are when you combine two different RAID levels onto a single machine. The most commonly used nested raid level is RAID 0/1.

In this implementation, you create a RAID 0 array of however many disks you require in order to provide for disk performance. Then, in order to implement some level of fault tolerance, you duplex the RAID 0 array on a separate controller. In the event that one disk fails, that entire side of the mirror is broken and the system is dependent on the other side until the defective disk is replaced. See **Figure 16.10**.

RAID 10 is stranger yet. RAID 10 requires a minimum of four hard disk drives. Two of these drives will be mirrored. The other pair will be striped in a RAID 0

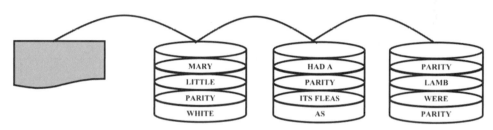

Figure 16.9   A RAID 5 Implementation. As with RAID 0, in actual practice all data blocks would be the same size.

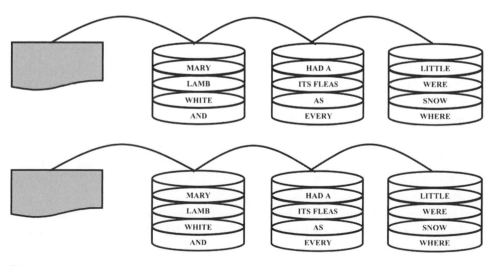

Figure 16.10   A RAID 0/1 implementation gives you the best of RAID 0 and RAID 1.

473

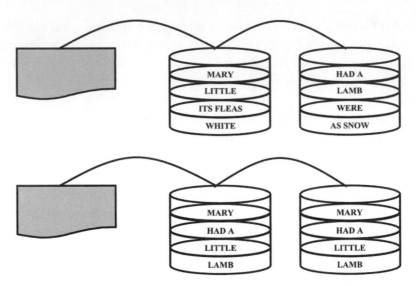

Figure 16.11 RAID 10 provides one striped pair for performance along with one mirrored pair for fault tolerance.

array for performance (see **Figure 16.11**). RAID 10 requires specialized hardware and software support, which adds to the cost of implementation. The advantage is that the machine benefits from a performance standpoint as well as enjoying a certain degree of fault tolerance. The disadvantage to this scheme is that the cost is somewhat high for the limited protection it offers.

RAID 50 is another combination of multiple RAID levels (**Figure 16.12**). Two separate RAID 5 arrays are implemented, using anywhere from three to thirty-two disks. Then, a separate, identical collection of disks duplexes that array. As you might imagine, implementing this configuration can be a more costly approach. However, your data is about as secure as it can get. In order for the data to be completely unavailable, a total of four different drives would have to fail at the same time. Failure of one drive in either array wouldn't generate so much as a flutter in the system. Should two drives in the same array fail simultaneously, the second array will automatically take over. To have a disaster resulting in total system failure, two drives in each array would have to go down at the same time. If this happens, you can only hope you have a good tape backup as well as a new server. You're most likely going to need both.

RAID levels 0, 1, and 5 can be done on either a hardware level or a software level. Windows NT 4.0, Advanced Server 2000, and Novel NetWare all support RAID 0, 1, and 5 in the operating system. Aside from the minimum number of hard

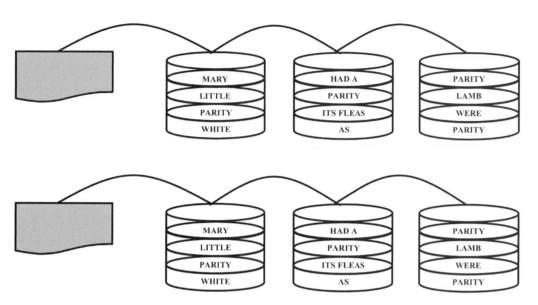

Figure 16.12 A RAID 50 Implementation duplexes a RAID 5 array.

drives required by the specific level, no special hardware is required. You can even do RAID 5 across IDE disks if you've got three of them available. However, the performance of software RAID is, at best, dismal.

Performance can be greatly enhanced if you use controllers that implement RAID in the firmware. There are a good number of these on the market. Adaptec, Mylex, Compaq, and many others all manufacture SCSI controllers that do RAID on a hardware level. These not only increase performance, but they make the initial setup of a RAID array as simple as it can be. And if you look into it, you'll find that, relatively speaking, the cost of hardware RAID doesn't add that much to the overall system cost when pricing out a new server. In other words, just do it!

For most of the nested RAID levels, you will not only need specialized hardware, you may need specialize software. Some controllers by Adaptec, Mylex, and others support RAID 10 in the hardware.

HOT SWAPPING COMPONENTS

Most midrange and high-end servers provide a certain degree of fault tolerance beyond RAID. Many support certain *hot-swappable* devices. A hot-swappable device is one that can be changed out without having to shut the computer system completely down.

The use of hot-swappable drives is one of the most commonly seen methods. If your computer is equipped with hot-swappable drive bays, the administrator can change out a defective hard drive without even shutting down the system. If one of the fault-tolerant RAID levels that I discussed in the previous section is being used,

a hard drive can completely fail, be replaced, and then go through the process of having information copied back to it, and the users logged onto the network won't even have to know that anything was going on.

Another technique that is frequently used in conjunction with hot swapping is the use of a *hot spare*. A hot spare is a drive that has been installed into the system, but not configured as part of the array. If one of the drives in the array happens to fail, the hot spare is called into service. It can automatically take over for the dead drive and rebuild the array. The advantage of this is that fault-tolerance levels are not compromised while the server is waiting to be repaired.

A component of the server that fails nearly as frequently as the hard drive is the power supply. *Dual-redundant hot-swappable power supplies* consist of a matched pair of power supplies that can be changed out on the fly without shutting the system down. An auto-switching circuit can detect a failure in a matter of milliseconds and the backup power gets a promotion. It becomes the primary power supply. The technician can pull the dead power supply and put a new one in its place, which then becomes the backup.

Hot-swappable power supplies and hard drives can be quite expensive, compared to their more conventional counterparts. Therefore, this solution isn't for everyone. On the other hand, if your company measures downtime in terms of how many thousands of dollars per hour it costs the company for a server to be out of commission, the few hundred extra dollars spent to avert downtime are minimal.

Two newer technologies that are helping increase the resiliency of our servers are hot-swappable PCI slots and hot-swappable memory. A hot-swappable PCI slot allows you to change out or add a PCI-based expansion card on the fly. Hot-swappable memory allows you to add or replace RAM on the fly.

There are three different levels of hot-swappable PCI. *Hot swap* allows you to remove a defective component and replace it with an identical, but working, replacement. This level does not require that device drives be added or replaced. It is the simplest form of hot-swappable PCI.

The next step up is the *hot upgrade*. Here, you are removing one device and replacing it with either a different model, or perhaps a different brand of a similar device. An example of this would to replace one brand of NIC with another. This level of hot-swap requires that you be able to change device drivers without requiring a system reboot.

A computer that supports the third kind of hot swap, the *hot add*, allows you to install a device that didn't previously exist in any form. To do this, the system and the device need to be able to install a new device driver from scratch without the necessity for a system reboot.

One thing that all of these levels have in common is that there must be some method of shutting off power to the slot in which the new device is to be installed, or the old device removed. Otherwise you would run a serious risk of shorting out your motherboard, the device, or both. To accomplish this task, there are two different methods available. Motherboards that support hot-swappable PCI usually ship with a utility that allows the technician to turn off a specific slot from a graphical display running on the OS. The fallback method is a switch adjacent to the slot that allows you to manually remove power.

One thing that should be kept in mind is that not all of the PCI slots on the board can be hot-swapped. Only one or two of the slots on the board are equipped with that capability. Should you attempt to play this trick on a conventional PCI slot, chances are extremely good that you will suddenly be in the market for a new motherboard, and your high-priced fault-tolerant system will be collecting dust until the replacement arrives. And so far they don't make hot-swappable motherboards.

Hot-swappable memory is the latest and greatest fault tolerance technology to hit the streets. Servers that support this feature allow the administrator to add or replace memory on the fly. As with hot-swappable PCI, for this to work the motherboard needs to support hot-swapping RAM sticks. This requires removing power from the slot. However, this technology also requires an OS that supports it. As of this writing the only currently available NOS that does so is Microsoft's .NET.

One technology that has been hovering in the background for the past few years is finally starting to get the attention it deserves. This is the technique of *clustering servers*. A server cluster consists of two or more machines that are seen by the network as a single entity. For example, you might have a huge database spread across a cluster of servers. The users on the network simply see a mapped drive called "DATABASE". If they make a request for data, that request might be fulfilled by any one of those machines. Clustering can be done for more reasons than fault tolerance. That big database I was just discussing might be spread across the machines in order to provide more efficient load balancing.

The server cluster that I'm interested in at this point in time is the fault-tolerant cluster. To play the game, you're going to need an OS that supports the technology.

Some of the server applications that currently support clustering include Unix, Novell, Windows NT 4.0 Enterprise Edition, Windows 2000 Advanced Server, and Windows 2000 DataCenter.

When clustering is properly deployed, two or more separate computers will work as if they were one. When a file is saved to SERVER, instead of just a single machine storing the file, they both will. Either computer can fail completely, and the network won't know the difference.

BACKUP DATA SITES

The ultimate in fault tolerance is to have a server or collection of servers physically located at another site where your organization's data is stored. Then in the event of a total disaster, the company has some chance of getting back on its feet in a minimal amount of time. The past few years have shown us the importance of such forethought.

Not all organizations have the same needs in terms of getting back up to speed. Some companies, such as financial institutions, intelligence organizations, and so forth are brought to their knees when the IT structure is crippled. Others can limp along for a couple of days until the cavalry arrives. Some small companies can wait even a week before they recover their data. Therefore the industry has developed the concept of hot, cold, and warm sites, in order to chart the need for recovery to the degree of fault tolerance the industry. The rest of this section covers these concepts in greater detail.

HOT SITES

Hot sites are used when speed of recovery is a bigger factor than cost. They are set up in such a way that in the event of disaster, a duplicate server array is ready, and the most recent data can be restored with just a few minutes notice. Hot sites maintain duplicate servers at a remote site, and the servers at your local site are constantly replicating data to those servers as it is modified. If a meteor strikes your building, you're pretty much out of luck. But your successor can use the hot site to get the organization back up and running in very short order.

The factors here are cost and bandwidth. There is the cost of maintaining the remote facility, the cost of the additional servers, and the cost of the dedicated secure line between the main location and the remote location. A third-party company that specializes in this service often provides the facility. Such companies often maintain banks of servers in hardened facilities that are protected from environmental disasters or catastrophic events. Bandwidth can become an issue if there is a substantial amount of data being replicated. You don't want your backup contingency imposing too much of a burden on network performance.

WARM SITES

The warm site is a step down from the hot site. All the servers are duplicated; however, data is not being replicated on an ongoing basis. Instead, periodic backups are made and transported to the remote location. Ideally, these backups would be daily full backups. For a smaller organization with less data to manage, intervals might be as much as a full week.

This eliminates the cost of a dedicated secure connection between the facilities. It also eliminates the performance overhead of constant data replication. The downside is the organization's data isn't already stored on a functioning server in the event of catastrophic failure. It will need to be loaded. In addition, any data added since the last backup was performed is lost forever.

COLD SITES

Cold sites are the cheapest to maintain but take the longest to get back up and running in the event of failure. Cold sites are locations that have equipment available for your company to use in the event that it ever needs their services. But there are no servers already configured with your software applications, NOS, and so forth. You periodically send them backups of your data and they store those backups in a secure location.

Should you ever require a system restoration, the company providing the offsite redundancy has several steps to perform before you are up and running again. First they have to configure a server to your specifications. Once the server is configured, all applications, such as Oracle, SQL server, email servers, and such, must be manually installed. Then your data is copied to the correct folders, and you have a machine that resembles your old server.

Cold sites operate in one of two fashions. The first of these is the most expensive, but takes the least time to initiate recovery. This is where the service provider keeps spare backup servers available for use by their clients. If your company experiences failure, the service provider pulls down a server, configures it, and loads your data. The thing to remember here is that it is highly unlikely that the provider will keep a spare server for each and every client. This is something to consider in view of the possibility of a catastrophic disaster such as the tsunami that hit Indonesia in 2005.

The second method is much slower. The service provider keeps no spare servers onsite, and it only acts as a storage facility for your data and a controlled environment for the servers you will buy when you need them. If you experience a failure, you will have to call the vendor of your choice and order a new server. When it arrives, your provider will get to work.

Chapter Summary

A key role of the network administrator is to make sure that the information stored on the network is always there when someone needs it. Loss of data is always a major inconvenience. In many cases, it may be a disaster.

Sometimes inadvertently deleted files can be simple to restore. Other times, the services of a third-party utility or even those of a professional data recovery service might be required. When the system goes down in its entirety, you can only hope that you've kept up with your backup routine to the letter of the law.

System or component failure is a primary cause of data loss. If you can limit the impact of either of these two events, you have taken a major step in the right direction. Most servers you work with these days will have, at a minimum, a RAID 5 implementation. If hot-swappable hard drives are also used, a hard drive in the server can fail, and the users won't even be aware of the failure while service is being performed on the server.

Many times the delineation between a so-so systems administrator and a first-class administrator is the ability to perform in the event of a major disaster. It is critical that any network engineer have a good understanding of backup/recovery methods and fault tolerance.

Brain Drain

1. Discuss in detail the difference between backup/recovery and fault tolerance.
2. On a sheet of paper, diagram the CHS geometry of a typical hard drive.
3. Think about the different ways a virus can corrupt the MBR of a hard drive and list them on a sheet of paper.
4. Describe in detail a complete backup/recovery strategy, beginning with the selection of hardware all the way through a system recovery.
5. Describe as many fault tolerance methods as you can think of.

THE 64K$ QUESTIONS

1. The BIOS call responsible for hard disk I/O operations is _____.
   a. Int13h
   b. Int19h
   c. LBA
   d. CHS

2. The original CHS geometry defined _____ cylinders, _____ heads, and _____ sectors per track.
   a. 1024, 16, 64
   b. 1024, 256, 64
   c. 1024, 16, 63
   d. 1024, 256, 63

3. The largest partition supported by FAT16 is _____.
   a. 2GB
   b. 4GB
   c. 64GB
   d. 64 exabytes

4. The road map that directs the read/write heads to the proper clusters that hold a file is the _____.
   a. Sector descriptor
   b. Registry
   c. File allocation table
   d. Master boot record

5. The backup device that uses helical scan read/write heads is _____.
   a. An optical drive
   b. DLT
   c. QIC
   d. DAT

6. An incremental backup makes copies of all files created or altered since _____.
   a. The last full backup
   b. The last incremental backup

    c. The last differential backup

    d. It backs up all files

7. DLT stands for _____.

    a. Dual linear tape

    b. Digital linear tape

    c. Dual level tape

    d. Digital level tape

    e. Dill pickle, lettuce, and tomato

8. The RAID level that provides no fault tolerance at all is _____.

    a. RAID 0

    b. RAID 1

    c. RAID 3

    d. RAID 5

9. The RAID level that equally distributes the data across all drives along with a mathematical model of data (also equally distributed across all drives) during that I/O operation is called _____.

    a. RAID 0

    b. RAID 1

    c. RAID 3

    d. RAID 5

10. Which of the following parts would not be hot-swappable?

    a. A PCI network card

    b. A hard drive

    c. A power supply

    d. A memory chip

    e. All of the above can be made hot-swappable.

11. Once a file has been deleted from a Windows server, that baby is gone for good.

    a. True

    b. False

12. Int13h initially provided hard drive manufacturers with a _____-bit address space.

    a. 12

    b. 16

    c. 20

    d. 24

    e. 32

13. Of the maximum address space provided by Int13h, _____ bits were reserved for addressing cylinders.

    a. 4

    b. 6

    c. 10

    d. 12

14. Because of the limitations of Int13h, the original ATA disks were limited to _____.

    a. 528MB

    b. 2GB

    c. 8GB

    d. 127GB

15. The partition tables on a hard drive are located in _____.

    a. The registry

    b. The master boot record

    c. The file allocation tables

    d. The second sector of the physical disk

16. In order to assure that your systems will be back up and running in the minimum amount of time after the failure of a single hard disk, which of the following is the best option?

    a. RAID 0

    b. RAID 3

    c. RAID 10

    d. RAID 5

17. Which tape format provides the fastest performance?

    a. QIC

    b. DAT

    c. AIC

    d. DLT

18. Which tape format has the most wear and tear on the tapes?

    a. QIC

    b. DAT

    c. AIC

    d. DLT

19. If you want to be sure your site is up and running in the fastest time after a disaster, you should employ the services of a _____.

    a. Hot spare

    b. Remote storage for backup tapes

    c. Hot site

    d. Dedicated backup specialist

20. A _____ backup only copies files that were changed since the last full backup.

    a. Full

    b. Daily

    c. Incremental

    d. Differential

TRICKY TERMINOLOGY

Backup strategy: A complete plan of action detailing the hardware and software configuration used throughout an organization as well as the backup method and frequency that will be used.

Boot sector: The sector or sectors on a hard drive that contains the master boot record (MBR). This holds information that defines the file system used by the OS, the layout of partitions on the drive, and a pointer to the OS.

CHS parameters: A description of a hard disk drive's geometrical layout. It defines the location and number of all cylinders and read/write heads and how many sectors are contained in each track.

Differential backup: A backup that copies all files added or changed since the last full backup.

Disk duplexing: Exactly duplicating the data on a system on two different drives, each hanging off of a separate controller.

Disk mirroring: Exactly duplicating the data on a system on two different drives hanging off of a single controller.

Disk slack: Wasted disk space caused by inefficient storage of data by the file system.

Fault tolerance: The capacity of a system or a network to experience a failure without it causing a significant impact on overall performance.

Full backup: A complete and total backup of all data on a hard disk. This does *not* necessarily include certain system files, including the registry, and will not include the MBR or FAT.

Hot swap: To change out a device without having to completely shut down the system on which it is installed.

Incremental backup: A backup that only copies files that were added or changed since the last incremental backup.

Logical drive: Another name for the volume created on a single hard drive when the disk was partitioned. To the end user, that partition appears as a separate disk drive.

Media set: The collections of tapes or other media that represent a complete image of the system.

Partition table: The portion of the MBR that defines the beginning and ending points of each logical division that was created on a hard drive.

Partition: A logical subdivision of a single hard disk drive. Partitions will be seen by the system as separate drives, or *volumes.*

Volume: A logical drive generated when a hard disk is divided into multiple partitions.

ACRONYM ALERT

CHS: Cylinders, Heads, Sectors per Track. A scheme that defines the geometric layer of a hard disk drive.

DAT: Digital Audiotape. One of several magnetic tape data storage options. It uses metal oxide tape and a helical scan transport mechanism.

DLT: Digital Linear Tape. A magnetic tape data storage option that uses metal film tape and a linear transport mechanism.

ECHS: Extended CHS. See CHS.

FAT: File Allocation Table. The file system originally used by MS-DOS. Also, the table used by file systems to identify the location of each FAU used by a file.

FAU: File Allocation Unit. The collection of sectors that houses the most basic collective unit of data on a hard drive.

IDR: Intelligent Disaster Recovery Backup Solution. A proprietary backup method developed by Compaq and HP that allows a full system, complete with MBR, FAT, and system files, to be restored in a single operation.

LBA: Logical Block Addressing. An extension to Int13h that numbers each FAU on the hard drive with a unique value.

MBR: Master Boot Record. This holds information that defines the file system used by the OS, the layout of partitions on the drive, and a pointer to the OS.

POST: Power On-Self Test. A program contained on the BIOS chip of most computers that brings the system from a cold start-up to operational condition.

QIC: Quarter Inch Cartridge. A magnetic tape storage mechanism that uses technology not much different that a standard audiocassette recorder.

RAID: Redundant Array of Inexpensive (or Independent) Disks. Describes several different techniques for storing data across multiple hard disks.

SMART: Self Monitoring, Analysis, and Reporting Technology. A technology that allows hard drives to predict imminent failure.

VBR: Volume Boot Record. Similar to the MBR, this is the descriptor for a specific volume on a portioned disk.

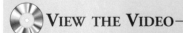 **VIEW THE VIDEO**

A video clip on Data Loss Prevention is available on the accompanying CD.

CHAPTER 17

PLANNING A NETWORK INSTALLATION

It has been said that the Network+ exam is heavy on theory and light on practical application. To a certain extent, that is true. CompTIA says in its policy statement that the exam is primarily targeted at those who have worked in the industry for twelve or more months.

However, you're not going to pass the exam without getting your hands at least a little dirty. The rest of the book will deal with practical application of the theory you have been learning. The best place to start is in planning and building a network. The key word here is planning. All too many organizations suddenly decide it's time to network the computers and just start ordering and installing equipment. If you want to minimize trouble later on down the road, a little planning in the early stages will go a long way. Exam topics to be either introduced or covered in this chapter include:

1.6 Identify the purposes, features and functions of key network components.

3.7 Given a connectivity scenario, determine the impact on network functionality of a particular security implementation (For example: port blocking/ filtering, authentication and encryption).

DEVELOPING YOUR PLAN

Okay, you've decided it's time to network the office. After reading this book, it is obvious that you need to make use of a client/server model, so you plunked down a pretty healthy chunk of change on a fancy new server. Now it's time to hook up all those machines.

Actually, no, it's not. It's time to take a step back, take a deep breath, and start making some decisions that will affect you for the rest of the time that your network is operational. Some of the things you should decide in advance include:

- Who will be the administrator, and who, if anyone, will be assigned additional administrative functions?
- Should there be a standard policy for naming user accounts?
- What kind of computer-naming convention should you use?
- What is your addressing scheme going to look like?
- What policies should be enforced on the network?

Making these decisions in advance provides a couple of safeguards. First of all, some of these things are a necessary part of user account management. They can be incorporated into the server configuration. Second, by adhering to a standard policy, as the network gets bigger, you avoid future conflicts. Here is a closer look at these issues, one at a time.

EXAM NOTE: Be able to select from a list some of the considerations of planning a network installation that should be worked out in advance.

CREATING ADMINISTRATIVE ACCOUNTS

In general, it is far better if only one person is fully responsible for the network. As networks get larger, and administering the network becomes too much for one person to handle, it is obvious that you will need to assign certain administrative chores to other people. Still, there should be only one pipeline through which administrative decisions flow. Therefore, on the day you first configure your new server, you want to create an administrative account.

Most NOSs include as a default a user account called either Administrator, or Supervisor or Superuser. One thing that all of these accounts have in common is that they have absolute power over the network. Another thing they have in common is that everybody who knows anything about networking knows that default user ID for these accounts. If security is an issue, the first thing you want to do is disable that account. Create a new account with a secure user ID and a complex password that has all the administrative privileges assigned. The reason for doing this is to add one more obstruction to the hackers who use dictionary attacks on the network.

Most NOSs also have some variation on the guest account. Even though a guest account carries only the most basic privileges, it can still be used as an entry to the network. Disable it.

If you do decide that you need a little administrative help with your network, instead of creating a second account with full administrative privileges, consider using one of the default groups or objects provided by the NOS. For example, if you want to assign somebody else the task of creating new user accounts in Windows 2000 Advanced Server, you can simply add that user to the Account Operators group. This is done in Active Directory Users and Computers, as seen in **Figure 17.1**.

There are several different built-in groups in most operating systems that have specific administrative functions assigned, but which do not give the members full run of the network. Some of these groups, along with the tasks that can be assigned simply by adding the user to that group or container, include:

- Account Operators – Adding and managing users
- Administrators – Full network privileges
- Backup Operators – Performing backups
- Guests – Limited access
- Printer Operators – Adding and managing printers

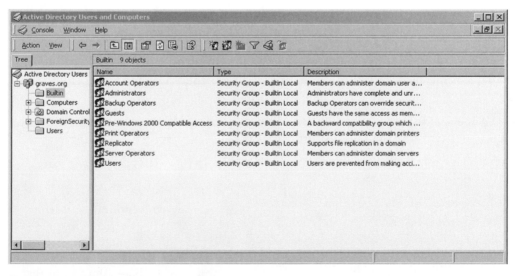

Figure 17.1 Most NOSs have a defined set of groups that endow certain privileges on their members. Adding a member to the appropriate group is more efficient and safer than trying to manage individual user rights.

- Replicators – Creating and managing replicas of objects on the network
- Server Operators – Managing network servers
- Users – All users currently logged onto the network

Creating more administrative accounts than are necessary on the network is really accomplishing more harm than good. Anyone with full administrative privileges has full access to all company information. This includes data on other employees as well as sensitive company data. In addition, those with full administrative privileges can create their own back doors into a network. Just disabling their accounts won't necessarily block them from accessing your network.

EXAM NOTE: Frequent appearances are made in the Network+ exam by questions relating to built-in Windows accounts. I strongly recommend memorizing those accounts.

A NAMING CONVENTION FOR USER ACCOUNTS

This is one area of network management that far too many organizations fail to consider. When a network is small and there are relatively few users, it is easy to simply create users IDs such as mgraves and dearreader. As more and more users are added the chances of a second mgraves or dearreader coming on-line increase exponentially.

You need to have a method of assigning user IDs that identifies the user to the network administrator as well as to the network security files. One of the more common approaches I've seen is to use some combination of the user's last name along with his or her initials. In a larger organization, this quickly breaks down as well. I once worked for a company in which there was a Michelle W. Graves, a Mark W. Graves, and myself. Since I was the last to come on board, my user ID was mwgraves3. I was in IT while the other two were each in different departments. Our user IDs did nothing to identify our function. And I never did find out if we were related.

A good naming convention will provide a unique user ID to each account, provide some hint at that user's function without sending the administrator skittering off to the database, and still be easy for the user to remember. MwgravesIT would have been a better user ID than mwgraves3.

BUZZ WORD

Naming convention: A predefined logical method for naming the users and the computers on a group. A good naming convention will provide some information that identifies the user or device.

CREATING A COMPUTER NAMING CONVENTION

Just like each user must have a unique name on the network, so must each device. The OS likes to assign a NetBIOS name based on the user account, followed by a randomly generated sequence of letters and numbers. Windows 2000 just slaps together a collection of random characters. This is about as useful as an ejection seat in a helicopter. Who is going to remember a computer name like 0ZBE13GHX? A good NetBIOS name will identify the type of device as well as the location. That way a user attempting to browse to that device on the network will be able to recognize its name. If the OS has already assigned a NetBIOS name, it isn't that difficult to change it. Simply find the Network Identification properties and change it. In Win9x applications it is the Identification tab in Network Properties (as in **Figure 17.2**). In Windows 2000 or XP, computer identification is done in the System Properties applet of Control Panel (as in **Figure 17.3**).

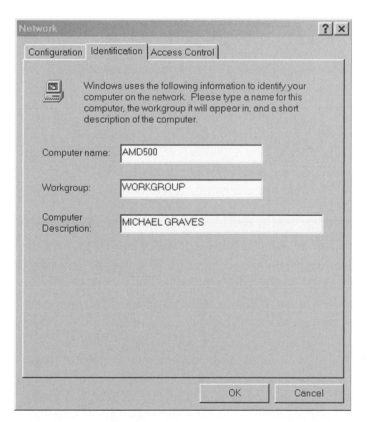

Figure 17.2 Setting the NetBIOS name in WIN9x operating systems.

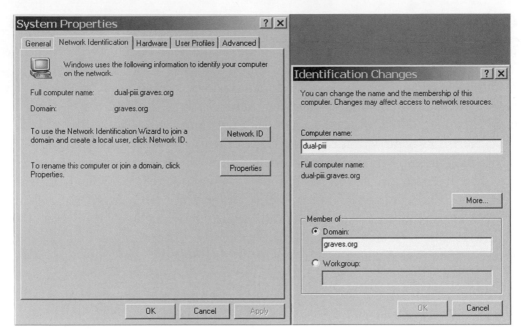

Figure 17.3 Setting the NetBIOS name in Windows 2000 or XP.

For example, in an office of fourteen users, you would not want to assign NetBIOS names such as workstation1 through workstation14. That tells you nothing. Nor would you want to use names such as MGRAVES and GBUSH on the computers. Eventually, Mr. Graves or Ms. Bush is likely to leave the company, and it is highly unlikely that you are going to let anyone take a computer when he or she leaves.

Just changing the NetBIOS name every time a new user takes over a machine isn't an ideal solution either. If anyone had mapped any of the resources on a computer you've renamed, those mappings are gone and will have to be re-created. Admittedly, this isn't a career-threatening problem, but if there are fifty-five users who mapped to Georgina Bush's customer database and you renamed her computer JOHNSMITH after he took over her position, you will have fifty-five irritated users on your hands.

A better routine is to identify the role of the machine along with its location. You have fourteen characters to work with. If your office of sixteen users is in Room 215, you could have names such as 215sales1, 215sales2, 215manager1, 215manager2, and so on and so forth. Now, if a network administrator is trying to trace a broadcast storm to its source, the packet headers will tell him or her exactly where to start.

DEVELOPING AN ADDRESSING SCHEME

Addressing schemes will differ somewhat, depending on whether you're using TCP/IP or IPX/SPX. In smaller networks using NetBEUI, this is a nonissue. In IPX, you can simplify matters dramatically. If you only have one network, do nothing. Matters will, for the most part, resolve themselves. If you have two networks, create unique network numbers for each subnet on the network and make sure your devices are all configured with the correct network number.

> **BUZZ WORD**
>
> **Scope:** A collection of IP addresses maintained by a DHCP server. Some of these addresses are reserved by the server for statically assigned devices, while the remainder are available for dynamic assignment.

TCP/IP is a little more complicated. You must decide whether to go with static IP addresses on each host or whether you should use DHCP. On a DHCP network, there will still be certain devices that require static IPs, and those devices must be taken into consideration.

Any server requires a static IP, whether it is a domain controller or not. Likewise, network printers configured for IP printing need a static IP. Any router or Layer 3 switch on the network will have interfaces configured with IP addresses. These will be static IP addresses.

If you put all of your static IP addresses into a contiguous block, you will be doing yourself a favor. On a DHCP server, IP addresses are configured into the server's *scope*. This scope consists of all the IP addresses available, either to be assigned or that are reserved for statically configured devices. When you configure the scope on your DHCP server (as in **Figure 17.4**) you can configure a single block of reserved addresses and be done with it. All the other addresses in your range can be doled out as needed.

If, for any reason, you do choose to go with static IP addresses across the board, do yourself a favor and make a complete list that shows every single IP address in your range followed by a blank line. As you assign an IP address, on the entry for that address, identify the device to which you assigned that address, along with its NetBIOS name. Include on the list any outside addresses that are relevant, such as routers and any other gateway devices installed. Make this list available to anyone responsible for configuring network settings anywhere on your network and enforce a strict policy that dictates the following:

- Any address that is used will be notated with the device and NetBIOS name of that device.

- IP addresses will not be assigned arbitrarily. I strongly recommend that you assign them in order.
- Any device reconfigured with a new address will have that information adjusted accordingly. The new address will be removed from the list of available addresses, and the old one will be indicated as available.
- IP addresses will not be changed by users.
- NetBIOS names will not be changed by users.

Unless there is some overpowering reason for not doing so, it is usually best if DHCP be properly configured and used. That eliminates the tedious task of keeping track of addresses. Also, should some element of the network change, such as a gateway or DNS server address, the scope options can be configured to reconfigure client devices for you.

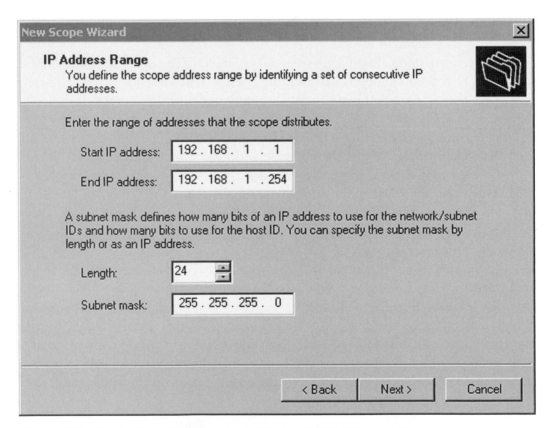

Figure 17.4 Configuring a DHCP scope in Windows 2000 Advanced Server.

CREATING A NETWORK POLICY

By necessity, this section will have to be only the briefest overview of what is possible for enforcing certain policies on a network. In previous sections of this chapter, I have given examples of how to configure certain things on Microsoft operating systems. I did this because nearly 90 percent of client machines in use today use Microsoft.

Network policies are enforced on the server. Each NOS is different on how this is accomplished, and Microsoft does not enjoy quite the numerical advantage in the arena of network servers. Therefore, I will discuss policies and not how they are set.

Network policy is also an area where your client or administration is going to want to play a significant role. After all, it is the responsibility of management to create and enforce rules, and that is what you are doing when you set up a network policy.

A good password policy is one of the first things that should be established. Discuss with the powers that be if a password policy is in order, and if so, how strict should it be? This is important enough that I gave password policies their own section in Chapter Sixteen, Working with Network Security. There are other policies that can further secure your network.

For example, a policy of logon hours can be enforced. Users can be assigned a block of hours during which they are allowed to log onto the network. This prevents them from using the organization's resources for their own purposes during off hours. This can be set up in one of two ways. One way is for users to get kicked off the network when their allocated time is over. The other way is to allow them to continue to work, but if they log off, they won't be able to get back onto the network until the beginning of the next time slot.

You can also specify what machines a person is allowed to log on to, should you so desire. By default, a user can log onto any workstation on the network. However, most NOSs have an option for limiting this. You can identify by either IP address or NetBIOS name specific computers to which a person may log on.

It is also possible to disable certain functions in some operating systems. For example, if you want to enforce the rule that no one is allowed to change IP settings, you can disable the network applet completely. You can enforce a uniform profile, so that every machine on the network always looks the same to every user.

> **BUZZ WORD**
>
> **Network policy:** A set of rules that defines access rights to the network as well as the behavior of those who use the network.

Each NOS has some specific policies that can be enforced and procedures on how to go about it. For further information on how to enforce policies on your particular NOS, refer to the documentation.

NETWORKING AND THE ENVIRONMENT

You finally get to do something fun that isn't bad for the environment. And wouldn't you know it? You have to be careful because, in this case, the environment can be bad for you. Computer systems and the components from which they are made are extremely sensitive to certain environmental factors, and this must be taken into consideration when you build your network. These factors include:

- Heat
- Humidity
- EMI and RFI
- ESD
- Pollution

On a smaller network with only a server and a few workstations—perhaps a printer or two—it is very likely that no one will consider environment to be an issue. Don't let yourself be fooled. Any one of these factors can raise its head at any time, and sometimes the problems they cause can be very difficult to troubleshoot, even in a small network.

EXAM NOTE: Don't slack off on environmental variables that affect the network. This is another favorite target on the exam.

HEAT

Every component in a computer system depends on electricity to function. And every component dissipates a certain amount of heat while it is running. CPUs and RAMDACs (*random access memory digital analog converter)* on video cards have required heat sinks and fans to help keep them cool for some time. Now it is getting to the point that the chips on the motherboard are coming equipped with heat sinks.

All that heat has to go somewhere. If it simply builds up in the case, the ambient temperature can get so high that the heat has nowhere to dissipate to. When micro-processors malfunction, they can do weird things. Generally, a CPU that overheats is not permanently damaged. It will simply shut down at a certain temperature.

However, having a CPU shut down is the same thing as turning your computer off without shutting down gracefully. That can have negative effects on the operating system. Temporary files aren't written back to the hard drive and data can be corrupted.

Therefore, you need to make sure that your server rooms and the areas around all other computers, routers, and other equipment in your network are well ventilated. If possible, the server should be in an air-conditioned room that can be kept a few degrees cooler than the rest of the office.

The maximum core temperature at which a CPU can operate varies considerably from brand to brand and from model to model. Intel design specs call for the Pentium 4 to operate at no higher than 70°C. AMD lists 90°C for its processors under 1GHz and 95° for processors over 1GHz . This disparity is not as great as it appears. Intel is suggesting maximum temperatures for the CPU case, while AMD is listing core temperatures.

Either way, without proper thermal control, a CPU will exceed these temperatures a few seconds after the machine is first turned on. With a well-designed heat sink/fan and a controlled ambient temperature, a CPU will run day after day, month after month with no ill effects. A good rule of thumb is, if you're uncomfortable in the room, so is your computer. Ideally, the room should be kept between 65° and 70°F.

> **CAUTION:** A lot of lip service is given to the importance of keeping a CPU cool during operation. Another related issue that isn't mentioned often enough is cold weather. Most CPUs are silicon wafers mounted on a ceramic substrate. Both of these substances are very brittle. If you ever need to transport a computer system on a very cold day and the computer cannot be kept warm, do not plug it in and turn it on as soon as you get it inside. Let it warm up to room temperature, even if it takes a few hours. When that CPU is turned on it will go from very cold to quite warm almost instantly. Imagine, if you will, what happens when you put a cold glass straight into boiling water. It shatters! CPUs have been known to do the same thing.

HUMIDITY

Another factor to watch is relative humidity. It seems to go hand in hand with heat. When it's cold, it's usually dry, and when it's hot, it's usually humid. This is, of course, a generality. If you've ever lived in the Southwest, you know what it feels like for the temperature to be 114° in the shade. But as everyone loves to tell you, it's a dry heat, so it doesn't bother you as much. (Yeah, right!)

Humidity can affect computers in two different ways. Many of the contacts inside of your computer are copper, many are tin, and some are gold. Gold isn't much of a concern, because it is a noble element. As such it does not corrode easily. Copper and tin both corrode quite easily. When that happens conductivity is lost, and it is conductivity that moves all our precious data from point A to point B. Corroded contacts in a computer system can cause the system to not work at all if the corrosion is bad enough. Unfortunately, before it gets that bad, it can cause little malfunctions like intermittent and unexplainable errors, random system reboots, and data corruption.

However, you don't want to get carried away with humidity control and make it too dry, either. If that happens, *electrostatic discharge* (ESD) can become a major problem. I'll be talking about that later in the chapter. Generally, if you can keep the air around your systems at 45-75 percent humidity, you'll be okay.

EMI AND RFI

Electromagnetic Interference (EMI) and *Radio Frequency Interference* (RFI) are basically two terms for the same phenomenon. For the rest of this chapter, I'll stick with EMI. Whatever you want to call it, it can cause a wide range of complications.

EMI is the disruption of an electrical signal caused by an electromagnetic field generated by another device. In other words, the other device is acting like a radio transmitter, and its emissions are interfering with your signal.

There are a wide variety of devices that cause EMI. The obvious culprits are radios and televisions. Less obvious sources of EMI surround you everywhere you go. Every computer and every monitor in your office is an EMI transmitter. Most of your more reliable manufacturers take great pains to minimize the amount of EMI that leaks from their devices. Still, the magnetic field is present and should be taken into account.

Don't forget other sources, either. A common method of routing network cables is to run them through the *plenum.* This is the space between your ceiling and the floor above you. Unfortunately, this is also where your fluorescent lights are located. Fluorescent lights depend on a device called a *ballast* to supply their electrical current, and ballasts are nasty generators of EMI.

If the ballast emits sufficient EMI, it could interfere sufficiently with the signal

BUZZ WORDS

Ballast: The power supply that provides current to a fluorescent light fixture.

Plenum: The space between the ceiling above you and next floor up.

on the network cable to keep devices on the other end from making connectivity. And even if connectivity is made, throughput can be seriously reduced. Therefore, it is definitely in your best interest to protect your network cables from the ballasts if they must share the same plenum. The best way to do this is to run your cabling through conduit made just for that purpose. If you can't do that, then make sure that the ballasts and cables keep a safe distance from one another.

A good troubleshooting tip relates directly to ballasts. Some brands throw out more EMI than others. Once in a while, you might have a user that comes into work in the morning and can't log onto the network. If you try to ping the server and get no reply, start asking around. If your maintenance crew recently switched brands of ballast and changed one out the night before, that might be the source of your problem.

Other sources of EMI include air-conditioning compressors, space heaters, hair dryers, and electric tools. Keep your server room a safe distance from the *heating, ventilation, and air-conditioning* (HVAC) equipment. The other side of the building would be nice. If your user who can't get onto the network is using a space heater in his or her cubicle, turn it off and try again. If you are now able to log on, confiscate the space heater and use it in your cubicle. At least you'll have the common sense to keep it a safe distance away from your computer.

ESD

Electrostatic Discharge (ESD), also called static electricity, is another one of those problems that surrounds you anywhere you go. It's that little spark that flies from your fingertips to the brass doorknob after walking across a new carpet. It's also that slightly larger spark that jumps from the clouds to the treetops during a ferocious thunderstorm.

ESD physically damages computer circuitry. What's more, it takes far less static voltage to damage a microchip than the average human can feel. That spark that jumped from you finger to the doorknob was probably in the 50,000V range. While that may sound frighteningly high, it didn't hurt you because there was very little amperage, or current, in the spark.

For the vast majority of humans to feel a spark of static electricity, it must be above 5000V. It only takes 2000V to fry a CPU or memory chip.

For the most part, computer systems are safe from EMI once they're installed. Don't, however, make the mistake of automatically assuming that is always the case. All of the ports on the back of a computer system, including the serial ports, the parallel port, USB or Firewire ports, and so on and so forth, are all direct connections to the motherboard. Someone attempting to hook up a peripheral can very easily make contact with a pin on a serial port and zap something on the system board.

A modem is a direct line to the outside world. Unless protected by a surge suppressor, it's also a direct line to all of the lightening bolts that can strike between hither and yon. You probably already know to make sure your computers are surge protected on the electrical lines, but you should also make sure than any computers with installed modems are equipped with surge protectors that provide RJ11 protection on the phone lines.

Any time you're swapping out components, be constantly aware of the dangers of ESD. Wear an ESD wrist strap whenever you're working on systems. If you find yourself in the position of swapping out some component in a system and do not have access to a wrist strap, keep the computer plugged in while you work and make sure that some part of your body (preferably bare skin) keeps in contact with the computer case. Don't worry. The power supply drops everything on your system down to 12V or less. You won't be in any danger. It does, however, go without saying that you won't want to indulge in this practice whenever it is the power supply itself that you are swapping out. And don't *ever* do any internal repairs on laser printers while they are plugged in.

POLLUTION

You'd almost think that computer systems would be immune to the effects of pollution. After all, they don't breathe the air and they don't drink the water. However, in extreme cases, your information infrastructure needs to be protected as well.

An excessively dusty environment is extremely dangerous to computer systems. Floppy disk drives and CD-ROM drives have motors that can be affected by the dust. And as it collects on the internal components of the system, dust acts like a blanket. Heat dissipation is restricted and your systems run hotter than normal. This can shorten the life of components, and in extreme cases, can cause intermittent system shutdowns.

Dust can also have an impact on optical wireless components. This includes both infrared personal area networks and point-to-point laser connections. If wireless technology is a must and dust is a factor, you definitely want to consider going with radio-based wireless equipment. Your point-to-point laser connections can also be affected by atmospheric pollution as well. In some cases, microwave transmissions are a better solution.

THE BASIC COMPONENTS

Most of today's networks weren't built from scratch in one huge project. They just sort of evolved over time, and as a result, the network administrator who inherits such a network simply has to work with what's there. As time and money permit, the network can be cleaned up and streamlined.

Once in a while, you may find yourself with the opportunity to properly design and implement a network from the ground up. For example, a new office building will need a new infrastructure. School systems occasionally add buildings and companies move from one location to another. Whenever this happens, you have the opportunity to do it right the first time. There are two parts to a good network infrastructure to consider. There is the cabling and there is the hardware. Throughout the book I've discussed what hardware does what and how it works. Here, I'll discuss how to keep herd on all the equipment that will end up in your server room.

NETWORK CABLING

For the most part, you as a network administrator will not be running the actual cabling. Zoning regulations in most, if not all, municipalities have very strict regulations concerning the installation of cabling, and one of these requirements is that certified technicians must install it. And this is one case where they're *not* looking for a Network+ certification. The cabling industry has its own certifications and standards.

It will, however, be the network engineers who draft the specifications. Therefore, you'll need a topological layout of the network drawn up in advance, complete with reasonable estimates of measurements for each *drop.* In cabling terminology, a drop is a run from some centralized location (usually the location of the hub or switch) to the specific device. I'll call the centralized location the server closet. Each device on the network will require a drop. Ideally, at the client end, that drop will be wired into a wall panel, like an electrical outlet, only made for your network cable.

Your contractor will be bringing several drops together and running the wire in bundles, usually through conduit. Where the wire comes into the server closet, the contractor will simply let it hang. Here is where you need to be very specific in your instructions. Most of the contractors I've

> **BUZZ WORD** ——————
>
> **Drop:** The run of cable that links a networked device to the central location, usually a hub or switch.

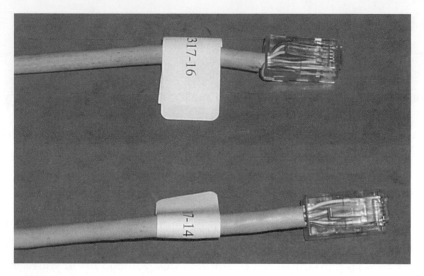

Figure 17.5 A good labeling scheme tells the network administrator exactly where a specific cable is coming from. This simplified scheme tells me that the cables come from Room 317 and are from jacks 16 and 14.

worked with in the past are very good about labeling the wires coming into the closet. However, unless you tell them otherwise, they'll use whatever method they're accustomed to for a labeling practice. That's not a bad thing as long as you understand the logic behind their method, but sometimes it's better to come up with a plan of your own.

The label on the end of the network cable needs to somehow identify the device that's hanging off the other end. A good method would involve some code that identifies the room in which a device is located, along with the station number. Take a floor plan of the office and identify each room with a letter or combination of letters, then number each jack. **Figure 17.5** illustrates what I mean.

Now, if you really want to avoid a lot of headaches in the future, you are not going to simply crimp an RJ-45 jack onto the end of each cable. You are going to use patch panels to terminate the cables and then run patch cables between the panel and your switch or hub as in **Figure 17.6**. Needless to say, you want your labels transferred from the network cable to the patch panel.

MANAGING THE HARDWARE

You've put together your basic plan and scouted a good location for your server room. The contractors are busy running your cabling, so now it's time to start

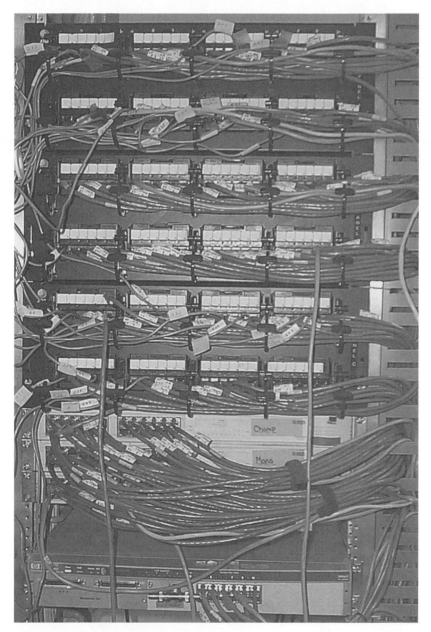

Figure 17.6 While the network rack shown in this illustration may not be the neatest you'll ever see, it does illustrate how much more efficiently one can manage the complex wiring of a network when using patch panels.

shopping for your necessities. Obviously, you're going to need a server. But there are a few other little things to consider.

First of all, you need to consider the geographic layout of the network. A small collection of devices located on a single floor has a dramatically different set of requirements than one spread out across three cities, each with offices spanning multiple floors. The latter will require, at a minimum, a certain degree of subnetting, and most likely need to be internetworked as well.

If you need to interconnect subnets or remote networks, you'll need enough router interfaces to do the job. Routers come in many different flavors, ranging from simple two-port WAN connections to the extreme. Cisco's Model 10008 router, when equipped with its Channelized OC-12 cards, can manage up to 2016 T1 connections.

Any network will benefit from the use of switches to segment the network. These days, the overall cost of a switch isn't substantially greater that that of a good quality hub. While a Layer 3 switch is a bit more costly, it can be used to enhance security.

The life of the network administrator is made much easier any time all of this equipment, along with the associated wiring, is in a single centralized location. Both troubleshooting and maintenance of the network becomes far less complicated. Many larger networks maintain *server farms*. Data and services are spread across several servers that are all located in a single room, along with routers, hubs, switches, and other networking equipment.

In networks of this nature, you will find that most administrators take advantage of racks on which their equipment is mounted. Most computer racks made today are modeled on the *Electronic Industry Association's* (EIA) RS310C-III specifications. RS310C-III strictly defines certain design factors to assure that all rack-mount equipment fits in all racks. **Figure 17.7** illustrates the key specifications.

The key point to note in Figure 17.7 is that the standard rack-mount *unit* (U) is 1.75". Devices designed for rack mounting carry a specification telling how many units they occupy. For example a 4U chassis for a rack-mount server would be 7" high.

Virtually anything you need for a network can be purchased in a rack-mount configuration. Servers are as small as 1U. Switches, hubs, routers, and patch panels all are available in rack mount. Racks make

---

Buzz Words

Server farm: A centralized location that houses all of the servers for a larger and more complex network.

Rack: A piece of furniture or fixture for mounting equipment built to standardized sizes.

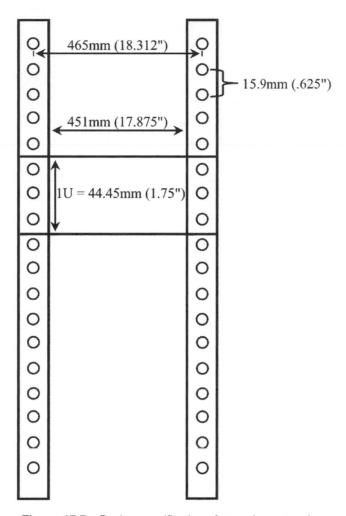

Figure 17.7 Design specifications for equipment racks.

for a very simple method of neatly organizing equipment and keeping the cabling from getting out of control.

FINALIZING THE NETWORK

Once your network is up and running, there are a few final points. Create a few user accounts and groups and run the network through its paces. Browse the network and make sure you have connectivity throughout. Try a few print jobs to networked printers. Send some emails to yourself at home. You want to work out as many bugs as possible before the users starting filing in on that first day. You might not get all the bugs, but the fewer glitches there are on opening day, the better you look.

CHAPTER SUMMARY

Designing a network from the ground up can be a very daunting chore if you let it. On the other hand, armed with enough knowledge and the right crew, it can be a very fulfilling experience. I've had the opportunity to work on several projects of this nature, and—speaking only for myself, of course—each one of those projects ranks as a high point in my career.

Presented with a project of this magnitude, you need to take a systematic approach to designing and building the network. Don't just start slapping equipment into place anywhere it fits. Start with the logical aspects of the network.

Decide on naming conventions, addressing schemes, and network policies before you even order the equipment. Have a professional cabling contractor run the drops for each station and maintain a logical labeling standard so that later on down the road you know what cable in the server room goes to what station on the network. And if the budget permits, use racks and rack-mounted equipment wherever possible.

BRAIN DRAIN

1. Working with a partner, design your own network from the ground up. Make a list of twenty users in at least four groups and outline your naming conventions, addressing scheme, and network policies.

2. List as many different options as you can for creating a secure password policy.

3. Define a good computer naming convention and describe as many reasons as you can why this is important.

4. Describe the environmental concerns facing a network administrator.

5. Describe your idea of the ideal server room and your reasons why.

THE 64K$ QUESTIONS

1. Which of the following is not an administrative account for any of the major brands of NOS?

    a. Superuser

    b. Administrator

    c. Manager

    d. Supervisor

2. Which of the following is not something that can be enforced by the NOS in a network policy?

    a. Password length

    b. Naming convention

    c. Logon hours

    d. The machine to which a person may log on

3. The spark that comes off of your finger after walking over a new carpet is a form of _____.

    a. ESD

    b. RFI

    c. EMI

    d. SED

4. The ballasts in your fluorescent lights are capable of emitting large amounts of _____.

    a. ESD

    b. RFI

    c. RPG

    d. SED

5. A standard rack-mount unit is _____ inches.

    a. 1.5

    b. 1.75

    c. 2.0

    d. 2.25

6. Which of the following items should be protected by a surge suppressor?

    a. The computer

    b. A hub

    c. A modem

    d. All of the above

7. As little as _____ volts of ESD can damage an IC.

    a. 500

    b. 1000

    c. 2000

    d. 50,000

8. It takes as much as _____ volts of ESD to make a human feel the spark.

   a. 500

   b. 1000

   c. 2000

   d. 5000

9. A network administrator can assign specific machines that a particular user can log on to.

   a. True

   b. False

10. The stretch of cable running from a workstation on the network to the server closet is called the _____.

    a. Segment

    b. Link

    c. Drop

    d. Span

11. Why is a computer naming convention so critical when planning a new network?

    a. Because computer names are limited to 8 characters.

    b. Computer names can only contain letters, so your options are limited.

    c. Who wants to try and figure out whether CS210334 has the files she needs instead of RDP12334?

    d. Who said it was important?

12. Which default account on a network should be immediately be disabled?

    a. Guest

    b. Administrator

    c. Host

    d. System Services

13. Why is a NetBIOS name so important to each device on a network?

    a. It is how devices find each other over the network.

    b. It used to be important because that was how NetBEUI located devices. No so anymore.

    c. A computer won't boot without a NetBIOS name configured.

    d. Who wants to remember that the computer that holds the needed file is 00011000 00001111 11010100 11110000?

14. Why would you choose to go with switches over hubs when installing a network?

    a. Switches offer each individual device more available bandwidth.

    b. Switches are cable of filtering packets based on the intended MAC address.

    c. Hubs tend to clutter up networks by sending all packets to everyone, rather than figuring out where they're supposed to go and sending them on a direct path.

    d. All of the above

15. The one aspect of network configuration that **should** be left for the users to reconfigure is the NetBIOS name.

    a. True

    b. False

16. Account operators are able to do the following with the server. (Choose all that apply.)

    a. Shut the server down

    b. Run daily backups

    c. Format hard disks

    d. All of the above

    e. None of the above

17. What addressing scheme should you use from the get-go, barring any mitigating circumstances?

    a. Static addressing

    b. BootP

    c. DHCP

    d. They're all about equal.

18. In a standard server room, which of the following environmental conditions is most likely to have an effect on a regular basis unless you take advance precautions?

    a. Humidity

    b. Static electricity

    c. EMI

    d. Heat

19. Why is it so hard to protect against ESD?

    a. Because you can't see radio waves. You simply have to assume they're there.

    b. Nobody can control climate changes.

    c. The current coming into the building isn't under your control.

    d. A spark you can't feel can seriously damage an IC.

20. When running cable drops, what is a key thing to make sure gets done and gets done accurately?

    a. Running the right kind of cable.

    b. Labeling the cables at the patch panel to match up to the correct wall jack.

    c. Assuring that the patch panels match the brand of server you're using.

    d. Keeping the switches isolated from the servers as much as possible.

TRICKY TERMINOLOGY

Ballast: The power supply that provides current to a fluorescent light fixture.

Drop: The run of cable that links a networked device to the central location, usually a hub or switch.

Naming convention: A predefined logical method for naming the users and the computers on a group. A good naming convention will provide some information that identifies the user or device.

Network policy: A set of rules that defines access rights to the network as well as the behavior of those who use the network.

Plenum: The space between the ceiling above you and next floor up.

Rack: A piece of furniture or fixture for mounting equipment built to standardized sizes.

Scope: A collection of IP addresses maintained by a DHCP server. Some of these addresses are reserved by the server for statically assigned devices, while the remainder are available for dynamic assignment.

Server farm: A centralized location that houses all of the servers for a larger and more complex network.

ACRONYM ALERT

EIA: Electronic Industry Association. One of the many governing bodies in the electronic industry.

EMI: Electromagnetic Interference. A magnetic field that can be generated by an electrical device that can interfere with an electronic signal.

ESD: Electrostatic Discharge. The technical term for static electricity.

HVAC: Heating, Ventilating, and Air Conditioning

RFI: Radio Frequency Interference. Just another word for EMI.

CHAPTER 18

NETWORK DOCUMENTATION AND SCHEDULED MAINTENANCE

If you've gotten this far through the book, you're beginning to realize that being a network administrator isn't just something you wake up one morning and decide you want to do. There is a lot of preparation and education that goes into the job. Your learning doesn't stop with the basics.

However, there are certain things a person just doesn't want to know, or at least doesn't want to keep sloshing around in the cranial juices all the time. There are also things you will learn, and then forget. For both of these cases a good collection of documentation is in order. There are three types of documentation that you need available for quick access. You need information regarding the equipment installed in your network, along with the NOS and other applications installed on the computers. Second, you need a thorough road map of your network that details the equipment, cabling, and configuration of the devices installed. And finally, a good reference library is a must for any networking professional.

The key phrase in the above paragraph is "available for quick access." When the server goes down, you don't want to spend the first three hours of the crisis trying to figure out where your predecessor left the CDs for the NOS. Nor do you want to have to walk around trying to look professional as you ask other people if they happen to remember what the IP address of the server happened to be before it went down. If you didn't learn anything else from the Scouts, be they Boy or Girl, the one thing that I hope stuck with you is summed up in two words. Be prepared.

The final topic I will discuss in this chapter deals with preventative maintenance. There are a few things you can do to keep trouble away. And I think you'll agree that keeping trouble away is definitely preferable to having to shoot it.

CompTIA exam objectives that will be covered in this chapter include the following:

3.10 Identify the purpose, benefits and characteristics of using antivirus software.

3.12 Identify the purpose and characteristics of disaster recovery.

HARDWARE AND SOFTWARE DOCUMENTATION

I cannot sufficiently emphasize the importance of maintaining a complete collection of vendor documentation for everything installed on your network. That includes both the hardware and the software. You never know when you're going to need it.

It is actually relatively rare these days for an NOS to ship with a big thick manual the way it used to. Even the hardware vendors are moving away from printed documentation. Printing costs and an impending shortage of trees has rendered hard copy a thing of the past. Therefore, much of your documentation resides on a CD that shipped with the product. **Figure 18.1** and **Figure 18.2** illustrate how extensive this documentation can be for a server class product such as Windows 2000 Advanced Server.

Don't stop looking once you think you've found the obvious. Late-breaking information is often contained on the CD in files such as *readme.txt* or *readme.1st*. Network operating systems will also have other critical text files that should be read prior to installing the OS, unless you've performed the installation so many times you've got these files memorized. These include *hardware compatibility lists* (HCL) and lists of *frequently asked questions* (FAQ). The HCL identifies hardware that has been specifically tested and certified to work with a particular OS. The FAQ lists commonly encountered problems and their solutions. There are also useful little pointers such as "If you want to install third-party device drivers during the installation process, these drivers must be available on a 3.5" floppy."

Exam Note: Be able to identify several different sources of software or hardware documentation other than the user's manual.

The manufacturers' web sites can provide a wealth of information, not only on just their products, but also on networking issues in general. Microsoft and Novell both have extensive on-line support sites that allow the IT professional to research

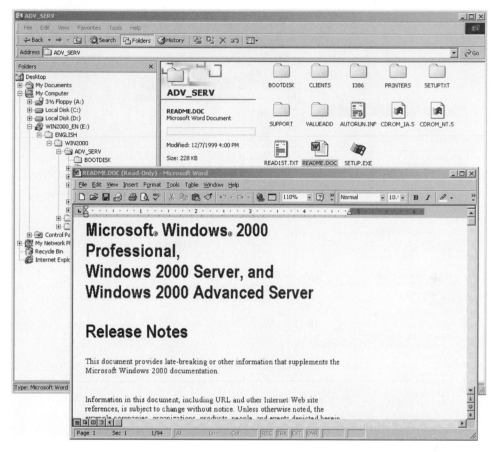

Figure 18.1 README.DOC in the Windows 2000 Installation CD is a ninety-four-page document with information you won't find anywhere else without having to do a very time-consuming search.

practically any issues that might arise with one of their products. Many companies even provide their manuals in PDF files so that you can download them and, if desired, print them out.

Using the manufacturer's Web site as a source of your information can provide you with abundant resources. This, of course, does presuppose that at the time you need the information you have a viable connection to the Internet conveniently available. This may not be the case if you're in the middle of disaster recovery mode and the only device with Internet access is the server you're working on.

A practice that I constantly preach to my clients is to download all of the relevant material now relative to their network and create a CDR for each server on the network. On this CDR you want any PDFs of manuals you might be able to

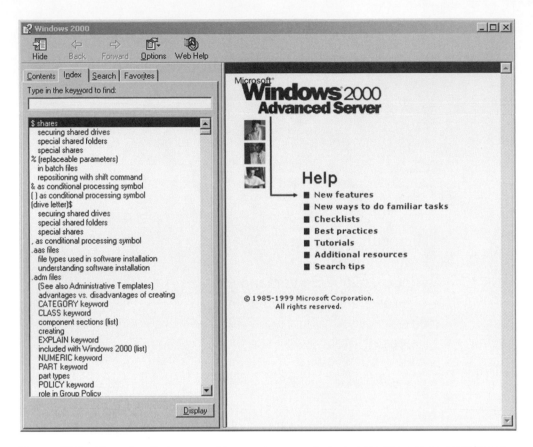

Figure 18.2 Once the file is opened in your browser, today's help files are as complex as any books written, and a whole lot easier to navigate.

find, critical read-me files, all updated device drivers, and a complete configuration report for that particular machine.

You should do this for every server, and make sure that all files are included on each CD, even if they all use the same NOS and have the same PDFs and read-me files. Trying to save a few moments of your precious time while preparing these disks can cost you a couple of hours of time during a critical recovery when you're scrambling around trying to find this information.

DOCUMENTING YOUR NETWORK

As I pointed out in Chapter Seventeen, Planning a Network Installation, most of you won't have the luxury of creating your network entirely from scratch. Most of the time you inherit something that evolved over time. From what I've seen with the majority of clients, it is very rare that anyone bothers to keep track of changes on the network.

A good network administrator has a record of every single device installed on the network. This includes servers and workstations, printers, hubs, switches, routers, WAN interfaces, and even repeaters, if any are used. Any time you find yourself in a position of building a network from scratch, create the documentation as you go.

This documentation should include a diagram of the network. On a very large and complex network, it will take several diagrams. You would start with an overview of the WAN, documenting the offices that are interconnected, and list all WAN interfaces along with IP addresses, the type of service connecting the locations, the carrier with whom you've contracted those services, and contact information for that carrier. **Figure 18.3** represents a simplified example of a WAN overview.

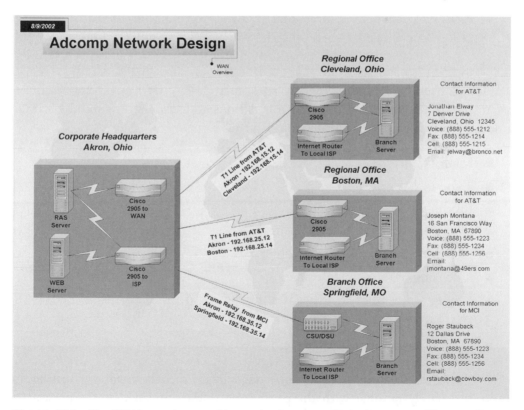

Figure 18.3 The WAN overview provides a simple schematic for how your different offices are connected.

Each of the separate offices would maintain more detailed diagrams of their autonomous networks. Copies from each office should be stored with the IT manager, wherever he or she works. This hardware list should include the following information:

- Manufacturer, model number, and type
- Serial number
- Place and date of purchase
- Contact information of vendor
- Account information (if any) for vendor
- Warranty information
- Technical support numbers and Web site
- List of software installed on each computer (if applicable)
- Configuration information (where needed)
- A list of passwords (stored securely away from publicly available documentation) for all servers and other network devices, such as routers

In addition to the hardware that accumulates on most networks, there is also a befuddling amount of software that accumulates. For both legal and utilitarian reasons, accurate records of software acquisitions and installations should be maintained as well. This information should include:

- Manufacturer
- Type of software
- Product key code or serial number
- Place and date of purchase
- Contact information for vendor
- Licensing agreement information
- Proof of the number of licenses purchased (if site licensing is used)
- Warranty information
- Technical support numbers and Web site

You also want a detailed report on your backup/recovery strategy. Just because you're intimately familiar with the procedures doesn't mean that the person who takes over for you while you're on vacation does. Always assume that there will come a day that someone without an iota of training will find him- or herself in the position of having to get the company's infrastructure back up and running. Include the following:

- Schedule for when backups are created and whose responsibility it is to oversee the process
- Location of device used for backup
- Detailed instructions on performing a backup
- Information on where backup copies are stored and for how long
- Location on the network where public files are stored to ensure data is backed up regularly
- Detailed instructions on how to perform a restore

If your network has Internet access (and these days, I think it's fairly safe to assume that most will), there is a list of information that should be maintained concerning this aspect of your network as well. It is as follows:

- Contact information for Internet Service Provider
- Account information
- Technical support numbers
- Type of connection
- Location of interface
- Login and password details for accessing the ISP
- List of usernames and passwords for all email accounts with the ISP
- IP addresses (if permanent connection is maintained)

Now that you've collected all of this information, collate it into a manageable form and make at least two copies. One of these copies (with sensitive information such as passwords removed) should be readily available to all members of your organization authorized to work on the network. The complete report, complete with passwords, should be stored in a secure site where only authorized personnel can access the information.

> **Exam Note:** It is possible that you might get a scenario in which a network installation is described and you are asked to identify what items should be documented and the best ways to do this. This scenario might represent more than one question on the exam.

MAINTAINING A TECHNICAL LIBRARY

Here is where I make some facetious remark about how this is the only book you'll ever need. The primary reason I'll avoid doing that is that it would be a blatant lie. My personal library consists of over sixty volumes accumulated over the span of several years. These books cover a variety of computer-related subjects. If you're going to call yourself a professional, you need to be well versed in hardware, operating systems, networking, and telecommunications. And then you need to pick an area and specialize.

Your reference library will serve as a support mechanism when you find yourself involved in a project for which you need a little additional help. I recommend books in the following categories. In a few cases, I'll even suggest some specific titles, although you shouldn't make the mistake of assuming I'm an expert on everything that's out there.

1. General Networking:
    a. This book
    b. *Exploring LANs for the Small Business* by Louis Columbo, Prompt Publications
    c. *The Complete Systems Administrator* by Curt Freeland and Dwight McKay, Onward Press
2. TCP/IP
    a. *TCP/IP Administration* by Craig Zacker, Hungry Minds, Inc.
3. Computer Hardware
    a. *PC Hardware Maintenance and Repair* by Michael Graves, Prompt Publications
    b. *The Complete A+ Guide to PC Repair* by Cheryl Schmidt, Delmar/Thomson Learning
4. Books specific to your NOS. Since I can't presume to know what NOS you'll be using, I prefer not to make suggestions in this area. Your local bookstore can be of assistance.

In addition to a collection of books, there is an abundant supply on the Internet of white papers written on specific subjects. These range from the subjects mentioned above to about anything you could imagine. Many are available for free download. Virtually any of the organizations responsible for implementing and maintaining standards that were mentioned in this book have very detailed papers concerning their activities. I rely heavily on these sources for advancing my own knowledge. Some are free; some require that you pay a fee. If you must pay a fee, before you get hostile and start cursing the audacity of corporate greed, consider this. Most of these organizations are not-for-profit. They get by on support from corporations and individuals who make use of their services. These papers are examples of those services.

PREVENTATIVE MAINTENANCE

My uncle always taught me that a pound of prevention was worth an ounce of cure. Unfortunately, like everything else he taught me, he got it backwards. But the concept was right, if the statement was awry.

Spending a few moments every now and again making sure everything is in order and functioning properly can be slightly annoying. Trying to restore a server that has suddenly blue-screened can cost you several hours of stress, loss of revenue, and perhaps your job. This too can be slightly annoying, but for a much longer period of time. So you want to avoid the latter scenario wherever possible. Much of your preventative maintenance can be scheduled to run unattended while you're home watching the playoffs.

NOS MAINTENANCE

Installing a network operating system doesn't end with electronic registration. It is a never-ending process that requires vigilance on your part. All of the major NOS manufacturers are constantly updating their different product lines. These updates range from simple *patches* to full-fledged *service packs*. There are several reasons for doing this.

Exam Note: Be able to distinguish between a patch and a service pack. Be able to describe a procedure for installing either.

First off, as much as the manufacturers would like to dance around the fact, the first release of just about any product is going to have some "undocumented features." (They never have bugs; mind you—simply undocumented features.) As inconsistencies or flaws in the programming are revealed, the companies provide fixes at no charge. If the problem is severe enough, they may make a public announcement. Usually, however, they simply post the update to the Downloads page on their Web site.

As an administrator, you need to visit these pages frequently, looking for any patches relevant to your needs. Some of these patches are specific to certain functions, while others relate to serious security holes in the NOS. My recommendation is this. If you can consciously think of one good reason to apply the patch after reading the manufacturer's reason for posting it, then do not hesitate. Download it, scan it for viruses (yes, even our major manufacturers have at one time or another fallen victim to the virus mongers), and apply it. Some patches require a reboot of the server, while others don't. Review any documentation that comes with the patch. There is usually a read-me file associated with it.

> **BUZZ WORDS**
>
> **Patch:** A fix to an OS or application that targets a specific flaw.
>
> **Service pack:** A major OS maintenance package that applies a large number of updates and fixes.

Service packs are another thing. A service pack is generally a virtual rebuild of an NOS that includes all patches from the last release date to the release data of the service pack. Because the service pack does rebuild the NOS, be aware of a couple of things. You will have to reboot your server for the service pack to take effect. You might want to do that during a quiet time when there are relatively few or no users on the network.

Second, if anything does go wrong during the installation of a service pack, there is the potential that your entire NOS can become corrupted. Therefore, before you begin, make sure you have a full and complete backup of your system in hand.

DEVICE DRIVERS

Device drivers are software files that provide instructions to the OS as to how to communicate with a specific piece of hardware. There isn't a piece of hardware in any machine that doesn't require a device driver. In many cases, these drivers are built right into the OS and are installed along with the OS. More specialized devices will ship with their own drivers. Once in a while drivers are modified and it becomes necessary to replace them.

> **Exam Note:** Be able to describe the purpose and function of a device driver. Also be able to describe times when it may be necessary to replace a driver.

When it comes to updating device drivers, there are two schools of thought. There are those who insist that any time a company updates a driver, the newest version should immediately be applied. There are others, myself among them, who firmly believe that if it ain't broke, you don't fix it.

There are times, however, when a change in drivers is in order. If the new driver supports some new function or feature that you can really use, then there is good reason for updating the driver. An example of this would be with color printers. Some of the newer drivers have color management options that allow you to assign profiles to your printers. This assures that color reproduction will be the same from one printer to another.

There are also times when a new driver addresses a specific issue with the older driver set. In this case, the manufacturer will usually specify precisely what changes were made to the driver and why. If the changes basically constitute a new set of bells and whistles and you don't need any more decorations, then leave it alone.

HARDWARE MAINTENANCE

As a computer gets older, you may notice that its performance begins to degrade. With electronic equipment powered by microchips, this is *not* because it is in need of a lube job. It's because your files are starting to get scrambled all over your hard drive. There are certain utilities that ship with your Microsoft NOSs that should used regularly. Two of these are ScanDisk and Defrag. If your NOS doesn't have their equivalents, then a third-party utility targeted for your NOS may be available.

ScanDisk

ScanDisk is a utility that looks for bad sectors on your disk drives. It can be used on hard disks, floppy diskettes, or most removable magnetic media. When ScanDisk finds what it considers to be a bad sector, it copies that data to a free space on the drive, compares the copy to the original, and once it confirms that the data is identical, deletes the data from the bad sector and marks that sector as *bad* in the file allocation tables.

It can also find certain problems with the files on the hard drive. Some of these problems pose potential hazards to the data on your drive, while others are merely annoyances.

Lost clusters occur when FAT can't find a file that is willing to claim the clusters. They belong somewhere, but FAT no longer

> **BUZZ WORD**
>
> **ScanDisk:** A utility specific to Microsoft operating systems that checks a hard disk for file system errors and surface irregularities, and where possible, fixes these problems.

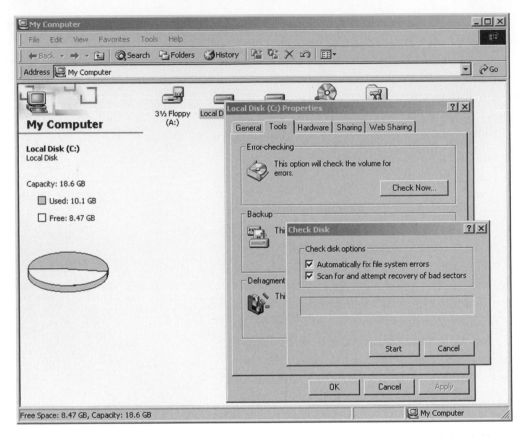

Figure 18.4   Running ScanDisk from time to time can help predict problems with hard drives.

can properly assign them to a file. Another error directly related to lost clusters is called an *invalid file*. This is when FAT is recording the file as a particular size, but the clusters add up to a different size. This renders the file unusable, but it is fixable. Another situation that can lead to the invalid file message is when a pointer that provides the location of a parent directory is lost. Files cannot exist without an associated parent directory, even if it is the root directory. If the pointer is missing, or points to an invalid directory, the file is unreadable. More critical are problems

BUZZ WORDS

Invalid file: A file on a disk drive that does not conform to FAT entries that define that file. These problems can include invalid size reporting, incorrect reporting of the number of clusters used, a missing entry identifying the parent directory, and others.

Lost cluster: A series of sectors on a disk drive that hold data but have no corresponding entries in the FAT identifying to what file these sectors belong.

with the file allocation tables. In some cases, ScanDisk detects the problem and can fix it.

Running ScanDisk periodically on your hard drives accomplishes two things. First of all, it keeps your data safe and prevents you from making backup tapes that consist of corrupted data. Second, it can give you a tip that your hard disk is about to fail when bad sectors start appearing at an accelerated rate.

DEFRAG

As files are opened, edited, closed, and then reopened, edited once again and closed, they start to find themselves being scattered all over the hard drive. The reasons for this are discussed in Chapter Sixteen, Data Recovery and Fault Tolerance. This is called *fragmenting* the file. When files become fragmented, they take more time for the hard drive to locate, read, and subsequently copy to memory. This can account for a substantial loss in performance.

Another negative aspect of a fragmented drive is that it reduces available space for your swap file. Modern OSs make use of a section of hard drive space that it treats as memory. This is known as either the swap file or the paging file. If these files get too small system performance is drastically degraded. The Defrag utility puts files back together onto contiguous sectors on a hard drive.

How much impact can this have on a system? I once had a client who brought a machine to me because she said it was unbearably slow. It took forever to boot, the client claimed. The first time I fired it up, it took seventeen minutes by the clock, from the time I pushed the power button to the time the hourglass finally disappeared from the desktop.

The first thing I did was back up the hard drive to an image server on our network. I had no idea when the customer had last done a backup. Then I ran ScanDisk. It found several problems with the file system, but no bad sectors. I then ran defrag. It reported the drive to be 73 percent fragmented and recommended that I defrag. That sounded like a fairly sound recommendation to me. So I started Defrag. I have no idea how long it took. I started it before lunch that day, and it finished some time during the night.

However, when I restarted the machine after the defrag was complete, it went from power-on to a useable desktop in a minute and fifteen seconds. I considered that to be somewhat of an improvement.

> **BUZZ WORD**
>
> **Defrag:** A utility specific to Microsoft operating systems that will take files that are scattered all over the disk and reassemble them into a contiguous order. Other OSs have similar utilities with different names.

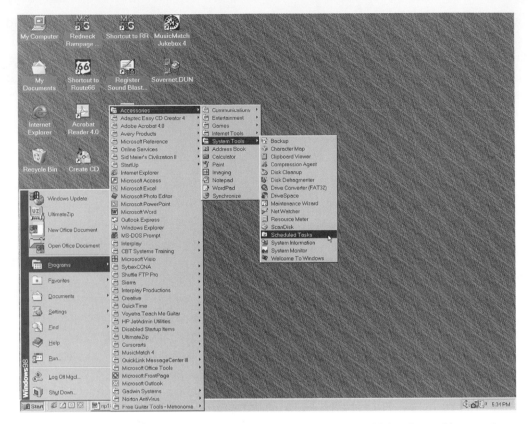

Figure 18.5 Getting to the Scheduled Tasks applet in Windows 98 involves taking a rather circuitous route. But once you get there you won't forget to do any of those tasks again. And keeping your system running smoothly assures that those critical apps, such as Redneck Rampage, run smoothly.

I demonstrated the improvement to the customer. I also showed her how to use the Scheduled Tasks applet.

SCHEDULED TASKS

Both of the above processes can be scheduled to run at a preconfigured time in Windows operating systems. In Win9x operating systems, you get there from the Start menu. The full sequence is Start>Programs>Accessories>System Tools>Scheduled Tasks, as seen in **Figure 18.5**.

It's a bit easier in Windows 2000. The applet was added to the Control Panel. You can get there from either the Start Menu or My Computer.

Once you're there, you can schedule any application on your system to run at any time, on any day you want. By scheduling such tedious functions as ScanDisk, Defrag, and a thorough virus scan to occur while you're asleep, it won't annoy you as much. The key is to make sure your machine is on at the time the event is scheduled to run.

OTHER MAINTENANCE ROUTINES

In addition to the ones I've already discussed, there are a few other routines that you can be performing on a regular basis to hold off disaster. Some procedures that it would serve you well to observe include:

- Regularly check logs in Event Viewer. Alerts here can point to specific problems.

- Check the logs in your UPS software to assure that the UPS is performing properly.

- Check your backup logs every day to make sure the backups are going right.

- Update and verify software licensing logs.

- Keep your antivirus signature files updated and run full scans at scheduled intervals.

- Check your server for old temp files, Zip files, and any other files that serve only to take up space.

- Regularly check and empty the Recycle Bin. The key here is *check first.*

- Make sure your emergency repair diskettes are kept up to date. For them to work properly, they must have an accurate snapshot of the system.

- Periodically reboot the server, whether you think it needs it or not. This clears the memory and restarts services that may have stopped responding.

- Clear the dust out of the systems. While the case is open make sure all cooling fans are functioning properly.

- Perform a practice restore of the server. Many organizations maintain a backup server just for this purpose, which in the event of a real emergency can be put into service.

While this not an all-inclusive list—nor is it intended to be—performing all of these preventative maintenance routines on a regular basis can alert you in advance to impending problems. In some cases they will prevent the problems from occurring with no other action required on your part. In other cases, you will simply be alerted to the problem and it will be up to you to take action. Either way, if you're able to keep the network running smoothly, you're keeping your clients happy. And that's what it's all about.

Chapter Summary

Anyone who's ever been put in charge of anything learns one key lesson early on. The primary responsibility is to keep the wolves away from the door. The wolves that threaten the existence of the network administrator are little things like crashed servers, lost data, and corrupted operating systems. Fortunately, technology has provided you with some key tools for defense against these and other disasters that might befall your system.

From the very start, you want a detailed analysis of your network, describing all cabling, topology, and hardware that is in place. Next, make sure you can get your fingers on any documentation you might need at a moment's notice. Unlike a good dog, manuals won't come when you call. And time spent searching for information is frequently time that a critical device is not working.

A good technical library is a must in any profession. Information Technology is such a diverse profession that developing and maintaining an up-to-date library is more important than it might be in many other professions. I know of very few technologies that evolve as quickly as information technology. Worse yet, while each subfield within the profession requires a unique knowledge base and set of skills, in our profession more than any other, network engineers find themselves forced to function outside of a specific area of specialty.

Keep your preventative maintenance up to date. Many organizations maintain checklists and check off each item of maintenance as it is performed. This is actually not just a good idea; you should make it a requirement. Create a checklist of weekly events, monthly events, and quarterly events to be performed and have the technician or engineer that performs the maintenance initial and date the checklist. If all this is done on a regular basis, most problems can be nipped in the bud before they happen.

Brain Drain

1. List the three forms of documentation a network engineer should maintain, and explain the importance of each.

2. How many different places might you look to find documentation specific to an operating system?

3. List as many different pieces of information as you can that you should record concerning pieces of hardware in your network.

4. What are the various ways in which an NOS must be maintained?

5. What are some hardware maintenance routines that can keep you out of trouble?

THE 64K$ QUESTIONS

1. Which of the following would *not* be something of interest to an engineer installing an NOS for the first time?

   a. HCL

   b. FAQ

   c. Readme.txt

   d. ARP

2. You're installing a network and plan on using DHCP. What devices will you need to record IP addresses for?

   a. Workstations

   b. Hubs

   c. Servers

   d. Routers

3. You've just gotten the message, "At least one Service Failed to Start." Where can you go to find out what service it was that failed?

   a. System Viewer

   b. Event Viewer

   c. Application Log

   d. Security Log

4. What is the easiest way to schedule an event to run automatically without intervention on the user's part?

   a. System Tray

   b. MSCONFIG

   c. Scheduled Tasks

   d. The Registry

5. Which utility puts files back into order and puts them into contiguous sectors?

   a. Defrag

   b. ScanDisk

   c. CheckDisk

   d. MemMaker

6. There is no reason for a network administrator to have a solid foundation in computer hardware.

   a. True

   b. False

7. Which of the following should be included in the documentation for a particular network?

   a. Vendor information

   b. An inventory of the hardware used throughout the network

   c. The dates specific changes were made to the network

   d. All of the above

8. Why does a fragmented hard drive degrade performance?

   a. Files must be pieced together by the OS before they are usable.

   b. The swap file or paging file must be on contiguous space.

   c. A fragmented hard drive is more prone to surface defects.

   d. It doesn't.

9. For antivirus software to do its job properly, the _____ must be up to date.

   a. Software version

   b. Registry entries

   c. INI files

   d. Signature files

10. ScanDisk can detect and fix which of the following? (Choose all that apply.)

    a. Lost clusters

    b. Deleted files

    c. Bad sectors

    d. Configuration errors

11. What is a key source of documentation that is frequently overlooked by users and administrators alike?

    a. The Installation CD for the NOS

    b. The Internet

    c. The manual always has "addendums" printed after the index.

    d. Third-party solutions

12. What are some things a network administrator is responsible for documenting?

    a. The path to the dump files

    b. The IP addresses assigned by DHCP

    c. Statically assigned IP addresses

    d. NetBIOS names assigned to computers

13. What are two devices that require static IP addresses, even in a DHCP network?

    a. The CEO's computer

    b. The administrator's computer

    c. Router ports

    d. A printer server

14. A list of administrative passwords should always be printed out and kept available for access when needed.

    a. True

    b. False

15. Where should copies of operating system CDs be kept located?

    a. At the desk of each user, so that the serial numbers don't get confused

    b. OS CDs aren't shipped by vendors, so this isn't an issue.

    c. At the administrator's desk

    d. In a centralized location

16. If you're looking for a good reference book on your NOS, how could you be assured that the book you were considering was accurate?

    a. **Only** buy books published by the manufacturer.

    b. Most manufacturers offer a seal of approval for third-party books that meet their expectations.

c. You can't.

d. Buy **only** books written by Michael Graves.

17. What is something that you should schedule to occur on a regular basis?

a. A registry backup

b. ScanDisk

c. A memory refresh

d. Defrag

18. What files will never by moved by Defrag?

a. Any device driver

b. Any user file that has been marked hidden/read-only

c. All open files

d. Only open system files

19. What is the difference between a service pack and a patch?

a. Service packs require a complete OS rebuild.

b. Patches are rarely that critical and usually only offer some new feature.

d. A patch is a full system configuration change.

d. Service packs are cumulative collections of patches over a period of time.

20. Service packs require that the server be restarted.

a. True

b. False

TRICKY TERMINOLOGY

Defrag: A utility specific to Microsoft operating systems that will take files that are scattered all over the disk and reassemble them into a contiguous order. Other OSs have similar utilities with different names.

Invalid file: A file on a disk drive that does not conform to FAT entries that define that file. These problems can include invalid size reporting, incorrect reporting of the number of clusters used, a missing entry identifying the parent directory, and others.

Lost cluster: A series of sectors on a disk drive that hold data but have no corresponding entries in the FAT identifying to what file these sectors belong.

Patch: A fix to an OS or application that targets a specific flaw.

ScanDisk: A utility specific to Microsoft operating systems that checks a hard disk for file system errors and surface irregularities, and where possible, fixes these problems.

Service pack: A major OS maintenance package that applies a large number of updates and fixes.

ACRONYM ALERT

FAQ: Frequently Asked Questions. A list of topics that are commonly asked by people having difficulty with a specific device or application.

HCL: Hardware Compatibility List. A list of hardware by different manufacturers that has been tested and verified to work with a specific OS.

CHAPTER 19

TROUBLESHOOTING THE NETWORK

Once a network is up and running, the administrator's job should run pretty smoothly. Except for minor little issues like users forgetting passwords, new users coming on, workstations that suddenly can't see the network, throughput that drops to a crawl . . . you know the routine. Finding out what went wrong when things don't work properly is known as *troubleshooting*. Many professionals will tell you that troubleshooting is an art and not a science. Others say it is a systematic process more akin to science.

I'm going to be a politician in this respect and straddle the fence. I agree with everybody. It's an art *and* it's a science. I can't teach you the art, but I can give you a head start in the science end. In many respects, troubleshooting is just one more aspect of life. If one starts with a systematic approach, the whole process can be a whole lot less drawn out and painful.

CompTIA exam objectives that will be covered in this chapter include:

3.3 Identify the appropriate tool for a given wiring task (For example: wire crimper, media tester/certifier, punch down tool or tone generator).

4.1 Given a troubleshooting scenario, select the appropriate network utility.

4.2 Given output from a network diagnostic utility (For example: those utilities listed in objective 4.1), identify the utility and interpret the output.

> **BUZZ WORD** ─────────────
>
> **Troubleshooting:** The process of identifying and subsequently fixing a problem that exists on a piece of hardware, in an application, or on the network.

4.3 Given a network scenario, interpret visual indicators (For example: link LEDs (Light Emitting Diode) and collision LEDs (Light Emitting Diode)) to determine the nature of a stated problem.

4.4 Given a troubleshooting scenario involving a client accessing remote network services, identify the cause of the problem (For example: file services, print services, authentication failure, protocol configuration, physical connectivity and SOHO (Small Office/Home Office) router).

4.5 Given a troubleshooting scenario between a client and a server environment, identify the cause of a stated problem.

4.6 Given a scenario, determine the impact of modifying, adding or removing network services (For example: DHCP (Dynamic Host Configuration Protocol), DNS (Domain Name Service) and WINS (Windows Internet Name Service)) for network resources and users.

4.7 Given a troubleshooting scenario involving a network with a particular physical topology (For example: bus, star, mesh or ring) and including a network diagram, identify the network area affected and the cause of the stated failure.

4.8 Given a network troubleshooting scenario involving an infrastructure (For example: wired or wireless) problem, identify the cause of a stated problem (For example: bad media, interference, network hardware or environment).

4.9 Given a network problem scenario, select an appropriate course of action based on a logical troubleshooting strategy.

THE NETWORK+ TROUBLESHOOTING METHOD

Scour the books on computer hardware and networking and you'll find as many variations on this theme as there are books. Since most of the people who wrote these books are like me and actually *worked* on computers before they sat down to write a book, they provide some pretty good approaches. They all boil down to basically the same approach, though, once you strip away the veneer. They involve a series of steps that one follows in solving problems. This list usually involves:

- Identifying the problem
- Re-creating the problem
- Isolating the cause of the problem
- Deciding on a solution

- Testing the solution
- Applying the fix
- Following up

> **EXAM NOTE:** It is definitely in your best interest to be able to describe in detail both the CompTIA and the Novell troubleshooting methods. While very similar, they do differ in certain respects, and the exam may cover both.

BUZZ WORDS

Open-ended question: A question formulated in such a way that the answer must provide an opening for further queries.

Closed-ended question: Questions that can be answered by "Yes" or "No" or that otherwise abruptly end the line of query.

IDENTIFYING THE PROBLEM

It almost seems like identifying the problem should be the easiest part of the process. The users call you up and say with great frustration, "I can't get on the network!" And they think that they've given you all the information you'll ever need to get them back up and running. Unfortunately, they haven't even given you a decent head start. There are dozens of things that can happen that all show the same symptoms.

A few leading questions will usually help you target the real problem. Several of the books I read when I was in training all suggested that first question you should ask a client is, "What changed since the last time it worked?" It took a couple of years for me to figure out that this was a useless question. The answer was always, "Nothing."

The problem with that approach is that the leading question was closed-ended. It was easy for users to provide an answer that was simple for them, but provided you with no information. You need to be more specific, and keep your questions open-ended. Ask questions that require the user to provide specific replies.

Perhaps someone has called you up because a computer is giving him or her problems. If the computer still works, but is simply acting up, a good question might be, "What were you doing when this happened?" This is the type of question that the user will most likely be very hesitant to answer by saying "Nothing."

If a specific device, such as a sound card or a modem, is exhibiting peculiarities, you might ask if any new software has been installed, or if another device was installed on the system. Admittedly, it is possible that something may have been added without the user's knowledge. But it is unlikely.

Once in a while, you get lucky and the customer is able to be specific about the problem. That's always a nice head start.

Re-creating the Problem

The next thing you want to do is make the problem happen for you. The best way is to simply stand over users' shoulders while they do whatever it is they were doing. User errors are a very common source of problems and wherever possible should be ruled out at the offset before a lot of unnecessary effort is put into fixing a problem that doesn't really exist.

If there is indeed really a problem, you want to see the malfunction take place, if possible. For any given failure, there will most likely be an error message generated that will point you in a specific direction. Many messages will provide the memory address at which the error occurred, and if you can find out what was running at that address, it might give you some ideas. For example, device drivers frequently load to the same memory address each time. Therefore, if the error repeats itself over and over and the address is always the same, it might be that device driver that is generating the error. It could also mean that the RAM stick is bad as well.

Whether it's hardware failure or network problems, it is essential that the problem be observed on-site. Localized issues may well be the problem. For example, maybe the computer doesn't power up at all. Plug something else into the same outlet and see if it works. Is the customer using a surge suppressor (and you hope he or she is)? Is the suppressor switched off? Is it plugged in? I once got called out on an eighty-mile round trip for a computer that wouldn't power up. I asked what I thought were all the leading questions. When I got out there, the cord for the surge suppressor snaked back and was plugged into itself. So I added one more question to my list of leading questions.

Isolating the Cause of the Problem

This is the part of the process where you put knowledge, training, and experience to work. You need to figure out what's causing the problem. First off, eliminate the obvious, such as user error, disconnected cables, and such. Never underestimate the value of those little LEDs I always refer to as "blinky lights." They're not simply there for cosmetics. They actually *mean* something. If you have link light, you can eliminate connectivity as an issue. If you have no light at all where a light is supposed to be, you either have no power to the devices, or in the case of a link light, you have no connection.

If the problem doesn't jump right out at you, it's time to get to work. Later in the chapter, I will be discussing some very valuable troubleshooting tools that no respectable network administrator should ever be without. Some of these are hardware tools, and some are diagnostics utilities. Depending on the nature of the problem, you will most likely find yourself putting one of these into action.

If you can't isolate the problem on your own at this point, it's still not time to panic. Sometimes, you've successfully re-created the problem on the computer and you and your colleagues are standing around scratching your head and saying, "Never seen anything like *that* before!" Sadly enough, this is one of those industries that, no matter how many things you've seen go wrong and how many things you've fixed, there is always something new to go wrong.

That's when it's time to find somebody who *has* seen the problem before. A good start is the manufacturer's Web site. Most, if not all, manufacturers maintain a FAQ list. Chances are, if you're having a problem, you won't be the first person who's ever had that problem.

If you can't find an answer on your own, call the people who made the device or the software and pick their brains. If it's a known problem, they'll probably be familiar with it. I've been in situations where I didn't even get halfway through my description of the problem before the telephone tech cut me off and began to explain the solution to my problem.

You don't necessarily have to be dealing with major name-brand equipment to benefit from technical support. Even if the computer is a white-box clone made by the mom-and-pop store that went out of business last year, all hope is not lost. Mom and Pop had to have bought the parts somewhere, and that means somebody manufactured them. Try to isolate the problem to a specific component. Then go to the Web site of the company that manufactured that component.

I have already established that error messages are a good way to start the problem-solving process. I've done Web searches simply by typing in the error message into my browser's search field and gotten help.

DECIDING ON A POSSIBLE SOLUTION

Once you've gotten this far in the process, you probably already have a possible solution in mind. This is your *hypothesis.* Think about that solution carefully before you implement it. In some respects, troubleshooting hardware has a few different approaches than that of software or networking issues. For example, if your proposed solution calls for formatting the customer's hard drive, you might want to make sure there are backups of any critical data. If there aren't any, you might want to think about possible ways of getting that data off the disks *before* you destroy it.

Networking issues can be caused by environmental factors as well as hardware failure. Therefore, don't automatically assume that, because the NIC can't connect, it is bad. Look at all the issues that affect connectivity.

TESTING YOUR IDEA

Once you're certain you know the cause of the problem, try out your solution. You think it's a bad NIC, but you're not 100 percent certain. Install a spare. If necessary, borrow one from another computer. Most organizations keep a collection of "known-good" components just for this purpose.

BUZZ WORD

Hypothesis: A fundamental theory as to why a particular situation exists the way it does.

One thing you probably want to avoid doing is simply ordering in new parts randomly. Distributors are justifiably reluctant to take back opened computer components. They have no way of knowing what precautions you may or may not have taken to protect those components from ESD while they were in your possession.

In some cases, testing your hypothesis will lead to fixing the problem. Issues such as incorrect configuration, corrupted drivers, or a protocol that needs to be reinstalled will require no additional work.

FIXING THE PROBLEM

Once you're comfortable that your hypothesis is correct and that it fixes the problem, go ahead and implement your solution. Apply the fix and then test the solution. Let the user run some applications for a while. Do your best to replicate the original problem, but keep watching for new problems while you're doing that. It is not at all uncommon for a new problem to appear once the original problem has been fixed. Whatever you do, don't just fire the machine up and be on your way. That's a good way of having the problem come flying back in your face. Have the user verify that he or she can no longer replicate the original problem and that there are no new problems apparent.

FOLLOWING UP

Just because the computer is now working perfectly doesn't mean your job is done. One of the things they teach you in the military is that no job is complete until the paperwork is done. That holds true of computer repair as well. You need to document exactly what you did. For a larger organization, it would be a good idea to implement one of the many help-desk software solutions that allow you to create a searchable database of problems and their solutions. The larger that database becomes, the more frequently you can simply turn to it for solutions during Step 2 of the troubleshooting process.

You also need to provide customers with proof that you've fixed their problems. And by this, I don't simply mean an invoice that lists what you did and how much it's going to cost them. When they pick up their system, *show* them it's fixed. Let them poke around on it and try to re-create the original problem themselves. Then have them put their initials on a checklist.

Doing this accomplishes two things. First off, you demonstrate to the customer that your solution has worked. It gives them a greater degree of confidence that whatever it is you fixed will continue to work once the door closes behind you on your way out.

Second, in the event that the problem recurs, you will be able to point out the fact that it was working when it left. While this admittedly does provide for a very good method of covering your own bases (in the industry, that is called the CYA solution. Don't ask why, and don't look for it in the glossary), it also might be providing some insight into what might be going on over on the customer's side. Is there an environmental issue causing the problem? I once had a computer system that kept coming back with bad power supplies. I finally got on my horse and rode over to the customer's site. I tested the outlet and found that it required immediate attention. You're not supposed to get 140V out of a standard AC outlet!

OTHER TROUBLESHOOTING APPROACHES

Not all companies recognize the official CompTIA method. Novell is one of those companies that has its own published approach, and there is the famous *Collect, Isolate, and Correct* method. When you come right down to it, there isn't a whole lot of difference between the three methods. However, an introduction to these two additional approaches is in order.

THE NOVELL TROUBLESHOOTING MODEL

Novell's approach differs from CompTIA's only in semantics. Both use the same logical assault on the problem. If there is any difference at all between the two procedures, it is that Novell's approach is targeted specifically at network issues, while CompTIA's troubleshooting method attacks hardware, software, and networking issues. Problems that occur across an entire network take on a completely different degree of complexity than something isolated to a single machine. Novell's list of procedures involves:

- Try the obvious first
- Gather basic information

- Develop a plan of attack
- Execute the plan
- Verify user satisfaction
- Document the problem and its solution

TRY THE OBVIOUS FIRST

This initial approach recognizes the fact that a very large percentage of problems that you see on a day-to-day basis are common problems. And common problems have obvious solutions. Some of the obvious items to check include:

- Eliminate user error. Issues like Caps Lock and Num Lock keys can prevent the user from logging on.
- Check for power.
- Check the cables. Sure the power cable is plugged into the wall. But is it plugged into the computer? And what about the network cable? The user will find it difficult to log on if that is lying loose on the floor.
- Check for indicator lights. Link lights on hubs and NICs indicate that you have electrical connectivity. Lights on devices can have varying meanings.
- Check for logical connectivity. Ping the server. If that fails, ping the router interface (if one exists). Then ping the NIC itself. Pinging the IP address tells you that TCP/IP is working. Pinging 127.0.0.1 tells you the NIC is working.

GATHER BASIC INFORMATION

This process combines into one three of the steps outlined in the Network+ procedures. If none of the obvious worked, you should then try to identify the problem more specifically as it is described by the user. You will then try to make the problem happen for you, and from there, collect data on error messages and personal observations.

DEVELOP A PLAN OF ATTACK

This step directly corresponds to the CompTIA step of formulating a correction. Using the information gathered in the previous step, develop a strategy that will solve the problem and prevent it from happening again.

EXECUTE THE PLAN

This step basically combines the Network+ procedures of Implement the correction and Test the solution. In either case, simply applying a fix does not end the process. Once again, with network failures, problems can be far more complex than those associated with a stand-alone machine. It is far more common on a network than it is on a stand-alone computer for the failure of one service to cause another service to fail.

That is why testing the success of your solution may require a more drawn-out process. For example, if your problem is that you are experiencing a series of security breaches, just applying a patch that supposedly seals the leak is only the beginning. You now need to constantly monitor the situation and use some of the tools I will discuss later in the chapter to see if you can detect any further attempts, and hopefully failures, to penetrate the network.

VERIFY USER SATISFACTION

User satisfaction can be a hard thing to identify on a network. If the problem simply involves a single user who cannot log on, it is a simple matter. You figured out why he or she couldn't log on, identified the problem, and figured out how to fix it. Now your user is happy.

In the case of the security problem discussed earlier, the user you are trying to satisfy is the data itself, and of course, the people who pay your salary in order to keep that data secure. Therefore, user satisfaction becomes an ongoing issue.

DOCUMENT THE PROBLEM AND SOLUTION

This is the same as the Network+ strategy. Once the job is finished, write down what went wrong and how you fixed it. That way, later on, when the same problem occurs, you know exactly what to do.

THE COLLECT, ISOLATE, AND CORRECT MODEL

This is called the CIC method for short. Once again, this method differs from the CompTIA approach only in semantics and organization.

During the *Collect* phase, you will identify the problem, eliminate the obvious problems, and gather as much information as you can that is related to the problem. It is also during this phase that you check with other sources to see if there are already solutions to the problem readily available. Once you've done that, you can gather any tools, software, and/or parts needed to fix the problem.

The *Isolate* phase involves more detailed research using the information collected. This is where you develop your hypothesis as to what is causing the problem and how you might fix it. You develop a plan of action and ask yourself two questions. "What might keep my theory from working?" and "If my theory does *not* work, what detrimental side effects should I be prepared for?"

During the *Correct* phase, you implement your plan of action. Here is an area where the CIC gets a bit more specific than other methods. I made it clear earlier that sometimes there is more than one problem that will evidence the same symptom. Never apply more than one fix at a time. This is bad for two reasons. If the problem does go away, which solution provided the fix? You won't know. Were both solutions required?

Second, if the problem continues to rear its ugly head, or worse yet, you see some new problems, once again, you don't know which of your proposed solutions to back out. Therefore, I cannot emphasize enough—only apply one "fix" at a time.

As with both of the other methods, just fixing the problem does not end the procedure. Part of the Correct phase involves demonstrating to the user or client that the problem is actually solved and then documenting everything.

TROUBLESHOOTING REMOTE CONNECTIONS

When remote connections fail, it is generally because of one of three things.

- The terminal equipment on the remote host is not working properly.
- The remote host is configured improperly.
- The remote access server is configured improperly.

You can also consider the terminal equipment of the server when all remote access users are affected. However, this is not an issue in the event that you are troubleshooting an individual who cannot log on while others can.

You can sometimes check for indicator lights, such as when the remote host's terminal equipment consists of a modem. However, internal modems rarely have lights that indicate a connection. Those lights are located on the back of the computer and offer little assistance in troubleshooting.

External modems and DSL/Cable routers have a variety of lights that mean different things. While there is some variation among different brands as far as the order in which the lights appear, there is good consistency in the labeling and function of those lights. **Table 19.1** lists these functions. (Note that not all lights listed may appear on all equipment.)

Table 19.1 The Function of External Modem Lights

Marking	Meaning	Modem functiGlows
PWR	Power On	Glows when power is applied to the modem
MR	Modem Ready	Glows when the modem has completed its self-check
TR (DTR)	Terminal Ready	Glows when DTR signal (from PC) is active
TD (DT)	Send (Transmit) Data	Glows while modem is transmitting data
RD	Receive Data	Glows while data is streaming into the modem
OH	Off Hook	Glows when modem is off hook
HS	High Speed	Glows when connected to high-speed link
AA	Auto Answer	Glows when modem is configured to answer calls
CD	Carrier Detect	Glows when remote carrier has been detected
RS	Request to Send	Glows while RTS signal is active
CS	Clear to Send	Glows when it is OK to transmit

Each light on an external modem has a specific function.

If PWR fails to light, the obvious first step is to make sure the modem is plugged in to a working outlet. If it is, you might have either a failed AC adapter or a failed modem. Unfortunately, the latter is most likely. Modems are just as susceptible to power surges as computer systems, yet they are rarely protected. Make sure that they are protected.

Failure of MR or TR to light can mean that the driver either has not been installed or has gone corrupt. Reinstall the driver and see if the problem goes away. If that doesn't work, don't automatically assume the modem is bad. It could be that the ISP is having difficulties.

If there is no sign that there is any trouble with connectivity, it is time to check the configuration of the remote computer. Obvious issues, such has having the incorrect protocol or IP settings, are the first things to check. If those settings are all correct, you may have to get your ISP involved. Advanced settings such as a custom initialization string for the modem or a specialized logon script may be required.

On the server side, the administrator can check the user's account. Was that account disabled after a preconfigured number of failed logon attempts? Is the user attempting an unauthorized logon? An example of an unauthorized logon would be if a user tries to log in from a motel room to an account that is configured so that the server hangs up on initial connection and dials back to a specific telephone number. If the user would be rejected because the server wouldn't dial the unapproved phone number.

TROUBLESHOOTING TOOLS

For the network administrator, there are a variety of tools available to assist in the troubleshooting process. Some of these are pieces of hardware that you use and others are applications that you can run. Also, as a network administrator, most of the time you will be called on to fix network-related problems. However, the biggest flaw I find with most network training programs is that they always assume that "someone else" will be responsible for hardware fixes. In the real world there is nobody by that name. All too frequently you are that someone else.

Therefore, I am going to include in this discussion tools for troubleshooting the network as well as aids for troubleshooting hardware. I will go over both physical tools as well as logical tools.

HARDWARE-BASED TROUBLESHOOTING TOOLS

There are certain tools you can't live without. Every technician needs a good set of screwdrivers, a pair of needle-nosed pliers, a 16-ounce ball peen hammer, and some duct tape. You may think I'm kidding about the hammer and duct tape, but I'm not. You'll find out what I'm talking about the next time you try to install a double-height tape drive into a pair of 5.25" bays. That little shelf they put in most server cases to keep the drives properly seated really gets in the way.

The duct tape comes in handy as well. When you add a drive, you need to remove a cover panel from the case. Many people make the mistake of simply throwing that panel away. Then, when they decide to move the drive over to a different computer, it's got this big gaping hole in the front. Not only is that unsightly, but it also affects how well your system dissipates heat. Things like cover panels and drive bay hardware can be taped to the inside of the case. That way, they're out of the way and always around when you need them.

But then, these aren't really troubleshooting tools are they? Troubleshooting tools are the ones that help you solve problems. And there are some good ones on the market.

THE POST CARD

Unfortunately, this is not the one you send to your mother-in-law when you go on vacation. These are a bit expensive for that. In Chapter Sixteen, Data Recovery and

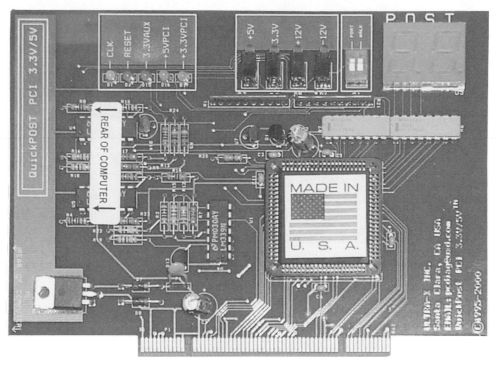

Figure 19.1 This POST card by Ultra-X is one of the most formidable tools you can have in your arsenal. It identifies problems that occur during the POST process.

Fault Tolerance, I discussed in great detail the process of *Power On/Self Test,* or POST. The POST card I'm talking about is used to diagnose problems that occur during the boot process that prevent the computer from starting properly. It mounts into an empty expansion slot and while the computer is booting (or trying to, anyway), it's zipping off light patterns on an LED readout so fast that you can't possibly read them. Don't worry about that. The ones you can't read are the ones you don't care about. They represent components that passed.

At the point that the boot process fails, the readout will display a pattern of lights that represents a specific component. The POST card ships with a booklet that itemizes all of those error messages. All you have to do is look up the number displayed and it tells you what part of the POST process failed. JDR Microdevices, in San Jose, California, offers several different options. It has standard POST cards in both PCI and ISA form. But it also has a combination card that works in either ISA or PCI slots that tests the BIOS as well as the POST process.

Another company that specializes in these devices is a company called Ultra-X (see **Figure 19.1**). It ships complete solutions that include a very advanced POST card along with some diagnostic utilities.

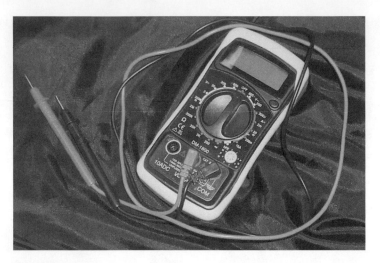

Figure 19.2 A good multimeter will let you know if your problems are electrical in nature.

A combination of tools such as this can go beyond the POST test and continue to test RAM, drive operation including CD-ROM drives, and much more. Ultra-X's Professional Kit includes an impressive array of diagnostics software utilities, a collection of loopback plugs, and the PCI card.

A rather interesting option, offered by PCWiz out of Clearwater, Florida, offers a single card that has an ISA connector on the top and a PCI connector on the bottom. Unless, of course, the device is mounted in an ISA slot, and then the ISA connector is on the bottom, and the PCI is on the top. But you get the idea.

POST cards aren't exactly the cheapest devices you can buy. But technician time isn't free, either. A midsized to larger organization with a large IT infrastructure will save a substantial amount of money in the long run by investing in one or more of these devices.

THE MULTIMETER

Sometimes simply testing for power or continuity can tell you a lot about what's going on. A simple and inexpensive tool for that is a multimeter (see **Figure 19.2**). I recommend that you spend a few extra bucks and get a digital version. It is easier to work with.

The multimeter will tell you if you have proper power coming out of the connectors coming from your power supply. You can use it to test a wire for continuity. It is also useful for testing those ceramic fuses that don't let you see the wire.

MEMORY TESTERS

Several times during this book, I've pointed out that error messages frequently include a hexadecimal address that indicates an address in memory where the error occurred. The addresses are **always** memory locations. But it isn't always the memory that's at fault. The error message could simply be telling you what address was active when the fault occurred. Therefore, it could be an I/O address, or the address in memory in which a device driver was running when that device suffered an unhappy event.

It is also very difficult to identify memory as to the type of DRAM it is made of. So just what kind of memory do you have in your hand? Will it work in the machine you're trying to upgrade? Just counting the number of pins doesn't really help. There are a number of different methods RAM uses for addressing functions as well as data retrieval. Very few types of memory are compatible with one another. Fortunately, in most cases, when you mix SDRAM with DDR, the system simply won't boot. No harm, no foul. If this occurs, your motherboard will issue a series of beeps that is the BIOS's way of telling you that you have a memory mismatch.

Mixing certain forms of memory won't prevent the system from booting properly. There are versions of SDRAM that, during POST, appear to the system as being identical to ECC. But even though the system boots perfectly well, using the system in that state can lead to a slow process of data corruption that eventually leads to disaster.

Specialized devices designed just to test memory are a valuable addition to your collection of troubleshooting tools, if you can afford one. The problem is that they tend to be pretty expensive. And RAM is getting to be where it isn't. However, if you can justify the expense, a memory tester is able to identify memory by type, speed, and density. However, they can also do more specialized tricks. Some of the better ones can detect and locate broken solder joints, bad cells on DRAM chips, and more. Cool toys, if you can afford one.

CABLE TESTERS

This is one of the tools in your collection that is specifically a networking tool. It can come in very handy. Cable testers can test for continuity, do a signal test on each conductor along the cable, and even detect a break in the cable. Some of them not only detect the break, but also tell you how far down the cable from the tester that the break occurs. This greatly enhances your ability to fix the problem.

The cable tester may or may not come with a remote unit. If it doesn't, there will be two sockets so that you can plug both ends of the cable in at once. These can be of limited use when testing an installed cable. One with a remote unit provides a second smaller unit that can be plugged onto the cable at the user's end. Then, from the hub or patch panel, you can perform your tests.

Cable testers come in several different varieties, but they pretty much boil down to one of two types. There are those that simply test for continuity and there are the advanced cable testers. Some of the less expensive ones sell for under a hundred dollars.

> **EXAM NOTE:** The advanced cable tester is a tool that frequently shows up on the exam. Be able to describe its function. Equally importantly, be able to describe the function of the TDR.

Advanced cable testers sell for a whole lot more than that, but can perform more sophisticated tricks. Some employ a *time domain reflectometer* (TDR). The TDR sends a signal down the wire, and when it encounters any condition that affects the signal in any way, such as a break, a crimp in the cable, or a dead short, it reflects a signal back. The device measures the total time elapsed for the round trip and can calculate within a few percentage points how far down the cable a break occurs. Even if there is no break, it is useful in telling the network engineer how long a particular run of cable is.

SOFTWARE-BASED TROUBLESHOOTING TOOLS

Most NOSs come with a fairly elaborate collection of software tools built in. Before you start talking about spending large amounts of money on some third-party utility, you should probably consider whether one of these built-in tools might do the job.

Some of these are the TCP/IP utilities that I discussed in Chapter Twelve, Using TCP/IP on the Network. To review, these utilities include:

- Ping
- Trace Route
- Netstat
- Route
- Nbtstat
- Ipconfig

For a more detailed discussion on these utilities, refer to Chapter Twelve. However, most NOSs also offer a few more sophisticated tools as well. Two of the ones offered by Microsoft are Network Monitor and Performance Monitor.

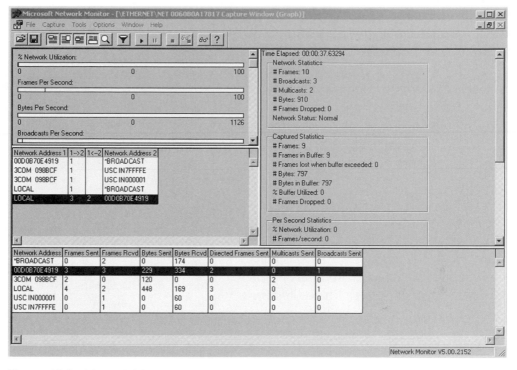

Figure 19.3 Network Monitor captures frames off of the network and provides the tools by which an engineer can analyze the frame.

NETWORK MONITOR

Most of Microsoft's OSs, since the days of Windows 9x, have shipped with a utility called Network Monitor (see **Figure 19.3**). Network Monitor is a diagnostics tool that monitors traffic on the LAN and collects information. It collects this information by capturing packets and analyzing the headers and, in some cases, the contents of the packets.

Basic information displayed includes:

- The source address of the frame
- The destination address of the frame
- The protocols used in sending the frame
- The payload

In order for Network Monitor to work, the NICs installed in the computers need to work in *promiscuous mode*. This term is a colorful way of describing a mode of operation in which a NIC will accept all packets that arrive, regardless of intended destination.

While Network Monitor will capture all packets passing through the NIC in a default configuration, it can be configured to filter packets on a large number of criteria. These criteria include addresses, protocols, NetBIOS name, and the list goes on.

Unfortunately, Network Monitor that comes with Windows OSs is much like some of the evaluation software that can be downloaded off the Internet. Many of the functions displayed are disabled, working only on the version that ships with Microsoft's *Systems Management Server* (SMS).

> ## BUZZ WORDS
>
> **Promiscuous mode:** An operating mode for any network interface in which all incoming packets will be accepted, even if they are not intended for that specific interface.
>
> **System object:** On a system in general, it is any hardware or software entity to which specific properties can be assigned. In Performance Monitor, it is a category of events that can be monitored.
>
> **Object counter:** In Performance Monitor, it is the specific property or variable for which data is being collected.

PERFORMANCE MONITOR

Performance Monitor is an application that ships with Microsoft server products that can monitor a huge number of system variables. Variables are broken down into groups called *system objects.* Within these objects are the counters themselves. The actual number of items that can be monitored is vast, and to attempt to cover them all would require a complete volume in and of itself. However, a few items are of sufficient value to the network engineer to justify a brief discussion.

While Performance Monitor is not necessarily limited to monitoring hardware statistics, it is very useful in that respect. It can measure certain statistics concerning your processor, your memory, and the network interface. **Figure 19.4** is a graphic of Performance Monitor trying to keep track of memory and CPU functions while a brief round of Pinball went on in the foreground. As you can see, this is a resource-intensive little game. I think it illustrates rather well why your server shouldn't be used for running any nonessential applications.

Performance Monitor can be used in this way to generate a report that can let you know if it is time to increase the amount of memory installed in a server, if a second processor is in order, or if your bandwidth is insufficient for your needs. To do this there are several key functions to watch.

There are two system objects with very similar names that are not very similar in what they do. One is *Process* and the other is *Processor.* Process keeps tab of the

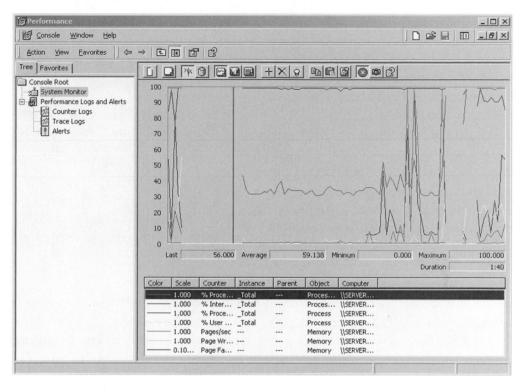

Figure 19.4 Performance Monitor allows you to collect data on the amount of strain specific aspects of your system's software or OS are being put under.

different processes from different applications running on the server, while Processor watches certain performance variables of the CPU. Both are useful to monitor if you think that your CPU can be a bottleneck.

Under Process, one of the key counters to watch is *% Processor Time*. *% Processor Time* is the percentage of elapsed time that all of the threads of a specific process used the processor to execute instructions (the basic unit of execution in a computer). A thread is the object that executes instructions, and a process is a virtual object that is created when a program is run. If this value continually runs much higher than 60 percent, you should get a noticeable increase in performance if you add a second process. On that note, if you already have multiple processors, it is possible to get values beyond 100 percent. Maximum percentage totals would be 100 percent times the number of processors installed in the system.

Another counter that can indicate the need for an additional processor is found in the Processor object. Unfortunately for beginners the counter has the same name as the one we just discussed—*% Processor Time*. The difference here is that under the Process object, the variable described the amount of processor time used by specific processes. Under the Processor object, it describes the amount of processor time used by *all* non-idle processes on the machine. Each processor has an Idle thread that consumes cycles when it has no other threads to run.

Under the Memory object, there are two key counters to watch. One is *Pages/sec*. Pages/sec is the number of pages read from or written to disk to resolve hard page faults. A hard page fault occurs when the CPU requires code or data that is not resident in physical memory and was not found in the page file. This indicates that, somewhere along the line, the processor expected to

> ## BUZZ WORDS
>
> **Page Read/Write:** When physical RAM in a system becomes full, data will be temporarily stored in a file called the paging file. A Page Read is a read operation from this file, while a Page Write is when data is moved from RAM to the paging file.
>
> **Page fault:** When the system does not find the data it needs in RAM, it will search the paging file. If it fails to find that data in the paging file as well, that is a page fault.

need that data, but there was insufficient memory to store it in RAM. Any time this happens, the CPU experiences extensive and unnecessary delays.

Page Faults/sec is somewhat like pages per second, but lets you know how many times the system hit the paging file looking for the data, and it wasn't there. There are two types of page faults. A *soft fault* is where the data was actually present in memory, but not part of the working set. They generally don't affect the system too badly. A *hard fault* requires a search and retrieval by the hard drive and is an even more significant delay than a simple page read. Excessive Pages/sec and Page Faults/sec are indications that you need to install more RAM in your system.

The *Network Interface Object* can let you know how heavily the interface to the server is being hit. Two counters to monitor are *Bandwidth* and *Output Queue Length*. Bandwidth suggests how much of your available bandwidth is being used. Output Queue Length shows how many packets are resident in the buffer. You want this to be zero. One is acceptable, but two or more means there is a problem and you need to locate the source of the bottleneck.

As I said earlier, there are literally hundreds of different counters in Performance Monitor. A good network engineer will make a more detailed study of this handy little application and put it to use.

EVENT VIEWER

A very handy tool Microsoft provides in its NOSs is something called the *Event Viewer*. Event Viewer monitors and maintains logs of three different aspects of OS performance (see **Figure 19.5**). These three areas are system performance, application

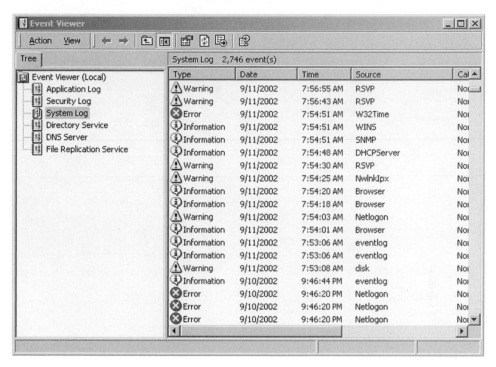

Figure 19.5 Here, I manipulated the OS so that Event Viewer would have several things to report. Each little symbol in front of an event has its own particular significance.

performance, and security. Windows 2000 Server adds three other logs as well. These include Directory Services, the DNS Server, and File Replication Services.

Events will be flagged for significance with one of three icons. These are a blue speech balloon with the letter *i*, a yellow triangle with an exclamation point (*!*), and a red circle with an *X*. The blue *i* is benign. It simply means that a monitored event has occurred and that Windows just thought you should know.

The yellow triangle is a caution. This event informs you that something has occurred that may or may not be of significance. It is up to the administrator to decide if the situation requires action or not.

The red *X* means something bad has happened. Either a configured service has failed to start, a device driver has failed to load, or something else necessary to the operation of the OS as configured isn't working right. Generally speaking, these events require action by the administrator.

If you open an event, you will get a screen similar to that shown in **Figure 19.6**. This screen tells you exactly what failed, and, if there is another service on which this particular event depended that also failed, it will tell you what service that is.

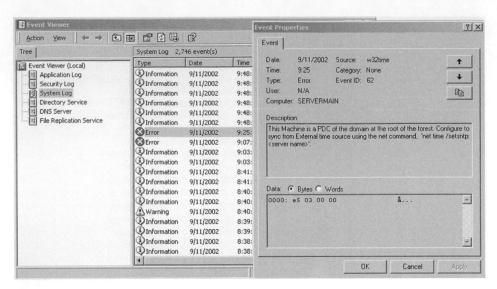

Figure 19.6 Event Viewer gives you some good background information on what exactly failed, and in many cases, why it failed.

In some cases, you might be given a memory address. This information can all be used to assist you in troubleshooting why your NOS isn't working properly. Get to know Event Viewer well. It can be your friend.

A SESSION IN TROUBLESHOOTING

Consider this situation. You've just been called into a client's office where the network speed has dropped to a crawl. It takes several minutes to log on, whereas it once took the blink of an eye. Browsing to a particular host on the network is an excuse to take a coffee break, and should a user decide to retrieve any file larger than an icon for the desktop, it's time to go to lunch. What are the different things you should look for?

Here's an opportunity for you to check the lights referenced in Chapter Nineteen, Troubleshooting the Network. Check the lights on the hub. There are two types of lights for each port: a link light and a collision light. A link light tells you whether or not you have connectivity, but in this situation, connectivity is not the issue. The collision lights (usually amber or red) flash every time a particular port is involved in a collision. On a busy network, it's not unusual for several of those lights to be flickering. In a situation as described above, you might see the collision lights constantly glowing. That is not good. But at least you know what the problem is. Network congestion has increased beyond the capacity of the infrastructure.

Once you determine the problem, then you need to determine its cause. If it just happened suddenly, you want to find out if anything in the environment changed. Is there any new equipment in the network? Nearly all NICs shipping today are 10/100 auto-sensing devices. If all workstations have 10/100 cards and the office manager decided to splurge on a new 100MB hub, then the whole network will try to shift into 100MB mode. As long as the cabling throughout the building is Cat5 or better, it will succeed. With cabling older than Cat3, you will experience the symptoms described.

You may need to consider other scenarios, such as the following: Did the maintenance crew install new ballasts in the ceiling? Was a new air conditioning compressor installed in the building? Did the power company just bring a new substation online in the client's backyard? EMI is very good at introducing noise onto the network that causes many problems such as extremely slow bandwidth or a complete disability to connect.

If you can't isolate anything of that nature, it is now time to engage one of the software utilities. If the NOS is a Microsoft product, the best one to call on at this point is Network Monitor. Other NOSs have similar utilities, as do several third-party network management packages. Take your pick. I'm going to use Network Monitor in this example because it is the one the majority of readers will have access to.

Open Network Monitor and start a capture on the network address affected. Look for an excessive outpouring of packets from a single interface. This is called a broadcast storm. Use Network Monitor to isolate the NetBIOS name of the guilty interface. Locate that host and change out the NIC. Chances are extremely good that you have solved the problem.

But what if you don't see any evidence of a broadcast storm? What if, according to Network Monitor, everything looks normal? Another good thing to check would be the bandwidth usage of the server's NIC. To do so, open Performance Monitor, and select Network Interface from Performance Object. Then select the server's NIC from the Select instance from list screen (lower right). In the Select counters from list screen, select Bytes total/sec, Current Bandwidth and Output queue length. Let that run for several seconds to a minute and watch the output. If your bandwidth is constantly saturated and the queue length stays higher than 3 to 4 frames, it is the server's NIC that is the culprit. One solution is to dual-home the server. In other words, give it a second NIC. A better solution is to install a switch and buy a couple more hubs. Put each hub on a separate switch port and divide the hosts among the hubs. Put the server on its own port.

If the problem isn't at the server, perhaps it's from the hub. From one of the affected machines, ping the server using the –t trigger. An example of this is ping 192.168.0.165 –t typed at a command prompt. Let the ping run for several seconds to a minute. Watch the time it takes for packets to return and watch for an excessive number of timeouts. There is a problem if the network is dropping more than 2-3 percent of the packets. In that case, one of the first things you want to look at is the hub. If you can beg or borrow a spare hub from another office that you know is good, put it in place and see if the problem goes away.

Then again, there's always the possibility that something has happened to cause the wiring infrastructure to fail. For example, in an older building it's possible that rodents in the wall have chewed through a wire. Or a maintenance person working on something else might have dislodged a wire or even accidentally cut one. Try to determine if these are possible causes.

While this doesn't cover all the possible causes of the problem described, it does account for the most common. And my goal here wasn't to actually solve this specific problem, but rather demonstrate an approach to solving problems in general.

TROUBLESHOOTING THE SMALL NETWORK

Generally there are no real differences between the methods of troubleshooting small networks and large networks. In smaller networks, there are different situations that might arise to cause problems. These include the following:

- User error/intervention
- Network topology
- Type of media
- ISP connection

Issues surrounding the ISP connection are discussed in the section on remote connections. Also note that while these issues are more common on smaller networks, they can certainly plague larger networks as well. Especially networks with smaller satellite branches.

USER ERROR/INTERVENTION

It's useful to remember that user error is a common reason for failure. This is not to say that you should assume that all users are inept. Such an assumption can easily get you in trouble. The accountant who uses a PC is likely far better at accounting than you'll ever be.

Failures also occur due to user intervention. Unless appropriate measures are taken, the so-called "computer guru" of the office can often do more harm than good. I have been onsite to several locations where the only problem was that someone tried to tweak the system. These attempts have included activities such as installing "modem optimizers" on the server, accessing the server and changing permissions, and even changing the passwords to routers. On a secure network you want to make sure that the bare minimum number of people have the necessary permissions to perform these functions. Be judicious when handing out administrative permissions. None of the situations just mentioned would have been possible had someone not begged, borrowed, or stolen the administrator's password, or been granted administrative privileges.

NETWORK TOPOLOGY

This is a gray area that, while not unique to the small network, is more commonly seen there. Conversely, the issues dealing with router and switch configurations are more likely to be related to larger networks, but may appear on smaller ones.

An infrequent problem is that of connectivity issues unique to bus networks. For a bus network to function properly, all hosts on the network must be connected, and the chain must be properly terminated on both ends of the network. The entire network goes down if just one person kicks the cable out of the NIC or if the person with the last computer on the chain pulls the terminating resistor off the NIC.

The star network is not without its problems. Smaller networks are frequently configured these days in a star configuration using Ethernet. As the network grows, it may be subnetted using routers. I discussed how adding additional routers could result in infinite loops in Chapter Seven, The Network Layer, pointing out methods of addressing these problems, such as poison loop and split horizon. A problem that is not addressed by these methods is when a router either fails, or is pulled from the network without notice.

Generally, when there are other routers on the network, these devices will quickly become aware that the network configuration has changed and start rebuilding their routing tables to reflect that change. However, sometimes one or two subnets are removed that had been directly connected to the router. Devices on those subnets will have been effectively removed from the network. Obviously if you were the person that removed the router, you would know what the problem was. You'll be trying to put those hosts back on the network if the router simply failed.

The solution is simple when it was the router directly connected to the subnets. Ping the gateway. If you get the "Host not found" reply, try to telnet into the router if you have the appropriate permissions and password. However, when you can't see the router in any way, shape, or form, it's time to get on your horse and ride out to the router's location. If somebody pulled it, the gaping hole where it used to be will probably tell you what the problem is. If it simply failed, use all the previously discussed troubleshooting methods. Check the indicator lights. Lack of any lights at all is a pretty easy diagnosis. The router isn't powered up. If it's plugged in and switched on and there's still no power, it's pretty safe to assume a failed router.

The problem is most likely with the router's configuration if it is powered up and all connections are secure. Perhaps it simply needs to be reset. Try that first. If that fails, then it may be necessary to clear the CMOS and reconfigure the router.

MEDIA TYPE

Problems relating to the media are not at all uncommon. I mentioned in another part of this chapter that when all hosts are equipped with 10/100 NICs and a 10/100 auto-switching hub is installed, the network immediately switches into 100MB mode. If CAT3 cable is installed, the results will be disastrous. Because of the number of collisions, dropped packets, and re-sent data, network speed will drop to a fraction of what it was before you made the changes. Configure the NICs to run in 10MB mode (or the hub, if it offers that option), and the problem will go away.

A more common problem these days occurs because more and more networks are going wireless. Wireless networking has its own issues to deal with. For one, all hosts must be able to connect to one of the wireless access points (WAP). Networks spread out over a larger area might have more than one WAP. You must make sure that first of all, all users are connecting to a WAP, and second, they are connecting to the correct WAP. To find out if the host is connecting to the correct WAP, ping it. WAPs have IP addresses just like every other device on the network. If it doesn't respond, you're not connected.

WHEN NETWORK SERVICES GO WRONG

Network services can cause as many headaches as unruly applications or corrupted device drivers. For example, without DNS, browsing the Internet is impossible. More importantly, without DNS, Windows 2000 Active Directory and other directory services models by Unix/Linux and Novell won't work at all. Be aware of the impact that these services and others have on your network.

On NT 4.0 and earlier Microsoft products, it is possible to remove DNS if you so desire. The LAN will continue to function as long as WINS is operational (for a full discussion of these services and the functions they perform, see Chapter Twelve, An Introduction to TCP/IP). Users won't even know anything happened until they try to access the Internet.

A good rule of thumb is to never change the IP address of any server on the network. But that isn't always possible, and it isn't always under your control. It's likely that a smaller network uses the services of their ISP's DNS servers. And you might note details such as organizations change ISPs fairly frequently, or the unlikely chance that your ISP may change the address of their DNS.

Users will be able to browse Internet sites when you roll out the IP addresses for the new servers. For example, the network administrator may install a new WINS or DNS server when the current server is overtaxed. In that case, all the workstations on the network need to be reconfigured for that change before users can access those services.

That's where DHCP really shines. Reconfigure the DHCP options to include the new IP addresses and reset the IP lease to zero. Now send out a blanket email to all users to restart their machines. You could simply have them use IPCONFIG or WINIPCFG to release and renew their IP addresses. But trust me when I tell you—in a larger organization, attempting the latter will result in anywhere from several dozen to several hundred hours handholding a large number of users through the process. Restarting a machine is something with which nearly all users will have no difficulty.

This brings up the importance of keeping DHCP running properly on your network at all times. Once DHCP is properly configured, it generally causes no problems. However, DHCP is a service, and services are really nothing more than applications running on a server. Applications can and do occasionally crash. If DHCP appears to have stopped functioning on your network, your first step would be to go to the server, and stop and then restart the DHCP services. This will solve the problem ninety-nine times out of a hundred. That hundredth time will require an uninstallation of DHCP followed by a reinstallation.

The most common DHCP problem occurs when a new server is added to the network with DCHP installed. Using multiple DHCP servers is not a bad idea on a larger network. It greatly reduces the burden from a single DHCP server. However, it is critical that the DHCP scopes not be identical, and that DHCP servers whose scopes service different network addresses not be on the same segment.

In the first situation, two DHCP servers on the network with identical scopes can result in users not being able to log onto the network. One DCHP server doles out an address and tags that address as being in use. But the other DHCP server has that same address as part of its scope and hands it out to another user. The first user with that address to log onto the network is a happy user. The second user to try will be on the phone with you in mere moments. For best performance, divide your block of addresses evenly between the various DHCP servers on the network. A crucial note here, however, is that you want your list of address exclusions to be identical on all servers. You don't want your new DHCP server handing out IP addresses that are supposed to belong to router interfaces and IP printers, now do you?

Inadvertently putting two DHCP servers whose scopes belong to different network addresses on the same segment can be even more disastrous. If you recall, a network segment consists of all hosts on a single broadcast domain. And remember that DCHP clients obtain their address by sending out a broadcast and then accepting the first address that is offered. If the workstation responds to the DHCP server that is on the wrong network, then users cannot access the resources they require. And they may, perhaps, if security is not the best, be able to access resources they shouldn't.

MACHINES THAT CAN'T GET ONTO THE NETWORK

One of the most common maladies diagnosed by the network engineer is the machine or group of machines that can't get onto the network. The sheer variety of problems that can result in this symptom is what makes it troublesome to diagnose. Therefore a logical approach is in order.

The first step is to determine the magnitude of the problem. Is it just one machine or is it several? If it is more than one machine, are they on the same segment?

In the case of one machine, first determine that there is no user error causing the problem. Watch users log in and see what happens. Make sure Caps Lock is off and Num Lock is on. If a user's attempt fails, watch for the error message that is returned at that point. If it doesn't fail while you're standing there, go back to your office. The majesty of your very presence was enough to solve the problem.

A failed logon may occur when the authentication server couldn't be found or the user ID or password was incorrect. An invalid user ID and password means that you need to reset the password on the account and verify the user ID. Use your credentials and see if you can log on. If neither of you can properly log on, use Ipconfig to check the address bound to the NIC. On a subnetted network, it is possible that a machine has either been configured to the wrong subnet or that a rogue DHCP server is handing out addresses.

The sign of a connectivity issue is when the server can't be found. Connectivity issues can be the result of a physical problem or a configuration problem. If the client machine is running TCP/IP, run Ipconfig to view the interface settings. An IP address in the range of 169.*.*.* indicates that the machine is configured as a

DHCP host and that a DHCP server could not be found. Ping the DHCP server. If it can be seen, there is no problem with the infrastructure.

Keep in mind, however, that it's not definitive proof of an infrastructure problem when you can't see the DHCP server. If it can't be seen, ping the address 127.0.0.1. That is the internal address of all NICs. If the ping is unsuccessful, one of two things is wrong. It could be that the driver needs to be reinstalled. If reinstalling the driver does no good, there is a very strong possibility that you need a new NIC.

A successful ping to that address means the card works. First double-check the network configuration in the OS. Even if the configuration proves to be correct, you're still not ready to start tearing into the walls looking for bad wiring. Before you get that drastic, uninstall and reinstall TCP/IP. Remember that the protocols are just applications running on the system, and the files that make them work can become corrupted just like any other application.

If your configuration is accurate to the letter and reinstalling TCP/IP does no good, it's time to start considering physical issues. If there is a direct connection between the PC and the hub or switch, you can use a cable tester to see of you have continuity. Most larger networks run wiring drops from the server room to wall jacks located near each station. Patch cables connect the PC to the wall jack. If possible, swap out the patch cable running from the PC to the wall jack. Next try a different drop, if one is available. If the PC works fine on one drop but not the other, you have a problem with the cable that runs from the wall jack to the server room.

This is where an advanced cable tester comes in handy. It will tell you exactly how for the "end" of the cable is from where you measure it. If you know the length of the run, it helps immensely. But even if you don't, you should be able to make a reasonable estimate as long as you have a decent knowledge of your infrastructure. If the cable tester comes up with a length that is abnormally short, there is a break in the cable somewhere. If not, the problem is either at the wall jack or the patch panel. Check the connections at both ends.

If the user can log onto the network but cannot connect to a specific device, the first thing you want to do is make sure that user has permissions to do what he or she is trying to do. Insufficient permissions or lack of permissions to access a device is *supposed* to block the user. If a user has sufficient rights to access the resource, ping it. Next, make sure DNS is working. You can do that by pinging a resource by its NetBIOS name. For example, if the user can't access a server named SERVERMAIN, type `ping servermain` from the command prompt. If you receive a message that says Unknown host servermain, ping the server by IP address. If that succeeds, then DNS isn't working. See all of the above steps in troubleshooting connectivity if you can't see the server either.

CHAPTER SUMMARY

When it comes to troubleshooting, there seems to be two types of people. There are those who have nightmares about being called on to figure out a problem, and there are those who thrive on the challenge. One would think that the former type would want to find a job in a different career field, but that doesn't seem to be the case. In any event, like it or not, troubleshooting is a key role for the network administrator.

Having a good knowledge of your trade and then following a rigid set of procedures are the keys to success. You'll gain the knowledge over time, but you can start applying the procedures from the start. You don't want to get into bad habits early in your career.

A good set of tools doesn't hurt much either. When troubleshooting hardware issues or when fighting with the network, there are hardware-based tools and software applications that assist in the troubleshooting process. Be prepared to use any of these when the time arises.

BRAIN DRAIN

1. List each step of the Network+ Troubleshooting Model, along with a brief description of each step.

2. Describe the differences between the Network+ Troubleshooting Model and the Novell Troubleshooting Model.

3. Describe the differences between a hardware-based troubleshooting tool and one that is software based.

4. What are three key variables to monitor when tracking the performance of your server?

5. Explain when you would use Network Monitor to help out with a problem and when Performance Monitor would be the application of choice.

THE 64K$ QUESTIONS

1. The best way to begin identifying a problem is to _____.
   a. Ask the user general questions about what was happening when the problem occurred.
   b. Sit down at the machine and log on as administrator.
   c. Ask the user specific open-ended questions about the problem at hand.
   d. Run Performance Monitor.

2. Which of the following is an example of an open-ended question?

    a. What changed since the last time you logged on?

    b. Did you install any new software or screen savers?

    c. What were you doing when the failure occurred?

    d. Did you receive any error messages before it locked up?

3. What are reasons for re-creating a problem before tackling the problem itself?

    a. You should always assume that users are less knowledgeable than you and have no idea of what they're talking about.

    b. You should always assume that the user is less knowledgeable than you and may have inadvertently missed something.

    c. You're billing by the hour, and this process generates more billable income.

    d. There may be error messages specific to the problem that will point you in a specific direction.

4. Why should you re-create the problem on-site?

    a. So that, if you can't re-create it, the user will be present to see that a problem doesn't exist.

    b. So that, if there is something specific that the user is doing, you can determine this and correct the situation.

    c. The problem may be a result of some environmental variable specific to the user's area, such as a space heater positioned right next to the computer.

    d. You want to avoid bringing the system back to the shop.

5. Which of the following troubleshooting steps is unique to the Novell Troubleshooting Model?

    a. Try the obvious first

    b. Information gathering

    c. Developing a plan of attack

    d. Documenting the problem and its solution

6. A POST card is _____.

    a. A hardware-based troubleshooting tool

    b. A software-based troubleshooting tool

    c. Used only by hardware technicians

    d. Used only by network engineers

7. You suspect that your server needs a second processor installed. In order to confirm your suspicions, you run a series of tests using _____.

   a. An advanced cable tester

   b. Netstat

   c. Network Monitor

   d. Performance Monitor

8. Network Monitor can do which of the following for you?

   a. Capture packets

   b. Identify bottlenecks in a network interface

   c. Locate the source of a broadcast storm

   d. Confirm that your NIC is defective

9. What is the easiest tool for identifying the logical address of a computer?

   a. Netstat

   b. Network Monitor

   c. Performance Monitor

   d. Ipconfig

10. Which of the following parts of a packet are not displayed in a captured frame?

    a. CRC information

    b. The source address of the frame

    c. The destination address of the frame

    d. The protocols used in sending the frame

11. Before you even begin to try and figure out a problem on a system or the network, you should _____.

    a. Document the problem

    b. Give the user a full CAT Scan

    c. Recreate the problem, if possible

    d. Form a hypothesis for what might be causing the problem

12. The best way to lock in onto what might be causing the problem is to ask the user what changed since the last time the system worked properly.

    a. True

    b. False

13. The real reason you want to recreate a problem in the user's presence is _____.

    a. To catch the user doing something wrong

    b. To see what error messages appear

    c. To make sure the problem isn't profile-specific

    d. To instill confidence in the user

14. Why do you test for hardware problems onsite whenever possible?

    a. To eliminate ID-ten-T errors.

    b. In case there might be environmental factors causing the problem.

    c. To instill confidence in the user.

    d. To make sure it's not an OS-related problem.

15. The best screwdrivers for working on computers are magnetized.

    a. True

    b. False

16. You have a system that is getting just so far into the boot process and is then shutting off. Which of the following tools would be useful in figuring out if the problem is memory-, video- or CPU-related?

    a. A multimeter

    b. A logic probe

    c. An advanced cable tester

    d. A POST card

17. What function of an advanced cable tester allows it to determine how far away a break in the cable occurs?

    a. A sonar generator

    b. A laser reflectometer

    c. Voltage reflectance

    d. A time domain reflectometer

18. One of the routers in your network is down. Which of the following tools can help you figure out which one?

    a. Netstat

    b. Network Monitor

    c. Ipconfig

    d. Tracert

19. You have a broadcast storm that is crippling your network. Which of the following tools can help you isolate the source of the problem?

    a. Netstat

    b. Network Monitor

    c. Ipconfig

    d. Tracert

20. Which of the following tools is the best one for helping you decide if your server needs a second CPU?

    a. Performance

    b. Network Monitor

    c. Ipconfig

    d. Remote System Monitor

TRICKY TERMINOLOGY

Closed-ended question: Questions that can be answered by "Yes" or "No" or that otherwise abruptly end the line of query.

Hypothesis: A fundamental theory as to why a particular situation exists the way it does.

Object counter: In Performance Monitor, it is the specific property or variable for which data is being collected.

Open-ended question: A question formulated in such a way that the answer must provide an opening for further queries.

Page fault: When the system does not find the data it needs in RAM, it will search the paging file. If it fails to find that data, that is a page fault.

Page Read/Write: When physical RAM in a system becomes full, data will be temporarily stored in a file called the paging file. A Page Read is a read operation from this file, while a Page Write is when data is moved from RAM to the paging file.

Promiscuous mode: An operating mode for any network interface in which all incoming packets will be accepted, even if they are not intended for that specific interface.

System object: On a system in general, it is any hardware or software entity to which specific properties can be assigned. In Performance Monitor, it is a category of events that can be monitored.

Troubleshooting: The process of identifying and subsequently fixing a problem that exists on a piece of hardware, in an application, or on the network.

ACRONYM ALERT

CIC: Collect, Isolate, and Correct. One of the generally accepted troubleshooting models used in the computer industry.

TDR: Time Domain Reflectometer. A sophisticated cable testing device that works by sending a signal down the cable and measuring the amount of time it takes to return.

CHAPTER 20

NAVIGATING THE INTERNET

Since this is basically a book about networking, it certainly wouldn't be complete without a rundown on the biggest network of all: the Internet. Everybody uses it. In fact, everybody these days pretty much takes it for granted. It's one of those things that is just there and always was, right? However, calling the Internet just another network is like calling the space shuttle just another airplane. And as difficult as it may be to believe, the Internet hasn't always been around, although some of us old-timers might find it difficult to believe just how long it *has* been in place.

For the most part, there won't be a lot from this chapter on the Network+ exam. This information is being provided primarily as a service to the reader. You could hardly consider yourself to be a networking professional if you have no concept of how the Internet came to be. If you're only reading this book in order to pass the Network+ exam, you can get away with skipping this chapter if you want. There is nothing in here specific to the exam. But you'll miss a lot of interesting material if you do.

THE HISTORY OF THE INTERNET

While this may come as a disappointment to some, it is my grievous duty to report that Al Gore did not actually invent the Internet. The Internet is one of those multi-headed entities that came about as the result of the work of thousands of individuals developing protocols and hardware that would allow different systems running on different platforms to communicate. However, if you want to give any one specific individual credit for the concept, let's give it to Joseph Carl Robnett Licklider of MIT.

In 1962, he wrote a paper entitled *On-Line Man Computer Communication*. In this paper, he described what he called the *Galactic Network*. This galactic network was composed of a worldwide conglomeration of computer systems interconnected in order to share and distribute information. Sound familiar? As the head of the Computer Research Program for the *Defense Advanced Research Projects Agency* (DARPA), he was given the opportunity to put form to some of his concepts, although the work would eventually be completed by his successor, Lawrence Roberts.

Another MIT alumnus, Leonard Kleinrock, had written a paper entitled *Information Flow in Large Communication Nets* that described how information could be broken down into packets for communication over a wire. Roberts brought Kleinrock on board, and in 1965 they had their first success. They interconnected MIT's TX-2 mainframe to a Q-32 in California. To illustrate what a remarkable achievement this was for the time, the TX-2 was a computer system built by academics that used a 38-bit word and had no operating system as we know it. Instead, programmers had to compile their own programs or data. The Q-32 was a machine custom built for the military by IBM and used a 48-bit word. The two systems made their first connection over a telephone line.

The following year, Roberts presented his plan for interconnecting a number of different computer systems scattered across the country into an integrated network. In 1969, there were a total of four computers linked together in the network now known as ARPANET. ARPANET became global in 1973 when The University College of London was successfully added to the network.

Two things happened in 1974 that provided momentum for the Internet to become the medium it is today. First and foremost was the publication of *A Protocol for Packet Network Intercommunication* by Vincent Cerf and Robert Kahn. It was in this paper that the Transmission Control Protocol was defined. The other significant event of that year was the release of the first commercial implementation of a packet-based data service. Bolt, Berenek, & Newman gave us Telenet.

Other global networks quickly began to emerge. In 1980, the Computer Science Network (CSNET) and the Because It's Time Network (BITNET) arrived. 1982 saw the European Unix Network (EUNET). A major step toward interlinking all of these networks occurred in 1983 when a gateway between CSNET and ARPANET was created.

In order to keep track of who was who in this ever-growing collection of entities, the Domain Name System (DNS) was ratified in 1984. This provided a more user-friendly way by which humans could locate computers over the wire. DNS provided each entity with a host name and created the domains that identified the type of organization. At first, there were only six primary domains—

education (edu), commercial (com), government (gov), military (mil), organization (org), and network (net). That has been expanded over the years.

From there, it was only a matter of time. In 1987, there were approximately 10,000 hosts on the Internet. Two years later, the number exceeded 100,000. But for most of us, the pivotal year was 1991. This was the year that the European Organization for Nuclear Research (CERN) unveiled the World Wide Web. One of its researchers, a man named Tim Berner-Lee, developed a method of linking documents to one another electronically called the *Hypertext Markup Language* (HTML).

I give you the Internet. But I didn't invent it.

FOUNDATIONS OF THE INTERNET

In the early days of development, it was apparent that the Internet was going to be a collection of internetworked networks rather than one of individual computers. A few key issues had to be resolved early on before serious development could begin. For one thing, if you wanted an organization to become a part of this global movement, you had to earn its trust. Therefore, it was decided that each network would stand alone. The process of internetworking would not require that any modifications to network structure or administration be implemented. Second, on an operational level, there would be no control of the network permitted by outside sources.

Multiple networks would be linked together by routers or gateways. These devices would not retain data once a transmission was completed. Routers had to be platform-independent.

Another key issue, once the World Wide Web was implemented, dealt with how to get individual users onto the network. The following section explains the different intermediate levels that occur from the end user's machine up to the actual source of data being accessed by that user (**Figure 20.1**).

- User's PC
- User's datacom
- The local loop carrier
- The ISP point of presence
- User services
- ISP backbone
- On-line content
- Origin of content

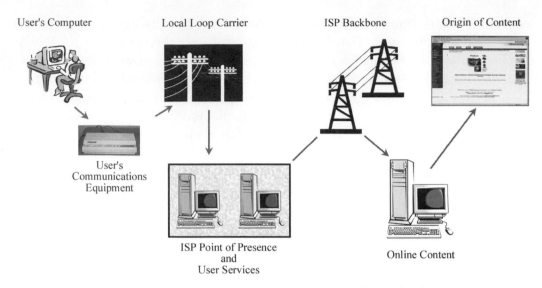

User's Computer Local Loop Carrier ISP Backbone Origin of Content

User's
Communications
Equipment

ISP Point of Presence
and
User Services

Online Content

Figure 20.1 While your Web browser makes it seem easy, getting on-line is actually a pretty complicated process.

THE USER'S PC

Of these different links, the user's PC should be the one that requires the least explanation (see **Figure 20.2**). However, it should be noted that there are different hardware requirements for different applications. If you're involved in any activity requiring sound, it might be nice if you have the appropriate equipment installed. A sound card, speakers, and very likely a microphone are in order. Applications such as tele-conferencing will require this sort of setup. If you work with streaming video, an appropriate graphics adapter is in order. Obviously, you will also need some form of software interface. Most people use Web browsers such as Internet Explorer or Netscape Navigator. Other software packages that are useful include some form of FTP client, a mail client, and perhaps a Telnet client.

THE USER'S DATACOM

More simply put, this is the communications equipment that allows the user's PC to hook up to another PC over a communications link of some sort. In the old days this was a simpler matter. Everyone used modems (see **Figure 20.3**). These days the choices include:

- Public Switched Telephone Network (PSTN) – Dial-up networking as we know it. ~53.3K

Figure 20.2 Internet connections start with the user logging onto the Internet.

- Integrated Services Digital Network (ISDN) – Sometimes called digital modem. ~128K
- Digital Subscriber Line (DSL) – High-speed broadband. ~384K – 6MB

> **BUZZ WORD** ───────────
>
> **Datacom:** A term coined to describe any equipment used in data communications.

- Cable Modem – Internet over cable television services. Speed varies
- Satellite Internet – Broadband Wireless Internet. ~400K

Which choice you make impacts on your speed of service, as you might imagine. However, be aware that not all services are available in all areas.

Figure 20.3 The user's telecommunications equipment makes the connection.

THE LOCAL LOOP CARRIER

Somebody has to maintain the circuits that carry the signal between you and your service provider (see **Figure 20.4**). Depending on your choice of datacom, these options include your local telephone company, cable television company, or an independent contractor.

Your selection here not only impacts performance, but security as well. Some carriers are less secure than others. For example, if you use a cable modem, when you log on you become part of a local segment for the company. Any files you have shared on your computer can be browsed by others on the same segment simply by visiting Network Neighborhood. A good firewall is in order here if you have any sensitive data at all.

Other carriers, such as satellites, can be impacted by external conditions. These would include elements such as the weather, solar flares, or other conditions beyond your control. If a constant connection is critical to your organization, you should consider this before investing in the equipment needed.

THE ISP POINT OF PRESENCE

People can't just hook themselves up to the Internet arbitrarily. They need some sort of service that provides an access point to the Internet. This provides the control necessary to prevent the presence of identical IP addresses on the net at once, as well

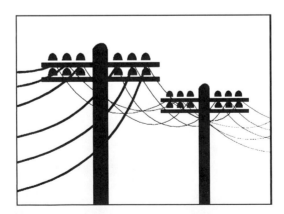

Figure 20.4 Your local communications services provider connects you to your ISP

as providing a certain degree (although a very limited degree) of security. Your *Internet Service Provider* (ISP) provides this function. Larger ISPs will have more than one POP. For every metropolitan area they serve, in order to provide local dial-up services, they will provide a separate POP. This POP controls your connection type and speed as well as providing user logon and authentication services.

The ISP also provides certain supplementary services, such as POP and SMTP services. These are the protocols for sending and receiving email. They act as your DNS server, greatly expediting your search for locations on the Internet. They also control the presence of IP addresses on the Web.

They do this because when they first established their services, they obtained a block of IP addresses from an administrative organization assigned to administer IP addresses. In the old days, this was InterNIC, or the *Internet's Network Information Center.* It used to be the sole administrator of IP addresses and domain names. These days, it only does domain names. IP addresses are allocated by *The Internet Corporation for Assigned Names and Numbers* (ICANN). Any given ISP has a certain number of addresses it can hand out and no more. In order to efficiently manage its pool of addresses, they are usually handed out by the DHCP protocol. However, dedicated links require static IP addresses. Therefore, you must use the IP address assigned to you by your ISP.

THE USER SERVICES

User services can be administered either on a local level or through your ISP. They might also be provided by a third party. Most end users depend on their ISP for the majority of their services, but not always. These services include:

- Domain name services
- Email hosting services
- Wcb hosting
- FTP services
- Newsgroup services
- Bulletin board services

Many of these services can be quite resource intensive and require dedicated servers in order to implement them. Therefore, even many companies and organizations depend on an ISP for these services. However, in a larger organization, Internet traffic can be minimized if the services are administered locally.

THE ISP BACKBONE

ISPs are not islands alone. Many of the larger companies, such as AT&T, Sprint, PSINet, and others, maintain their own infrastructure and lease it out to smaller ISPs. The signals are routed over high-speed broadband fiber circuits maintained by the major telecommunications corporations. These would include AT&T, Sprint, MCI, and others. The different providers link their services together over banks of routers and switches.

Most major metropolitan areas have one or more *Network Access Points* (NAP). These provide the entry point to a *Large Capacity Circuit*. This is one of those fiber circuits mentioned above. ISPs lease fiber-optic connections to link each of their POPs together. However, if that is as far as anyone went, the customers of one company would have communications with all other customers of that company if they so desired, but not with other ISPs of the world. Therefore, the various ISPs set up gateways between their networks through these NAPs.

From there, data moves over large-capacity circuits to its destination NAP. Large capacity circuits range everywhere from T1 lines operating at 1.544Mb/s over the smaller connections to an OC-48 line capable of moving 2.488 gigabits of data every second. Each of the major communications carriers maintains its own backbone infrastructure. Through various international arrangements, these corporations have agreed to intercommunicate with one another, allowing the unobstructed passage of the data moving over the lines.

ON-LINE CONTENT

The material you're searching for generally resides on a *Web server*. Web servers are particularly potent computers running an NOS specifically designed for maintaining multiple incoming virtual connections. These operating systems include Apache, UNIX, Microsoft's Data Center, and several others.

Web servers are likely to host hundreds or even thousands of sites on a single machine—or to be more accurate, a single cluster of machines. It is unlikely that any business seriously involved in Web hosting would entrust their future to a single box. Web sites are identified by their *domain name.* Any site created and published out to the Internet must be properly registered with one of the various agencies. When your computer wants to find a specific Web

> **BUZZ WORD**
>
> **On-line content:** The overall availability of resources across an intranet or the Internet.

site it will make use of DNS to find it. (See Chapter Twelve, An Introduction to TCP/IP, for a detailed explanation of DNS.) Once a specific site has been found, you now have access to any data for which you have the appropriate permissions to access.

> **BUZZ WORD**
>
> **Origin of content:** A specific resource available to users of an intranet or the Internet.

ORIGIN OF CONTENT

This is the part of the chain that is providing much of the legal battleground for the Internet. The material that is actually made available for consumption constitutes origin of content (see **Figure 20.5**). This consists of pretty much every form of medium that can be stored digitally. Hundreds of thousands of books, movies, images, musical recordings, and what have you have been converted to digital format and made available to the public.

Figure 20.5 A single Web page created by an individual or organization makes up the origin of content, which is the final data you receive.

A huge stir of controversy has erupted over several issues relating to this. For one thing, how do we protect our children from viewing unsuitable material? Or for that matter, is some information suitable for public distribution at all? Do we really want detailed instructions on how to make your own nuclear warhead generally available to the public? Fortunately, this book does not have to confront these issues head on. However, as a Web page designer, they are issues that might confront you.

Know your copyright laws well. The laws that protect written materials are just as valid over the Internet as they are in the public library. Just because you have the technology and the resources to copy and publish another person's creations doesn't mean you have the right.

ADMINISTERING THE INTERNET

As of 2002, a crude estimate on the Internet population put it at approximately a half-billion people per day. At that time, there were a little over 170 million Web sites competing for their attention (see **Figure 20.6**). In order to prevent this from being total chaos, someone needs to be responsible for keeping track of things like IP addresses, domain names, security, and enforcement.

This is far too much for a single agency to keep track of. Therefore, several agencies are assigned different tasks. Domain naming and the distribution of IP addresses on a global level fall under the jurisdiction of the *Internet Assigned Numbers Authority* (IANA). To make things run a little more smoothly, this organization has delegated much of its responsibility to regional groups. Agencies that handle domain naming include InterNIC, RIPE-NCC, and Asia-Pacific NIC. IP addresses are managed regionally by the American Registry for Internet Numbers (ARIN), the Asia-Pacific Network Information Center (APNIC), and Réseaux IP Européens (RIPE NCC).

Even so, should you require an IP address, you would not approach any of these organizations directly. The proper procedure is to approach your ISP and make your request. It will contact an intermediate agency known as an upstream register in order to fill your request.

Operational control of the Internet falls under the watchful eye of the Internet Engineering Planning Group (IEPG). The American organization charged with this responsibility is the North American Network Operators Group (NANOG). It is an evolutionary offshoot of the National Science Foundation Network (NSFNET). This organization oversees the development of new Internet segments, maintains acceptable use policies, and, until it was retired in 1996, maintained the NSFNET

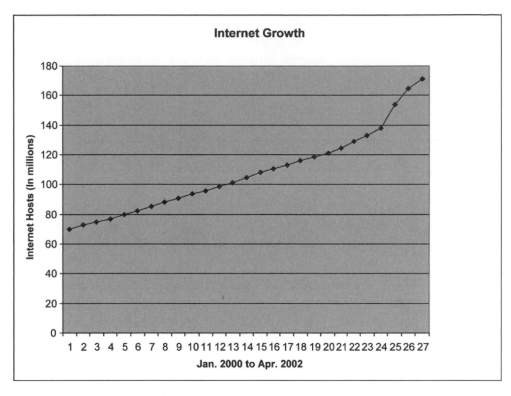

Figure 20.6 Internet growth from January 2000 to April 2002.

backbone. The European entity that manages this is called EOF, and in the Asian-Pacific region it is AP-NG.

The rash of critical viruses that erupted in 2001 brought to the spotlight another group that has been around for years. This is the Forum of Incident Response and Security Teams (FIRST). FIRST oversees a group of Computer Emergency Response Teams (CERT) in eight countries and a large number of ISPs that monitor the Internet and respond to these types of incidents. In an outbreak such as the Nimbda virus, these organizations respond quickly in an attempt to isolate the virus and stop its propagation. And then they work on finding its origin.

In addition to these organizations, there are literally hundreds of others focused on more granular issues. There are groups that oversee the development of protocols, and other groups that come up with the names that we're going to call those protocols. There are legal organizations calling the shots and lobbying for various and sundry laws governing the Internet. There are organizations overseeing the dispersal and movement of email, newsgroups, and the World Wide Web. It goes on and on. One organization that does a wonderful job of overseeing a large number of these groups is the Internet Society (ISOC). To get a good overview of its responsibilities and ongoing projects, visit its Web site at http://www.isco.org.

CHAPTER SUMMARY

By now, I'm sure you realize that the Internet is an extremely complex entity. In some respects, it has taken on a life of its own, perpetually growing and occupying more virtual space. In this chapter, I examined a bit of the infrastructure of the Internet. Key features covered in this chapter are some of the administrative procedures involved in acquiring and maintaining an Internet presence, as well as how the millions of interconnected devices around the world make the concept of the Internet a reality.

BRAIN DRAIN

1. List the intermediate levels across which two machines communicating over the Internet must travel.
2. Describe in as much detail as you can the structure of an ISP backbone.
3. Discuss the differences between origin of content and on-line content.
4. List as many organizations as you can that are involved in administering, policing, and protecting the Internet.
5. Think of as many people as you can who have claimed to invent the Internet.

THE 64K$ QUESTIONS

1. Who invented the Internet?
   a. Al Gore
   b. JCR Licklider
   c. ISOC
   d. Nobody. It just grew.
2. Which of the following was the first network to span a nation?
   a. CSNET
   b. ARPANET

    c. NFSNET

    d. BITNET

3. The intermediate level that moves user data from the modem to the ISP is called _____.

    a. The user's datacom

    b. The ISP's POP

    c. User services

    d. The local loop carrier

4. The distribution of IP addresses in handled by _____.

    a. InterNIC

    b. ISOC

    c. ICAN

    d. CERN

5. The page you view when browsing the Internet is an example of _____.

    a. On-line content

    b. Origin of content

    c. User services

    d. Host services

6. Information posted on the Internet automatically forfeits all copyright protection.

    a. True

    b. False

7. Network Access Points are _____.

    a. The links between the user and the ISP

    b. Entry points to the Internet backbone located in major metropolitan areas

    c. A link between every ISP and the Internet backbone

    d. The major companies who provide the infrastructure used by the Internet

8. The local telephone company is considered to be _____.

    a. The user's datacom

    b. The local loop carrier

    c. The Network Access Point

    d. The regional provider

9. A major virus has just struck the Internet, bringing many servers down. Which organization is likely to be the first to jump into action?

   a. IEPG

   b. NANOG

   c. IANA

   d. CERT

10. The user-friendly name given to a particular Internet site is the _____. (Choose all that apply.)

    a. ISBN

    b. Domain name

    c. Web page address

    d. URL

11. Because of the work of Leonard Kleinrock, the Internet was developed by private companies without any intervention from the government.

    a. True

    b. False

12. The Transmission Control Protocol was first described by _____.

    a. Leonard Kleinrock

    b. Cerf and Kahn

    c. Vincent Price

    d. Lawrence Robers

13. The programming language used to build most Web pages is _____.

    a. HTTP

    b. C++

    c. Java

    d. HTML

14. A DSL modem is a perfect example of _____.

    a. Origin of content

    b. The local carrier loop

    c. The user's PC

    d. The user's datacom

15. Which of the following services must be provided by your ISP?
    a. An email client
    b. Your web browser
    c. FTP services
    d. All of the above

16. Most major metropolitan areas contain at least one _____.
    a. POP
    b. Backbone
    c. NAP
    d. LCP

17. An Apache server is a form of origin of content.
    a. True
    b. False

18. The minute a major virus infestation is detected on the Internet, _____ will hop on its horse and get on the job.
    a. CERF
    b. ICAN
    c. IANA
    d. FIRST
    e. Your ISP

19. You want a block of IP addresses for your company. Who should you approach?
    a. CERF
    b. ICAN
    c. IANA
    d. FIRST
    e. Your ISP

20. You don't have a clue what organization can help you with a particular problem. Which of the following groups can help you figure that out?
    a. CERF
    b. ISOC
    c. IANA
    d. LANA
    e. Your ISP

TRICKY TERMINOLOGY

Datacom: A term coined to describe any equipment used in data communications.

Local loop carrier: A communications service provider. They provide the electronic link between geographically separated devices.

On-line content: The overall availability of resources across an intranet or the Internet.

ACRONYM ALERT

FIRST: Forum of Incident Response and Security Teams. An organization charged with maintaining the security of the Internet.

IANA: The Internet Assigned Numbers Authority. The organization that currently hands out IP addresses to those that need them.

ICANN: The Internet Corporation for Assigned Names and Numbers. One of several organizations involved in the administration of the Internet.

IEPG: The Internet Engineering and Planning Group. An organization involved in overseeing the operational control of the Internet.

InterNIC: Internet's Network Information Center. One of several organizations involved in the administration of the Internet.

ISOC: The Internet Society. The organization that oversees all the other organizations involved in managing the Internet. (Who oversees them?)

ISP: Internet Service Provider. The end user's gateway to the Internet.

NAP: Network Access Point. The entry point to one of the several large capacity circuits that transport data across the Internet.

POP: Point of Presence. The physical connection supplied by an ISP that provides access to the Internet.

APPENDICES

ANSWERS TO CHAPTER EXERCISES

Here are the answers to the odd-numbered Brain Drain and 64K$ Questions throughout the book.

CHAPTER ONE

BRAIN DRAIN

1. **In your own words, describe a bus network in detail, including its advantages, disadvantages, and limitations.**
    Answer should include, at a minimum, the following concepts:
    a. Advantages: Easy to set up and configure; minimal amount of cabling
    b. Disadvantages: Disconnection of any client on network can bring entire network down; Not very scalable, network size is limited
    c. Characteristics: Systems are linked together in a chain, one to the other; Both ends of chain must be terminated
    d. Limitations: Because of the coaxial cable used, you can only install a 10Mb/sec network; Overall size of the network will be limited by the type of cable used. If using RG58U, the total segment length, including all stations on that segment, cannot exceed 180 meters.

3. **Why would I describe Token Ring as being logically a ring, but physically a star?**
    While the data on a Token Ring network flows from one device to another in a circular fashion, the devices are hooked up through an MAU. The MAU creates the ring topology internally, whereas the devices are connected to the MAU in a star fashion, similar to that of a typical hub.

5. **Discuss why segmenting a network using switches is superior to using hubs.**

    Each port on a switch is considered a separate network segment. Each port is on its own collision domain, and data circulating the devices linked to one port cannot collide with data circulating on another port. The devices on each segment will be competing for bandwidth only with the other devices on that segment. In other words, if there is a 100Mb/sec switch, each port is a 100Mb segment. On a 100Mb/sec hub, every device hanging off of every port is competing for the same 100Mb bandwidth and has the potential to collide with every other device on the hub.

THE 64K$ QUESTIONS

1. C. A router. It is the only device on this list that can interconnect two autonomous networks. A switch can separate a larger network into smaller segments, but it is still all one network. A hub interconnects devices on a single segment, and a repeater only extends the distance capabilities of a single length of medium.

3. A. Ethernet. Technically speaking, Ethernet is a proprietary name for a technology introduced by Digital Equipment Corporation, Intel, and Xerox, many years ago. However, the name has stuck, and that is what is commonly used.

5. D. Bayonet Neil-Concelman. You'll see both A. Bayonet Nut Connector, and B. British Naval Connector used a lot. They're just not correct.

7. B. Beaconing. Beaconing is a process by which each computer on a Token Ring network summons both its upstream neighbor and its downstream neighbor, asking if it's hogging the token.

9. B. 802.3

11. C. Mesh

13. A. Unshielded twisted pair

15. B. To reduce crosstalk

17. D. IEEE

19. B. A bridge

CHAPTER TWO

BRAIN DRAIN

1. **In your own words, describe the differences between a peer-to-peer network and a client-server network.**

   Answers should indicate an awareness that peer means equal. On the P2P network, at any given moment any machine might be acting in either the client role or the server role. On a client-server network, dedicated computers or pieces of software handle the role of server.

3. **Define as best you can the concept of a domain.**

   A domain is best described as all network resources and facilities that are under the administrative control of a single administrative unit.

5. **What do I mean by pass-through authentication and how does it work?**

   Pass-through authentication occurs when a trust relationship exists between two domains. If the local domain cannot resolve a logon request, before denying access to the user, that user's credentials are forwarded to the trusted domain for authentication.

THE 64K$ QUESTIONS

1. D. An application or device requesting services on a network.
3. C. Share level permissions
5. C. IPX/SPX
7. B. Nontransitive
9. D. The NOS uses a unique number assigned to each account to identify that account. Re-creating the account generated a new number.
11. B. Outlook Express
13. B. A workgroup and D. Peer-to-peer
15. D. A unique set of credentials
17. D. Active Directory
19. B. Passthrough Authentication

CHAPTER THREE

BRAIN DRAIN

1. **Describe in your own words the difference between bounded and unbounded media.**

   At a minimum, the answer should include that unbounded media are those that have no direct physical connection between hosts. In other words, these are the wireless media. Bounded media directly connect the host by way of some form of cabling. More detailed answers would include that bounded media includes fiber-optic or copper cable, and unbounded media includes infrared, laser, radio, and microwave.

3. **How many transmission modes can you think of for sending encoded data over an electrical signal running on copper wire?**

   These would include simplex, half duplex, and full duplex.

THE 64K$ QUESTIONS

1. Answers B. Scatter infrared and C. Microwave are both correct. These are unbounded, or wireless media. A is copper cabling and B uses fiber-optics cable.

3. B. Wireless networking.

5. A. Radio

7. B. Analog. While the data being sent may be in digital form, the carrier signal that transports it is analog. The same can be said of A. Physical. Crosstalk is a phenomenon that occurs *because* you're moving the signal over an electrical current, but it does not represent the signal itself.

9. C. Connect fiber optics to a transceiver.

11. D. Networks are limited to 10MB/s throughput

13. B. Frequency modulation

15. B. False

17. C. Crosstalk

19. B. EIA/TIA

CHAPTER FOUR

BRAIN DRAIN

1. **Develop your own analogy that best describes what a protocol is and what its functions include.**

   Protocols translate data into a format that is mutually acceptable to both ends of the communication, and also incorporate procedures and methods of transmitting and receiving that both parties understand.

3. **Why would understanding the OSI layers give you a head start in troubleshooting network issues?**

   Different processes occur at each layer. By knowing what goes on at each layer, when a process fails you can begin by checking the devices and protocols that operate in the same layer.

THE 64K$ QUESTIONS

1. A, C, and D are all correct. Who or what company developed a particular standard has nothing to do with layering.

3. E. The Network Layer. In a way, this is a trick question. As you will see in later chapters of the book, there are a number of different methods of logical addressing, including network and host addresses, port numbers, and sockets. The answer that CompTIA would be looking for here though, would be the Network Layer. Those are the logical addresses that network administrators assign.

5. F. The Data Link Layer

7. F. The Data Link Layer

9. None of them, actually. D. 802.5 is the committee that used to oversee Token Ring, but that committee is now in permanent hibernation.

11. D. Network

13. B. The transport layer

15. B. False

17. B. Data Link

19. C. Data Link

CHAPTER FIVE

BRAIN DRAIN

1. **List as many functions of the Physical Layer as you can think of.**

   The physical layer turns data into energy for transmission. The Physical Signaling component defines electromagnetic or optical properties and encoding schema. The Physical Medium Attachment component defines the properties of transceivers.

3. **Explain in your own words the differences between synchronous and asynchronous communication.**

   Asynchronous communication does not require a defined logical circuit to be established, nor does it wait for acknowledgments of each packet that goes out. It just throws its data onto the wire and hopes it gets there. Synchronous communication sets up a logical circuit and employs some form of transmit-reply mechanism through which the receiving device acknowledges the receipt and integrity of each packet it receives.

THE 64K$ QUESTIONS

1. A. PLS

3. C. PMA

5. Both B. Parity information is used for error checking, and D. The transmitting device throws data out onto the medium and hopes that it gets there, are correct. Note that parity is only an error checking mechanism and can do nothing to correct errors.

7. B. It is more accurate.

9. C. Several microwave carriers are managed by a single transponder.

11. A. Defining the physical cables used by the network and B. Determining an encoding mechanism

13. A. Pulse signaling

15. B. Asynchronous

17. D. Asynchronous communications sends only one byte at a time. It just adds extra bits.

19. A. Adding up all the 1s in a packet and storing the value in the trailer.

CHAPTER SIX

BRAIN DRAIN

1. **In your own words, list and describe the various functions of the Data Link Layer.**

    Answers should include physical addressing, network topology, network access mechanisms, error correction, and flow control.

3. **Write out an example of a typical MAC address and define what the two components of this address are.**

    A MAC address consists of six pairs of hexadecimal characters, such as 01 0B 00 C6 B1 00. These characters represent a 48-bit address. The first three pairs, or 24 bits, are the Organizational Unique Identifier; the remaining three pairs are a serial number assigned by the manufacturer.

5. **Describe the process of beaconing, as used by Token Ring.**

    When a device on the ring has not received the token for a time that exceeds the token's TTL, it sends a directed signal to both its upstream neighbor and downstream neighbor. These devices in turn transmit to their upstream and downstream neighbors until the offending device has been located. The MAU will then bypass the port to which the offending device is attached. The active monitor will then generate a new token.

THE 64K$ QUESTIONS

1. Both A. Switches and C. Bridges are Layer 2 devices.
3. D. APs (Access Points)
5. C. Round-robin
7. A, C, and D are all forms of error detection. B. Transmitting a NACK, is a form of error notification not detection.
9. D. Sliding window
11. B. Network topology, C. Error notification, and E. Flow control
13. C. Bridges and E. Switches
15. A. The hard-coded address on a NIC
17. B. Organizational unit numbers and D. Interface serial numbers
19. A. Only one device can occupy the medium at a time.

CHAPTER SEVEN

BRAIN DRAIN

1. **List as many functions of the Network Layer as you can.**
   The answers should include logical addressing of hosts, routing, best path determination, address translation, and congestion control.

3. **What are the minimum fields necessary to build a routing table, and what additional fields can be added by some protocols?**
   A minimum of two fields is needed. The IP Address Prefix and the Next Hop are required fields. Some protocols also include other fields such as a metric field, a netmask field, or a gateway address.

5. **Explain how a router using EGP begins the process of building its routing tables.**
   As soon as a router is up and running for the first time, it sends out a broadcast with a neighbor acquisition packet. This packet includes its hello interval and its poll interval. Neighboring routers will respond with similar information and then transmit their routing tables.

THE 64K$ QUESTIONS

1. C. 10
3. C. 65,534
5. C. It plays no role in routing at all. The process of routing involves finding the correct network. Once the packet arrives at the destination, the MAC address will be used on a local level to identify the correct machine.
7. C. 255.255.0.0
9. B. Run a neighbor acquisition function.
11. D. Packet
13. A. Latency
15. C. 48
17. D. Multicast addresses
19. C. 128

CHAPTER EIGHT

BRAIN DRAIN

1. **List as many of the functions of the Transport Layer as you can.**

   Insertion of port numbers (logical end-to-end addressing), disassembly and reassembly of messages into segments, flow control, end-to-end error detection and recovery, directing the transmission of ACKs and NACKs.

3. **Discuss the differences between connection-oriented and connectionless services.**

   A connectionless service is not concerned with reliability of data transfer. It throws its data out onto the wire and just assumes it will get there. A connection-oriented service wants to be sure the data gets there. It will establish a virtual connection between the communicating devices, and receiving devices will acknowledge the receipt of all frames that arrive.

5. **Describe in detail how sliding window flow control works.**

   Several frames are transmitted before waiting for the ACKs to come flooding in. If the ACKs received represent only a portion of the frames transmitted, the transmitting device can adjust its window downward, transmitting only the number of frames for which it received ACKs.

THE 64K$ QUESTIONS

1. C. A logical address of a process or application
3. C. Encapsulation
5. B. Connection-oriented
7. B. False. In the Transport Layer, errors that occur in the transmission of frames are detected and corrected. Bit level detection is done in Data Link.
9. B. The client sends a SYN packet
11. B. Adding a CRC trailer to the end of the packet
13. D. Inserting port numbers for applications
15. C. A socket embeds the IP address of the intended recipient
17. A. A 16-bit port
19. D. It cleans up its own mess before sending it out to the world.

CHAPTER NINE

BRAIN DRAIN

1. **List as many functions of the Session Layer as you can.**
   Answers should indicate that the student understands that the Session Layer establishes and releases connections between hosts and also provides dialogue management and synchronization.

3. **Discuss the differences between a session and a dialogue.**
   A session is defined by the entire time two devices maintain the same virtual link, exchanging information. A dialogue is an exchange of information between the two devices. Several dialogues can occur during a session.

THE 64K$ QUESTIONS

1. C. A primitive
3. A. True
5. Both B and D. Synchronize Major and Resynchronize both reestablish connection IDs.
7. Both A. A server reset, and D. A system crash, are unexpected events
9. C. Tokens
11. D. Providing dialogue management and synchronization
13. B. Dialogue
15. B. Network
17. D. A randomly generated number
19. A. The next number in a sequential list of numbers that begins with a randomly generated number

CHAPTER TEN

BRAIN DRAIN

1. **List as many functions of the Presentation Layer as you can.**
   The Presentation Layer does data format conversion, file format determination, compression, and encryption.

3. Define in your own terms the difference between abstract syntax and transfer syntax.

Abstract syntax describes the type of data that you are dealing with. A sound clip and a graphics file are both examples of abstract syntax. Transfer syntax is the format the data will take as it makes its way from host to host, including any compression and encryption that may be applied.

5. In as much detail as you can, describe how an application differs from a process.

An application is a program that a user installs on a computer and runs in order to perform a specific function (or play a game). A process is a specific thread of code *from* any given application that is being run at that moment in time.

THE 64K$ QUESTIONS

1. E : Transfer syntax
3. B. Run length encoding
5. A. CASE, or Common Application Specific Element
7. D. A thread of code from an application currently being run.
9. C. .rll. As far as I know the .rll file extension does not exist. Jpg and gif are file extensions that represent graphics files, while mpeg (or .mpg) are combined audio/video clips. The extensions themselves are acronyms for the compression scheme used. JPG is a three-letter derivation of JPEG, which is the Joint Photographic Experts Group. MPEG stands for Motion Picture Expert Group and GIF is short for Graphics Interchange Format.
11. B. Telnet
13. B. False
15. B. Presentation
17. D. .tif
19. Which of the following file formats uses lossy compression?

    C. .jpg

CHAPTER ELEVEN

BRAIN DRAIN

1. **Discuss the differences between the TCP protocol and the IP protocol and how they relate to one another.**

   TCP is designed to provide end-to-end services, assuring that data moves from one device to another in an orderly fashion, at an acceptable speed, and intact. IP provides the internetworking functions required to locate devices on the network.

3. **Explain how the subnet mask differentiates between the host portion of an IP address and the network portion.**

   The subnet mask consists of a series of 1s followed by a series of 0s. The network portion of an IP address hides behind the 1s and the host portion hides behind the 0s.

5. **How do the Process/Application protocols differ from the other protocols in the TCP/IP suite?**

   Process/Application protocols and utilities are not concerned with moving data over the wire. They are concerned with preparing data for its journey.

THE 64K$ QUESTIONS

1. B. DARPA, the Defense Advanced Research Projects Agency
3. C. Internet
5. C. 192.168.0.1
7. Both B. IMAP4 and C. SMTP are email transmission protocols.
9. B. IP
11. C. TCP
13. B. 1981
15. B. 4
17. B. 4
19. B. The address of the wire

CHAPTER TWELVE

BRAIN DRAIN

1. **Write out on a sheet of paper as many items as you can think of that can be configured into your TCP/IP settings in the Windows Network Applet.**

    IP Address and Subnet Mask are required. Other optional items include WINS Server, DNS Server, and a Gateway.

3. **You have network address of 142.15.0.0. You want to subnet it down into a minimum of twelve networks. What is your subnet mask? Also list each new network address along with its range of host addresses and its broadcast address.**

    This is a Class B address. To get 12 addresses, you need to borrow 4 bits from the Host portion of the address and move it over to the network portion, therefore your new subnet mask is 255.255.240.0. We have 4 bits remaining in the first octet assigned to hosts, so our network addresses will increment in units of 16. Our first network address will be 142.15.16.0 and move up from there. You should have a table of addresses identical to the one below.

Subnet	Mask	Subnet Size	Host Range	Broadcast Address
142.15.0.0	255.255.240.0	4094	142.15.0.1 to 142.15.15.254	142.15.15.255
142.15.16.0	255.255.240.0	4094	142.15.16.1 to 142.15.31.254	142.15.31.255
142.15.32.0	255.255.240.0	4094	142.15.32.1 to 142.15.47.254	142.15.47.255
142.15.48.0	255.255.240.0	4094	142.15.48.1 to 142.15.63.254	142.15.63.255
142.15.64.0	255.255.240.0	4094	142.15.64.1 to 142.15.79.254	142.15.79.255
142.15.80.0	255.255.240.0	4094	142.15.80.1 to 142.15.95.254	142.15.95.255
142.15.96.0	255.255.240.0	4094	142.15.96.1 to 142.15.111.254	142.15.111.255
142.15.112.0	255.255.240.0	4094	142.15.112.1 to 142.15.127.254	142.15.127.255
142.15.128.0	255.255.240.0	4094	142.15.128.1 to 142.15.143.254	142.15.143.255
142.15.144.0	255.255.240.0	4094	142.15.144.1 to 142.15.159.254	142.15.159.255
142.15.160.0	255.255.240.0	4094	142.15.160.1 to 142.15.175.254	142.15.175.255
142.15.176.0	255.255.240.0	4094	142.15.176.1 to 142.15.191.254	142.15.191.255
142.15.192.0	255.255.240.0	4094	142.15.192.1 to 142.15.207.254	142.15.207.255
142.15.208.0	255.255.240.0	4094	142.15.208.1 to 142.15.223.254	142.15.223.255
142.15.224.0	255.255.240.0	4094	142.15.224.1 to 142.15.239.254	142.15.239.255
142.15.240.0	255.255.240.0	4094	142.15.240.1 to 142.15.255.254	142.15.255.255

5. **Explain why, on a network running DHCP, Ipconfig can help a Network Administrator roll out a network configuration change more rapidly.**

   The network administrator can add many configuration changes to the DHCP options and have DHCP reconfigure the client workstations automatically the next time a new IP address is assigned. The network administrator can force the workstations to be reconfigured by resetting the IP address lease to 0. The next time each machine on the network restarts, it will get its new configuration.

THE 64K$ QUESTIONS

1. Both A. An IP address, and C. A subnet mask, are required. D. A DNS server address is an option. DHCP servers are found through broadcast messages.

3. B. 255.255.240.0

5. C. Tracert

7. B. From the command prompt, type IPCONFIG /RELEASE_ALL, then type IPCONFIG /RENEW_ALL

9. C. /T

11. C. WIN95

13. C. Device A will be denied access.

15. C. $2^x - 2$

17. C. Classless interdomain routing

19. A. NAT

CHAPTER THIRTEEN

BRAIN DRAIN

1.   **Describe in detail a complete IPX/SPX address.**

     An IPX address consists of a 32-bit network address assigned by the administrator, a 48-bit host address derived from the MAC address of the interface, and a 16-bit socket number.

3.   **Explain why NetBEUI would not be the protocol of choice in a larger network.**

     NetBEUI is not routable. Therefore, you would be limited to the number of hosts allowed by your network class. Also, even if you have a Class B address, all of your hosts would have to be on a single subnet. Not good.

5.   **Compare and contrast the AppleTalk Suite to what you learned about TCP/IP.**

     Both suites have protocols that provide network messaging services and utilities that use those services that can help the network administrator troubleshoot problems on the network. Both suites have protocols that are used for both connectionless and connection-oriented communications. However, the logical address schemes used by the two suites are not at all similar. And while both suites use a function that they call a port, the two terms mean different things.

THE 64K$ QUESTIONS

1.   C. Internetwork Packet Exchange/Sequenced Packet Exchange
3.   B. Sockets
5.   C. 127
7.   D. Datagrams
9.   A. DDP. Use of the long header provides routing information. RTMP handles routing table management functions.
11. D. Xerox
13. A. True
15. D. Socket
17. A. Datagram
19. B. The Name Binding protocol

CHAPTER FOURTEEN

BRAIN DRAIN

1. **List as many protocols as you can that are specific to remote communications.**

   Your list should include, at a minimum, PPP, SLIP, VPN, and PPTP. For more complete lists, include RDP and ICA.

3. **Why is CHAP a better protocol to use than PAP if security is an issue?**

   CHAP requires the client requesting logon services to provide a predefined "secret." If this information is not provided, authentication is denied. Also, the logon server can be configured with a maximum number of failed attempts, after which the account will be locked out.

5. **Explain the concept of the VPN.**

   A virtual private network, or VPN, is a secure virtual connection over the Internet. Connections are made using the PPTP protocol and all data transmitted or received is encrypted and encapsulated into IP packets.

THE 64K$ QUESTIONS

1. C. PPTP
3. D. Packet switching
5. E. None of the above. The correct answer would be two 64K B-channels and one 16K D-channel.
7. B. Layer 2
9. B. DUN and D. PPP
11. C. PPTP
13. B. It transmitted logon credentials in plain text.
15. D. All processing and storage is done on the server side. Only screenshots are passed on to the client computer.
17. B. 128Kb/s
19. B. DUN

CHAPTER FIFTEEN

BRAIN DRAIN

1. **How many ways can you think of in which your network is in danger?**

   Penetration from the outside (both known and unknown users), penetration from the inside (both known and unknown users), viruses, physical loss of data, corruption of data, theft of data (through unauthorized copying, printing, or transmission of data), and physical destruction of the equipment housing the data.

3. **Describe in as much detail as you can a good password policy.**

   A good password policy should define the minimum length a password must be, how frequently passwords must be changed, and how many changes must occur before a given password can be reused. For even more security, the administrator can also require that a combination of letters and numbers be used and that letters be a combination of upper-case and lower-case.

5. **Describe the different ways a firewall can protect your network.**

   Firewalls can block incoming or outgoing transmissions based on a very large number of criteria. These include IP address, domain, protocol, port number, and many others. They can hide internal IP addresses behind that of the firewall device. The three forms of firewall are Packet Filtering, Stateful Inspection, and Proxy.

THE 64K$ QUESTIONS

1. E. These are all security issues

3. D. User level security

5. B. Packet filtering

7. Both C. A combination of upper-case and lower-case letters, and D. A combination of letters and numbers. A is not possible because the maximum password length is fifteen characters.

9. C. Stateful Inspection

11. B. False

    C. Only if you'll lose your job if you don't. Looks tempting, but look how many CEOs went to jail last year.

13. D. You need to train the users in security measures.

15. D. The SID

17. C. Full Control allows the user to take ownership of files.

19. D. They don't require a password at all.

Chapter Sixteen

Brain Drain

1. **Discuss in detail the difference between backup/recovery and fault tolerance.**

    Backup/recovery is the process of creating copies of critical data so that in the event of data loss it can be recovered. Fault tolerance defines a number of different steps that can be taken to prevent data loss to begin with.

3. **Think about the different ways a virus can corrupt the MBR of a hard drive and list them on a sheet of paper.**

    A virus could alter the code that defines the file system in use. It can alter or delete fields from the partition tables, and it can alter or delete the pointer to the OS.

5. **Describe as many fault tolerance methods as you can think of.**

    Software fault tolerance strategies include RAID and duplicate FAT and DET. Hardware fault tolerance can include hot-swappable components, including hard drives, power supplies, and certain types of PCI devices. One might also use hot spares in some cases. Fault tolerance can also include cluster servers and/or backup servers.

The 64K$ Questions

1. A. Int13h

3. A. 2GB

5. D. DAT

7. B. Digital linear tape

9. D. RAID 5

11. B. False

13. C. 10

15. B. The master boot record

17. C. AIC

19. C. Hot site

Chapter Seventeen

Brain Drain

1. **Working with a partner, design your own network from the ground up. Make a list of twenty users in at least four groups and outline your naming conventions, addressing scheme, and network policies.**

    The plan should include a description of the topology and an addressing scheme. Look for useful naming conventions in both the user accounts and computer names used.

3. **Define a good computer naming convention and describe as many reasons as you can why this is important.**

    The naming convention should identify the device and its function, and provide a hint as to its location.

5. **Describe your idea of the ideal server room and your reasons why.**

    This will vary greatly, but I'm looking for answers that describe protection from environmental concerns and easy access to cable harnesses and equipment for fast maintenance.

The 64K$ Questions

1. C. Manager. This is the only term on this list not used by a common NOS for a built-in account.

3. A. ESD

5. B. 1.75

7. C. 2000

9. A. True

11. C. Who wants to try and figure out whether CS210334 has the files she needs instead of RDP12334?

13. D. Who wants to remember that the computer that holds the needed file is 00011000 00001111 11010100 11110000?

15. B. False

17. C. DHCP

19. D. A spark you can't feel can seriously damage an IC.

CHAPTER EIGHTEEN

BRAIN DRAIN

1. **List the three forms of documentation a network engineer should maintain, and explain the importance of each.**

   Documentation for the hardware and applications installed on your network, in case problems arise with either. A good reference library for looking up what little information you don't already have stored in your own head. And finally, a detailed description of your network showing the topology of the network; location of devices on the network; addressing schemes; RAS, WAN, and Internet connections (with IP addresses); and all contact information for all vendors.

3. **List as many different pieces of information as you can that you should record concerning pieces of hardware in your network.**

   Type and brand of hardware, serial number, where purchased, contact information for vendor, warranty information, contact information for tech support, and Web site.

5. **What are some hardware maintenance routines that can keep you out of trouble?**

   ScanDisk and Defrag.

THE 64K$ QUESTIONS

1. D. ARP. When you are installing an NOS for the first time, you are not really ready to start resolving other addresses on the network just yet.

3. B. Event Viewer

5. A. Defrag

7. D. All of the above

9. D. Signature files

11. A. The Installation CD for the NOS

13. C. Router ports and D. A printer server

15. D. In a centralized location

17. B. Scandisk and D. Defrag

19. D. Service packs are cumulative collections of patches over a period of time.

CHAPTER NINETEEN

BRAIN DRAIN

1. **List each step of the Network+ Troubleshooting Model, along with a brief description of each step.**

   The steps are as follows:
   - Identifying the problem
   - Re-creating the problem
   - Isolating the cause of the problem
   - Deciding on a solution
   - Testing the solution
   - Applying the fix
   - Following up

3. **Describe the differences between a hardware-based troubleshooting tool and one that is software based.**

   A hardware-based tool is one that you can hold in your hand and/or carry around in your briefcase and that is usable wherever you happen to be, even if where you happen to be is nowhere near a computer, such as on a ladder with your head above the ceiling panels. A software-based tool is run from the server or a workstation and requires access to a computer, and probably to the network.

5. **Explain when you would use Network Monitor to help out with a problem and when Performance Monitor would be the application of choice.**

   Network Monitor is useful in diagnosing issues related to protocols, identifying the source of particular packets, and other items related to the packet structure. Performance Monitor deals with hardware and service-related issues.

THE 64K$ QUESTIONS

1. C. Ask the user specific open-ended questions about the problem at hand.

3. Both B. You should always assume that users are less knowledgeable than you and may have inadvertently missed something, and D. There may be error messages specific to the problem that will point you in a specific direction. It is not inherently bad to assume that the end users are less knowledgeable than you are. A little tact is in order, however. You should not assume that they don't know what they're talking about. A user with good computer knowledge can be a vast help in the trouble-shooting process. And even experienced users may fail to take note of error messages.

5. A. Try the obvious first

7. D. Performance Monitor

9. D. Ipconfig

11. C. Recreate the problem, if possible

13. A. To catch the user doing something wrong

15. B. False

17. D. A time domain reflectometer

19. B. Network Monitor

CHAPTER TWENTY

BRAIN DRAIN

1. **List the intermediate levels across which two machines communicating over the Internet must travel.**

   User's PC, user's datacom, the local loop carrier, the ISP, point of presence, user services, ISP backbone, on-line content, and origin of content.

3. **Discuss the differences between origin of content and on-line content.**

   On-line content is a general description for everything out there that is available to the Internet user. Origin of content represents a specific resource or document on the Internet.

5. **Think of as many people as you can who have claimed to invent the Internet.**

You didn't really expect a serious answer to this one did you?

THE 64K$ QUESTIONS

1. This can be either B or D, but not both. Essentially the Internet evolved over time. However, if you want to credit a specific individual with the concept, it would be J. C. R. Licklider.

3. D. The local loop carrier

5. B. Origin of content represents the actual resource accessed by the user.

7. B. Entry points to the Internet backbone located in major metropolitan areas

9. D. CERT, or the Computer Emergency Response Teams, will be on the job long before the average user even knows there's a problem.

11. B. False

13. D. HTML

15. C. FTP services

17. B. False

19. E. Your ISP (IANA is responsible for assigning them, but they don't talk to individual users.)

COMPLETE LISTING OF WELL-KNOWN PORTS

While some of the most commonly used ports were described in the text, there comes a time when TCP/IP or some other application or protocol will inform you that an error has occurred on this or that port. There isn't space in the book for me to discuss all 65,536 ports, but I do think that a list of the well-known ports is in order. This information was extracted directly from IANA's Web site and translated into something the average human could understand. For more details, including how to have a port assigned to an application you may be developing, visit www.iana.org/assignments/port-numbers.

A few comments are in order concerning the following list. IANA did not identify the purpose of each and every service, daemon, or protocol for which it assigned a port. It simply assigned the port and recorded to what function that port had been assigned. Many of these ports were assigned for proprietary functions, and information was simply not available for some. Where I was able to trace a port's function down to a particular source, but not specifically identify the function, I indicated that the port was proprietary. Where I could find no information whatsoever on the port, or where the information I do have is incomplete or ambiguous, I marked that port with a (?).

Why is this information useful? Hackers use specialized software called *port scanners* or *port sniffers* to identify open ports on a target machine. When you configure a firewall, some ports are left open by default. If you have no need for a particular service, then that port should be closed.

Complete Listing of Well-Known Ports

Port	Protocol	Port	Protocol
0	Reserved	29	Message Internet Cache Protocol (MSG-ICP)
1	TCP Port Service Multiplexer (TCPMUX)	30	
2	Management Utility	31	MSG Authentication
3	Compression Process	32	
4		33	Display Support Protocol
5	Remote Job Entry	34	
6		35	Any private printer server
7	Internet Control Messaging Protocol Echo Reply	36	
		37	Time Protocol (TIME)
8		38	Internet Route Access Protocol (RAP)
9	Discard		
10		39	Resource Location Protocol (RLP)
11	Systat, A Statistical Analysis Program	40	
		41	Graphics
12		42	Name/Nameserver Host Name Server
13	TCP's Daytime protocol		
14		43	Whois
15	TCP/IP's Network Statistics (NETSTAT) protocol	44	Multi-media Mail (MPM) FLAGS Protocol
16		45	Message Processing Module (receive)
17	Quote, Quote of the Day		
18	Remote Write Protocol (RWP), Send Message – Send Protocol	46	MPM (default send)
		47	Network Independent (NI) FTP
19	Character Generator Protocol (CHARGEN)	48	Digital Audit Daemon
		49	Terminal Access Controller Access Control System (TACACS) login host protocol
20	File Transfer Protocol (FTP), Data		
21	File Transfer Protocol (FTP), control	50	Remote Mail Checking Protocol RCMP
22	Secure Shell (SSH)		
23	Telnet	51	Internet Messaging Programs (IMP) Logical Address Maintenance
24	Any private mail system		
25	Simple Mail Transfer Protocol (SMTP)	52	Xerox Network Services (XNS) Time Protocol
26		53	Domain Name System (DNS)
27	National Software Works (NSW) User System	54	XNS Clearinghouse
		55	Information Sciences Institute (ISI) Graphics Language protocol
28			

Port	Protocol	Port	Protocol
56	XNS Authentication	86	Micro Focus Cobol
57	Mail Transfer Protocol (MTP)	87	Any private terminal link
58	XNS Mail	88	Kerberos
59	Network File Access (NFILE)	89	SU/MIT Telnet Gateway
60		90	DNSIX Security Attribute Token Map (90 is being used unofficially by Pointcast)
61	NERS Internal (NI) MAIL		
62	Access Control Area (ACA) Services	91	MIT Dover Spooler
63	Whois	92	Network Printing Protocol
64	Communications Integrator (COVIA)	93	Device Control Protocol
		94	Tivoli Object Dispatcher
65	TACACS-Database Service	95	Super Duper (SUPDUP) Telnet
66	Oracle Sequenced Query Language (SQL)	96	DIXIE Protocol
		97	Swift Remote Virtual File Protocol
67	Bootstrap Protocol (BootP) server	98	Terminal Access Controller (TAC) News
68	Bootstrap Protocol client		
69	Trivial File Transfer Protocol (TFTP)	99	Metagram Relay
70	Gopher	100	(unauthorized use)
71	Remote Job Service	101	Hostname Server
72	Remote Job Service	102	ISO Transport Service Access Point (TSAP)
73	Remote Job Service		
74	Remote Job Service	103	Genesis Point-to-Point Trans Net
75	Any private dial-out service	104	American College of Radiology/ National Electronic Manufacturers Association (ACR-NEMA) Digital Imaging & Communications 3.00
76	Distributed External Object Store		
77	Any private Remote Job Entry (RJE) service		
78	Virtual Environment Testbed (VET) TCP	105	Computing and Communications Services Organization (CCSO) Name Server Protocol
79	Finger	105	Mailbox Name Name Server
80	HyperText Transfer Protocol (HTTP)	106	3COM-TSMUX (TS Multiplexing)
81	HOSTS2 Name Server	107	Remote Telnet Service
82	XFER Utility	108	Systems Network Architecture (SNA) Gateway Access Server
83	Massachussetts Institute of Technology Modeling Laboratory (MIT ML)	109	Post Office Protocol, version 2 (POP2)
84	Common Trace Facility	110	Post Office Protocol, version 3 (POP3)
85	MIT ML Device	111	Portmapper

Complete Listing of Well-Known Ports *(continued)*

Port	Protocol
112	Man-Computer Interactive Data Access System (MCIDAS) Data Transmission Protocol
113	Identification Protocol
114	Audio News Multicast
115	Simple File Transfer Protocol (SFTP)
116	Advanced System Network Architecture Remote Extensions (ANSA REX) Notify
117	Unix to Unix Copy Program (UUCP)
118	SQL Services
119	Network News Transfer Protocol (NNTP)
120	Coherent File Distribution Protocol (CFDP)
121	Encore Expedited Remote Procedure Call
122	SMAKYNET
123	Network Time Protocol (NTP)
124	ANSA REX Trader
125	Locus PC-Interface Net Map Server
126	Unisys Unitary Login
127	Locus PC-Interface Conn Server
128	Generic Security Services (GSS) X License Verification
129	Password Generator Protocol (PWDGEN)
130	Cisco FNATIVE
131	Cisco TNATIVE
132	Cisco SYSMAINT
133	Statistics Server (STATSERV)
134	INGRES-NET Service
135	Distributed Computing Environment (DCE) endpoint resolution

Port	Protocol
136	PROFILE Naming System
137	NETBIOS Name Service
138	NETBIOS Datagram Service
139	NETBIOS Session Service
140	Employee and Facility Information System (EmFIS) Data Service
141	EmFIS Control Service
142	Britton-Lee Intelligent Database Machine (IDM)
143	Interactive Mail Access Protocol (IMAP)
144	Universal Management Architecture
145	User Authentication and Access Control (UAAC) Protocol
146	Transport Protocol 0 (TP0) bridge between TCP and X25
147	Industry Standards Organization Internet Protocol (ISO-IP)
148	Jargon
149	AED 512 (a model of color graphics terminal) Emulation Service
150	Sequenced Query Language over the Network (SQL-NET)
151	High-level Entity Management System (HEMS)
152	Background File Transfer Program (BFTP)
153	Simple Gateway Monitoring Protocol (SGMP)
154	NETSC™ Products
155	NETSC Development
156	SQL Service
157	KNET/VM™ Command/Message Protocol
158	Distributed Mail Service Protocol (DMSP)
159	Netscape Security Services (NSS) Routing

Port	Protocol	Port	Protocol
160	SGMP Traps	190	Gateway Access Control Protocol
161	Simple Network Management Protocol (SNMP)	191	Prospero Directory Service
		192	OSU Network Monitoring System
162	SNMP traps	193	Spider Remote Monitoring Protocol
163	Common Management Information Protocol (CMIP) TCP Manager	194	Internet Relay Chat Protocol
		195	Department of Defense Intelligence Information System Network Security for Information Exchange (DNSIX) Network Level Module Audit
164	CMIP TCP Agent		
165	Xerox		
166	Sirius Systems		
167	Netware Asynchronous Messaging Protocol (NAMP)	196	DNSIX Session Mgt Module Audit Redir
168	Rapid Sequential Visual Display (RSVD)	197	Directory Location Service
		198	Directory Location Service Monitor
169	SEND	199	SNMP Multiplexer (SMUX)
170	Network PostScript	200	IBM System Resource Controller
171	Network Innovations Multiplex	201	AppleTalk Routing Maintenance
172	Network Innovations CL/1	202	AppleTalk Name Binding
173	Xyplex	203	AppleTalk Unused
174	Mail Queue (MAILQ)	204	AppleTalk Echo
175	VMNET™	205	AppleTalk Unused
176	GENRAD™ MUX (multiplexer)	206	AppleTalk Zone Information
177	X Display Manager Control Protocol (XDMCP)	207	AppleTalk Unused
		208	AppleTalk Unused
178	NextStep Window Server	209	The Quick Mail Transfer Protocol
179	Border Gateway Protocol (BGP)	210	Z3950 (Refers to the Information Retrieval Application Service Definition and Protocol Specification)
180	Intergraph		
181	Unify		
182	Unisys Audit Security Information Transfer Protocol (SITP)	211	Texas Instruments 914C/G Terminal
183	OCBinder	212	ATEXSSTR (A now-defunct file-sharing protocol. No more information could be found.)
184	OCServer		
185	Knowbot Information Service		
186	Kellogg Information Systems (KIS) Protocol	213	Internetwork Packet Exchange (IPX)
187	Application Communication Interface	214	Virtual Managed Programmable Workstation Communication Services (VM PWSCS)
188	Plus Five's MUMPS™		
189	Queued File Transport	215	Insignia Solutions

617

Complete Listing of Well-Known Ports *(continued)*

Port	Protocol	Port	Protocol
216	Computer Associates Int'l License Server	266	SCSI on ST
217	dBASE Unix	267	Tobit™ David Service Layer
218	Message Posting Protocol (MPP)	268	Tobit David Replica
219	Unisys ARP	269–279	
220	Interactive Mail Access Protocol, version 3 (IMAP3)	280	HTTP Management (HTTP-MGNT_0)
221	Berkeley rlogind with SPX authentication	281	Personal Link
222	Berkeley rshd with SPX authentication	282	Cable Port A/X
223	Certificate Distribution Center	283	Resource Capability Protocol (RESCAP)
242	Direct	284	CORERJD (?)
243	Survey Measurement	285	
244	Dayna	286	Foreign Exchange Protocol, version 1 (FXP-1)
245	LINK	287	K-BLOCK
246	Display Systems Protocol	288–299	
247	Subnet Broadcast over TFTP (SUBNTBCST_TFTP)	300–307	
248	Bellhow File Handling System (BH-FHS)	308	Novastor Backup
249–255		309	EntrustTime
256	Route Access Protocol (RAP)	310	Bellhow Monitoring and Directory Service (BHMDS)
257	Secure Electronic Transaction	311	AppleShare IP WebAdmin
258	Yak Winsock Personal Chat	312	Virtual Software Library Multilink Protocol (VSLMP)
259	Efficient Short Remote Operations (ESRO)	313	Magenta Logic
260	Openport	314	Opalis Robot
261	Internet Inter-ORB Protocol (IIOP) Name Service over TLS/SSL	315	DPSI™
262	Army Company Information Systems Defense Message System (ARCISDMS)	316	decAuth
		317	Zannet
263	Heavy Directory Access Protocol (HDAP)	318	Time Stamp Protocol (TSP)
264	Border Gateway Multicast Protocol (BGMP)	319	Packet Transfer Protocol (PTP) Event
		320	PTP General
265	X-Bone Common Text Language (CTL)	321	Presence Information Protocol (PIP)
		322	Real Time Signal Processing System (RTSPS)
		323–332	

Port	Protocol	Port	Protocol
333	Texar Security Port	376	Amiga Envoy Network Inquiry Proto
334–343		377	NEC Corporation
344	Prospero Data Access Protocol	378	NEC Corporation
345	Performance Analysis Workbench	379	TIA/EIA/IS-99 modem client
346	Zebra server	380	TIA/EIA/IS-99 modem server
347	Fatmen Server	381	HP performance data collector
348	Cabletron Management Protocol	382	HP performance data managed node
349	Multicast File Transfer Protocol (MFTP)	383	HP performance data alarm manager
350	Mapping of Airline Traffic over Internet Protocol, Type A (MATIP)	384	A Remote Network Server System
351	MATIP Type B	385	IBM Application
352	Deutsche Telekom AG (DTAG)	386	ASA Message Router Object Def
353	NDSAUTH™	387	AURP, AppleTalk Update-based Routing Protocol
354	bh611	388	Unidata LDM Version 4
355	DATEX-ASN	389	LDAP, Lightweight Directory Access Protocol CLDAP, Connection-less Lightweight X500 Directory Access Protocol
356	Cloanto Net 1		
357	bhevent		
358	Shrinkwrap		
359	Tenebris Network Trace Service		
360	scoi2odialog	390	Unix Integrated Services (UIS)
361	Semantix	391	SynOptics SNMP Relay Port
362	SRS Send	392	SynOptics Port Broker Port
363	RSVP Tunnel	393	Data Interpretation System
364	Aurora CMGR	394	EMBL Nucleic Data Transfer
365	DTK	395	NETscout Control Protocol
366	SMTP, Simple Mail Transfer Protocol ODMR, On-Demand Mail Relay	396	Novell NetWare over IP
		397	Multi Protocol Trans Net
367	MortgageWare	398	Kryptolan
368	QbikGDP	399	TP2 over TCP
369	rpc2portmap	400	Workstation Solutions
370	codaauth2	401	Uninterruptible Power Supply
371	Clearcase	402	Genie Protocol
372	ListProcessor	403	Decapulization (DECAP)
373	Legent Corporation	404	NCED (?)
374	Legent Corporation	405	NCLD (?)
375	Hassle	406	Interactive Mail Support Protocol

Complete Listing of Well-Known Ports (continued)

Port	Protocol	Port	Protocol
407	Timbuktu	434	Mobile IP agent
408	Prospero Resource Manager System Manager	435	Mobile IP MN
409	Prospero Resource Manager Node Manager	436	Digital Network Architecture (DNA) CML
410	DEC Ladebug Remote Debug Protocol	437	COMSCM (?)
		438	DSFGW (?)
411	Remote MT Protocol	439	DASP (?)
412	Trap Convention Port	440	Simple Gateway Control Protocol (SGCP)
413	Storage Management Services Protocol (SMSP)	441	Digital Equipment Corporation Virtual Memory System System Management (DECVMS-SYSMGT)
414	InfoSeek		
415	BNet	442	CVC_HOSTD (?)
416	Silverplatter	443	HTTP over SSL/TLS (HTTPS)
417	Onmux	444	Simple Network Paging Protocol (SNPP)
418	Hyper-G		
419	Ariel	445	Microsoft Denial of Service (DS)
420	Society of Motion Picture and Television Engineers (SMPTE)	446	Distributed Data Management Relational Database (DDM-RDB)
421	Ariel	447	DDM Reply to Flagged Message (RFM)
422	Ariel		
423	IBM Operations Planning and Control Start	448	DDM Secure Socket Layer (SSL)
		449	Apache Server (AS) Server Mapper
424	IBM Operations Planning and Control Track	450	Terminal Server (Tserver)
		451	Cray Network Semaphore server
425	ICAD™	452	Cray SFS configuration server
426	Smart Session Description Protocol (SMARTSDP)	453	CreativeServer
		454	ContentServer
427	Service Location Protocol (SLP)	455	CreativePartnr
428	Open Communication Systems Control Access Unit (OCS_CMU)	456	Macon™ TCP
		457	Santa Cruz Operations (SCO) Help
429	OCS Access Management Unit (OCS_AMU)	458	Apple Quick Time
		459	Amateur Packet Radio Remote Command (AMPR-RCMD)
430	UTMPSD (?)		
431	UTMPCD (?)	460	Skronk™
432	IASD (?)	461	DataRampSrv
433	News Server to News Server Protocol (NNSP)	462	DataRampSrvSec

Port	Protocol	Port	Protocol
463	Alpes™	493	Transport Independent Convergence for FNA
464	Kerberos change/set password	494	POV-Ray
465	SMTP TLS/SSL	495	Intecourier
466	Digital VRC (proprietary)	496	PIM-RP-DISC (proprietary)
467	Mylex mapd (proprietary)	497	DANTZ™
468	Photuris™	498	Society for Industrial and Applied Mathematics (SIAM)
469	Radio Control Protocol (RCP)	499	ISO InterLibrary Loan (ILL) Protocol
470	Scattercast (SCX) Proxy	500	Internet Key Exchange (IKE)
471	Mondex™	501	Simple Transportation Management Framework (STMF)
472	LJK-LOGIN (?)	502	ASA-APPL-PROTO (?)
473	HYBRID-POP	503	Intrinsa
474	TN-TL-W1 (TCP) AND TN-TL-W2 (UDP) (proprietary)	504	Citadel
475	TCPNETHASPSRV (proprietary)	505	MAILBOX-LM
476	TN-TL-FD1 (proprietary)	506	OHIMSRV (?)
477	Signaling System 7 Name Server (SS7NS)	507	Certificate Request Syntax (CRS)
478	Standard Products and Services Classification (SPSC)	508	XV Time Triggered Protocol (XVTTP)
479	Internet Address Finder Server (IAFSERVER)	509	SNARE
480	IAF Database (IAFDBASE)	510	FirstClass Protocol
481	PH SERVICE	511	MYNET-AS (proprietary)
482	BGS-NSI (?)	512	Remote process execution; Used by mail system to notify users of new mail received
483	ULPNET (proprietary)		
484	Integra Software Management Environment	513	Remote Login (Rlogin)
485	Air Soft Power Burst	514	Security Issues in Network Event Logging (Syslog) Command (CMD)
486	Avian	515	Line Printer (LPR)
487	Simple Asynchronous File Transfer (SAFT)	516	Videotex
		517	
488	Generic Security Services (GSS) HTTP	518	Ntalk: An on-line "chat" protocol
489	NEST Protocol	519	unixtime
490	MICOM-PFS (proprietary)	520	Routing Information Protocol (RIP) Extended file name server
491	GO-LOGIN		
492	Transport Independent Convergence for Fujitsu Network Architecture (FNA)	521	RIP Next Generation (NG)
		522	Universal Logging Protocol (ULP)
		523	IBM-DB2

Complete Listing of Well-Known Ports (continued)

Port	Protocol	Port	Protocol
524	Network Control Protocol (NCP)	554	Real Time Streaming Protocol (RTSP)
525	Timeserver		
526	Newdate	555	Data Storage and Formatting (DFS)
527	Stock IXChange	556	Remote File System (RFS) Server
528	Customer IXChange	557	Openvms-sysipc (proprietary)
529	Internet Relay Chat Server (IRC-SERV)	558	SDNSKMP (?)
		559	TEEDTAP (?)
530	Remote Procedure Call	560	Remote Monitor data (RMONITORD)
531	Chat		
532	Readnews	561	Monitor
533	Emergency broadcasts	562	Command Character (CHCMD)
534	MegaMedia Admin	563	Network News Transfer Protocol (NNTP) over TLS/SSL
535	Internet Inter-Orb Protocol (IIOP)		
536	Opalis-rdv (proprietary)	564	Plan 9 file service
537	Networked Media Streaming Protocol (NMSP)	565	Whoami
		566	Streettalk
538	Gdomap (?)	567	Banyan RPC
539	Apertus Technologies Load Determination	568	Microsoft Shuttle
		569	Microsoft Rome
540	Unix to Unix Copy Protocol Data (UUCPD)	570	Demon
		571	Unix Demon (UDEMON)
541	UUCP-RLOGIN	572	Sonar
542	COMMERCE	573	Banyan Virtual Internet Protocol (BANYAN-VIP)
543	Kerberos Login (KLOGIN)		
544	Kerberos Remote Command (KRCMD)	574	FTP Software Agent System
		575	Versatile Multi-Media Interface (VEMMI)
545	APPLEQTCSRVR		
546	DHCPv6 client	576	Internet Protocol Device Control (IPCD)
547	DHCPv6 server		
548	AppleTalk Filing Protocol (AFP) over TCP	577	Virtual Network Access Server (VNAS)
549	Internet Discussion Forum Protocol (IDFP)	578	Internet Paperless Direct Debit (IPDD)
550	New-who	579	DECBSRV
551	Cybercash	580	SNTP Heartbeat
552	Deviceshare	581	Bundle Discovery Protocol
553	Public Information Retrieval Protocol (PIRP)	582	SCC Security

Port	Protocol	Port	Protocol
583	Philips Video-Conferencing	616	SCO System Administration Server
584	Key Server	617	SCO Desktop Administration Server
585	IMAP4+SSL	618	DEI (?) Integrated Cached Disk Arrays
586	Password Change	619	Digital Error Vector Magnitude (EVM)
587	Submission	620	SCO WebServer Manager
588	CAL	621	Errored Second, CP-bit Parity (ESCP)
589	EyeLink	622	Collaborator
590	Transparent Network Substrate (TNS) CML	623	Aux Bus Shunt
591	FileMaker Inc—HTTP Alternate Port	624	Crypto Admin
592	Eudora Set	625	DEC Data Link Monitoring (DLM)
593	HTTP RPC Map	626	ASIA
594	Transaction Processing over IP (TPIP)	627	CKS & TIVIOLI (proprietary)
595	CAB Protocol	628	Quick Mail Queuing Protocol (QMQP)
596	SMS Sending Subsystem (SMSD)	629	3Com AMP3 (proprietary)
597	PTC Name Service	630	Remote Database Access (RDA)
598	SCO Web Server Manager 3	631	Internet Printing Protocol (IPP)
599	Aeolon Core Protocol	632	Bulk Mail Preferences Protocol (BMPP)
600	Sun Inter-Process Communications (IPC) server	633	Service Status update (Sterling Software)
601	Security Issues in Network Event Logging (SYSLOG)	634	GINAD (?)
602–605		635	Realizer (RLZ) DBase
606	Cray Unified Resource Manager	636	Interdomain Access Protocol (IDAP) protocol over TLS/SSL
607	Network Queuing System (NQS)	637	Lanserver
608	Sender-Initiated/Unsolicited File Transfer	638	Multi-media Cable Network Systems (MCSN)
609	Network Peripheral Management Protocol (NPMP) trap	639	Multicast Source Discovery Protocol (MSDP)
610	NPMP local	640	Entrust-sps
611	NPMP Graphical User Interface (GUI)	641	REPCMD (?)
612	Home Network Management Protocol (HMMP) Indication	642	Efficient Mail Submission and Delivery (EMSD) over Efficient Short Remote Operations (ESRO)
613	HMMP Operation		
614	SSLshell		
615	Internet Configuration Manager	643	SANity (proprietary)

Complete Listing of Well-Known Ports *(continued)*

Port	Protocol	Port	Protocol
644	Domain-Wide Multicast Group Membership Reports (DWR)	673	CIMPLEX (Proprietary)
645	Personal Service Session Control (PSSC)	674	Application Configuration Access Protocol (ACAP)
646	Label Distribution Protocol (LDP)	675	Data Control Transfer Protocol (DCTP)
647	DHCP Failover Protocol	676	VPPS Via (Proprietary)
648	Registry Registrar Protocol (RRP)	677	Virtual Presence Protocol (VPP)
649	Aminet (proprietary)	678	GNU Generation Foundation NCP
650	Object Exhange (OBEX)	679	Multicast Reachability Monitor (MRM)
651	Institute of Electrical and Electronic Engineers Manufacturing Message Specification (IEEE MMS)	680	Entrust-aaas
		681	Entrust-aaas
652	Dynamic Tunnel Configuration Protocol (DTCP)	682	Transfer (XFR)
		683	CORBA IIOP (Proprietary)
653	Replicate Command (RepCmd)	684	CORBA IIOP SSL (Proprietary)
654	Ad hoc On-Demand Distance Vector (AODV)	685	MDC Port Mapper (Proprietary)
		686	Hardware Control Protocol Wismar
655	There is no Cabal (TINC)	687	AppleShare IP Registry (ASIPREGISTRY)
656	Software Project Management Plan (SPMP)		
		688	REALM-RUSD
657	Reliable Multicast (RMC)	689	Networked Messaging Application Protocol (NMAP)
658	TenFold		
659	URL Rendezvous	690	Vector Adaptive Transform Processing (VATP)
660	MacOS Server Admin		
661	Host Access Protocol (HAP)	691	MS Exchange Routing
662	Parallel FTP (PFTP)	692	Hyperwave-ISP
663	PureNoise	693	P-connection end (CONNENDP)
664	Secure Aux Bus	694	HA Cluster (proprietary)
665	Sun DR	695	IEEE MMS over Secure Socket Layer (IEEE-MMS-SSL)
666	Doom, Id Software		
667	Campaign contribution campaign contribution disclosures—SDR Technologies	696	RUSHD (?)
		697	Unix User ID Generator (UUIDGEN)
668	MeComm	698	Optimized Link State Routing (OLSR)
669	MeRegister		
670	VACDSM-SWS (Proprietary)	699	Access Network
671	VACDSM-APP (Proprietary)	700–703	
672	VPPS-QUA (Proprietary)	704	errlog copy/server daemon
		705	AgentX

Port	Protocol	Port	Protocol
706	Secure Internet Live Conferencing	766	
707	Borland DSJ	767	Phone
708		768	
709	Entrust Key Management Service Handler	769	Video (VID)
		770	CADlock
710	Entrust Administration Service Handler	771	Real Time Internet Protocol (RTIP)
		772	Cycleserv2
711	Tag Distribution Protocol	773	Submit
712–712		774	Rpasswd acmaint_dbd
729	IBM NetView DM/6000 Server/ Client	775	Entomb acmaint_transd
		776	Wpages
730	IBM NetView DM/6000 send TCP	777	Multilingual HTTP
731	IBM NetView DM/6000 receive TCP	778	
		779	
732–740		780	WPGS (?)
741	netGW	781–785	
742	Network based Rev Cont Sys	786	Concert
743		787	QSC (proprietary)
744	Flexible License Manager	788–799	
745		800	Multi Database Systems Daemon (MDBS_DAEMON)
746			
747	Fujitsu Device Control	801	Device
748	Russell Info Sci Calendar Manager	802–809	
749	Kerberos Administration	810	Fiber Channel Protocol (FCP)
750	Kerberos Version IV	811–827	
751	Pump	828	ITM-MCELL-S
752	Group Handling (GRH)	829	Certificate Management Protocols (CMP)
753	Remote Route Handling (RRH)		
754	Send	830–846	
755–757		847	DHCP-failover 2
758	Nlogin	848–872	
759	Connect (CON)	873	Remote Synchronization (RSYNCH)
760	Negative Send (NS)		
761	Receiver Empty (RXE)	874–885	
762	Quotad	886	ICL coNETion locate server (proprietary)
763	Cycleserv		
764	Omserv	887	ICL coNETion server info (proprietary)
765	Webster		

Complete Listing of Well-Known Ports *(continued)*

Port	Protocol	Port	Protocol
888	AccessBuilder CD Database Protocol (proprietary)	993	IMAP4 protocol over TLS/SSL
889–899		994	IRC protocol over TLS/SSL
900	OMG Initial Reference	995	POP3 protocol over TLS/SSL (was spop3)
901	System Monitoring Protocol Name Resolution (SMPNAMERES)	996	Virtual Switch Interface Network (VSINET)
902	IDEAFARM-CHAT (proprietary)	997	MAITRD (proprietary)
903	IDEAFARM-CATCH (proprietary)	998	BUSBOY PUPARP (proprietary)
904–910		999	APPLIX AC (proprietary)
911	xact-backup	1000	CADLOCK2 (proprietary)
912–988		1001–1007	
989	FTP data over TLS/SSL	1008	Sun Solaris
990	FTP control over TLS/SSL	1009	
991	Netnews Administration System (NAS)	1010	Surf
		1011–1022	
992	TELNET protocol over TLS/SSL	1023	Reserved

Note: Listings without an assignment were not yet assigned as of June of 2002.

GLOSSARY

Abstract syntax The type of data that is to be moved or stored. For instance, a music or video clip is one form of abstract syntax, while a text document is another.

Access list A collection of statements mapped to a router interface that define conditions under which packets will be permitted to pass, or denied access.

Acknowledgment number A sequence of numbers, beginning with a randomly generated number, that identifies each packet in a transmission and the order in which it goes.

Activity The most basic transfer of information that occurs in the course of a session.

Administrator The user and/or account that has full and complete privileges to do anything and everything on the network.

Agent In TCP/IP terminology, this is an application or utility that fulfills requests by gathering the information requested by a manager application.

Amplitude The relative strength of an electrical signal.

Backoff timer A logical mechanism that tells a device how long it must wait to retransmit after a collision occurs.

Backup strategy A complete plan of action detailing the hardware and software configuration used throughout an organization as well as the backup method and frequency that will be used.

Ballast The power supply that provides current to a fluorescent light fixture.

Beaconing A process Token Ring uses to find out what station has dropped from the network. Each device sends a beacon frame to both its upstream neighbor and its downstream neighbor. Once the culprit has been found, the MAU can bypass that station internally.

Bit stuffing Adding non-data information to a frame in order to bring it up to a minimum size.

Bit timing A method used by transceivers to accurately extract encoded data from an analog signal using clock cycles as a basis.

Boot sector The sector or sectors on a hard drive that contain the master boot record (MBR). This holds information that defines the file system used by the OS, the layout of partitions on the drive, and a pointer to the OS.

Bounded media Material that moves data and that is directly connected to the devices, such as copper cable or fiber optics.

Bridge A device that interconnects two different networks using two different hardware protocols or two different computing platforms.

Broadcast A data transmission directed at all hosts on the network.

Brouter A hybrid device that combines the functions of both a router, which can interconnect two disparate networks, and a bridge, which can interconnect two different topologies.

Bus In general terms, a bus is simply the path data takes to move from one location to another. In network topology, it refers to a layout that connects all devices in line with one another.

Cell The 53-byte fragment of data transmitted over an ATM connection. Frames generated by upper-level protocols will be broken down into multiple ATM cells.

Channel aggregation protocol A protocol that binds two or more signals of lower bandwidth into a single signal of higher bandwidth.

Checksum A method of error detection that simply keeps track of the number of 1s in the packet. If the receiving device calculates a different checksum than that stored in the trailer, the packet will be rejected and a NACK returned to the sender.

Chipping code A pattern of several changes in the signal carrier to represent a single bit. These changes can be either frequency, amplitude, or pulse modulated.

CHS parameters A description of a hard disk drive's geometrical layout. It defines the location and number of all cylinders and read/write heads and how many sectors are contained in each track.

CIDR Block A network address that includes the number of 1s used in the subnet mask as part of its format.

Circuit switching A telecommunications technology that selects the best route for data to take, based on current network conditions, and then creates a virtual circuit over which all data from that session will flow.

Client Any device or piece of software requesting the services of another device or piece of software.

Client-server A network in which one or more master computers keep a database of users and/or dole out files on an as-needed basis.

Closed-ended question Questions that can be answered by "Yes" or "No" or that otherwise abruptly end the line of query.

Cluster addressing The ability to identify the topological location of a host by its IP address.

Coaxial A conductor that has both the signal conductor and the ground running along the same axis.

Congestion control Managing the overall flow of data between all hosts on the network.

Connection ID A randomly generated number that the server application assigns to each session to assure that data is kept together and in sequence.

Connectionless service A networking service that establishes no virtual link between transmitting devices and makes use of no error control.

Connection-oriented service A networking service that does establish a virtual link between transmitting devices and incorporates end-to-end error control.

Contention window The number of time slots a device will wait after a collision occurs. This is the value used to set the backoff timer.

Copyleft A coined term that decribes the lack of a copyright applied to open-source software.

Credentials Users' logon IDs and passwords, along with the permissions they have been assigned.

Crossover cable A twisted-pair cable that has the transmit and receive signals reversed from the conventional wiring standard. This allows two devices to talk directly to one another without the need for a hub or switch in the path.

Crosstalk The tendency of an electrical current to "leak" from one conductor to another when they are run alongside one another.

Data format The structure that your data will assume as it is moved over the wire.

Datacom A term coined to describe any equipment used in data communications.

Datagram The format of the data fragment used by AppleTalk to send information over the network.

Default gateway The address to which a host will dump any packet whose address it cannot resolve.

Defined context set The complete set of transfer syntaxes used in the transfer of data along with the abstract syntaxes to which they are associated.

Defrag A utility specific to Microsoft operating systems that will take files that are scattered all over the disk and reassemble them into a contiguous order. Other OSs have similar utilities with different names.

Demultiplexing The separation and resequencing of multiple messages coming off of a single communications link.

Deterministic Any approach that is guaranteed to achieve the desired results.

Dialogue The two-way transfer of data between devices, including control data used to maintain the session.

Dictionary attack An attempt by a hacker to break into a network by barraging the server with a database of user IDs and passwords.

Differential backup A backup that copies all files added or changed since the last full backup.

Disk duplexing Exactly duplicating the data on a system on two different drives, each hanging off of a separate controller.

Disk mirroring Exactly duplicating the data on a system on two different drives hanging off of a single controller.

Disk slack Wasted disk space caused by inefficient storage of data by the file system.

Domain All network resources, including devices, software, and users, that fall under a single administrative unit of the network.

Drop The run of cable that links a networked device to the central location, usually a hub or switch.

Dynamic Any variable that allows itself to be configured or edited on the fly by a device or protocol.

Encapsulation The process of dividing a stream of data into smaller pieces for transmission and then adding layer-specific information to each segment as it passes from layer to layer.

Entity name A user-friendly host name used by NBP for identifying hosts on the network.

Ephemeral port A port created by a client application that identifies the place where all incoming data intended for that application will go.

Fault tolerance The capacity of a system or a network to experience a failure without it causing a significant impact on overall performance.

File format The structure your data assumes while stored on the system.

Firewall A device or piece of software that examines all traffic going in or out of a network and uses a preconfigured set of rules to determine whether or not that data is allowed to pass.

Flat addressing model A method of addressing in which there is only one level of address for every node on the network. All addresses get thrown into the same pool, and a network device has to dive in to find a specific address.

Flow control Maintaining a mutually acceptable data transfer speed between two devices on the network, making sure that all data arrives intact.

Fractional T1 A telco service that allows users to select how much bandwidth they needwithout having to pay for the services of an entire T1 line.

Frame Relay A packet-switching WAN protocol that makes use of Layer 2 networking services.

Frequency How many times in a specifically defined timer interval an event occurs. Usually measured in hertz.

Full backup A complete and total backup of all data on a hard disk. This does not necessarily include certain system files, including the registry, and will not include the MBR or FAT.

Full duplex The ability to send and receive data in either direction, both directions at the same time.

Fully qualified domain name An identification of an Internet location that completely describes the path to that location, including the root domain, the top-level domain, and all subdomains.

Gateway The default address to which all packets with unknown network addresses will be forwarded.

Go Back N A flow control method that requires that all packets arrive in sequence. If one packet is rejected, then all subsequently received packets must be retransmitted by the sending device along with the offending packet.

Half duplex The ability to send and receive data in either direction, but in only one direction at a time.

Handshaking The process two devices go through in order to agree on protocols used, connection speeds, and a number of other issues.

Header Information placed at the beginning of a segment/packet/frame by the layer protocol or device processing the data.

Hexadecimal A Base 16 counting method that makes use of the 10 numeric characters plus 6 alphabetical characters as well.

Hierarchical address model A method of addressing in which there are multiple levels of addressing, such as a network address and a host address. A network device can find the network it's looking for and let that network figure out which host is supposed to get the data.

Hop An intermediate stop, dictated by the chosen path of the router, that data must make as it travels from its source to its destination.

Hot swap To change out a device without having to completely shut down the system on which it is installed.

Hub An unintelligent device that distributes data across a subnet. What goes in one port goes out all ports, including the one from whence it came.

Hybrid A network that consists of two or more different topologies. For example, a star/bus network is relatively common.

Hypermedia Any resource on the network or local system that can automatically redirect the user to another resource simply by clicking on a link.

Hypothesis A fundamental theory as to why a particular situation exists the way it does.

Incremental backup A backup that only copies files that were added or changed since the last incremental backup.

Interactive logon An authentication procedure in which the user is prompted to enter his or her user ID and password.

Invalid file A file on a disk drive that does not conform to FAT entries that define that file. These problems can include invalid size reporting, incorrect reporting of the number of clusters used, a missing entry identifying the parent directory, and others.

Ipconfig The TCP/IP utility that displays all TCP/IP configuration information for any given interface or for all interfaces on a system.

Iterative query A request that must be fulfilled on the local server, providing whatever information it has, if any.

Lease In TCP/IP, this is the amount of time a client that has received its IP address over DHCP can keep that address.

Local collector ring The network of end users with their different bandwidths that interconnect to a single regional network.

Local loop carrier A communications service provider. It provides the electronic link between geographically separated devices.

Local procedure call A request for services that can be performed by or resources that reside on the machine from which the request was made.

Logic bomb A piece of code programmed to run at either a specific time or when a specific action is performed. Until then, it sits dormant.

Logical drive Another name for the volume created on a single hard drive when the disk was partitioned. To the end user, that partition appears as a separate disk drive.

Logon authentication In this process, a user's logon ID and password are transferred to the host providing the requested service. It is compared to a security database, and if confirmed, the user is allowed in.

Lost cluster A series of sectors on a disk drive that hold data but have no corresponding entries in the FAT identifying to what file these sectors belong.

Manager In TCP/IP terminology, this is an application or utility that initiates requests for information to be gathered.

Media set The collections of tapes or other media that represent a complete image of the system.

Mesh A network in which all devices directly interconnect with all other devices. Also sometimes called a "mess" network.

Message The format of data, or PDU, processed by the Application, Presentation, and Session Layers and sent downward to the Transport Layer.

Metric A value placed in a routing table that defines the relative cost, in time, of taking that particular hop.

Multicast A data transmission directed at selected multiple hosts.

Multiplexing The combining of multiple signals from different sources to be transferred over a single communications link.

Multipoint A communications link in which several devices set up a logical connection in order to communicate among themselves.

Naming convention A predefined logical method for naming the users and the computers on a group. A good naming convention will provide some information that identifies the user or device.

Nbtstat The TCP/IP utility that displays information for all NetBIOS over TCP/IP connections.

Netstat The TCP/IP utility that displays TCP/IP statistics for a specific interface on the system.

Network number A number used by IPX/SPX and AppleTalk to identify the network on which a device resides. In IPX/SPX it is a 32-bit number; in AppleTalk it is a 16-bit number.

Network policy A set of rules that defines access rights to the network as well as the behavior of those who use the network.

Network Any two or more devices connected either directly or indirectly and configured to communicate with one another.

Node address A unique number assigned to an individual host on the network. In IPX/SPX, this number is derived from the MAC address of the interface.

Node ID A number assigned by the AppleTalk protocol that identifies a specific host on the network.

Noninteractive logon Once a user is logged onto the network, subsequent access authentication is done in the background, transparent to the user.

Nontransitive Trusts begin at Point A and end at Point B. They will not automatically pass through to Point C.

Object counter In Performance Monitor, it is the specific property or variable for which data is being collected.

Octet Any collection of eight bits. In the context of TCP/IP, it represents one of the four sections of an IP address, which will be represented by one to three decimal characters.

On-line content The overall availability of resources across an intranet or the Internet.

Open-ended question A question formulated in such a way that the answer must provide an opening for further queries.

Packet switching A telecommunications technology that selects the best route for each packet of data to take, based on current network conditions. There is no single path used throughout the session and packets may not arrive in sequence.

Packet The format of data, or PDU, processed by the Network Layer and sent downward to the Data Link Layer by the transmitting computer, or up to the Transport Layer by the receiving computer.

Page fault When the system does not find the data it needs in RAM, it will search the paging file. If it fails to find that data, that is a page fault.

Page Read/Write When physical RAM in a system becomes full, data will be temporarily stored in a file called the paging file. A Page Read is a read operation from this file, while a Page Write is when data is moved from RAM to the paging file.

Parity An error detection mechanism that simply counts the number of 1s in a byte and indicates in a unique bit whether there is an even number of 1s or an odd number.

Partition table The portion of the MBR that defines the beginning and ending points of each logical division that was created on a hard drive.

Partition A logical subdivision of a single hard disk drive. Partitions will be seen by the system as separate drives, or volumes.

Pass-through authentication The procedure by which one domain hands off the responsibility for logon authentication to another domain.

Patch A fix to an OS or application that targets a specific flaw.

Payload The actual information carried in the frame that is the reason for the frame being transmitted to begin with. This may include user or application data or protocol-specific information.

Payload The part of a frame that actually consists of user or application data, separate from header and trailer information.

Peer entity Any two devices, protocols, or services that operate on the same layer that can communicate with one another.

Peer-to-peer A network in which there is no single controlling device. All devices act as both client and server, depending on circumstances.

Permissions Access rights a user has been given to network resources.

Ping Not only is Ping an acronym, it has been universally adopted as a term that can be either a noun or a verb. As a noun, it represents the packets sent when pinging another host. As a verb, it represents the process of pinging another host.

Plenum The space between the ceiling above you and the next floor up.

Point-to-point A communications link in which two devices set up a logical connection in order to communicate one to the other.

Port A logical address added to each segment of data transmitted that indicates what application or protocol is expecting the data.

Presentation context The collection of syntaxes that will be used to move data during a session.

Privileges The rights a user has been given to perform certain functions on the network, such as to add or administer user accounts.

Probabilistic Any approach that is likely to achieve the desired results, but is not guaranteed to achieve them.

Process entity The protocol or application on a host that is actually requesting or transmitting data during a network session.

Promiscuous mode An operating mode for any network interface in which all incoming packets will be accepted, even if they are not intended for that specific interface.

Protection ring A secondary circuit used by SONET to provide a backup path for data in the event that the primary ring fails.

Protocol A set of predefined rules and formats used to allow two unlike devices or applications to communicate.

Proxy server A device or piece of software that provides a singular point of entry for an Internet connection, masking IP addresses of internal users. It also caches Web pages for faster access.

Rack A piece of furniture or fixture for mounting equipment built to standardized sizes.

Recursive query A request for information that can be forwarded to other locations for fulfillment.

Redirector An application process that distinguishes whether a requested resource is local or remote. It then initiates a local procedure call for localized services and a remote procedure call for those that reside outside the local system.

Regional network The portion of the SONET network that provides services to users at varying bandwidths and collates the signals into a single high-speed pipeline.

Remote procedure call A request for services that can be performed by or resources that reside on a machine other than that from which the request was made.

Repeater A device that takes a signal, cleans it up, amplifies it back to its original strength, and then sends it along its way.

Retry counter A value maintained by a RAS server that increments with each attempt to log on. When configured with a specific value, once that value is reached, the account will be locked out.

Ring A topology that keeps data moving in a logical circle around the network.

Root server One of several collections of servers scattered around the world that maintains the databases of all domains that reside in any given top-level domain.

Round-robin algorithm A media access method in which a centralized device, such as an intelligent hub, scans each interface, searching for a device that wants to send data. It skips devices that do not need to transmit. If two or more devices need to transmit on the same cycle a priority method is used to determine who gets to go first.

Router A device that interconnects two autonomous networks.

S/T interface A device that allows access to the ISDN signal by multiple other devices.

ScanDisk A utility specific to Microsoft operating systems that checks a hard disk for file system errors and surface irregularities, and where possible, fixes these problems.

Scope A collection of IP addresses maintained by a DHCP server. Some of these addresses are reserved by the server for statically assigned devices, while the remainder are available for dynamic assignment.

Segment In reference to the Transport Layer, it is the PDU of the Transport Layer. The term can also be used to define a specific length of cable or the network devices that all share a singular collision domain.

Selectively repeat A flow control method that allows only offending packets to be retransmitted.

Server farm A centralized location that houses all of the servers for a larger and more complex network.

Server Any device or piece of software that processes requests for services and/or information by clients and subsequently provides services that another device or piece of software requires.

Service access point A predefined address that is used to transfer data between OSI layers.

Service pack A major OS maintenance package that applies a large number of updates and fixes.

Service primitive A specific function or activity that is performed by any specific layer entity.

Session A virtual connection created between two devices for the purpose of transmitting data.

Signature file The data file used by antivirus software to compare known viruses to code embedded in your system. Without an up-to-date signature file, newer viruses can go unnoticed.

Simplex The ability to send data in only one direction, but not the other way.

Sliding window A flow control method that allows two transmitting devices to adjust the number of packets that can be sent before waiting for ACKs as line conditions and congestion states change over time.

Sniffer A device or piece of software that is used to capture data packets off the network for analysis.

Socket number A 16-bit number assigned to a specific process or function that is accessing the network in IPX/SPX.

Source encoding A file compression scheme that introduces compression onto the file itself, regardless of whether or not that file will be transmitted.

Source routing The ability of the host to maintain its own routing tables and make route selections before transmitting data.

Spread spectrum The transmission of data by spreading it across several different radio frequencies.

Star A topology in which a central device interconnects all other devices on a segment of the network.

Stateful inspection A process by which a firewall can inspect the contents of a packet to determine whether or not it will be allowed to pass through the interface.

Static window A flow control method that allows a fixed number of packets to be sent. The transmitting device will then wait for ACKs for each of those packets to return before sending any more data.

Static Any variable that must be manually configured and/or updated.

Station address In IPX/SPX, this is the combination of the network number and node address. A socket number is added to create the complete IPX/SPX address.

Stop-and-wait A flow control method that requires that the transmitting device wait for the acknowledgment of each packet transmitted before it can send the next packet.

Subnet mask An entry into the TCP/IP configuration, formatted similarly to an IP address. This is a 32-bit value that defines which portion of the address is network and which portion is host.

Subnet Noun: A smaller network that exists within a larger network. Verb: To break a larger network down into smaller networks.

Supernetting The use of Classless Interdomain Routing to combine multiple blocks of contiguous IP addresses into a single network.

Superuser The administrator account for a Unix or Linux system.

Supervisor The administrator account in a Novell network.

Switch An intelligent device that distributes data between subnets. Packet filtering keeps unwanted data from cluttering up segments where it is not intended to go.

System object On a system in general, it is any hardware or software entity to which specific properties can be assigned. In Performance Monitor, it is a category of events that can be monitored.

Telco A generic term for any provider of telecommunications services.

Terminating resistor Small device that absorbs the electrical signal at the end of the conductor to prevent it from rebounding in the opposite direction.

Topology Physical or logical configuration. For example, the topology of a network shows the pattern in which the computers are interconnected. Common network topologies are the star, bus, and ring.

Trace Route The utility used by TCP/IP to generate a report of all intermediate devices between a source and a destination.

Trailer Information placed at the end of a segment/packet/frame by the layer protocol or device processing the data.

Transceiver Any device that can both transmit and receive.

Transfer syntax The form that data will assume as it moves over the wire.

Transitive Trust relationships can pass from one domain to another, through a third domain, simply on the basis of trusts that already exist.

Trojan horse A malignant program designed to look like a conventional program that induces the user to perform certain functions.

Troubleshooting The process of identifying and subsequently fixing a problem that exists on a piece of hardware, in an application, or on the network.

Trust A virtual link between two domains that allows one domain to perform authentication and provide resources to another domain.

Trusted domain The domain that contains the security database that is providing authentication and/or resource access to another domain.

Trusting domain A domain that is requesting authentication services or access to the resources from another domain.

Twisted pair A form of cable that consists of multiple strands of wire. The strands are separated into pairs and each of these pairs is twisted together.

U interface The device that accepts an incoming ISDN signal and brings it into the building.

Unbounded media Typical wireless media, such as radio waves, infrared, laser, or microwave transmissions.

Unicast A data transmission directed at a single host.

Virus A string of code embedded into a legitimate file that, when released, performs a mischievous or malignant function.

Volume A logical drive generated when a hard disk is divided into multiple partitions.

Well-known port A port used by common applications and processes through which data specific to that application or process will be sent.

Window size The amount of data a given host is capable of absorbing before its buffers overflow.

Worm A executable program that enters your system through another route and performs mischievous or malignant functions.

X-on/X-off A flow control method in which the transmitting device will continue to send data until the recipient tells it to stop. Once the recipient is once again ready to receive data, it will send a message to the transmitting device that it is okay to resume.

NETWORKING ACRONYMS

ABM Asynchronous Balanced Mode. An HDLC communications mode in which there is no specific master/slave relationship.

ACK Acknowledgment. Thank you, it arrived safe and sound.

ACL Access Control List. The security database used by Directory Services.

ACSE Association Control Specific Element. The Application Layer process that keeps track of the logical connection between two communicating applications.

ADSP AppleTalk Data Streaming Protocol. A connection-oriented protocol used by AppleTalk for sending large groups of data. It does not require the maintenance of transactions in order to function.

AEP AppleTalk Echo Protocol. AppleTalk's answer to ICMP.

AM Amplitude Modulation. A method of sending signals over an analog medium that encodes data by changing the relative strength of the signal without affecting the frequency.

AMI Alternate Mark Inversion. A modification of RTZ.

ARM Asynchronous Response Mode. An HDLC communications mode that allows the "slave" device to transmit with permission from the "master" under certain circumstances.

ARP Address Resolution Protocol. A protocol that can determine the MAC address of any host by sending a query to the IP address.

ASP AppleTalk Session Protocol. The AppleTalk protocol that establishes, maintains, and breaks down logical connections between devices.

ATM Asynchronous Transfer Mode. A high-speed telecommunications protocol that breaks down upper-level protocol packets into 53-byte cells and transmits them over a high-speed link.

ATP AppleTalk Transaction Protocol. A connection-oriented protocol used by AppleTalk for sending small pieces of data.

BCP Base Cryptographic Provider. A Windows service that generates user keys for encrypting data.

BDC Backup Domain Controller

BGP Border Gateway Protocol. A routing protocol that takes up where the Exterior Gateway Protocol left off. Advanced algorithms allow for more sophisticated routing decisions.

BNC Bayonet Neil-Concelman. A connector used in coaxial cable that attaches in a simple twist-and-lock motion.

BootP Bootstrap Protocol

BRI Basic Rate ISDN. An ISDN service that provides two 64K B channels and one 16K D channel.

CASE Common Application-Specific Element. An Application Layer process that is required of most, if not all, transfers of data.

CCR Commitment, Concurrency, and Recovery. An Application Layer process that makes sure that once a transaction begins, it is either completed or discarded if not complete.

CDDI Copper Distributed Data Interface. A dual-ring network topology that uses two redundant rings of copper cabling, capable of sending data in opposite directions.

CDPD Cellular Digital Packet Data. A packet-switching technology used to send voice communications.

CHAP Challenge Handshake Authentication Protocol. A password authentication protocol that makes use of a three-way handshake to provide authentication.

CHS Cylinders, Heads, Sectors per Track. A scheme that defines the geometric layer of a hard disk drive.

CIC Collect, Isolate, and Correct. One of the generally accepted troubleshooting models used in the computer industry.

CIDR Classless Interdomain Routing. A technology that allows multiple smaller network addresses to be bundled into a single network.

CIR Committed Information Rate. The minimum bandwidth guaranteed to a Frame Relay subscriber. Depending on network conditions, subscribers may actually enjoy the benefits of even higher bandwidths than those for which they subscribed.

CRC Cyclical Redundancy Check. The error correction algorithm most commonly used in networking protocols today. It performs a mathematical calculation on the stream of data and stores the results as a numerical value.

CSMA/CA Carrier Sense, Multiple Access/Collision Avoidance. The media access method frequently used by wireless networking.

CSMA/CD Carrier Sense, Multiple Access/Collision Detection. The media access method used by Ethernet.

CSU/DSU Channel Service Unit/Data Service Unit. This is the device that interconnects a network to a communications carrier.

DAP Directory Access Protocol. An early incarnation of directory access based on the OSI model.

DARPA Defense Advanced Research Projects Agency. The government agency that first began the research that would eventually lead to the Internet.

DAT Digital Audiotape. One of several magnetic tape data storage options. It uses metal oxide tape and a helical scan transport mechanism.

DDF Data Decryption Field. A header field that is added to any file encrypted by EFS that allows the decryption of that file.

DDP Datagram Delivery Protocol. The AppleTalk protocol that provides end-to-end support services.

DES Data Encryption Standards. A secure set of methods by which data can be securely encoded on one side and decoded on the other.

DHCP   Dynamic Host Configuration Protocol

DLCI   Data Link Communication Identifier. A specific circuit assigned to a Frame Relay subscriber. It may consist of either a virtual circuit or a permanent virtual circuit, depending on the level of service selected by the subscriber.

DLT   Digital Linear Tape. A magnetic tape data storage option that uses metal film tape and a linear transport mechanism.

DN   Distinguished Name. The complete network path to any object on a network using Directory Services.

DNS   Domain Name System

DPLL   Digital Phase Locked Loop. A clock signal carried in an electrical transmission of data.

DRF   Data Recovery Field. A header field that is added to any file encrypted by EFS that allows a recovery agent to decrypt the data in the absence of the original user.

DSAP   Destination Service Access Point. The address a layer uses to send data to the next layer in the flow.

DSSS   Direct Sequence Spread Spectrum. One of the frequency-hopping methods used in radio-based wireless networking.

DUN   Dial-Up Networking. A method for interconnecting a remote user to a network using a modem and a conventional telephone or an ISDN line.

ECHS   Extended CHS. See CHS.

EFS   Encrypting File System. In NTFS 5.0, this is the portion of the file system that allows individual files and folders to be encrypted for local storage by the user.

EGP   Exterior Gateway Protocol. The first of the border gateway protocols to be released.

EIA   Electronic Industry Association. One of the many governing bodies in the electronic industry.

EMI   Electromagnetic Interference. A magnetic field that can be generated by an electrical device that can interfere with an electronic signal.

ESD Electrostatic Discharge. The technical term for static electricity.

FAQ Frequently Asked Questions. A list of topics that are commonly asked by people having difficulty with a specific device or application.

FAT File Allocation Table. The file system originally used by MS-DOS. Also, the table used by file systems to identify the location of each FAU used by a file.

FAU File Allocation Unit. The collection of sectors that houses the most basic collective unit of data on a hard drive.

FCC Federal Communications Commission

FCS Frame Check Sequence. A field in the trailer of a frame that holds error correction data.

FDDI Fiber Distributed Data Interface. A dual-ring network topology that uses two redundant rings of fiber-optic cabling, capable of sending data in opposite directions. Like Token Ring, it uses the concept of attaching data to a token in order to avoid collisions.

FEK File Encryption Key. The 128-bit value used by encrypting software to scramble the code.

FHSS Frequency Hopping Spread Spectrum. One of the frequency-hopping methods used in radio-based wireless networking.

FIRST Forum of Incident Response and Security Teams. An organization charged with maintaining the security of the Internet.

FM Frequency Modulation. A method of sending signals over an analog medium that encodes data by changing the frequency of the signal without affecting the relative strength.

FTP File Transfer Protocol. Protocol used for transferring critical data.

GFSK Gaussian Frequency Shift Keying. A scheme for determining shift patterns and frequency in spread-spectrum radio networking.

GID Group Identification. Identifies a group account, of which several users might be members.

GPRS General Packet Radio Service. A packet-switching technology used to send voice communications.

HCL Hardware Compatibility List. A list of hardware by different manufacturers that has been tested and verified to work with a specific OS.

HDB3 A modification of AMI that prevents more than four 0s from occurring in sequence.

HDLC High Level Data Link Control. A networking protocol that works at the Data Link Layer.

HPSF High-Power Single Frequency. A radio wave-based networking technology using high-powered, assigned radio frequencies.

HTTP HyperText Transport Protocol

HTTPS Secure HyperText Transport Protocol

HVAC Heating, Ventilating, and Air Conditioning

IANA Internet Assigned Numbers Authority. The organization responsible for TCP/IP address and port number assignments.

ICA Citrix's thin-client protocol.

ICANN The Internet Corporation for Assigned Names and Numbers. One of several organizations involved in the administration of the Internet.

ICMP Internet Control Message Protocol

IDR Intelligent Disaster Recovery Backup Solution. A proprietary backup method developed by Compaq and HP that allows a full system, complete with MBR, FAT, and system files, to be restored in a single operation.

IEEE The Institute of Electrical and Electronic Engineers. One of several organizational bodies devoted to the development and ratification of international standards in various industries.

IEPG The Internet Engineering and Planning Group. An organization involved in overseeing the operational control of the Internet.

IETF The Internet Engineering Task Force. An organization charged with technological development of the Internet.

IMAP4 Internet Message Access Protocol

InterNIC Internet's Network Information Center. One of several organizations involved in the administration of the Internet.

IP Internet Protocol

IPCP IP Control Protocol. One of the lower level protocols of PPP.

IPSEC IP Security. A security protocol for standard TCP/IP transmissions. While optional on IPv4, it is built into IPv6.

IPv6 Internet Protocol, Version 6. The latest release of IP that supports 128-bit addresses and several advanced features.

IPX/SPX Internetwork Packet Exchange/Sequenced Packet Exchange

ISDN Integrated Services Digital Network

ISO Industry Standards Organization. One of several organizational bodies devoted to the development and ratification of international standards in various industries.

ISOC The Internet Society. The organization that oversees all the other organizations involved in managing the Internet. (Who oversees them?)

ISP Internet Service Provider. The end user's gateway to the Internet.

ITU The International Telecommunications Union. An organization that deals primarily with communications protocols.

JPEG Joint Photographic Experts Group. An organization that developed compression techniques for digital graphic images.

L2TP Layer 2 Tunneling Protocol. A more recent implementation of PPTP that works exclusively at the Data Link Layer.

LBA Logical Block Addressing. An extension to Int13h that numbers each FAU on the hard drive with a unique value.

LCP Link Control Protocol. One of the subordinate protocols of PPP.

LD Laser Diode. A small electrical device that emits pulses of laser light.

LDAP The Lightweight Directory Access Protocol. A more recent directory access protocol based on TCP/IP.

LED Light Emitting Diode. Small electrical device that emits conventional light waves (usually in the visible spectrum).

LLC Logical Link Control. One of the sublayers of Data Link.

LLC2 Logical Link Control, Type 2

LPSF Low-Power Single Frequency. A radio wave-based networking technology using weak, publicly available radio frequencies.

LSA Local Security Authority. A Windows service that manages internal security on a local machine or server.

MAC Media Access Control. One of the sublayers of the Data Link Layer.

MAU Multistation Access Unit. A device used on the Token Ring network that interconnects hosts in a physical star, but maintains the logical configuration of a ring.

MBR Master Boot Record. This holds information that defines the file system used by the OS, the layout of partitions on the drive, and a pointer to the OS.

MDI The Media Dependent Interface component of the Physical Layer.

MMDS Multipoint Microwave Distribution System. A technology for sending broadband signals over microwave.

MTU Maximum Transmission Unit. The largest size a packet can be in order to be used by a specific protocol.

NACK No Acknowledgment. It arrived, but there's something wrong. Can you retransmit?

NAP Network Access Point. The entry point to one of the several large capacity circuits that transport data across the Internet.

NAT Network Address Translation. A technology that hides a private addressing scheme from the public view.

NBP Name Binding Protocol. The AppleTalk protocol that handles name resolution.

NCP Network Control Protocol. One of the lower level protocols of PPP.

NDS Novell Directory Services

NetBEUI NetBIOS Enhanced User Interface

NFS Network File System

NIC Network Interface Card

NLM NetWare Loadable Module

NLSP NetWare Link Services Protocol

NOS Network Operating System

NRM Normal Response Mode. A communications mode of HDLC in which one or more devices are involved in the exchange of data, but only one machine controls the session.

NRZ Non-Return to Zero. An analog signaling scheme in which zeros and ones are each represented by a different voltage.

NT1 Network Termination-1. The interface of an incoming ISDN line that converts the incoming two-wire circuit to a four-wire ISDN circuit.

OCx Optical Carrier Level. A method of defining the different levels of transmission speed over high-speed networks. The x represents the specific level.

OSI Open Standards Interconnect. The seven-layer model of networking defined by ISO.

OSPF Open Shortest Path First. An interior gateway protocol that uses a link state method of route determination.

OU Organizational Unit. One of the container objects used in Novell's Directory Services model.

OUI Organizational Unique Identifier. Half of a MAC address that has been assigned to the manufacturer by the IEEE Registration Authority.

P2P Peer-to-Peer

PAP Password Authentication Protocol. A nonsecure protocol for providing user credentials between hosts on a network. It is nonsecure in that passwords are transmitted in plain text.

PDC Primary Domain Controller

PDU Protocol Data Unit. The format of data as it moves between OSI layers.

PING Packet Internet Groper. A TCP/IP utility that sends ECHO packets and waits for the reply.

PLS The Physical Signaling component of the Physical Layer

PMA The Physical Medium Attachment component of the Physical Layer.

POP In reference to TCP/IP, it refers to the Post Office Protocol, which is responsible for managing and delivering electronic mail over networked systems. Can also refer to the Point of Presence, when discussing Internet connectivity. This is the physical connection supplied by an ISP that provides access to the Internet.

POST Power On-Self Test. A program contained on the BIOS chip of most computers that brings the system from a cold start-up to operational condition.

POTS Plain Old Telephone Service

PPP Point-to-Point Protocol. A networking protocol that works at the Data Link Layer. It is the default protocol of dial-up networking.

PPTP Point-to-Point Tunneling Protocol. A protocol that allows the encapsulation of encrypted packets for secure transmission over the Internet.

PRI Primary Rate ISDN. An ISDN service that provides twenty-three 64K B channels and one 64K D channel.

PSTN Public Switched Telephone Network

PVC Permanent Virtual Circuit. A dedicated circuit assigned to a subscriber of Frame Relay services.

QIC Quarter Inch Cartridge. A magnetic tape storage mechanism that uses technology not much different that a standard audiocassette recorder.

RAID Redundant Array of Inexpensive (or Independent) Disks. Describes several different techniques for storing data across multiple hard disks.

RARP Reverse Address Resolution Protocol

RAS Remote Access Services. A method of authenticating and controlling access to the network by remote users.

RBS Robbed Bit Signaling. A technology used in voice communications in which a bit is "borrowed" from every eighth byte of data going over the wire for use by the telco.

RDP Remote Desktop Protocol. Microsoft's thin-client protocol.

RFC Request for Comment. The method by which TCP/IP protocols and utilities are introduced and subsequently defined.

RFI Radio Frequency Interference. Similar to EMI, except that it specifically defines wavelengths in the Radio/Television area of the Electromagnetic Spectrum.

RIP Routing Information Protocol. One of the earlier interior gateway protocols.

RJ-45 Registered Jack number 45. An 8-conductor connector used with twisted-pair cable that looks very similar to a standard telephone jack, only larger.

ROSE Remote Operation Specific Element. The Application Layer process that provides for remote procedure calls when necessary.

RPC Remote Procedure Call. The request for services that a system will present when it requires support of nonlocal resources.

RST Reset. Field or packet that initiates the breakdown of a session.

RTMP Routing Table Maintenance Protocol. The AppleTalk protocol that dynamically maintains routing table information.

RTS/CTS Ready to Send/Clear to Send. A type of packet that indicates a device using CSMA/CA is about to transmit data.

RTSE Reliable Transfer Specific Element. The Application Layer process that makes sure the data that arrives is the same data that was sent.

RTT Round Trip Time. The amount of time it takes a packet to go from host to host, and for the resultant ACK or NACK to return.

RTZ Return to Zero. A pulse signaling method used when moving data over copper wire.

SAM Security Accounts Manager

SAP Can refer to the Service Addressing Protocol, a protocol used by network operating systems to identify services offered by a particular device. When discussing OSI, the same acronym refers to a Service Access Point. This is the logical address that moves data between OSI layers on the same machine.

SASE Specific Application-Specific Element. An Application Layer process that is used only in certain circumstances and will be called by the program or protocol when needed.

SDH Synchronous Digital Hierarchy. A high-speed telecommunications technology, very similar to SONET, that combines multiple signals of different speeds into a single high-speed signal that moves over a fiber-optics backbone.

SLIP Serial Line IP. An early protocol used to transmit IP packets over a serial connection.

SMA Subminiature Assembly. One of several forms of connector used with fiber-optic cabling.

SMART Self-Monitoring, Analysis, and Reporting Technology. A technology that allows hard drives to predict imminent failure.

SMTP Simple Mail Transport Protocol

SNMP Simple Network Management Protocol

SOHO Small Office/Home Office. A generic term for offices used either by a single individual or a small group.

SONET Synchronous Optical Network. A high-speed telecommunications technology that combines multiple signals of different speeds into a single high-speed signal that moves over a fiber-optics backbone.

SPDU Service Protocol Data Unit. A small package of data used between OSI layers to request a specific service or activity.

SSAP Source Service Access Point. The address from which a layer will receive data from an adjacent layer.

SSPI Security Support Provider Interface. A Windows service that handles user authentication transparently after initial logon.

ST Generally refers to a Straight Tip connector. This is one of several forms of connector used with fiber-optic cabling. However, it is also occasionally seen in reference to the Internet Streaming Protocol, a protocol that never really got off the ground, which would have been IP version 5.

SWAP Shared Wireless Access Protocol. A protocol that uses the same technology as cordless telephones to interconnect network devices.

SYN Synchronization. Field or packet type that establishes transmission speeds.

T1 Digital Trunk Line. A circuit that combines up to twenty-four signals into one.

TCP/IP Transmission Control Protocol/Internet Protocol. The protocol suite of the Internet.

TCP Transmission Control Protocol

TDM Time Division Multiplexing. The technology used by SONET and SDH to combine different signals of different speeds into a single high-speed transmission.

TDR Time Domain Reflectometer. A sophisticated cable testing device that works by sending a signal down the cable and measuring the amount of time it takes to return.

TFTP Trivial File Transfer Protocol. Protocol used for transferring files that are smaller or not necessarily critical.

TTL Time to Live. A built-in countdown timer put into packets. If the transmitting device counts down to zero before receiving an ACK, it will automatically resend the packet.

UDP User Datagram Protocol. Connectionless protocol that simply throws data onto the network and hopes that it gets there.

UHF Ultrahigh Frequency

UID User Identification. Identifies a specific user's account.

VHF Very High Frequency

VPN Virtual Private Network. A secure connection between two devices over the Internet.

WINS Windows Internet Name Service

INDEX